CORPORAL PUNISHMENT IN AMERICAN EDUCATION

TEMPLE UNIVERSITY PRESS • PHILADELPHIA

CORPORAL PUNISHMENT IN AMERICAN EDUCATION

READINGS IN HISTORY, PRACTICE, AND ALTERNATIVES

Edited by
Irwin A. Hyman
and
James H. Wise
Preface by Nat Hentoff

Temple University Press, Philadelphia 19122
© 1979 by Temple University. All rights reserved
Published 1979
Printed in the United States of America

Library of Congress Cataloging in Publication Data
Main entry under title:
Corporal punishment in American education.
Includes index.
1.   Corporal punishment—United States—History—
Addresses, essays, lectures.   I.   Hyman, Irwin.
II.   Wise, James H.
LB3025.C67   371.5'4'0973   79-17
ISBN 0-87722-147-2

To
Nada, Nadine and Debbie

Contents

•

Contents

Preface

Nat Hentoff

•

In 1853, the Indiana Supreme Court expressed a state of consternation that is just as topical now:

> The public seems to cling to the despotism in the government of schools which has been discarded everywhere else . . . The husband can no longer moderately chastise his wife; nor . . . the master his servant or his apprentice. Even the degrading cruelties of the naval service have been arrested. Why the person of the schoolboy . . . should be less sacred in the eyes of the law than that of the apprentice or the sailor, is not easily explained.

The fact that schoolchildren remain the last Americans who may legally be beaten is still not easily explained.

First, in 1971, as an investigator for the American Civil Liberties Union on the state of students' rights in the schools; and then, in the years since, as a reporter on education, I have interviewed many beaten children and their parents. They are as bewildered as the 1853 Indiana Supreme Court.

In the spring of 1978, for instance, I spoke to a woman in North Little Rock, Arkansas, whose eighth-grade son had been hospitalized for two days after a lusty beating by his principal. The boy's offense: he had been talking in class when he hadn't been asked to.

The mother had come to this place from Appalachia years before, but the proud, lonesome sound and cadences of West Virginia were still in her. "The man who hit my boy," she told me, "should be abandoned from children. Why, he·took another boy and slammed him into the locker. I cannot understand how they let people like this teach children. It's like letting people from a crazy institution take over a school, throw children against the wall, beat them with boat paddles, and they say they're teaching them."

After some silence, the mother said, "My child has been abused. And not only him. Good lord, not only him. But you cannot whip a child and make him learn anything. I may be old-fashioned, but I do believe that if you give a child some love, even a little love, and let him know you care for him, he'll learn. What a child needs is confidence in grown-ups. Not to fear them."

In a small Texas town, a ten-year-old boy was dying of a blood disease. He didn't know it, but school authorities had been told. Yet the boy was whacked, more than once, for talking in class. "I have given up trying to understand how people could do that," his father told me after the boy had died. "People who say they are educators. They have a sickness that is beyond me. But what still makes me furious is that there wasn't a damn thing I could do about it." (The boy would not have understood his being kept home; he wanted to be with his friends).

"They told me," said the father, "they had the right to beat my boy. And there it was, right in the law."

There it still is, right in the law, in the vast majority of school districts in the country. And the beatings keep being administered not by "crazy" people but by officials who, having this weapon, use it rather than work out alternatives. And some ("hitting freaks," the kids call them) use it with particular vehemence, resulting in no little damage. To the psyche as well as the body.

Yet corporal punishment makes no sense—educationally, psychologically. And its results are long-lastingly pernicious. As the *New York Times* has pointed out editorially: "Youngsters are being taught the efficacy of rule by bully. It is hardly surprising that such children subsequently apply that rule in their own dealings with others, weaker than themselves."

Or, as a member of the National Advisory Committee on Child Abuse noted, after the committee voted to recommend total abolition of corporal punishment in the schools: "In junior high and high school classes to prepare youngsters for parenthood, we teach them not to beat kids but to reason with them. How can we, at the same time, say it's okay for school officials to beat kids? It makes no sense."

It is significant, in the growing national effort to finally bring sense to this subject, that this book is the first comprehensive volume on corporal punishment in American education. We have been very late in attending to this routine abuse of schoolchildren. But this book is so full of sense that it should considerably accelerate the awakening of American educators, and all other citizens, to the normative violence against children in our schools.

"What dismays me most," a Dallas teacher opposed to corporal punishment told me, "is how routinely most of the kids accept having their bodies violated by principals and teachers. The kids are so used to it that they beileve it's normal. They've been successfully beaten down. Just as *their* kids will be."

Unless—

Contributors

•

Luis Alvarez
New York City

Maxine Antell
Assistant Clinical Professor of
    Psychiatry
Albert Einstein College of Medicine
New York City

The Honorable Gertrude Bacon
President
Parents Anonymous, Inc.
New York City

Leopold Bellak
Albert Einstein College of Medicine
New York City

Anthony F. Bongiovanni
National Center for the Study of
    Corporal Punishment and
    Alternatives in the Schools
Temple University
Philadelphia

Vincent L. Broderick
New York City

Kenneth Cassie
High School Teacher
Ocean Township, New Jersey
Brielle, New Jersey

Kenneth B. Clark
Former President
Metropolitan Applied Research
    Center
New York City

Richard Elardo
University of Iowa
Iowa City, Iowa

Clifford B. Freeman
Librarian (Retired)
Institute of Education
University of Hull
Great Britain

Alma S. Friedman
Pupil Services Counselor
Los Angeles City Schools
Los Angeles, California

David B. Friedman
Professor of Pediatrics
University of Southern California
    School of Medicine
Los Angeles, California

Robert Friedman
School Psychologist
Somerset, New Jersey

Phyllis Harrison-Ross
New York City

Irwin A. Hyman
Director, National Center for the
    Study of Corporal Punishment
    and Alternatives in the Schools
Temple University
Philadelphia

Maurice A. Jackson
Woodrow Wilson High School
    Principal
Washington, D.C.

xiii

Jacob S. Kounin
Professor of Educational Psychology
Wayne State University

Edward T. Ladd (*deceased*)
Emory University
Atlanta, Georgia

John Lamberth
National Center for the Study of
    Corporal Punishment and
    Alternatives in the Schools
Temple University
Philadelphia

Virginia Lee
Formerly with The Center for Law
    and Education
Cambridge, Massachusetts

Professor John Manning
Department of Humanities
Michigan State University
East Lansing, Michigan

Eileen McDowell
Research Associate
National Center for the Study of
    Corporal Punishment and
    Alternatives in the Schools
Temple University
Philadelphia

Executive Director Adah Maurer
End Violence against the Next
    Generation
Berkeley, California

David J. Owens
University College
Cardiff, Wales
Great Britain

Philip K. Piele
Associate Professor and Director
University of Oregon ERIC Clear-
    inghouse on Educational Manage-
    ment
Eugene, Oregon

The Honorable Justine Wise Polier
New York City

Francis J. Reardon
Research Associate
Division of Research
Pennsylvania Department of Educa-
    tion

Donald R. Raichle
Professor of History
Kean College of New Jersey

Lansing K. Reinholz
Superintendent Burlington
    Public Schools
Burlington, Vermont

Alan Reitman
Associate Executive Director
American Civil Liberties Union

Robert N. Reynolds
Research Associate
Pennsylvania Department of Educa-
    tion

Stanley G. Sanders
Associate Professor
Department of Educational
    Administration and Supervision
University of Houston
Houston, Texas

Carolyn Sutcher Schumacher
Research Associate
Department of Applied History and
    Social Sciences
Carnegie-Mellon University
Pittsburgh, Pennsylvania

B. F. Skinner
Professor Emeritus,
Harvard University
Cambridge, Massachusetts

Murray A. Straus
Professor, University of
  New Hampshire
Durham, New Hampshire

James S. Wallerstein
Director
The Council of Orenda
Mount Kisco, New York

Robert C. Weaver
New York

Ralph S. Welsh
Clinical Psychologist in Private
  Practice
Bridgeport, Connecticut

Gertrude J. Williams
Clinical Psychologist in Private
  Practice
St. Louis, Missouri

James H. Wise
Child Protection Center
Children's Hospital National
  Medical Center
Washington, D.C.

Janis S. Yarbrough
Public Information Officer
Alief Independent School District
Alief, Texas

PART I

•

INTRODUCTION

An Overview

Irwin A. Hyman

Eileen McDowell

•

A great Nez Perce Indian chief was once on a peace mission to a white general. The story goes that as he was riding through the white man's camp he observed a soldier hitting a child. The chief reined his horse and said to his companions, "There is no point in talking peace with barbarians. What could you say to a man who would strike a child?" His observation was tragically prophetic for his own tribe and perhaps an accurate assessment of American society in that place and time. The event he witnessed was not an unusual one then, nor is it unusual or illegal now. It was and is accepted practice to beat children in the United States.

On April 19, 1977, the United States Supreme Court, in a five to four decision, ruled that corporal punishment as a disciplinary tool in public schools did not constitutionally constitute cruel and unusual punishment and that the children so disciplined were therefore not guaranteed protection by the Eighth Amendment to the Constitution of the United States (*Ingraham* v. *Wright*). The Court noted that "public school teachers and administrators are privileged at common law to inflict only such corporal punishment as is reasonably necessary for the proper education and discipline of the child; any punishment going beyond the privilege may result in both civil and criminal liability." That is considerably less protection than criminals enjoy. The minority opinion of the Court in fact suggested that by restricting the Eighth Amendment's protection to criminals, children in school would have to commit criminal acts in order to be protected from harsh physical punishment by school authorities. The minority opinion also pointed out that the ruling, by denying schoolchildren due process in cases of physical punishment, has deprived them of even rudimentary assurance "against unfair or mistaken findings of misconduct."

Educators and parents responded variously, but none without passion. The Supreme Court decision did not settle the issue of using corporal punishment in schools; on the contrary, it sparked a new controversy raising questions basic to American education. If, as repeated Gallup polls suggest, discipline is regarded as the major problem in the schools, then the use of physical punishment as a means of maintaining discipline must be examined. This book is intended not as a dispassionate examination of the issue; rather, it is a brief for rational alternatives to corporal punishment. The editors have brought together essays by a variety of experts whose research and reflection may or may not have begun in the conviction that corporal punishment in a democratic society is intolerable, but—with one exception—did result in that conviction. Moreover, there are few who willingly defend in print the use of corporal punishment as a suitable method for maintaining discipline in the schools. The Supreme Court justices are a notable exception. The essays in this book then are meant to inform the discussion and to counterbalance the effect of the Supreme Court decision by proposing alternatives to physical punishment. The editors see no evidence to support its use or to prove its efficacy as a tool of education.

The general definition of the term *corporal punishment* indicates it to be the infliction of pain, loss, or confinement of the human body as a penalty for some offense (Barnhart, 1963). The legal definition is similar. *Black's Law Dictionary* (1968) defines corporal punishment as "physical punishment as distinguished from pecuniary punishment or a fine; any kind of punishment of or inflicted on the body, such as whipping or the pillory. The term may or may not include imprisonment according to the individual case." Educationally, corporal punishment has been generally defined as: the infliction of pain by a teacher or other educational official upon the body of a student as a penalty for doing something which has been disapproved of by the punisher (Wineman & James, 1967). The infliction of pain is not limited to striking a child with a paddle or the hand. Any excessive discomfort, such as forcing the child to stand for long periods of time, confining one in an uncomfortable space, or forcing a child to eat obnoxious substances, fits the description. Laws forbidding the use of corporal punishment do not include the teacher's use of force (1) to protect himself or herself, the pupil or others from physical injury; (2) to obtain possession of a weapon or other dangerous objects; (3) to protect property from damage (National Education Association, 1972).

Currently, forty-seven states through state legislation allow or specifically endorse the use of corporal punishment as a means of disciplining children in public schools (Friedman & Hyman, 1977). Some states, such as Hawaii, are reviewing their statistics and have imposed temporary bans on the use of physical punishment. Maine, Massachusetts, and New Jersey have laws against corporal punishment in schools, and Maryland has a permissive regulation that leaves the decision to local districts. The states and local districts permitting corporal punishment vary in determining the appropriate time, place, extent, and form of the administration of physical punishment. Despite some differences in due process and the severity of punishment allowed, the fact remains that corporal punishment is an officially sanctioned form of institutionalized child abuse in the United States. That is not true in a number of other countries. Among those that have abolished corporal punishment altogether are Luxembourg, Holland, Austria, France, Finland, Sweden, Denmark, Belgium, Cyprus, Japan, Ecuador, Iceland, Italy, Jordan, Qatar, Mauritius, Norway, Israel, The Philippines, Portugal, and all Communist bloc countries (Reitman, Follmann & Ladd, 1972; Bacon & Hyman, 1976).

Why has the practice persisted in the United States? The question is probably unanswerable. Corporal punishment is an old and ingrained method of discipline in American homes and schools. Manning (1959) reports that a schoolhouse, constructed in 1793 in Sunderland, Massachusetts, had an ominous whipping post built into the schoolhouse floor. Erring young students were securely tied to the post and whipped by the schoolmaster in the presence of their classmates. Manning also reports that paddling devices were prominently displayed in the classrooms of the 1800s, conspicuous reminders of the wages of sin. Bakan (1975) suggests, in fact, that corporal punishment was a method of literally beating the "devil" out of errant children.

The notion that children might have rights is of recent origin. It was not until about 1900 that American law began to recognize that anyone except the father and husband had any rights whatsoever (Hyman, 1976b). Currently, there are a number of laws on the books that uphold the rights of children—and few Americans believe that children are inhabited by evil spirits or the devil—yet children may be physically assaulted in schools. Those who founded the New York Society for the Prevention of Cruelty to Children in 1874—ten years after the founding of a similar society for the prevention of cruelty to animals—were addressing a serious issue that remains unresolved one hundred years later. Is it possible, as Keniston suggested (1975), that Americans do not really like children? At the least, our society has not always been aware of a gap between what it claims to do for its children and what it does to them. On the one hand we are child oriented and, some accuse, permissive; on the other child abuse accounts for more childhood deaths than any other single factor (Hyman & Schreiber, 1975).

In a survey of the literature on the relationship between cultural mores and the institutionalization of corporal punishment, Babcock (1977) found that among more complex societies there is a tendency toward more punitive child-rearing practices, although more orthodox and repressive societies, whether primitive or complex, tend to favor the use of corporal punishment. Significant exceptions are the Soviet Union and most Communist countries, which have abolished physical punishment. It is difficult to correlate social order with the use of corporal punishment; more studies are needed. It is possible, however, and necessary to address the problem of freedom and discipline in our own society.

The problem is central to the conflict between what is taught and how it is taught. Democracy is taught as a subject but seldom as a process, even though some educational and psychological theorists—John Dewey most notably—have urged the application of democratic processes to help children internalize controls. Unfortunately for education, Dewey's basic concepts have been distorted to such an extent that the term "democratic teaching" has come to be linked with an absence of teacher control in the classroom. Permisiveness, progressiveness, open education, and democratic teaching have all become synonymous with softness and a lack of discipline. The opposite is being "tough" on kids. The relevant issue is not one of degree but rather one of source. Classes in a democratic society should have as much discipline as in authoritarian societies, but the controls should be internalized. In a democratic atmosphere, the attempt should be made to reduce a child's anxiety so that he is free to learn, rather than to induce anxiety with punitiveness and guilt (Sandford, 1956). Further, there is research evidence to support the use of democratic disciplinary methods without resort to force (Hyman, 1964).

What, however, do we mean by corporal punishment in the schools? Is it mainly a matter of applying a ruler to young knuckles or a switch to the buttocks? Following are examples of punishments that are not exceptional, although they are clearly excessive.

In Vermont, in 1974, a young sixth grade student was seriously beaten by the principal for striking another student. The principal struck the child repeatedly, knocking him from his seat to the floor. He then kicked the child in the abdomen, back, and legs, and pulled his hair. The child suffered severe bodily bruises (*Roberts* v. *Way*, 1975).

In Missouri, after being caught with cigarettes, three boys were given the choice of receiving a paddling or eating their cigarettes. The prospect of the beating was more distasteful than the cigarettes, and the boys ate eighteen of them. The ingestion of tobacco resulted in three-day hospitalizations for the boys. One suffered aggravation of an existing ulcer, and another developed a kidney infection (*Hub*, 1976).

In a shop class in Pittsburgh, in one of the "best" elementary schools, a seventh grade student allegedly mumbled something under his breath. Whatever it was he said, the teacher became enraged, grabbed the student by the throat, and slammed him against the wall (Schumacher, 1971).

During the 1971–72 school year, the Dallas public schools reported an average of two thousand incidents of physical punishment per month (NEA, 1972). In the Houston public schools, it was reported by Dr. J.

Boney, an administrator, that during a two-month period in 1972 there were 8,279 paddlings administered (Elardo, 1977).

The message—that violence is a way to solve problems—is surely not lost on children. Kempe (1962) has suggested that parents who were beaten as children end up beating their own children. Teachers who attended schools in which corporal punishment was an accepted practice may in a like manner find it natural to turn to it themselves, although other people, beaten as children, react adversely to the notion of using physical force themselves. There are no simple solutions. Kempe feels that the parents of children who are victims of the "battered child syndrome" are mentally ill. While corporal punishment applied by teachers is usually not so extreme in intent or result as the abuse inflicted on children by their own parents, its use by teachers who experienced corporal punishment as children suggests a tendency to "identify with the aggressor" which characterizes the authoritarian personality (Adorno, Frendel-Brunswick, Levinson & Sanford, 1950). Gil (1971) suggests that the use of force on children stems from an inherent cultural belief that violence is an acceptable way to solve problems. Carried far enough, that position could suggest that the society itself is "mentally ill," judged by its approach to violence.

The more serious question relates to the mental health of the teachers acting on behalf of society. Several theorists (Bakan, 1970; Wohlford & Chibucos, 1975) have deduced from national estimates the incidence of mental illness among teachers. Consider the following conclusion reached by David Bakan (1970):

> Nor can we be assured of wisdom in connection with the *use* of corporal punishment, even if one were to accept the *principle* of corporal punishment. I have no data on mental health of teachers . . . [but] it is estimated that one in every ten persons is suffering from some form of mental illness; and the probability is one in twenty that any given individual will, at some point in his lifetime, be a patient in a mental hospital. If we add to this the observation of the Celdric Report that approximately one in every ten children is in need of special psychological and psychiatric services, the probability that either an ill teacher or an ill child or both will be involved in an incident involving corporal punishment is simply too high to allow it to go on at all. (p. 2)

Wohlford and Chibucos (1975) attempted to make a statistical estimate of mental health among teachers. Using figures compiled by others, they estimate that 9 percent of the teachers in the United States are "seriously maladjusted." Projections indicate that there are probably 180,000 teachers who are seriously disturbed; by extrapolation, there could be

4,500,000 students exposed yearly to maladjusted teachers. "Tens of thousands of these teachers may act out their problems with mental abuse, sarcasm, ridicule, etc., if not physical abuse" (Wohlford & Chibucos, 1975, p. 11). This may be an extreme estimate of the possible dangers of corporal punishment, but those on the receiving end of the paddle are not concerned with statistical rarity.

What are the effects of punishment on learning? Bongiovanni (1977) casts doubt on the efficacy of punishment under the conditions encountered in public schools. Punishment appears to result in the temporary reduction of undesirable behavior. To be effective in the long run, however, the retribution must be extremely harsh and repeated—and even then the research results are inconclusive. At issue is "traumatic avoidance learning": it is sometimes necessary to spank a two-year-old to keep the child from wandering into the street. That is the theory, and it may be effective for the short term. The spankings will have to become more frequent and severe as the child grows older and develops more complex reasons for crossing the street, if the physical force is to be the primary educational tool. It is likely to be more effective in the long run to teach the child the danger he faces in heedlessly crossing the street and present him with a viable alternative, such as learning to look both ways.

A review of the literature revealed no adequate studies of the effects of corporal punishment on achievement, although a significant body of literature exists on the effects of teacher behavior on learning. Rosenshine (1968), for example, reviewed studies of the relative effects of praise, mild criticism, and strong criticism. It is clear that strong criticism had statistically negative correlations with achievement (Perkins, 1965; Wallen, 1966). This relationship held across socio-economic classes and among teachers otherwise rated as superior, according to the usual criteria.

A later review by Rosenshine and Furst (1971) considered seventeen studies which were based on a more extensive tabulation of the use of criticism. In all studies, criticism was characterized by the use of negative or demeaning statements and/or threats. Most of the studies reviewed indicated a relationship between teacher criticism and less student achievement. In ten of the seventeen studies, stronger forms of criticism were more clearly correlated with less achievement. Rosenshine and Furst concluded that "teachers who use extreme amounts and forms of criticism usually have classes which achieve less in most subject areas" (1971, p. 51). More recent studies are reviewed by Lamberth later in this book. The results cast doubt on the value of "traumatic avoidance learning" in the classroom.

There is evidence that suspensions and corporal punishment are used most frequently against a select group of children (Bakan, 1970; Polier et al., 1974; Children's Defense Fund, 1974, 1975). The children in this group are often emotionally disturbed, black, Hispanic, or otherwise disadvantaged: they represent a "discipline problem." Corporal punishment tends to reinforce their alienation from the white middle-class system of learning into which they had been thrust. A number of other studies supports that contention, including the work of Rosenthal and Jacobson (1968). Their study of the self-fulfilling prophecy, *Pygmalion in the Classroom*, was seriously questioned at the time (Thorndike, 1968); a more recent series of studies, however, lends support to the original hypothesis (Mackowsky, 1973).

Some educators, black and white, seem to believe that hitting ghetto children is the only discipline they understand (Polier, 1974; Schumacher, 1971). But such attitudes may merely increase a child's sense of his lack of worth. Once a person develops a particular self-image there is a tendency to cling to that concept (Rogers, 1951). If, as research on locus of control suggests (Battle & Rotter, 1963; DuCette, Wolk, & Soucar, 1972), lower-class children tend to feel they have little power to control their own destinies, then the attitudes of teachers and their approach to discipline can seriously affect the children's abilities to improve themselves and their situation. Lower-class children, who are paddled most frequently among schoolchildren, are likely to contine the behavior physical punishment was meant to eliminate. Teachers expect them to misbehave, and the children meet that expectation.

Corporal punishment, as we suggested earlier, derives its justification from past beliefs rather than current knowledge. Despite the existence of a variety of research evidence that can be interpreted as support for the elimination of corporal punishment, there is actually little hard data on the subject. Within the present federal framework of research with human beings, it is improbable that state or federal funds will be used for experimentally controlled research on corporal punishment. Such research would have to include a group of children regularly beaten under controlled circumstances. That of course is out of the question. Almost all research to date on corporal punishment has been confined to surveys of incidence and attitudes. Some correlational studies have been conducted but the nature of the data limits the conclusions one can draw.

It is useful, however, to have a sense of the extent to which corporal punishment is used in schools. We can assume that the incidence has decreased since 1850, where in Boston it took "sixty-five beatings a day to sustain a school of four hundred" (Hapkiewicz, 1975), and since 1889, when 11,768 children in the same city were physically punished. The Vermont State Department of Education conducted a state survey of the use of corporal punishment in Vermont schools (Corcoran, 1975). Responses from 415 school districts with a total enrollment of 109,294 children are presented in Table 1.

The data in Table 1 do not reveal the frequency of corporal punishment per child or by particular teachers. That limitation aside, the figures indicate that one child out of every 379 could have been a recipient of corporal punishment. Interestingly, the reason most often given for using corporal punishment, correction, is the one least justified by available research.

In 1968, the Pittsburgh Board of Education commissioned a survey of corporal punishment, which was conducted by its Office of Research (Shaffer, 1968). Their data are reported in terms of percentage reponse to a twenty-one-item questionnaire distributed to teachers through their building principals. A 72.8 percent return yielded interesting data which is too extensive to present in full here. Table 2 provides some idea of the frequency of the use of corporal punishment.

The data indicate that 60 percent of the responding teachers hit children at least once during the year; most incidents occur in grades one

*Table 1. Reported Incidents of Corporal Punishment
in Vermont for the 1974–1975 School Year**

				REASON FOR CORPORAL PUNISHMENT		
Grade	*Girls*	*Boys*	*Total*	*Obedience*	*Correction*	*Control*
K	0	1	1	0	1	0
1	3	29	32	9	9	14
2	4	15	19	2	9	8
3	3	20	23	6	8	9
4	4	41	45	4	27	14
5	2	24	26	6	8	12
6	5	50	55	17	22	16
7	1	30	31	4	20	7
8	0	40	40	8	20	12
9	1	11	12	1	6	5
10	0	3	3	3	0	0
11	0	1	1	0	1	0
12	0	0	0	0	0	0
TOTAL	23	265	288	60	131	97

*C. Corcoran. Report of suspensions and corporal punishment. Vermont State Department of Education, July 29, 1975, p. 2.

Table 2. *Percentage Responses of Pittsburgh Teachers*
to Corporal Punishment Survey in 1968*

Question	N	K	1–4	5–8	9–12	Total
Have you ever paddled or hit any students in the classroom?						
Never	108	45	10	60	65	38.6
Once a year or less	67	40	10	20	20	23.9
Several times a year	74	10	65	15	5	26.4
Every month or more	25	0	15	5	5	8.9
No response	6	5	0	0	5	2.2
TOTAL	280	100	100	100	100	100.0
When did you last paddle or hit a student?						
Within the past 2 months	65	5	60	15	15	23.2
Within the past 6 months	25	15	5	5	5	8.9
Within the past year	37	5	25	15	0	13.2
Within the past 10 years	33	10	0	25	15	11.8
Within the past 15 years	4	0	0	0	0	1.4
Not applicable	101	60	5	40	60	36.1
No response	15	5	5	0	5	5.4
TOTAL	280	100	100	100	100	100.0

*S. M. Shaffer. Corporal punishment survey. Pittsburgh, Pennsylvania, Board of Education, Office of Research, June 13, 1968.

through four. Over 60 percent of the teachers, grades five through twelve, reported they never paddled children. An analysis of other data by Shaffer indicates that 61 percent of the teachers wanted to allow corporal punishment to be administered at their own discretion. Lest that be judged as a belief in the effectiveness of corporal punishment, 60 percent felt that teachers needed inservice training to provide for more effective ways of dealing with problem children. Another finding was that a significantly greater number of paddlings occurred in large schools receiving Title I funds; the implication is clear. Schools receiving Title I funds are those with a large population of disadvantaged and minority students. This finding supports previously stated evidence that poor children are hit more often. Shaffer points out that 38 percent of the teachers administering punishment in grades one through four at large Title I schools have less than three years' teaching experience. That is well below the district average when non-Title I schools are included in the calculations. Additionally, 40 percent of the teachers in smaller Title I schools have less than three years' experience.

Adah Maurer analyzed the results of a survey of corporal punishment mandated by the state of California during the 1972–73 school year (California State Assembly, 1973). Results indicated that there had been 46,022 cases of the use of corporal punishment, not including Los Angeles and eighty other school districts that failed to report. Of these 46,022 cases, almost 30,000, or 65 percent, occurred in the intermediate and junior high schools. Only 2,225 high school students were beaten, whereas 10,000 children in kindergarten and the primary grades received some form of physical punishment. Punished boys outnumbered punished girls 18 to 1: 37,594 males, 2,146 females, and 6,282 unidentified by gender. Boys between the ages of eleven and fourteen took the brunt of the paddlings. Seven cases charging excessive, abusive punishments resulting in injury were taken to court. There were 63 serious complaints to school boards, and 535 families registered complaints with the administration.

Reardon and Reynolds (1975) have completed what is probably the best-designed survey of corporal punishment to date. It is presented in greater depth later in this book. The survey was requested by the Pennsylvania State Board of Education to clarify questions concerning beliefs about corporal punishment. Of the 292 school districts responding, 269 indicated official approval of the use of corporal punishment. Sixteen prohibited it, and seven were undecided. Guidelines varied; about one-third of the responding districts had no guidelines, apparently leaving the practice up to the judgment of individual teachers. Among the adults responding, 71–81 percent approved the use of corporal punishment.

Elardo (1977) interviewed a group of elementary schoolchildren to determine their attitudes toward corporal punishment. Some of the children preferred paddling to other forms of punishment to "get it over with." They also felt a paddling did little to change behavior. Some, however, had more sophisticated responses. One articulate child said, "Sometimes you get accused falsely of doing something. If you get paddled and later prove you did not do it, you can't get unpaddled. But if you lose an activity, maybe by the time the activity should occur you can prove your innocence and still get your activity" (Elardo, 1977, p. 18).

Studies of the incidence of corporal punishment only go so far. They tell us that corporal punishment is widely used and generally approved. Even the psychologists conducting the studies appear to approve the practice (Anderson & Anderson, 1976).

> It was found that the majority of the respondents spank their own children, felt that children need to be spanked sometimes and have no regrets about

spanking their own children. About one half of those questioned felt that school personnel should have the option to spank children in school. (p. 46)

What is needed are direct naturalistic studies to determine correlations among behavior, achievement, and attitudes in schools that use corporal punishment and those that do not.

Even more important, however, than increasingly sophisticated studies of incidence is the development and understanding of the use of alternatives to corporal punishment. In a sense, the need is for a program to educate teachers, parents, and school administrators, beginning perhaps with Clarizio's exploration and disproof of the four most common assumptions used to support corporal punishment.

The first assumption is that physical punishment is a tried and true method: "It is good for students. It helps them develop a sense of personal responsibility, learn self-discipline and develop moral character" (Clarizio, 1975, p. 3). The second assumption is that "occasional paddling contributes substantially to the child's socialization." Both of these assumptions find little support in research or practice.

The third assumption Clarizio discusses is that "corporal punishment is the only recourse in maintaining order." In our program to educate educators, this assumption deserves special attention, and we will return to it in a moment. The fourth assumption is that "educators favor the use of corporal punishment." Some figures in fact support the assumption, but there is far from an overwhelming belief among educators that corporal punishment is a good thing. There is no question, however, that many educators are beleaguered, especially in inner-city schools, and turn to corporal punishment because nothing else seems as likely to work. There are, however, alternatives; corporal punishment is not necessarily the only discipline some children understand. It may only be the primary form that they have been exposed to. Physical punishment may be in fact the only thing that some teachers understand.

Citizens for Creative Discipline conducted a survey among South Carolina educators and found that good teachers also tended to be creative disciplinarians (Survey: Good teachers, 1976). The survey reports that the educators identified the following techniques as most successful in preventing disciplinary problems: (1) consistent application of rules; (2) respect for students; (3) strong administrative leadership; (4) low ratio of students to teacher; (5) skillful diagnoses of and approach to academic weakness.

In the same survey, educators polled described a particular teacher or practitioner of creative discipline in the following terms: (1) the teacher respects the students; (2) the teacher is creative in his/her approach to teaching; (3) the teacher plans carefully for his/her class and keeps students involved in active and interesting work; (4) the teacher is adept at developing appropriate curriculum involvement.

In January 1972, a Task Force on Corporal Punishment was appointed by the National Educational Association. The members represented students, teachers, and all regions of the country. The final report of the Task Force was presented to the delegates at the annual meeting in 1972. While the report recommended the elimination of corporal punishment in American schools, it also stressed the need for preservice and inservice training in effective methods of discipline and proposed specific alternatives to corporal punishment. That section of the NEA report follows:

Short-Range Solutions

The first step that must be taken is the elimination of the use of punishment as a means of maintaining discipline. Then, the ideas below can be used as temporary measures to maintain discipline while longer-range programs are being put into effect.

1. Quiet places (corners, small rooms, retreats)
2. Student-teacher agreement on immediate alternatives
3. Teaming of adults—teachers, administrators, aides, volunteers (parents and others)—to take students aside when they are disruptive and listen to them, talk to them, and counsel them until periods of instability subside
4. Similar services for educators whose stamina is exhausted
5. Social workers, psychologists, and psychiatrists to work on a one-to-one basis with disruptive students or distraught teachers
6. Provision of alternate experiences for students who are bored, turned off, or otherwise unreceptive to particular educational experiences:
    a. Independent projects
    b. Listening and viewing experiences with technological learning devices
    c. Library research
    d. Work-study experience
7. Inservice programs to help teachers and other school staff learn a variety of techniques for building better interpersonal relations between themselves and students and among students:
    a. Class meetings (Glasser technique)
    b. Role playing
    c. Case study—what would you do?
    d. Student-teacher human relations retreats and outings
    e. Teacher (or other staff)—student-parent conferences

8. Class discussion—of natural consequences of good and bad behavior (not threats or promises); of what behavior is right; of what behavior achieves desired results; of causes of a "bad day" for the class

9. Privileges to bestow or withdraw

10. Approval or disapproval

11. Other staff members to work with a class whose teacher needs a break.

Intermediate-Range Solutions

1. Staff-student jointly developed discipline policy and procedures

2. Staff-student committee to implement discipline policy

3. Parent education programs in interpersonal relations

4. Staff inservice program on interpersonal relations, on understanding emotions, and on dealing with children when they are disruptive

5. Student human relations councils and grievance procedures

6. Training for students and teachers in crisis intervention

7. Training for students in student advocacy

8. Training for teachers in dealing with fear of physical violence

9. Regular opportunities for principals to experience classroom situations.

Long-Range Solutions in Schools

1. Full involvement of students in the decision-making process in the school

2. Curriculum content revision and expansion by students and staff to motivate student interest

3. Teacher inservice programs on new teaching strategies to maintain student interest

4. Alternate programs for students

5. Work-study programs

6. Drop-out—drop-back-in programs

7. Alternative schools within the public school system

8. Early entrance to college

9. Alternatives to formal program during last two years of high school

10. Few enough students per staff member that staff can really get to know students

11. Adequate professional specialists—psychiatrists, psychologists, social workers

12. Aides and technicians to carry out paraprofessional, clerical, and technical duties so that professional staff are free to work directly with students more of the time

13. A wide variety of learning materials and technological devices

14. Full implementation of the *Code of Student Rights*

15. Full implementation of NEA Resolution 71–12: "Student Involvement"—

The National Education Association believes that genuine student involvement requires responsible student action which is possible if students are guaranteed certain basic rights, among which are the following: the right to free inquiry and expression; the right to due process; the right to freedom of association; the right to freedom of peaceful assembly and petition; the right to participate in the governance of the school, college, and university; the right to freedom from discrimination; and the right to equal educational opportunity.

Long-Range Solutions with Other Agencies

1. Staff help from local and regional mental health and human relations agencies
2. More consultant staff to work with individual problem students
3. Long-range intensive inservice programs to prepare all staff to become counselors
4. Mass media presentations directed to both the public and the profession on the place of children in contemporary American society
5. Some educational experiences relocated in business, industry, and social agencies
6. Increased human relations training in preservice teacher education and specific preparation in constructive disciplinary procedures.

There is a growing literature in educational research based on empirical findings that offers alternatives to corporal punishment. Jacob Kounin (1970) has discovered common mistakes made by poor classroom managers. Hyman (1972, 1976) has developed Kounin's work into a system for training teachers to be better managers in order to avoid the need for paddling. Further research by Schultz and Hyman (1971) suggest certain personality and teacher characteristics which affect teachers' management style as measured by Kounin's system. Marino (1975) trained teachers to recognize their ineffective management techniques. He was able to demonstrate improved management and thereby obviate the need to rely on physical punishment.

This introduction has touched on the themes developed in more detail by the papers included in this book. In it the editors have tried to outline the research and experience that leads to the conclusion that corporal punishment is not a useful educational tool. At base, however, is their conviction that humane education does not require reinforcement by physical abuse. We believe that a case can be made, using the available empirical evidence, for alternatives such as those proposed by the NEA to maintain discipline in the classroom.

It is also our conviction that children are entitled to the same guarantees accorded adults. Their status should not leave them vulnerable to the whims of harried teachers in overcrowded schools. The Supreme Court has ruled that within limits it is the privilege of the teacher to inflict physical punishment on students, but that is a privilege teachers and educators may and should decline to exercise. A legal decision does not make good educational practice; the debate should center not on what is legal but on what is likely to produce whole, well-educated adults who think before they strike another person. This book is intended to stimulate further efforts in that direction.

REFERENCES

Adorno, T. W., Frenkel-Brunswik, E., Levinson, D., & Sanford, R. N. *The authoritarian personality.* New York: Harper and Brothers, 1950.

Anderson, K. A., & Anderson, D. E. Psychologists and spanking. *Journal of Clinical Child Psychology*, Fall, 1976, 46–49.

Aron, P. S., & Katz, M. L. Corporal punishment in the public school. *Harvard Civil Rights–Civil Liberties Law Review*, 6(19/1), 538–594.

Babcock, A. A cross-cultural examination of corporal punishment: An initial theoretical conception. Paper presented at the Conference on Child Abuse, Children's Hospital National Medical Center, Washington, D.C., February 19, 1977.

Bacon, G. & Hyman, I. *Brief of the American Psychological Association task force on the rights of children and youth as Amicus Curiae in support of petitioners.* The Supreme Court of the United States, No. 75–6527, 1976.

Bakan, D. On corporal punishment. Paper presented to the Board of Toronto Education, October 1, 1970.

Bandura, A. *Aggression: A social learning analysis.* Englewood Cliffs, N.J.: Prentice Hall, 1973.

————, Ross, D., & Ross, S. A. Imitation of film-mediated aggression. *Journal of Abnormal and Social Psychology*, 1963, 66(1), 3–11.

Barnhart, C. L. *American college dictionary.* New York: Random House, 1963.

Battle, E. S., & Rotter, J. B. Children's feelings of personal control as related to social class and ethnic group. *Journal of Personality*, 1963, 31, 482–490.

Black, H. C. *Black's law dictionary* (4th ed.). Minnesota: West Publishing Company, p. 408.

Bongiovanni, A. A review of research on the effects of punishment: Implications for corporal punishment in the schools. Paper presented at the Conference on Child Abuse, Children's Hospital National Medical Center, Washington, D.C., February 19, 1977.

Buttons, A. Some antecedents of felonies and delinquent behavior. *Journal of Clinical Child Psychology*, 1973, 2, 35–37.

California State Assembly. *Report on the administration of corporal punishment in California Public Schools for the year 1972–73 as required by concurrent resolution no. 69.* Sacramento: Author, 1973.

Chase, N. F. Corporal punishment in the schools. *Wall Street Journal,* March 11, 1975.

Children's Defense Fund. *Children out of school in America.* Cambridge, Mass.: Author, 1975.

_____. *School suspensions, are they helping children?* Cambridge, Mass.: Author, 1975.

Clarizio, H. *Some myths regarding the use of corporal punishment in the schools.* Paper presented at the annual meeting of the American Educational Research Association, April 2, 1975.

Coles, R. Growing up in America. *Time,* December 29, 1975, 27–29.

Corcoran, C. *Report on suspensions and corporal punishment.* Vermont State Department of Education, July 29, 1975.

Dewey, J. *The public and its problems.* New York: Henry-Holt Company, 1927.

DuCette, J., Wolk, S., & Soucar, E. A typical pattern in locus of control and non-adaptive behavior. *Journal of Personality,* 1972, *40*(2), 287–297.

Duffy, J. B. The relationship between authoritarian democratic classroom climate and teacher managerial success. Manuscript, Department of School Psychology, Temple University, 1971.

Ebel, R. L. The case for corporal punishment. Paper presented at the annual meeting of the American Educational Research Association, Washington, D.C., April 2, 1975.

Elardo, E. Implementing behavior modification procedures in an elementary school: Problems and issues. Paper presented at the annual meeting of the American Educational Research Association, New York City, April 1977.

Feshbach, S., & Feshbach, N. Alternatives to corporal punishment. *Journal of Clinical Child Psychology,* Fall 1973, *2,* 46–49.

Friedman, R. & Hyman, I. An analysis of state legislation regarding corporal punishment. Paper presented at the Conference on Child Abuse, Children's Hospital National Medical Center, Washington, D.C., February 20, 1977.

Gil, D. G. Violence against children. *Journal of Marriage and the Family,* 1971, *33*(4), 637–648.

Gallup, G. H. Eighth annual Gallup poll of the public attitudes toward the public schools. *Phi Delta Kappan,* October 1976, 187–200.

Goss v. *Lopez,* 95 S. Ct. 729 (Ohio 1975), 5.6.

Gwertzman, B. Human rights: The rest of the world sees them differently. *New York Sunday Times,* March 6, 1977, PE5.

Hapkiewicz, W. G. Research on corporal punishment effectiveness: Contributions and limitations. Paper presented at the annual meeting of the American Educational Research Association, Washington, D.C., April 2, 1975.

Hentoff, N. A. Parent-teachers' view of corporal punishment. *Today's Education,* May 1973, *62,* 18–24.

Hub (Kearney, Nebraska), October 20, 1976.

Hyman, I. A bicentennial consideration of the advent of child advocacy. *Journal of Clinical Child Psychology*, Winter 1976, *5*(3), 15–20. (b)

_____. Some effects of teaching style on pupil behavior. Doctoral dissertation, Rutgers University, 1964.

_____. Consultation in classroom management based on empirical research. Paper presented at the annual meeting of the American Psychological Association, Honolulu, September 3, 1972.

_____. (Producer). *School psychology consultation using the Kounin managerial system.* Philadelphia: Temple University, 1976. (a) (Videotape)

_____ & Schreiber, K. Selected concepts and practices of child advocacy in school psychology. *Psychology in the Schools*, 1975, *2*(1), 50–58.

It's time to hang up the hickory stick. *Nations Schools*, November 1972.

Ingraham v. *Wright*, 95 S. Ct. 1401, at 1406, citing 525 F. 2d 909 (1976), at 917.

Kempe, C. H. et al. The battered child syndrome. *Journal of the American Medical Association*, 1962, *18*(1), 17–24.

Keniston, K. Do Americans really like children? *Today's Education*, November–December, 1975, 16–21.

Kounin, J. S. *Discipline and group management in the classroom.* New York: Holt, Rinehart, and Winston, 1970.

Mackowsky, H. The effects of teacher's locus of control, teacher's knowledge of intellectual potential and informational source status of teacher's judgments of children's expected academic ability. Doctoral dissertation, Temple University, 1973.

Manning, J. Discipline in the good old days. *Phi Delta Kappan*, December 1959, 114.

Marino, M. The effectiveness of teacher centered versus case centered consultation in the reduction of classroom management errors and negative classroom behavior of students. Doctoral dissertation, Temple University, 1975. *Dissertation Abstracts International*, 1975.

Maurer, A. All in the name of the "last resort." Paper presented at the Conference on Child Abuse, Children's Hospital National Medical Center, Washington, D.C., February 20, 1977.

Marberry v. *Pennsylvania.* 91, S. Ct. 499, 504–505, 1971.

Meyers, J., Martin, R., & Hyman, I. *School consultation.* Springfield, Ill.: Charles C. Thomas, 1977.

Miller, N. E. & Dollard, J. *Social learning and imitation.* New Haven, Conn.: Yale University Press. 1941.

National Education Association. *Report of the task force on corporal punishment.* Washington, D.C.: Author, 1972. (Library of Congress No. 22–85743).

Nussbaum, M., Hilmer, L., & Precup, R. *Brief of the National Education Association as Amicus Curiae in support of petitioners. Ingraham* v. *Wright*, US No. 75–6527, 1976.

O'Leary, K. D. & Drabman, R. Token reinforcement programs in the classroom: A review. *Psychological Bulletin*, 1971, *75*, 379–398.

Patterson, J. How popular is the paddle? *Phi Delta Kappan*, 1975, *56*, 707.

Perkins, H. V. Classroom behavior and underachievement. *American Educational Research Journal*, 1965, *2*, 1–12.

Peyton, H. G. A comparison of classroom managerial success between authoritarian and democratic teachers. Masters project, Department of School Psychology, Temple University, 1972.

Polier, J. W., Alvarez, L., Broderick, V., Karrison-Ross, P., & Weaver, R. *Corporal punishment and school suspensions: A case study*. New York: Metropolitan Applied Research Center, 1974.

Radbill, S. X. A history of child abuse and infanticide. In R. E. Helfer, & C. H. Kempe (Eds.), *The battered child* (2d ed.). Chicago: University of Chicago Press, 1974.

Reardon, F. J. & Reynolds, R. N. *Corporal punishment in Pennsylvania*. Department of Education, Division of Research, Bureau of Information System, November, 1975.

Reitman, A. Corporal punishment in the schools: The civil liberties objections. Paper presented at the Conference on Child Abuse, Children's Hospital National Medical Center, Washington, D.C., February 19, 1977.

————, Follmann, J., & Ladd, E. T. *Corporal punishment in the public schools: The use of force in controlling student behavior*. New York: American Civil Liberties Union, 1972.

Reshov, J. Child abuse: What the educators should know. *NJEA Review*, November 1973, *47*(3), 14–15.

Roberts v. *Way*. 398, F. Supp. 856 (D. Va. 1975), CIV A, No. 74, 302, 1975.

Rogers, C. R. *Client centered therapy*. Boston: Houghton-Mifflin Company, 1951.

Rosenshine, B. Teaching behaviors related to pupil achievement. Paper delivered at the annual meeting of the National Council for the Social studies, Washington, D.C., 1968.

———— & Furst, N. Research in teacher performance criteria. In B. O. Smith (ed.), *Research in teacher education*. Englewood Cliffs, N.J.: Prentice-Hall, 1971.

Rosenthal, R. & Jacobson, L. *Pygmalion in the classroom: Teacher expectations and pupils intellectual development*. New York: Holt, Rinehart and Winston, 1968.

Sanders, S. G. & Yarbrough, J. S. Bringing order to an inner city school. *Phi Delta Kappan*, 1976, *58*(4), 333–334.

Sandford, N. The approach to the authoritarian personality. In J. L. McGary (ed.), *Psychology of personality*. New York: Grove Press, 1956.

Schumacher, C. *Report of incidents*. Pittsburgh: Committee for the Abolition of Corporal Punishment, 1971.

Schultz, N. & Hyman, I. Consistency of classroom climate of high school teachers for different ability groups. Paper presented at the annual meeting of the New Jersey Education Association, Atlantic City, November 5, 1971.

Shaffer, S. M. *Corporal punishment survey.* Pittsburgh: Board of Education, Office of Research, June 13, 1968.

Skinner, B. F. *Beyond freedom and dignity.* New York: Alfred A. Knopf, 1971.

_____. *The behavior of organisms.* New York: Appleton, Century, Crofts, 1938.

_____. The science of learning and the art of teaching. *Harvard Educational Review,* 1954, *24,* 86–97.

Solomon, D., Houlihan, K. A., & Parelius, R. J. Intellectual achievement responsibility in negro and white children. *Psychological Reports,* 1969, *24,* 479–483.

Survey: Good teachers also creative disciplinarians. *Emphasis* (South Carolina Education Association), August 20, 1976, *1*(31).

Task force on alternatives to school disciplinary and suspension problems. *Alternatives to school disciplinary and suspension problems.* Columbia, S.C.: South Carolina State Department of Education, 1976.

Thorndike, R. L. A review of pygmalion in the classroom. *American Educational Research Journal,* 1968, *5*(4), 708.

Wallen, N. B. *Relationships between teachers' characteristics and student behavior—part 3.* Salt Lake City, Utah: University of Utah, 1966. (U.S. Office of Education, Research Project No. SAEOE 5–10–181.)

Welsh, R. Severe parental punishment and delinquency. *Journal of Clinical Child Psychology,* 1974, *3.*

Wineman, D., & James, A. *Policy statement: Corporal punishment in the public schools.* Detroit: Metropolitan Detroit branch of the American Civil Liberties Union of Michigan, 1967.

Wohlford, P., & Chibucos, T. Research evidence on corporal punishment in schools: Needs and roadblocks. Paper presented at the annual meeting of the American Psychological Association, Chicago, September 1975.

PART II

•

HISTORICAL PERSPECTIVES

The information presented in the Introduction and in many of the essays which follow clearly demonstrates that corporal punishment in American homes and schools is a firmly entrenched tradition. However, as with many traditions, the true historical context may be either unknown or poorly understood. While many advocates of corporal punishment preach "moderation and love" it is obvious that the major intent of the practice is to inflict pain upon the body of the recipient. While the putative purpose is to change children's behavior, an examination of historical evidence reveals that the end result of this practice has often been disaster for children. The first essay by Gertrude Williams documents the historical precedents for extreme physical cruelty which is now considered child abuse. Dr. Williams attempts to demonstrate how the history of childhood in Western society is a chronicle of familial, religious, economic, and politico-legal sanctions for violence against children. Dr. Williams's presentation is somewhat polemical and tends to represent her own view of child advocacy. However, it is also a scholarly attempt to relate, through historical analysis, one course of child abuse in our society, the acceptance of hitting children.

While the Williams's article speaks of the Anglo-Saxon tradition of violence against children, the essay by C. B. Freeman presents a brief history of attempts to eliminate the flogging of English schoolchildren in the seventeenth century. While evidence of authorship is not clear, it is apparent that in 1669 and in 1698 petitions against the flogging of schoolchildren were presented to Parliament. C. B. Freeman, an Englishman and librarian, offers an interesting analysis of the unsuccessful movement to end flogging of English schoolchildren. Corporal punishment, although under more control and for the most part less severe than in the seventeenth century, is still practiced in English schools.

John Manning's article, "Discipline in the Good Old Days," was written in 1959 when the public was concerned about gang violence in the schools. The context of his writing of historical practices in American education is interesting when one considers the current concern of "newly discovered" violence in American schools. Manning's description of the schools of early New England clearly demonstrates the continued Anglo-Saxon religious and educational belief in the use of physical punishment on children.

The final essay in this section provides a detailed description of the statutory banning of corporal punishment in New Jersey schools in 1867. This detailed analysis is important for several reasons. While educators were beginning to forgo the use of the rod and local schools were forbidding its use, New Jersey was the first state to make it illegal. It was not until 1972 that the next of four states (as of 1978) passed similar legislation. Also, it is interesting to consider the reasons for the New Jersey action which may surprise the reader. Finally, Donald Raichle provides a continuing chronicle of the abuses of the practice and the reactions of educators to those abuses.

The section on historical perspectives provides the reader with an overview of the practice of corporal punishment in the home and school as a tradition in Western culture. While historical material offers the reader actual circumstances and cases, all of the articles also suggest etiology. To some extent this overlaps with the next section of the book which examines the roots of the practice from psychological, anthropological, and sociological perspectives. Therefore, by providing a constant interface between theory and practice, the overlap should enhance the reader's comprehension of the problem.

1

Social Sanctions
for Violence against Children:
Historical Perspectives

Gertrude J. Williams

•

Since the dawn of humanity, children have been treated with incredible cruelty and have had little recourse to the law which regarded them as things, not persons. They have been tortured, burned, dipped in ice water and rolled in the snow in order to "harden" them, flogged daily, starved, worked to death, sexually abused, and buried alive with their dead parents. Swaddled babies have been thrown around like balls for amusement. The upper-class child was not spared from socially sanctioned abuse; indeed, the brother of King Henry IV was dropped and killed as a child when he was being passed like a toy from one window to another. Children have been forced to observe public hangings and to examine rotting corpses to teach them what happens to bad children when they become adults. Special dummies have been used to terrorize children into being good, and several of them died of fright during these graphic lessons.

Laws against child abuse had rarely been enforced until 1874. In that year the director of the Society for the Prevention of Cruelty to Animals, which had been founded nine years earlier to enforce animal protection laws, petitioned the New York Supreme Court to remove an abused child, Mary Ellen Wilson, from her parents. *The New York Times* gave the case extensive coverage, and the ensuing public support led to the founding of the Society for the Prevention of Cruelty to Children several months later. Since that time, except for the investigations of Caffey, Kempe, Helfer, Gil, and a few other pioneers, child abuse continued to be a socially repressed, scientifically and professionally unfashionable topic for the last one hundred years.

This essay first appeared in the *Journal of Clinical Child Psychology*, Winter 1973, Vol. V, No. 3, 2–11. Reprinted by permission, *Journal of Clinical Child Psychology*, 1100 N.E. 13th, Oklahoma City, Oklahoma, 73117.

Suddenly in the seventies, child abuse has been rediscovered amidst much fanfare, media coverage, political attention, and publicity regarding the alleged vast amounts of federal funds spent on projects purporting to prevent and eliminate it. The message we are apparently expected to receive from all the clamor is that this burgeoning child abuse industry demonstrates that America is a child-caring nation.

It is my thesis that the long overdue furor over this centuries' old practice is a red herring which diverts attention from two threatening realities. First, the hullabaloo obscures the fact that parental child abuse is a manifestation of deeply rooted Anglo-Saxon traditions and American social institutions and ideologies which reinforce filicidal impulses. Secondly, the exclusive definition of child abuse as parental violence against children deflects the public's focus away from the child-wrecking supported by the sins of omission and commission of industry, government, organized religion, schools, and other social structures in America.

A critique of the case-oriented, remedial strategies applied to individual children and families and emphasis on the filicidal ethos in America in no way demean the contributions of countless devoted workers who are saving the lives and improving the quality of life of many abused children. These workers are especially aware of the social context of child abuse as they observe every day the child-wrecking influences of the socially sanctioned use of physical force in child rearing, legally endorsed child battering in schools, unemployment and dehumanized employment, housing rip-offs and other stressors which represent business as usual in America and which contribute to parental child abuse. Furthermore, children whose parents do not batter them to brain damage are being brain-damaged by lead paint in FHA-approved hovels and brain-damaged *in utero* from pollutants permitted by the industries where their parents work; then there are the "Kentucky-fried children" in whose brains the light is being extinguished in many of the franchised baby bins often used as a last resort by parents who have been denied developmental day care by the government in order, incredibly, "to preserve family life."

Moreover, filicidal impulses appear to be a significant component of adult, especially parental, impulses, but it has been examined primarily within the context of severe parental child abuse. Although compassion for children—what I term filiphilic impulses—is also a significant component of adult emotions, it does not appear to neutralize filicidal impulses and appears to require strong social supports to maintain it. There is little evidence that the American way of life—its institutions, ideologies, and practices—can tip the balance in favor of reinforcing filiphilic impulses and extinguishing, or at least attenuating, filicidal impulses.

Beneath the surface of severe parental child abuse is a violence-ridden society which sanctions, contributes to, or is indifferent to pandemic violences against children. As Gil (1970) stated, "The choice of symptoms through which intra-psychic conflicts are expressed by members of a society tends to be influenced by the culture of that society. Symptoms of personality deviance involve exaggerated levels of culturally sanctioned trends" (p. 8). Freud contended that we need sensational, socially disruptive, destructive events in order to shock the public into awareness of the extent to which a society has failed to meet the human needs of its citizens. Thus, despite the fanfare, the myriad expressions of violence against American child-citizens will continue to increase until the carnage, perhaps, shocks the public into radical transformations of the American way of life.

Let us briefly examine some of the historical roots of filicidal impulses in the Anglo-Saxon literary heritage and in Western religious and politico-legal institutions.

Childhood, a Chronicle of Cruelty

The history of childhood reveals the extent to which filicial impulses have been woven into the fabric of the daily lives of children. Familial, religious, economic, and politico-legal institutions sanctioned violence against children and supported a view of them as chattels of parents or the state, as things—indeed, evil things, demons born of original sin—for whom compassion was irrelevant. Furthermore, as G. B. Williams (1976) has stated:

> . . . a child was worthless as a child; he attained his worth when he reached adulthood. His importance as a child was identical with his future importance as an adult. Thus, strict guidelines as to what qualities made up an admirable adult evolved and varied slightly from culture to culture. The purpose of childhood was to bring out these qualities so that they would be emphasized as an adult and to do away with "the foolishness bound up in the heart of a child." Since children were considered worthless individuals, the means of achieving a respectable adult did not matter, and the ends could always justify the means in any case. (p. 224)

The filicidal side of parenting has been investigated only recently in publications on the history of childhood, especially in the work of deMause (1974). This work gives evidence against myths of childhood as inherently happy, of instinctive parental love of children, and of child abuse as a rare twentieth-century expression of individual psychopathology. Let us take a brief excursion into the chamber of horrors that has often characterized the history of childhood.

Literary Heritage. Anglo-Saxon literature often transmitted a role expectation of the child as victim and recipient of unquestioned violence in the child-adult relationship. This literary heritage is so reflexively accepted that we fail to be horrified by legends, children's stories, even nursery rhymes that express filicidal impulses. Reflect on the message of helplessness conveyed to the drowsy child by this favorite lullaby (Iona and Peters, 1951):

> Rockaby, baby, on the treetop,
> When the wind blows, the cradle will rock,
> When the bough breaks the cradle will fall,
> And down will come baby, cradle and all. (p. 377)

The old Anglo-Saxon *Fable of the Bees* (Mandeville, 1970) tells children:

> It is our Parents that first cure us of natural Wildness and break in us the Spirit of Independency we are all born with; It is to them that we owe the first Rudiments of our Submission; and to the Honour and Deference which children pay to Parents, all Societies are obliged for the principle of Human Obedience. (p. 51)

Children in sixteenth-century England were described as possessing a stubbornness and natural pride which should be broken and beaten down in order that the foundation for their education might be based on humility, tractability and other virtues (deMause, 1974).

The unquestioned acceptance of corporal punishment by children themselves is expressed in this verse you may have sung as you jumped rope as a child or which your children are singing now (Abrahams, 1969):

> Down by the ocean, down by the sea,
> Johnny broke a milk bottle
> And blamed it on me.
> I told Ma, Ma told Pa.
> Johnny got a spanking. Ha! Ha! Ha!
> How many spankings did he get?
> [Count till the jumper misses (p. 101)]

Here is another jump rope rhyme in which filicidal impulses are openly expressed (Abrahams, 1969):

> Fudge, Fudge, call the judge! Mama has a newborn baby.
> It isn't a boy; it isn't a girl. It's just an ordinary baby.
> Wrap it up in toilet paper!
> Throw it down the elevator!
> First floor, miss! Second floor, miss! Third floor, miss!
> [Jumper continues till misses and baby hits (p. 51)]

Do you recall Goldilocks, the eternal child-symbol? The storybook says, "She was a naughty girl who jumped out the window, and whether she broke her neck in the fall, or ran into the woods and was lost there, or found her way out and got whipped for being a bad girl and playing truant, no one can say." We can say, however, that all Goldilocks's options involve pain. Here is a quaint verse from the *Oxford Dictionary of Nursery Rhymes* (Iona & Peters, 1951):

When I went up to Sandy Hill
I met a sandy boy;
I cut his throat, I sucked his blood
And left his skin a-hanging-o. (p. 377)

Thus, part of our Anglo-Saxon literary heritage expresses an unquestioned, often sadistically humorous violence against children which, until very recently, had not even been examined, let alone questioned.

Religious Traditions. Another significant part of our literary heritage, a hallmark of Anglo-Saxon religious institutions, is the Bible whose references to inflicting pain on and killing children are numerous and which often provides justification for violence against children by today's parents, teachers, and other child caretakers. Although many clerics offer various interpretations to these references and while religious sentiment often stimulates filiphilic impulses, as psychoanalyst Rheingold (1964) contends, ". . . the destructive mother and the authoritarian church have two things in common: their power is founded on fear and both are cloaked in sanctity."

Biblical sanctions of violence against children extend far beyond Proverbs (13:24): "He that spareth the rod hateth his son, but he that loveth him chasteneth him." Chronicles (28:3; 33:6) refers to burning children; Joshua (6:26) and Kings (16:34) refer to the common early practice of putting live children in the foundations of buildings; Deuteronomy refers to stoning children to death; Kings 2 describes disobedient children being torn apart by bears. Cannibalism of children is sanctioned in Leviticus (26:28, 29); God tells the Jews that if they fail to follow his commandments, ". . . then I will walk contrary unto you in fury; and I, even I, will chastise you seven times for your sins. Any ye shall eat the flesh of your sons, and the flesh of your daughters shall ye eat." According to Jewish commentary, Adam's first wife, Lilith, attacked children in their sleep. In some homes children who laughed too hard were slapped lest jealous Lilith murder them.

Christianity began with the "slaughter of the innocents" from which Jesus is presumed to have been saved. According to Matthew (2:16), when Herod was mocked, he became ". . . exceeding wroth and sent forth and slew all the children that were in Bethlehem and in all the coasts thereof, from two years and older." In commemoration of this slaughter, Innocents Day was celebrated in most Christian countries until recently by ritually whipping children.

The biblical association of children as inherently pain-inducing to women prior to and during childbirth may have an important relationship, according to Rheingold (1964), to the pain inflicted in turn by the mother, an especially thought-provoking hypothesis in light of recent research suggesting a relationship between child abuse and difficult pregnancy and delivery. Dick-Read (1972), author of *Childbirth without Fear*, reported that the authority of the Bible was used to oppose the introduction of obstetric anaesthesia because it would "rob God of the deep, earnest cries of women in labor."

In short, although new-thought religions, humanistic clergy, and such parts of the Bible as The Prodigal Son advocate compassion toward children, the apperceptive mass of Western so-called civilization still contains ideologies which support filicidal impulses: the doctrine of original sin, parental destructiveness sanctioned by a diety that is often a model of violence to his own figurative children, the association of femaleness with wickedness and children with pain, and a view of children as wild and satanic who need to have the devil literally beaten out of them.

Political Institutions. Throughout history, politico-legal and economic institutions influenced the development of filicidal impulses through the definition of children as chattel. Indeed, domination of children by parents has been used to justify slavery, colonialism, and tyranny, for the family has often been viewed as the model for the state. Even Aristotle, ancient proponent of democracy, stopped short of applying democratic principles to children and slaves: "The justice of a master or a father is a different thing from that of a citizen, for a son or slave is property, and there can be no injustice done to property" (Russell, 1969, p. 186). Seneca, stoical political philosopher, concluded that the mutilation of children to exploit them for money was not only not wrong but was a service to children whose parents had abandoned them, especially since the practice did no harm to the state, precious Rome. Said Seneca (deMause, 1974):

> Look on the blind wandering about the streets leaning on their sticks, and those with crushed feet, and still again, look on those with broken limbs. This one is without arms, that one has had his shoulders pulled down out of shape in order that his grotesqueries may excite laughter. . . . Let us go to the origin of all those ills—a laboratory for the manufacture of human wrecks—a cavern filled with the limbs torn from living children. . . . What wrong has been done to the Republic? On the contrary, have not these children been done a service inasmuch as their parents had cast them out?
> (p. 31)

So unquestioned is the chattel status of children that those who justify dominance over others "frequently employ a familial imagery: they analogically transform themselves into parents and, simultaneously . . . infantalize their inferiors . . . . black, yellow, and red people have been transmuted by whites into children; colonized peoples have been called children by imperial powers; and many a monarch ruled over children subjects" (Wallace, 1974). It is instructive to reflect on our own status as children in the eyes of Britain prior to the American Revolution. The American colonists were "Children of one common Mother, and embarked in one common cause, the Welfare of their Parent." Regarding taxation of the colonists, the British contended that "to lay even a heavy Burden upon faithful and dutiful children . . . must at all times be allowed to be praiseworthy."

Having been raised by authoritarian parents, the colonists, despite their rebellion, perhaps transmitted, as many formerly abused parents transmit to their children, a tradition of minority group abuse in their treatment of Indians and blacks. Rogan (1971) postulated that somehow a feeling of paternal benevolence of a father for his children, also supported a policy of death and dispossession for Indians and blacks who were only children in the eyes of the colonists. Child destruction was accomplished by the white father whose maturity enabled him to accept actions which led to Indian extinction. There were few feelings of regret or responsibility.

Apologists for racism in the nineteenth century used the model of unquestioned family tyranny for explaining the role of the whites to black slaves. Black slaves were always "boys," no matter how old. The masters were parents and guardians of the "children." Perhaps, he absorbed this ideological heritage long before America came into existence from such viewpoints as that of a seventeenth-century British theorist who said that fathers of families governed by no other law than their own will, not the wills of their sons or servants (Burrows & Wallace, 1972).

Thus, the family scenario of authoritarian parent and child-chattel was part of the paternalistic heritage of our founding fathers to which our founding mothers were often exposed, for they too were chattels of their husbands. This is the heritage that continues to shape our treatment of children, women, and minority group child-surrogates. Let us examine the current institution of the family.

The Family: Breeding Ground for Violence

Like Charity, Violence Begins at Home. Just as the myth of unalloyed parental love provides an erroneous model of the parent-child relationship and obstructs awareness and investigation of filicidal impulses, so the "Walton's myth," initiated by a popular TV show about the Walton family, perpetuates an erroneous model of the family as harmonious haven and obstructs awareness and investigation of family disruption and violence. The facts of intra-family violence fly in the face of the "Walton's myth" of two gently loving partners who kiss and make up after an occasional love-enhancing tiff, who never beat or wish to kill their children, all of whom look like the cherubs in toilet paper ads, whose earnest John-boy adolescents never use acid or shove their parents around and are ever eager to contribute to endless, hopelessly constructive family conferences. FBI and police data expose this fatuous myth: violence in the home is the major source of violence committed in the United States. Twenty-five percent of all homocides occur within the family. About half of these are spouse murders; about one-seventh are child murders. Between 1960 and 1965 more policemen were killed responding to domestic disturbances than to any other calls (FBI, 1966). Clearly, the family that stays together often slays together.

Referring to findings that child abuse occurred within all socio-economic classes and in normal families, Gil (1973) stated:

> This should surprise no one as the use of physical force in the rearing and disciplining of children is widely accepted in our society. Common sense suggests that whenever corporal punishment is widely used, extreme cases are bound to occur and children will be injured. Quite frequently, acts aimed at merely disciplining children will, because of chance factors, turn into serious accidents. Our studies indicate that the widespread acceptance in our culture of physical discipline of children is the underlying factor of physical child abuse. (p. 8)

Another centuries' old expression of family violence has been rediscovered now that child abuse has come out of the closet, namely, wifebattering, a socially sanctioned practice euphemistically referred to as "a family dispute." Again, violence is word-magically disguised as discipline. As the old Anglo-Saxon proverb advised: "A wife, a spaniel, and a walnut tree; the more they're beaten, the better they be." The Anglo-Saxon-derived term "rule of thumb" is based on a husband's right to beat his wife with a weapon no thicker than his thumb "in order to enforce the salutary restraints of domestic discipline."

Aggression and Intimacy: An Enduring Dyad.   Although Freud did much to dispel the myth of unalloyed filial and sibling love and emphasized the importance of becoming aware of negative feelings toward parents, the myth of the abnormality of hostility—and certainly murderous impulses—toward children persisted. Parents are inadequately prepared for the reality that, whether or not intimacy breeds contempt, it does breed aggression and puts the loved one at risk for violence. The greatest personal violence occurs in families where it appears that aggressive behavior may be closely tied to emotional contingencies associated with the daily stress which may be part of complex interpersonal relations with family members (Singer, 1971).

A variety of other investigators have observed that intimacy and aggression seem to be an enduring dyad. In the early twentieth century the social theorist George Simmel conceptualized the paradox of intimate relationships. He hypothesized that the more people have in common with each other as whole persons, the more readily they become involved in each other's behaviors; therefore, there is also a disproportionate amount of violence as the closeness of relationships increase (Simmel, 1955). Anthropologist Malinowski (1948) contended that close social relations increased the probability of violent behavior. Ethologist Lorenz (1967) observed that among animals intraspecific aggression can certainly exist without its counterpart, love, but conversely there is no love without aggression. Lorenz discussed the fragility of aggression-inhibiting mechanisms among animal mothers with respect to their offspring. He indicated that all livestock breeders are aware that seemingly slight disturbances of animal mothers may disrupt the aggression-inhibiting mechanism. He cites as an example a case when an airplane, flying low over a silverfox farm, caused all the mother vixens to eat their young (Lorenz, 1967). In the laboratory, the application of stress to post-partum mother rats elicited violent behavior including cannibalism toward their offspring. It may be that ferocity is a part of mothering and may have survival value in that it is elicited by attackers of the offspring but that it gets misdirected to the offspring when the mother is under stress.

"The Settled Tradition"—Legalized Child Battering in American Schools

Another American institution in which violence against children is sanctioned is the schools (Williams, 1975). All over America public schools permit corporal punishment. Children are beaten with rattans, straps, fists, belts, and boards; they are slapped, forced to eat cigarettes, pinched and thrown against walls. For what crimes? Not paying attention, talking without permission, chewing gum, smoking, refusing to leave the cloakroom, not trying hard enough . . . and now, playing kickball after the schoolbell has rung, the crime for which the U.S. Supreme Court legally sanctioned corporal punishment of a psychologically fragile sixth grader. In its retrogressive ruling last year, it let stand without comment a federal court decision to allow teachers to use corporal punishment on children against parental objections.

Just when the Child Abuse Protection Act is being implemented amidst all the be-kind-to-children clamor in the United States, the Supreme Court sanctions violence against children at school. It maintained that "the State's interest in maintaining order must be balanced against the mother's right to control the means of disciplining her child . . . outlawing corporal punishment bucks a settled tradition of countenancing such punishment when reasonable." What is reasonable? If an adult continued playing kickball after the coach had blown the whistle and the coach had beaten him or her on the buttocks with a foot-long wooden drawer divider, the coach would be viewed as unreasonable if not demented. When the same action is taken against the plaintiff, an eleven-year-old schoolboy, the action is viewed as reasonable.

Other irrationalities emerge from the decision. The Child Abuse Protection Act legally requires employees who have contact with children to report immediately their "reasonable suspicions" of parents who batter their children. Bruises on a child inflicted by a parent are examples of "suspected child abuse"; bruises inflicted on a child by a teacher are examples of "the settled tradition of corporal punishment." This paradox is discussed by Chase (1975) in *A Child is Being Beaten*. The author questions the long-term value of taking a parent to court for hitting a child when teachers may perform the same act with virtual immunity. If courts may remove children from parents because of abuse, Chase asks, why does society allow those same children to be handed over to the public schools for abuse? Furthermore, who will report the teachers who are subject to the same mandatory reporting laws as parents? Certainly not the parents, for the Court has upheld the teachers' abuse of the child. Will reporting a teacher do any good? Chase commented that a teacher kept trying to report a pattern of repeated beatings of children in his school in New York City, but school authorities did not respond. Finally, the teacher went to *The New York Times* with a wooden paddle as evidence. The result? The teacher was suspended for going outside school channels.

Medical data document spinal and whiplash injuries, sciatic nerve damage, CNS hemorrhage as well as interference with the psychological developmental tasks of childhood by corporal punishment (Friedman, 1976). Innumerable investigators have emphasized the irrationality of corporal punishment and have suggested effective, growth-inducing alternatives (ACLU, 1972; Bakan, 1971; Button, 1973; Divoky, 1973; Feshback, 1973; Feshback & Feshback, 1973, 1976; Hagebak, 1973; Kozol, 1967; Maurer, 1973, 1974; Meier, 1976; NEA, 1972; Skinner, 1976; Valusek, 1974, Welsh, 1976a, 1976b). Despite evidence and research-based recommendations, corporal punishment against children continues in the schools. Just as battering parents serve as a model of violence to their children, so the schools, a primary social institution, serve as a model of violence to parents, especially brutal, marginal parents who receive legal sanction through the schools to batter their children.

Assaults on teachers and vandalism by students have often been used to justify physical coercion of children, another irrationality, for the issue of self-defense by a teacher against assault by a student is an entirely different issue from the use of corporal punishment of children by teachers. Furthermore, data indicate that the children who are hit at school are the younger, smaller elementary school children, many of them handicapped or emotionally fragile, a significant number of them from the ghettos and barrios. What teacher is going to strike a husky, healthy, middle- or upper-class high school adolescent who is able to strike back? One writer suggests that cruel individuals are attracted to professions which offer them the possibility to act out their cruelty; therefore, a considerable percentage of teachers may be attracted to the profession since it gives them power over helpless individuals (Rothman, 1971). Welsh's (1976a) findings suggest that children who received corporal punishment in school when they are too weak to defend themselves may retaliate when they are older and stronger by assaulting teachers and vandalizing schools.

Corporal punishment in schools is not a universally required "teacher tool": it has been abolished in Denmark, Finland, Norway, Sweden, Holland, the Soviet Union, Israel, and Japan. It is practiced in English-speaking countries such as Australia, Britain, and the United States. In 1853, a judge of the Indiana Supreme Court noted that it was illegal for a master to beat his apprentice and an officer an ordinary sailor, and he wondered "why the person of a schoolboy should be less sacred." Responding to the Anglo-Saxon "settled tradition" of violence against children, the United States Supreme Court failed to ask in 1975 why the person of an American school child should be less sacred.

It is obvious that the extent of violence against children at school and at home is irrationally denied in the face of evidence. Violence against children by parents and teachers is discipline; violence against parents and teachers by children is assault. A teacher's lack of discipline—it is the least competent teachers who resort to corporal punishment—is magically transformed into discipline. A child who strikes a teacher creates disorder; a teacher who strikes a child creates order in the classroom.

Why America Needs a Child Abuse Industry

The reasons for the current clamor over the centuries' old practice of child abuse and the focus on individual sensational cases of parental child battering become clear. Severe parental child abuse in America is the tip of the iceberg (Gelles, 1973). The glacier from which that iceberg cracked off is the violence-ridden American way of life. The child abuse industry merely gets beneath the tip of the iceberg but creates the illusion that the glacier is nonexistent. By denying its existence, we exclude from awareness a multitude of threatening realities. We can avoid the pain of getting in touch with the darker side of parenthood which is manifested, not merely in sensational child abuse, but in the resentments, hostilities and filicidal impulses of normal parents who, often guilt-laden, repress such socially reprehensible feelings. Glimpses of the cultural expression of filicidal impulses are revealed in the assertion of 70 percent of mothers polled that they would not have had children if they could choose again; in the glib acceptance by all too many parents and other adults of marijuana and other drugs as "youthful experimentation" in the face of evidence that usage during adolescence is psychologically destructive and probably medically harmful; in the depiction of the child, as in early times, as satanic expressed in such recent fiction as *Rosemary's Baby, The Exorcist*, and *The Omen* (Maynard, 1976); in the ironic reality that the most neglected variable in the child abuse field is the abused children themselves; in the fact that investigations relating specifically to abused children and their best interests have significantly lagged behind other noteworthy advances in the field (Williams, 1976); in the passive public acceptance of television violence which is known to have harmful effects on children (Cater & Strickland, 1975) and which probably enhances violence among adults.

The National Commission on the Causes and Prevention of Violence drew some interesting conclusions from their study (Steinmetz and Straus, 1974). They suggested that the United States, among advanced industrial states is not only a leader in technology, but is also pre-eminent in the level of violence. The high level of violence has existed since colonial days. This early history of violence may be related to the harsh realities of the frontier but may also be a function of people who were the inhabitants of the frontier. Many were from the lowest and most violent strata of British society. Many were actually convicted criminals who were punished by banishment to the American Colonies. The child abuse industry helps to deflect attention from our violent history and social sanctions for violence against children through the Anglo-Saxon literary heritage and institutions and to preserve the fiction that the American way of life is nonviolent and authentically child-caring.

America needs a child abuse industry to help us ignore the contributions of industry and government to the stresses associated with parental child battering and to institutionalized child abuse. By focusing on the red herring of severe parental child abuse, we can refrain from redefining child abuse within the social context emphasized by Gil (1973, p. 8): "Any act of commission or omission by individuals, institutions or society as a whole, and any condition resulting from such acts of inaction which deprives children of equal rights and liberties and/or interferes with their optimal development." Alvy (1975) contends that such a comprehensive approach:

> . . . indicts us for not protecting the bodies of four million children who are estimated to be physically or sexually abused or severely neglected by parents or other individual caretakers. It indicts us for impeding the overall development of the seven million children who we allow to be reared in the abusive child rearing conditions of poverty. It indicts us for denying certain rights of our 67 million youths. (p. 36)

As has been asserted elsewhere (Williams, G. J., 1974a), a nation that truly stands for child advocacy would oppose such child-wrecking influences in America as:

> . . . bureaucratic logrolling, police harassment, harmful policies of archaic social agencies, violations of health and safety codes, anachronistic school systems and entrenched school boards, illegal consumer practices, slum landlords who are powerful bulwarks of the community. . . . Child advocacy in action means changing the odds against the powerless child by actively challenging and remaking diabolical structures within our society. (p. 48)

Even the focus on parental child abuse is threatening to reveal its social supports. Senator Mondale, author of the 1974 Child Abuse Prevention and Treatment Act which kicked off the child abuse industry, expressed deep concern about this. Mondale's reservations center around the use of the legislation to promulgate laws that do not really help abused children. His concern was so strong that he threatened that inadequate implementation by H.E.W. would result in his writing to all state legislatures recommending that they not adopt the Child Abuse Prevention and Treatment Act. The Model Child Protective Services Act to which he objects includes within the definition of child abuse "substantial risk of physical or mental injury to the child, including excessive corporal punishment" or failure "to supply the child with adequate food, clothing, shelter, education or medical care." Perhaps a well-publicized cottage industry is what the senator had in mind for abused American children.

Severe parental abuse and neglect are the extremes along the continuum of filicidal impulses reinforced by the American way of life. The child abuse industry preserves the illusion that massive improvements are being made in this one sensational area, and that no other major changes need to be made in an otherwise harmonious social order. Lulled by the mock harmony, America remains silent to the sufferings of millions of its children. As Dostoevsky wrote in The Brothers Karamazov (1958, p. 306):

"Listen, if all must suffer to pay for the eternal harmony, what have children to do with it, tell me please? It's beyond all comprehension why they should suffer, and why they should pay for the harmony."

REFERENCES

Abrahams, R. D. (ed.) *Jumprope rhymes.* Austin: University of Texas Press, published for the American Folklore Society, 1969.

Alvy, K. T. On child abuse: values and analytic approaches. *Journal of Clinical Child Psychology*, Spring 1975, 4 (1), 36–37.

American Civil Liberties Union. *Report of the national conference on corporal punishment in the public schools.* New York, 1972.

Bakan, D. The effects of corporal punishment in school. *Journal of the Ontario Association of Children's Aid Societies*, November 1971.

Baring, W. S. and Gould. *The annotated mother goose.* New York: Bramhall House, 1962.

Burrows, E. G. and Wallace, M. The American Revolution: The ideology and psychology of national liberation. *Perspectives in American History*, 6, 1972.

Button, A. Some antecedents of felonious and delinquent behavior. *Journal of Clinical Child Psychology*, Fall 1973, 2 (3).

Cater, D. and Strickland, S. TV violence and the child: The evolution and fate of the Surgeon General's report. New York: Russell Sage Foundation, 1975.

Chan, I. Head Start in the Socialist way. *New China*, January 1976, 1 (4).

✓ Chase, N. *A child is being beaten.* New York: Holt, Rinehart and Winston, 1975.

deMause, I. (ed). *The history of childhood.* New York: The Psychohistory Press, 1974.

Dick-Read, G. *Childbirth without fear.* New York: Harper & Row, 1972.

Divoky, D. Corporal punishment in U.S. schools. *Learning*, February 1973.

Dostoevsky, S. M. *Brothers Karamazov: collected works.* Vol. 9. Moscow: Gosuizdat, 1958.

Drabman, R. S., Thomas, M. H., and Jarvie, G. J. Will our children care? New evidence concerning the effects of televised violence on our children. Paper, University of Mississippi Medical Center, 1976.

Federal Bureau of Investigation. *Uniform crime reports*, 1966. Washington, D.C., U.S. Government Printing Office, 1967.

Feshbach, N. D. The effects of violence in childhood. *Journal of Clinical Child Psychology*, Fall 1973, 2 (3) 28–31.

―――― and Feshback, S. Parent rites vs. children's rights. In G. P. Koocher (ed.), *Children's rights and the mental health professions.* New York: Wiley & Sons, 1976.

Feshback, S. and Feshback, N. D. Alternatives to corporal punishment: Implications for training and controls. *Journal of Clinical Child Psychology*, Fall 1973, 2 (3), 46–48.

Friedman, D. B. Corporal punishment in the schools—Discipline or abuse? Paper presented at the annual convention of the American Psychological Association, September 1976, Washington, D.C.

Gelles, R. J. Child abuse as psychopathology: A sociological critique and reformulation. *American Journal of Orthopsychiatry*, July, 1973, 43, 611–621.

————. *The violent home.* Beverly Hills, Calif.: Russell Sage Publications, 1974.

Gil, D. G. Child abuse prevention act: Testimony before U.S. Senate Subcommittee on Children and Youth, March, 1973. Reprinted in *Journal of Clinical Child Psychology*, Fall 1973, 2 (3), 7–10.

————. *Violence against children: Physical child abuse in the United States.* Cambridge: Harvard University Press, 1970.

Gordon, G. Psychology and the worker. Paper presented at the annual convention of the American Psychological Association, September 1976, Washington, D.C.

Hagebak, R. Disciplinary practices in Dallas contrasted with school systems with rules against violence against children. *Journal of Clinical Child Psychology*, Fall 1973, 2 (3), 14–16.

Kozol, J. *Death at an early age.* Boston: Houghton Mifflin Company, 1967.

Lee, D. Nurseries in Factories? *New China*, January 1976, 1 (4).

Lorenz, K. *On aggression.* New York: Bantam Books, 1967.

Malinowski, B. An anthropological analysis of war. In *Magic, science and religion.* Glencoe, Ill.: Free Press, 1948.

Mandeville, B. *Fable of the bees.* London: Penguin Books, Ltd., 1970.

✔ Mauer, A. Corporal punishment. *American Psychologist*, August 1974, 29 (8), 614–626.

————. Spare the child! *Journal of Clinical Child Psychology*, Fall 1973, 2 (3), 4–6.

Maynard, J. The monster children. *Newsweek*, July 26, 1976.

Meier, J. H. Corporal punishment. Paper presented at the annual convention of the American Psychological Association, September 1976, Washington, D.C.

National Education Association. *Report of the task force on corporal punishment,* Washington, D.C., 1972.

Opie, I. and Opie P. (eds.). *The Oxford dictionary of nursery rhymes.* London: Oxford University Press, 1951.

Resnick, P. J. Child murder by parents: A psychiatric review of filicide. *American Journal of Psychiatry*, 1969, 126.

Rheingold, J. C. *The fear of being a woman: A theory of maternal destructiveness.* New York: Grune and Stratton, 1964.

Rickot, A. *Working for your life,* 1976, in press.

Rogan, M. P. Liberal society and the Indian question. *Politics and Society I*, May 1971, 269–312.

Rothman, G. *The riddle of cruelty.* New York: Philosophical Library, 1971.

Russell, B. *The history of western philosophy.* London: George, Allen and Unwin, 1969.

St. Louis Post Dispatch. PCBs and cancer. August 27, 1976, 2B.

✓ Sears, R. R., Maccoby, E. C., and Levin, H. *Patterns of child rearing.* New York: Harper and Row, 1957, 255–263.

Simmel, G. *Conflict and the web of group affiliations.* Glencoe, Ill.: Free Press, 1955.

Singer, J. L. (ed.). *The control of aggression and violence.* New York: Academic Press, 1971.

Skinner, B. F. Corporal punishment of children in the schools. Paper presented at the annual convention of the American Psychological Association, September 1976, Washington, D.C.

Soman, S. C. *Let's stop destroying our children.* New York: Hawthorn Books, 1976.

Steinmetz, S. K. and Straus, M. A. *Violence in the Family.* New York: Dodd, Mead and Company, 1974.

✓ Valusek, J. E. *People are not for hitting.* Wichita, Kan.: Valusek, 1974.

Wallace, M. Paternalism and violence. In P. P. Weiner and J. Fisher, *Violence and aggression in the history of ideas.* New Jersey: Rutgers University, 1974.

Welsh, R. S. Severe parental punishment and delinquency: A developmental approach. *Journal of Clinical Child Psychology,* Spring 1976, 5 (1), 17–23.

Williams, G. B. From brutality to humanity: A history of the maltreatment of children. Paper, St. Louis, Mo., 1976.

Williams, G. J. Abused children: Neglected variable in the child abuse field. Guest editorial. *Journal of Pediatric Psychology,* Spring 1976, 1 (2), 3–5.

———. Legalized child battering in U.S. public schools: An editor's reflections on pain. *Journal of Clinical Child Psychology,* Fall 1975, 4 (3), 56–57.

———. The psychologist as child advocate: Reflections of a devil's advocate. In G. J. Williams and S. Gordon, *Clinical child psychology: Current practices and future perspectives.* New York: Behavioral Publications, 1974a.

2

The Children's Petition of 1669 and its Sequel

C. B. Freeman

•

The prevalence of brutal flogging in seventeenth-century English schools is amply attested by the protests against it that have survived. John Brinsley of Ashby-de-la-Zouch, Milton's friend Samuel Hartlib and Charles Hoole of Rotherham are among a considerable band of writers on education who deplore the use of flogging except as a last resort and with severe restraint.[1] Still another Puritan, Hezekiah Woodward, tells how he learnt from his own bitter experience that "harshness loseth the heart and alienates the affections," and also retards scholastic progress; for he says of his own days at the grammar school, "I know not which lost me most time, feare or play. I know I played away much of the time (for all the sorrow) but, I know also, fear hindred me most, and cast me farthest back."[2]

To protest against the abuse was one thing. To promote an agitation for legislative action against it was quite another. Special interest attaches to the Children's Petition of 1669 and its sequel of 1698–9 because they represent two determined attempts to bring the matter into the arena of Parliament. The evidence of the first attempt is to be found in a very scarce little duodecimo of seventy pages, of which a copy may be seen in the British Museum: *The Children's Petition: or, A modest remonstrance of that intolerable grievance our youth lie under, in the accustomed severities of the school-discipline of this nation. Humbly presented to the consideration of the Parliament . . . Printed for Richard Chiswell . . . 1669.*

The petitioners describe themselves as "we the children of the land," and they deplore the fact that it is the custom to entrust to men who have no qualifications but a knowledge of Latin and Greek "the liberty to use such a kind of discipline over us, as that the spring-time of humane life, which in all other creatures is left at the greatest freedom to be sweet and

This essay first appeared in *The British Journal of Educational Studies*, 14 (May 1966), 216–223.

jocund, is defloured and consumed with bitterness and terror, to the drying up the very sap which should nourish our bodies, and those more lively spirits which should animate our minds in our future life, unto brave actions" (pp. 5–6).

It then becomes apparent, however, that this is no childish effort, and that the protest is not only against cruelty, but against sadism:

> And if it were only the evil of our suffering we had to complain of, feeling our unadvertent parents do give us up to this carnage, we should bear it: But when our sufferings are of that nature as makes our schools to be not meerly houses of correction, but of prostitution, in this vile way of castigation in use, wherein our secret parts, which are by nature shameful, and not be uncovered, must be the anvil exposed to the immodest eyes, and filthy blows of the smiter; We are confounded with the horror, and could wish we had some such way, as by turning up the soal of our schoe (which they use, they say, among the Turks) to present to you our grievance. (P. 7.)

The writer quotes *Hudibras*:

> The pedant in the school-boyes breeches
> Does claw and curry his own itches.

He complains that, whereas natural appetites find satisfaction, "the appetite which is unnatural, is infinite," so that the masters seek punishment for its own sake, and no respite can be hoped for.

The writer admits that there are some masters who do not punish their pupils in this way, and that there are some who have taken over the traditional method of punishment for no other motive than the good of their pupils. He recognizes, too, that discipline presents a genuine problem in the schools, and he has his own proposals for dealing with it. His most radical suggestion is that the man who "is not able to awe and keep a company of youth in obedience, without violence and stripes, should judge himself no more fit for that function, than if he had no skill in the Latin and Greek," and should not be chosen for the office of schoolmaster. No doubt many teachers of today, struggling through the blackboard jungle of our tougher urban areas, would be particularly interested in his next piece of advice:

> If any boy shall be negligent, or do unworthily, let him be turned out of the school to trap in the fields, or to nine-pins in the streets, amongst those rude and illiterate boyes who are no scholars. (P. 59.)

On the other hand, the reward of the diligent should be admission "to some more intimate converse of their master in reading of history, or other delightful studies."

When some offence arises which cannot be overlooked, the master is to take care not to punish in anger, but to consider the matter on the following day, when the boy shall undergo "a solemn kind of judicature," which may take the form of judgement by his peers. (One seems to remember that certain modern writers reject such a scheme on the grounds that boys would judge each other too harshly!) If the boy is found worthy of punishment, it may then be administered in the form of three strokes on the back, his doublet only being removed. The suggestion is made that "one of the vilest boys" should be picked out for executioner, and so be shamed. At the end of his tract, the writer re-affirms his petitionary purpose:

> We humbly implore the higher powers, that this impure practice, which hath continued in our schools hitherto, without controul or detection, (unless what hath been private only) may come under public censure, and consequently prohibition, and extermination.

Here, then, is a highly interesting little book, issued under the imprint of Richard Chiswell, who was to become one of the most reputable booksellers of his time, especially in the field of theological publications. Beyond that it contains no clue to its origins. The question of its ultimate fate, however, provokes our curiosity even more than the question of its authorship, and in this matter we have rather more evidence to go on. Our most important internal clue consists in some words printed opposite the title-page in one of the Bodleian copies. (In the British Museum copy the fly-leaf is missing, and in the other Bodleian copy it is blank.) The passage reads: "It is humbly desired this book may be delivered from one hand to another: and that gentleman who shall first propose the motion to the House, the book is his; together with the prayers of posterity." This gives the impression that the booklet was not a petition in the formal sense, but was printed primarily for circulation among Members of Parliament, in the hope that one of them would attempt to introduce legislation on the subject with which it dealt. (Presumably copies lacking the words addressed to M.P.s were issued for public sale.)

A later publication, *Lex Forcia* (1698), provides evidence that the Children's Petition was brought to the attention of Parliament in a more formal manner than the internal evidence would lead us to suppose. The author of this pamphlet writes:

> In the year 1669 these ensuing papers for the most part, not altogether (for there are many passages intermingled, not before in them, some changed, some left out) were printed in a little book in duodecimo, and licensed by Roger Le Strange, they being brought him by a knight of his acquaintance, and the book was presented by a lively boy (with a servant of that knight attending him) to the Speaker, and to several members of

the House, as a petition in behalf of the children of this nation; a quantity of them being paid for, and designed to that end.

From the same source we learn that at least one M.P. was aroused to interest:

> One of the members, and an active gentleman and schollar, had the thoughts (if not the resolution) to make a motion in regard to the petition, or purpose of it: But thinking it wise to consult with that Doctor at Westminster School, with whom he had conversation, it was a wrong box he went to, and it is no wonder if one so much concern'd (though there was not the least mention of him then in the book) should effectually disswade him from it. (P. 4.)

Dr. Busby of Westminster was, of course, a notorious flogger. Nor was the Member of Parliament wrong when he went on to suggest that the Cavalier Parliament was unlikely to take any action against the "long prevalency of a base, wicked, and injurious custom." Neither the Commons' nor the Lords' Journals make any reference to the matter, and the House of Lords papers calendared by the Royal Commission on Historical Manuscripts are equally silent. Nor, for that matter, do the registers of the Stationers' Company (in the printed transcript) make any reference to the licensing of the book by Roger L'Estrange, although the term catalogue, *Mercurius Librarius*, records its publication in its issue for Hilary Term, 1669–70.

We are thus left with many unsolved questions about the Petition of 1669. Who wrote it? Was it the Knight who took it to be licensed, and in any case who was he? Who was the lively boy (who, we are told, died shortly afterwards) who presented it to the Speaker on behalf of the nation's children, and was there any reaction apart from the ineffectual interest of one M.P.?

One thing we do know is that there was a sequel to all this in the publication nearly thirty years later of the pamphlet already mentioned: *Lex Forcia: being a sensible address to the Parliament, for an Act to remedy the foule abuse of children at schools, especially, in the great schools of this nation . . . Printed for R.C. and are to be sold by Eliz. Whitelock, 1698.* It is interesting to note that this was not published by some obscure bookseller, but, like the earlier book, by Richard Chiswell, who had by now risen to the top of the trade. Plainly a further attempt was to be made to exercise a direct influence upon Members of Parliament, for the imprint of another edition (or rather reissue) reads: "London: printed for a number to be sent, or presented to Parliament-Men. And the rest to be sold only by the booksellers in Westminster-Hall, (when such come) and no other-where else; there being but a few copies in all to be sold, 1699." On the back of the title-page in this edition is a paragraph which states: "For the fundamental discouraging of vice, according to the King's most gracious speech, Decemb. 9. 1698 and the Reformation of Manners (set a foot of late in the nation) a Bill . . . is *Id quod desideratur*." This paragraph is shared with yet another edition, which has the following quite different title page:

> Lex Forcia: being an address to the several Societies for the Reformation of Manners . . . That such a care may be taken of the education of young schollars, that a more ingenuous, modest, and virtuous disiplining [*sic*] them . . . may be brought into our schools, so as the beginning of that reformation may be put in practice there . . . By their timely endeavours to get a Bill prepared (and some Members to countenance and move it) against the sitting of Parliament, to that end. Published and propagated, but not written by *W.C.* Gent. London, A. Baldwin.

The last edition described is undated, but it was presumably issued about the same time as the one dated 1699, the two title-pages representing a two-pronged attack. One edition was to be distributed among the Members of Parliament themselves. The other was addressed to the members of the Societies for Reformation of Manners in the deliberate hope that they would approach such M.P.s as they were able to influence. Unfortunately, what we know of the work of the Societies suggests that they were much more interested in the promotion of punishment than in its abatement, although it is true that the suggestion that cruel flogging was a form of sexual perversion might have been thought to bring it within the scope of their campaigns against vice. Parliament also might have been presumed to have an interest in this aspect of the matter, since it was in response to a petition from the House of Commons that the King had issued the proclamation against vice dated 24 February 1698, which was followed later in the same year by his speech of 9 December. It looks as if the two editions of our pamphlet in 1699 were a deliberate attempt to use the occasion of the King's speech in order to make a weightier impression with a tract which had fallen flat in 1698. In the pamphlet itself the author asserts: "There is nothing but an Act of Parliament about the education of children can deliver the nation from this evil" (p. 17).

Two puzzles arise from a perusal of these title-pages: the anonymity of the work and its curious title. We are told explicitly in one edition that "W.C., Gent.," although he published and propagated the pamphlet, did not write it. Nevertheless, if we could discover his identity it might give us a clue. As it is, the only clue we have is a passage in which the author says that he started at a dame school, and later "went to the Free School where

I was born." This is meagre indeed. Since passages from the Children's Petition are interspersed quite freely among the new matter, it would seem reasonable to suppose that what we have is the original author doing a rehash of his own work, but this is far from certain.

For the significance of the title we have clear guidance in *The Children's Petition*, where the author says (p. 33): "We read of Marcus Portius, in the Roman story, who established a law, that no Roman citizen should be beaten by the magistrates with rods. He should be a tribune of the people by our vote, that could prefer a Lex Porcia in our schools, and some work-houses, where poor children are employed in this nation." Why this should have been altered to *Lex Forcia* in the title page and text of the later work is a mystery. The law in question is referred to by Livy, and by Sallust in his *De Coniuratione Catilinae*.[3] It was passed at the instance of M. Porcius Cato the elder, probably in 198 B.C.

In *Lex Forcia* the sexual aspect of flagellation is stressed even more than in *The Children's Petition*. It is suggested that "our lewd sparks' common prancks in late days" should have enlightened even those who formerly could see nothing sinister about school flogging.

> And certainly (I must needs say) for an accidental loose gentleman, to be tempted once or twice to using this sport, while their whores are at liberty to endure but so much as they list, it is not half so damn'd a mischief, as for the masters and dames doing the same wickedness, with the adding the hypocrisie, lye, and mask of a pretended justice, righteousness, and that holy thing discipline, in the doing. (P. 10.)

The author describes an incident in his own boyhood, when the master called him out, determined to find occasion for flogging him. When he did not stumble over reciting his lesson, the master was driven to find fault with his new stockings. If the mastery of a school gives such wonderful opportunities for satisfying impure appetites, we need not wonder "that Busby that transcending Rabbi . . . should not, at King Charles's coming in, be won to change this province, for any other tendered to him by the highest bounty."

On another page we read of "a spruce, generous, brave spirited lad," who, after a somewhat lenient regime at home, goes to Westminster and, "coming to see, and feel, what doings was there, is not long under the regiment of that Doctor, but his spirits are cowed, his parts lost, and he returns a mope home." Others, reacting differently, got pistols, and were only accidentally prevented from killing their master.

> There are such stories that might be told out of Westminster School, now the dreadful venerable Bard thereof is dead, Eaton School, Pauls School, formerly, and the like noted schools, that would make a heart of stone to

bleed. There have been masters arraigned at bar for the death of some boys. There are children have been ready to drown themselves, or make away themselves . . . rather than go to such masters. (P. 15.)

It is not, however, only the "foundation-schools" that are mentioned. Dame schools are alluded to much more than in the *Children's Petition*, and there are specific references to ill-treatment of girls.

A woman, that used to teach, and set girls to work, took a poor neighbour of mine's daughter to prentice, and finding some occasion, whips the girl, till she was stark dead; whereupon, the other girls crying out, she was dead! *Is she* (says the woman) *I'll fetch her alive again*: and whips on, from the first beginning to the end, a whole hour by the clock. (P. 16.)

The author is highly indignant that teachers should be allowed to wield such absolute power, when in truth theirs is only a subordinate power, derived from the natural power of the parents. He would have flogging abolished, but if "the major vote of the wise shall be for letting this custom still obtain," then control should be exercised over three things: the age of the scholar, the measure of the weapon, and the number of the stripes. He proposes that boys shall be exempt from such punishment after fourteen, and girls sooner; that the length of the rod shall be limited (say to half an ell); and likewise the number of stripes (say to three). "I say, if there were nothing more (though in a Bill concerning the Education of Youth, many a thing more would be thought on, and put in) could be done, such as an Act yet would be a good act, and to compass it, a very worthy exploit."

In a concluding outburst of indignation, the author condemns the current practice as the greatest of all evils which have public allowance:

The corruption of discipline. The bane of all good education. The infection of the school-master: the dishonour of their function. The infandum of the teacher: the horrendum of the taught. The stupid man's idol: a Tophet to those that have their eyes open. To the one a ludicrous matter: to the other, an iniquity to be punish'd by the judges. (P. 29.)

Epilogue

"Once and again, but Satan hindred," runs the colophon to *Lex Forcia*. It is well that the author could not know how much longer Satan was to hinder the extension of Christian mercy to the children of a Christian country—as if the text, "He that spareth the rod hateth his son," had been singled out by some special revelation as more important than the whole of the New Testament. Dr. Keate, Headmaster of Eton (1809–34), was considered by Gladstone to be the last of the line of flogging masters in the

Busby tradition, but to compare with Busby is to compare by a high standard. Lord Taunton's Schools Inquiry Commission, reporting as late as 1868, gave figures for boys' and mixed schools which showed that 75 percent used public flogging as a punishment.[4] The fact that, two centuries after the Children's Petition, there were still those who thought that parliamentary action was needed to control corporal punishment—and not only in the endowed schools—was shown in 1863 when Viscount Raynham and Mr. Dunlop introduced into the House of Commons the Corporal Punishment in Schools Bill, "to put an end to the irregular and cruel treatment of pupils by schoolmasters and tutors, especially in national schools."[5] The Bill was said by Sir George Grey to be "of an unnecessary and almost a ridiculous character," and did not get a second reading. In the House of Lords, in the parliamentary sessions of 1867–8, 1868–9 and 1870, the Marquess of Townshend again brought up the control of corporal punishment in three Bills for the Better Protection of Children, Servants and Apprentices. Two were withdrawn, and the other failed to get a second reading.[6]

In the end, control over the abuse of corporal punishment was not brought about by Act of Parliament. A current manual on the law of education has only one index-entry under "Punishment," and that refers to an administrative memorandum requiring the keeping of a punishment book.[7] In practice, corporal punishment is controlled in the state schools by the regulations of local education authorities, and (in the case of Approved Schools) by Home Office rules. Doubtless the accumulation of cases under the Common Law, and the development of public opinion, have also had their effect. The seventeenth-century campaigners would probably feel today that the battle they fought has been won, though not quite in the way they envisaged.

NOTES

1. John Brinsley, *Ludus Literarius, or the Grammar Schoole*, 1627, chaps. 27, 29; Samuel Hartlib, *The True and Readie Way to Learne the Latine Tongue* (1654), quoted in E. B. Castle, *Moral Education in Christian Times*, London, 1958, p. 97; Charles Hoole, *A New Discovery of the Old Art of Teaching School* (1660), ed. E. T. Campagnac, 1913, pp. 276–8.

2. Hezekiah Woodward, *A Childes Patrimony*, 1640, Part I, Preface, pp. 6–7.

3. Livy, X. 9, 4 (Loeb edition, vol. 4, p. 388 and note); Sallust, *op. cit.* LI, 21–2.

4. Statistics derived from information in the Taunton Report by E. B. Castle, *op. cit.*, p. 291.

5. Hansard, 3rd series, vol. 171, col. 1842.

6. Hansard, 3rd series, vol. 193, col. 169; vol. 197, col. 1865; vol. 202, col. 1593.

7. M. M. Wells and P. S. Taylor, *The New Law of Education*, 5th ed., London, 1961.

3

Discipline in the Good Old Days

John Manning

•

*Wanting elbow room, the chair would be quickly
thrust on one side, and Master John Todd was to be seen
dragging his struggling suppliant to the flogging ground
in the center of the room. Having placed his left foot
upon the end of a bench, with a patent jerk peculiar to
himself, he would have the boy completely horsed across
his knee, with his left elbow on the back of his neck to
keep him securely on. . . . Having his victim thus completely at his command . . . , once more to the staring
crew would be exhibited the dexterity of master and
strap. . . . Moving in quick time, the fifteen inches of
bridle rein would be seen, . . . leaving on "the place beneath" a fiery streak at every slash.*

"Does it hurt?"

"Oh yes, Master! Oh don't Master!"

*"Then I'll make it hurt thee more. . . . Thou shan't
want a warming pan tonight."*[1]

Such were the memories of school life from one American school. These
were the "good old days," but I suspect that very few of us would care to
go back to this particular type of discipline. We would not feel completely
at ease watching Master Todd's face assume a deep claret color, or admire
the grimace of his face as the long pen, which, in the passion of the
moment, he gripped in his teeth, was diabolically bent downward at both
ends, paralleling his chin. It is no wonder that little George Fudge took the
only means of defense open to him—that of wearing a pair of leather
breeches against which Master Todd's strap flailed in vain.

Similarly, the *Memoir of William Ellery Channing* recounts the discipline which was enforced in the dame school of his boyhood, by means of

Reprinted by permission of *Phi Delta Kappan.* "Discipline in the Good Old
Days," by John Manning, December 1959.

the long round stick which stood at the right arm of the Dame's soft easy chair like a "watchful, sleepless being of ancient mythology."[2] In the same vein, Sam Seton, assistant superintendent of schools, New York, could look back to Master Young's Parish School of Old Trinity, where a small ladder, inclined beside the master's desk, was climbed by each juvenile delinquent, and a severe application of the master's cane upon the culprit's flesh inevitably followed.[3] A schoolhouse, erected about the year 1793 in Sunderland, Massachusetts, had, solidly embedded in the schoolhouse floor, an ominous whipping post, to which erring humanity was securely tied and whipped by the master in the presence of its classmates.[4]

Elizabeth Montgomery, in her *Reminiscences* of 1851, recounts practices in the girls' school of a Mrs. Elizabeth Way. For permitting her head to fall forward, a girl was forced to wear a necklace of sharp Jamestown weed-burrs, strung on tape. If tasks were slighted, a girl was forced to wear leather spectacles, "but a morocco spider worn on the back, confined to the shoulders by a belt, was more usual."[5] In 1833, the delinquent girls in Burton's district school, were "obliged to sit on the masculine side of the aisle with crimsoned necks and faces buried in their aprons."[6]

Today, many teachers and psychologists insist that school should be made so interesting that many disciplinary problems do not arise. But this does not mean that all are against the use of corporal punishment, nor that all teachers have been deprived of the right to administer it. Opinion among America's 1,100,000 teachers was sampled in 1956 by the National Educational Association. In the field of elementary education, only 77 percent believed that they should have authority to administer corporal punishment, whereas, in actuality, 86 percent already had been given such authority. On the other hand, in the junior high school group, 63 percent of the teachers thought they should have such authority, whereas, in actuality, only 30 percent of the teachers had been given it.[7]

Whatever else may be said about the discipline practiced in the "good old days," the regulations were usually clear enough. The principal of the Chauncey Hall School, Boston, in 1840, required the boys to scrape their feet on the scraper, to be punctual, to bow when entering or leaving the room, when reciting, or when accepting anything. They were also required to sit erect, to stand when speaking, and to carry their books in a satchel. They were forbidden to borrow or lend, to climb, to carry a pen on the ear, to leave their seats without permission, or to spit on the floor. The latter practice was said to be far too prevalent among the parents to be winked at.[8] Regulations in most schools of Rhode Island included cleaning of shoes, personal cleanliness, payment for damage to school property, and abstinence from smoking or chewing tobacco.[9] A century ago, a school in North Carolina enforced the following: "For boys and girls playing together, four lashes; for failing to bow at the entrance of strangers, three lashes; for blotting copy book, two lashes; for scuffling, four lashes; for calling each other names, three lashes," and so on.[10] An earlier code, drawn up at Deerfield, Massachusetts, provided an economic penalty, viz., for the mingling of the sexes other than at prayers, one dollar; for missing church service, one dollar; for playing cards or checkers, one dollar; for being absent from 5 A.M. prayers or from a study period, six cents, and so on.[11] Most academies posted a set of rules prohibiting attendance at parties with members of the opposite sex or "corresponding by letter or otherwise with any member of the opposite sex except that it be a near relation."[12]

One speculates what the reaction would have been to our modern coeducation, to high school dating, to teen-age petting, or "going steady." Yet the Lansing, Michigan, *State Journal* of December 4, 1957, reported a request from the Teachers' Federation at Grand Rapids to its board of education for a disciplinary code to deal with defiance of authority, fighting, drinking, and the carrying of obscene literature or pictures.

Strict disciplinary practice in the old days often received wholehearted parental, administrative, and public support. Benjamin Silliman, a professor at Yale, 1805–1851, takes pains in his *Reminiscences* to indicate that good manners and respect for one's elders were *de rigueur*. "If we received a book or anything else . . . a look of acknowledgment was expected. . . . We must not interrupt anyone who was speaking. . . . We were taught always to give place at door or gate to another person, especially if older."[13] Today, the significant verdict of ten thousand representative teachers (sampled by the NEA and reported in their *Research Bulletin*, April 1956) was that parental irresponsibility accounts for "a large proportion of all the misbehavior in school."

"The private and judicious use of corporal punishment should have a place," wrote the Reverend Sam Hamill, of Lawrenceville, New Jersey, in 1855. "No judicious Board of Trustees should put a person into a school room, to train and govern and keep in order a company of youth, and yet tie his hands on his subject. . . . Surely it is enough for a teacher to endure the vexation, weariness, anxiety, and toil incident to his position without being thus trammelled."[14]

The compulsory school attendance laws which hold many unwilling students in high school today undoubtedly add to school disciplinary problems. Few school superintendents today, however, would care to express the sentiments uttered by the superintendent of schools in St. Louis in 1838: "Public opinion is in favor of a fearless performance of duty. . . . The Board prescribes conditions upon which any and all can enjoy the benefits of public instruction: Those who will not comply with these conditions, must forego the privileges; and for no man, it matters not what his station, or how great his wealth, will these conditions be changed."[15]

Many a present-day teacher, too, probably wishes that he had support such as the following: "Do not listen to every tale of childish grievance against the master. The presumption is that nine times out of ten the grievance is imaginary: in truth, the presumption is always so, generally the fact is so. . . . The parents' cooperation is important. . . ."[16]

A century ago, we find strong censorship of reading materials. Having examined the textbooks used in the Kensington schools, and having found considerable fiction therein, a would-be censor opined: "The mind that feeds on fiction becomes bloated and unsound, and, already inebriated, still thirsts for more." Awe and quietness, she went on to say, diffuse ideas among children which tend to good order.[17] Such comments probably befitted a woman whose father, Sam Hart, was a direct descendant of Thomas Hooker, one of the founders of Connecticut. One can envision her comments on modern radio, motion pictures, and television, where the supply of material is in such staggering amounts.

Another writer, from Massachusetts, complained that those papers which were least scrupulous in moral tone often had the widest circulation. The popular amusements of his day, he lamented, were adapted "to low and vulgar tastes in order to . . . be made profitable." That has a more modern ring, but the following perhaps does not: "A large proportion of the support they [popular amusements] receive comes from children for whose injury the fond but inconsiderate parent pays the price more freely than he does his school tax."[18]

A century ago, stress on parental supervision for enforcement of a strict disciplinary code was apparent. A writer from Ohio deplored the temptations suffered by students who were obliged to attend a distant high school. "In the parent's fond anticipations, he never dreams that dice and cards, drinking, gaming, midnight debauchery, and every species of recreation and amusement, frivolous and dangerous, occupy his son's time, instead of sober industrious study. . . . Deeds, which in his native town he would never think of doing, . . . he can do with impunity, when far away and comparatively unknown."[19]

The foregoing illustrations should not blind us to the fact that there were, of course, many schools which were conducted along admirable disciplinary lines. Woody mentions a school conducted by a Mrs. Rowson of Boston "who governs by the love which she always inspires in her scholars." John Poor's Academy at Philadelphia, attended by one hundred girls in the 1780s, used no bodily punishments. The school kept by Miss Grant at Ipswich, Connecticut, maintained control through "sweet reasonableness."[20] Channing remembered that William Rogers avoided flogging in his school, especially following the memory of a very small boy trying to shield with his arms the body of a larger boy whom the master was about to whip. The great heart and the small frame resisting tyranny was a picture that refused to be erased.[21] A Mrs. Lucy Lane Allen could not remember any corporal punishment during her summer school days at Scituate, Massachusetts, nor during the three winters she spent under Harvard students at Sudbury; and during the four years which she herself taught school at Medfield, she did not use corporal punishment. George B. Emerson, who taught at the Boston Latin School from about 1821, managed to maintain both study and discipline without recourse to the rod.[22]

There were also those who took the middle ground, as expressed by Francis Gardner, who taught at the Boston Latin School between 1852 and 1862: "He is the best teacher who produces the best results with the least application of force. But force of some kind must lie in the teacher, or good results cannot be produced."[23] Like Ichabod Crane, the teachers might temper justice with mercy and take it out on some of the bigger rather than the smaller fellows, but they did what they considered to be their "duty to the parents"!

What has brought about the change in attitude? Some writers lay most of the commendation (or blame) on modern educational theory. There is probably some truth in this. But there are other factors, such as the obvious rise and popularization of psychology. One school argues that teachers and educators have adopted and popularized so much of this thought that they must be held responsible. Two other factors, however, are involved: the change of conditions under which schooling is acquired, and the rise of humanitarianism.

The latter expressed itself in many ways, not only in agitation to abolish Negro slavery, but also to increase religious toleration, to improve conditions in prisons, to end brutal treatment of the insane, to lessen the incidence of capital punishment, to end flogging in the navy, to set up "charity schools," to get popular education for all, to introduce the "natural" educational methods advocated by Rousseau or the "kindly" school practices of Pestalozzi. It was a movement for the betterment of all humanity. The severity of the use (or abuse) of corporal punishment certainly felt this moderating influence of "enlightened" humanitarianism.

Disciplinary measures, moreover, reflect the conditions under which schooling is acquired. These conditions, in turn, are influenced by the personality of the teacher. What were the teachers like a century or more ago? "Cimon" in *The American Mercury*, April 14, 1794, explains that district schools were generally kept by a man who had managed to learn to read, spell, and cypher. "When he has arrived at the age of nineteen, with his head well-stocked with ignorance, and himself too lazy to sled wood, or dress flax in winter, he gladly makes the exchange, and enters the schoolhouse for the winter months, and keeps school."[24] Edward Everett thus described his teachers about 1800:

> The reading school was under Master Little . . . , and the writing school was kept by Master Tileston. Master Little, in spite of his name, was a giant in stature—six feet four at least. . . . I acquired under his tuition what was thought in those days a very tolerable knowledge of Lindley Murray's abridgement of English grammar, and at the end of the year [he was nine years of age] could parse almost any sentence in the American Preceptor. Master Tileston was advanced in years. . . . The fingers of his right hand had been stiffened and contracted in early life by a burn. . . . They served as a convenient instrument of discipline.[25]

Peter Parley has left a fairly typical description of a teacher whose school he began to attend when he was about six years old. "My teacher was Aunt Delight, that is Delight Benedict, a maiden lady of fifty, short and bent, of sallow complexion and solemn aspect. I remember the first day. . . . I went alone. . . . There were seventeen scholars seated upon thin planks known as slabs." Peter's own little legs dangled in mid-air. He continues:

> The children were called up, one by one, to Aunt Delight, who . . . with a buck-handled penknife pointed one by one to letters of the alphabet, saying, "What's that?" . . . I looked upon these operations with intense curiosity and no small respect, until my own turn came. . . . And when she said, "Make your obeisance" my little intellects all fled away, and I did nothing. . . . Gazing at me with indignation, she laid her hand on the top of my head, and gave it a jerk which made my teeth clash. . . . And when she pointed to the letter A and asked me what it was, it swam before my eyes dim and hazy, and as big as a full moon.[26]

Some of the teachers, by 1850, were young women. Whipping of big, strapping boys was postponed until the district superintendent made his routine visit. Kennedy, whose father was a horseback-riding superintendent, mentions this practice as common in Indiana. Teachers hunted rabbits or coons during the noon hour. Others, such as Scroggins, both smoked and chewed tobacco.[27] Frothingham remembered a "Mr. Caper, a poor humped-back cripple who . . . kept on his table a cowhide which was pretty generously exercised"; while Town remembered his teacher as "a large slab-sided man who always sat in an oldfashioned chair, about the center of the room," and by whose side was a small round table and the usual birch rod.[28] Similarly, Robert Mack remembered his first few days at Londonderry, New Hampshire, under a gentleman named Sam Bell who on the opening day of school struck each pupil over the head with his hickory cane, with a "blow heavy enough to fell an ox," which apparently had no particular significance. However, Squire Bell, father of Sam Bell the teacher, saw to it that when Sam started for school the following Monday morning, the hickory cane was not to be found high or low.[29]

Some idea of the qualifications of these teachers may be gleaned from the story of an examiner who asked a candidate for a teaching certificate a problem involving the multiplying of twenty-five cents by twenty-five cents; the answer, since it was not in the book, was merely debated upon! Another would-be teacher (obviously so stupid that even the incompetent examiner demurred) insisted so much on being given a certificate that the examiner wrote: "This is to certify that Mr. Amaziah Smith is qualified to teach a common school in Washington Township, and a damned common one at that!"[30] Apparently, if a person was over sixteen years of age, could read the Scriptures without too much stumbling, write well enough to set a line of copy, mend a broken quill pen, cypher passably, and above all "keep order," then such a person "would do" for a teacher.

The discipline enforced by such teachers may well be envisioned, and when the actual classroom procedures and conditions of a century ago are revealed, it becomes obvious why disciplinary problems arose. The education given in a common school was very meager; the subjects taught were usually reading, spelling, and writing. Some arithmetic was taught, usually as far as the rule of three (three is to six as four is to what?), and of course the little "beginners" were taught their ABC's. Aunt Delight used the common method, calling upon the little tykes twice a day, and pointing with a penknife: "What's that?" ("A") "What's that?" ("B") "No! It's D. Take your seat." The pupil eventually proceeded to explore the hornbook a little further, learning the letters, the numerals, and perhaps the Lord's Prayer therefrom. Elizabeth Montgomery, in her *Reminiscences of Wilmington, Delaware* (1851), describes such a hornbook as a piece of paper containing the above information "fastened on a thin board, about the size of a small spelling book page," and "securely nailed to it was a strip of bright brass for a margin, and covered with a plate of horn so transparent as to render the text to be clearly read, yet fully defended from the unwashed fingers of the pupils."

No two pupils were likely to be at the same stage, and seldom did any two pupils have identical texts—if indeed they owned any text at all. "Our school books," wrote H. Humphrey in 1863, "were the Bible, Webster's Spelling Book and [Webster's] Third Part, . . . but no maps, no globes; and as for blackboards, such a thing was never thought of. . . . Arithmetic was hardly taught at all. . . . Spelling was one of the leading daily exercises. . . . The public exercises (on Quarter Day or on Spring Exhibition) were reading, spelling, and speaking pieces."[31] The Webster Speller, of course, carried not only columns of words, but also many pious precepts as well.[32]

The usual routine in a district school began with reading from the Scriptures by the first class, followed by a writing lesson. The latter necessitated the thawing out of ink, the mending of pens, and for the older pupils the writing of a line of copy by the master, such as "The road to Hell is paved with good intentions," or "Procrastination is the thief of time." Reading from the Scriptures by the second and third classes and from the hornbook by the beginners usually followed. After recess, there was a "general spell" during which the teacher gave out a word and the class then spelled it, in syllables, in unison. The afternoon, similarly, was spent in reading, until the final hour, when spelling occurred again, with perhaps some incidental instruction in weights, measures, currencies, etc. Following final roll call, there were reminders as to behavior on the way home, and a check on those pupils whose responsibility it was to light the morning fire next day.

The latter practice was a more desirable form of discipline. The fire had to be lighted half an hour before school, and has been described thus: "The boy whose turn it is to make the fire has crowded the six-plate stove . . . with a plethoric quantity of unseasoned wood . . . and the smoke is oozing from the crevices. . . . At length we are allowed to thaw ourselves . . . Having become red as lobsters, we are sent back to our seats. . . . A strange lassitude comes over us . . . , the vision is suddenly broken by another call to 'come up and recite.' "[33]

Edward Everett gave a similar picture of the Boston Latin School, about 1805: "The boys had to take their turns in winter in coming early to the schoolhouse, to open it; to make a fire sometimes out of wet logs; . . . to sweep out the room, and, if need be, to shovel a path through the snow to the street. . . . Such a thing as a school library, a book of reference, a critical edition of a classic, a map, or a blackboard, an engraving of an ancient building, or a copy of work of ancient art, such as now adorn the walls of our schools, were as little known as the electric telegraph."[34]

If we are to take the word of Henry K. Oliver, who began Latin at the age of nine in the Boston Grammar School under the rod of schoolmaster Pemberton, the routine of an urban Latin school was just as dreary as that of a district school. Oliver reached the age of ten knowing little of the syntax of Dr. Adam's *Latin Grammar*. Of geography, and arithmetic he says he knew literally nothing, and "less than nothing" of the grammar of his own language. Perhaps nothing less than corporal punishment could have roused the weary under such conditions. Small wonder that Oliver remembered that "we sat, we studied, we idled, or we recited, or we were flogged as the case might be," and looking back at the job of the teachers— mending pens, watching this boy or that, setting copies, answering questions, hearing recitations, keeping order—Oliver wondered how any of them "lived a twelve-month outside the walls of an insane asylum."[35] Yet, and this is worth noting, in spite of these conditions, pupils learned a great deal; Oliver eventually attended Harvard, and later taught, and still later served the government of Massachusetts well.

Flogging, dreary routine, impossible teachers, odd jobs of kindling fires or shoveling snow, all contributed a measure of discipline. To this may be added preparations for the public exercises given by the pupils on Examination Day, or as it was sometimes known, on Quarter Day, or the Spring Exhibition. A description is given by I. Kingsley of such a day, in 1834, at Mrs. Eames's School in Providence, Rhode Island. The public examination lasted two days. On the second day, as many more people were invited as could be comfortably seated in the hall. "On each day, the examination last five hours . . . , gazing at planets and distant worlds, discoursing on kings and queens . . . , showing conclusively that A.B.C. equalled D.E.F., and our acquirements in Latin and Greek."[36] The positive disciplinary measure served as incentive to students and parents; it usually closed with a "grand finale," described by Kingsley as "each one reading a composition, the Valedictory calling forth . . . a great display of white handkerchief. And each member of the class was presented with a testimonial."[37]

The geographic and temporal aspects of this more positive discipline (as well as earlier examples of milder methods) appear to have significance. On the frontier, schooling was utilized to snatch new pioneering communities from savagery, materialism, and uncouthness. As the pioneering conditions moved further and further westward, however, it was natural for both life and schooling to become less violent, less brutal, and less individualistic. It would appear, also, that education in the East tended to be used less for assimilating minority groups (and expediting social or economic mobility) and more for bolstering the *status quo* of the social class structure.

Individualized instruction and punishment, of course, continued even in the East, as witness the experience of a young teacher from England who took over a private school in New York in 1831:

> The noise and uproar of my school had been increasing every day. . . . I reprimanded such as appeared most riotous, but some of them told me that they would not be restrained by any English tyrant; so I visited one of them with a stroke. Hereupon . . . I was pelted on all sides with books, and slates, and copies . . . I was compelled to take refuge behind a pillar, against which I placed my back, and protected myself in front by a chair. Such as approached near enough I knocked down. . . . At last snatching a piece of wood out of the hands of the oldest, I put my pupils on the defensive.[38]

This sounds like *Blackboard Jungle* in reverse. On the frontier, discipline took the following forms: a tobacco-chewing student was deliberately asked a question by his teacher which was not amenable to a nod or a shake of the head. In two gulps, the pupil "swallowed everything—quid, saliva and all."[39] Within three minutes the subsequent nausea sent the delinquent dashing for the door. On other occasions, a giggling student was actually pitched out of the window as the button on his shirt-collar gave way in the hand of the teacher; a time-waster ended up being stuffed head-first into the box stove; a delinquent girl of eighteen, who insisted there was no place to which her teacher could "remove her," ended up under the school floor with a broad puncheon placed over the trap door. On hearing a small fellow-pupil remark: "They's rattlesnakes under that floor!" a very repentant girl was quickly extricated amid fervent promises "to be good" henceforth![40]

It is perhaps significant that the improvised punishments common in the Midwest about the middle of the nineteenth century scarcely reached the barbarous improvisations found in New England in the eighteenth, which included: the use of solitary confinement within some dark recess beside the chimney, standing on one foot placed within a wooden shoe with sharp pegs projecting upward from the sole, standing before a class with the nose wedged into the split end of a sapling, flogging the boy *next* to a pupil who was delinquent in his recitation, watching a suspended wire until a fly alighted upon it, forcing a pupil to hold out heavy objects at arm's length or to stoop over touching a peg in the floor aided by sundry sharp taps on elbow or knee to keep sagging limbs rigid, inserting a chip of wood perpendicularly between a pupil's teeth to hold the jaws apart, or having a girl balance herself on a one-legged stool for an hour or so.[41] Perhaps such stern and brutal discipline could only have been tolerated within a culture which was characterized by a spirit of self-reliance and by austere repression within the family circle. The crude but happier improvisations of the Midwest probably reflected the free, adventurous, yet relentless spirit of the westward expansion.

These incidents were not necessarily typical of all schools during the nineteenth century. Common sense dictates that discipline must be clearly justifiable, that it must not be excessive, and that it should be meted out in good faith, *in loco parentis* as the lawyers say, as by a wise and judicious parent.[42] Discipline—as practiced in the old days—may now be clouded with our attempts to idealize the past, and we have come a long way since the unfolding of the West. The use of corporal punishment when not combined with more positive disciplinary measures may often have been a too frequent confession of failure. On the other hand, no one doubts that it was an old-fashioned way of preparing youth to meet life's problems.

NOTES

1. John F. Watson, *Annals of Philadelphia and Pennsylvania* (Philadelphia, 1870), pp. 290–92.

2. *Memoir of William Ellery Channing* (Boston, 1851), I: 23.

3. *American Journal of Education*, April, 1978, 18:555.

4. Clifton Johnson, *Oldtime Schools and Schoolbooks* (New York, 1925), p. 123.

5. Elizabeth Montgomery, "Reminiscences of Wilmington Delaware," *American Journal of Education*, September, 1867, 17:189.

6. Thomas Woody, *A History of Women's Education in the United States* (New York, 1929), I: 148.

7. "Opinion Poll," *The Nation's Schools*, July 1956, 58:57–58.

8. "A Lecture on Courtesy," by the principal of Chauncey Hall School, Boston, 1840.

9. *American Journal of Education*, December 1863, 23:857.

10. Charles L. Coon, *North Carolina Schools and Academies*, 1790–1840 (Raleigh, 1915), p. 763.

11. Clifton Johnson, ibid., pp. 148–150.

12. E. N. Vanderpool, *Chronicles of a Pioneer School*, 1792–1835 (Cambridge, 1903), pp. 231ff; *American Journal of Education*, December 1863, 23:857; and Woody, *History of Women's Education*, I: 435–41.

13. "Reminiscences of Benjamin Silliman," MSS in Yale University Library. Quoted in American Journal of Education, April, 1876, 26:226.

14. *American Journal of Education*, August 1855, I:123–33.

15. Ibid., p. 351. Yet, the chips being down, the board of education in New York suspended several hundred troublesome students with the support of Mayor Wagner and Governor Averell Harriman.

16. Ibid., December 1859, 7:348.

17. Ibid., March 1859, 6:163.

18. Ibid., December 1856, 2:503.

19. Ibid., December 1856, 2:540.

20. Woody, *History of Women's Education*, 1: 158, 205, 334, 351.

21. Channing, I: 44.

22. *American Journal of Education*, July 1878, 28:265.

23. Ibid., December 1862, 29:554.

24. Ibid., June 1859, 6:381.

25. Ibid., December 1859, 7:344.

26. S. G. Goodrich, *Recollections of a Lifetime* (New York and Auburn, 1856), pp. 34–39.

27. F. M. Kennedy et al., *Schoolmaster of Yesterday* (New York, 1940), pp. 72–77.

28. Goodrich, *Recollections* (New York, 1891), p. 19; and *American Journal of Education*, December 1863, 23:737.

29. *American Journal of Education*, July 1878, 28:358.

30. Kennedy, *Schoolmaster of Yesterday,* pp. 75–76.

31. *American Journal of Education,* March 1863, 30:125ff.

✔ 32. Johnson, *Oldtime Schools and Schoolbooks,* chaps. 9 and 10; Montgomery, *Reminiscences,* pp. 227–30, 269–70; and K. F. Leidecker, *Yankee Schoolteacher* (New York, 1946), mention books common in early schools.

33. *American Journal of Education,* September 1856, 2:380.

34. Ibid., December 1859, 7:344–45.

35. Ibid., April 1876, 26:209–24.

36. Ibid., June 1858, 5:25.

37. Ibid., June 1858, 5:25.

38. Isaac Fidler, *Observations on Professions . . . in the United States . . . in 1832* (London, 1833), pp. 75–80.

39. Kennedy, *Schoolmaster of Yesterday,* pp. 334ff.

40. Ibid., pp. 248ff; 250–51, 18–21.

41. W. H. Small, *Early New England Schools* (Boston, 1914); cf. also ✔ H. A. Falk, *Corporal Punishment* (New York, 1941), pp. 48, 71, 107.

42. Lee O. Garber, *The Nation's Schools,* June 1956, 57:79–80. Cf. Falk, ✔ *Corporal Punishment,* 145–47, cf. Garber, "The Teacher's Right to Administer ✔ Corporal Punishment," *The Nation's Schools,* February 1954, 53:83; also J. M. ✔ Spinning, "Discipline Today," ibid., December 1956, 58:454.

4

The Abolition of Corporal
Punishment in New Jersey Schools

Donald R. Raichle

•

In 1867 New Jersey became the first state to abolish corporal punishment
in its schools by statute and remained the *only* state to do so for more than
a hundred years. Not until 1972 when Massachusetts passed equivalent
legislation was she emulated by any sister state.[1] The unique statutory
restraint in New Jersey appeared as a relatively minor element of a wide-
reaching law which sought to strengthen a school system that had not yet
attained development comparable to that of other states. Not that the legislature went very far, for even in 1867 the law neither compelled the establishment of schools nor children to attend them. Still, the additional funds
provided state-wide coordination, and more sophisticated administration
showed that New Jersey had embarked on its most ambitious state school
project up to that time. New Jersey's reluctance to provide the educational
system sought by the schoolmen was pointed up in the addition of the ban
on corporal punishment to the then new school law. It was no coincidence
that the statutory ban came exclusively in New Jersey; it illustrated the gap
between the schoolmen on the one hand and the citizens and legislators on
the other. For, however popular the ban may have been among parents it
found virtually no support among educators.

Of course, the mitigation of corporal punishment *per se* was nothing
new as the nineteenth century progressed. Throughout the country schools
increasingly found themselves circumscribed in the time-honored use of the
rod. The unique feature in New Jersey was the prohibition by statute rather
than the more familiar state or local school board regulation. Whatever the
method, Americans grew increasingly reluctant to wreak physical pain
routinely on their children. Lloyd deMause, arguing a progressive improvement in child care through two thousand years of Western history,[2] is
certainly borne out in the United States experience. In colonial Connecticut

This essay first appeared in the *History of Childhood Quarterly*: *The Journal of
Psychohistory*, II, no. 1 (Summer 1974), 53–78.

and Massachusetts, the penalty for disobedience of the parent could reach as far as capital punishment.[3] Family and state united in grim refusal to tolerate rebellion from the young. That American settlement coincided with the development of the Enlightenment induced progressive distaste for disciplining children by inflicting physical pain. DeMause finds that of over two hundred statements of advice on child rearing prior to the eighteenth century, most approved beating children severely, while only three forbade beating altogether. The earliest lives of children who may never have been beaten, he puts in the period 1690–1750.[4] America swung away from the corporal tradition much more than did England as the experience of the two peoples widened.

The American Home

From the first, the American experience corroded forms brought from the European past. The "patriarchal" family apparently was not nearly so extensive in kinship group as earlier had been thought, yet it contained within it, for the most part, the educational functions later assumed by the school. Elementary socialization as well as vocational education had been the responsibility of the colonial family and, as Bernard Bailyn shows, the education of children extended to family, church, and community in a continuous web until the American Revolution.

With the disruption of the old order, the movement of the child from the family out into society becomes sharper, losing the earlier ease and naturalness[5] and inviting, particularly in an increasingly mobile society, anxiety on part of both child and parent. By the early Jacksonian period this break was best illustrated by the child's entry into school.

The patriarch himself, of course, had begun to disappear. Tocqueville observes that "the family in the Roman and aristocratic signification of the word does not exist" in the United States and that as the psychological distance between family members lessens, so, too, with parental authority at the same time that the father develops more intimate and affectionate relations with his children.[6] No wonder Frances Grund, Marryat, Dickens, and Sir Charles Lyell, along with other British travelers, found in American schools an air of permissiveness which they put down to "republican spirit," a term they equate with hostility to authority.[7] Arthur W. Calhoun made the nineteenth century a revolution in the status of the child with increasing valuation of the child, leading to the "reign of youth" and the "century of the child."[8] The most repeated consensus of British travelers was that the American character itself was the character of the child.[9]

John F. Walzer has shown the eighteenth century in America to be a period of ambivalence in the development of the child.[10] Although the nineteenth century was different in many ways, ambivalence continues and, of course, reaches to our own times. There is not one but rather a range of patterns. Still if crusty John Adams, as vice president of the United States, could be prevailed upon by his grandson to draw him about in a chair for a half-hour, to the delight of grandfather and the derangement of Abilgail Adams's carpet, one can more readily appreciate Tocqueville's comment that in early America even those of the most conservative persuasion invited from their children addresses of easy, colloquial familiarity.[11] The trend was clear in the age of Jackson, even to the point that the concept of the "developmental" child as the sociologist sees him today had begun to supplant the "traditional" concept of childhood. The "traditional" child as seen in the twentieth century keeps clean and neat, obeys, pleases, and respects adults, respects property and so on. The "developmental" child is healthy, cooperative, happy, contented, loves and confides in his parents, "grows as a person," and so on.[12] Now although the study setting forth this dichotomy was made about the time of World War II, some of these same elements in the concept of childhood were vying with one another in Jacksonian America. "Kisses, hugs, and frequent embraces were recommended [by the popular writers on child nurture of the time] and the mother's kisses were given magical power over the child's destiny." To be sure, the substitution of love and example for authority and precept in the early period aimed essentially at producing a child who would obey, respect, and please adults, but it also contained wider objectives. The child was expected to love back and "confide" and, Bernard Wishy notes, to develop his own free individualism. Fundamentally, those travelers to America who spoke of "the republican spirit" in American childhood were observing the beginnings of the developmental child. America in the nineteenth century wrestled with the conflict of attempting to pass on its heritage of Christian morality and faith in democratic ideals in much the same form it knew them both while at the same time to allow for the contradictory development of the free individual, eager to carve his own destiny in his own way.[13] In many homes the old orthodoxies led to infant depravity. These orthodoxies came to be replaced by an image of the child as a being of almost limitless expectations for the future. As a result the need to flog the "future" rested on shakier and shakier philosophical grounds. The child appeared with less sin and the parents with more hope. So corporal punishment began to play a smaller, but still significant role in the American home. Even Bronson Alcott, philosophically as well as temperamentally opposed to physical punishment, spanked his growing daughters as "a last resort."[14] Where the gentle Alcott fell back on the traditional methods, we may be sure that few of his contemporaries showed greater restraint. On the other hand, a new emphasis on alternatives after Beccaria and Bentham appear: "isolation, maintenance of physical decencies, reflection on the crime, change of heart, return to society."[15]

The American School

The classic notion of the place of corporal punishment in the nine-teenth century American school is summed up in the opening page of Edward Eggleston's *The Hoosier School-Master* published in 1871. The local trustee issued the young, slightly built teacher aspirant a stern warn-ing. "Want to become a school-master, do you? You? Well, what would *you* do in the Flat Creek deestrick, *I'd* like to know? Why, the boys have driv off the last two, and licked the one afore them like blazes. . . . They'd pitch you out of doors, sonny, neck and heels, afore Christmas."[16]

The great thing about this for the boys was that it was often a heads-I-win, tails-you-lose for them. If one bested the teacher, he was immortal but even if he took a beating, he was a kind of hero simply because he had engaged the enemy. But the free, mutual exchange of blows could be en-gaged in, obviously, only by the older boys. More typically, the teacher was school*master* of the physical encounter quite as much, or even more than he was master of the knowledge he engaged to teach. Nathan Hedges, the dean of teachers of the state at the time New Jersey legislated an end to corporal punishment, was as famed for his ability with the rod as for his teaching. One source, crediting him with having taught "most of the men in Newark who were in active business" at the close of the century, adds that they "doubtless held him in awe to the latest moment of his life."[17] Hedges himself had felt the rod cruelly when, in 1799 as a boy of seven in a school outside Morristown, he studied under a master known as "Club-ber Blair." In 1865 Hedges recalled the barbarities of the classroom he had known.

> I well remember that when I could not multiply by even one figure, he would give me a sum in multiplication, with four figures for a multiplier, and from day to day would pound my bare feet with his hickory club for not doing the sum correctly. He furnished no help, no instruction, no kind encouragement to a beginner, but relied entirely on the severity of his pun-ishment. Children in those days were not allowed to complain to parents of the unreasonable severity of teachers.[18]

No "Clubber Blair" himself, Hedges developed his own, ruthlessly playful style. He ordered the pupil to be chastised to line up his toes on a crack in the floor, to bend over, to touch another crack with his fingers and then, whack! Remembered by a former pupil, such an exercise was "fun" for the veterans in the class but an abomination for him who was being baptized into the rite. The aura of "fun" that Hedges infused into this punishment appears in a variation, cheerfully known as "Going to London." The victim was forced to crawl, on hands and knees, under the legs of the schoolmaster who stood like the Colossus of Rhodes, feet wide apart to permit the passage, meanwhile rewarding the victim with a shower of blows. Nor was there any escape in an attempt to scoot through in a hurry; the burst of speed merely caused the schoolmaster's legs to close and pin the victim while the punishment proceeded at leisure. On one occasion a particularly muscular lad, held fast by the schoolmaster's legs, simply stood up and toppled Colossus in what was surely the high point of delight in the school careers of those students present. Hedges must have been a very considerable man merely to live down the story. However little the redoubtable Hedges amused his victims with his lighthearted approach, he seems infinitely less menacing than another Newark teacher, the physician William P. P. Sanford, who simply smiled grimly as he brought down the rattan.[19]

No one speaks of any restraint on the part of Hedges; his students remembered the dramatic and told stories for effect. His remark that in his boyhood pupils could not complain of undue severity suggests that by mid-century they could and did. But they probably did not have to complain about him; he knew and felt affection for his pupils as his speech at Elizabeth in 1847 shows.[20] His overriding reputation, in the profession and outside it, the reputation that brought the sons of his former pupils to his private school, argues that the man had more good sense than muscle. It argues, too, that Hedges could do what many schoolteachers could not. To explain why Americans have been and are less willing than their English cousins to expose their children to school whipping, M. A. Eckstein has written that the English have more confidence in the competence of their teachers, which may well provide more sanction for corporal punishment than in America where "the teacher's status is subject, not superior or independent, not professional." As Edgar W. Knight put it, "the American school-teacher as a type has a shady past."[21] Knight referred to early nineteenth century schoolmasters who were often shiftless, lazy, and even inebriate. Moreover, in England the traditional independence of the school as an authority for the proper ways of educating the young is entrenched as it has not been in the American experience. There is also in the English tradition a rather clear mutual understanding of the procedures used. Exceptions notwithstanding, a proper caning is a proper caning wherein a familiar, however formidable, weapon is applied to the buttocks. Americans, more individualist, used a larger variety of weapons in a variety of ways, thereby increasing the anxieties of the equally individualist parent. At least one Teachers Institute sought to set forth some ground rules, forbidding such practices as blows to the head, pulling the ear or hair, etc.[22] In addition to these considerations, there are the somewhat different perceptions of the English and the Americans as to just who it is they discipline. A more class-structured society the more easily accepted the role of the "master" in the authority role.

In nineteenth century America, the Calvinist view of man as corrupt continuously gave ground to the Enlightenment view of human perfectibility. Horace Mann, defending his advice to minimize the use of corporal punishment, shrewdly seized upon his opponent's belief in infant depravity to discredit him. Mann knew how to appeal to his constituency; by citing infant depravity he could put down his opponent by tying him to a discredited concept.[23] The Enlightenment view of "natural goodness," best represented in the writings of Rousseau, was introduced into the schools by the followers of Pestalozzi. By the end of the century, the "child study" movement had clearly projected an image of a child to be loved, not beaten. And, of course, it was those American parents who were least likely to use corporal punishment at home who pushed the fight against it in the schools. As a former president of the Newark Board of Education noted in 1893, not only do parents not rebuke their children, they do not wish them rebuked. "We have homes," he said, "in every part of the city where the children have no home government whatever but where the slightest interference of the liberty of the child at school is resented."[24]

Bronson Alcott, beginning his teaching in a Connecticut district school in 1823, stepped completely out of the role of the ferule-bearing schoolmaster and anticipated Charles Silberman by establishing a classroom that was not without joy. Remembering that his ungraded classroom contained about eighty children of varying ages, his achievement was no mean one. Unhappily for both children and Alcott he was premature; the community wanted no such school and Alcott was dismissed.[25]

As the nineteenth century progressed, the trauma of the child stepping from the nuclear family to the outer community seemed to increase with the development of the school system. Less and less was the American prepared to surrender *carte blanche* his parental rights to the school no matter what the common law might hold. Increasing development of the schools by no means increased the confidence of parents that the same love and warmth that he sought to provide in his home flourished in the schoolroom. Two years after the close of the Civil War, the new edition of the popular textbook on school teaching by David Page still alluded to the fact that corporal punishment in the schools was "debated with great zeal and warmth in almost every educational meeting that is held." An ex-principal of the Albany State Normal School, Page was no doubt the veteran of many such meetings and he exemplifies the most common approach of the educational community—the teachers and the administrators—to corporal punishment.

First, there must be qualifications: in Page's case he cautioned against ever using corporal punishment harshly, never in the heat of passion, always in public in order that the pupil may not later misrepresent the incident to the detriment of the teacher (addressing himself to teachers, Page is at least as much concerned with the protection of the teacher as he is of the child), delay the punishment so that there can be no doubt that anger has subsided and use the proper instrument—a light ruler for the hand, a rod for the back and lower extremities. Second, there are no suitable alternatives. Confinement (isolation) is not possible, for example, in a one-room schoolhouse, and expulsion only deprives the child who most needs it from the school which is the means to provide him with correction. Page admits that there are better ways, but none so promising that corporal punishment can be abandoned entirely for the child must be brought to obey.[26] On the primal need for obedience—the community insistence on the preservation of the heritage—there was little dissent. But if obedience was elemental, so too was the heritage of freedom. Foes of corporal punishment argued that it could not develop the moral character consistent with liberty. Lyman Cobb's book attacking corporal punishment is full of this argument but Morrill Wyman sums it up best. "American youth for the reason that they are born to an inheritance of unparalleled individual freedom, stand in peculiar need of the early acquisition of a reverence for law and its administrators."[27]

Lyman Cobb who wrote what Bernard Wishy has called an "influential book" on "the evil tendencies of capital punishment" illustrates the foe of corporal punishment. Typically, he called for its diminution, not its extinction. Repelled by the harshness and the routine nature of whipping both in homes and schools, Cobb devoted half of his book to pointing out the shortcomings of whipping and, attempting to forestall his opponents, the other half to alternative methods. Cobb accepted corporal punishment as "a last resort."[28] Aimed at the home, Cobb's approach had a great deal of merit; parents could be introduced to alternatives that, left to their own devices, might not have occurred to most of them. Less effective was the thrust at the school where, not only was the policeman, judge, jury, and executioner all the same person, but no blood relation to the accused. Where such authority was being routinely abused, Cobb and others had their work cut out to stop it. One attempt to balance the scales, however ineffectual, was the requirement to record each instance of whipping in order to allow some oversight.[29]

Opponents of corporal punishment made what they could of sex differences—both of teacher and pupil. Cobb cited a New York superintendent of schools who would not subject "delicate females" (teachers) to the unpleasant task and trial of physical strength.[30] A minority report of the Massachusetts Education Committee in 1867 thought women teachers, being "more excitable," would be protected from wrong by a ban on corporal punishment.[31] But the stronger case, of course, rested on the prohibition of the whipping of girl students, more apt to suffer injustice, it was argued, from unwise teachers, as girls were "more sensitive, more excitable, more subject to change and diseased actions during their school life."[32] Indeed, why flog a creature who "instinctively knows that upon the good impression she makes on others is based her hopes for the future"?[33]

The extent to which the daily clash of egos entered into school whippings is illustrated in the case of a girl in a Massachusetts school who whispered and, as she was thought to be defiant, sent by her teacher, a woman, to the recitation room to be whipped. The teacher could not hold her so the principal instructed her to get another woman teacher to help. This made the whipping possible but the girl screamed and brought an angered principal to the scene in person. He proceeded to whip the girl until she stopped screaming after which he left in triumph but the teacher told the girl she had "submitted" to the principal and now she would have to "submit" to the two women. So a third beating ensued. An investigating committee, looking into corporal punishment, found, in this instance, no "improper" motive.[34] As one of the contemporary reformers pointed out, a young woman could receive punishment by a man in the public schools of Massachusetts which could not legally be inflicted in a state penitentiary or, if inflicted by a husband on his wife, would be cause for divorce.[35]

No doubt one of the factors checking corporal punishment was the feminization of the teaching profession. Early nineteenth century schools employed men during the winter terms, but in the summer when the older children were busy with farm chores, women served to teach the younger ones. With the rise of the public schools the call for increasing numbers of teachers revolutionized the system. School systems quickly learned that the same low salaries that attracted few capable young men brought large numbers of quite capable young women. By no means excluding corporal punishment entirely, women probably tended to emphasize it less, partly because they encountered grave disadvantage in physical confrontation with adolescent boys, but also because it was considered less seemly in their sex. This is not to say women were inferior to men as disciplinarians or even thought so by school officials. In the mid-nineteenth century, the state superintendent of schools surveyed the New Jersey school officials to find men only "slightly" preferred to women as disciplinarians. Successive city superintendents in Newark staffed its schools for incorrigibles with women exclusively.[36] Sometimes, women abandoned flogging but were nonetheless corporal as was Marion Patton, a teacher in Camden, who in 1892 disciplined an occasional unruly youngster by popping a handful of pepper in his mouth. Her defense at the hands of her principal significantly illustrates the great quality of loyalty within professions. He explained that she used neither red pepper nor ginger, only black pepper, and by the handful, never a whole pot, and added that by the practice some of his "wildest boys had been tamed into obedience."[37]

Testimony of the recipients of the beatings reveals interesting, if predictable, patterns. Sado-masochism emerges in John Griscom, an associate high school principal from New York, who wrote Lyman Cobb that he remembered as a child "having, after a well-merited flagellation from my father, felt a glow of regard for him, far beyond what I had enjoyed while in a state of rebellious feeling." As a teacher, Griscom had seen the same phenomenon in pupils.[38] One father beat his son with such severity that the family physician had to intercede.[39] Cobb reported a little girl who had never before either been whipped or seen anyone whipped develop a "frightful and alarming tremor" terrifying both her teacher and the other pupils.[40] Apparently not unusual was the lad who shrugged that it was worth a licking to go fishing.[41] Another reported that he was completely paralyzed by the threat of flogging and, although he knew his lessons, could never say them and so was flogged daily. There was no relief for him until he was transferred to another school.[42] Toward the close of the century, one school observer reported a story illustrating the most complete flight to fantasy. A boy described a schoolmate, Harry Custer, the son of a cowboy, a fourth-grader who owned a revolver and shot and killed another boy. When the teacher threatened to whip Harry he held her off with his revolver. Harry Custer, of course, was wholly a figment of the boy's imagination.[43]

Richard Henry Dana exemplifies the "battered child" that resulted from the unrestrained use of force on schoolchildren.[44] At the age of seven Richard was provoked by another boy to laughter as he was reciting. Rebuked, he could not control himself and had his ear pulled. Twice more his tormenter succeeded in making him laugh and each time the enraged teacher spent more force on the ear, the last time tearing the skin connecting it to the head. Richard's father later succeeded in bringing an end to ear pulling in the school, leaving discipline to be handled by the ferule. But young Richard some years later experienced an even more harrowing episode which he recorded himself.

> Mr. W. kept [school] but a fortnight. He was very unfortunate in all his plans and notions. He also inflicted some violent corporal punishments. One inflicted upon myself was the cause of his being turned out of office.
>   He (the schoolmaster) had placed me in the middle of the floor for

some offence or other, and my station being near the stove, and the room very hot, I became faint and asked to be allowed to go out and gave my reason, but to no purpose. In a few minutes we had our usual recess of a quarter of an hour, and I went out. Here I came very near fainting again, looked very pale, and asked leave to go home. This was refused. As I was really sick, at the suggestion of the boys, I went home, which was but a few minutes' walk, to get a written excuse. My father saw that I was ill and kept me at home, and sent me the next morning with a written excuse for my non-appearance, alleging faintness and sickness. Mr. W. was mortified and angry at this and said that the excuse only covered my not returning, while the chief offence was my going home without leave, which he could not excuse, and calling me out, took his ferule and ordered me to put out my left hand. (He also intimated that my sickness was all a sham.) Upon this hand he inflicted six blows with all his strength, and then six upon the right hand. I was in such a frenzy of indignation at his injustice and his insulting insinuations that I could not have uttered a word for my life. I was too small and slender to resist, and could show my spirit only by fortitude. He called for my right hand again, and gave six more blows in the same manner and then six more upon the left. My hands were swollen and in acute pain, but I did not flinch or show a sign of suffering. He was determined to conquer and gave six more blows upon each hand, with full force. Still there was no sign from me of pain or submission. I could have gone to the stake for what I considered my honor. The school was in an uproar of hissing and scraping and groaning, and the master turned his attention to the other boys and left me alone. He said not another word to me through the day. If he had I could not have answered, for my whole soul was in my throat and not a word could get out. . . . I went in the afternoon to the trustees of the school, stated my case, produced my evidence and had an examination made. The next morning but four boys went to school, and the day following the career of Mr. W. ended.[45]

Thomas Wentworth Higginson recalled in his *Cheerful Yesterdays* some not so cheerful schooldays, described by his classmate in later years simply as "My dears, it was hell." While Higginson chose not to express himself so bluntly, he found his school in which the schoolmaster constantly carried a rattan "degrading to boyish nature."[46]

Cobb remembered one boy whose genius for mischief resulted in frequent and severe beatings and whose family concluded that he was mentally deficient. When Cobb knew the boy some years later the beatings had stopped and in his judgment the boy had more talent than anyone else in the family.

Almost an American version of "Dotheboys Hall" apparently flourished for a time in Girard College if even part of the sickening record is true that included pupils showing purple welts and the marks of cruel stripes upon their persons; boys incarcerated under lock and key, for weeks upon weeks, in midwinter, in the topmost rooms of the college building, where no heat was allowed them, no light permitted when evening came, no books given them to read; stripped of their clothes, in some instances partially, and in others almost entirely; obliged to answer all the calls of nature in these rooms, and fed upon bread and water; children condemned to the House of Refuge, on the application of the President, without knowledge of their mothers or friends, and without any opportunity of appeal; new and ingenious modes of punishment, which were but the synonym of torture; utter want of sympathy for the mute appeals of orphanage; and disregard for the feeling and rights of mothers, as shown in the denial of their most innocent requests.[47]

There is little doubt, then, of the excesses. Moving in humanitarian directions in such areas as prison reform, care for the mentally ill, treatment of labor, America had responded to appeals like those of Herman Melville in *White Jacket* and abolished corporal punishment on shipboard in 1853. (The strong pull of tradition is underlined in Richard Henry Dana's refusal, despite his long history as a victim of the excesses of corporal punishment, to advocate its ban on shipboard in his classic *Two Years before the Mast*.) By 1890, Richard Humphreys could point not only to the New Jersey ban but also to school board prohibitions on corporal punishment in both New York and Chicago as he sought to convince Boston to follow those examples.[48] There was to be no final or complete victory; ambivalence still reigns in the United States. As far as one can generalize, the home still wars with the school. Parents, or large numbers of them, wish to retain the exclusive rights to whip or not to whip their children's bodies. The schoolmen claim, almost invariably as "a last resort," that they must share the right as a necessary consequence of their vocation. The mid-nineteenth century Massachusetts debate underscores the division between home and school on the subject.[49]

The New Jersey Ban

Exceptions to the general schoolteachers' attitude include that of Professor David Cole of the New Jersey State Normal School who argued that "God never intended pain to be connected with the acquisition of knowledge, but only moral delinquency." Cole, one of the most outstanding educators in New Jersey at mid-century, unfortunately, could gush on occasion with sentimentality. One can understand that a teacher might, as Cole said he did, "sicken at the thought of imposing restraint on the joyous little children."[50] But, of course, Cole at the Normal School taught not children but fairly adult students and, as every parent knows, no one imposes restraint on "the joyous"; it is the mischievous who provoke irritation and the rebellious who invite retaliation.

Cole had a good case but did not make it and, in any event, did not speak for the profession. Throughout the nineteenth and into the twentieth century schoolmen as a body continued to articulate their faith in the desirability of corporal punishment.[51] Herbert Falk found during World War II that a small sample of faculty members of graduate schools of education divided about equally on the necessity for the use of corporal punishment in the schools. On the other hand, Rotarians and school administrators favored its use much more.[52] For, however permissive Americans might have been as compared with the English, they were by no means entirely so, neither at school nor at home. Frederick W. Ricord, New Jersey State Superintendent of Schools during the Civil War, pointed out that corporal punishment cast a pall of fear over the classroom that interfered with chilren's education, particularly as he found it to be the custom for parents to warn their children that if they were whipped in school they would be whipped even harder when they came home, a practice which dated back to colonial times. But Ricord did not ask for the abolition of corporal punishment, objecting to it only when "injudiciously administered."[53] This was long received doctrine with New Jersey teachers, as with teachers elsewhere. The New Jersey Society of Teachers in 1845 had passed a resolution "to dispense with physical force as far as is consistent with the maintenance of wholesome discipline" which is to say that they would never use it unless they thought they should.[54]

George B. Sears, city superintendent of schools in Newark from 1859 to 1877, took a similar view although early in his tenure as superintendent he sought to reduce school floggings. Group singing, he thought, should be practiced more in the schools for its therapeutic effect inasmuch as it "calms, quiets and gladdens the heart, subdues the passions," and prepares the way for "kindly suggestions." "I should not," he wrote, "expect to find a prosperous Primary School where there was no singing." The mood produced, he maintained, was precisely the opposite of that produced by corporal punishment which "only exasperates and sours unless administered by a master hand." Note the escape clause which virtually always accompanies the schoolman's criticism of corporal punishment. The evidence that these exponents of the rod had the best of motives is overwhelming. By their lights, the public school was a moral crusade which would preserve the state, mold the good citizen, and honor God. Moreover, they were humanitarian in the sense that they sought to mitigate, if not abolish, the use of force. When they were faced with the choice of whipping a child or suspending him from school, they whipped him in the firm conviction that suspension, driving the child into the streets, would destroy him as well as imperil the state.[55] In this they had distinguished precedent: Horace Mann defended corporal punishment as a lesser evil than to turn out thousands of children "to be marauders and freebooters on society 'free' from all salutary restraints."[56]

In response to public criticism the Newark Board of Education recorded its disapproval of "any corporal punishment whereby wounds or other marks of violence are inflicted." That was enough for Superintendent Sears. Newark classrooms in the middle of the nineteenth century routinely numbered between seventy-five to a hundred students. Those numbers called for strong deterrents to high spirits and Sears had no mind to ban the rod although he conceded that if classes should be reduced to twenty-five to thirty and "proper houses of correction for the incorrigible" provided he might alter his view.[57]

Sears, moreover, accommodated himself to constant violation of board of education regulations which specified that only principals could administer corporal punishment. Classroom teachers ignored the regulations and wielded the rod on their own, a practice which eventually called forth a rebuke from the president of the board. The superintendent officially put himself on record not as determined to enforce board regulations, but as in favor of recording each instance of corporal punishment *by whomsoever inflicted* as a means of moderating its use. This flouting of the law by schoolteachers with the cooperation of the superintendent continued under Sears's successor, William N. Barringer. In 1881 Barringer told his principals to pass word on to the classroom teachers that "frequent" resort to floggings was no credit to the school. By 1888, under pressure from parents, he finally told his principals that the violations must stop.[58]

Flogging in Newark schools during Sears's tenure was quite common. Complaints sometimes appear in board minutes of beatings of undue severity. Terms such as "brutal whipping" or "indications on the person of the child of excessive severity" indicate that passion often accompanied punishment. In 1876 the board became sufficiently exercised to instruct the superintendent to report the number of cases of corporal punishment in each school. Sears reported that teachers recorded a total of 9,408 beatings in Newark schools in the year ending 30 June 1876. In that year there were 10,153 students in average daily attendance in the city schools (not counting the high school which is not mentioned in Sears's report) so that there was an average of almost one whipping a year for each child in the system.[59] Not much in comparison to English public schools, where Dean Keate, headmaster of Eton, flogged eighty boys in a single evening, but that was in 1832, a particularly boisterous period of school life in England. Not long before, George III, on meeting some Eton boys at Windsor, had been prompted to ask, "Have you had any mutinies lately, eh, eh?"[60] The Newark figures, however, roughly compare with Boston, which in 1866 recorded 20,000 whippings.[61] The population of Boston in 1870 was roughly a quarter of a million compared to Newark's which was slightly over a hundred thousand. It must be remembered that these are *recorded* beatings and about as accurate as the police blotter for crime statistics. In Boston, for example, substitute teachers did not record their exploits, and contemporary observers report even experienced teachers omitted to record severe floggings.[62] However Newark floggings compare with exploits elsewhere, it remains true that in that city the threat of the rod was the major means of maintaining order. Nor did schoolmen elsewhere in the state take a stand against corporal punishment. In the first place, most schools outside the cities were ungraded and in a one-room school such as that in the Hilton section of South Orange (now a part of Irvington) seventy to eighty pupils ranging from four to twenty years of age could keep a teacher in such a state of siege that little, if any, learning took place. Only a master with the skill of Frank H. Morrell, who later became superintendent of schools in Irvington, or his brother William marked a regime given to study. Lesser men found themselves locked in the outhouse, held on the pot-bellied stove, or assaulted by a barrage of ink bottles. Under such conditions, it was unthinkable to abandon corporal punishment. As a "reserve force," it could be used quite legally or not, as the schoolmaster determined, so long as school boards and legislatures left it alone.[63]

School board regulations, rather than statute, became the usual basis for restraints on the practice of corporal punishment. In this regard Newark early exemplified what came to be national practice. When, in 1855, a public school system was established in that city, the board prescribed that only the principal could legally administer such punishment and then only for offenses of willful neglect or insubordination. Protests against this system were frequent but sporadic and quite unorganized. Indeed, nowhere in the state appeared any concerted movement or public debate against corporal punishment nor does it seem that New Jersey abused corporal punishment more than other states. Unfortunately for the New Jersey public school teachers in the nineteenth century, they were notoriously ineffectual politically and almost powerless to counter legislative moves they opposed. When, quite casually, the ban was introduced, schoolmen were caught surprised and impotent. The occasion was the consideration by the legislature of a general school law in 1867. On 14 March, Assemblyman A. O. Evans of Hudson County arose to amend the law to prohibit corporal punishment absolutely in all of the schools of the state, private as well as public. Evans's amendment might have been provoked by an incident in a Hudson County public school a day or so earlier where a mother came and asked to see her child's teacher. When the teacher presented herself, the mother gave her what the newspaper called a sound "cowhiding." The principal, hearing the row, rushed to the rescue but apparently the irate mother was a match for teacher and principal together and she thrashed him as well. Her child, she felt, had been punished too severely, and she took matters firmly into her own hands.[64]

Assemblyman Evans, however strongly he may have felt about the incident, if indeed he was influenced by it at all, led no crusade and certainly did not consult with school officials about his amendment. He did argue at some length that there were better ways to get along with children, and his proposal found spontaneous support in the legislature. Representatives from all parts of the state spoke in favor of it while the opposition proved wavering. Elias M. White of Morris County threw in the obvious quotation about sparing the rod and spoiling the child—inevitably, someone had to—but the heart of the opposition centered really in the fear that the people would not sustain the action and such fear did not loom large enough to prevent passage.[65]

On 21 March the bill came before the Senate for final action. Senator August G. Richey of Mercer spoke the last word for the lost cause, arguing that corporal punishment was "often necessary for the well being of the scholars." Senator Alexander Wurtz of Hunterdon answered with the viewpoint that carried the day. Many teachers are "perfect brutes," he held, adding that nothing so irritated parents as having their children beaten, and the best course lay in prohibiting such punishment in the schools. Should some pupils prove incorrigible, he proposed that they be sent home with the responsibility shifted to parents who were the proper persons to inflict the punishment.[66] Therein lay one of the bones of contention between schoolman and layman. The schoolman wanted the child off the streets and in school and therefore (what he considered to be) adequate scope to deal with him.[67] When Senator Wurtz suggested sending the child home he ignored the fact that many of these children were "incorrigible" because of parental neglect. To send them home might well mean to turn them into the streets which was precisely what the schoolman sought to avoid.

But the striking thing is the casual approach to the ban. It had been before the legislature only a week. Apparently no one thought to ask the state superintendent of schools, Ellis A. Apgar, or any other expert on the matter if, indeed, the legislature thought there *were* any experts on a subject like the public schools that we all know so much about. To be sure, the nineteenth century produced fewer specialized experts than the twentieth and, hence, never became quite so habituated to consult them. Even if one takes this into account, all the evidence shows the law to be a careless gesture: a vote for the sanctity of the home and against the teacher with his disreputable past, to use Knight's term. There was no attempt to spell out anything more than the widest blanket prohibition which even the legislature must have known would be flouted in private schools. There was no provision even to define what corporal punishment was. For example, corporal punishment has been variously defined to mean punishment *of* the body such as imprisonment, as well as punishment *on* the body such as whipping. What of popping pepper in the pupil's mouth? Was that corporal? The New Jersey refusal to set forth a definition is in sharp contrast to the minority report of the Massachusetts education committee which in 1868 clearly made it "any punishment which produces physical pain."[68]

But the nineteenth century New Jersey legislature had learned to show more interest in its own image than in reality. Seven years later, when it made school attendance compulsory it carefully avoided any machinery for enforcement.[69] In the face of inadequate facilities statewide, the law was impossible to enforce. Yet to the casual observer it gave the impression of a legislature that brooked no nonsense about education. So, in banning corporal punishment, we need not assume that the legislative purpose was really to eliminate the beating of children.

Nor does the record show litigation to enforce the law until the twentieth century when the ban was construed rather favorably to school disciplinarians. For example, a commissioner of education held in 1913 that a teacher who pulled a pupil's hair had violated the law but found himself overruled by a board of education who maintained that this was not corporal punishment but only a way of attracting the pupil's attention.[70] Nor did a janitor violate the law who, catching some lads in an act of misconduct, slapped each of them "on the behind" as they ran out of the building.[71] But these were twentieth century cases; the nineteenth century proved less litigious. Despite an increasing sensitivity to humanitarianism, the abolition of corporal punishment in New Jersey sprang from no intensive effort of an organized movement, nor was it a response, in any direct sense, to the industrialization or urbanization that had begun to change the face of New Jersey. Rather, it was the compound of New Jersey apathy toward the public schools and low esteem for teachers together with a shrewd political judgment that the ban on corporal punishment would have some superficial popularity while it antagonized no group with enough political power to worry about. The schoolmen objected, of course, only to demonstrate again the little political power at their command. After the law had been enacted, Superintendent Apgar recorded his grave reservations, articulating the received position of the educators. Conceding that some county superintendents had reported improved discipline since the ban, he noted that others reported "disorder and insubordination." Despite his hope that the time would come when corporal punishment could be eliminated altogether, he doubted that the schools were ready then for prohibitory legislation. However, the first step had been taken; "it may be well to let the section remain." But on one point he was adamant; "there certainly should be no exceptions in favor of the cities"; to make them is to create "inconsistent legislation."[72]

The New Jersey Ban and the Cities

His point was well taken. New Jersey's absolute ban on corporal punishment had not lasted a month. On 12 April the legislature approved a joint resolution which nullified the effect of the ban on those cities already empowered by the legislature to make regulations for the government of their schools.[73] (The nearly ten thousand beatings in the city of Newark in 1876 were all quite legal.) Not a single dissenting voice in the legislature decried the slipping back into the corporal tradition.[74] What more eloquent testimony to the irresolution of a legislature and the careless drafting of legislation than the short, sweet life of the absolute ban in the cities? To be sure, by its ban on corporal punishment the legislature had circumscribed the powers it had earlier granted the cities of New Brunswick, Newark, and Elizabeth.[75] But, in logic, if the ban were justified for the rest of the state, then that made the case for the necessity of taking back to the state a part of the powers it had earlier granted the cities. Superintendent Apgar was right; the legislators had written "inconsistent legislation" and beyond that, had passed legislation which they had not only not thought through; they were perfectly willing to abandon unanimously their high ground with the first breath of political opposition against it. Only in the cities was there sufficient organization to rise against the law and, once it did, legislative resolution collapsed with neither bang nor whimper. No hero of humanitarianism immortalized himself with a vote of dissent.

The ban on corporal punishment in New Jersey produced some grumbling a year later. Apgar polled the county superintendents to get their view of the 1867 law establishing a statewide school system. Only one complaint of the law emerged in the poll: apprehension about the prohibition of corporal punishment expressed by six of the twenty-one county superintendents. Not a single one approved the ban. Superintendent Ralph Willis of Middlesex commented revealingly that an absolute prohibition covering all cases and all places must be modified or it would be violated. The prohibition, if not disregarded, he pointed out, was "overruled" by the impossibility of repressing disorder and maintaining the authority of the teacher by any other means than the use or fear of the rod.[76] The state had been put on notice that in some schools the law would be observed more in the breach than the observance; for apparently Newark was not alone in its cavalier attitude toward obeying the law. Here, by the way, we are considering only public schools and public school officials; parochial school teachers continued to swing the ferule far into the twentieth century in imperious disdain of secular dicta on classroom discipline.

Beatings, then, continued in the cities under color of the law. A writer for the Newark *News* remembered early in the twentieth century that each Newark principal kept a long, black walnut ruler within ready reach, to be applied to the outstretched hand of the hapless child, and, should maximum punishment be indicated, the hand first dipped in a basin of water and the principal bending back the fingers to make a taut surface.[77] No doubt some principals practiced this particular device but by no means all. A janitor gave J. Wilmer Kennedy, principal of Miller Street School in 1892, a piece of rattan from an old chair. Kennedy, who later became a Newark assistant superintendent of schools, used the rattan on a boy named James Cork six or eight times on the hand and across the back of the leg for having thrown a wad of paper at a girl, striking her in the eye and inflaming it. Charged by the boy's father with "unjust and severe punishment," Kennedy faced a hearing by a subcommittee of members of the board of education. Although young James bore at least one mark on his leg, the committee and the board of education exonerated Kennedy. It is interesting that in a hearing that stretched over three sessions and entailed lengthy questioning, no one asked whether Kennedy thought the boy had displayed willful insubordination, the only offense that permitted corporal punishment under Newark regulations.[78]

But the hearing merely punctuated the ending of the old order. The following year, in 1893, the legislature extended the statutory prohibition on corporal punishment to include even the city schools.[79] Uneasiness stirred in the Newark school system. City Superintendent of Schools William N. Barringer reported that one of the Newark principals remarked, "Well, corporal punishment is abolished. What shall we do now? What shall be done with the defiant and persistently disobedient? We must obey the law of the state."

"Certainly," replied Barringer, "you must obey the law. You say corporal punishment is forbidden, but punishment for wrongdoing is not prohibited. Have you no other means of correction but the rod?" One cannot help reading this conversation as a question from principal to superintendent, asking if the law need be obeyed. The answer was emphatic and must be understood to represent as well the city superintendent's official warning that no violator of the law might look to him for defense irrespective of earlier practice. The principal at once proposed that the ban would lead both principal and teacher to examine other approaches to the problem and he went on to point out that at least one result of the law would be that more study would enlighten "the whole subject of punishments as related to the reformation, training, and education of the young."[80] Had the law done nothing else than to stimulate this kind of thinking in the schools, its justification might well be established.

In December 1894 the board directed Barringer to survey the schools to determine the effects on discipline after a year of the latest statutory restraint on the schoolmen's power. At the February 1895 meeting of the board, Barringer presented his report. He had asked the thirty-eight principals of the Newark system four questions. First, what had been the experience of discipline in your school since the abolition of corporal punishment? Thirteen noted no change. Twenty had encountered difficulty with parents; that is, they had had to spend too much time meeting with parents settling paltry differences. This was the most universal complaint. The second question asked the principals what their experience had been prior to the ban. No consensus developed; the principals significantly did not wish to illustrate the experiences of the past golden age. Barringer also wanted to know their opinion of corporal punishment. Of the thirty-eight, twenty-two found it necessary while fourteen opposed it. Two responded that some other provision should be made. The final question asked what measures the principal would recommend for improvement. Various suggestions followed but a clear majority opted for an ungraded school for "incorrigibles" which certainly did not antagonize Barringer. He and his predecessor had been trying to persuade the board to provide one for twenty years.

Barringer, who in the past year had gathered data on wayward children from sixty cities throughout the country, swept aside the silly objection that too much time had to be spent with parents. As for Barringer, he knew no better way for principals to spend their time. Then he returned to the refrain that his predecessor, Sears, had raised twenty years earlier. The large size of classes continued. In this context, there remained three ways of dealing with the "incorrigible." A return to corporal punishment "under rigid limitations" apparently looked to possible modification of the state statute. Alternatively, the board might expel or suspend the recalcitrant but it should understand that, in effect, this was to turn the child into the street and meant, for Barringer, the destruction of the pupil. Finally, he reiterated the recommendation of the establishment of a reformatory school with suitably equipped shops and staffed with a "strict" faculty.[81]

A last voice spoke for the continuation of the use of corporal punishment. Citing United States Commissioner of Education William Torrey Harris, "one of the two or three foremost educators of the country," the *Newark Sunday Call* reminded its readers that corporal punishment had wide support among educators. The *Call* argued, too, that the twenty principals who favored use of corporal punishment were conceded to be at the head of their profession in the city. (These, it will be remembered, were the principals who found too much of their time wasted talking to parents.) Barringer's report, the *Call* held, ought to open the eyes of "the anti-rod shouters"; either there must be a return to corporal punishment or face the burden of maintaining a costly school for "incorrigibles." That is what it came down to in the end. Spare the purse but not the rod.

Probably the extension of the statute to the cities was better enforced than Newark board regulations had been in the past. In the fifteen years after the ban reached Newark, extant records disclose only three cases touching corporal punishment. One constituted a scuffle between teacher and pupil in which the teacher seems to have emerged second best. The second resulted in the censure and subsequent transfer of a teacher who used corporal punishment. Officials dismissed a third charge, probably with justification, although the standards of evidence sought by the superintendent seemed to embrace only the most severe encounter. Had the witness "ever seen a child with clothing torn, or nose bleeding, or otherwise showing *signs* of corporal punishment"? Nonetheless, the censure and transfer of the only teacher on record as breaking the law suggest a hostility to corporal punishment and a resolve to enforce the law not characteristic of the past.[82]

Conclusion

In nineteenth century New Jersey—even in Newark—restraint marked the use of corporal punishment in the school system. Compare the regulations in Newark with twentieth century Dallas, and Newark does not fare badly. Dallas instituted its program after consultation with B. F. Skinner, investing it with the most recent psychological thought in a way that Newark could not equal. But Newark gave authority of the rod—without power to delegate—solely to the principal. Dallas not only empowered the principal to delegate his authority to the assistant principal, but in addition it opened the door for any teacher to do his or her own flogging if the "Pupil Personnel Committee" so determined. After such determination, a teacher may administer the corporal punishment only in the presence of an adult after written consent from the parent. But in giving the teacher *any* powers and in permitting the principal to delegate his, twentieth century Dallas went further than did nineteenth century Newark. To which, unhappily, must be added the observation that neither nineteenth century Newark nor twentieth century Dallas respected its own rules.[83]

On the other hand, the sheer numbers dwindle. Dallas chalked up 5,358 cases in 1971;[84] a century earlier Newark, a city only a sixth as large, had nearly twice as many. The city superintendent of Newark claimed a need for flogging because of large classes, but as the ninteenth century closed, the argument shifted to where it lies basically today: flogging as a last resort and for the unusual case.[85]

A question lingers about the educator's perception of the child as he decides whether or not to flog. In nineteenth century Newark, that perception was at least in part because of "the influx of a foreign element . . . so great that it is impossible to bring it at once under the higher and better influences. Many of these children have very little idea of obedience to authority of any kind." So said Superintendent Barringer who further believed that the time had "fully come when this large and lawless class of children should be taught obedience to righteous authority." To be sure, corporal punishment was to be used only "in very, very rare instances."[86] The "foreign element" further complicates the image of him to be beaten. While nineteenth century America increasingly turned away from corporal punishment of its own children, it was rather more certain that other people's children needed a good hiding, particularly if they were of another race, ethnic group, or class.[87] In this sense the flood of immigration to industrializing America nurtured traditional belief in corporal punishment. Happily, not always. Reconstruction Freedmen's Schools in the South on occasion could lead the country in abandoning the rod. Reverend J. F. Ware of Maryland reported that "in dealing with a degraded race we took at once a stand *against the rod*" and it worked.[88]

The Newark argument for continued use of corporal punishment was badly flawed. If the case rested on the need to teach obedience to constituted authority, then both Barringer and his predecessor, Sears, might have begun with good example, obeying the regulations of the board by enforcing the ban on classroom teachers. Moreover, no evidence appears that the ban on corporal punishment subverted discipline in New Jersey schools, but on the contrary, despite the gloomy forebodings of the educators, they came to admit that discipline did not suffer. After the first full year that the statutory ban applied to the cities, Barringer reported to the state superintendent that *"discipline and government of the schools throughout all classes and grades have decidely improved."*[89] Charles B. Gilbert, the able city superintendent who succeeded Barringer in 1896, had no taste for corporal punishment in education and Addison B. Poland who followed in the same post in 1901 found that the segregation of the "incorrigibles" in ungraded schools—the substitute for corporal punishment proposed since 1874—reduced disobedience to authority to a minimum in Newark schools.[90]

For the historian, the significance of the use of corporal punishment may be in the way it emphasizes the monumental difficulties in the establishment of the public schools in the first place. Why should teachers traditionally have associated the whip as the *sine qua non* of their profession?

Does not corporal punishment forever establish the psychic insecurity of the schoolman and his own anxiety about the monotony, the irrelevance, and the haunting inhumanity of so many of the things he taught and the way he taught them? To be sure, America had to be literate, and progressively larger numbers yearned for the achievement not only of a democracy, but an industrialized society, and also for the appreciation of the deeper meanings of the religious heritage. The values in so rich a bequest filled the educator with such a crusading spirit that the public school became a value in itself and woe to him, either outsider or recalcitrant child, who did not accept it and accord with it.

But the realization of the public school dream fell short of its aspiration and none sensed this better than the children. For the school in the end also had to serve in Morrill Wyman's phrase, "an inheritance of unparalleled individual freedom," that is, that the end purpose was neither government, economy, or church, but the child himself. Sometimes the truth of things is seen by the children first as the Reverend Bradford Frazie wrote Lyman Cobb in 1847.[91] They knew something was wrong, not just in the use of corporal punishment, but the essential operation of the school as institution which fell short, so lamentably short, of achieving the reconciliation of individual freedom and the transmission of the heritage. Perhaps the goal itself was unreal, expectations beyond the hope of realization. To the extent that the schoolmen swung the rod, energetically dedicated to keeping order, doing what they could as best they could in what Thoreau saw as "lives of quiet desperation" and without investing the children with the sense of mutual respect and affection, the goal was missed.

In the New Jersey experience the schools withstood the statute banning corporal punishment which has remained essentially unchanged down to the present. Unconsulted by the legislature, the schoolmen had no recourse but to swallow their medicine only to find it had quite different results from what they had expected. They did not need the ancient power of the rod that had been wrested from them and they found themselves better examples of the obedience to authority, the ideal that they sought to instill in the young. The law is an ironic example of educational reform. Born of a political gesture as much as a humanitarian's dream, it remains in the second century of its establishment in far better repute than so many more earnestly felt and more carefully reasoned reforms that have characterized American schools.

NOTES

I am indebted to Lloyd deMause, Robert J. Fridlington, and my wife, Elaine, for comments on this article.

1. Massachusetts *Annotated Laws*, ch. 71, sect. 37G.

2. Lloyd deMause, "The Evolution of Childhood," *History of Childhood Quarterly* 1 (Spring 1974): 504–575, 542–543.

3. Bernard Bailyn, *Education in the Forming of American Society: Needs and Opportunities for Study* (New York: W. W. Norton, 1960) p. 23.

4. DeMause, "The Evolution of Childhood," p. 544.

5. John Demos, *A Little Commonwealth: Family Life in Plymouth Colony* (New York: Oxford University Press, 1970) pp. 62–81; Bailyn, *Education*, pp. 15–29.

6. Demos, *Little Commonwealth*, p. 100; Alexis de Tocqueville, *Democracy in America*, 2 vols. (New York: The Century Company, 1898) 2:233–239.

7. Lawrence Cremin, *The American Common School: An Historic Conception* (New York: Teachers College, 1951) p. 217.

8. Arthur W. Calhoun, *A Social History of the American Family*, 3 vols. (Cleveland: A. H. Clark, 1915–1918, reprinted New York: Barnes and Noble, 1960) 2:51, 56, 77.

9. Richard L. Rapson, "The American Child as Seen by British Travelers, 1845–1935," *American Quarterly* 17 (Fall 1965): 520–534.

10. John F. Walzer, "A Period of Ambivalence: Eighteenth Century American Childhood," in Lloyd deMause, ed., *The History of Childhood* (New York: The Psychohistory Press, 1974) pp. 351–382.

11. Calhoun, *American Family*, 2:54; Tocqueville, *Democracy in America*, 2:237.

12. Evelyn Millis Duvall, "Conception of Parenthood," *American Journal of Sociology* 52 (1946) 193–203, cited in Ruth Shonle Cavan, *The American Family* (New York: Thomas Y. Crowell, 1958) pp. 511–513.

13. Bernard Wishy, *The Child and the Republic: The Dawn of Modern American Child Nurture* (Philadelphia: The University of Pennsylvania Press, 1968) p. 10.

14. Charles Strickland, "A Transcendentalist Father: The Child Rearing Practices of Bronson Alcott," *History of Childhood Quarterly* 1 (Summer 1973) 4–51.

15. Wishy, *The Child*, p. 46, but see Wishy's whole chapter "Spare the Rod and Save the Child," pp. 42–49.

16. Edward Eggleston, *The Hoosier School-master* (New York: Grosset and Dunlap, 1889) p. 37.

17. Frederick W. Ricord, ed., *Biographical and Genealogical History of the City of Newark and Essex County*, 2 vols. (New York and Chicago: Lewis Publishing Company, 1898) 1:492–3.

18. Hedges to editor of the *American Journal of Education* 16 (1866): 738.

19. *Newark Sentinel*, 2 September 1890.

20. Excerpts are in Lyman Cobb, *The Evil Tendencies of Corporal Punishment as a Means of Moral Discipline in Families and Schools, Examined and Discussed* (New York: Mark H. Newman & Company, 1847) pp. 129–130n, 161n.

21. Cited in Herbert Falk, *Corporal Punishment: A Social Interpretation of Its Theory and Practice in the Schools of the United States* (New York: Teachers College, 1941) p. 65.

22. M. A. Eckstein, "Ultimate Deterrents: Punishment and Control in English and American Schools," *Comparative Education Review* 10 (October 1966): 433–41; *Newark Daily Advertiser*, 1 June 1889.

23. Horace Mann, *Sequel to the So-Called Correspondence between the Reverend M. H. Smith and Horace Mann Surreptitiously Published by Mr. Smith; Containing a Letter from Mr. Mann, Suppressed by Mrs. Smith with the Reply Therein Promised* (Boston: William B. Fowler, 1847) pp. 27–28.

24. "Hearings on Franklin Street School," 20 February 1893, reported in a manuscript book in the office of the Superintendent of Schools in Newark. I am indebted to Dr. John Anderson of Edison High School for bringing this document to my attention and to Mr. Bernard J. Reilly, Jr., of the superintendent's office for assistance in locating it.

25. Maxine Green, *The Public School and the Private Vision: A Search for America in Education and Literature* (New York: Random House, 1965) pp. 42–43.

26. David Page, *Theory and Practice of Teaching or the Motives and Methods of Good Schoolkeeping* (New York: A. S. Barnes, 90th ed., 1867) pp. 194–215.

27. Dr. Morrill Wyman, *Progress in School Discipline, Remarks of Dr. Morrill Wyman, of Cambridge, in support of the resolution to abolish the corporal punishment of girls in the public schools of the city made in the Republican caucus, November 16, 1866* (Cambridge: James Cox, 1866) p. 5.

28. Cobb, *Corporal Punishment*, Appendix.

29. Falk, *Corporal Punishment*, p. 79.

30. Cobb, *Corporal Punishment*, p. 260.

31. Massachusetts Education Committee, *Reports on the Abolition of Corporal Punishment in the Public Schools*, House Document 335 (Boston: Wright and Potter, 1868) p. 15.

32. Massachusetts Education Committee, *Reports*, p. 14.

33. Wyman, *Progress in School Discipline*, p. 6.

34. Ibid., p. 5.

35. Ibid., p. 40.

36. New Jersey State Board of Education, *Annual Report*, 1861, p. 18; Newark Board of Education, *Annual Reports*, 1901, p. 59; 1910, p. 75.

37. *Newark Evening News*, 25 March 1892.

38. Cobb, *Corporal Punishment*, p. 225.

39. Ibid., p. 61.

40. Ibid., p. 30.

41. Richard C. Humphreys, *Corporal Punishment: Reply to the Majority Report of Committee on Rules and Regulations of Boston School Board* (Boston: George H. Ellis, 1890) p. 14.

42. Cobb, *Corporal Punishment*, p. 71.

43. J. P. Gordy, *Rise and Growth of the Normal School Idea in the United States* (Washington, D.C.: Government Printing Office, 1891) p. 83.

44. For a discussion of "battered children," see deMause, "The Evolution of Childhood" pp. 543ff.

45. Cited from Charles Francis Adams, *Richard Henry Dana*, in Falk, *Corporal Punishment*, pp. 57–58.

46. Falk, *Corporal Punishment*, p. 59.

47. Massachusetts Education Committee, *Reports*, pp. 26–27n.

48. Humphreys, *Corporal Punishment*, pp. 15, 19.

49. Massachusetts Education Committee, *Reports*, p. 45; Wyman, *Progress in School Discipline*, p. 4, citing the *Massachusetts Teacher*.

50. "Address at the State Normal School" *American Journal of Education* 5 (July 1867): 835.

51. See the poll in National Education Association *Journal* 50 (May 1961): 13 in which 71.6 percent of teachers favored corporal punishment; a poll in *Nation's Schools* 87 (May 1971): 39 showed an increase from 25 percent to 74 percent in five years in schools using corporal punishment. Sixty-four percent of teachers approved. A shocking development in collective bargaining is the "negotiation" of the right to beat children's bodies; 7.3 percent of teacher's contracts had corporal punishment clauses, National Education Association *Bulletin* 47 (May 1969): 59.

52. Falk, *Corporal Punishment*, pp. 36–7.

✓ 53. Alice Morse Earle, *Child Life in Colonial Days* (New York: Macmillan Company, 1899) p. 197; New Jersey State Board of Education, *Annual Report*, 1863, pp. 10, 15.

54. Cobb, *Corporal Punishment*, p. 253n.

55. Newark Board of Education, *Annual Report*, 1860, p. 16. Lyman Cobb preceded Sears as a believer in singing as a corrective for the need for corporal punishment, *Corporal Punishment*, pp 148–151; for a colonial precedent of the same type see Alice Morse Earle, *Child Life in Colonial Days*, p. 202; *Newark Daily Advertiser*, 1 June 1889; *Newark Evening News*, 25 May 1890.

56. Mann, *Sequel*, p. 26.

57. Newark Board of Education, "Minutes," 31 May 1861; *Annual Report*, 1874, pp. 54–56; 1876, p. 58.

58. Newarak Board of Education, *Annual Report*, 1864, p. 41; "Minutes" principal's meeting, 2 March 1881, 7 March 1888.

59. Newark Board of Education, "Minutes," 27 October 1876; *Annual Report*, 1876, p. 19.

60. James McLachlan, *American Boarding Schools: A Historical Study* (New York: Scribner's, 1970) p. 152; Philippe Ariès, *Centuries of Childhood: A Social History of Family Life* (New York: Random House, 1962) p. 319.

61. Wyman, *Progress in School Discipline*, p. 25.

62. Humphreys, *Corporal Punishment*, p. 12. For figures in the 1880s for Boston, see Falk, *Corporal Punishment*, p. 93.

63. *Newark Sunday Call*, 28 September 1909; the common law makes the teacher *in loco parentis*; the parent in the act of sending the child to school

delegates parental power of such correction as may be necessary to accomplish the purpose of education; Michael Arthur Travis, "New Jersey School Law as Applied to Classroom Teachers and Teacher Relationship," doctoral dissertation, Rutgers University, 1943, p. 107.

64. *Trenton Daily True American*, 18 March 1867.

65. Ibid., 16 March 1867.

66. Ibid., 21 March 1867.

67. The view survives in John A. R. Wilson, "Sometimes Teachers *Should* Spank Students," *Educational Forum* 24 (January 1960): 217–19.

68. Massachusetts Education Committee, *Reports*, p. 4.

69. *Trenton Daily True American*, 27 March 1874.

70. *School Law Decisions of Commissioner of Education and (New Jersey) State Board of Education* (Trenton:McCrellish and Quigley, 1938) pp. 585, 586, 588.

71. Carl Graydon Leech, *The Constitutional and Legal Basis of Education in New Jersey* (Philadelphia, privately printed, 1932) pp. 419–420.

72. New Jersey State Board of Education, *Annual Report*, 1867, p. 665.

73. New Jersey *Acts*, 1867, Joint Resolution No. 12, p. 1028.

74. *Trenton Daily True American*, 12 April 1867.

75. New Jersey *Laws*, 1855, ch. LXX, sect. 3, p. 160; 1857, ch. LII, sect. 61, p. 147; 1860, ch. CXXIV, sect. 62, p. 314, for New Brunswick, Newark, and Elizabeth, respectively.

76. New Jersey State Board of Education, *Annual Report*, 1868, pp. 755–783.

77. *Newark Evening News*, "Neighborhood Editorial Corner," 30 May 1913.

78. "Hearings," 24 February to 8 March 1892; *Newark Evening News*, 26 March 1892.

79. New Jersey *Laws*, 1893, ch. 109, pp. 194–195.

80. Newark Board of Education, *Annual Report*, 1894, "Corporal Punishment," pp. 98–103, p. 100.

81. *Newark Evening News*, 26 January 1894, 18 February 1895; *Newark Daily Advertiser*, 28 February 1895.

82. Newark Board of Education, Committee on Teachers, "Minutes," 28 January 1898, 30 November 1900; my italics, Committee on Instruction and Educational Supplies, "Minutes," 13 September 1909.

83. *Ware* v. *Estes* 328 F. Supp. 657 (1971) at 658. Incidentally, the opinion of the court that teachers in Dallas abused the practice of corporal punishment did not lead it to declare the practice including such abuse a violation of any constitutional rights. The Supreme Court, 20 November 1972, upheld the opinion, denying certiorari.

84. *Time* 99 (12 June 1972): 37–38.

85. L. C. Hickman, "Corporal Punishment: Relegated to Last Resort Discipline, Survey Shows" *Nation's Schools* 76 (1965): 48–50; see also Francis Keppel and others cited for the same view in National Education Association *Journal* 52 (September 1963): 19 20.

86. Newark Board of Education, *Annual Report*, 1895, p. 101.

87. Earl Barnes, "Corporal Punishment as a Means of Social Control," 13 (March 1898) *Education*, 387–395.

88. Massachusetts Education Committee, *Reports*, p. 29.

89. New Jersey State Board of Education, *Annual Report*, 1894, Appendix A, p. 115, my italics.

90. Gilbert to G. M. Brant, 1897 in Letterbooks, Office of the Newark Superintendent of Schools; Newark Board of Education, *Annual Report*, 1911, p. 115.

√91. Cobb, *Corporal Punishment*, pp. 240–241.

PART III

•

CAUSES AND CONSEQUENCES

The preceding section of this book presented historical information regarding the practice of corporal punishment in schools within the larger context of cultural and societal attitudes regarding discipline and children. While the writers in that section emphasized historical information and speculated about causal factors, the writers in this section deal with various theories to explain the continued use of the practice. Overlap between the sections is inevitable.

The first essay by Philip Piele is an edited version of a longer article which considers the Supreme Court decision discussed more thoroughly in Part IV. Piele analyzes the Supreme Court's dependence on historic precedents as a major rationale in their decision in Ingraham v. Wright. *Historic precedent, based more in tradition and social practice than actual law, reflects the Supreme Court's belief in traditional conservative values. Piele then presents a wide-ranging anthropological, socio-biological, and ethological discussion of the roots of our adherence to the practice of hitting children. Piele's excellent theoretical essay is complemented by the different approach of the next one by Owens and Straus, "The Social Structure of Violence in Childhood and Approval of Violence as an Adult." The latter attempts to utilize data collected in a national survey by the Commission on the Causes and Prevention of Violence. The survey suggests that those who experience violence as children tend to favor the use of violence to achieve both a political and a personal end when they are adults. The authors conclude that there seems to be a relationship between the use of violence in childhood and the maintenance of violence as a method for solving problems in adulthood. This essay points out the necessity of an educational system which not only does not support the use of violence for solving problems but educates children to the rational use of other methods for changing behavior.*

In the following essay, Welsh presents a more dramatic case for the theory of "modeling" which is supported in the sociological studies of

Owens and Straus. Dr. Welsh discusses the aggression-inducing properties of punishment which result in repeated cycles of receiving and giving aggression from one generation to the next. This essay offers a balanced combination of clinical observation and psychological research. Welsh's work must be extended to the schools in order to test the hypothesis that violence against children will result in counterviolence against school property, other children, and even teachers. One study linking school vandalism and the use of corporal punishment is reported in the Introduction and the experimental evidence for Welsh's theory is detailed by Bongiovanni in Part VI.

The final essay in this part presents a cross-cultural study which again supports the theory of modeling to account for the continuing use of corporal punishment on children. Bellak and Antell conducted a direct observational study of aggression by parents and consequent displaced aggression by children toward other children. The interesting aspect of this inter-cultural study is that it reflects cultural attitudes. The studies conducted in Germany where corporal punishment is used in the school, and in Italy and Denmark where it is not, found a greater tendency among German parents to use physical punishment against their children and a consequent greater tendency for German children to use the same methods against other children than was observed by the children of the other two countries.

These four essays offer some suggestions as to the roots of the practice of corporal punishment and reasons for its continued use. They are just a representative sample of the vast literature on the subject of human aggression and the use of physical force to change behavior and solve problems. The next part deals with legal issues which reflect the consequences of corporal punishment.

5

Neither Corporal Punishment Cruel
nor Due Process Due:
The United States Supreme Court's Decision
in *Ingraham v. Wright*

Philip K. Piele

•

> *Between the idea*
> *And the reality*
> *Between the motion*
> *And the act*
> *Falls the Shadow.*
>
> *T. S. Eliot,*
> Journey of the Magi

In April of this year, the United States Supreme Court handed down its decision, in the case of *Ingraham* v. *Wright*,[1] that corporal punishment of students in the nation's public school system does not violate the Eighth and Fourteenth amendments of the United States Constitution. If the Court had been disposed to reach just the opposite conclusion and to ban corporal punishment as an option that teachers and administrators can exercise in maintaining discipline in the public schools, the Court could likely have found no better case on which to base its judgment. The evidence heard by the Court in this case cannot help but shock the sensibilities of even the most clinical observer. In reaching its decision, the majority of the Court was quite obviously looking beyond the circumstances of this particular

This essay is a condensed version of the original paper which was presented at a conference on "Problems of Law and Society: Asia, the Pacific, and the United States," Institute for Cultural Learning, The East-West Center, Honolulu, Hawaii, July 25–August 11, 1977. Reprinted from *Journal of Law and Education*, Vol. 7, No. 1. (728 National Press Building, Washington, D.C., 20004.)

case, which developed in a junior high school in the school system of Dade County, Florida. What the Court had in mind was that the issue was not merely how corporal punishment was applied by the officials of one particular school system but rather whether corporal punishment as a principle is inherently inconsistent with the tenets of constitutional law, and thus whether school officials throughout the nation have the authority to administer corporal punishment in any degree at all. On the basis of evidence pointing to its misuse in one particular case, the Court apparently was not willing to say no to the use of corporal punishment in general. Aware that its ruling in this case would set a precedent for the entire nation, the Court considered as evidence more than just the facts of this case. It looked at the cultural and historical setting as a background for viewing the position corporal punishment occupies in American education. Thus, the Court intended to base its decision governing the nationwide practice of corporal punishment in the schools, in part at least, on a balanced understanding of national attitudes and values pertaining to corporal punishment and on the historical wellsprings from which those values flow.

As we shall see, these current national attitudes and values, as well as their historical counterparts, reflect two diametrically opposed concepts of the nature of man. In this paper, I want to focus particularly on the development, in the American context, of these two quite different views of man, each of which reaches different conclusions as to the proper role of physical punishment in controlling behavior. This analysis will afford the necessary basis for understanding how the Court reached the decision it did.

The majority opinion contains numerous references to the traditional conservative values of many white, middle-class Americans, particularly those living in the South and the Midwest. This comes as no great surprise, given the Court's present conservative disposition. Since the judicial process is an important aspect of our cultural milieu, which both influences and is influenced by contemporary social, political, and economic conditions and by public opinion, it is hardly surprising that the rebirth of conservative values in American society as a whole is reflected in the constitutional interpretation the Court adopts in any specific case.

The very emphasis the majority opinion places on the importance of understanding history and tradition in *Ingraham* itself reflects white, middle-class, conservative values, which stress the importance of heritage. At least two dozen times the Court invokes "history" and "tradition" in its arguments. In determining that the Eighth Amendment does not apply to corporal punishment of schoolchildren, the Court's majority draws on "the way in which our traditions and our laws have responded to the use of corporal punishment in public schools."[2] The majority cursorily outlines the historic precedents for the practice, citing the colonial period as its source in America. The majority's reasoning here is clear: because corporal punishment in the schools has historic precedents both in social practice and in common law, which of course reflects social practice, that heritage cannot be tampered with, especially since corporal punishment is still in use today. A similar line of reasoning is evident in the majority's assertion that the Eighth Amendment applies only to criminals. The majority found "an inadequate basis for wrenching the Eighth Amendment from its historical context and extending it to traditional disciplinary practices in the public schools."[3]

The Court's affinity for conservative values is also to be seen in the acceptance of the following tenets implied in the majority opinion:

• The historically close relationship of the school to the community, emphasizing local control and the influence of local norms on the learning environment behind the schoolhouse door ("The openness of the public school and its supervision by the community afford significant safeguards. . . .")[4]

• Respect for established institutions of government ("[R]espect for democratic institutions will . . . dissipate if they [teachers] are thought too ineffectual to provide their students an environment of order.")[5]

• Respect for traditional authority figures ("Teachers, properly concerned with maintaining authority in the classroom. . . .")[6]

• The minimal intrusion of the federal government into areas of traditional state and local concern ("Elimination or curtailment of corporal punishment [should be the result of] the normal process of community debate and legislative action. . . .")[7]

To elaborate further on these commonly understood values of American conservatism is, for me at least, to belabor the obvious. What is perhaps less obvious and by far a more intellectually provocative line of inquiry is to examine the historical and contemporary assumptions regarding the social and educational context of the use of corporal punishment on children. As we shall see, these assumptions relate closely to the Calvinist concept of the nature of man, a concept deeply rooted in America's Puritan heritage. The Court's implicit sanction of these assumptions, without provision for even minimal due process in the public schools, is of course the essence of *Ingraham*.

In America, the historical roots of the use of corporal punishment can be traced to the Puritan settlement of the Massachusetts Bay Colony in the seventeenth century, although other American colonies imported penal practices in wide use at that time, including severe corporal punishment of criminals. But the conjunction between the Calvinist philosophy of innate depravity and the practice of physical punishment intended to curtail man's evil nature achieved its most obvious expression in the Bay Colony. The punishment of children was but one manifestation of the Puritan view that man was basically weak, sin-ridden, and incapable of truly moral, independent action. According to Jonathan Edwards, man was but "a spider or some loathsome insect," which God abhorred and, at the slightest provocation, would "cast into the fire" of hell.[8] Man viewed in such odious terms could find redemption only through strict obedience to the doctrine of the Puritan religion.

The authority of the Puritan governors, who strove to control the secular as well as the religious affairs of their flock, was believed to emanate from and reflect God's ultimate authority. This belief, coupled with the conviction that man was in need of strong direction to keep him from indulging his depraved nature, led to the development of a theocratic government, which employed tight, autocratic control. Thus, church and state conjoined to enforce the value of obedience to authority—both of God and of his ministers. Cotton Mather both articulates the need to regulate profligate tendencies among Puritan adherents and indicates the high value placed on reverence for authority: "There is a liberty of corrupt nature, which is affected both by men and beasts, to do what they list; and this liberty is inconsistent with authority, impatient of all restraints; by this liberty, *sumus omnes Deteriores*; 'tis the grand enemy of *truth* and *peace*, and all the ordinances of God are bent against it."[9]

Puritan belief in the sanctity of authority and the virtue of obedience was amply evident in their attitude toward children, who were hardly held in high esteem. The progeny of this innately depraved creature called man was also, quite naturally, possessed of the same loathsome characteristics. Thus, children were regarded as "young vipers and infinitely more hateful than vipers,"[10] who must have the devil beaten out of them.[11] The theocracy's legal sanctions against a child not responding to correction imposed on him by his parents were severe indeed:

> If a man have a stubborn or rebellious son, of sufficient years and understanding, viz, 16, who will not obey the voice of his father or the voice of his mother, and that when they have chastened him will not harken unto them, then shall his father and mother, being his natural parents, lay hold on him, and bring him to the magistrate assembled in Court, and testify unto them, by sufficient evidence, that this their son is stubborn and rebellious, and will not obey their voice and chastisement, but lives in sundry notorious crimes, *such a son shall be put to death.* (Emphasis added.)[12]

While there is no evidence that the law was ever applied, still it is little wonder, in light of this colony-mandated punishment for extreme cases of youthful disobedience of the Fifth Commandment, that all but the most

brutal parental application of corporal punishment to children was regarded as reasonable by our Puritan forefathers. The same obedience demanded of children was likewise expected of servants. The early laws and
ordinances provided that "[m]agistrates may punish disorderly children or
servants on complaint, by whipping or otherwise, as they see cause."[13]

The whipping of children must have seemed in most cases mild indeed
in comparison to the widespread corporal punishment inflicted on criminals,
including such methods of punishment as the pillory, the whipping post, and
the stocks, all of which were considered quite "reasonable." Any Puritan
parent having second thoughts about the rightness of rod-enforced discipline of his or her child could turn for reassurance to the Bible: "Foolish-
ness is bound up in the heart of a child, but the rod of correction shall drive
it far from him."[14]

The Puritan belief that man's depravity must be rigidly controlled
through strict adherence to the rule of God among men encouraged the
development of an educational system intended to perpetuate Puritan doctrine and values. In the "Old Deluder Satan Act," the governors established
a system of public instruction intended to provide "knowledge of the scrip-
ture," and to ensure "that learning may not be buried in the graves of our
forefathers."[15] Furthermore, according to John Calvin, whose theology
formed a basis for Puritan beliefs, "Children are inherently evil and must
be trained rigorously in developing good habits. Education is to be a complete regimentation of the child to suppress his evil nature and build good
living and thinking."[16] The instrument for the realization of Calvin's proposition concerning the goal and method of education was the rod. Rules
drawn up for the Free Town School of Dorchester in 1645 established the
rationale and procedure for the logical extension of rod-enforced training
of children in the home by parents to that same but more formalized purpose in the school by the master *in loco parentis*:

> And because the Rodd of Correction is an ordinance of God necessary
> sometymes to bee dispenced unto Children. . . , [i]t is therefore ordered
> and agreed that the schoolmaster for the tyme beeing shall haue full
> power to minister correction to all or any of his schollers without respect
> of p'sons according as the nature and qualitie of the offence shall require
> whereto, all his schollers must bee duley subject and no parent or other
> of the Inhabitants shall hinder or goe about to hinder the master therein.[17]

While this paper focuses on the Puritan roots of the use of corporal
punishment in the public schools, it would be entirely misleading to suggest
that all the early colonists ascribed to the same point of view. Quite the
contrary. Although corporal punishment was used in Quaker schools, it
was not assigned the importance that it received in Puritan schools, prob-

ably because the Quakers were not so inclined to view children as essentially depraved and therefore did not see so much need to govern them by fear—of God and of authority. The school overseers recommended (in 1796) that "the children under your care be governed, as much as possible [by love]. This will make the use of the Rod in a good degree unnecessary, and will induce the Children to love and respect rather than to fear."[18]

The Quaker overseers promulgated a set of rules bearing on student behavior, which they printed, distributed to the schools, and read publicly "at least every three months, and as much oftener as fit occasion may present, and a printed copy thereof put up in a conspicuous place in each of the schools."[19] The rules contained no mention of consequences, should one of them be violated, though obviously some disciplinary measure would be taken. Positive reinforcement was also employed "[a]s an incentive for scholarship, it was customary to give 'premiums' or awards." Even though philosophically the Quakers objected to such a course, "the policy of rewards was approved by the overseers, and ways and means to accumulate funds for these purposes were sought."

Games and hazing were common, as were practical jokes, sometimes even played on schoolmasters. Student newspapers and magazines were also quite common, and apparently they were not subjected to strict censorship. It is apparent that Quaker school life and attitudes toward children and their discipline were often in sharp contrast to what was occurring in Massachusetts at approximately the same time.[20] The freedom of expression given students and the publication of laws (as opposed to authoritarian caprice) might be taken to suggest the roots of democratic/humanistic influence in public schools in this country. While the principles of Jeffersonian democracy were obviously a more powerful and lasting force in American education than were the ideals and practices of the Quakers, it is noteworthy that two contrasting (and frequently conflicting) religious and educational philosophies were established in America about the same time.

The democratic/humanistic view of man has had an obvious influence on the public school disciplinary practices deriving from the Puritan view that mankind and his progeny are essentially depraved and therefore to be governed by fear of God and civil authority. One needs only to read some of the voluminous writing on the history of childhood and of the use of corporal punishment in the schools to see how the democratic/humanistic influence has resulted in the gradual waning (particularly during the past several decades) of the use of corporal punishment in American schools and in the increasing rejection of the implicit assumption (that children are not reasonable and, therefore, must be governed by fear) on which its use is based.[21]

Still, the practice persists. The Court is indeed correct in asserting that the use of corporal punishment in the schools "survived the transformation of primary and secondary education from the colonials' reliance on optional arrangements to our present system of compulsory education and dependence on public schools, . . . [and] continues to play a role in the public education of schoolchildren in most parts of the country."[22] And so it does, with the exception of three states: New Jersey (which outlawed its use in the schools in 1867), Maryland, and, ironically, Massachusetts.[23] Several cities, including Chicago, Baltimore, New York, Philadelphia, and the District of Columbia have also forbidden its use. The survival of corporal punishment in American public schools is all the more noteworthy, considering that many other countries around the world have abandoned its use.[24]

Perhaps corporal punishment in American schools remains an important vestige of our Puritan heritage because its use is sustained by the beliefs of a considerable number of Americans (particularly in the South and Midwest) who hold fundamentalist religious convictions and of still others who consider that man is innately aggressive and therefore, according to this argument, bad. It is this latter notion, buttressed by considerable scientific and pseudoscientific evidence, that holds a particular fascination to many Americans. Popularized in the sixties by a number of books (Robert Ardrey's *The Territorial Imperative*, Desmond Morris's *The Naked Ape*, and Konrad Lorenz's *On Aggression* were three of the best-selling books of this genre), the thesis that man and animals share certain common innate behavior patterns, such as territoriality, aggression, and dominance, strikes a particularly responsive chord in many Americans.

"Human sympathies, moral convictions, political absolutes, philosophical certainties—none, whatever the discomfort their frustration may cause us, will suborn or suppress the territorial imperative, that biological morality which will still contain the behavior of beings when *Homo sapiens* is an evolutionary memory."[25] Those dramatic words, by dramatist *cum* ethologist[26] Robert Ardrey, are from one of the most popular books of this genre, *The Territorial Imperative*. Ardrey's message to the world is that man is innately territorial and aggressive, a behavior pattern he shares with his animal ancestors. "We act as we do for reasons of our evolutionary past," says Ardrey, "not our cultural present, and our behavior is as much a mark of our species as is the shape of a human thigh bone or the configuration of nerves in a corner of the human brain."[27] Man's biogenetically derived aggressiveness is constantly at odds with his culturally derived capacity "for tenderness, sympathy, charity, [and] love."[28]

Adopting Herbert Spencer's phrases "code of amity" and "code of enmity" to describe this dual nature of man, Ardrey asserts that man must follow them "unthinkingly, since he has no alternative. Let enough members of society disobey the code of amity, and the society will fragment; let enough disobey the code of enmity and society will be crushed."[29]

It is quite predictable that Ardrey would find Spencer, the original social Darwinist, an appealing source. Darwin's theories offered determinism a scientific justification, which social theorists like Spencer hastened to apply to human social interaction. Thus, on two levels (the biological and the social), man was seen as subject to the same natural forces as those determining the course of the rest of nature. Man's lot, like that of the other beasts, was cast irrevocably, not by God as the Calvinist Puritans had believed, but by natural scientific law. But what Puritan theology and social Darwinism (as well as Ardrey's neo-naturalism) have in common is determinism. Man is governed by forces beyond his control, whether those forces are seen as deific (as the Puritans believed) or naturalistic and genetic (as Ardrey believes).

Obviously, if man must follow his innately aggressive (and therefore, destructive) course "unthinkingly," he can hardly be conceived to possess the free will and independence of action central to the democratic/humanistic conception of man. In Ardrey's scheme, man is as weak and helpless as Jonathan Edwards's "spider" dangled over the fires of hell. As M. F. Ashley Montagu has said of the works of Ardrey, Morris, and Lorenz, they represent "the new litany of 'innate depravity' " and a contemporary version of "original sin."[30]

Although Ardrey does not himself acknowledge his Calvinist propensities, he is certainly aware that his philosophic roots differ from Montagu's. According to Ardrey, Montagu represents a new "scientific romanticism" much akin to Rousseau's philosophy (man is innately good), but restated in scientific terms. Thus Ardrey accuses Montagu of cloaking "the original goodness" in a "scientific vocabulary." The irony of his rejection of Montagu's position is that Ardrey follows exactly the same process to express his philosophical biases in favor of determinism and innate depravity.

Desmond Morris's *The Naked Ape* emphasizes the links between man and his fellow primates. Morris, a zoologist, draws on material from paleontology and ethology, including "direct observation of the most basic and widely shared behavior patterns . . . of the naked ape itself."[31] One of these "widely shared behavior patterns" is the sexually related "appeasement gesture" in the fighting behavior of primates. In man, this gesture has been culturally adapted to become the spanking ritual:

[T]he more specific case of the adoption of the female sexual rump-presentation as an appeasement gesture has virtually vanished, along with the disappearance of the original sexual posture itself. It is largely confined now to a form of schoolboy punishment, with rhythmic whipping replacing the rhythmic pelvic thrusts of the dominant male. It is doubtful whether school-masters would persist in this practice if they fully appreciated the fact that, in reality, they were performing an ancient primate form of ritual copulation with their pupils.[32]

If Morris is correct, then it is indeed ironic that corporal punishment, intended to instill in children a respect for authority and other values we associate with civilized behavior, is at base a most primitive (and certainly uncivilized) ritual. Morris's implicit message is that, try as we might, we are still no different (and no better) than the so-called lower primates. Far from being "in action how like an angel, in apprehension how like a god!"[33] man is in nature no different from the creatures ("beasts") he has for so long scorned. Morris's argument, like the Calvinist argument of innate depravity, is hardly calculated to bolster man's self-esteem.

Morris grants, however, that we do indeed differ from our hairy cousins in our cultural development and aspiration toward ideals. But he cautions that "in acquiring lofty new motives, [man] has lost none of the earthy old ones."[34] What man needs, Morris argues, is a reconciliation between these two sides in order to become a "less worried and more fulfilled animal."[35] But notice that even with resolution of the duality, man will still be an "animal." There is no transcendence here.

Konrad Lorenz comments on man's dual cultural/biogenetic nature in terms similar to those of Morris. In *On Aggression*, Lorenz posits (like Ardrey) that man is innately aggressive; at the same time, though, man can apprehend and pursue "the very highest moral and ethical values": "[T]he Janus head of man: The only being capable of dedicating himself to the very highest moral and ethical values requires for this purpose a phylogenetically adapted mechanism of behavior whose animal properties bring with them the danger that he will kill his brother, convinced that he is doing so in the interests of these very same high values."[36]

But Lorenz sees rapid social and technological change causing the maladaptation of social norms and rites derived from this so-called "phylogenetically adapted mechanism of behavior" as one of the major factors "threatening to interrupt the continuity of our Western culture."[37]

While many disagree with the basic arguments of Ardrey, Morris, Lorenz, and others that man is an innately aggressive creature subject to biological forces beyond his control,[38] their view of man has achieved considerable acceptance by American lay readers. Why? One plausible explanation is provided by Montagu:

> The layman is bewildered. Two World Wars, the breakdown in political, public, and private morality, the ever-increasing crime rates, the development of a climate and a culture of violence, together with the consciousness of an apocalyptic realization of irreversible disaster, are quandries enough to cause men to look desperately about them for some sort of an answer, for some explanation of the meaning, of the causes which seem to be leading man to destruction.[39]

Perhaps Montagu is right, perhaps not. Whatever the explanation, the Puritan concept of man is an innately depraved creature whose fate is preordained appears to have been transformed by the scientific revolution into the concept of man as an innately aggressive creature whose fate is genetically determined. These notions seem to be well entrenched in the subconscious of many Americans, finding cultural expression in times of social change and unrest.

Another modern reappearance of the Puritan belief in man's innate depravity, particularly the idea of the child as evil, is to be found in a number of recent American films. *The Exorcist, Rosemary's Baby, The Omen*, and *The Devil within Her* are but a few of the more popular recent motion pictures that have treated the devil-in-child or devil-as-child theme. The hugely successful film *The Exorcist* depicts an innocent twelve-year-old girl whose body is suddenly and inexplicably invaded by the Evil One. Defying the best efforts of science and medicine, the Devil remains in control of the child until driven out by the exorcist rites of a Catholic priest. *Rosemary's Baby* is a film about a married woman who bears a child fathered by Satan. Conventional medicine, bewildered by the strange aspects of her demonic pregnancy, is powerless to help her. A child born of Satan is also the subject of both *The Omen* and *The Devil within Her*.

The seemingly endless film variations on the child-as-demon theme expressed in these films moved one movie critic to remark that "[t]he babies in them are easy customers for cinema's feeble conception of badness, which is as puny an approximation of evil as Pollyanna is of virtue."[40] Puny or not, there seems to be something emotionally and aesthetically compelling about supreme evil invading (or being embodied in) supreme good. The most handy archetype here is the snake (evil, knowledge, experience) in the garden (good, blissful ignorance, innocence).

The same juxtaposition of extremes occurs in the image of the child-demon. When rendered in fictional terms as in the motion pictures mentioned, this dichotomous image—of the child as demon or devil/the child as innocent, or the child as actively evil/the child as passively good, or the child as the source of evil/the child as the victim of evil—serves as a focal point for adult anxieties, with fear of rebellion by children being one of the primary ones.

Two themes stand out in these movies: the straight-line reincarnation of the child-as-evil belief of the Puritans and the inability of modern science to control evil forces. This latter notion has prompted one critic to observe in his review of *Rosemary's Baby* that "[t]he film, like the culture, is part of the challenge to science, for if God-concepts are ship-wrecked on the problem of evil, neither does science provide us with answers."[41]

In terms very much like Ashley Montagu's explanation of the contemporary popularity of the biogenetic, deterministic concept of "innate aggression," Forshey explains the immense popularity of the child-as-devil, antiscience films as a derivative of

> [t]he events of our day, the seemingly uncontrollable forces existing in the world, [which] have opened up the occult again. We are coming to believe in powers and principalities again and are trying to find the language to express that belief. Wars, the increasing number of violent crimes against persons, the devastating undermining of our political institutions, the energy and environmental crises, etc.—all these seem to be out of the hands of human beings. It seems as if the devil himself has control of the forces which shape us.[42]

The widespread attention paid in the news media to juvenile crime indicates both the adult anxieties about uncontrolled or evil children and the seeming insufficiency of social science to cope with such children. The author of *Time* magazine's cover article "The Youth Crime Plague" (July 11, 1977) suggests the insecurities that adults experience when confronted with the seemingly purposeless violence and mayhem wreaked by child criminals: "How can such sadistic acts—expressions of what moral philosophers would call sheer evil—be explained satisfactorily by poverty and deprivation? What is it in our society that produces such mindless rage? . . . Or has the whole connection between crime and society been exaggerated? Some of the usual explanations seem pretty limp."[43]

If traditional social scientific explanations of youthful deviance fail adequately to explain such behavior, and if social science has no workable solutions to youth crime, then it makes a kind of emotional sense to attribute such inexplicable violence to supernatural, or at least mysterious, forces. "Sheer evil" in youthful criminals is perhaps ultimately comprehensible to many Americans only in the superstitious or occult context of celluloid child-devils.

Like the relationship between man and society, the relationships between parent and child and between teacher and student are seemingly beyond our control. In contemporary American society, the "youth rebellion" of the 1960s aroused extreme anxiety among parents, teachers, and other representatives of established authority. Likewise, the "repression" of youth by adult authority brought about extreme anxiety among the young. As long as we look only at the surface issues and occurrences of this period, the anxieties of both sides seem widely out of proportion and inappropriate. But if we view the social disruption of this decade in historic and cultural context, we can perhaps glimpse the underlying primitive currents of the tension between teacher and student—between parent and child.

The basis for the parent-child relationship is biological, and, as F. S. C. Northrop notes,[44] this biological relationship finds expression in "law of status." Northrop maintains that such law-of-status relationships are the basis for the most primitive kind of government predicated on inheritance and the rule of primogeniture. Power relationships based on law of status are of necessity, according to Northrop, authoritarian and vertical. In the parent-child relationship and (since the teacher traditionally stands *in loco parentis*) the teacher-student relationship, the adult's authority over his or her children emanates from his biologically determined status, not from his fitness to govern according to democratic, contractual criteria.

Such absolute power as that of a parent over a child, based not on merit but on biology, has provoked various cultural anxieties, which find expression in our mythology and art. It can be argued that the absolute, biologically determined relationship of parent to child is both the source and the expression of such collective cultural anxieties as fear of repression and fear of rebellion. In Western culture, these fears and anxieties are reciprocal—child fears parent (usually father) and parent fears child. In mythology, these fears are almost always couched in terms of violence— physical coercion and violent death. Greek mythology, the source of many archetypes fundamental to Western culture, is replete with patricide and infanticide. Cronus (one of the Titans and the father of Zeus) eats his children so that they will not supersede him; Zeus escapes this fate, in turn poisoning Cronus and taking his place. Oedipus kills his father and succeeds him as king of Thebes and husband of Jocastro.

Given that early Western mythology and literature portrayed parent-child relationships in terms of bloody conflict, it is hardly surprising that Freud drew on such myths to describe the anxieties plaguing modern man— anxieties centering around the parent-child relationship. And whether or not one endorses Freud's theories, their impact on the course of modern thought cannot be denied.

Western culture from its earliest Greek sources abounds with children who fear repression by parents and parents who fear rebellion by children. These cultural anxieties are even expressed in the language we use to describe our own American history. The colonies rebelled against "the mother country" and became "the fledgling republic" because of repression by England. Note that, as in Greek mythology, the repression and the rebellion were violent.

In reaction to the "violent 60s," many adults are now calling for a return to the "good ole days" when children respected their parents (and others in authority) and were obedient and well disciplined—in other words, a return to what Northrop calls the law of status. Corporal punishment, as the most obvious expression of the ascendancy of parent over child, teacher over student, is an important symbol of law-of-status authority and, therefore, is an important element of the desire for return to the "good ole days."

Despite the progress and reform of child-rearing practices during the last century, the basic relationship between parent and child remains the same, at least at a very primitive level of our collective unconscious (to borrow from Jung). Perhaps we are so loath to give up corporal punishment for children (though not for adults) partly because physical coercion is the most immediate and explicit expression of a very important authority relationship—parent and child. Control of children through corporal punishment symbolizes not only other more subtle forms of adult control of children, but also represents the absolute nature of the biologically determined relationship between parent and child—a vertical relationship in which one party (parent) rules autocratically and absolutely over the other (child).

We should remember, however, that our cultural heritage also contains the concept of what Northrop calls "liberal contractual democracy," a concept "which depends on consent rather than biology and breeding" for authority. This tradition has helped to shape all aspects of American life, including the parent-child relationship in the home and the teacher-student relationship in the school. It offers a counterpoint to primitive law of status and prescribes a relationship of basic equality between the governors and the governed—between parent and child, teacher and student. Physical coercion is obviously an inappropriate symbol of democratic law of contract.

The Supreme Court's decision in *Ingraham* suggests some of the tensions between these two strains of American thought and actually perpetuates, rather than resolves, these tensions. Indeed, the majority and minority opinions indicate that the Court itself, as part of the cultural milieu, reflects the biases and tensions that have long plagued (and will probably continue to plague) Western thought in general and American thought in particular.

The Court's decision upholding the use of corporal punishment in our public schools will not exorcise from our society the moral and spiritual

confusion, business and governmental corruption, or violence and lawlessness on our city streets and in our national parks and public schools, phenomena that unfortunately many of us have come to regard as symbolic of
life in contemporary American society. Nor will the Court's decision likely
even restore conservative values of respect for authority, love of learning,
and fear of God.

But perhaps the character and vitality of contemporary American
society lies in the continual balancing of extremes of authoritarianism and
humanism, control and freedom, hate and love. If such be the case, then the
Court's decision, coming as it does after the youth-oriented, revolutionary
spirit of the sixties, is but one manifestation of our societal balancing act,
which some suggest is beginning to bring about America's return to the
relative tranquility of the fifties.

NOTES

1. *Ingraham* v. *Wright*, U.S., 97 S. Ct. 1401 (1977).

2. Ibid., *supra* note 37 at 1406.

3. Ibid., at 1411.

4. Ibid., at 1412.

5. Ibid., at 1418.

6. Ibid., at 1417.

7. Ibid., at 1417–18.

8. M. Tyler, *A History of American Literature*, 1710–1765, vol. 2 (1890),
p. 191.

9. *Magnalia Christi Americana: Or, the Ecclesiastical History of New-
England, Etc.* (1855), p. 127.

10. Jonathan Edwards, quoted in P. Ford, *The New-England Primer 1*
(1879).

11. *Records of the Governor and Company of Massachusetts Bay in New
England*, vol. 2 (June 14, 1642), p. 90.

12. Ibid. (November 4, 1646), pp. 179–80.

13. Ibid. (June 14, 1642), p. 9.

14. Proverbs 22:15.

15. Quoted in E. Cubberley, *Readings in Public Education in the United
States* (1934), p. 18.

16. W. Walker, *John Calvin* (1906), p. 211.

17. Dorchester Town Records (January 14, 1645), quoted in *Fourth Report of the Record Commissioners of the City of Boston* (1883), vol. 41, p.56.
These 1645 rules prohibiting parental interference with the schoolmaster's power
to inflict corporal punishment were sustained 331 years later in the Supreme
Court's summary judgment in *Baker* v. *Owen*, affirming the court of appeal's
ruling that parents have no constitutional right to control the means of discipline

their children receive while enrolled in the public schools. 423 U.S. 907, *aff'g* 395 F. Supp. 294 (M.D.N.C. 1975).

18. J. Straub, "Quaker School Life in Philadelphia before 1800." *The Pennsylvania Magazine of History & Biography* 89 (October 1965), p. 451.

19. Overseers Minutes, vol. 32 (February 11, 1796), p. 68.

20. One cannot resist pointing out the small irony (already apparent to some) of having an American president (Nixon), whose religious upbringing was in the Quaker faith, appoint four justices to the Court during his term of office, all of whom supported the majority view in *Ingraham*.

21. See H. Falk, *Corporal Punishment* (1941); N. Edwards and H. Richey, *The School in the American Social Order* (1947); K. James, *Corporal Punishment in the Public Schools* (1963); A. Reitman, J. Follman & E. T. Ladd, *Corporal Punishment in Public Schools* (ACLU Report 1972); Cubberley, *Public Education in the United States* (1934 ed.).

22. *Ingraham* v. *Wright*, 97 S. Ct. at 1407.

23. Twenty-one other states have enacted legislation providing for the moderate use of corporal punishment in public schools. Id. at 1408.

24. Among them are Poland, Luxembourg, Holland, Austria, France, Finland, Sweden, Denmark, Belgium, Cyprus, Japan, Ecuador, Iceland, Italy, Jordan, Qatar, Mauritius, Norway, Israel, The Philippines, Portugal, and all Communist bloc countries. Brief of the American Psychological Association Task Force on the Rights of Children and Youth as Amicus Curiae in Support of Petitioners [James Ingraham and Roosevelt Andrews], filed July 22, 1976, in the Supreme Court of the United States, at 3.

25. R. Ardrey, *The Territorial Imperative* (1966), p. 294.

26. Ethology is the study of innate behavior patterns in animals "pioneered by Austria's Konrad Lorenz and Holland's Niko Tinbergen in the 1930's." Ibid., p. 20.

27. Ibid., pp. 4–5.

28. Ibid., p. 262.

29. Ibid., p. 263.

30. Montagu presents his argument in an article in *Man and Aggression* (A. Montagu, ed., 1968) along with the contributions of several experts who share Montagu's desire "to put the record straight, to correct what threatens to become an epidemic error concerning the causes of man's aggression, and to redirect attention to a consideration of the real causes of such behavior," p. ix.

31. D. Morris, *The Naked Ape* (1967), p. 11.

32. Ibid., p. 137.

33. Shakespeare, *Hamlet* II.ii.317.

34. Morris, *The Naked Ape*, p. 9.

35. Ibid.

36. K. Lorenz, *On Aggression* (1966), p. 265.

37. The other factors mentioned by Lorenz are "[d]iminishing cohesion of the family group and decreasing personal contact between teacher and pupil. Ibid., p. 251.

38. There is an extraordinary amount of research, both theoretical and empirical on the causes of man's aggressive behavior, the distinguishing feature of which is its absence of consideration of innate aggression. The anthropologically derived theories of cultural stress are one example. A representative work in this field is R. Naroll, *Data Quality Control: A New Research Technique; Prolegomena to a Cross-Cultural Study of Culture Stress* (1962). Another example comes from psychological theories of political violence. For an excellent synthesis of the empirical research and partial theories in this field, see T. R. Gurr, *Why Men Rebel* (1970).

39. Lorenz, *On Aggression*, p. viii.

40. P. Gilliatt, "Vivat Satans!" *The New Yorker* (July 19, 1976), p. 81.

41. G. Forshey, "A Vision of Evil," *The Christian Century* 91 (February 13, 1974), p. 183.

42. Ibid.

43. "The Youth Crime Plague," *Time*, July 11, 1977, p. 25.

44. F. Northrop, "Comparative Philosophy and Science in the Light of Comparative Law," in *Philosophy and Culture East and West* (C. Moore, ed., 1962).

6

The Social Structure of Violence in Childhood and Approval of Violence as an Adult

David J. Owens

Murray A. Straus

•

A national survey conducted in 1968 for the President's Commission on the Causes and Prevention of Violence (Baker and Ball, 1969) revealed that one out of four agreed that "groups have the right to train their members in marksmanship and underground-warfare tactics in order to help put down any conspiracies that might occur in the country"; and one out of ten Americans said that they would "participate in a physical assault or armed action against a group of people who are deliberately blocking rush-hour traffic to protest the war in Vietnam." As might be expected, the number of Americans who approve of using violence against people of other nations is much greater. In fact, two out of three citizens agreed that "in dealing with other countries in the world, we are frequently justified in using military force."

Another national sample survey found that one-half to two-thirds of American men approved of shooting in situations such as ghetto riots or campus disturbances, and 20 to 30 percent advised the police to shoot to kill under such circumstances (Blumenthal, et al., 1972; p. 243). Findings of this type, plus a homicide rate which is seven times that of the next highest industrial nation, have led some observers to characterize the United

Paper presented at the 1973 meeting of the American Orthopsychiatric Association. This essay is based on the M.A. thesis of D. J. Owens (1973). The preparation of this essay and part of the data analysis were supported by NIMH grant number 15521. The authors are indebted to Professor Sheldon G. Levy for providing a copy of the data tape containing the results of the survey conducted for the Media Task Force of the National Commission on the Causes and Prevention of Violence (1969) and to Richard J. Gelles for suggestions in revising the paper. This version appeared in *Aggressive Behavior*, 1 (1975), 193 211.

States as having a "culture of violence." This is correct up to a certain point. If, however, one comes to use the idea of a culture or a subculture of violence as an explanation for the high level of actual violence that occurs in American society, there are problems. One problem we see is that such an explanation does not account for the existence of these cultural norms. How did American culture come to approve of or to value violence? Why does it continue to do so? Such a question is not only important for theories of violence; it is also important in determining national policy in respect to violence. If "culture" is a main cause, then educational and other policies designed to modify this culture, such as the current mass media campaigns against drug use, are in order. But if, as we believe, the cultural norms concerning violence primarily reflect an adaptation to certain aspects of American social structure, then alterations in these underlying social structure elements are a more appropriate mode of response to the problem of violence.

The study reported in this essay will not settle this important issue. But it does provide some evidence relevant to a social-structure theory of violence. Specifically, rather than starting with the premise that there are cultural norms that approve of violence and investigating the extent to which such norms are correlated with actual violence, we take the opposite approach. That is, the focus of this paper is on how people learn to approve of violence. We start with the violence that occurred in the childhood of our respondents. The data analysis examines the question of whether such childhood violence is associated with the extent to which, as adults, those respondents approve of violence.

There are a large number of factors that can and probably do influence the extent to which societies and their individual members approve or disapprove of violence. The present paper is limited to only one group of such causal factors: violence experienced in childhood through having observed violence, having committed violence, and having been the victim of the violent acts of others.

A fundamental assumption underlying this investigation is that the disposition to use violence is a learned behavior and that much of this takes place in childhood through the actual experience of violence. Thus, the general hypothesis of the study is that the more a person experiences violence as a child, the more likely he is as an adult to approve of the use of violence as a means of social control.[1]

Evidence to support this "experience theory" of violence is admittedly scanty. However, certain studies hint at its plausibility. Studies of child-abusing parents, for example, consistently show that these parents tended to have been victims of abuse or severe physical punishment (Gelles,

1973). The research of Bandura and his colleagues on imitative and modeling behavior show that children and young adults imitate the behavior of aggressive models in experimental situations. For example, Bandura and Houston (1961) and Bandura et al. (1961) show that children who watched the models attacking a Bobo doll were significantly more aggressive in their own play than the two control groups. Indeed, there was often remarkable direct imitation of the actual aggressive play of the model. Studies of violence shown on television have echoed these findings. Children learn behavior, at least in part, by the process of imitating someone else's behavior—even though no normative guidelines are put forth (Singer 1971). In fact, in most situations the norms taught to and known by the children would probably run counter to the behavior exhibited.

Observing and experiencing violence tends to provide a powerful learning situation because (among other things) such experience provides the entire script for behavior, not just attitudes of approval or disapproval. Among the important elements of this script are the specific types of situations in which violence is used, the appropriate affective states, and the appropriate response to such situations, that is, the type and intensity of violence. Thus, the experience theory perspective that guides this research, especially the concepts of role modeling and role practice, indicates that attitudes and behavior modalities may be acquired independent of cultural prescriptions and proscription. People tend to practice that behavior which is in evidence around them, even though the behavior may conflict with cultural standards. If the conflict between the behavior practiced and the cultural standards is too great, the behavior may be dropped. But our guess is that the more common resolution of this discrepancy is for the individual to resolve the conflict by adopting attitudes that approve of violence (Bem, 1967). If enough people do this, then of course, the societal norm changes. Behavior, therefore, can exert a powerful influence upon attitudes, beliefs, and cultural norms.

Methodological Considerations

Shortcomings of Studies on Imitation and Modeling. The previously-mentioned experimental studies have several serious shortcomings. First, such experiments, while enjoying the benefits of rigorous control over the relevant variables, suffer from the fact that the experimental treatments and the effects measured are short term. Given the nature of the experimental situation, long-term influences cannot be estimated. Thus, critics have questioned the value of the "one shot" film of an aggressive model. It is quite possible that viewing television daily makes the situation very much more complex. Repeated exposure to violent films could have either a cumulative effect in building up the potential for imitation or a "cathartic" effect.[2]

A second shortcoming of the experiments on modeling is related to the first. Ethical controls on the experimental situation mean that practically every study involves play situations and attack on inanimate objects. It remains an unanswered question whether aggressive play is at all the same as a direct assault upon another child. Indeed, the studies tend to confuse aggressive fantasy, healthy anger, and hostile wit or sarcasm with direct violence. Yet, if we are to fully understand the effects of observing violence, there must also be evidence of direct aggression on others, taken directly from real life.

Third, almost all of the experimental studies involve nursery school children of predominantly middle-class backgrounds. Such children may provide compliant imitators of adults or other children in an experimental setting, but the question of whether lower class children would manifest comparable patterns remains open. Moreover, these studies do not provide us with much information on adolescents or adults. It is hazardous therefore, to make broad generalizations about reactions to observation of violence from such a select sample.

The Violence Commission Survey.   The research to be reported is a reanalysis of the nationwide sample survey data collected for the National Commission on the Causes and Prevention of Violence (Baker and Ball, 1969).[3] These data have their own set of limitations, notably problems connected with the accuracy of self-reported behavior. However, they have two advantages over the laboratory studies just discussed. First, the data cut across social classes, sexes, ethnic groups, and age groups. Second, unlike the laboratory studies, they enable us to analyze the effects of experiencing real-life violence. Thus, the Violence Commission data can provide information on a representative sample of the population and on critical aspects of violence needed to complement the experimental studies.

Hypotheses

Observation of Violence in Childhood.   Attitudes may be acquired in a number of ways. It is most common to think of them as being learned from the attitudes held by significant others in a person's life, especially parents. For example, it has repeatedly been shown that most young adults support the same political party as their parents (Nelson and Tallman, 1969). But attitudes can also be formed out of specific experiences. That is, a person can come to accept and approve of much of the behavior around him because he sees others engaging in that behavior—especially

if he sees other people obtain desired goals by using that behavior. We believe that children are extremely prone to acquire attitudes and beliefs in
this way. Exposure to violent behavior in childhood will have deep seated
and lasting effects on attitudes toward violence. As Singer (1971, p. 31)
points out,

> in new situations where a child is at loss for what to do he is likely to re-
> member what he saw his parent do and behave accordingly, even occa-
> sionally to his own detriment. Indeed, adults when they become parents
> and are faced with the novelty of the role revert to the type behavior they
> saw their parents engage in when they were children sometimes against
> their current adult judgment.

On the basis of the studies of imitation, which show that in the short
term, observation of violent behavior leads to imitation of that violent behavior, and of the well-established fact that children are extremely quick
to adopt behavioral patterns in evidence around them, and finally because
attitudes toward behavior may be set up to justify that behavior despite
cultural guidelines to the contrary, the first major hypothesis is:

 • Hypothesis 1: The greater the observation of violence as a child,
the greater the approval of violence in adult life.

Physical Involvement in Violence and Approval of Violent Behavior.
Observation of violent behavior is only one aspect of participation in a
violent social structure. Exposure may take a more immediate form. One
could be actively involved in the violence as a victim or instigator. In either
case, we would expect the learning situation to be an extremely intense one
and to exert considerable influence on the individual's subsequent attitude
toward violence. Involvement with violence, it is argued, leads to acceptance of that violence. Sheer familiarity with violence inures one to its
harmful effects. In most cases, the physically harmful effects are temporary.
The victim or the loser soon gets over the physical damage. In the process,
he may well see that his assailant has obtained what he wanted by violent
means. If the victim is a child, then he will see the value of spanking in
controlling behavior, even though he might resent it. If he is a teenage boy,
even as the loser of a fight he may well realize the value of success in a
physical confrontation. These considerations lead to the second and third
major hypotheses of the study.

 • Hypothesis 2: The more a child is a victim of violence in childhood,
the greater his approval of violence in adult life.
 • Hypothesis 3: The more a child commits violent acts, the greater
his approval of violence in adult life.

Approval of Violence as a General Concept

Violence is a multifaceted phenomenon. Situations in which violent behavior occurs can be as widely varied as that of a parent spanking a child, two teenage boys in a knife fight, a vigilante mob, or a massacre in a war. In each case violence is present, but the context and meaning of the violent behavior is different. There are, therefore, arguments for and against grouping all of these behaviors under the single heading of "violence." Such behaviors could be different aspects of a single underlying dimension—approval of violence, or they could be so dissimilar in meaning for most individuals that the single dimension of violence does little to relate them. If the latter is the case, they may well have a dissimilar etiology.

In this study, in order to take account of some of the different types of violence, we have subdivided approval of violence into approval of three types of violence and computed indexes for each type as follows: interpersonal violence approval, national violence approval, and political violence approval.

The interpersonal violence approval index deals primarily with those acts of violence that take place at a face-to-face level, most often between friends and acquaintances. The national violence approval index is concerned with acts of international aggression and includes questions on the Vietnam War. The political violence approval index focuses on acts of violence as means for achieving local and national political ends.

Measurement of Violence Experience and Violence Approval

Within the limitations of a brief paper we can only summarize the measurement procedures employed (complete information may be found in Owens, 1973). The general procedure was (1) select from the available data sets of items which, in our judgment, indexed the variables listed above, (2) convert the responses to ordinal form if they were not originally in that form, and (3) sum the resulting responses for each respondent. (4) The resulting indexes were then subject to item analysis. (5) Items which did not show a correlation with the total score of 0.2 or higher were dropped from the index.

Exposure to Violence Indexes. The three aspects of exposure to violence in childhood that are used as the independent variables in this study are shown in Table 1 along with the results of the item analysis.

After completion of the item analyses of these indexes, the intercorrelation of the three indexes measuring these different aspects of exposure

Table 1. Item-Total Correlations for Exposure to Interpersonal Violence

Question no.*	Name of item	Correlation (r) with index
A. Interpersonal violence observed as a child		
27A1–R	Ever seen anyone slapped	0.80
27A2–R	Ever seen anyone punched	0.81
27A3–R	Ever seen anyone choked	0.68
27A4–R	Ever seen anyone knifed	0.76
27A5–R	Ever seen anyone shot	0.75
B. Interpersonal violence received as a child		
25A–R	Ever been spanked	0.34
26A1–R	Ever been slapped	0.72
26A2–R	Ever been punched	0.76
26A3–R	Ever been choked	0.55
26A4–R	Ever been knifed	0.67
26A5–R	Ever been shot	0.63
C. Interpersonal violence committed as a child		
29A–R	Slapped/kicked	0.87
30A–R	Beat	0.83

*R denotes that the variable has been recoded and may be a combination of two or three variables. Information concerning the recording and combining of these variables will be found in Appendix B, Parts 1 and 2 on Construction of Indices in Owens (1973).

to violence was computed. The resulting correlations indicate that although the three aspects are clearly related to each other (and hence can be considered part of a pattern that we will call the social structure of violence in childhood), the correlations are low enough (0.41 to 0.63) to make it important to examine each aspect of this structure separately when testing the general hypothesis of the study.[4]

Approval of Violence Indexes. Far more data were available in the Violence Commission interview schedule on approval-disapproval of violence than on the experience of violence in childhood. This made it possible to construct indexes with more items and presumably greater reliability. The items for each index and their correlations with the total scores are shown in Table 2.

The intercorrelation of the three measures of violence approval is particularly crucial since, as previously noted, there are some grounds for

Table 2. Item-Total Correlations for Violence Approved Indexes

Question no.*	Name of item	Correlation (r) with index
A. National violence approval		
11C–R	Government too ready to use force	0.60
11L–R	We are too ready to use force	0.56
11Q–R	Killing civilians is unavoidable in war	0.62
11H–R	Human nature means war is inevitable	0.45
9A–R	Vietnam opinion	0.67
B. Political violence approval		
18A–R	Arms against tax law	0.48
19A–R	Arms against suppression of criticizing government	0.66
20A–R	Arms against imprisoning negroes	0.66
21A–R	Arms against shooting innocent people	0.76
22A–R	Arms against war protestors	0.50
23A4–R	Tomatoes against senator	0.44
23A5–R	Empty bottles against senator	0.29
23A6–R	Gun against senator	0.22
C. Interpersonal violence approval		
33A–R	Approve of spanking	0.31
33B1–R	Approve of spanking if child is noisy	0.28
33B2–R	Approve of spanking if child is disobedient	0.31
33B3–R	Approve of spanking if child is expelled	0.30
33B4–R	Approve of spanking if child has broken law	0.34
34A–R	Approve of beating	0.19
34B3–R	Approve of beating if expelled	0.17
34B4–R	Approve of beating if broken the law	0.22
35A–R	Approve of husband's slapping wife	0.46
35B1–R	Approve of husband's slapping wife if argument	0.24
35B2–R	Approve of husband's slapping wife if wife insults him	0.34
35B3–R	Approve of husband's slapping wife if wife flirting	0.41
35B4–R	Approve of husband's slapping wife if wife unfaithful	0.48
36A–R	Approve of husband shooting wife	0.25
36B4–R	Approve of husband's shooting wife if unfaithful	0.20
37A–R	Approve of wife's slapping husband's face	0.48
37B1–R	Approve of wife's slapping husband's face if argument	0.27
37B2–R	Approve of wife's slapping husband's face if husband insults her	0.40

Table 2 (continued)

Question no.*	Name of item	Correlation (r) with index
37B3–R	Approve of wife's slapping husband's face if husband flirting	0.39
37B4–R	Approve of wife's slapping husband's face if husband unfaithful	0.49
38A–R	Approve of wife's shooting husband	0.26
38B4–R	Approve of wife's shooting husband if unfaithful	0.20
39A–R	Approve of teacher's hitting student	0.52
39B1–R	Approve of teacher's hitting student if noisy in class	0.32
39B2–R	Approve of teacher's hitting student if disobedient	0.44
39B3–R	Approve of teacher's hitting student if destructive	0.44
39B4–R	Approve of teacher's hitting student if he hit the teacher	0.51
40A–R	Approve of teacher's punching student	0.26
40B4–R	Approve of teacher's punching student if he hit the teacher	0.29
41A–R	Approve of policeman's striking citizen	0.54
41B1–R	Approve of policeman's striking citizen if obscene	0.30
41B2–R	Approve of policeman's striking citizen if demonstrating	0.30
41B3–R	Approve of policeman's striking citizen if suspected murderer	0.52
41B4–R	Approve of policeman's striking citizen if escaping	0.52
42A–R	Approve of policeman's striking citizen if attacking police	0.52
42B4–R	Approve policeman's shooting citizen	0.48
42B5–R	Approve policeman's shooting citizen if escaping	0.37
41B5–R	Approve policeman's shooting citizen if attacking	0.52
42B6–R	Approve policeman's shooting citizen if threat of gun	0.55
43A–R	Approve of teenager punching teenager	0.24
43B1–R	Approve of teenager punching teenager if dislikes him	0.50
43B2–R	Approve of teenager punching teenager if ridiculed	0.47
43B3–R	Approve of teenager punching teenager if challenged	0.57
43B4–R	Approve of teenager punching teenager if hit	0.62
45A–R	Approve adult male's striking adult male	0.24
45B2–R	Approve adult male's striking adult male if drunk	0.54
45B3–R	Approve adult male's striking adult male if he hit child	0.57

Table 2 (continued)

Question no.*	Name of item	Correlation (r) with index
45B4–R	Approve adult male's striking adult male if beating woman	0.62
45B5–R	Approve adult male's striking adult male if broke into man's house	0.51
46A–R	Approve man's choking stranger	0.39
46B3–R	Approve man's choking stranger if he hit child	0.45
46B4–R	Approve man's choking stranger if beating woman	0.48
46B5–R	Approve man's choking stranger if committing assault and robbery	0.50

*See footnote to Table 1.

expecting that the three aspects will be correlated and some for expecting the opposite. For example, research in the "authoritarian personality" tradition (Adorno et al., 1950; Lewis, 1971) suggests a personality type that tends to favor violence of all kinds, ranging from spanking children to dropping atom bombs. Yet, as is apparent from the event of past years, there are many Vietnam War "doves" who favor domestic political violence as a means of ending the war.

Our results are consistent with both the authoritarian personality theory and the behavior of the militant doves. Consistent with the militant dove phenomenon is the essentially zero correlation between the measures of national violence approval (pro-war attitudes) and political violence approval (0.02 for the total sample, 0.00 for males, and -0.07 for females). At the same time, the remaining two sets of correlations are consistent with the authoritarian personality theory. This is because interpersonal violence approval was found to have low but consistently positive correlations with both national violence approval ($r = 0.20$, 0.23 and 0.16 for the total sample, the males, and the females, respectively) and political violence approval ($r = 0.28$, 0.31, and 0.28).[5] In all cases, however, the correlations show that each of these aspects of violence approval is sufficiently independent of the other to make it necessary to treat each one as a separate dependent variable.

The Social Structure of Violence. The data on the intercorrelation of the violence experience measures with each other and on the violence approval measures with each other have more than methodological importance. The fact that the violence experienced measures have substantial correlations with each other suggests that certain people are simultaneously confronted with several different aspects of violence: They see violence between others, they receive violence from others, and they themselves act violently toward others. Thus, there seems to be what we called a "social structure of violence," even if not a culture of violence. These correlations also have implications for the central issue of this paper: the effects of experiencing violence. Our reasoning is that if experiencing violence forms a pattern or syndrome, each element of the syndrome is likely to have long-term consequences because it tends to be consistent with the other two elements. It is time then to turn to the evidence on the central issue: To what extent the experience of violence in childhood is associated with approval of violence in adulthood.

Exposure to Violence and Violence Approval

This section will examine the relationship of each of the three aspects of exposure to violence (observed, received, and committed) to approval of each of the three types of violence (interpersonal, political, and national). Since it was shown in the previous section that approval of each of the three types of violence tends to be relatively independent of approval of the other types of violence, we will examine the childhood antecedents of each type separately, starting with approval of interpersonal violence.

Interpersonal Violence Approval. Figure 1 shows that each of the three aspects of exposure to violence in childhood is moderately correlated with approval of interpersonal violence as an adult. Our major hypothesis is, therefore, substantiated. Furthermore, although the correlations are moderate, they are higher than might have been expected, since the time separation between the independent and dependent variables is so great. Clearly, the causes of approval of interpersonal violence are many and varied. In the years between exposure to childhood violence and adulthood, a multiplicity of factors are operating to influence the level of approval of violence. In these terms, therefore, a correlation of 0.3 assumes a different importance. Given that over time the effects of exposure to childhood violence will be substantially reduced by the operation of other variables, the relationship found is of considerable interest.[6]

Victimization and Approval. One might think that the victims of violence would be unlikely to favor further violent acts. Contrary to this line of reasoning, our data show that being a victim of violent acts is as much associated with approval of violent acts as seeing or committing violence. These findings become plausible if one assumes that the victim observes the likelihood of the instigator's obtaining what he wants through violent means.

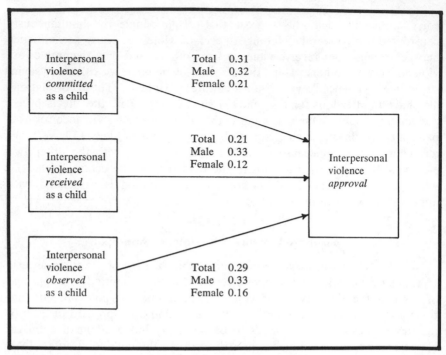

Figure 1. Correlation between exposure to violence and approval of inter-personal violence for total sample and by sex.

The equal relation of the three different aspects of childhood exposure to violence to approval of violence may be due to the fact that all three (initiating, observing, receiving) are learning situations for the individual. If the victim observes that the instigator obtains his ends by violent means, he may be inclined to use violence himself. Further, if he feels that "it does you good," or that he is "the better man for it," then subsequent approval of violent acts can also take on overtones of moral correctness.

Control for Sex.   Figure 1 also reveals that there is consistently less of a relationship between exposure to violence and interpersonal violence approval for women than for men. There are at least two possible reasons for these lower correlations. First, women are subject to more societal pressure to disapprove of violence than are men. As a result, the effects of exposure to violence as learning situation may be considerably dampened for women by the operation of normative factors that tend to suppress approval of violence. A second and equally plausible reason for the lower female correlation derives from the fact that women are less able to defend themselves against violent acts or to employ violence. Thus, the correlation between violence experienced and subsequent approval of violent acts could be lower for women than for men simply because women feel more threatened by violence and because violence is less useful to women.

Control for Socioeconomic Status. Two different measures of socioeconomic status were available. The first of these, the social class of parents of the respondent (as self-reported), did not discernably affect the correlations between exposure to violence and interpersonal violence approval. The correlations for each class are almost identical with those shown in Figure 1 for the total sample.

When the correlations between experiencing violence and approving violence were repeated within each of three educational levels, there was a tendency for the middle educational group (completed high school through some college) to have slightly lower correlations. We do not have a plausible explanation to offer at this time. However, the more important fact seems to be that despite this difference, one would not conclude that the relationship between experiencing violence and approval of violence is substantially different for persons of low or high education level.

National Violence Approval. Our measure of national violence approval indexes the extent of approval of warfare as a means of settling disputes between nations. Exposure to interpersonal violence as a child was found to have little relation to national violence approval. Correlations between the indexes of exposure to violence and national violence approval for the total sample and with controls for sex and socioeconomic status ranged from -0.05 to 0.13, with a mean of 0.05. With regard to national violence, therefore, our hypothesis that exposure to violence leads to approval of violence was not substantiated.

The lack of relationship between the indexes of exposure to violence and national violence approval is probably due to the large difference in the type of violence measured by each of the indexes. The exposure-to-violence indexes focus on acts of face-to-face interpersonal violence committed primarily among family members and friends. The index of national violence approval, however, is concerned with acts of war. Thus, the types of violence measured by each index are clearly distinct. To hit or kick a friend or family member is a far cry from engaging in acts of war. Therefore, learning derived from exposure to interpersonal violence has substantially less effect on attitudes toward war than on attitudes toward interpersonal violence. It is possible that if our childhood experience indexes had measured exposure to acts of war, then we might have found a greater relationship between childhood violence and national violence approval.

Controls. Neither the sex of the respondents, nor the parents' social class, nor the level of education had any appreciable effect upon the relationship of childhood violence to national violence approval.

Political Violence Approval.   Exposure to interpersonal violence as a child was found to be moderately correlated with political violence approval (Figure 2), especially among men. Furthermore, the correlations remained roughly the same when controls were introduced for parents' social class and respondent's level of education. The subgroup correlations ranged from 0.24 to 0.44 with a mean of 0.29.

Why was approval of political violence found to be associated with violence experienced in childhood, whereas approval of war was found to have no such association? We suggest that these differences stem from differences in the mode of expressing violence: What is learned by observing, committing, and being the object of acts of interpersonal violence does not provide a direct script for the kind of actions that dominate modern technological warfare—operating computers, arming bombs, or even driving a tank. On the other hand, the acts of violence carried out as political protest most often do involve direct person-to-person confrontation. Consequently, exposure to interpersonal violence in childhood can (and, as these

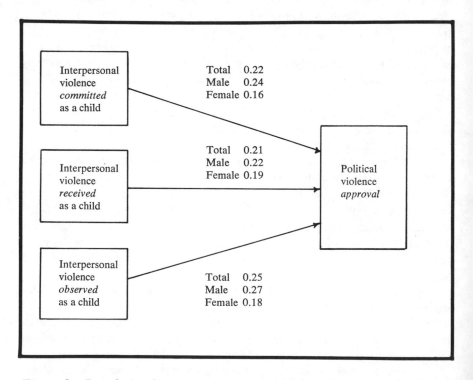

Figure 2. Correlation between exposure to violence and approval of political violence for total sample and by sex.

data suggest, does) provide a more direct model for acts of political violence.

Summary and Conclusions

This paper reports a test of the idea that the experience of violence in childhood is one of the factors that leads to approval of violence as a means of achieving such socially desirable goals as preserving national honor and integrity, securing desired political ends, and maintaining social control in face-to-face situations such as those between parent-child, husband-wife, and student-teacher. The data were obtained from a national sample survey conducted in 1968 (N = 1175).

Measures were constructed to index three different aspects of violence experienced in childhood: observing violence, carrying out violent acts, and being the victim of violence. The hypothesis that violence in childhood is related to adult approval of violence was tested by computing the correlation of each of these measures of "violence experienced" to three indexes of "violence approval."

It was found that approval of *interpersonal* violence is the aspect of violence approval most highly related to experiencing violence as a child. Approval of violence for political ends was almost as highly correlated, but approval of violence in international relations, that is, approval of war, was uncorrelated with violence experienced in childhood. The correlations tended to be slightly higher for males than for females and to be essentially similar for different socioeconomic status groups.

At the individual level the finding that childhood violence experiences are most highly correlated with approval of interpersonal violence seems to support the role-model theory of violence that the study was designed to test. This is because the kind of violence experienced as a child, as measured in this study, is primarily face-to-face violence between intimates. At the other extreme, the near-zero correlations between childhood violence and approval of war, reflect the fact that the face-to-face violence indexed by our measures of violence experienced does not provide a role model for acts of war. These findings suggest that a reduction in the interpersonal violence experienced by children in the United States would not importantly affect American attitudes toward war, but it could well lead to a reduction in the level of approval of interpersonal violence on the part of the adult population when these children reach maturity. This, in turn, would be one factor which could bring about a reduction in the high level of violence that characterizes American society.

It is always hazardous to move from data at the individual level to conclusions that embrace society in toto. But since violence is a societal as well as an individual phenomenon, it is imperative that such linkages be developed. As a start in this direction, we suggest that the findings of this study are most consistent with what we have called a social-structure theory of violence, as contrasted with a culture of violence theory. The two theories are more complementary to each other than opposed, but they differ in their causal emphasis. This difference has important implications in terms of the steps that can be taken to reduce violence.

The structural theory of violence is developed more fully in another paper (Straus, et al., 1973). The aspect of the theory considered in this paper is the social learning and role modeling that take place in childhood. In propositional form, this part of the theory is as follows:

1. The greater the presence of violence in the social structure during childhood, the more the person learns to use violence.

2. For any set of behaviors characteristic of a population, there will develop a normative counterpart that rationalizes and justifies that behavior.

3. Assuming the validity of proposition 2, and taking the data presented in this paper as evidence supporting proposition 1, we conclude that the culture of violence characterizing American society is, at least in part, attributable to the high level of violence experienced during the formative years of childhood.

It follows from the foregoing that a society or a segment of society that has a high level of violence will also have a culture that justifies and supports violence. This is the "culture of violence." However, it also follows from these propositions that efforts to alter the level of violence in such societies by "educational" and other activities designed to change the culture are not likely to be successful unless the underlying "social structure of violence" can also be altered.[7]

NOTES

1. Although this hypothesis and the reasoning underlying it places the emphasis on the social structure of interpersonal relations as the causal factor, rather than on the cultural norms and values to which the child has been verbally exposed, the two elements can not be clearly separated in our research. This is because those respondents who had a high exposure to actual violence may also have been exposed to norms approving violence. However attitudes and behavior are by no means the same. The typical correlation in fact is quite low. Our structural explanation is, at the minimum, a plausible hypothesis that has not yet been empirically tested.

It will take a longitudinal study to nail down more definitively the relative roles of cultural norms and structural factors. More specifically, a cross-lagged correlation design is called for in which factor A is some measure of norms approving violence and factor B is a measure of violence actually experienced.

A further limitation of the scope of this study is indicated by the phrase "violence as a means of social control." Physical violence is a complex phenomenon, whose elements or aspects must be clearly specified to enable knowledge to advance. In the case of violence, we have elsewhere indicated (Steinmetz and Straus, 1974) that at least two major dimensions must be considered: (a) Whether the use of physical force is an end in itself—"expressive" violence, or whether physical restraint, pain, or injury is intended as a means of inducing another person or group to carry out some act—"instrumentall" violence; (b) whether the violence under consideration is required or authorized by the rules of the society or social group of the violent actor—"legitimate" violence, or whether it is prohibited or depreciated by the society or group—"illegitimate" violence. The combination of these two dimensions produces a fourfold taxonomy of violence (Straus et al., 1973): expressive-legitimate, expressive-illegitimate, instrumental-legitimate, and instrumental-illegitimate. By means of this taxonomy this paper is limited to what we have called instrumental violence, and even more specifically, to the question of the degree of approval that would place such violence in the instrumental-legitimate cell of the taxonomy.

2. However, one longitudinal study, which measured exposure to television violence in the third grade, found that the amount of such violence observed is correlated with aggression scores obtained at age 18 (Lefkowitz, et al., 1972).

3. The interviewing was conducted in October 1968 by Louis Harris and Associates, Inc. The following is a description of the sample provided by Baker and Ball (1969). "The total sample comprised 1,176 interviews with persons 18 years of age and older. Respondents were selected by means of an area probability sampling procedure which involved 100 sampling points, or "clusters," of approximately 12 interviews each. Instructions from the Harris home office directed interviewers to specific blocks or other geographical units and then designated systematic procedures for determining which individual within the household should be interviewed. No callbacks were employed; if no interview was obtained at an address, the interviewer attempting an intereview at the next residence, following a prescribed route. Interviewing among adults took place October 1–8."

4. The correlations are somewhat higher for the males and lower for the females:

	SAMPLE		
Interpersonal violence indexes	*Total*	*Male*	*Female*
Experienced X observed	0.59	0.60	0.44
Experienced X committed	0.59	0.63	0.41
Committed X observed	0.52	0.49	0.43

5. A similar pattern of correlations was found when socioeconomic status was controlled by computing the correlations within each of three educational levels.

6. At the same time, even with the assumption of the validity of the causal interpretation of the correlations found in this analysis, coefficients in the range of 0.25 can only show that experiencing violence in childhood is but one of the factors explaining the degree to which violence is approved. A more complete explanation must include such factors as belief in the need for social change or in the need to defend the status quo, belief in the equity of the society, and belief in the goodness or badness of specific groups and of humanity in general —all of which have been shown to be related also to the justification of violence (Blumenthal, et al., 1972). In addition, any attempt to account for most of the variance in pro-violence attitudes must take into account the demand character-istics of the specific situation in which people find themselves. Among the most important of such situational determinants are the probability of being the victim of violence in the family and community in which one lives, the expectations of significant others with whom one interacts, and the availability of alternative nonviolent means for bringing about either the social changes that one sees as crucial, or for maintaining the level of social stability that is regarded as essential.

7. Of course, the elements making up the social structure of violence are far more numerous than the role-model aspects considered in this paper. See Straus, et al., (1973) for an outline and Straus (1973) for an example of a general systems theory used to put some of these elements into a cybernetic model.

REFERENCES

✓Adorno, I. W., Frenkel Brunswick, E., Levinson, D. J., and Sanford, N. (1950), "The Authoritarian Personality." Harper & Row, New York.

Baker, R. K., and Ball, S. J. (1969). "Mass Media and Violence: A Report to the National Commission on the Causes and Prevention of Violence." Government Printing Office, Washington, D.C.

Bandura, A., and Houston, A. C. (1961). Identification as a process of in-cidental learning. Journal of Abnormal and Experimental Psychology 63: 311–318.

Bandura, A., Ross, D., and Ross, S. A. (1961) Transmission of aggression through imitation of aggression. Journal of Abnormal and Social Psychol-ogy 63:575–582.

Bem, D. J. (1967). Self perception: An alternative interpretation of cognitive dissonance phenomena. Psychological Review 74:183–200.

Blumenthal, M., Kahn, R. L., Andrews, F. M., and Head, K. B. (1972). "Justi-fying Violence: The Attitudes of American Men." Institute for Social Re-search, Ann Arbor, Mich.

✓ Gelles, R. J. (1973). Child abuse as psychopathology: A sociological critique and reformulation. American Journal of Orthopsychiatry 43:611–621.

Lefkowitz, M. M., Huesmann, L. R., Walder, L. O., and Eron, L. D. (1972). Environmental variables as predictors of aggression. Paper presented at the American Association for the Advancement of Science Meetings. Wash-ington, D.C.

Lewis, R. A. (1971). Socialisation into national violence: Familial correlates of hawkish attitudes toward war. Journal of Marriage and the Family. Nov: 699–708.

Nelson, J. I., and Tallman, I. (1969). Local-cosmopolitan perceptions of political conformity: A specification of parental influence. American Journal of Sociology 75:193–207.

Owens, D. J. (1973). Experience with Violence in Childhood and Adult Violence Approval. Unpublished Master's Thesis, University of New Hampshire, Durham, N.H.

Singer, J. L. (1971). The influence of violence portrayed in television or motion pictures upon overt aggressive behavior. In "The Control of Aggression and Violence." J. L. Singer (Ed.) Academic Press, New York.

Steinmetz, S. K., and Straus, M. A. (Eds.). (1974) "Violence in the Family." Dodd, Mead, New York.

Straus, M. A. (1973). A general systems theory approach to the development of a theory of violence between family members. Social Science Information 12:105–125.

Straus, M. A., Gelles, R. J., and Steinmetz, S. K. (1973). Theories, methods, and controversies in the study of violence between family members. Paper presented at the American Sociological Association meeting.

7

Severe Parental Punishment and Aggression: The Link between Corporal Punishment and Delinquency

Ralph S. Welsh

•

This essay is a summary of the work my assistant and I have been doing with juvenile delinquents for more than nine years, culminating in the formulation of a theory[1] of juvenile delinquency. Although the "Belt Theory" of juvenile delinquency has been viewed by some of my colleagues to be too simplistic, we are becoming increasingly certain that the theory has far-reaching implications for the ultimate reduction of juvenile delinquency in particular, and human aggression in general.

Early in my clinical career I became alarmed to discover an unusual number of juvenile delinquents who were reporting severe parental punishment (SPP)[2] when giving their development histories. When I began carefully to question the delinquents or their parents, and tabulate the information regarding parental punishment practices, I was astounded to find that the recidivist male delinquent who had never been exposed to a belt, board, extension cord, or fist was virtually nonexistent. Although puzzled and skeptical viewing my own data, I was, nevertheless, intrigued. I began to explore the ramifications of the relationship between SPP and delinquency. With the help of several associates and consultants, to date we have surveyed more than four hundred subjects, including juvenile delinquents, their parents, high school service club youths, PTA members, adult education students, and laundromat patrons. Armed with information obtained from the above studies, and utilizing supportive data from the literature, I constructed a behavioral model which I frequently refer to as my "Belt Theory of Juvenile Delinquency" (Welsh, 1976*a*).

126

SPP and Aggression: The Growing Evidence of a Relationship

For years learning theorists have known that punishment, as a means of behavior control, is highly complex. In fact, the same punishing stimulus may accelerate or retard performance of the same behavior, depending upon whether it is given in such a way to produce responses that are compatible or in conflict with the behavior (Fowler & Miller, 1963). In other instances, punishment may serve virtually no purpose because its inhibiting effects tend to wear off (Skinner, 1938). Recently, its aggression-inducing effects began to be appreciated by those working in the animal laboratory; Ulrich (1966) and Azrin (1964) showed that experimentally induced pain can produce a violent aggressive attack in a wide variety of animal species, including rats, pigeons, and monkeys. Of course, the pain-induced aggression they observed was reflexive, and delinquent aggression is not. However, field studies with humans are starting to show that SPP might be a potent precursor to the development of habitual instrumental aggression.

Sears, Maccoby, and Levin (1957) found that mothers who severely punished aggressive behavior in their children had more aggressive children than mothers who lightly punished aggressiveness, and Eron et al. (1971) found that schoolchildren who were rated by their peers to be the most aggressive in the classroom tended to have parents who used the most corporal punishment. When studies of criminals and juvenile delinquents are made, the findings are similar. In a multidisciplinary approach to violence, among 158 female prisoners Climent et al. (1973) found five nonmedical variables associated with violence, one of which was severe parenting; and Langner et al. (1976) were able directly to implicate the belt and the stick when they found that punitive parenting (the use of a stick or belt, and the frequent withholding of privileges) was the most powerful predictor, and the behavior it predicted best was antisocial misconduct.

Cultural Differences and Severe Parental Punishment

If SPP is a significant variable in the development of socially aggressive behavior, other cultures should reveal a strong relationship between cultural childhood disciplinary practices and the level of aggression in that particular culture. Whiting (1963) has shown that cultures with a high crime rate invariably use corporal punishment as their chief socialization technique, but in cultures with a low crime rate, corporal punishment is de-emphasized. Sollenberger (1968) and Porteus (1951) report two practically crime-free cultures, both of which were almost free of SPP.

Bolton (1973*a*) initially implicated hypoglycemia as the primary factor contributing to the high level of aggression in the Qolla Indians of Peru; yet, in a private communication, Bolton (1973*b*) confirmed my suspicions that the Qolla are unusually aggressive parents. O'Hanlon (1975) suggests that the violence in Northern Ireland, exemplified by the Irish Republican Army's terrorist tactics, can be traced back to the brutal child-rearing practices of the tense, distressed, and remarkably aggressive parenting of the poor Irish Catholic mothers and fathers.

In our own society non-whites have consistently shown higher crime rates than whites (*Time*, 1975). If socio-economic status is the primary reason white and non-white crime rates differ, non-white and whites matched for class status should exhibit similar crime rates. However, Wolfgang et al. (1972) found that lower socio-economic status non-white delinquents had committed more than twice as many crimes as the lower SES whites, and higher-socio-economic status non-white delinquents had committed more than twice as many crimes as higher socio-economic status whites. In fact, for every age level from ten to seventeen years, lower SES whites committed fewer crimes than higher SES non-whites (Wolfgang et al., 1972). Since we have no reason to believe one race is inherently more aggressive than another race, we have a strong hunch that aggressive child-rearing practices peculiar to the non-white culture may be a more important variable than socio-economic class, per se, in the development of delinquent and criminal misconduct.

The Problem of Aversive Conditionability in Psychopathy

It has been known for some time that adult psychopaths and delinquents condition poorly (Hare, 1965, 1968; Lykken, 1955, 1957; and Franks, 1961). Eysenck (1964) has argued that the psychopath is a neurotic extrovert whose poor conditionability is probably an innate personality trait. The psychopath's general impulsivity, insensitivity to others, lack of moral values, and failure to profit from past experience or respond favorably to psychotherapy are well known. Schachter and Latané (1964), Schlichter and Ratliff (1971), and Hare (1968) have all shown that the psychopath is particularly poor in learning pain-avoidance tasks, although he seems to learn with positive reinforcement as well as normals. Hare (1974) writes: "The picture of psychopathy that emerges, therefore, is of a disorder in which there is ready activation of psychophysiological defense mechanisms when aversive stimulation is threatened or anticipated."

Since we are relatively confident from our own findings that all recidivist male delinquents have been exposed to SPP, we immediately began to suspect that SPP might be the environmental precursor that causes this blunting of autonomic reactivity which apparently services to reduce the emotional impact of a situation. Unfortunately, this may result in a person who fails to profit from aversive experiences, producing a person who habitually engages in behavior for which he has previously been punished.

The Search for a Theory of Delinquency Based on SPP

In our first controlled attempt to investigate the prevalence of SPP among delinquents, we sampled nineteen juvenile court–referred girls and twenty-nine juvenile court–referred boys (Welsh, 1974). We were surprised to find that all twenty-nine boys had been exposed to SPP, although only twelve of the nineteen girls had. Since we had no idea how prevalent SPP was in the general population, we constructed and administered a multiple-choiced questionnaire to 132 laundromat patrons, specifically asking them what kind of discipline they would use on an eight-year-old child who had seriously misbehaved. We found that 54 percent of the minority non-college subjects and 33 percent of the minority subjects with some college were willing to use a strap on their child. Only 15 percent of the white, non-college subjects and 11 percent of the white subjects with some college were willing to use the belt if they were parents of an eight-year-old child. The difference between the two groups was statistically significant. Apparently our uneducated black and Puerto Rican subjects were three times more willing to use a belt on their children than were uneducated white subjects, and the same ratio (3 to 1) held for our educated subjects. These data, showing a higher use of SPP by educated minority subjects than uneducated whites, strikingly parallel the puzzling delinquency statistics reported earlier by Wolfgang who found higher crime rates among higher SES non-whites than among lower SES whites.

Since we later realized that the question asked of the laundromat sample was too indirect (we were a bit restrained in our early probing), we feel that data obtained on a later group of subjects probably reflect the use of SPP by the general population better than the data obtained from the laundromat sample. However, we still feel that the relationship among SPP, race, and socio-economic level obtained from the laundromat sample is still valid.

To obtain a better estimate of the use of the belt in a typical white middle-class community, we asked fifty members of the PTA of a medium-sized, industrial Connecticut town if they felt they had ever been pushed to the point where they had to use the strap on one of their children. Twenty-one of the fifty subjects (42 percent) admitted having used the strap at least once on their child, but twenty-nine of the subjects (58 percent) had not.[3] We also found that significantly more of those who had used the strap on their children reported having at least one aggressive child than those who had not used the strap. In even a smaller sample, eleven inner-city high school service club students, the three subjects reporting that they had been suspended from school or had been arrested on at least one occasion, all had been raised on a belt, but none of the five subjects free of exposure to SPP had ever been suspended or arrested. We now feel confident in stating that any group of subjects who use a belt on their children will report having significantly more aggressive children than a comparable group of subjects who do not use SPP, even in small samples barely large enough to make statistical comparisons.

Since our first study with juvenile delinquents was rather crude, the decision was made to gather additional data on seventy-seven consecutive juvenile court referrals, including fifty-eight boys and nineteen girls. The sample included nineteen black and Puerto Rican males, and seven black and Puerto Rican females, thirty-nine white males, and twelve white females. The blacks and Puerto Ricans were grouped together because of their minority group status.

As a group the sample exhibited the same discouraging characteristics so commonly found in other groups of delinquent children. Approximately 60 percent had at least one alcoholic parent, 84 percent were reading below expected grade level, and 34 percent were representative of a minority group. On the other hand, nine of the fifty-eight males had parents classified as professional-managerial, including five of the most aggressive subjects in the delinquent sample. Rather surprisingly, fifty-six out of the fifty-eight male subjects were found to have been raised on a belt, board, extension cord, fist, or the equivalent, with only two exceptions, representing only 3 percent of the sample. The two non-SPP youngsters, moreover, were inappropriate referrals and could not readily be considered delinquents.

Two independent judges were asked to classify the subjects according to severity of parental punishment. Severe was defined as the parental use of the belt to the rear, the belt having been terminated prior to referral; very severe punishment was defined as the continuing use of the belt, or anything more severe than a belt to the rear, including frequent beatings, the use of extension cords, boards, fists, or the equivalent. The SPP data was obtained by simply asking the subjects to specify what their parents normally did when they misbehaved. When the subject failed to mention anything more severe than a hand, the subject was asked if he had ever been struck with a belt. If the answer was positive, the subject was asked to explain the circumstances under which it was used, and was also asked to recall at what age his parents stopped using SPP. If the subject claimed that he had never been hit with anything other than a hand, he was pressed no further.

Aggressive level was determined from the offense record provided by the juvenile court. The subjects were placed, according to their crimes, into one of the three following categories: very aggressive, including crimes against persons (assaults, purse snatchings, constant fighting in school, etc.); moderately aggressive, including crimes involving objects or property (auto theft, bicycle theft, shoplifting, vandalism, etc.); and mildly aggressive (parental defiance, running away from home, suspensions from school for nonphysical defiance, etc.). Two independent judges were asked to place the subjects into their appropriate aggressive categories. Interjudge agreements on aggressive categories were 87 percent. Where there was a disagreement, the lesser of the aggressive categories was chosen. The relationship between aggressive level and severity of corporal punishment in male delinquents was highly significant, and SPP was found to be related to delinquent aggression, as we had defined it for the purposes of this study. On the other hand, the same relationship was not significant within the sample of delinquent girls, although the trend was in the expected direction.

Perhaps there are common correlates to SPP and aggression yet undiscovered, but at present it is difficult for us to believe that a parent can have a delinquent male child if SPP was not used on that child during the developmental years.

Since we have long suspected that SPP is a better predictor of aggressive level than is socio-economic class, we compared our minority subjects and our white subjects along the dimension of severity of discipline. As predicted, significantly more of the minority subjects were found to have been exposed to SPP than whites, consistent with the laundromat data. Our delinquent subjects were then separated into two SES levels, those whose parents were blue collar workers or in the trades, and those who had parents in the professional-managerial area. A comparison was made between those who had received severe parental punishment, but the difference was not significant. Clearly, within our sample of delinquents, SPP was related to minority group status, but not social class. We are now quite confident that minority group subjects are more aggressive because more of their parents use SPP than do the parents of whites. Delinquent aggressive level would appear to be no respecter of class, but of SPP.

Since delinquency appears to follow a developmental pattern, we were curious to find the age at which SPP terminates. Within our sample of fifty-eight boys, thirty-eight subjects were no longer receiving SPP, two subjects were never exposed to SPP, and eighteen subjects were still receiving SPP. Coincidentally, SPP appears to terminate[4] at precisely the same time the delinquent is building up aggressive steam. Violent crime appears to reach its peak at fifteen (*Time*, 1975), and trails off thereafter (West, 1968). We also found that fewer girls received SPP than did the boys, but girls tend to be hit longer when they are exposed to SPP.

The Belt Theory of Juvenile Delinquency

Although the belt theory of delinquency was developed primarily for its heuristic value, it has proven to be of considerable value in my clinical practice in formulating treatment plans for my patients, working with schools, and for advising the parents of aggressive children. Essentially, the theory states that delinquency develops in three stages: from zero to three the hitting is minimal, except for the rare aberration of true child abuse; from about three to five, the parent believes the child is old enough to understand, and, therefore, can now learn from hitting, which usually involves the open hand. The first sign of aggression and defiance tends to surface at this age. During the early school years, from five to about thirteen, the child may exhibit hyperactivity and behavior problems in the home and school, but criminal activity is rarely seen during this period. Yet, it is during these years that parents tend to escalate from using the open hand to wielding a tool of discipline such as a belt, board, extension cord, or the fist. In fact, many of my delinquent patients report exposure to the belt for a few short years just prior to the onset of adolescence. Coincidentally, SPP tends to terminate around the 14th year, according to our data, or at approximately the same time the delinquent is building up aggressive steam. (See West, 1968, and *Time*, 1975.)

Prior to the termination of SPP, the delinquent has already started to habituate to the punishment, and starts to exhibit the poor conditionability to aversive stimuli which has so frequently been seen in the psychopath (Schachter & Latané, 1964; Schlichter & Ratliff, 1971; and Hare, 1968 and 1970). Having been physically punished so often, and having grown insensitive to the social expectancies of our society, he is now unable to gauge the effect his negative behavior has on others, and is even unable to understand the embarrassments and anxieties others experience (see Widom, 1976). If the child is beaten enough, he may become the cold, impersonal psychopath described by Cleckley (1955).

The various studies I have conducted suggest that the following propositions are true:

1. The level of reported aggressive behavior in males is a function of the severity of their corporal punishment histories.
2. Severity of corporal punishment in the home is more important than socio-economic class as a precursor to delinquency.

3. Corporal punishment produces both fear and anger; when the fear habituates, anger is left in its place.

4. The more aggressive a culture, the more probable the members of that culture will be found to utilize corporal punishment as their chief socialization technique.

5. Since the effects of corporal punishment are no respecter of group, race, or social class, so-called normal parents will have aggressive children proportional to the severity of corporal punishment they utilize on their offspring.

6. Parents of delinquents are, contrary to popular opinion, "hard liners" on discipline rather than overpermissive, although they are often neglectful; permissiveness and neglect are not the same.

7. Although SPP appears to be a necessary precursor to delinquent aggression, family violence, especially between the parents, produces a powerful modeling effect, accentuating the anger already implanted in the child.

8. The well-documented differences in conditionability between delinquents and normals are probably due to fear habituation, reducing the delinquent's ability to rely on anticipatory fear responses, and avoid potentially delinquent situations. It is speculated that this process of habituation or "negative perception" is primarily due to the delinquent's early exposure to severe parenting.

9. Poverty appears to be a major source of frustration in families with high rates of delinquency. However, poverty probably produces crime indirectly, apparently acting as a catalyst for aggressive parenting.

What Corporal Punishment Probably Does to a Person's Ability to Cope with Stress

Although many of our colleagues are not so convinced as we are of the detrimental effects and ubiquitousness of severe parenting in our society, our work with delinquents has convinced us that corporal punishment, and to a lesser extent other types of parental punishment, exerts a profound effect on the young child's ability to cope later on in life. Although we admit that a link has yet to be established between the poor conditionability of delinquents on pain-avoidance tasks, Hare's work (1974) suggests that the psychopath seems to be unusually adept in modulating aversive cues, which, in turn, reduces the emotional impact of a situation. Lykken (1967) has also noticed this, calling it "negative perception." It would appear then that the delinquent's inability to respond normally to threats of punishment may be an adaptive response to a punitive environment. One has to eat and sleep, and if home is likely to be miserable, one learns to ignore the misery. Unfortunately, this seems to produce a human being unable to profit from punishment, and unable to avoid it.

In most cases of delinquency, the following scenario appears to unfold. As the child gets bigger, more menacing, and is able to grab the belt out of the parent's hand, the corporal punishment ends, and the child has dramatically been reinforced for aggressive behavior. With the lid off the pressure cooker, the anger pours out. At this point, total alienation can occur between parent and child with a youngster growing into adulthood full of angry frustration that his parents never understood, and parents who want nothing to do with him for having spoiled their lives. Everyone expects the child to fail, including himself, so he does.

The school situation parallels the home. The child shows his defiance, and the school retaliates. Often, when the child arrives home, the parents retaliate, too. It is probably less than coincidental that those who have studied high school dropouts find that most of them are budding delinquents (see Liehter et al., 1962).

Societal Supports for SPP

When the above findings and theory have been discussed with my colleagues, they are often met with either skepticism, or, on occasion, contempt. Interestingly, my most vehement critics are usually forced to admit that their own parents had thrashed them with a belt quite soundly when they were young, but they usually insist that the thrashings did them no harm. They also point out, as do the parents of my delinquents, one can only expect that the most violent youngsters were hit the most; after all, they were the bad ones who invited their parents' wrath. There may be a grain of truth in this argument, but I seriously doubt that a child is born bad. Rather, it would appear that the studies showing that delinquents more commonly exhibit evidence of neurological dysfunction than other groups (see Razavi, 1975, pp. 223–25) implicate hyperkinesis as the behavioral condition that most commonly invites SPP. Since our data clearly indicate that parents of delinquents are, contrary to popular opinion, the antithesis of permissiveness in their disciplinary practices, hyperactive youngsters raised in these high punishment families probably have an unusually high probability of becoming delinquent. In fairness, it should be emphasized that the SPP parent is not an ogre, however. He or she is frequently a well-respected member of the community who simply believes that his child needs firm discipline—in fact, a rather typical American. No matter what the media say, the American parent is not permissive now, wasn't even permissive during the so-called Spock era of the forties and fifties, and apparently has never been permissive from the time the dreaded schoolmaster first brought the birch rod with him from England, when he came to this continent to settle (see Welsh, 1976c).

Also, we currently have one of the most punitive criminal justice procedures in the world, and there is a growing fear of crime in America that far exceeds the amount of personal injury that Americans risk each day from sources other than crime (Brooks, 1974, p. 241). The fact is that an enormous myth exists, the myth that hell-raisers are raised by parents who let their children do as they please, which is clearly an outgrowth of the all-too-common practice of ignoring the child while he knocks all the cereal boxes off the supermarket shelf, but later thrashing him soundly behind closed doors in the home.

Another interesting discovery that parallels the findings of those working in the child abuse area is the fact that at least one of the parents of a delinquent male child was exposed to SPP during his or her childhood (Welsh, 1975). I am now gathering data on more than 100 parents of juvenile delinquents (mostly mothers); these parents of delinquents have reported having been beaten with such items as: belts, fists, sticks, cat-o'-nine-tails, extension cords, wooden spoons, broom handles, 2 x 4s, rubber hoses, and "anything my parents could pick up." Clearly parents learn to discipline from their own parents and not from child-rearing manuals. One of my patients was a fifteen-year-old-boy who had broken into four houses, stolen a gun—shooting it randomly into several houses, and tied a boy to a tree with wire, then beat him with a stick. In describing her childhood, his mother reported, "My father was an alcoholic, worked at a rubber company, and made a cat-o'-nine-tails out of rubber strips he brought home. He was very abusive, and we were all terrified of him. My husband was just beaten with the belt." The mother of a fifteen-year-old boy who had stolen two cars, broke into a house, and claimed to have had fist fights with his father, reported, "My mother knocked my teeth out with a hairbrush. She used to hit me with a belt, a wooden spoon . . . anything she could get her hands on." The businessman father of a twelve-year-old boy arrested for breaking and entering, and vandalism recalled, "I was raised in an orphanage. They used to beat me every day for wetting the bed," and the mother of a drug-dependent fifteen-year-old boy who had been arrested for breaking and entering and car theft, said, "My mother used to use a wide leather belt with diamonds on it which she would then monogram our rears with."

A factor I had failed to emphasize in my earlier work was the strong effect of modeling. Although my data on more than one hundred delinquents and their parents are not yet fully analyzed, it appears that the child who was exposed to SPP, and also observed his mother being battered by his father, is the most aggressive youngster of all. Typical is a fifteen-year-old, Puerto Rican youth who has repeatedly been involved in breaking and entering, had verbally challenged a police officer, and had assaulted a teacher. His passive, meek mother was raised in a happy, pleasant home, but married a man who had been brutalized by his father with "an extension cord or anything he could pick up." The father episodically beat up the mother in front of the children, putting her in the hospital on one occasion. Another eleven-year-old boy who had frequently watched his father brutalize his mother smashed numerous windows in the school after his teacher had grabbed him by the hair, and said she was going to beat him if he didn't behave. It is, of course, ironic that the child who starts to become aggressive invites further aggression from the home, the school, and the community. The fact that the poor, the mistreated, and the children most in need of understanding and support are those most often singled out by the punishment-oriented school personnel, has been observed before (see Glasser, 1969; Foster's remarks in Welsh, 1976*b*; and Welsh, 1978).

What about the Effects of SPP versus the Effects of Violence on TV?

A highly popular area of research and public interest has been the effects of violence on TV and in the media. We suspect that this interest is probably unwarranted. Although the portrayal of violence may temporarily increase a child's aggressive play, and decrease his sensitivity to the problems of others, I must agree with Singer (1971) whose exhaustive survey of the literature led him to conclude: "A careful scrutiny of the formal scientific literature does not yield evidence that warrants a judgment linking the increased violence in the United States to the portrayal of violence in fiction or news reporting on T.V. or movie film" (Singer, 1971, p. 54).

Kaplan and Singer (1976) in a more recent survey of the literature are even more skeptical about the influence of TV on violent behavior, stating:

> It is unikely that war, murder, suicide, and the battered child syndrome, other violent crimes, and man's inhumanity to man stem to any marked degree from television viewing. . . .
>
> Instead of castigating the networks, it might be more useful to ask why the public is so fascinated by programs portraying violence. (Kaplan & Singer, 1976, p. 64)

Further, Gelles (1974) has shown us that violence in the American home is remarkably common (57 percent of his agency families and 37 percent of their neighbors reported at least one violent act of one family member against another). Our work leads us to suspect that SPP is the most significant precursor to violent behavior, and general family violence is next. Other family factors may also be important, but we doubt that TV viewing numbers among the more significant ones. It should not be too surprising that real-life violence, not contrived Hollywood violence, is the factor that most directly influences a child's aggressive behavior.

What Can Be Done

If we are correct that the single most important factor in the development of delinquency is severe parenting, then the direction is clear. In recent years the social cost of crime has become enormous, costing business alone more than 23.6 billion dollars per year, and homicide claims 20,000 people annually. The vandalism rate in our schools is estimated at 500 million dollars a year, and crime continues unabated. If a dent could be made in these statistics by teaching our society less punitive parenting, a strong effort in this direction should probably be made. Unfortunately, recent societal attitudes are not in keeping with this philosophy. People are scared, they are clamoring for a return to corporal punishment in the schools, tougher laws, and a return to capital punishment. We find this trend very alarming, and one that can only exacerbate the delinquency problem, with the juvenile delinquent becoming the one with the most to lose.

Assuming the belt theory is essentially valid, a community assault on the problem is needed. The following recommendations are suggested:

1. The negative effects of corporal punishment must be well publicized, and recognized by the public at large as well as the clinical community, resulting in a social atmosphere condemning it.[5]

2. Therapists need to make a clear distinction between different types of corporal punishment; spankings on the rear with the open hand are probably not so damaging as the belt and stick, and the therapists who hysterically condemn all corporal punishment, thereby losing the patient's confidence, probably help the patient no more than the therapist who ignores the parents' punitive disciplinary practices. The fact that we found 42 percent of the parents surveyed at a PTA meeting in a medium-sized, New England factory community admitting that they had used a belt on their children, gives one pause (see Welsh, 1976b).

3. Schools need to be well staffed with family therapists who can enter the home when a child has been found to be unusually aggressive, or has shown other evidence of parental maltreatment. The dangers of severe parenting must be pointed out, and other alternatives to discipline provided. Other family stresses could then be identified and reduced. The schools are in a unique position to provide this service, since they see, practically every day, the consequences of bad parenting.

4. The aggressive-hyperactive child should not be medicated and then forgotten if his behavior improves. If SPP continues, puberty could very well bring the anger to the surface again.

5. Schools that still practice corporal punishment and other punitive practices must be encouraged to stop these destructive procedures immediately, the 1975 and 1977 Supreme Court rulings allowing corporal punishment in the schools notwithstanding. A school cannot provide supportive services if the school, itself, is also an aggressor.

6. Training for parenthood should be government-mandated and should begin in the early grades. The use of corporal punishment should be repeatedly and resoundingly condemned in these programs, with appropriate alternatives to discipline being provided. Of course, this does result in a dilemma. The U.S. government has traditionally avoided becoming involved in local education, and the general public appears to be oblivious to the insidious long-term effects of corporal punishment exemplified by the growing "back to basics" movement, pressing for the old-fashioned discipline (see Egerton, 1976, and Hand, 1975). In the present climate, local school boards are likely to be slow in implementing such programs, unfortunately.

7. Police need to be better trained in handling and understanding delinquent misconduct. Many a policeman has told a parent of a delinquent, "What your kid needs is a good crack on the ass!" Frequently, the youngster has a parent who is at his or her wits' end, and open to any and all suggestions. The policeman who quietly tells the parent to go a little easier on the kid, rather than harder, would be probably doing everyone more of a service.

8. Battered wives, and to a lesser extent battered husbands, need assistance. The fact that a group of battered wives recently banded together in New York because of the cavalier way the criminal justice system had treated them, exemplifies a serious problem that exists in every American community (see Barden, 1977). It is clear that every time an angry parent strikes another, their children's aggressive thresholds drop a little more (see Gelles, 1974).

9. Family therapists need to teach parents of delinquents to express hurt rather than anger when their child misbehaves. If the child is to learn guilt, and to love the parent, he must not be treated in such a way that alienation is guaranteed.

10. All poor, minority, and other high-risk SPP groups in our society urgently need to be apprised of the risks involved in severe parenting. Ethnic leaders should be enlisted to lead the educational campaign.

It is our suspicion that the most effective way of eliminating the aggression that fuels juvenile delinquency is to prevent the problem from ever starting, rather than dealing with it later on. In fact, Langner et al. (1976), suggests that early punitive parenting, even when it is eliminated before the child grows up, will still contribute to a child's later aggressiveness. Our work suggests the same. There are many adults who are "hotheads" who were raised by aggressive parents and are now unhappy with their acting out, but unable to control themselves. We have growing evidence that many alcoholics are physically punished people who have tried to deal with their angry and inadequate feelings by tranquilizing themselves with alcohol, which unfortunately often causes that anger to break through.

It would appear that we will have to work harder if we ever expect to achieve the highly advanced society psychohistorian Lloyd deMause thinks we have been heading toward where "children are neither struck nor scolded, and are apologized to if yelled at under stress" (see deMause, 1974, p. 52). It is hoped that this country's recent retreat from permissiveness to a more "hard line" approach is only a momentary pause, as does Dr. David Friedman who strongly urges that we all work toward the development of alternatives to striking children (see Welsh, 1976*b*). In response to *New York Times* reporter Richard Flaste (1977), Friedman remarked, "I just don't think adults have any right to hit children. And in the best of all possible worlds, they wouldn't."

We strongly suspect the term *permissive parenting* will have to be eliminated from the clinical literature because of its present strong negative connotation, and possibly this is for the good. Parents never seem to have been able to discriminate between permissiveness and neglect. Perhaps "consensual parenting" might be a good alternative term, since it implies a cooperative relationship between the parent and child which many of the "modern" parents of the permissive era failed to understand. Obviously, all children need values, direction, and guidance, but they also require a liberal amount of freedom to make choices and find their own way. "Modern" permissive parents may have made a few mistakes, but they never deserved the ridicule and denunciations the antipermissive advocates heaped upon them. A national reversion to strict, authoritarian child-rearing patterns in response to the permissive strawman would be an American tragedy indeed.

NOTES

1. Perhaps the use of the term *theory* is presumptive. Nevertheless, my data force me to conclude that the relationship between severe parental punishment and delinquency is strong, has been largely neglected in the literature, and needs to be better documented, explored, and understood.

2. Severe parental punishment (SPP) is defined as any type of physical discipline utilizing an object capable of inflicting physical injury. Included are belts, boards, extension cords, fists, or the equivalent. Excluded are open hands, switches, and minor forms of corporal punishment.

3. This was slightly higher than the data obtained by Adah Maurer who found that 32 percent of a sample of college freshmen reported previous exposure to the strap during their development years (Maurer, 1975). We consider either figure too high, however.

4. The mean age of termination of SPP among the thirty-eight boys no longer being hit was 14.14 years (SD = 1.29).

5. I have repeatedly suggested that all belt manufacturers stamp on the back of their belts, "Caution: The use of this belt on your child is dangerous to his mental health."

REFERENCES

Azrin, N. H. Aggression. Paper read at the American Psychological Association convention, Los Angeles, 1964.

Barden, J. C. 59 battered wives join suit against New York police and courts. *New York Times*, 6–12–77.

Bolton, R. Aggression and hypoglycemia among the Qolla. *Ethnology*, 1973a, 12, 227–257.

_____. Personal correspondence from Cusco, Peru, 10–28–73b.

Brooks, J. The fear of crime in the United States. *Crime and delinquency*, vol. 20, no. 3, July 1974, 241–244.

Cleckley, H. *The mask of sanity*. St. Louis: C. V. Mosby, 1955.

Climent, C. E., Rollins, A., Ervin, F. R. & Plutchik, R. Epidemiological studies of women prisoners, I: Medical and psychiatric variables related to violent behavior. *Am. J. of Psychiatry*, 1973, 9, 985–990.

The crime wave. *Time*, June 30, 1975, 105 27, 10–24.

deMause, L. (ed.) *The history of childhood*. New York: Harper Torchbook, 1974.

Egerton, J. Back to basics. *Current*, no. 186, October 1976, 27–33.

Eron, L., Walder, L. O. & Lefkowitz, M. M. *Learning of aggression in children*. Boston: Little, Brown & Co., 1971.

Eysenck, H. J. *Crime and personality*. London: Routledge and Kegan Paul, 1964.

Flaste, R. Corporal punishment at home and school: Assessing its value. *New York Times*, 5–6–77, A27.

Fowler, H. & Miller, N. E. Facilitation and inhibition of runway performance by hind-and-forepaw shock of various intensities. *J. of Comparative and Physiological Psychol.*, 1963, 56, 801–805.

Franks, C. M. Conditionability and abnormal behavior. In Eysenck, H. J. (ed.), *Handbook of abnormal psychology*. New York: Basic Books, 1961, 457–487.

Gelles, R. J. *The violent home*. Beverly Hills: Sage Publications, 1974.

Glasser, W. *Schools without failures*. New York: Harper & Row, 1969.

Hand, J. Teachers call for that old-time discipline. *New York Daily News*, 11–12–75, p. 48.

Hare, R. D. Anxiety, stress, and psychopathy. Paper presented at the conference on dimensions of stress. Symposium on the physiological aspects of stress and anxiety, Athens, Greece, September 1974.

————. A conflict and learning theory analysis of psychopathic behavior. *J. Res. in Crime and Delinq.*, 1965, 1, 12–19.

————. *Psychopathy*. New York: Wiley, 1970.

————. Psychopathy, autonomic functions, and the orienting response. *J. Abnorm. Psychol. Monogr. Supp.*, vol. 73, no. 3, 1968, part 2, 1–24.

Kaplan, R. M. & Singer, R. D. Television violence and viewer aggression: A reexamination of the evidence. *J. of Social Issues*, vol. 32, no. 4, 1976, 35–70.

Langner, T. S., Gersten, J. C. & Eisenberg, J. G. The epidemiology of mental disorders in children: Implications for community psychiatry. Paper presented at the fourth international symposium of the Kittay Scientific Foundation, New York, N.Y., March 1976.

Liehter, S. O., Rapien, E. B., Seibert, F. M. & Sklinsky, M. D. *The drop-outs*. New York: The Free Press, 1962, 144–147.

Lykken, D. T. A study of anxiety and the sociopathic personality. *J. of Abnorm. Social Psychol.*, 1957, 55, 6–10.

————. A study of anxiety in the sociopathic personality. Doctoral dissertation, University of Minnesota, 1955.

————. Valin's emotionality and autonomic reactivity: An appraisal. *J. Experimental Res. in Personality*, 1967, 2, 49–55.

Maurer, A. Personal correspondence, March 11, 1975.

O'Hanlon, T. J. *The Irish*. New York: Harper & Row, 1975.

Porteus, S. D. In *Annual report, the juvenile court, Honolulu*, First Judicial District, T. H., 1951.

Razavi, L. Cytogenetic and somatic variation in the neurobiology of violence: Epidemiological, clinical and morphogenetic considerations. In Fields, W. S. & Sweet, W. H. *Neural bases of violence and aggression*. St. Louis: Warren H. Green, 1975, pp. 205–270.

Schachter, S. & Latané, B. Crime, cognition, and the autonomic nervous system. In Levine, D. (ed.), *Nebraska symposium on motivation*. Lincoln: University of Nebraska Press, 1964, 221–273.

Schlichter, K. J. & Ratliff, R. G. Discrimination learning in juvenile delinquents. *J. Abnorm. Soc. Psychol.*, 1971, 77, 46–48.

Sears, R. R., Maccoby, B. & Levin, N. *Patterns of child rearing*. New York: Harper & Row, 1957.

Singer, J. L. The influence of violence portrayal in television or motion pictures upon overt aggressive behavior. In Singer, J. L. (ed.), *The control of aggression and violence*. New York: Academic Press, 1971, pp. 19 60.

Skinner, B. F. *The behavior of organisms.* New York: Appleton, 1938.

Sollenberger, R. T. Chinese-American child-rearing practices and juvenile delinquency. *J. of Soc. Psychol.,* 1968, 74, 13–23.

Ulrich, R. Pain as a cause of aggression. *Am. Zoologist,* 1966, 6, 643–662.

Welsh, R. S. Delinquency, corporal punishment and the schools. *Crime and delinquency,* vol. 24, no. 3, July 1978.

_____. Delinquency and parental exposure to severe parental punishment. Symposium paper presented at the American Psychological Association convention, Chicago, 1975.

_____. Delinquency, levels of aggression, and parental punishment: A developmental approach to aggression. Unpublished study, 1974.

_____. Severe parental punishment and delinquency: A developmental theory. *J. Clin. Child Psychol.,* vol. 5, no. 1, Spring 1976a, 17–21.

_____ (chairman). The Supreme Court spanking ruling: An issue in debate. Symposium-debate with Fallon, M., Fontana, V. J., Foster, H., Friedman, D., Newbold, K., Reinholz, L., Westmoreland, D., Williams, G., Vanore, A., and comments by Gil, D. Presented at the annual convention of the American Psychological Association, Washington, D.C., September 1976. Available through the Clearinghouse for Counseling and Personnel Services, School of Education, University of Michigan, Ann Arbor, Spring 1978 (1976b).

_____. Violence, permissiveness, and the overpunished child. *J. Pediatric Psychol.,* vol. 1, no. 2, Spring 1976c, 68–71.

West, D. J. *The young offender.* Baltimore: Penguin Books, 1968.

Whiting, B. (ed.). *Six cultures.* New York: Wiley, 1963.

Widom, C. S. Interpersonal and personal construct systems in psychopaths. *J. Consult. Psychol.,* vol. 44, no. 4, 1976, 614–623.

Wolfgang, M. E., Figlio, R. M. & Sellin, T. *Delinquency in a birth cohort.* Chicago: The University of Chicago Press, 1972.

8

An Intercultural Study of Aggressive Behavior on Children's Playgrounds

Leopold Bellak

Maxine Antell

●

A number of books in the early seventies have signaled, as well as contributed to, a revival of interest in the history of the Nazi period in Germany and in German character. Prominent among these were Langer's book on Hitler's mind,[1] Speer's memoirs,[2] and Fest's series of biographies of twelve Nazi leaders.[3] Reading these books inevitably calls up questions of a repetition of similar behavior and activities: how could they, what made them, do it? With these questions in mind, one is struck by the fact that nearly all of the Nazi criminals had suffered some sort of serious mistreatment or cruelty in childhood. Perhaps this is a partial answer, perhaps, as previously suggested by Bellak, "Man's inhumanity to man is his revenge for the indignities he suffered in his childhood."[4]

In order to study this plausible generality in a somewhat controlled fashion, it seemed profitable to compare German playground behavior with playground behavior in other cultures. The simple hypothesis was that if indeed there is any validity to the above line of reasoning, the German adult would show more aggression toward children on the playground than would parents of other nationalities, and that in turn the German children would show more aggressive behavior to their peers than would children in other countries.

This hypothesis certainly accorded with some impressionistic data gleaned while one of us (LB) wandered through some playgrounds in several European countries. In several hours spent on the banks of the Main River in a regular playground in Frankfurt, Germany, the following incidents were observed:

This essay appeared in the *Journal of Orthopsychiatry*, 44 (4), July 1974.

Two boys, about seven or eight years old, threw their stilleto-like knives into the ground, each in increasing proximity to the other one; then one threw his "accidentally" quite close to a sleeping man, then cut into the branch of a tree. Two other boys, probably older and younger brothers of seven and five, were first throwing gravel into the river, and then at each other until the little one started to cry, after which they threw some at the ducks in the water. A boy of about five chased another one for fifteen or twenty minutes with a toy rifle; eventually the latter obligingly played dead, pretending to be shot out of a tree. At one point, the mother of one of the boys came over and shook her finger threateningly. On another playground, in a group with a predominance of girls, one boy bounced a pretty seven-year-old rather heavily on the seesaw so that she left with a somewhat drawn face but rejoined various games, including some with him later on. A pre-adolescent girl of about twelve started to twist the arm of a seven- or eight-year-old girl, and this set off a whole chain of aggressive interplay with tickling, arm-twisting, and the sadistic and sexual handling of the girl who had started the arm-twisting with the smaller girl.

During a day of observing the playground at the Tivoli Gardens, Lange Line, and other playgrounds in Copenhagen, not a single aggressive act was seen. An attempt at more systematic observation seemed warranted.

Method

Italy and Denmark were chosen to be compared with Germany. Accordingly, two German, two Italian, and two Danish psychologists* from three cities of roughly comparable size and character (Frankfurt, Copenhagen, and Florence) were engaged to make the observations. They were given identical directions as follows:

Your task consists of observing children and adults on a playground during six half-hour units, using a tape recorder to dictate your observations and a notebook for additional information. You will first conduct two trial sessions to familiarize yourself with the procedures and to confer with your co-observer and discuss possible disagreements in coverage.

Choice of playground: Find out from the city housing or renting department, or from some other official agency that keeps renting records, what the overall average per room rent is in your city, and determine the districts or neighborhoods where this amount of rent is being paid by the dwellers. Select a public playground in such a district that may be con-

*We are grateful to the following psychologists for participating in the study: Dr. Laura Mori and Dr. Rosemarie Morossi of Florence; Dr. Poul Pedersen and Dr. Leif Pedersen of Copenhagen; and Dr. Antje Bultmann and Dr. Grete Osterwald of Frankfurt. The study was supported by the Esther Simon Foundation.

sidered of average socio-economic level. It should provide playground equipment, such as slides, swings, sandboxes. As we are also interested in child-adult interactions, it is important that parents or other significant persons related to the children be present. Please give a brief description of the chosen setting.

Time of observation: A time when the playground is frequently crowded with children and adults—probably best on Saturday and holiday afternoons between 3 and 4 p.m.

Subjects: Together with your co-observer, choose the *first* five boys and five girls between the ages of five and ten within your sphere of observation in order to avoid unintentional selection of hyperactive children, which would bias the sample. Make a list of the selected subjects, identifying them by some outstanding characteristic that will permit unequivocal recognition throughout the session (tall, blond, brown shirt, pigtails, etc.). Write down their sex and approximate age. Assign each child a small letter (a, b, c) and, as adults intervene, use the corresponding capital letter (A, B, C) to designate them. If you are not sure of the relationship of the adult to a child, name the adult X1, X2, etc.

Observation: When you and your co-observer feel ready to begin the actual observation session, agree on a precise starting time (synchronize your watches!). Dictate a flowing account of all verbal and behavioral interactions occurring during the following 30 minutes, independently from your co-observer. At the same time, write down any additional notes implementing your verbal account. Pay special attention to the aggressive interactions among the children and between children and intervening adults. Keep track of the time of the described events.

Report of the observation sessions: Transcribe the taped observations and combine them with your written notes to produce a complete protocol of the six sessions with a minimum of editing and a maximum of accurate details. If your preliminary report is not in English, please submit a typed translation together with your original draft.

The psychologists were also given an example of a report of an observation session (see Sample Observation Report). The protocols received were rated blindly in conference by two American graduate students, according to the scale given below.

Scoring Scheme

The aggressive acts are divided into two groups—those carried out by adults, and those by children. The acts themselves are given point values from one (least aggressive) to four (most aggressive). A description of those score values follows:

One point: verbal aggression, in which the subject verbally expresses scorn, contempt, or disdain and is quarreling, swearing, or threatening.

Two points: physical coercion—games that if done with a "real" object would cause injury or death, but done as a game are without intent to harm.

Three points: physical aggression not expected to cause death, but with intent to harm—fighting, struggling, hitting, causing injury, rape, robbery, deliberate destruction of property.

Four points: Physical aggression that usually results in death—shooting, choking, knifing, inflicting severe injury, murder.

The scores were summed over each half-hour session, separately for children and adults.

Sample Observation Report

Date of observation: ————
Playground: (name, location, description of neighborhood, attendance playground equipment)

SUBJECTS

CHILDREN
(Note: This part should be prepared together with your co-observer before starting the observation session of 30 minutes.)

Sex	Approximate Age	Identifying Characteristics
a female	7	Ponytail, red gloves, tall
b male	9	Curly hair, white sneakers
c female	6	Blue coat and matching hat

ADULTS
(Fill in as they intervene during the observation session.)

A	female	early 30s	Probably mother of "a"
B	male	60	Grandfather
C	female	18	Older sister or maid
X1	female	40	Mother of unselected child
X2	male	55	Onlooker

OBSERVATIONS

Starting time: 15:00
Time of described event:
15:03   a and c peacefully playing in sandbox;
        b intentionally rides bicycle over the sandcastle they were building;
        a gets up, runs after b, trying to kick him unsuccessfully;
        c remains in sandbox weeping softly at first, then louder;
15:06   C, sitting on nearby bench, finally notices her crying child and interrupts
        her conversation with another mother to scream in an exasperated tone:
        "Will you stop crying like a baby, or we'll go home."

Limitations

A word may be said here about shortcomings in the design. The major one, perhaps, is that the observers differed from country to country so there remains the possibility, at least in theory, that observer differences account for any differences in the results. Psychologists equally fluent in German, Danish, and Italian are hard to come by, and this did not seem a good enough reason *not* to do the observations. While it does not really solve this problem, it may be mentioned here that the independently recorded protocols of each pair of observers were highly correlated (r being in the .90s in each case) so at least the instructions could be understood with some consistency.

Secondly, there were a number of unforeseen practical difficulties that compromised the rigor of the procedure. (1) In Copenhagen, as it turned out, average neighborhood rental was not a good criterion for establishing the socio-economic status of the people in the neighborhood because throughout the city there is a mixture of rent controlled and uncontrolled dwellings next to each other. Thus the class matching of the Danish playgrounds with the German and Italian playgrounds was probably a good deal less than perfect. (2) Because of the time of the year, certain Danish holidays were approaching which would have left the city playgrounds depleted of children (many would be taken to the country); therefore the Danish psychologists submitted protocols for only four (rather than six) half-hour sessions. (3) Again in accord with the dictates of practicality rather than the instructions given them, the German psychologists did not always observe groups of ten children. When on two occasions groups of 8 or 9 presented themselves, the observers simply made do with these groups; on two other occasions, the groups were slightly larger than ten. Therefore their data had to be pro-rated on the basis of ten children per observation session. (The data for the interacting adults were also pro-rated.) It is unlikely that these inconsistencies tarnish the significance of the results.

Results

To give an idea of how the actual protocols read, two samples follow:

Sample 1 (Danish)
14:31   i plays in pond;
   e seesaws with a girl;
   b runs to the swings with i who swings the two boys (b and y);
14:34   a leaves the playground with A;
   b, i, and y are still swinging;
14:35   i plays tag with h and y;

e goes to the swing with x (a small sister?);

j and f are paddling together in the pond;

14:38 g plays with z (a girl); they have played together for some time;
they fetch sand in the sandbox and put it on the edge of the pond;

e rides the rocking horse with x;

g washes the sand down from the edge of the pond;

14:40 g and z paddle together;

14:42 i swings alone;

b swings with y;

14:43 j paddles and f runs to her;

j stands up and runs ashore; f runs after her;

f and j run into the sandbox, where they roll in the sand;

14:45 g is playing with a plastic boat;

f and j run out into the pond where they throw themselves down;

14:46 b is still swinging with y; B (their father?) has come and plays with
them;

i is swinging with another girl.

Sample 2 (German)

12:15 f pushing e;

e yelling, shouting to f;

k on the top of the grating, laughing at d, singing: "Silly little Pet-
rus!" repeated several times;

d coming up to the grating, interested in climbing;

e and f and k stop playing, jump down;

d tries to climb;

e flogs d brutally, laughing;

d tries to escape, confused;

12:17 e looking whether d's trousers are wet, laughing, shouting at d;

e pushes d into the sandbox, throws sand in d's face;

d weeping softly, throws a little bit of sand back to e;

e and f and k laughing at d;

k kicking on the ground and with her feet pushing sand at d;

f doing the same as k;

d doesn't defend himself anymore, standing immobile, weeping;

e and f and k take an elastic and a ball. They have a discussion, can't
agree on any game;

d running away;

k pursues d, catches him, flogs d brutally, pulls his arm, pulls him
back to e and f;

d resigned, weeping softly;

fused situation follows;

e proposes to play with the elastic;

12:20 k takes the elastic, doesn't agree to play;

k pulling the elastic, which is breaking;

k shouting with joy, laughing;
e laughing too;
When the elastic was breaking, k was stumbling and kicking m a little, inadvertently;
m was sitting in the sandbox playing;
m astonished to be kicked, retires a little;
k notices m, very content to have kicked m, laughs ironically and points at m with a finger.

The aggression scores averaged for the two protocols for the German, Italian, and Danish adults and children in the six, six, and four observation sessions are presented in Table 1. It should be noted that approximately the same number of adults interacted with the groups of children, and that in no case was the aggression score for a session contributed by a single aggressive child alone, or even a single pair of children. As can be seen, there were no acts of aggression by Italian and Danish adults, while the German adults produced a combined aggression score of over 73.

Table 1. Playground Aggression Scores

GERMAN		ITALIAN		DANISH	
Adult	*Child*	*Adult*	*Child*	*Adult*	*Child*
10	36	0	20	0	9.5
33	31	0	3	0	2
0	29	0	.5	0	4
2	75	0	10	0	4
9.5	35	0	10		
19	52	0	4.5		
73.5	258	0	48	0	19.5

These scores were rank ordered, and the Mann-Whitney U test was performed comparing the German and Italian adults, the German and Danish adults, the German and Italian children, and the German and Danish children. (The Italian and Danish parents and children did not differ from each other significantly.) The results are given in Table 2.

Discussion

Clearly these results show an association between adult aggression and child aggression, not an etiology. They are consistent with the dynamic hypothesis suggested at the beginning of this paper, that people avenge the abusive and humiliating treatment they receive from their own parents by

Table 2.   Validity of Score Differences

Comparison	U Statistic	P
German vs. Italian adults	6	.032
German vs. Italian children	0	.001
German vs. Danish adults	4	.057
German vs. Danish children	0	.005

All differences are significant at the .05 level.

mistreating others. They are equally consistent, however, with a learning type hypothesis such as Bandura and Walters[5] have put forth, that children learn aggressive behavior by modeling themselves on aggressive parents. They are also certainly consistent with the hypothesis of Sanford in regard to the development of the authoritarian personality from a type of harsh and threateningly applied discipline:

> An authority that is at once stern, rigid, unreasonable, and unloving arouses hostility, which, instead of being directed against the strong and (as the child must believe) "good" people who wield such authority, is suppressed and displaced onto substitutes and eventually, with some assistance from parents and educators, onto outgroups. Though submitting to this kind of authority, the child does not accept it in the sense that it finds a place in the formation of his own conscience. Authority remains, as it were, out there—to be obeyed self-pityingly, if it is strong enough and unavoidable enough, and to be ignored when it is possible to get around it.[6]

However, what these hypotheses have in common is the attempt to understand and account for aggressive behavior as a product of the interaction between parent and child in the child's upbringing.

The dramatically greater aggressiveness of the treatment of German children shown in this experiment fits the notion widely held by Germans themselves that German culture is *kinderfeindlich*, or hostile to children. A West German poll showed recently that "up to 60 percent of parents believe in beating, not slapping or spanking, but beating their children."[7] Munich psychologist Rolf Luckert has said, "We beat our children dumb in this nation."[8]

Our study was concerned with child aggression as a correlate to aggressive treatment of children by parents and presumed cause of aggression of those children later grown into adults. Other indices of a great need for aggressive discharge exist—for instance, the rate of motor vehicle accidents, the rate of all other accidents, the rate of suicide and self-inflicted injuries, and the rate of homicide—and all are much higher in Frankfurt than in Florence or Copenhagen.[9]

These observations should realert us to the importance of studying patterns of child-rearing with the potential goal of intervening in an educative way. Are there certain ethnic or social groups in the United States, for instance, whose methods of discipline and harsh handling of their children are creating people who as adults will be easily prone to express hatred, aggression, and prejudiced attitudes toward others or toward other groups? The method described lends itself easily to replication and modification for inquiry into any subgroup.

We are aware of the limitations of this method. It does not imply that all aggression is of experiential origin and does not negate biological factors. It simply describes *some apparent relationships between aggression endured and aggression meted out.* We also understand that aggression so stimulated in children need not necessarily relate directly to aggressive behavior in adults. In keeping with psychoanalytic ego psychology, it is obvious that neutralization, reaction formation, and other characterological and defensive devices may modify aggression.

As a matter of fact, at the beginning of the currently described project it seemed desirable to supplement the study of overt behavior on playgrounds by studies of preconscious and unconscious aggression in the three cultural groups of children and adults by studying their responses to selected pictures of Murray's Thematic Apperception Test[10] and of Bellak's Children's Apperception Test.[11] The circumstances of the current experiment made it impossible to obtain these tests from the subjects observed: the playground groups were approached unobtrusively to avoid contamination by obvious observation, and it seemed risky to ask for their later cooperation. Hostile reactions had to be expected. This attempt, and a parallel one to obtain and study TATs and CATs from unrelated groups in each country, were discarded.

It might well be feasible in the future to study school playgrounds and attempt to get permission to obtain CATs on the children observed and TATs on their parents. Intercorrelations should be interesting and could be of various natures.

Finally, however, such refinement was neither necessary nor relevant for the current study. We were interested in manifest behavior as precipitated by the concern with the facts of Nazi crimes. The fact seems to be that German treatment of children, as still practiced today and consistent with what is known of past German attitudes toward child-rearing, is strongly correlated with cruelty exhibited by these children and likely to be related to behavior of adult Germans in everyday life, such as driving. Both

Germans and other national groups might do well to examine their practice of child-rearing in the light of these findings.

Summary and Conclusions

We described a small pilot study that consisted of observation in a natural setting of children and adults on playgrounds in three different countries. Observers were skilled professionals, unaware of the nature of the hypothesis, whose independent, verbatim recordings showed a high level of agreement. Judges unaware of the hypothesis rated their protocols. Statistically significant differences in degree of aggression, expressed verbally and behaviorally, were found, that is, there was much more aggression on the German playground than on the Danish or Italian ones.

Methodological limitations are inherent in the definition of the setting. While gaining the advantage of a naturalistic setting without the contamination by artifacts, we lose the advantages of controlled and videotaped observation for replication. By observing only three playgrounds during only several half-hour sessions, we take a chance that these playgrounds or these children may not be representative. All observers were female, and some critics may feel that that would influence the data. What is most important, Danes observed Danes, etc., when methodological rigor would demand that the same trilingual observers report on all three countries.

Many more methodological objections could be raised and suggestions offered. In addition, one should exercise conceptual caution. Though the study finds a close correlation between adult aggression and that of children, this correlation need not be a causal one, but might be due to some other factor. Psychodynamically, we know that aggression by parental figures need not lead to manifest aggression—or manifest aggression solely—in children. A vast number of defensive formations, neutralization and character transformations might result instead. Finally, investigators are loath to think in terms of national character because it constitutes a statement of intragroup similarity without allowing sufficiently explicit statements for deviation from that possible central tendency. The above considerations and the difficulties generally encountered in cross-cultural and developmental studies make it stringently necessary to consider the results reported merely as suggestive and very tentative and in need of replication by larger and more controlled studies.

NOTES

1. Langer, W. 1972. *The Mind of Adolf Hitler.* Basic Books, New York.
2. Speer, A. 1970. *Inside the Third Reich.* Macmillan, New York.

3. Fest, J. 1970. *The Face of the Third Reich.* Pantheon, New York.

4. Bellak, L. 1970. The *Porcupine Dilemma.* Citadel Press, New York.

5. Bandura, A. and Walters, R. 1963. *Social Learning and Personality Development.* Holt, Rinehart, & Winston, New York.

6. Sanford, N. 1971. Authoritarianism and social destructiveness. In *Sanctions for Evil,* N. Sanford and C. Comstock, eds. Jossey-Bass, San Francisco.

7. Torgerson, D. 1973. *Daily Times,* Mamaroneck, New York. (February 20, p. 4)

8. *Ibid.*

9. United Nations Demographic Yearbook, 1969.

10. Murray, H. 1972. *The Thematic Apperception Test.* Harvard University Press, Cambridge, Mass.

PART IV

•

LEGAL PERSPECTIVES

This section of the book presents information describing the problem of corporal punishment in the context of constitutional rights. The first essay by Friedman and Hyman presents a description and content analysis of state laws regarding the maintenance of discipline in schools. This study was conducted by writing to all state commissioners of education and receiving actual copies of the state legislation regarding the maintenance of discipline. The analysis of state regulations presented in Table 1 of this essay should be helpful to those interested in conducting their own research.

Much of the publicity and concern about the problems of corporal punishment in recent years has occurred within the context of judicial decisions regarding the rights of children. Until recently, the Supreme Court had rendered a number of decisions which indicated a growing belief that children are entitled to the same constitutional rights as adults. In more recent years, under the influence of the Nixon appointees, a number of cases regarding corporal punishment in the schools have been extensively publicized. The most prominent is the Ingraham v. Wright *case which was decided by the United States Supreme Court on April 19, 1977. Because this case presents some of the major issues regarding corporal punishment, most of this section of the book is devoted to an analysis of this case.*

The next essay is the short brief presented to the Supreme Court on behalf of the American Psychological Association's Task Force on Rights of Children and Youth. This is offered as a example of how a national organization expended resources to support a resolution against the use of corporal punishment in the schools. The following extensive analysis by Virginia Lee deals in depth with the Supreme Court decision. This essay will provide the reader with a rather complete understanding of the case short of reviewing the original case material. An interesting follow-up would be to turn to the essay by Hyman and Lee entitled "A Social Science Analysis of the Supreme Court Decision in Ingraham v. Wright" *which appears in Part VII of this book.*

Alan Reitman, associate executive director of the American Civil Liberties Union, has been a member of the ACLU staff since 1949. His brief analysis of Ingraham v. Wright *somewhat overlaps the preceding article but was included because it represents a view of an evolving civil liberties conceptualization of children which contrasts sharply with the material presented in Parts II and III of this book.*

Finally, James H. Wallerstein offers a layman's view of the Ingraham v. Wright *decision. While not couched in "legalese," this essay articulately rebuts the argument of the Supreme Court's majority.*

9

Corporal Punishment in the Schools: A Descriptive Survey of State Regulations

Robert H. Friedman

Irwin A. Hyman

•

"Spare the rod and spoil the child" has been a philosophy of child rearing strongly held by both professional educators and laymen. Historical reports are replete with representations of disciplinary measures which relied on physical punishment (Manning, 1959).

Today, those feelings continue to be securely embedded in the minds of what is probably a large percentage of educators, students, and laymen. Newspaper reports provide us with glaring examples of public approval of corporal punishment. In an editorial supporting the Supreme Court decision on *Ingraham* v. *Wright*, a West Virginia newspaper describes children as being "born into this world as wild and unruly little animals who have to be trained in order to fit into a civilized society" (*Martinsburg Journal*, 1977). In Virginia, a newspaper took an informal poll of its readers to determine the local attitude toward corporal punishment. The results of their survey showed an equal number both for and against the practice (*Norfolk Star Ledger*, 1977).

It does not appear that the Court's intention was either to condone or to encourage the use of corporal punishment. In effect, the Court merely *preserved* the rights of states to develop their own rules and regulations regarding the disciplining of school children. If they wish, state lawmakers may reject corporal punishment entirely. Or they may write legislation which permits, or in some way restricts, the extent of its imposition. Regardless, the Supreme Court decision was a reaffirmation of the power of

This is an edited version of an essay which appeared in *Proceedings*: *Conference on Corporal Punishment in the Schools*, National Institute of Education, 1977.

state governments to deal with educational issues, and thus their power to legislate on corporal punishment.

Given the Supreme Court decision, it becomes increasingly important to examine state legislation to determine the current status of corporal punishment regulations. To date, there have been few compilations of what individual states have legislated. Brown (1971) examined state statutes regarding corporal punishment as an adjunct to her exploration of the rationale behind various forms of school discipline. The New Jersey Department of Education (1976) commissioned a study which examined the wording in all state legislation concerning corporal punishment. More recently, Friedman and Hyman (1977) examined various dimensions of corporal punishment legislation. However, that analysis was hampered by a limited number of responses to requests made for copies of each state's legislation regarding corporal punishment.

Purpose

The purpose of the present study was to evaluate existing state legislation and attempt to discover the intent and meaning of the laws in each state by use of a content analysis. Toward this end, the following questions were explored:

1. Which states allow corporal punishment, which do not allow it, and which are silent on the issue?

2. In those states where corporal punishment is permitted, who may inflict it?

3. Which states defer the ultimate decision regarding corporal punishment to local governments?

4. What are the procedural requirements in the administration of corporal punishment?

5. What type of language is used to justify or limit the use of corporal punishment?

6. Which states specify or reject channels of recourse for those interested in taking legal action against excessive use?

A further purpose was to examine actual practices of corporal punishment as they relate to the described legislation.

Method

In order to obtain the necessary data, a letter was sent to the commissioner of education in each state. The letter briefly described the study and requested a copy of the law in their states which related to corporal punishment. Responses to the initial inquiry were received from thirty-six states. An analysis of this data was presented in a prior paper by Friedman and Hyman (1977). Subsequent to the recent *Ingraham* v. *Wright* decision, a second inquiry was sent to the fourteen states which had not replied. At the time of this writing, responses have been received from forty-eight states.

Examples of corporal punishment practices were gathered by surveying compilations of pertinent newspaper articles.

Results and Discussion

A content analysis of the results is presented in Table 1. It should be noted that necessary information presented for Arkansas and Nebraska, the two states from which information was not received, was obtained by consulting the New Jersey survey of 1976. This has limited the analysis of legislation from these two states.

Permissibility. Massachusetts and New Jersey are the only states which clearly and functionally prohibit the use of corporal punishment in the schools. Within Article 1 of New Jersey's legislation it is stated that "no person employed or engaged in a school or educational institution . . . shall inflict or cause to be inflicted corporal punishment upon a pupil attending such school or institution" (New Jersey 18A: 6–1). In Massachusetts, the language of its prohibition is equally clear: "The power of the school committee to maintain discipline upon school property shall not include the right to inflict corporal punishment upon any pupil" (Massachusetts C71). Clearly, with the exception of its use for the physical protection of oneself or others, corporal punishment cannot be used by teachers in Massachusetts or New Jersey as a method of discipline.

In the two other states which limit the use of corporal punishment, the effect of legislation does not appear to be as restrictive. Although Maryland abolished corporal punishment as a statewide disciplinary measure (Maryland 741:2), an article in its Public School Laws clearly indicates that regardless of any regulation approved by the State Board of Education, administrators in twenty-one of its rural counties may use such disciplinary measures (Maryland 77). There are twenty-four counties in Maryland.

In Maine, a new criminal code which recently became effective (Maine, 1976) mandates that a student cannot be punished corporally, yet physical force may be used to bring a disturbance under control or to remove a student who is causing a disturbance. In a memorandum issued from the state's Attorney General's Office (1976), it is indicated that what constitutes a disturbance must be dealt with on an individual basis. Thus, in New Jersey, quelling a disturbance would involve breaking up a fight but not hitting a child who is being noisy. In Maine, it is not so clear.

Table 1. Content Analysis of State Legislation Regarding Corporal Punishment

STATE	PERMISSIBILITY			WHO MAY INFLICT				LOCAL DISCRETION	PROCEDURAL REQUIREMENTS										JUSTIFICATIONS					RECOURSE	
	Permitted	Silent	Not Permitted	Administrator	Teacher	Other Certified Employee	Noncertified Employee		Approval of Principal	In Presence of Another Person	Without Undue Anger	Reasonable	Not Deadly Force	Approval from Parents	Provide Parents with Explanation	Not on Head or Face	Not in Presence of Other Students	Restraint	Correction	To Maintain Discipline	Promote Welfare of Child	To Quell Misbehavior	To Increase Obedience	Yes	No
Alabama		X						X																	
Alaska		X																							
Arizona	X			X	X							X													
Arkansas	X			X	X	X				X															
California	X					X		X		X		X	X						X						
Colorado	X			X	X	X						X								X	X				
Connecticut	X			X		X																			
Delaware	X			X	X	X	X	X												X					
Florida	X			X	X	X	X		X	X															
Georgia	X			X	X			X	X	X		X													X
Hawaii	X				X			X				X													
Idaho		X																							
Illinois	X			X	X			X		X				X								X			
Indiana		X																							
Iowa		X																							

State														
Kansas	X													
Kentucky	X													
Louisiana	X			X	X									
Maine						X	X							
Maryland						X	X							
Massachusetts			X			X								
Michigan	X				X	X								
Minnesota	X				X	X								
Mississippi				X		X	X							
Missouri				X		X	X							
Montana	X		X	X		X		X	X	X				
Nebraska	X					X		X		X				
Nevada	X	X		X	X	X	X	X						
New Hampshire				X										
New Jersey		X												
New Mexico	X		X	X	X	X	X	X	X	X	X			
New York	X		X	X	X	X	X	X	X	X	X	X		
North Carolina	X		X	X		X	X	X	X	X	X	X		
North Dakota	X		X	X	X	X		X	X	X	X			
Ohio	X		X	X	X			X	X	X				
Oklahoma	X		X	X	X	X		X	X	X				
Oregon	X		X	X	X	X		X	X	X	X			
Pennsylvania	X		X	X		X	X	X	X	X				
Rhode Island		X												
South Carolina	X			X										
South Dakota			X			X		X		X				
Tennessee	X		X											
Texas	X	X		X	X	X		X		X				
Utah	X		X											
Vermont	X		X	X	X	X	X	X	X	X	X	X		
Virginia	X		X	X	X	X		X	X	X		X		
Washington	X	X	X	X	X	X	X							
West Virginia	X	X	X	X										
Wisconsin	X													
Wyoming	X													

Other states have shown legislative interest in the abolition of corporal punishment. Illinois has a statewide policy which allows administrators and teachers to inflict corporal punishment at local discretion. In 1977, a bill was introduced into the Illinois House of Representatives which would have banned its use in public schools. The House Elementary and Secondary Education Committee rejected the measure by a fourteen to seven vote, reiterating the need for local discretion (*Aurora Beacon-News*, 1977).

Many cities also forbid corporal punishment. Among the larger ones are Chicago, Los Angeles, New York, San Francisco, Washington D.C., and Baltimore (*Last Resort*, 1977). In Pittsburgh it is also forbidden, yet public sentiment almost led to it being reinstated. Arguments for each side were heard at a board meeting, and by a nine to six vote the school board refused to reinstate it (*Pittsburgh Post Gazette*, 1976).

Sixteen states are silent on the issue of corporal punishment. That is, there is no specific mention of the use of physical force in the disciplining of pupils. However, six of these states issued qualifying comments as part of their replies. Kansas and Kentucky indicated that limitations on the use of corporal punishment generally follow current case law, more specifically *Baker* v. *Owen* (1975). In this decision, the United States Supreme Court issued a summary judgment which affirmed the lower court's ruling. While upholding the rights of teachers and school officials to administer corporal punishment, the decision requires that students be accorded minimal procedures of due process. Officials in Idaho (Idaho, 1976) and West Virginia (West Virginia 18A) commented that their states typically have followed "In Loco Parentis" guidelines, while officials in Missouri (Missouri 171.011) and Wyoming (Wyoming 21.1) authorize local school boards to make needful rules and regulations on the maintenance of discipline.

The remaining thirty states clearly allow for the use of corporal punishment, and newspaper reports suggest that where it is sanctioned it invariably tends to be practiced. Consider the following examples:

• Florida's legislation indicates that any person within the schools, certified or not, may inflict corporal punishment upon a pupil, provided that the school principal has approved and it is done in the presence of another person. In Sarasota, Florida, an incident is reported which involves a physical education teacher and five nine-year-old boys. The instructor became incensed when these youths caused him to waste time. In response to those angry feelings, the instructor used a rope to tie the boys together, subsequently fastening the rope to his motorcycle and dragging them through the parking lot. He was later charged with a misdemeanor (*San Francisco Examiner-Chronicle*, 1976).

• Louisiana permits the infliction of corporal punishment by either the classroom teacher or school administrators. The *Shreveport Times* (1977) tells of a sixth grade teacher who allegedly whipped a child with a section of a rubber hose. Parents of other children in this class claim that this is not an unusual practice, as the teacher regularly carries a piece of black garden hose in his pocket with which to discipline children.

• South Carolina is another state which permits corporal punishment (at local discretion), and one teacher in the state had an interesting method of administering it. This particular teacher assigned to her students a group of math problems which were due in two weeks. As a punishment for those students who did not complete the assignment, they were each given one whack with a paddle by every student who did complete it (*Charlotte Observer*, 1975).

• As was mentioned previously, Illinois permits corporal punishment as a method of quelling misbehavior, provided that local approval is given. It is reported that a teacher in Ottawa, Illinois, had at one time used a battery operated cattle prod to discipline her sixth grade students. The teacher was later dismissed (*Champaign-Urbana Courier*, 1977).

• Texas is another state which permits corporal punishment as a method of maintaining discipline, provided that local approval is given. A principal of an El Paso elementary school disciplined a five-year-old kindergarten boy by placing him in the school vault for several minutes. When people became angered by this, the principal submitted a letter of apology to district officials, and no action against him was taken (*El Paso Herald Post*, 1977).

Who May Inflict.   Of the thirty-six states which allow corporal punishment, thirty authorize the classroom teacher to use such methods. Twenty states authorize administrators, nine authorize other certified employees, and two permit noncertified employees. One even allows school bus drivers (South Dakota SDCL 13). Each state which authorizes administrators also gives the same permission to teachers. Six states permit teachers to punish corporally while excluding the administrator from such permission.

State or Local Issue.   The duty to educate has historically been an issue relegated to local governments. The very nature of financing education through local property taxes clearly supports the concept of local rule. As such, educational legislation at a statewide level very often delegates authority to local districts. A minimum of twelve states either place the responsibility for the establishment of policies which govern punishment at the local level, or set minimal procedures around which local districts may operate.

Procedural Requirements.   An argument used by the United States Supreme Court in its *Ingraham* v. *Wright* (1977) decision, and one which is proferred by many supporters of physical punishment, is that there is no trend toward the elimination or control of corporal punishment by state governments. However, twenty-two of the thirty states which endorse the use of physical punishment have imposed procedural safeguards which attempt to limit its inherently capricious nature. Sixteen states either infer or directly state that punishment must be administered in a reasonable manner. Other restrictions placed on the punishment dictate that deadly force not be used (1 state), that it may not be administered with undue anger (2 states), and that the child cannot be hit in the head or the face (1 state). Only one state, New Mexico, has recognized and acted upon the well-documented social-psychological theory which holds that children who witness an adult physically aggress upon another will tend to imitate that behavior (Bandura, Ross, & Ross, 1961). In New Mexico's statute it is stated that "corporal punishment shall not be administered in the presence of other students" (New Mexico, 1976).

Many educators from those states which condone the use of corporal punishment feel that sufficient limitations and procedural safeguards can be imposed so as to prevent harm from being done to children. However, an angry teacher does not always follow procedural requirements. The following examples help to illustrate this point.

- Fifteen-year-old David Drum refused to do extra pushups during a junior high school physical education class. Angered by this, the physical education teacher (also athletic director) allegedly picked up David by the neck and slammed his head into the bleachers. North Carolina's law indicates that corporal punishment may be used to restrain, correct, or maintain discipline, and further that it must be done in a reasonable manner (*Gastonia Gazette*, 1977).

- Georgia's law also requires corporal punishment to be reasonable. A music teacher in Americus, a city outside of Plains, seems to have overlooked that procedural requirement. When her class became unruly, she gave them a choice—the writing of a sentence one hundred times or five licks with a paddle. Twelve children in this elementary school class chose the latter. Consequently, the music teacher is facing a $5,000 damage suit (*Atlanta Constitution*, 1977).

Justifications for Its Use. A primary purpose of this paper was to determine by content analysis rationales behind the use of corporal punishment in the states where it is endorsed. Toward this end, six categories were identified: for purposes of restraint, for correction, to maintain discipline, to promote the welfare of the child, to quell misbehavior, and to promote obedience. Twenty-one of the thirty states which authorize the use of corporal punishment mention those times when it may be used.

The word *restraint* is mentioned in the statutes of six states. Although the concept of restraint implies self-defense, and as such would not be contained in the most widely used definitions of corporal punishment, no state uses the word *restraint* by itself. Five states combine "restraint" with "correction," and "correction" remains undefined.

It should be noted that the maintenance of discipline is the most frequently used reference in statutory discussion of corporal punishment. When the maintenance of control is used, a justification used by Montana (Montana 75–6109), fifteen states make mention of it as a justification for the use of corporal punishment. Another reference to discipline is in Vermont's statute which indicates that it may be used for "the purpose of securing obedience on the part of any child" (Vermont 1161).

Basing their rationale perhaps on the biblical belief that the devil must be beaten out of the child, three states indicate that corporal punishment may be administered when such is necessary to promote the welfare of a child. Those states are Colorado, New York, and Oregon.

Channels of Recourse.   The liability of school personnel who misuse corporal punishment is clearly stated in the legislation of three states. Montana (Montana 75–6109) indicates that any teacher who administers undue or severe punishment "shall be deemed guilty of a misdemeanor and, upon conviction of such misdemeanor by a court of competent jurisdiction, shall be fined not more than $100." Washington provides a similar clause (Washington 28A). Georgia (Georgia 32–838) takes a contrasting position by exempting those teachers and principals who act in good faith from legal action.

When the Supreme Court upheld the rights of educators to use corporal punishment when disciplining children, the majority felt that current law provides sufficient civil and criminal sanctions to deal with those educators who abuse their disciplinary powers (*New York Times*, 1977). If a particular case of corporal punishment is either unjustifiably severe or unreasonable, damages can be sought in court. The basis of argument would be the current common law.

An increasing number of corporal punishment cases are reaching the courts, and not only in those states where official sanctions are provided. Consider the following examples:

• The *Oskaloosa Herald* (1976) reports of a suit being filed in Mehasaka County District Court (Iowa) by a father and his son against a second grade teacher. The suit, which seeks $20,000 in actual and compensatory damages, as well as $25,000 in punitive damages, alleges that the boy's second grade teacher "willfully, intentionally, and maliciously" caused injury to the student by "slamming his head onto his desk." Allegedly, this caused the young boy to suffer mental and physical pain, as well as permanently disabling him. Iowa is one of the sixteen states whose legislation is silent on the issue.

• A Lacrosse, Wisconsin, newspaper (*Eau Leader Telegram*, 1976) reports of a lawsuit brought by a sixteen-year-old youth and his father against a junior high school principal. The principal, accused of assault and battery, allegedly threw the boy against a wall and struck him, causing his ear drums to puncture. The suit asks for $20,000 in damages. Wisconsin statutes are also silent on the issue.

• Arizona is one of the thirty states which officially sanction corporal punishment as a method of discipline. The only limiting factor is that it must be done in a reasonable manner. The *Tempe News* (1976) reports of a $20,000 lawsuit being filed against a high school teacher and a school system for an alleged assault. The suit contends that the male teacher recklessly grabbed the student around the neck, causing possible permanent injury that resulted in a $6,000 medical bill.

Decisions have varied. In Buhl, Minnesota, a seventh grade student was accused of taking five dollars from the room of a fourth grade teacher. The teacher then humiliated the boy in front of his classmates by manhandling and frisking him, and subsequently proceeded to have him strip in another room so that it could be seen if the money was hidden. A suit was brought against the teacher and two administrators who witnessed the incident. Even though Minnesota officially sanctions the use of corporal punishment, a $4,000 out-of-court settlement was made (*Deluth News Tribune*, 1977).

However, a judge in the Houston area was not so sympathetic with another plaintiff. In Texas, corporal punishment is permitted in order to maintain classroom discipline. Local discretion is also permitted. When a special education student from the Deer Park School District arrived home complaining of pain and showing bruises on his buttocks, a complaint was filed with local authorities. Since corporal punishment is permitted, and deadly force was not used, the district attorney and municipal court prosecutor said criminal charges could not be filed (*Pasadena Star News Citizen*, 1977).

Conclusion

The results of our study show that only four states have current legislation limiting the use of corporal punishment (excepting its use for self-defense, to protect a child from hurting himself, or to protect others). A content analysis which examined the wording of statutes reveals (1) the classroom teacher is the person most frequently given power to inflict the punishment, although administrators are often mentioned, (2) the most common procedural requirement is that the punishment must be reasonable. Other requirements include obtaining administrative permission, having a witness present, and notifying the child's parents. (3) Twelve states delegate the authority to establish laws pertaining to corporal punishment to local districts, (4) corporal punishment is most often justifiable when it is used to maintain discipline. Other frequently mentioned justifications are to promote the welfare of a child, for purposes of restraint, and for purposes of correction. (5) Two states mention criminal sanctions which can be taken against those who administer excessive corporal punishment, and one state exempts teachers and principals who act in good faith from legal action.

REFERENCES

Atlanta Constitution, May 5, 1977.

Aurora Beacon News (Illinois), March 9, 1977.

Baker v. *Owen* 395 F. Suppl. 294 F. Suppl. 294 (M.D.N.C. 1975), off'd U.S.— 96 S. Ct. 210.

Bandura, A., Ross, D., & Ross, S. A. Transmission of aggression through imitation of aggressive models. *Journal of Abnormal and Social Psychology*, 1961 63; 527–34.

Brown, Joan G. Law and punishment: Status of state statutes. *Clearing House*, 46, 1971, 106–109.

Champaign-Urbana Courier (Illinois) January 5, 1977.

Charlotte Observer (South Carolina) January 5, 1975.

Deluth News Tribune (Minnesota) January 29, 1977.

Eau Leader Telegram (Wisconsin) November 20, 1976.

El Paso Herald Post (Texas) January 5, 1977.

Friedman, R. & Hyman, I. An analysis of state legislation regarding corporal punishment. *Proceedings: Conference on corporal punishment in the schools*, National Institute of Education, U.S. Department of Health, Education, and Welfare February 20, 1977.

Gastonia Gazette (North Carolina) January, 1977.

Idaho, personal communication, December 3, 1976.

Ingraham v. *Wright*, 45 U.S.L.W. 4364, 4371 (1977).

Last ? Resort 5, May/June 1977.

Maine Criminal Code, revised, May 1, 1976, chap. 5.

Maine Laws, 17 AMRSA; 106; sut; 2.

Manning, John. Discipline in the good old days. *Phi Delta Kappan* 3, December 1959, p. 94. See Chapter 3 above.

Martinsburg Journal (West Virginia) April 22, 1977.

Maryland State Board of Education, bylaw 741:2.

Maryland State Law, article 77, section 98B.

Massachusetts General Laws, C 71, 5, 376.

Missouri School Operations, section 171.011.

Montana School Laws, section 75–6109, p. 145.

New Jersey Department of Education, *NJSA*, 18A: 6–1.

New Jersey Department of Education, Rulings for corporal punishment in the
    United States, by state. 1976, unpublished survey.
New Mexico, Regulation Number 76, Rights and responsibilities of the public
    schools and public school students, discussion draft, December 7, 1976.
New York Times April 20, 1977.
Oskaloosa Herald (Iowa) October 23, 1976.
Pasadena Star News Citizen (Texas) March 4, 1977.
Pittsburgh Post Gazette March 24, 1976.
✓Reitman, A., Follman, J., & Ladd, E. *Corporal punishment in the schools: The
    use of force in controlling student behavior.* New York: American Civil
    Liberties Union, 1972.
San Francisco Examiner Chronical March 14, 1976.
Shreveport Times (Louisiana) January, 1977.
South Dakota, *SDLC*, 13–32–2.
Tempe News (Arizona) December 31, 1976.
Vermont Statutes, number 1161.
Washington, Revised Code of Washington, 28A.87.140.
West Virginia Code, 18A–5–1.
Wyoming Statutes, section 21.1–64A.

10

Brief of the American Psychological Association Task Force on the Rights of Children and Youth as Amicus Curiae in Support of Petitioners In the Case of *Ingraham* v. *Wright*

Gertrude M. Bacon

Irwin A. Hyman

●

Statement

We respectfully submit this brief based on the following resolution passed by the Council of Representatives—the governing body of the American Psychological Association: "The American Psychological Association opposes the use of corporal punishment in schools, juvenile facilities, child care nurseries, and all other institutions, public or private, where children are cared for or educated."

The right of protection afforded to every human being against physical encroachment on their bodies without their consent is one of the most important protections afforded by the Constitution.

The wisdom of the Supreme Court cautiously to consider any decision permitting violence is well evidenced by its overruling mandatory enforcement of capital punishment—and specifically permitting this Writ of Certiorari—opposing corporal punishment in schools.

It is clear that the constitutional issue of "cruel and unusual punishment" must be periodically reconsidered as it applies to any form of officially sanctioned physical violence.

This essay was submitted as an amicus curiae in support of petitioners to the United States Supreme Court in the case of *Ingraham* v. *Wright*.

It is especially relevant since the public school is the *only* institution which permits corporal punishment. For example, the armed forces, the prisons, and state hospitals, et al., specifically forbid corporal punishment.

Historically, many western cultures have used spanking, caning, paddling, whipping, and flogging as methods of "beating the devil" out of errant children. Most societies do not currently believe that devils inhabit the bodies of young children.

However this particular form of punishment continues although the original meaning has lost validity.

In fact, in the civilized world many countries have long since abandoned corporal punishment in schools. Among them are Poland, Luxembourg, Holland, Austria, France, Finland, Sweden, Denmark, Belgium, Cyprus, Japan, Ecuador, Iceland, Italy, Jordan, Qatar, Mauritius, Norway, Israel, The Philippines, Portugal, and all Communist bloc countries.

New Jersey, Massachusetts, and Maryland have state laws prohibiting corporal punishment in the schools, as have many cities including the District of Columbia, Chicago, Baltimore, New York, and Philadelphia.

It is therefore evident from a numerical point of view that corporal punishment is increasingly considered "unusual" as a practice to facilitate learning and improve behavior.

If a method of learning is effective it should be continued as a usual practice.

If it is not effective it should be discontinued and therefore is unusual.

Misbehavior in an educational setting, generally refers to behavior which impedes learning. However, educational and psychological research indicate that the use of corporal punishment and any punitiveness has a deleterious effect on learning.

The practice of corporal punishment provides a sanction for the use of violence as a solution to learning and behavior problems. Violence teaches counterviolence which encourages open hostility by children against schools.

A recent study conducted in Portland, Oregon, has shown that as corporal punishment increases in a particular school there is an increase in student vandalism against the school.

Where corporal punishment has been sustained and encouraged as an aid to the learning process, it has been found ineffective. In fact, there is substantial evidence from the research in positive reinforcement, that children learn much more effectively in the absence of corporal punishment.

Therefore it is clear that if a method is shown to work it should become the "usual" method. It would be "unusual" for educators, faced with scientific data and the opinion of experts, to endorse a practice which is ineffective as being the "usual" method of pedagogy.

The United States Supreme Court, in *Baker* v. *Owen*, stated that "corporal punishment of children is today discouraged by the *weight* of professional opinion."

The National Education Association Report on the Task Force on Corporal Punishment took a strong stand against the practice and offered many viable alternatives for motivating children to learn.

Despite the weight of professional opinion, some behavioral scientists maintain that there is not sufficient evidence to demonstrate the specific negative effects of corporal punishment. There never will be the type of controlled research that some require for scientific proof. Our laws, ethics, and morals forbid the practice of using human "guinea pigs."

From animal research we know that avoidance behavior is the first response to pain. If escape is impossible, the organism will attack anything available—an otherwise peaceable cagemate, a tennis ball, the cage, or even itself. If this is translated into human terms we find the child will first try to escape, by lying, by accusing others, by wriggling, or by truancy, daydreaming, or school phobia. If escape is impossible, he becomes aggressive and fights with his "cagemates." Biting and scratching at the cage are certainly vandalism and this too we find resulting from excessive punishment.

Lastly, when no other recourse is left the animal bites himself. We also see in some extreme cases child suicidal behavior, usually described as "self-destructive."

Why Is Corporal Punishment "Cruel"?

Corporal punishment is cruel because it is inflicted most often upon children who are struggling with a variety of developmental and social problems which are related to their self-image. The American Psychological Association has indicated in an official statement that "punishment intended to influence 'undesirable' responses often creates in the child the impression that he or she is an 'undesirable' person; and an impression that lowers self-esteem and may have chronic consequences."

It is "cruel" because it hurts. This is a fact recognized by all criminal statutes in evaluating assaults as crimes, differing only in degrees.

Most important, there is never assurance that the teacher or administrator conducting the punishment can always control his or her own feelings properly to separate them from the "degree" of pain involved as solely related to the "offense." As in the case of *Ingraham* v. *Wright* overzealous "punishers" can cause such physical damage that children may become severely injured and require hospitalization.

Does the United States Supreme Court feel that it can truly draw the line necessary for the welfare of children whom it has always protected?

Conclusion

In conclusion, the American Psychological Association's Task Force on the Rights of Children and Youth implores the United States Supreme Court to follow its wisdom of reversing its own decisions when their results have been proven ineffective.

Specifically, we request its reconsideration in reversing its former decisions permitting corporal punishment in schools.

We feel that this practice is ineffective as well as cruel and unusual and is disadvantageous to all the parties concerned.

11

A Legal Analysis of
Ingraham v. Wright

Virginia Lee

•

The Facts

Fourteen-year-old James Ingraham was an eighth grader attending Drew Junior High School in Dade County, Florida. On October 6, 1970, a number of students, including James, were slow in leaving the stage of the school auditorium when asked to do so by a teacher. The school principal, Willie J. Wright, Jr., took James and the other students to his office to be paddled. When James protested, claiming his innocence, Lemmie Deliford, the assistant principal, and Solomon Barnes, an assistant to the principal, were called in.[1]

Q. Do you remember if he told you how many times he was going to beat you?
A. Started off with five, then he went up to twenty.

. . .

Q. How did he paddle you, if you resisted it?
A. They took off their coats when they come in. . . .
Q. Who were "they"?
A. Mr. Deliford, Mr. Barnes and Mr. Wright.
Q. They took off their coats? . . .
A. Yes, and their watches.
Q. Then what did they do?
A. Told me to take the stuff off my pockets and take off my coat.

. . .

Q. Then what did they tell you to do?
A. "Stoop over and get your licks."

. . .

Q. Did you do that when they told you to do it?
A. No.
Q. What did you do? . . .
A. I stand up.

Q. Then what happened?
A. Then they grabbed me; took me across the table.
Q. Who were "they?"
A. Mr. Deliford, Mr. Barnes and Mr. Wright.

. . .

Q. You say Mr. Barnes and Mr. Deliford did what?
A. Put me across the table.
Q. Show me how they did that.

. . .

Mr. Feinberg. Let the record reflect the witness is lying prone, face down, across the . . . table, with his feet off the floor.

. . .

Q. Who held you there?
A. Mr. Barnes and Mr. Deliford.
Q. Who held what?
A. Mr. Barnes held my legs and Mr. Deliford held my arms.
Q. Who paddled you?
A. Mr. Wright.
Q. You said he was going to give you how many licks?
A. Twenty.
Q. How many did he give you?
A. More than twenty.

. . .

Q. Did it hurt?

. . .

A. Yes, it hurt.
Q. Did you cry?
A. Yeah.

. . .

Q. What happened after he finished paddling you? . . .
A. He told me to go wait.
Q. Did Mr. Wright say anything to you after you were paddled?
A. To put on my clothes.

. . .

Q. . . . Then what did he say to you? . . .
A. "Wait outside of the office."

. . .

Q. Did you have to open the door to get out of there?
A. He opened the door and told me if I move—I said I was going home—he said if I move he was going to bust me on the side of my head.[2]

James went home anyway and examined his injuries. According to James, his backside was "black and purple and it was tight and hot."[3] He was "ashamed" to show the injuries to his mother, and when he did she became hysterical and started "screaming and hollering."[4] James's mother took him to a local hospital where the examining doctor diagnosed the cause of James's pain to be a "hematoma." "The area of pain was tender and large in size, and . . . the temperature of the skin area of the hematoma was above normal which is a sign of inflammation often associated with hematoma."[5] The doctor prescribed pain pills, a laxative, sleep pills and ice packs, and advised James to stay at home for at least a week.[6] A different doctor examined James on October 9 when he returned to the hospital for treatment, and again on October 14. This doctor found "a hematoma approximately six inches in diameter which was swollen, tender, and purplish in color. Additionally, there was serousness or fluid oozing from the hematoma."[7] On October 14, eight days after the paddling, this doctor indicated that James should rest at home " 'for next 72 hours.' James testified that it was painful even to lie on his back in the days following the paddling, and that he could not sit comfortably for about three weeks."[8]

Roosevelt Andrews was another student attending Drew Junior High School. During his one year there he was paddled approximately ten times.[9] Roosevelt was beaten by Lemmie Deliford several times. Solomon Barnes, who nearly always carried a paddle with him, paddled Roosevelt four times within a twenty-day period.[10]

On one occasion, Roosevelt was headed for his physical education class.

Q. Who stopped you?
A. Mr. Dean.
. . .
Q. What did he say to you; do you remember?
A. He said I was late.
Q. What did you say?
A. "I got two more minutes, and I can make it."
Q. What did he do?
A. He said I couldn't make it, so he took me to Mr. Barnes.
Q. Where was Mr. Barnes at this time?
A. He was walking to the bathroom at the time.
Q. Did he have a paddle with him?
A. Yeah.
Q. Did you see it?
A. Yeah.
. . .
Q. You got to the bathroom; is that right?
A. Yeah.
Q. Then what happened?
A. When I got there there was lots of children, lots of boys.
Q. How many boys were there?
A. Maybe fourteen, fifteen.

Q. You say "there." Where do you mean by "there"?
A. In the bathroom, inside.
Q. What were they doing in there?
A. Standing up when I got in there.
Q. Where was Mr. Barnes?
A. Standing at the door.

. . .

Q. Then what happened?
A. He started beating them boys at first.
Q. Did he say anything to them before he beat them?
A. "Get over here," and that's all.
Q. How did he make them stand when he beat them?
A. I got to show that too?
Q. Sure. Show me how he made them stand when he beat them. Stand up and show me.

. . .

A. Well, you know how the squares are in the bathroom, the lines on the floor, he tell me to get . . . to a certain line and then bend over to the urinate thing.
Q. On the what?
A. He tell you to stand like the third line and like this is the bath urinate.
Q. That is what?
A. Urinate place.
Q. Then what did he say?
A. He says—like the line here going across, so he tell you to stand up and touch the urinal thing.
Q. Did you touch the urinal? Is that what he said, "Bend over and touch the urinal"?
A. Yeah.
Q. He said that to the other boys; is that right?
A. Yeah.
Q. Is that before he paddled you or after he paddled you?
A. Before.
Q. What did he do when they stood over and leaned against the urinal?
A. Beat them.
Q. With what? . . .
A. A board.
Q. Do you remember how many licks he gave?
A. All different kind of licks. I mean all different kinds of numbers.
Q. Did they say anything?
A. Yeah, they say something.
Q. What did they say?
A. All kinds of stuff. They say—some of them hollering, cry, prayed, and everything else.

. . .

Q. When did he paddle you; before, while he was paddling the fifteen boys, or after, or what?

A. After he paddle all of them, sending them out and then he paddled me.

Q. What did he tell you to do?

A. Same thing; stand behind the line and touch the urinate thing.

Q. Then did he paddle you?

A. No.

Q. Why not?

A. Because I ain't stand up there.

Q. Why is that?

A. I told him I could have made it if he . . . would have left me went.

Q. You mean made it to class? Is that what you mean?

A. Yeah.

Q. Then what happened?

A. Then he said something. I don't know what it was, and then he said, "Bend over," and I ain't want to bend over, so he pushed me against the urinate thing, the bowl, and then he snatched me around to it and that's when he hit me first.

He first hit me on the backsides and then I stand up and he pushed me against the bathroom wall, them things—that part the bathroom, the wall.

Q. The partition?

A. Between the toilets, he pushed me against that and then he snatched me from the back there and that's when he hit me on my leg, then he hit me on my arm, my back and then right across my neck, in the back here.

Q. Did those blows hurt?

A. Yeah, all of them hurt.[11]

Roosevelt's father angrily protested the punishment at a meeting with Wright, Deliford and Barnes. This apparently had no effect on them, as Wright paddled Roosevelt within the next ten days, striking his buttocks and wrist and causing him to lose the full use of his wrist and arm for a week.[12]

Student Rodney Williams was a victim of an auditorium number system at Drew Junior High School. The seats in the auditorium were numbered and if a student allegedly misbehaved the number was written on the blackboard by the teacher. Solomon Barnes would walk into the auditorium, call out the numbers, and administer four or five licks of the paddle to five to eight students daily. Rodney, who stood up from his seat to wipe off some grease, recalled the event:

A. . . . So he [the teacher] put my number on the board. So when Mr. Barnes came, he asked for me and took me to the office and told me to hook up.

Q. What did he mean by "hook up"?

A. Grab a chair, you know. The chair, he mean by hooking up on the chair.

Q. In preparation to being paddled.

A. So I refuse. I told him, I say, "Mr. Barnes, I didn't do nothing; that's why I refuse not to take a whipping."

Q. What did he do?

A. So he told me, say, "You are going to take this one."

I said, "Mr. Barnes, I didn't do nothing. I'm not taking no whipping."

So I was leaning over the table and I said "I'm not taking a whipping," and I was hit across the head with the board. He was hitting me across the head with the board, and my back and everything.

Q. He was whipping you where?

A. Across the head, with the board. He was hitting me all across the head and on the back. I was begging him for mercy to stop and he wouldn't listen.

So he had some chairs in there and I was falling in the chairs as he was hitting me with the board.

Then after a while he took off his belt and then started to hit me with the belt and hit me with the buckle part, and tears were coming out of me.[13]

Rodney's head became swollen a few days later. He was anesthetized and a protuberance was lanced. "Pus and water and blood shot out."[14] Rodney was out of school for a week and has a half-inch scar on the side of his forehead. Two other paddlings caused him to cough up blood.[15]

The Courts

The United States Supreme Court considered the constitutionality of these punishments in the 1977 decision of *Ingraham* v. *Wright*, 97, S.Ct. 1401 (1977). The Court held that the punishments administered to these and other students at Drew Junior High School did not violate the cruel and unusual punishment clause of the Eighth Amendment to the United States Constitution. The Court also held that the due process clause of the Fourteenth Amendment to the United States Constitution does not require notification of charges and an informal hearing prior to the infliction of corporal punishment. The students of Dade County, Florida, had lost their case.

The case was originally filed on January 7, 1971, by James Ingraham and Roosevelt Andrews in the United States District Court for the District of Florida. Their complaint contained three counts. Counts one and two were individual damages actions based on paddling incidents involving Ingraham and Andrews during October 1970. Count three was brought on behalf of the class of all students subject to the corporal punishment policies of the Dade County School Board. The students requested that the court enter a judgment declaring the School Board policy allowing corporal punishment, as well as all corporal punishment imposed on students attending the Dade County public schools, to be unconstitutional. The students also requested that the defendants be enjoined and restrained from inflicting any form of corporal punishment upon them. Named as defendants in all counts were Willie J. Wright (principal of Drew Junior High School), Lemmie Deliford (an assistant principal), Solomon Barnes (an assistant to the principal), and Edward L. Whigham (superintendent of the Dade County school system).

The plaintiff students presented evidence during a week-long trial before a judge and jury. Without submitting any evidence in their defense, the defendants moved to dismiss count three on the ground that, based upon the facts and the law, the plaintiffs had no right to relief. The defendants also moved for a ruling that the evidence would be insufficient to go to the jury on counts one and two. The district court judge dismissed all three counts without hearing any evidence on behalf of the school authorities.

The case was appealed to the Court of Appeals for the Fifth Circuit where three judges reversed the decision of the district court.[16] Two years later, the Fifth Circuit reheard the case with seven judges, reversed its earlier decision, and affirmed the decision of the district court. James Ingraham and Roosevelt Andrews had again lost.

Ingraham and Andrews sought review of the Fifth Circuit opinion by petitioning the United States Supreme Court. This petition was granted on May 24, 1976, but was limited to review of the following questions:

> Does the cruel and unusual punishment clause of the Eighth Amendment apply to the administration of discipline through severe corporal punishment inflicted by public school teachers and administrators upon public school children?
> Does the infliction of severe corporal punishment upon public school students, absent notice of the charges for which punishment is to be inflicted and an opportunity to be heard violate the due process clause of the Fourteenth Amendment?[17]

The Supreme Court specifically denied review of a substantive due process claim made by the petitioners:

> We denied review of a third question presented in the petition for certiorari:
> "Is the infliction of severe corporal punishment upon public school students arbitrary, capricious and unrelated to achieving any legitimate educational purpose and therefore violative of the Due Process Clause of the Fourteenth Amendment?" Petition for Certiorari 2.
> *Ingraham* v. *Wright*, 97, S.Ct. 1401, 1406, footnote 12.

Briefs were filed by the petitioners (plaintiffs) and respondents (defendants). Those filing briefs on behalf of the student petitioners were the

American Psychological Association and the National Education Association. The National School Boards Association and the United Teachers of Dade, Local 1974, AFT, AFL–CIO filed briefs on behalf of the respondent school authorities. The case was argued on November 2 and 3, 1977, and was decided on April 19, 1977.

The Legal Theories: The Eighth Amendment

The Petitioners.   Ingraham and Andrews did not argue that every act of corporal punishment violates the United States Constitution. Rather, they argued that "in this case we are talking about the infliction of severe, brutal, and excessive punishment."[18] The petitioners' legal foothold for attacking excessive corporal punishment was the cruel and unusual punishment clause of the Eighth Amendment to the United States Constitution: "Excessive bail shall not be required nor excessive fines imposed, nor cruel and unusual punishments inflicted."

Ingraham and Andrews argued that the cruel and unusual punishment clause applies to public school students punished by school officials.

> We begin with this principle:
>   In our system, State-invented schools may not be enclaves of totalitarianism. School officials do not possess absolute authority over children. Students in school as well as out of school are "persons" under the Constitution. They are possessed of fundamental rights which the State must respect, just as they themselves must respect their obligations to the State.
>   *Tinker* v. *Des Moines School District*, 393 U.S. 503, 511 (1969)

In considering Ingraham's and Andrews's case, the court of appeals had reasoned that the Eighth Amendment's application is limited to punishment invoked as a sanction for criminal conduct and is inapplicable to corporal punishment inflicted in public schools. In their appeal to the Supreme Court, petitioners argued:

> That decision created this anomalistic result: public school children may be savagely beaten and whipped by teachers acting under color of state law, yet they will have no Constitutional redress. But hardened criminals suffering the same beatings at the hands of their jailers will have Constitutional claims. Neither the Constitution nor common sense condones that conclusion.[19]

The petitioners cited numerous cases to support their contention that the Eighth Amendment applies to non-criminal conduct. Federal Courts of Appeals have applied the Eighth Amendment to mental institution inmates,

Knecht v. *Gillman*, 488 F.2d 1136 (8th Cir. 1973), as well as to runaway children in state training schools, *Vann* v. *Scott*, 467 F.2d 1235 (7th Cir. 1972). Numerous federal courts have applied the cruel and unusual punishment clause to pretrial detainees held in jails, not for punishment, but because of their inability to make bail, *Jones* v. *Wittenberg*, 323 F. Supp. 93, 330 F. Supp. 707 (N.D. Ohio, 1971); *Collins* v. *Schoenfiel* 344 F. Supp. 251 and 363 F. Supp. 1152 (D. Md., 1972 and 1973); and *Johnson* v. *Lark*, 365 F. Supp. 289 (E.D. Mo., 1973).[20]

Ingraham and Andrews argued that severe corporal punishment constitutes cruel and unusual punishment under two tests. They first argued that the severe corporal punishment meted out by the defendants at Drew Junior High School violated the "contemporary values" test of the Eighth Amendment. Secondly they argued that this excessive corporal punishment violated the concept of human dignity embodied in the Eighth Amendment.

To determine if a punishment is cruel and unusual under the contemporary values test, the Supreme Court must assess " 'contemporary values concerning the infliction of a challenged sanction,' looking to 'objective indicia that reflect the public attitude toward a given sanction.' *Gregg* v. *Georgia*, . . . 44 L.W. at 5235."[21] Petitioners argued that public tolerance for corporal punishment imposed upon public school students could be measured by legislative enactments. Id., 44 L.W. at 5240. Such legislation, they argued reflects the "moral consensus" concerning such punishment and its "social utility as a sanction."[22]

According to Ingraham and Andrews, only ten states specifically permitted corporal punishment in 1976. Two states expressly prohibited its use. Some large school systems had banned it. Comparing these statistics to the endorsements of *capital* punishment by at least thirty-five states, petitioners argued that public sentiment was ambivalent about the use of any corporal punishment on students.[23]

Furthermore, no statutes or rules authorize severe corporal punishment as used at Drew Junior High School. "No legislature has authorized the imposition of penalties like twenty brutally hard strokes with a paddle for tardiness in leaving a school auditorium . . . ; or the mass paddling of fifteen boys in a bathroom for being late to class or other minor transgressions. . . . Beatings requiring medical treatment . . . and causing the injured person to be unable to sit comfortably for three weeks . . . , or to miss school for two weeks with an injured hand . . . would be obnoxious to societal values even if inflicted by a parent."[24] Such behavior, petitioners argued, would be violative of the "contemporary values" test.

Ingraham and Andrews also argued that corporal punishment could be so "excessive" as to violate the "human dignity" test.

> A penalty also must accord with "the dignity of man," which is the "basic concept underlying the Eighth Amendment." . . . This means, at least, that the punishment not be "excessive."
>
> > *Gregg* v. *Georgia*, 44 L.W. at 5236[25]

They argued that punishment is excessive when it involves the unnecessary and wanton infliction of pain, and when the punishment is grossly out of proportion to the offense.[26]

In making their excessiveness/human dignity arguments, petitioners pointed out that nonphysical punishment is customarily imposed in school settings. "Suspensions are one of the traditional means—ranging from keeping a student after class to permanent expulsion—used to maintain discipline in the schools." *Goss* v. *Lopez*, 419 U.S. 565, 591 (1974) (Powell, J., dissenting).[27] Even if the petitioners had been tried in criminal or juvenile court, only nonphysical penalties of fines or imprisonment would have been imposed.

The petitioners argued that the defendant school officials had not shown a "compelling interest" which would justify the use of excessive corporal punishment. Dade County School Board policy stated that corporal punishment is a "penalty" designed to maintain discipline by "changing the behavior of the student."[28] The petitioners argued that corporal punishment accomplishes none of these stated objectives.

> I can't think of a renowned or leading authority in psychology, educational psychology, educational research, psychiatry who advocated corporal punishment in schools.
>
> > Testimony of Dr. Scott Kester[29]

Petitioners discussed the National Education Association's "Task Force Report on Corporal Punishment." This report concluded that:

> . . . it is an inefficient way to maintain order; that it may increase disruptive behavior; that it hinders learning. After examining "all reasons it could identify for the use of corporal punishment in both oral and written materials," the Task Force found "that the weight of fact and reasoning was against the infliction of physical pain as an attempt to maintain an orderly learning climate."[30]

Even if some valid reason to paddle existed, the petitioners argued that the paddling of Drew Junior High School students was "more than retribution, more than they 'deserved.' "[31] Such harsh measures would not deter future misconduct or maintain discipline, particularly in light of the fact that "innocent conduct, more than culpable conduct, prompted the harsh vengeance of the school administration."[32]

The Respondents.   The respondent school officials argued vigorously against interpreting the Eighth Amendment to offer constitutional protections to schoolchildren. They argued that the Eighth Amendment applies only to punishments arising out of criminal, and not school, settings. The correctness of their position, the respondents argued, is based on historical fact.[33]

> The critical historical fact is that the governmental limitations imposed by this clause on the infliction of punishment were exclusively directed toward the process of criminal proceedings.
>
> 4 W. Blackstone, *Commentaries* . . . 376–77.

That the Eighth Amendment applies only to criminal punishments, respondents argued, is supported by revelant case law.

> The order of deportation is not punishment for "crime" . . . . Therefore the provisions of the Constitution . . . prohibiting . . . cruel and unusual punishment, have no application.
>
> *Fong Yue Ting* v. *U.S.*, 149 U.S. 698, 730 (1893).[34]

See also *Gregg* v. *Georgia*, 428 U.S. 153, 96 S.Ct. 2909 (1976) (Death penalty imposed for armed robbery and murder); *Robinson* v. *California*, 370 U.S. 660 (1962) (crime to be addicted to narcotics); *Trop* v. *Dulles*, 356 U.S. 86 (1958) (penalty imposed as a direct result of a criminal conviction for desertion), and so forth.[35]

Finally, the school officials argued that if the Eighth Amendment does apply to schoolchildren the punishments were not "excessive." In their brief the respondents quoted from the district court's decision, which stated:

> Considering the system as a whole, there is no showing of severe punishment degrading to human dignity, nor of the arbitrary infliction of severe punishment, nor of the unacceptability to contemporary society of corporal punishment in the schools, nor of excessive or disproportionately severe punishment. . . .[36]

The Supreme Court.   The United States Supreme Court agreed with the respondent school officials, and held that the Eighth Amendment is not applicable to the imposition of disciplinary corporal punishment by public school teachers or administrators. The case was a five to four decision, with Justice Powell writing the majority opinion for Chief Justice Burger and Justices Rehnquist, Blackmun, and Stewart. Justices White, Brennan, Marshall and Stevens dissented from the majority's decision.

Justice Powell begins his analysis by stating:

> In addressing the scope of the Eighth Amendment's prohibition of cruel and unusual punishment this Court has found it useful to refer to "[t]raditional

common law concepts . . . , and to the attitude[s] which our society has traditionally taken." . . . We therefore begin by examining the way in which our traditions and our laws have responded to the use of corporal punishment in public schools.

Ingraham v. *Wright, supra,* p. 1406.

Justice Powell gives great weight to the historical bases of corporal punishment.

The use of corporal punishment in this country as a means of disciplining school children dates back to the colonial period . . . . Despite the general abandonment of corporal punishment as a means of punishing criminal offenders, . . . the practice continues to play a role in the public education of school children in most parts of the country . . . . Professional and public opinion is sharply divided on the practice, . . . and has been for more than a century. . . . Yet we can discern no trend towards its elimination.

Ingraham v. *Wright, supra,* p. 1407

Blackstone, an eighteenth century legal writer, appears to have been a key authority on corporal punishment in Justice Powell's view.

Blackstone catalogued among the "absolute rights of individuals" the right "to security from the corporal insults of menaces, assaults, beatings, and wounding," I Blackstone, Commentaries *134, but he did not regard it a "corporal insult" for a teacher to inflict "moderate correction" on a child in his care. To the extent that force was "necessary to answer the purposes for which [the teacher] is employed, "Blackstone viewed it as "justifiable or lawful." I Blackstone, Commentaries *453, III Blackstone, Commentaries *120.

Ingraham v. *Wright, supra,* p. 1407

Powell notes that "[o]nly two States, Massachusetts and New Jersey have prohibited all corporal punishment in their public schools."[37] He further notes that of the twenty-three states that have addressed corporal punishment through legislation, twenty-one have authorized its moderate use in public schools.[38]

Powell has little trouble in concluding that "the proscription against cruel and unusual punishment confirms that it was designed to protect those convicted of crimes."[39] He cites the English Bill of Rights of 1689 and states that "every decision of this Court considering whether a punishment is 'cruel and unusual' within the meaning of the Eighth and Fourteenth Amendments has dealt with criminal punishment."[40] In concluding that the Eighth Amendment applies only to criminal punishments, the Supreme Court rejected petitioners' contemporary values and human dignity tests as being irrelevant to a noncriminal punishment.

The four dissenting judges reach the opposite conclusion.

The Eighth Amendment places a flat prohibition against the infliction of "cruel and unusual punishments." This reflects a societal judgment that there are some punishments that are so barbaric and inhumane that we will not permit them to be imposed on anyone, no matter how opprobrious the offense. . . . If there are some punishments that are so barbaric that they may not be imposed for the commission of crimes, designated by our social system as the most thoroughly reprehensible acts an individual can commit, then *a fortiori*, similar punishments may not be imposed on persons for less culpable acts, such as breaches of school discipline. Thus, if it is constitutionally impermissible to cut off someone's ear for the commission of murder, it must be unconstitutional to cut off a child's ear for being late to class.

[T]he constitutional prohibition is against cruel and unusual *punishments*; nowhere is that prohibition limited or modified by the language of the Constitution.

The relevant inquiry is not whether the offense for which a punishment is inflicted has been labeled as criminal, but whether the purpose of the deprivation is among those ordinarily associated with punishment, such as retribution, rehabilitation, or deterrence. . . . [*Trop* v. *Dulles*,] 356 U.S., at 96

In fact, as the Court recognizes, the Eighth Amendment has never been confined to criminal punishments.

Dissenting opinion of Justice White, *Ingraham* v. *Wright*, 97 S.Ct., 1401 1419–1420.

It is difficult to understand why five justices would believe so strongly that the Eighth Amendment applies only to criminals, and why four justices would believe just as strongly that the Eighth Amendment applies to public school children as well as to criminals. Justice Powell's decision can in part be explained by his personal perceptions of public schools.

The schoolchild has little need for the protection of the Eighth Amendment. Though attendance may not always be voluntary, the public school remains an open institution. Except perhaps when very young, the child is not physically restrained from leaving school during school hours; and at the end of the school day, the child is invariably free to return home. Even while at school, the child brings with him the support of family and friends and is rarely apart from teachers and other pupils who may witness and protest any instances of mistreatment.

The openness of the public school and its supervision by the community afford significant safeguards against the kinds of abuses from which the Eighth Amendment protects the prisoner. In virtually every community where corporal punishment is permitted in the schools, these safeguards are reinforced by the legal constraints of the common law. Public school teachers and administrators are privileged at common law to inflict only such corporal punishment as is reasonably necessary for the proper education and discipline of the child; any punishment going beyond the privilege may result in both civil and criminal liability. As long as the schools are open to public scrutiny, there is no reason to believe that the common law constraints will not effectively remedy and deter excesses such as those alleged in this case.

Ingraham v. *Wright, supra,* p. 1412

To this author's knowledge, no evidence was presented concerning the "openness of public schools" or the effectiveness of "common law constraints." One can only conclude that Justice Powell effectively took "judicial notice" of these factors. Certainly, looking to our own experiences, many of us would disagree with these perceptions of public education. From a legal standpoint, moreover, it is bad practice to base decisions on standards for which no evidence is presented.

Due Process

The Petitioners.   The second issue which the Supreme Court agreed to review was:

Does the infliction of severe corporal punishment upon public school students, absent notice of the charges for which punishment is to be inflicted and an opportunity to be heard violate the due process clause of the Fourteenth Amendment.[41]

The Due Process Clause of the Fourteenth Amendment to the United States Constitution states: ". . . nor shall any state deprive any person of life, liberty, or property, without due process of law."

Petitioners Ingraham and Andrews argued that their due process "liberty" rights had been violated. "The intrusions upon the physical integrity of the Drew Junior High School students were severe, annoying, frightening and humiliating. . . . 'Liberty,' as a broad concept, or as a Fourth Amendment concept, is certainly the right which was lost by the Petitioners and their class."[42]

Citing *Goss* v. *Lopez*, 419 U.S. 565 (1975), the United States Supreme Court decision requiring rudimentary due process prior to the imposition of ten-day suspensions, the petitioners argued that they had also been denied "property" rights in violation of the due process clause of the Fourteenth Amendment. James Ingraham was absent from school for a "week and a few days"[43] as a result of respondent Wright's paddle. "Under the 'property' test of *Goss* v. *Lopez*, Ingraham's loss of schooling reached constitutional proportions."[44]

The petitioners limited their due process analysis to *severe* corporal punishment.

> In the due process sense, "severe" corporal punishment means the infliction of bodily pain by an instrument designed to cause such pain. That definition is drawn from the facts of this case. We do not include a brief hand spanking or a slapped face within the definition of "severe" corporal punishment. But one "lick" with a paddle, an instrument designed for the purpose of causing pain, is "a severe though brief intrusion upon cherished personal security." Cf. *Terry* v. *Ohio*, 392 U.S. 1, 24–25 (1968).[45]

Having argued that at least *severe* corporal punishment is a liberty and property right protected by the Fourteenth Amendment, the petitioners described the minimal procedures required. " '[T]he timing and nature of the hearing will depend on appropriate accommodation of the competing interests involved.' *Goss* v. *Lopez* . . . ." Due process is not necessarily elaborate or formal. At the very least, a student must be told " 'what he is accused of doing and what the basis of the accusation is.' *Goss* v. *Lopez*, 419 U.S. at 582. Essential to the notice requirement is some code of discipline so that a student will not be exposed to punishment for conduct which he did not know was improper."[46] The students argued that formal procedures should not be imposed, but that the hearing must be at least an "informal give and take between student and disciplinarian" prior to the imposition of punishment.[47]

The petitioners argued that due process requires that a neutral person decide the need for punishment and impose punishment if necessary. They asserted that such a requirement would protect students against harsh treatment inflicted in anger and hostility. A neutral person would, moreover, be more likely to arrive at an unbiased conclusion.

The Respondents. The respondent school officials argued that corporal punishment does not involve liberty or property rights protected by the Fourteenth Amendment. In contrasting the suspended students in *Goss* v. *Lopez*, they argued that the purpose of corporal punishment is to avoid exclusion from school, and does not deprive students of property rights. The respondents also rejected the petitioners' argument that liberty rights, in terms of reputation and stigma, were affected.

> There is nothing in the record, nor in common experience, to support the idea that a paddling brings upon the student anything more serious than the kidding of his friends. . . . Male chauvinists among us, if any are left, might remember a paddling by the principal as a mark of honorable achievement

in the eyes of one's boyhood friends. Not to be facetious, though, it passes belief that school spankings can be perceived as having *any* damaging or lasting consequences to reputation, honor or integrity.[48]

If one assumes, however, that corporal punishment does involve rights protected by the Fourteenth Amendment, the respondents argued that the issue is not whether the infliction of *severe* corporal punishment must be preceded by due process, but rather whether procedural requirements are necessary before *any* corporal punishment may be administered to public school students. "So understood, the issue . . . becomes clear in its dimensions, and, in its implications for state and local control of disciplinary measures in the schools."[49] "This notion can only be seen as expensive, time- consuming and needless in the context of public school operations."[50]

Looking to the effect on teachers and administrators the respondents argued:

If they are now to be told that the United States Constitution requires due process procedures prior to every use of corporal discipline, no matter how bland the description of the process may be, school officials are necessarily going to see each choice of corporal punishment as laden with the risk of being hauled into federal court on claims of procedural flaws. The results are likely to be in two directions, both undesirable. Conscientious educators, in order to protect themselves in using corporal punishment, will over-formalize and document the pre-spanking procedures, and thus prolong the anxiety of the students and defeat the proper function of the discipline as swift and nondisruptive of the educational process. This would have the added effect of further diverting school resources and administrative time from educational concerns, a factor recognized by both the majority and dissenting opinions in *Goss* v. *Lopez*, 419 U.S. 565 at 583, 594 (1975). On the other hand, less imaginative but still frightened administrators will find it simpler to discard corporal discipline as a viable measure, and either ignore misconduct or turn to more stringent penalties such as suspension or expulsion from school.[51]

The respondents suggested several other arguments supporting their contention that due process will be ill-advised prior to the imposition of corporal punishment. The respondents argued that procedural steps and their resulting delays would worsen, rather than avoid, mental distress for the candidate for corporal punishment.[52] In making this argument the respondents did not refer to any psychological or educational authorities to show whether or not such mental stress would occur, and if so, what its effect might be on principles of learning as well as on student's developing principles of justice. The respondents pointed to a rising concern over disorder and disruption in the public schools. "This is not to argue for more and harder beatings, but only to suggest that in a consideration of ordinary, garden-variety corporal punishment, the so-called liberty interest of the student has to be seen in the perspective of the needs of hard-pressed educators for effective and efficient disciplinary alternatives."[53] The respondent school officials, however, offered no evidence concerning the effect of corporal punishment on disruption nor did they offer any evidence concerning the effectiveness, generally, of the use of corporal punishment as a disciplinary technique.

The Supreme Court. The United States Supreme Court held that corporal punishment involves a constitutionally protected liberty right, the right to be free from unjustified intrusions on personal security.[54] Although a liberty right was identified, the Court held that the Fourteenth Amendment did not require procedures prior to the imposition of corporal punishment. The Court reasons that common law constraints and remedies were sufficient to satisfy the due process clause.

In his majority decision, Justice Powell indicates that the court's analysis required consideration of three distinct factors:

> "first, the private interest that will be affected . . . ; second, the risk of an erroneous deprivation of such interest . . . and the probable value, if any, of additional or substitute procedural safeguards; and, finally, the [state] interest, including the function involved and the fiscal and administrative burdens that the additional or substitute procedural requirement would entail." *Mathews* v. *Eldridge*, 424 U.S. 319, 335, . . . (1976).
>
> *Ingraham* v. *Wright, supra*, p. 1415

In describing the first factor, the "private interest affected," the court indicates that teachers and administrators have a common law privilege to use reasonable corporal punishment. A balance must be struck "between the child's interest in personal security and the traditional view that some limited corporal punishment may be necessary in the course of a child's education." *Ingraham* v. *Wright, supra*, p. 1415.

The second factor, risk of error and probable value of additional procedures, is treated by Justice Powell as follows:

> If the punishment inflicted is later found to have been excessive—not reasonably believed at the time to be necessary for the child's discipline or training—the school authorities inflicting it may be held liable in damages to the child and, if malice is shown, they may be subject to criminal penalties.
>
> Although students have testified in this case to specific instances of abuse, there is every reason to believe that such mistreatment is an aberration. The uncontradicted evidence suggests that corporal punishment in the Dade County school was, "[w]ith the exception of a few cases, . . . unremarkable in physical severity." App. 152. Moreover, because paddlings are usually inflicted in response to conduct directly observed by teachers in

their presence, the risk that a child will be paddled without cause is typically insignificant.

In those cases where severe punishment is contemplated, the available civil and criminal sanctions for abuse—considered in light of the openness of the school environment—afford significant protection against unjustified corporal punishment unnecessarily or excessively when a possible consequence of doing so is the institution of civil or criminal proceedings against them.

Ingraham v. *Wright, supra,* pp. 415–16

Additionally, the court reasoned that the Fourth Amendment proscription against seizures of a person without "probable cause" does not require that an arresting officer seek an advance judicial determination of the facts. Since advance procedural safeguards do not apply to the Fourth Amendment, the court reasoned that they should not apply to students who are corporally punished.

The third factor requires the examination of fiscal and administrative burdens on school systems.

Such a universal constitutional requirement would significantly burden the use of corporal punishment as a disciplinary measure. Hearings—even informal hearings—require time, personnel, and a diversion of attention from normal school pursuits. School authorities may well choose to abandon corporal punishment rather than incur the burdens of complying with the procedural requirements. Teachers, properly concerned with maintaining authority in the classroom, may well prefer to rely on other disciplinary measures—which they may view as less effective—rather than confront the possible disruption that prior notice and a hearing may entail. . . . Paradoxically, such an alteration of disciplinary policy is most likely to occur in the ordinary case where the contemplated punishment is well within the common law privilege.

Ingraham v. *Wright, supra,* p. 1417

In a footnote, the Court noted that Dade County school officials believed that the "effect of interposing prior procedural safeguards may well be to make punishment more severe by increasing the anxiety of the child." *Ingraham* v. *Wright, supra,* p. 1417, no. 51.

The four dissenting justices reject Justice Powell's analysis of due process. Justice White states:

Nor is it an adequate answer that school children may have other state and constitutional remedies available to them. Even assuming that the remedies available to public school students are adequate under Florida law, the availability of state remedies has never been determinative of the coverage or of the protections afforded by the Eighth Amendment. The reason is obvious. The fact that a person may have a state-law-cause of action against a public official who tortures him with a thumb screw for the commission of an antisocial act has nothing to do with the fact that such official conduct is cruel and unusual punishment prohibited by the Eighth Amendment.

Ingraham v. *Wright, supra,* p. 1422.

Justice Powell does not take into consideration the inadequacies of state tort remedies. As Justice White points out:

This tort action is utterly inadequate to protect against erroneous infliction of punishment for two reasons. First, under Florida law, a student punished for an act he did not commit cannot recover damages from a teacher "proceeding in utmost good faith . . . on the reports and advice of others," . . . the student has no remedy at all for punishment imposed on the basis of mistaken facts, at least as long as the punishment was reasonable from the point of view of the disciplinarian, uninformed by any prior hearing. Second, and more important, even if the student could sue for good faith error in the infliction of punishment, the lawsuit occurs after the punishment has been finally imposed. The infliction of physical pain is final and irreparable; it cannot be undone in a subsequent proceeding. . . .

The majority's conclusion that a damage remedy for excessive corporal punishment affords adequate process rests on the novel theory that the State may punish an individual without giving him any opportunity to present his side of the story, as long as he can later recover damages from a state official if he is innocent. The logic of this theory would permit a State that punished speeding with a one-day jail sentence to make a driver serve his sentence first without a trial and then sue to recover damages for wrongful imprisonment. Similarly, the State could finally take away a prisoner's good time credits for alleged disciplinary infractions and require him to bring a damage suit after he was eventually released. There is no authority for this theory, nor does the majority purport to find any in the procedural due process decisions of this Court.

Ingraham v. *Wright, supra,* 1424–25

Justice Powell's majority opinion regarding due process is even more difficult to understand than his opinion regarding the Eighth Amendment. Having found a protected "liberty" interest, he clearly ignores the mandate of *Goss* v. *Lopez, supra,* which requires at least minimal procedures prior to the imposition of the punishment. By reasoning that a student receives due process by going to court after he is corporally punished, Justice Powell rejects the concept of an informal give and take between student and disciplinarian which acts as a "meaningful hedge" against erroneous infliction of injury. *Goss* v. *Lopez, supra,* 583, 584.

Conclusion

In *Ingraham* v. *Wright*, the United States Supreme Court made it clear that students who have been corporally punished should not seek redress from the federal courts. Although the Supreme Court did not address the issue of substantive due process,[55] it is unlikely that the Court would find severe corporal punishment to be violative of substantive due process since it specifically declined to hear the substantive due process issue.

Students and their parents may want to consider seeking redress from their state courts. This can be pursued in a combination of three ways. First, students may challenge the legality of corporal punishment under their state constitutions. It is unlikely that state court judges would hold that their state constitutions prohibit the use of corporal punishment, where the federal constitution has been interpreted otherwise. Legally, however, the Supreme Court's ruling in *Ingraham* does not require a state court to interpret its state constitution in the same way as the federal constitution. Second, consideration may be given to state tort actions for assault and battery. In contrast to Justice Powell's view, such cases have not been particularly successful, nor have they acted as a deterrent to the academic community.[56] Such tort actions require great time and energy, and generally result in little financial gain to the plaintiff. Third, students and parents may want to consider criminal prosecution. Success in this attempt will, however, be further complicated by the political realities of their communities.

Another line of attack is to bring the struggle against the use of corporal punishment to local school boards, unions, state departments of education and state legislatures. Efforts should be made to enact legislation and regulations which would prohibit or at least discourage the use of corporal punishment.

New Jersey's corporal punishment statute provides:

> No person employed or engaged in a school or educational institution, whether public or private, shall inflict or cause to be inflicted corporal punishment upon a pupil attending such school or institution; but any such person may, within the scope of his employment, use and apply such amounts of force as is reasonable and necessary:
>
> (1) to quell a disturbance, threatening physical injury to others;
> (2) to obtain possession of weapons or other dangerous objects upon the person or within the control of a pupil;
> (3) for the purpose of self-defense; and
> (4) for the protection of persons or property;
>
> and such acts, or any of them, shall not be construed to constitute corporal punishment within the meaning and intendment of this section. Every resolution, bylaw, rule, ordinance, or other act or authority permitting or

authorizing corporal punishment to be inflicted upon a pupil attending a school or educational institution shall be void.

N.J. Stat. Ann. §18A:6–1 (1968).

Similar statutes have more recently been enacted in Maine[57] and Massachusetts.[58]

Legislation passed in California discourages the use of corporal punishment.

Corporal punishment shall not be administered to a pupil without the prior written approval of the pupil's parent or guardians. The written approval shall be valid for the school year in which it is submitted but may be withdrawn by the parent or guardian at any time.

California Reorg. Educ. Code §49001(a) (1977).

Students and their parents cannot look to the courts for meaningful protection against the abuses of corporal punishment. They should assess the political climates in their communities and should organize around discipline issues. Students and parents should push for humanistic, non-racist alternatives, including the elimination of corporal punishment from their school systems. In some instances school board elections could turn on the issue of corporal punishment. Some unions, such as the National Education Association, may be persuaded to oppose its use. Many school psychologists and members of the mental health profession already oppose the use of corporal punishment. For all practical purposes, the use of corporal punishment in the public schools has become a political, and not a judicial, issue.

NOTES

1. *Ingraham* v. *Wright*, 498 F.2d 248, 255, 256 (1974).
2. Testimony of James Ingraham, ibid., case no. 71–23, Relevant Docket Entries, United States District Court, Southern District of Florida (hereafter referred to as "Relevant Docket Entries"), pp. 70–72.
3. Ibid., p. 73.
4. Ibid., p. 74.
5. Stipulated testimony of Dr. Fernando Milanes, Relevant Docket Entries, p. 19.
6. *Ingraham* v. *Wright*, 498 F.2d 218, 256 (1974).
7. Stipulated testimony of Dr. Carlos Gomez, Relevant Docket Entries, p. 19.
8. *Ingraham* v. *Wright*, 498 F.2d 218, 256 (1974).
9. Ibid.
10. Brief for Petitioners, p. 12, *Ingraham* v. *Wright*, 97 S.Ct. 1401 (1977).

11. Testimony of Roosevelt Andrews, Relevant Docket Entries, pp. 108–113.

12. Brief for Petitioners, p. 13.

13. Testimony of Rodney Williams, Brief for Petitioners, pp. 14–15.

14. Ibid., p. 15.

15. Ibid.

16. *Ingraham* v. *Wright*, 498 F.2d 248 (1974).

17. Ibid., no. 75–6527, Supreme Court of the United States (October term, 1975). Relevant Docket Entries, p. 216, May 24, 1976.

18. Oral argument, Ibid., 45 L.W. 3337.

19. Brief for Petitioners, p. 25, *Ingraham* v. *Wright*, 97 S.Ct. 1401 (1977).

20. Reply Brief for Petitioners, p. 2., ibid.

21. Brief for Petitioners, p. 31.

22. Ibid.

23. Ibid., pp. 31–32.

24. Ibid., pp. 33–34.

25. Ibid., p. 36.

26. Ibid., p. 38.

27. Ibid.

28. Ibid., p. 40.

29. Ibid.

30. Ibid., pp. 40–41.

31. Ibid., p. 41.

32. Ibid.

33. Brief for Respondents, p. 19, *Ingraham* v. *Wright*, 97 S.Ct. 1401 (1977).

34. Ibid., p. 23.

35. Ibid., p. 24.

36. Ibid., p. 43.

37. *Ingraham* v. *Wright*, 97 S.Ct. 1401, 1408 (1977).

38. Ibid.

39. Ibid., p. 1409.

40. Ibid., p. 1410.

41. See note 17 above.

42. Brief for Petitioners, p. 44.

43. Ibid., p. 45.

44. Ibid.

45. Ibid., p. 44, footnote 19.

46. Ibid., p. 52.

47. Ibid., p. 52, citing *Goss* v. *Lopez*, 419 U.S. 565, 584.

48. Brief for Respondents, pp. 55–56.

49. Ibid., p .46.

50. Ibid., p. 64.

51. Ibid., p. 62.

52. Ibid., p. 55.

53. Ibid., p. 57–58.

54. *Ingraham* v. *Wright*, 97 S.Ct. 1401, 1413 (1977).

55. A substantive due process argument would proceed as follows:

(1) Corporal punishment, as used by the Defendants at Drew Junior High School, is too severe for the offenses allegedly committed by the plaintiffs.

(2) Severe corporal punishment is not reasonably related to any legitimate school objective.

(3) There are reasonable alternative means, other than severe corporal punishment, which would accomplish any legitimate school objectives.

56. Patricia M. Lines, "Corporal Punishment After Ingraham: Looking to State Law," *Inequality in Education*, Number 23.

57. "A teacher or other person entrusted with the case or supervision of a person for special and limited purposes is justified in using a reasonable degree of force against any such person who creates a disturbance when and to the extent that he reasonably believes it necessary to control the disturbing behavior or to remove a person from the scene of such disturbance." Me. Rev. Stat. Ann., Title 17–A §106(2) (1976).

58. "The power of the school committee or of any teacher or other employee or agent of the school to maintain discipline upon school property shall not include the right to inflict corporal punishment upon any pupil." Mass. Gen. Laws Ann., Chapter 71, §37 G (1976–1977 Supp.).

12

Corporal Punishment in the Schools: The Civil Liberties Objections

Alan Reitman

●

Those who proclaim the civil liberties creed have a very clear idea of why corporal punishment in schools is a civil liberties issue and why such punishment should be eliminated from our educational system. Their opposition focuses on two fundamental violations of constitutional rights which are imbedded in the practice of corporal punishment. These are the Eighth Amendment's prohibition against cruel and unusual punishment and the Fifth Amendment's protection of both substantive and procedural due process.

Acceptance of this civil liberties position hinges on acceptance of changes in the status of children in our society. The point has long passed where children are subject *only* to the control of their parents, a relic of a smaller, less complex society in which government played a less influential role. Children are now controlled by various institutions of the state, for example, schools, social agencies, and courts; and we have begun to think of applying to children the same rights which adults possess when they become involved with agencies of the state.

This move to define the rights of children, to assert that children are no longer a special class requiring special protection and different treatment from adults, was boosted by the turbulent and radical social changes of the 1960s. Highlighted by movements to secure individual rights for members of many disadvantaged groups, the decade left its mark on the courts' attitude toward the rights of children. When for the first time in the *Gault* case (1967) the Supreme Court said young people have the right of counsel and notice in juvenile proceedings; when the Court ruled in *Tinker* (1969; a

This essay first appeared in J. Wise (ed.), *Proceedings*: *Conference on Corporal Punishment in the Schools*: *A National Debate.* Washington, D.C.: National Institute of Education, 1977 (NIE–P–77–0079).

case upholding the wearing of a black armband to protest the Vietnam War) that "students in school as well as out are persons under our Constitution" —then the door was opened to say to school authorities that corporal punishment is a violation of constitutional rights.

What are the specifics of the two main constitutional arguments? The case against corporal punishment as a violation of the Eighth Amendment is based on the idea that such punishment *is* indeed cruel and unusual. This claim is asserted on several grounds: (1) Since corporal punishment has been eliminated from prisons and the military, schools are the one institution where, as a matter of legal right, children can be physically punished. (2) Many countries in the world have abolished the practice as an unhealthy and unnecessary part of the educational process. (3) It is psychologically cruel to teach children that violence is an appropriate means for handling differences or disputes. (4) Most importantly, the application of physical punishment to children contradicts the cardinal element of democracy, the dignity of the individual. The whole meaning of the Eighth Amendment is rooted in the concept of human dignity, a concept conceived as a humanistic reaction to the use of torture and other barbarous treatment by European nations in punishing people.

The case against corporal punishment as a violation of due process of law rests on two aspects. One is the idea of *substantive* due process, the deprivation of personal liberty, in the instance of corporal punishment invading the physical integrity of the individual. This is often done in an arbitrary or capricious manner by teachers and school administrators without a *reasonable relationship* to a societal purpose. The key words to bear in mind are "reasonable relationship." Despite the claims that corporal punishment is an essential educational mechanism, it does not foster education. To the contrary, it teaches violence, it breeds tension and frustration between student and teacher, and it defeats the purpose of education in a democracy.

The second due process concern is the absence of *procedural* rights. When punishment is inflicted by the state (the teacher or administrator is the state's agent) the individual is entitled to certain elementary procedural guarantees which are central to a fair hearing: notice of the charge, right to counsel, a chance to rebut the charge, and cross-examination of complaining witnesses.

To state so definitely that these civil liberties standards have been abrogated does not mean that the law, as interpreted by the courts, agrees with these approaches. The courts have declined, except in certain minimal ways, to adopt the civil libertarian position. Why?

The courts are great believers in the constitutional doctrine of separation of powers. In the area of education the courts have been especially loath to impose their authority on another branch of government, the local school authorities, in determining how to operate the schools. When one remembers that it took twenty-six years between the Supreme Court's *Barnette* (1943) decision (that the children of members of the Jehovah Witnesses' sect need not salute the American flag) and the *Tinker* decision on children's freedom of symbolic expression, one can see how strongly rooted is the Court's notion of federalism.

While some court decisions in the 1960s demonstrated a sensitivity to children's rights, and their importance should not be overlooked, a strong feeling persists that children are a special class which is not covered by the same blanket of constitutional protection that adults have. This attitude, often described as the "social worker" approach, seeks to shield the child from the harsh reality of adversary proceedings and courtroom conflict. The motivation behind this attitude is commendable, but the attitude permits abuses of rights to flourish.

But the most important reason for the courts not rallying behind the civil libertarian position is their concern that elimination of corporal punishment will rob school principals and teachers of the tool necessary to enforce school discipline, to maintain order in the classroom. In adopting the educators' claim, the courts reflect society's broader concern for physical security and protection against violence. Yet this is a shortsighted view. The method of allegedly assuring order, corporal punishment, only fosters further violence and disorder. As in other emotionally charged instances of societal tension and unrest, the simplistic view prevails. The fact that unruly behavior in schools is symptomatic of a deeper, festering sore which needs to be treated is glossed over in favor of temporary palliatives for surface symptoms.

Before turning our attention to how the United States Supreme Court has handled the challenge of corporal punishment, we should bear in mind that the weight of lower court decisions has rejected the constitutional arguments, even though there are some differences among the courts themselves. On the Eighth Amendment problem, the courts have divided into three camps: some have said that there is no violation of the cruel and unusual punishment guarantee, some have said yes there is, and others have made no decision on the basic constitutional point but ruled that as applied in particular cases no violation has occurred.

The two-prong due process argument has similarly failed except for agreeing that some attention should be paid to informing students of the reasons why corporal punishment is being imposed. However, the full array of procedural rights has not been given. And most important, since corporal punishment is perceived as a *reasonable* measure for maintaining order in schools and enabling them to carry out their educational function, substantive due process has not been infringed. One due process argument that has impressed a few courts is that of securing parental permission—a form of notice—before the punishment is applied.

All of these approaches blend in two cases before the High Court, one decided in the fall of 1975 and *Ingraham* v. *Wright*, decided in 1977. To comprehend fully the Supreme Court's action, the facts of each of these cases must be presented. In the North Carolina *Baker* v. *Owen* (1975) case Russell Carl Baker and his mother claimed that their constitutional rights were violated when Russell, a sixth grade student, was twice hit with a wooden drawer divider for allegedly violating his teacher's announced rule against throwing balls except during designated play periods. Mrs. Baker had previously requested of her son's principal and teachers that Russell not be corporally punished because she opposed it on principle. Nevertheless, the two licks were given by a teacher in the presence of a second teacher and in view of other students.

The three-judge federal court in the *Baker* case made a number of rulings. First, that the North Carolina law allows the "use of *reasonable* [emphasis added] force in the exercise by school officials of their lawful authority to restrain, correct pupils and maintain order." Second, while parents have the right to control the disciplining of their children, when there is a compelling state interest, the parental right is not absolute. The state does have a countervailing interest in maintaining order in schools, and in the *Baker* case the interest was sufficient to sustain the use of a reasonable amount of corporal punishment. In short, the two licks did not add up to cruel and unusual punishment.

However, the federal court did say that a minimal amount of procedural due process must be given a student before corporal punishment could be inflicted. The court relied on the Supreme Court's ruling in the 1975 *Goss* v. *Lopez* decision involving the suspension and expulsion of students from school. In that case, the High Court ruled that the suspension and expulsion amounted to a denial of education to the students. This constituted denial of a valuable property right, and therefore some degree of due process must be provided. Applying this approach to corporal punishment cases, the three-judge court held that (1) the punishment may never be used unless the student is informed "before hand that specific misbehavior may occasion its use"; (2) corporal punishment cannot be utilized as the first form of discipline; and (3) a second school official, the principal or other teachers, must be present and informed in the student's presence as to why corporal punishment is being used before the punishment can be inflicted. Before acknowledging these minimal protections, the court did note that Russell Baker did have an interest in avoiding corporal punishment as a matter of his personal liberty. The court held there is "personal security in small things of life as well as the obviously momentous" and that "the legal system, once quite tolerant of physical punishment in many contexts, has become less so."

The Supreme Court affirmed the *Baker* decision, but without any oral argument. This affirmance of a state statute was taken as the High Court's definitive stand on corporal punishment in schools. But to the surprise of corporal punishment's friends and foes, the Supreme Court accepted for review the case of *Ingraham* v. *Wright* (1977). The case concerned the use of corporal punishment in schools in Florida's Dade County, the sixth largest school system in the country.

The *Ingraham* (1977) case is different from *Baker* in a very significant way, the key point being the use of excessive, not reasonable, physical punishment. The final decision of the full U.S. Court of Appeals for the Fifth Circuit (*Ingraham* v. *Wright*, 1976a) described the issue as follows:

> Plaintiffs James Ingraham and Roosevelt Andrews, two junior high school students in Dade County, Florida, filed a complaint containing three counts on January 7, 1971. Counts one and two were individual actions for compensatory and punitive damages brought under 42 U.S.C. Sec. 1981–88, with jurisdiction claimed under 28 U.S.C. Sec. 1331 and Sec. 1343. Plaintiffs claimed that personal injuries resulted from corporal punishment administered by certain defendants in alleged violation of their constitutional rights, in particular their right to freedom from cruel and unusual punishment.
>
> Specifically, plaintiff Ingraham alleges in count one that on October 6, 1970, defendants Principal Wright and Assistant Principals Deliford and Barnes struck plaintiff repeatedly with a wooden instrument, injuring plaintiff and causing him to incur medical expenses. Plaintiff testified that this paddling was precipitated by his and several other children's disruption of a class over the objection of the teacher. Defendant Wright removed plaintiff and the other disruptive students to his office whereupon he paddled eight to ten of them. Wright had initially threatened plaintiff with five blows, but when the latter refused to assume a paddling position, Wright called on defendants Deliford and Barnes who held plaintiff in a prone position while Wright administisistered twenty blows.
>
> Plaintiff complained to his mother of discomfort following the paddling, whereupon he was taken to a hospital for treatment. Plaintiff introduced evidence that he had suffered a painful bruise that required the prescription of cold compresses, a laxative, sleeping and pain-killing pills and ten days of rest at home and that prevented him from sitting comfortably for three weeks.
>
> Plaintiff Andrews alleges two incidents of corporal punishment as the basis for his claim for damages in count two of the complaint. Plaintiff alleges that on October 1, 1970, he, along with fifteen other boys, was

spanked in the boys' restroom by Assistant Principal Barnes. Plaintiff testified that he was taken by a teacher to Barnes for the offense of tardiness, but that he refused to submit to a paddling because, as he explained to Barnes, he had two minutes remaining to get to class when he was seized and was not, therefore, guilty of tardiness. Barnes rejected plaintiff's explanation and, when plaintiff resisted punishment, struck him on the arm, back, and across the neck.

Plaintiff Andrews was again spanked on October 20, 1970. Despite denials of guilt, plaintiff was paddled on the backside and on the wrist by defendant Wright in the presence of defendants Deliford and Barnes for having allegedly broken some glass in sheet metal class. As a result of this paddling, plaintiff visited a doctor and received pain pills for the discomfort, which lasted approximately a week.

Count three is a class action brought by plaintiffs Ingraham and Andrews as representatives of the class of students of the Dade County school system who are subject to the corporal punishment policies issued by defendant members of the Dade County School Board. This count seeks final injunctive and/or declaratory relief against the use of corporal punishment in the Dade County School System and can be divided into three constitutional arguments.

First, plaintiffs claim that infliction of corporal punishment on its face and as applied in the present case constitutes cruel and unusual punishment in that its application is grossly disproportionate to any misconduct in which plaintiffs may have engaged. Second, plaintiffs claim that because it is arbitrary, capricious and unrelated to achieving any legitimate educational goal, corporal punishment deprives all students of liberty without due process of law in violation of the Fourteenth Amendment. Plaintiffs also allege that the failure of defendants to promulgate a list of school regulations and corresponding punishments increases the capriciousness of the punishment. Finally, plaintiffs claim that defendants' failure to provide any procedural safeguards before inflicting corporal punishment on students, including adequate notice of alleged misconduct, hearing, examination and cross-examination, representation and notice of rights, constitutes summary punishment and deprives students of liberty without due process of law in violation of the Fourteenth Amendment. (p. 911)

The *Ingraham* (1977) case was especially noteworthy because there was an earlier decision of the Fifth Circuit which reflected a partial civil liberties view. By a two to one vote the panel said that while corporal punishment per se could not be invalidated, its excessive use was not reasonable and thus violated the constitutional bar against cruel and unusual punishment. The majority said that when such punishment causes obvious physical and psychological injuries, and is systematically administered and inflicted on students who were not given a chance to explain the circumstances of their "crime," the Eighth Amendment guarantee could be invoked (*In-ghaham* v. *Wright*, 1974).

Sensing the importance of this legal decision, the school authorities in Dade County appealed for a re-hearing before the full bench of the Fifth Circuit. This time the decision went the other way, with ten judges finding nothing improper with the Dade County school policy or the actions of its school personnel. Three judges adhered to the earlier majority position.

What did the ten-judge majority say? On the key question of cruel and unusual punishment, the court held that this provision of the Constitution does not apply to the administration of educational discipline for two major reasons (*Ingraham* v. *Wright*, 1976a):

1. The background of the Eighth Amendment shows that it is concerned only with criminal actions. Historically, the Eighth Amendment reaches back to European practices centuries ago when confessions were extorted from criminal suspects through various forms of torture. A distinction, therefore, must be drawn between criminal behavior and civil penalties such as applied in school situations.

In this vein, while the Eighth Amendment is not applicable to wrongful behavior by school officials, if a teacher or administrator has meted out excessive punishment, there is no reason why the state courts cannot be asked to redress the grievance of such wrongful conduct in a suit for damages. In effect, child abuse can be challenged, but not as a constitutional issue.

2. The argument that since corporal punishment has been banned in prisons, similar punishment should be barred in schools is a poor analogy. In the context of the Eighth Amendment, the two situations are different because, as noted above, prisoners were involved in crimes while students and teachers were not.

The claim that substantive due process is infringed was turned down on the usual ground that the punishment in the *Ingraham* case was not "arbitrary, capricious or wholly unrelated to the state's purpose of determining its educational policy." The appellate court went on to say that "maintenance of discipline and order in public schools is a prerequisite to establishing the most effective learning atmosphere." Hence it is a proper "object" for state and school board regulation. Moreover, since the Florida education law provides guidelines for establishing standards in the use of corporal punishment, there is no evidence of arbitrary action.

The majority expressed no concern about the "individual" instances of punishment, stating that it is not the court's function to determine the difference between applying five or ten licks of the paddle. This section of the majority decision concludes with a subjective statement on the value of paddling, which seems to contradict its view that courts have no right to judge the wisdom of particular school regulations. The majority said, "Paddling of recalcitrant children has long been an accepted method of promoting good behavior and instilling notions of responsibility and decorum into the mischievous heads of school children. We do not here overrule it." (Compare this statement with that of the three-judge federal court in the *Baker* case which said, "And though we accept Mrs. Baker's assertion that corporal punishment of children is today discouraged by the weight of professional opinion, we are also cognizant that the issue is unsettled and probably incapable of categorical resolution.")

The contention that procedural due process was also violated fared poorly in the majority decision. It was rejected on three basic grounds:

1. Due process guarantees are rooted in the idea of fairness measured against the total circumstances of the case, especially the extent to which an individual suffers a *grievous loss* (emphasis added). Since the paddling of students does not amount to a grievous loss, due proceess standards don't apply.

2. Reliance on the North Carolina *Baker* decision providing some degree of due process is faulty legal analysis. That decision drew from the Supreme Court's statement in the *Goss* case concerning due process in suspension and expulsion situations. But there is an important distinction between the harm suffered by students who are suspended or expelled and students who face corporal punishment, defined by the court "as a much less serious event in the life of the child." The majority also noted the technical point that since the only question before the Supreme Court in *Baker* was whether parental objection could bar the use of corporal punishment, and the defendant school officials did not appeal the lower court's decision on procedural safeguards, the Supreme Court's affirmance of *Baker* did not cover the due process elements in the case.

3. The value of corporal punishment as a tool for maintaining discipline and order would be undermined if it were diluted by a series of elaborate procedural due process protections. The court said, "To require, for example, a published schedule of infractions for which corporal punishment is authorized, would serve to remove a valid judgmental aspect from a decision which should properly be left to the experienced administrator. Likewise, a hearing procedure could effectively undermine the utility of corporal punishment for the administrator who probably has little time under present procedures to handle all the disciplinary problems which beset him or her."

The three dissenting judges, while a small minority, provided a powerful rebuttal which was grounded in many areas on a strong civil liberties rationale.

The minority saw an important distinction between the two licks of the paddle applied in the *Baker* case, which it called "reasonable" punishment, and the kind of excessive beatings noted in the *Ingraham* record. The latter were so severe as to constitute cruel and unusual punishment.

Sharp issue was taken with the majority's position that the Eighth Amendment standard does not apply to school discipline. This is wrong, the minority said, because the Constitution must be seen as a document based on evolving standards. While in 1791, when the Bill of Rights was adopted, government punished "solely in retribution for crimes," the scope of the Eighth Amendment is much broader today, since it is applied to a variety of state actions. "Today, government has greatly expanded and provides a multitude of social institutions and public services. The administration of punishment is no longer confined to a criminal setting. It is now employed in public schools." To substantiate its contention that the Constitution is a "living" constitution, the court said that at one time the Supreme Court held the view that "separate but equal" facilities in education was constitutional. Yet in 1954, in the *Brown* case, this ruling was rejected because of new knowledge available about the status of education and the psychological development of children.

Rejecting the majority argument that corporal punishment might be viewed as child abuse to be dealt with in damage suits in local courts, the minority stressed the responsibility of federal courts to uphold constitutional rights. Citing the precedential case of *Marbury* v. *Madison* in 1803 which asserted the authority of the federal judiciary over congressional statutes, the three judges wrote, "School children have a constitutional right to freedom from cruel and unusual punishment when applied under color of state law: Our duty as federal judges is to enforce that right."

The dissent also differed with the majority's view of the due process interests in *Ingraham*. It said that cruel and severe corporal punishment was never justified and the undisputed evidence in the case "amounted to arbitrary and capricious conduct unrelated to the achievement of a legitimate educational purpose." Such conduct contravened substantive due process. Procedural due process was denied in light of the standards set down in the *Baker* case. Heavy emphasis was placed on the fact that there was a grievous loss of rights and a hearing of some kind should have been held, especially in light of the students' protestations of innocence, deprivation of their liberty, and the psychological injury suffered.

When the Supreme Court heard argument in the *Ingraham* case in the fall of 1976, opposing counsel debated sharply the underlying philosophy in the majority and minority opinions of the Fifth Circuit opinions. Bruce Rogow, attorney for the paddled children, argued that the Eighth Amendment's prohibition against corporal punishment did apply to the school setting (*Ingraham* v. *Wright,* 1976*b*). Rejecting the notion that the amendment is reserved only to actual crimes, Rogow said that while the ban on cruel and unusual punishment was enacted in the context of proscribing barbarous methods of punishing criminals, the Supreme Court "has recognized that for a principle to be vital it must be capable of wider application than the mischief which gave it birth." Noting that the corporal punishment inflicted in the *Ingraham* case should be measured against contemporary values, he cited the Supreme Court's decision in *Robinsion* v. *California* (1962) which prohibited the imprisonment of persons for drug addiction. This showed the flexibility inherent in the Eighth Amendment.

Rogow emphasized to the Court the excessive and severe punishment involved in the case, adding that whenever an instrument is used to inflict bodily pain upon public school children, the Eighth Amendment is invoked and due process guarantees apply. The children were denied their property right to an education because of time missed from school, the paddling being, in effect, "suspension."

Frank A. Howard, counsel for the Dade County School Board, stressed that the case offered the Supreme Court the opportunity to clarify the scope of the Eighth Amendment by confining it "to punishment collateral to the criminal process" (*Ingraham* v. *Wright*, 1976b). He said that corporal punishment in a public school setting involves neither imprisonment nor a deprivation of liberty. He also denied that the punishment imposed on the children was so severe that it approached the level of an Eighth Amendment violation.

Howard also challenged the contention that procedural due process is required before *any* punishment could be inflicted on public school students. He distinguished between the due process protections set down by the Court in the *Goss* v. *Lopez* decision, and the *Ingraham* case (1976a). The former dealt with suspension from the school, whereas corporal punishment is an alternative to suspension. The Florida students suffered no future deprivation, either in schools or in finding jobs.

This summary of the most current legal developments would not be complete without reference to the Supreme Court's decision in the *Ingraham* case, decided on April 19, 1977. However, a full and detailed analysis is provided in this section of the book. The essay by Virginia Lee analyzes both the majority and minority position, and therefore only a brief comment follows.

The narrow five to four majority in support of the Florida school board answers in the negative, at least for the moment, the two key constitutional issues: does corporal punishment violate the cruel and unusual punishment clause, or offend due process of law? But the door is not completely closed to further legal tests. The due process parts of the Court's decision dealt primarily with procedural matters. Another case could raise the other part of the due process coin, substantive due process. Moreover, there are elements in the majority opinion which may lead to further challenges, such as Justice Powell's statement negating the severity and extent of corporal punishment or applauding its value as a useful form of discipline in schools.

The record in *Ingraham* lacked adequate documentation of these areas, and research, such as initiated by the National Center for the Study of Corporal Punishment and Alternatives in the Schools, could authenticate the number of schoolchildren subject to physical beatings and whether corporal punishment really is an effective disciplinary tool in the educational process. With such data, new cases can be brought, especially if the facts of these cases parallel the serious physical injuries noted in the *Ingraham* case. But even with the slim one-vote margin in *Ingraham*, there is no certainty that the Supreme Court will soon review its ruling. The High Court is loath to decide constitutional issues generally, and having declared itself so recently in this sensitive area, they probably will want to let time pass and see what the schools do under the *Ingraham* decision. So, while the legal battle must be continued wherever possible, the issue must also be carried into the political arena where school boards, state legislatures, and parents must be persuaded that regardless of constitutionality the practice of corporal punishment is wrong, ineffective, and should be abandoned.

REFERENCES

Baker v. Owen, 423 U.S. 907 (1975).
Barnette v. *State of West Virginia Board of Education*, 319 U.S. 624 (1943).
Brown v. *Board of Education*, 347 U.S. 483 (1954).
Goss v. *Lopez*, 419 U.S. 565 (1975).
Ingraham v. Wright, 498 F.2d 248 (5th Cir. 1974).
———, 525 F.2d 909 (5th Cir. 1976)(a).
———, 45 U.S.L.W. 3337 (11/9/76)(b).
———, 45 U.S.L.W. 4364 (4/19/77).
In re Gault, 387 U.S. 1 (1967).
Marbury v. *Madison*, 1 Cranch 137, 2 L.ed. 60 (1803).
Robinson v. *California*, 370 U.S. 660 (1962).
Tinker v. *Des Moines Independent Community School District*, 393 U.S. 503 (1969).

13

A Youth Worker's Opinion of the Majority Decision in Ingraham v. Wright

James S. Wallerstein

•

The confused opinion by the Supreme Court majority upholding corporal punishment in *Ingraham* v. *Wright* can hardly be the final judgment of the Court.

The Court could have held that school kids *are* protected by the Eighth Amendment, but that "paddling" is not a cruel or unusual punishment. Or, they could have held that "the proscription against cruel and unusual punishment . . . was designed to protect those convicted of crimes," and stopped right there. Either of these positions would, at least, have the merit of clarity.

If protection against cruel and unusual punishment were limited only to "those convicted of crimes," there would be a dangerous threat to many persons under the control of the state or its institutions. Mental patients, material witnesses, youth drafted for national service, neglected children, or old people in public institutions—anyone held in protective detention for his own welfare or under civil, as opposed to criminal, custody—would have no constitutional safeguard against cruel or unusual punishment.

The Russian grand inquisitors who allegedly have been sending political dissidents to insane asylums, would feel quite comfortable with the Supreme Court ruling. Those who criticize the Communist system are not "criminal," just "crazy." If it happened over here, the political dissenters would be "patients," not convicts, unprotected by the Eighth Amendment. Any treatment or mistreatment they received would be quite constitutional.

The Court majority makes much of the history of the Eighth Amendment derived from the English Bill of Rights in 1689. It was designed to curb the excesses of the English judges under James II. Big Brother, however, has become a good deal more sophisticated in his tyranny and in the twentieth century has mastered using the *civil* powers of the state for oppression and abuse.

Perhaps conscious of these dangers, the Court majority proceed to restrict and qualify their ruling.

First, it is limited to pupils in the public schools. "We have no occasion in this case to consider whether and under what circumstances persons involuntarily confined in mental and juvenile institutions can claim to the protection of the Eighth Amendment."

Second, it is confined to day schools "where the openness of the school prevents abuse."

Third, the punishment must be "moderate" and "reasonable."

Fourth, "it must be reasonably necessary for the proper education of the child and for the maintenance of group discipline."

Further, the Court majority claims, school pupils do not need the protection of the Eighth Amendment. "The laws of virtually every State forbid the excessive physical punishment of school children." In Florida, corporal punishment was limited to "paddling," which could not be "degrading or unduly severe." There were requirements for the consent of the principal, for adult witnesses, etc.

In *Goss* v. *Lopez*, 419 U.S. (1974) the Court held that students may not be suspended from schools without a hearing. But there is no need to hold a hearing—even an informal one—before hitting a kid. Because schools are open and pupils go home every night, there is little possibility of abuse. The right of a youth to be protected against abuse, contends the Court majority, is less important than the trouble a school would incur if they had to hold hearings.

"The benefits of an additional safeguard . . . that the action is just, may be outweighed by the cost."

The Court majority does not contend that schoolchildren are not entitled to "due process"; rather, it contends that they are already getting as much due process as they need.

"It is fundamental that the State cannot hold and physically punish an individual except in accord with *due process of law*. This constitutionally protected liberty is at stake in this case."

However, *due process* "is satisfied by common law constraints and remedies." No prior hearing is required before imposing corporal punishment in the public schools.

The petitioners are accused of "wrenching the Eighth Amendment out of its historical context." But the Court majority seems to wrench the English language out of its common sense meaning. The Eighth Amendment says *no cruel or unusual punishment. Period.* The language is nonrestrictive. It says "punishment," not just "criminal punishment."

In his dissenting opinion, Judge White points out (and the Court majority at one point agrees) that "paddling" is punishment imposed for violating the rules of a State agency (the public schools) for the purpose of deterrence, retribution, or reform. It is indistinguishable from criminal punishments.

Certainly the founding fathers did not think of the Eighth Amendment as applying to the schools. But schools were then private, local, and voluntary. A parent sent a child to school and could withdraw him.

Today, the police power of the state licenses teachers and enforces school attendance. An absent youngster can be (and sometimes is) locked up for truancy. A parent who keeps his child out of school can be jailed for neglect.

The school is now a function of the state, supported by criminal sanctions. If children are mistreated in the public schools, it is the *state* that does it. The Court majority does not question this. "Although the early cases viewed the authority of the teachers as derived from the parents, the concept of parental delegation has been replaced by the view . . . that the State itself may impose corporal punishment."

The Court majority seems troubled that "school children could be beaten without constitutional redress, while hardened criminals, suffering the same beatings at the hands of their jailors, might have a valid claim under the Eighth Amendment." They insist, however, that corporal punishment is approved by the common law and is "the law of the land."

However, the common law approves only *moderate* and *reasonable* corporal punishment. In the case of *Ingraham* v. *Wright*, both boys, James Ingraham and Roosevelt Andrews, were seriously injured. At Drew Junior High School, the Court concedes that "the regime was exceptionally harsh." Sixteen youngsters testified that they had been severely beaten.

The majority opinion here approaches a non sequitur.

Moderate and *reasonable* corporal punishment is not unconstitutional because it is permitted by the common law.

Therefore, *excessive* corporal punishment *not* approved by the common law is also without constitutional restraints.

It is urged that because school youngsters are protected by the common law, they don't require the protection of the Constitution. But such an argument is never made for any of the constitutional rights and privileges of grown-ups. Constitutional rights are clear, definite, and enforceable. Common law rights, like common law marriages, are hard to get recognized and even harder to preserve.

The Court majority contends that the mistreatment of school pupils is "rare" and the risk of abuse is "minimal." Public schools are "*open.*" "The child is not physically restrained from leaving school during school hours."

The Court majority is hardly being realistic. A youth might walk out of school to avoid a beating. But he would have to go back the following school day and face the likelihood of something even worse. A pupil who stayed out of school could be, and sometimes is, committed to an institution as a "habitual truant." A school pupil has as much freedom to stay out of school as a draftee has to escape the military service, or a taxpayer to avoid his income tax.

Nor is it always true that a schoolboy (or girl) is not physically restrained from leaving. In New York City some years ago, an eighth grader named Keith tried to sneak out of the junior high school and play "hookey." A gym teacher, lurking in ambush, pounced on Keith. In the ensuing confrontation, Keith was taken to a hospital, bleeding badly. The gym teacher, a wrestling champion, was unmarked. The authorities, however, arrested Keith for assaulting the teacher! Keith ran away and went into hiding. Keith was a member of my youth group, The Council of Orenda. I found him with a friend whose parents were away. Keith told me gloomily, "It's a teacher's word against a kid's, and who is going to believe the kid?"

I made a Fourth of July speech about American justice. Keith went back home. In juvenile court, Keith was acquitted. The teacher, however, was unchallenged.

The Court majority's low estimate of child abuse in the schools is based on the infrequency of lawsuits by pupils and their parents. But this low frequency may be due not to the absence of abuse, but to the high cost of litigation and fear of reprisals. If a youth becomes known as a troublemaker, the schools have the power to make a good deal of trouble for *him*. After all, how many slaves sued their masters? Dred Scott did, but who else?

Even so, the number of alleged school mistreatments are by no means negligible.

From November 1976, to June 1977, fifty-five new cases and six previous cases were reported by a clipping service.[1] Not all cases involved paddling. Incidents involved also cutting a youngster's hair, locking a child in a "coffin-like" box, taping children's mouths, and forcing a boy to eat cigarettes.

Not all the cases went to court. When they did, more often than not, the decision was in favor of the teacher. Thus, in Tennessee, a ten-year-old who "took two desserts" was paddled and badly bruised. The judge found the paddling teacher had not acted "with malice" and dismissed the case.

The Court majority emphasizes that "a majority of teachers and of the general public [adults, of course] have consistently favored moderate corporal punishment in the lower grades."

It is uncertain how much of this approval is the result of confusion between true physical punishment (paddling, whipping, slapping) and the use of physical force by a teacher to break up a fight or to make a kid sit down.

As a youth group leader, I have frequently used *physical force* to stop a dangerous activity, or break up a fight. The kids accept this and are relieved to have a grown-up step in. None of the combatants ever turned around and took a poke at me, though some of the youths were quite capable of flattening me.

Corporal punishment is quite different. It is not to stop misbehavior that is happening, but to subject a youth to physical pain or distress for something that is now over and done with.

The Court majority quotes from the Florida statute permitting corporal punishment. It permits "the moderate use of physical force or physical contact by a teacher or principal as may be necessary to maintain discipline or to enforce school rules."

Now, the interesting thing is that the statute does not mention corporal punishment at all, but instead, the use of "*physical force.*" There is no distinction between physical force needed to restore order and the deliberate infliction of pain for deterrence or reprisal.

The advocates of corporal punishment keep confusing the two and perhaps are confused themselves.

What the Court majority finally comes up with is a "balance of interests" doctrine. "Reasonable corporal punishment . . . represents the balance struck by the country between the child's interest in personal security and the traditional view that some limited corporal punishment may be necessary in the course of a child's education."

However, "the deliberate infliction of corporal punishment on a child who is restrained for that purpose" is an "intrusion of the child's liberty." It must be "*justified*" and "*reasonable*" to be lawful. "*Unjustified*" corporal punishment is "*unlawful.*"

The decision in *Ingraham* v. *Wright* was heralded by both friend and foe as permitting unrestricted school corporal punishment. A cartoon shows a stupid-looking ape-like teacher marching forth with an enormous paddle. It is entitled *Open Season on American Kids.* The Supreme Court is shown handing the goon a hunting license.

The Court decision may have encouraged some "brainless beating" but was clearly not intended to. Corporal punishment is lawful only if it is "justified," "reasonable," "moderate," and to "serve an educational purpose."

This is the balance between the schoolchild's interest in "*liberty,*" and the state's interest in "*orderly education.*"

In *Ingraham* v. *Wright*, the Court majority considered the Eighth Amendment and the due process clause of the Fourteenth Amendment. They refused, however, to consider the third issue raised by the petitioners:

"Is the infliction of severe corporal punishment arbitrary, capricious and unrelated to achieving any legitimate educational purpose?"

However, this question is indeed germane for, on the balancing theory of the Court majority, the curbing of a youngster's liberty must be balanced by some positive benefit.

It is fitting to inquire whether corporal punishment does serve any genuine educational purpose. If the results are uniformly negative, the schoolchildren's liberty and security are weakened in exchange for *nothing*.

Corporal punishment was abandoned for criminal offenders and, indeed, everywhere but in the schools, because it proved to be not only ineffective but harmful.

Corporal punishment, at best, turns schools into a circus. At worst, it is shameful, degrading, and brutalizing. It is a very temporary deterrent and may even incite the very behavior it is supposed to prevent.

If school is boring enough, it may be a welcome relief to "play chicken" with the paddle. You do something you could be hit for, without being caught. Then you win the game. If they do catch you—well, no game is any fun without the risk of losing.

"High corporal punishment" was found to be negatively correlated with school achievement.[2]

Corporal punishment has a ripple effect on the entire class, not just on the pupil who is hit. Respect for the teacher and the school is undermined. Instead of a wise guru, the teacher becomes like a policeman in a hostile neighborhood. The disruptive pupil becomes a hero instead of a bum. There is a ripple effect also in the community. Even mild school corporal punishments encourage the more violent kinds of child abuse.

There is abundant evidence that hitting kids in school promotes student violence—perhaps not immediately, but in the later grades.

Paired schools in Oregon, for example, showed a vandalism rate three times as high in the schools practicing corporal punishment.[3] Thus, the taxpayers are getting hit too—in the pocketbook.

One hundred percent of all violent prison inmates[4] surveyed and 64 percent of juvenile delinquents[5] generally were found to have been subjected to "extreme corporal punishment."

"Violent crime," says Dr. Welsh, "is commited only by people who were beaten as children. And the more they were beaten, the more violent their crime will be."[6]

Hitler,[7] Mussolini, Stalin, and Napoleon were all subjected to severe childhood beatings.

The mass killer, Charles Manson, was a shy, lonely child who changed after being violently beaten in a juvenile institution.[8]

A beaten youngster loses self-esteem and strikes back to regain it when he is strong enough.

Corporal punishment permits no inner controls to develop. After being flogged in school, writes the philosopher Rousseau, young people were no longer bound by ties of respect, intimacy and confidence to their guardians. They became less ashamed of doing wrong and more afraid of being caught. If they were treated as rogues, they were entitled to behave as rogues.[9]

Girls subjected to corporal punishment lost respect for the purity of their bodies and were inclined toward sexual promiscuity. Girls who became prostitutes were often the victims of childhood beatings.[10]

It is among the common law rights of a school pupil that the punishment he receives cannot be "degrading." By this the Court means, presumably, that you can't be held up to shame and ridicule by being clobbered in public. They have to hit you in private. The Court fails to consider whether *any* corporal punishment may not be deemed as "degrading."

Corporal punishment may stimulate unhealthy sexual impulses. Paddling and whipping may stimulate sadism and masochism in both teacher and pupil. Indeed, the resentment felt by some paddled students suggest that they sense the linkage between paddling and sodomy. Thus, one youth allegedly shot an assistant principal who "wallopped" him.[11] A particularly nasty paddling teacher was "jumped" and severely beaten by his students after which, we are told, he carried a gun to school.[12]

Supporters of corporal punishment insist that nobody gets hurt by a paddling. "There are only bruises and they heal." But this is increasingly doubtful as our knowledge of physiology grows. The buttocks are the seat of the spine. From the buttock region, vital nerves go to the bladder, the genitals, and the lower limbs. Distortion of the vertebrae of the buttock area will bring about nerve pressures that can seriously affect vital organs of the body.[13]

A blow with a hard paddle could be damaging, especially if a youth has a spinal weakness to begin with. Far from healing, with the bruises, the injury might develop many years later.

In every community there is an elderly gentleman who waxes wroth about "permissiveness" in the schools. "I was paddled as a boy," he insists, "and it didn't hurt me!" This same gentleman is suffering from acute lower back pains, so perhaps it is hurting him *now*.

Indeed, the Florida corporal punishment law (which the Court quotes with approval), "cautioned against using corporal punishment against a student under psychological or medical treatment.' Thus, the Court majority implicity admits that corporal punishment may be damaging to many pupils. The authorities failed to consider how many kids who do get hit might be *in need of psychological and medical treatment*, but are not getting it.

Has the Supreme Court closed the doors on future litigation to restrict or abolish corporal punishment in the public schools? The Court itself says it has not: "We have no occasion in this case to decide whether and under what circumstances corporal punishment of a public school child may give rise to a Federal cause of action to vindicate substantive rights under the due process clause."

The majority decision in *Ingraham* v. *Wright* is by no means completely negative. It establishes or confirms:

1. That every schoolchild has a constitutional right to liberty and security of person.
2. That corporal punishment is a curb on a child's liberty and security of person. It must be carried out *with due process* (even though hearings are not required).
3. That corporal punishment must be "moderate," "justified," "reasonable," and for an educational purpose. It cannot be "degrading."
4. That a schoolchild may sue if his common law rights (which are identical with his constitutional rights) are violated.

"If the punishment is excessive—not reasonably believed at the time to be *necessary* for the child's discipline or training, the school authorities inflicting it may be held liable for damages . . . and if malice is shown . . . subject to criminal penalties."

It may be that the Court majority, like the old gentleman with a backache, is hopelessly committed to combating school "permissiveness" with paddle and rod. But such a conclusion is unwarranted on the basis of *Ingraham* v. *Wright*. The tone of the majority opinion is almost apologetic. The Court keeps insisting that school pupils have all the protection they need. Indeed, their way of protecting youngsters is the best. It "may be viewed as affording substantially greater protection to the child."

Sue if your common law rights are violated, suggests the Court majority. And the only way to test the Court will be to try it. The seeing will be in the suing.

But talk the language of the Court which means *common law* rights rather than *constitutional rights*. Ultimately, they amount to the same thing. For *due process* is getting your common law rights and *due process* is guaranteed by the Constitution.

The Court majority grants that school pupils have a constitutional right to liberty and security of person. This right can be restricted only by corporal punishment that is "moderate," "reasonable," "justified," "non-degrading," and designed to serve an educational purpose.

Thus, you have a case if the beating you got was severe and/or degrading, unreasonable, unjustified and/or without any educational purpose.

Sue in the state courts if your common law rights are violated. Even suits that are thrown out seem to impress the judges and make it easier for the next petitioner.

If you lose in the state courts, *then* you can go to the federal court. The state courts have not protected your common law rights which are also your due process rights under the Constitution. Such an appeal is quite consistent with *Ingraham* v. *Wright*.

There is another possible attack on corporal punishment in the federal courts. In *Ingraham* v. *Wright*, the Court considered only the Eighth Amendment and the due process clause of the Fourteenth Amendment.

The Court did not consider the "equal protection" clause of the Fourteenth Amendment, "No State shall make or enforce any law which shall abridge the privileges and immunities of the citizens of the United States . . . nor deny to any person within its jurisdiction equal protection of the laws."

If school youngsters are not protected against cruel and arbitrary punishments, their privileges and immunities are being violated and they are being denied the equal protection of the laws.

No one could have realistically expected the Supreme Court to outlaw corporal punishment. That might happen at some future time, but only after setting forth the overwhelming evidence—medical, sociological, psychological—that school corporal punishments damage not only the individual but the community.

NOTES

1. I am indebted for these data to Dr. Adah Maurer, director of the Committee to End Violence against the Next Generation, Berkeley, California.

2. Barton, K., Dielman, T. E. and Cattell, R. E., Child rearing practices and achievement in school. *Journal of Genetic Psychology*, 1974, 155–65.

3. Hardy, G. L., *The Last Resort*, 3/4:7 (1975).

4. Maurer, Adah, *The Last Resort*, 4/5:4 (1976). A similar finding was reported by the late Robert R. Hannum of the Osborne Association, N.Y.

5. Welsh, Ralph, and Button, A., *The Last Resort*, 4/5:4 (1976).

6. Welsh, Ralph, *The Last Resort*, 4/4:11 (1975).

7. Waite, Robert, *The Psychopathic God*, New York: Basic Books, 1977, pp. 137–38.

8. Wooden, Kenneth, *Weeping in the Playtime of Others*, New York: McGraw Hill, 1976, pp. 50ff.

9. Rousseau, Jean-Jacques, *Confessions, book I*. London: Penguin, 1953.

10. From a report by the late Robert R. Hannum, Youth Counselor, 1951.

11. *The Last Resort*, 4/3:4 (1976).

12. Ibid, 5/1:14 (1976).

13. Chresomales, Dr. James A., *Mental Calisthenics*, New York: Bellamy Press, 1955, p. 27.

PART V

•

CASE STUDIES

The first three essays of this part offer in-depth studies and examples of the use of corporal punishment in American schools. By way of contrast, the last essay presents the experiences of an American teacher who taught for a limited period within the Soviet Union. This latter article was selected since it is representative of the Communist educational ideology which forbids the use of corporal punishment in the schools.

The first essay by Adah Maurer chronicles the recent history of the excessive use of corporal punishment in the schools as represented in the press. The cases presented offer a rather convincing argument against the assumption that corporal punishment is practiced with moderation and concern in American schools. The many cases of abuse presented are further documented by an ongoing case book kept at the National Center for the Study of Corporal Punishment and Alternatives in the Schools. There is a strong suspicion from informal data collection that these only represent the tip of the iceberg. The preponderance of cases which are reported in the press as occurring in the South and Southwest should be considered in relation to the data presented in the essay by McDowell and Friedman in Part VI on editorial opinion regarding the Supreme Court decision in Ingraham v. Wright.

The essay by Polier et al. was chosen for its detailed documentation of efforts to eliminate corporal punishment where it had already been banned! The analysis of racial, political, and community social standards provides the reader with a good understanding of how community feeling and educational bureaucracy interfaces in the arena of discipline.

The essay by Schumacher describes the ongoing battle between the Pittsburgh Board of Education and the teachers' union. The teachers have been waging a continual war to reestablish their prerogative to use corporal punishment. An understanding of their attitudes is presented in the Introduction of this book in its discussion of research. The liberal board has banned corporal punishment by a slim majority. This becomes a major issue each year during contract negotiations. The delicate majority will be lost with the election of one more "conservative" board member.

This part ends with the essay by Cassie which illustrates that the elimination of corporal punishment must be preceded by training teachers in humane and effective alternatives. The shaming through official and peer pressure used in the Soviet system can be as damaging to the ego as is the paddle to the buttocks.

14

It Does Happen Here

Adah Maurer

•

The custom of caning schoolboys was memorialized throughout the English-speaking world in the literature of the nineteenth century with its bitter vignettes of unjust and pointless cruelty that left psychic and physical scars on the whole society. Dickens, Thackeray, Lamb, John Stuart Mill, Auden, D. H. Lawrence, Kipling, and more recently Freud, Adler, and Einstein, and from earlier times Plato, Plutarch, and Montaigne—the whole star-studded pantheon of intellectual leadership of our civilization—all have written eloquently of the folly of beating children and of the advantages of enlightened persuasion in educating youth. Orwell modeled his chilling prophecy of a robot-watched world in 1984 on his perception of the British schoolroom of his childhood. The authority of the schoolmaster was absolute and each child was terror-marked. Out of this school tradition had come the colonizers who enslaved with whips. They were adept because they had been taught physically that power brooks no back talk and that democracy is a dream available only to those who wield the weapons. The Prussian version of the same system kept the continent in turmoil. Our century has seen the result in wars, genocidal exterminations, and cruelties beyond counting.

Now that our technology has made possible the destruction of the whole planet by the pushing of a few buttons, the realization is beginning to dawn that a peaceable world has advantages that savagery cannot match. And one of the essentials in building a nonviolent world is the nonviolent education of the children who will administer that world. But not all are aware. Cultural lag or inadequate education, or psychic scars from the battlefields on which they fought, or some vestigial remnants of primitive reflexes have far too many school administrators clinging to the anachronism of corporal punishment in American schools in the space age. True, it has softened a bit. They have almost abandonned the pants-down public thrashings and not all boast publicly of their severity. The most common

Parts of this essay appeared previously in *Proceedings: Conference on Corporal Punishment in the Schools: A National Debate*. National Institute of Education, 1977.

defense of the paddle is even a bit apologetic and defensive at times. "It is used rarely and with thoughtful discretion and only as a last resort after all other means of correction have failed."

This is a dearly held delusion. Definitive data cannot be produced to prove or disprove such claims since no national survey has been made. There are few statistics and what few there are, are suspect since confessions of having minimized the numbers on reports to prevent possible criticism are fairly common. What might be learned from a complete study is suggested by a look at three mini-surveys done in Dallas, Texas; Miami, Florida; and in the state of California. In 1972, the city of Dallas recorded 24,305 paddlings for a school population of approximately 330,000. The number of unreported incidents may have been many times that number according to student stories (Duncan, 1973). In 1974 a report mandated by a resolution of the legislature of the state of California included responses from 92 percent of the school districts but not including the city of Los Angeles. Reported were 46,022 cases of the use of corporal punishment with only 5 percent of these in the high schools (Riles, 1974). The third and most recent survey was made at the behest of the Office of Civil Rights of the Department of Health Education and Welfare. The figures and details for the city of Miami, Florida, were reported in the *Miami News* (1976). Since the survey was undertaken primarily to discover whether minority students were subjected to corporal punishment more than white students, the first finding was that indeed black students took the brunt of the paddlings. Although only 28 percent of the student population is black, 67 percent of those punished was black. But one could make a case that the overall number of incidents was of far greater import than particulars of skin color.

The Miami survey covered the first forty-five days of school in the fall of 1975. During those forty-five days, Northwestern Senior High School recorded 193 paddlings, or 4 to 5 every school day. At Westview Junior High the self-reported score was 307; that means that if there is a seven-period day, not a class period went by without someone taking a beating. On the other hand, 99 schools out of 242 reported no instances. Either they managed to conduct school without fear, force, and pain, or they were ashamed of their occasional lapses and chose not to confess them. Considerable publicity went to a Mr. "K." who proudly displayed a fan of paddles from the closet where he kept the old ones after they had been fully inscribed with the signatures of the victims. He claimed he paddled with "love," although psychologists have labeled the paddling of the anal erotic area as symbolic sodomy. His words? "Like a mother stroking her little child."

So much for surveys. The United States Office of Education, the Office of Civil Rights and a number of other federal agencies were approached by the Task Force on Children's Rights of the American Psychological Association with the suggestion that a nationwide assessment be made of the amount and kind of corporal punishment in use. We realize what we are asking is presumptuous. Educators are known to be difficult to motivate and some school boards are less than cooperative. The form requested by the Office of Civil Rights has drawn fire from school officials. The Houma, Louisiana, *Courier* (1976) covered a local school board meeting and reported one member complaining, "You got to go through an act of Congress just to give a kid a little spank!" A Pennsylvania board member said, "The question really is—Should we teach the three R's or fill out federal forms. It's that bad" (*Daily Local News*, 1977). One sympathizes. But would they rather the FBI fan out over the country spying on them? Branches of commercial firms would not dare object to reporting their losses. Self-examination is good for mental health.

Lacking better data we have turned to other sources in our effort to document that corporal punishment is used often and harshly. Since November of 1972 our organization, End Violence Against the Next Generation, Inc., has published the *Last ? Resort*, a newsletter with the avowed purpose of collecting and disseminating information about corporal punishment. Sponsors, readers, and well-wishers have responded with descriptions of incidents known to them; with newspaper articles, editorials, and letters to the editor; as well as with reports of bills introduced into legislatures, and local school board debates and decisions. To add to this we subscribed to a clipping service in November 1976 that produced an avalanche of articles from all over the country. Every Monday morning there arrives in my mail a packet of clippings which I sort, continually amazed at the ingenuity with which school people create new forms of baiting to induce bad behavior in children. The *Tucson Star* (1976) told a "hilarious" story about a retired home economics teacher overly sensitive to noise, who was assigned to substitute with a class of fifty-eight band members. She demanded pin-drop quiet while calling the interminable roll. A chair collapsed; she accused them of throwing chairs and turned off the lights. Naturally, chaos erupted. Fifty-eight suspensions and angry parents caused a day's work to be lost. A tempest for nothing: "We would have been quiet if she'd let us play music," said a sophomore.

Winnowing through this mass of material, we have retrieved enough tales of scabrous behavior on the part of presumed educators to convince all but those who most determinedly refuse to see. Corporal punishment in American schools is a national disgrace. It is not rare. It is not used only as a last resort—and as bad discipline it drives out good. Some of the stories are distributed by the news services and are used by those of their subscribing newspapers that choose to run them. Others are purely local dispatches by the education editor on the deliberations of the school board in the area served. Some incidents appear and reappear in succeeding editions, often with embellishments and sequels, although the final disposition of cases is hard to find. The most popular stories are those that permit the punning propensities of the headline writer to move into high gear. I have also made the observation that when the circulation is small, joking takes precedence over seriousness. In other words, rural America still treats spanking as scatological humor. That is one reason I doubt the findings of those who see paddling as racist. Rural America is predominantly Caucasian, and unless you label "poor white" as a minority, I think we shall find that it is the children of poor and undereducated families who are physically punished rather than the children of black families per se.

The most widely reported story was the cigarette-eating case. Told with a variety of humorous headlines was the incident involving Principal Hightower of the Hume High School of Hume, Missouri, whose standard response to boys caught with cigarettes in their pockets was: Eat them or bend over. In all the years of his little joke, no boy had ever chosen to do anything but to accept the swats. But Bill Adkins and Terry Weatherman were made of sterner stuff. They took the dare and ate eighteen cigarettes between them. Both became ill. Bill had to be hospitalized for ulcers. His mother, Katherine Adkins, demanded that Principal Hightower be fired. The school board predictably backed him, and he announced that the penalty would continue unchanged. A week or so later, the president of the Student Council was caught in the same delictum. He not only took his swats but at a press conference announced his total loyalty to Principal Hightower and Hume High. My guess is that he thinks such toadying constitutes first steps up the political ladder. Maybe he is right.

Mrs. Adkins has been subjected to harassment from the community. Night riders buzzed her home in the woods and attempted to nudge her car off the road. The Adkins family has no well or other source of water except by truck delivery. The water supplier, a member of the Hume Board of Education, refused to haul their weekly supply and persuaded his competitor not to serve them either. She refused to send Bill to school and said she had been warned that he could be sent to a state training school. The American Civil Liberties Union asked for an injunction to prevent further impositions of the penalty of ingesting poisons (*Nevada Herald*, 1976). The principal resigned to go back to farming and the superintendent moved to another town. The two young victims and their mothers brought suit for two million dollars.

A majority of the cases that go public are accusations of cruelty by coaches. Raymundo Castro was required to do push-ups over an open knife by Coach Bill Vanhorbiekc, claims the Asociacion Educativa de Padres Mexicanos (*Fresno Bee*, 1974). A follow-up story recounted the outrage of Fresno, California, coaches at a presentation on ABC television which dealt with high school football injuries. In the documentary, a Florida high school coach was shown slapping and tossing his players around physically. The anger of the Fresno coaches against ABC was for using an "extreme example" and for making all coaches look like "oafs, dummies and unconcerned with the welfare of the players." The *Fresno Bee* chided them for not recognizing an "extreme example" and oafishness in their own back yard. They then added to the story the fact that Raymundo had been told that the knife would be used every day until he did the push-ups. But it was the reporter, not the coach, who discovered that the nine-year-old had had an accident some years before and one arm could no longer be fully extended.

In Detroit, Michigan, the state court of appeals reversed the manslaughter conviction of a swimming instructor who was charged in the drowning of an emotionally disturbed student at a special school. Testimony at the trial showed that the boy drowned after the coach had thrown him into the pool three times on the "sink or swim" theory (*Holland Evening Sentinel*, 1975).

Another example of an overzealous coach causing death occurred at the college level. A freshman at Virginia Tech, Robert Vorhies, allegedly broke down a door while roughhousing. Penalty? Yes, but a death penalty? Running extra laps is standard punishment for athletes, but Bob Vorhies was required to do ten 50-yard dashes, ten 100-yard dashes, two 100-yard bear crawls, 50 sit-ups, 50 push-ups and four other 100-yard drills. And that was only the beginning. Bystanders watched as he desperately struggled through the mammoth series of punishment drills, fell, was ordered up, fell again and yet had to run the entire field both ways twice. Teammates said Vorhies went to his dormitory room too tired to shower or undress and vomited blood. At 11 P.M. he was found on the floor, dead. The coach was fired, not for being too hard on his students, but because he had a losing season (United Press, Blacksburg, Va.).

In Sarasota, Florida, a coach at an elementary school was incensed because five boys caused him to waste fifteen minutes of class time. He required them to stay after school. If this had been taken as time to have a confidential talk about cooperation, the uses of team time, or some such pertinent topic, there could have been little objection. Instead, Coach McGary used a gym class rope to tie the nine-year-olds together by attaching it to their belts. He "strung them up like clothes on a line," said the state attorney's office. McGary then allegedly fastened the rope to his motorcycle, started the engine, and dragged the boys through the parking lot. He later treated them for cuts, scrapes, and bruises. Their clothes were torn. The coach was charged with a misdemeanor (*San Francisco Examiner*, 1976).

In Brunswick, Georgia, a new school board ruling requires that if any physical punishments are to be administered, it must be by the principal or assistant principal and there must be a witness. Coaches sometimes think they are a law unto themselves. Coach Ben Young, without attention to protocol, felt free to paddle a fifteen-year-old who had forgotten his gym shorts. His reasoning? The boy had asked for it. Therefore it was not punishment. It was just a reminder. When the father brought pictures of the bruises, the coach said, "If there were any marks on him they were the result of scabies. He was always scratching himself." Was the coach suspended for breaking the rules? No, the boy was (*Brunswick News*, 1976).

With coaches, corporal punishment seems more in the nature of an initiation or coming of age rite than a serious effort to inculcate learning. In Washington State the penalty for the last man in a cross-country squad was a "hacking" (*Seattle Post*, 1976). In Corry, Pennsylvania, for kicking the ball high enough to hit the ceiling during the game of kickball, a paddling was in order (*Times-Observer*, 1976). When a father complained, he was assured that this was not considered punishment; indeed it was nothing more than a harmless diversion. The coach described it as "ritual purely for laughs," even though it resulted in raised welts and bruises. No one asked the recipients if they thought it was funny.

Some coaches have heard the word and are changing. From Renton, Washington: "The old discipline method of coaches giving an obnoxious kid a whopping with the tennis shoe is gone. . . . The philosophy behind the [new] procedure . . . is to have a student take responsibility for his or her own behavior" (*Record*, 1977). And from Alexandria, Louisiana, "It has been traditional to whip junior high school football players at Buckeye High for making poor grades, but the practice has been discontinued" (*Daily Town*, 1977).

The tales of coaches misinterpreting their mandate to develop character by "hardening" their charges is giving way far too slowly. But they are not the only ones who misuse their authority over children. The custom of cruelty as a deterrent begins before kindergarten.

In Prosperity, South Carolina, the Independent Bible Baptist Church was sued for severe corporal punishment of an infant under one year of age. The attorney for the Church Day Care Center responded by quoting *Ingraham* v. *Wright*: "Because he was slow to respond to his teacher's instruction, Ingraham was subjected to more than twenty licks with a paddle while being held over a table in the principal's office. The paddling was so severe that he suffered a hematoma requiring medical attention and keeping him out of school for eleven days." Since it had been decided by the Supreme Court that the student Ingraham had not been deprived of his rights, it was argued in the case of the infant under one year of age that he also had no rights against excessive corporal punishment when this is done in a school setting and the administrator reasonably believes it to be necessary for the child's proper control, training, or education. However, at the request of the presiding judge, the attorney for the day care center presented a policy statement for future guidelines for "reasonableness." He recommended for infants from 18 months to 2½ years, one lick; from 2½ to 4 two licks, and from 4 to 6 three licks and not oftener than twice a day for: lying, cheating, stealing, hitting, spitting, playing with electric sockets, matches, or a vaporizer.

Tony Johnson was two years old and it was his first day at nursery school. He cried when mother left, a not uncommon behavior for two-year-olds. That evening as his mother prepared him for bed she discovered that his back was covered with twenty-five to thirty welts, red and swollen. The teacher, Mrs. Webb, was miffed at having to explain to a judge, "I have never received a complaint before and I've been in the business for 15 years!" She had switched him "a time or two" for crying. The grand jury in Shelbyville, Tennessee let her explain (*Nashville Tennessean,* 1976).

From the *Memphis Scimitar* (1976) comes the tale of two kindergarten teachers who used a tacking iron to laminate name tags. It seemed a handy weapon and thus they began to use it as a "lesson on telling stories." Several children had their hands burned before the principal called a halt and fired them. At the hearing the attorney for the dismissed teachers cross-questioned the children, all four years old, and tried to make much of their shy reluctance to speak up. He even accused the principal of having coached them and implied the dismissal had been racially motivated.

From the *Oskaloosa Herald* (1976) we read of a second grade Iowa boy whose face was slammed down onto his desk so hard as permanently to disable him. His father was suing. In Guadalupe, California, Mexican-American children described before a Senate committee how they hated lunch because they had to eat in silence but the lunch lady blew a whistle right into their ear (Dymally, 1973). Children have been locked in the school vault, made to lie in a coffin-shaped box, and been shut away from light and air in a variety of "time-out boxes" (Associated Press, 1975*b*).

Retarded children are not immune. Those who live at home and attend school are not as hideously tortured as are some institutionalized handicapped. One such child was given a pants-down spanking on the driveway as he entered the school for the first time (*Sunday Bulletin*, 1977). Retarded children, in spite of inadequate language and understanding, are subject to the same paddling and slamming about as normal children. In Martinez, California, some children are even subjected to electric shock with the infamous cattle prods for grinding teeth, and may have a squirt of hot pepper sauce shot into their mouths for disobedience (*Los Angeles Times*, 1977).

Leslie Ellefson and his father sued a high school principal in La Crosse, Wisconsin, for having thrown Leslie against a wall and punctured his ear drum (*Leader*, 1976). The *Tempe News* (1976) reported another suit in Phoenix, Arizona, which charges that a teacher recklessly grabbed Aquila Scott around the neck causing her injuries and a $600 medical bill.

The family of a ninth grade student at Gaskill Junior High in Niagara Falls, New York, sued the school district and mathematics teacher Joseph R. Rizzo for $100,000. They claimed that their son Dino Primerano suffered a fractured coccyx when his teacher struck him with a wooden paddle. The coccyx is the vestigial tail bone at the base of the spine; injury there can cause a draining cyst and permanent inability to sit comfortably. Dino had failed to turn in his homework on time.

In Mount Clemens, Michigan, an assistant principal ordered seventeen eighth grade boys to strip naked for a search for a lost master key. Two girls in the class had to strip in an adjacent room. The key was not found (United Press, 1976).

Most startling of all to people outside the ambiance of the Old South and unaware of how the purity of southern womanhood is protected there were the stories that began to filter out about male administrators paddling nubile young women for trivial offenses. For example: High school girls in Tecumseh, Oklahoma, are paddled for the first offense of missing a class. When asked what position he required these young women to assume to accept blows on the buttocks, Principal Mihura found the question very funny and said, "I've considered several positions and rather lean toward stringing students up by their ankles, but since simply having them stand on their heads has such merit, we are still somewhat flexible on that matter" (Maurer, 1976).

That this is an exercise in pornographic amusement for the perpetrators becomes clear in the description given by Tamara May of Mesquite High School in Mesquite, Texas. She told a reporter for the New York *Star*: "They make you spread your legs, bend over and put your hands on the desk. Then they rub the paddle lightly on your rear and bring it back as far as they can and hit you. It hurts real bad." Even a normal person could be unavoidably aroused by spanking a member of the opposite sex, said Dr. Alvin Burstein, professor of psychology at the University of Texas

Medical School at San Antonio. "We all have unconscious sexual fantasies," he said, "and the problem becomes more acute as the child victim grows older." Tamara was fifteen. Her mother was in tears but eventually yielded to the pressure of the principals who argued that the least-motivated 5 percent would think they could get away with anything without taking licks if Tamara were excused after having refused to bend over. A compromise was reached. Tamara bent over for her mother in the presence of the voyeurs and took the three licks from a gently wielded belt. The petition for an end to swats in the high school that Tamara's mother attempted to circulate was eclipsed by another petition in favor of strong discipline which the teachers were required to sign. They were also required to obtain signatures from students and their families. They dared not protest. A last despairing cry escaped the mother: "If they can take the prayer out of the schools, surely they can take the beatings out too."

Rhonda Davis of Jones, Oklahoma, also refused to bend over, but she succeeded in her resistance. Security was less tight than in Texas, and townspeople rallied with letters to the editor biting in their sarcasm. Rhonda's story was more widely publicized and letters poured in from across the country. Wrote one: "In a place where young adults can still be spanked . . . anything can happen. One is left wondering only whether the principal would have turned the captain of the football team over his knee for the same offense?" Rhonda had been tardy.

Still more unbelievable is the story of Kimberley Jones of Bartow High School near Tampa, Florida, as told in the Tampa Tribune of February 23, 1978. The principal had gone to the funeral of his wife's mother. The assistant principal, Ralph Anthony, found nine cars improperly parked and, bursting with the temporary authority, he called the students in and offered each a choice: three licks or three days' suspension. Some of the young men insisted upon an appeal to Principal Bill Bryan when he should return.

Kimberly Jones, honor student and never before reprimanded, did not want to miss three days' school since she was a candidate for yearbook honors. Reluctantly she chose a paddling. Her father protested to the school board that the penalty was too severe for the infraction. He wanted the charge of "open defiance of authority" erased from her record and Mr. Anthony reprimanded and required to apologize to his daughter.

Kimberly had parked her car on the grass.

Bill Henry, lawyer for Werner Jones, Kimberly's father, said they would not sue if the requested relief were granted.

Superintendent Homer Addair insisted that Anthony was within the scope of his authority and refused to reprimand

Principal Bill Bryan wrung his hands. "To me, the mere publicity is probably the worst thing that has happened in our county in 28 years. I did announce the restriction on parking two times over the P.A. system. I don't know what you do after you tell students two times!"

Sixteen other people testified. Students, parents, the PTA president, a juvenile court judge, an administrator, and a psychologist stood up to plead and denounce.

Honor student David Altman, attending as a reporter for his school newspaper, Auburndale High, said he had been paddled for talking in class. "You can't imagine the humiliation of being told, 'Bend over.' I was in shock." He went on, "If you want to know something, three licks don't reform a student. All it does is place in their minds a spirit of rebellion." With tears in his eyes, he pleaded with the administrators to take time for the students they see. "We're people too, and would like to treated as such."

Judge E. Randolph Bentley, speaking also as a parent, said, "I'm against paddling high school students for one simple reason. It is the least effective punishment I've seen. It's an easy cop-out. The principals don't have to think. The concept of self-dignity is what many of the cases before me don't have. If you don't think paddling destroys self-dignity, let's try it in adult court. The next time you have a parking violation, we'll ask you to bend over."

An assistant principal claimed, "If paddling were taken out of the schools, the borderline students would have no effective deterrent."

Ralph Anthony, the paddler, said, "I don't consider paddling any more severe than a verbal reprimand. There is no distinction in my opinion."

A Lakeland psychologist, in response to an accusation that discipline problems (elsewhere) range from rape to murder, said: "I'd like to ask: Would spanking deter rape and murder? If capital punishment can't, would spanking?"

Board member Dan Moody emphasized the importance of keeping order and the need to take a firm stand. "I fear the greatest problem in America today is that the whole idea of right and wrong is being lost. Everything is 'situation ethics' which means you can justify anything you want to." Then he turned right about and advised the use of "discreet judgment in the application of punishment." He did not explain the difference between "situation ethics" and "discreet judgment." There is none.

Board Chairwoman Nancy Simmons argued that the county disciplinary policy wasn't followed. "Why wasn't she charged with parking in the wrong place? It's absurd to charge a child with something more than what they've done. Later she added: "Spanking a student is a sign of an undeveloped, immature and uncreative administrator."

The *Lakeland Ledger* editorialized: ". . . Stone Age approach to discipline. . . . If students are to learn to respect authority, authority must be reasonable."

But some Florida educators had not learned. Another school year brought the story of the mass paddling of all seventy-one of the sixth grade boys because none would confess to the scribbling of a dirty word on the lavatory wall (Jacksonville *Post*, 1978).

I could go on. The tales are endless, each one more bizarre than the one before. Yet what percent of the total instances of corporal punishment they represent is anybody's guess. We think of them as a tip of the iceberg phenomenon, but tip of the volcano might be a better simile. The rolling fury beneath this turbulent outpouring is reflected in our juvenile delinquency statistics, in the violence and vandalism that is wracking our schools, and in the enormous dissatisfaction with our schools that is evident on every hand.

It should be made very clear that most parents would not dream of going to the law to protect their children. That is truly a last resort. The steps usually taken include the following:

1. Good parents usually produce good, that is, cooperative, courteous, and studious children. Most parents depend upon their children's good behavior to protect them from abuse in school. Such children are not free from anxiety, however, since their sense of fairness and compassion may also make them highly sensitive to and unhappy about the punishments of others.

2. When a child is punished in school, old-fashioned parents simply assume that the school is right and that the child deserves whatever he gets. It is expected that swats in school are doubled when the child gets home. The faith of the American people in educators as the gatekeepers of the door to success is no longer quite so implicit and unquestiong as of yore.

3. If the parents listen to the child or look closely at bruises, they will usually go first to the teacher for an explanation. Sometimes this is enough. If the parents have status, the teacher may attempt to placate them. In Berkeley some years ago a kindergarten teacher raised in another tradition was assigned to a school attended by the sons and daughters of university professors. Within a week of her regime with a whip on display the faculty wives descended upon her, not with condemnation but with enlightenment. "No, we didn't complain to the administration," one of those involved explained to me, "we taught her how to teach gently."

4. If the parents in any community have slightly less clout than faculty wives they may volunteer to be parent representatives on a committee for discipline. This worked for one woman with whom I am acquainted, who moved when her husband transferred from Montgomery

County, Maryland, to Seminole, Florida. She volunteered and won agreement to a three-year phase-out of corporal punishment in her new community, although this was later nullified by a state law forbidding school boards from stopping teachers' use of paddles.

5. Another escape is to move. Andy finished sixth grade but told his father: "Nuh uh! I'm not going to that junior high. They whip kids there!" His unbelieving father checked it out and reported to me that he had arranged for his son to attend the school of his choice. Sometimes whole families decide to move. Dr. Newhard, his wife Martha, and five children stayed with the Ohio schools as long as they could. They worked for improvement; Dr. Newhard even won a place on the school board. The children were not paddled since they were bright and courteous, but they began to feel less and less comfortable with the screams and cries of paddled classmates. In the end, despairing of effecting any fundamental changes in the punitive atmosphere, Dr. Newhard left a flourishing practice and moved across the continent to a California community more to their liking (*Last ? Resort*, 1976).

6. If changing the system or escape are both impossible, harassed parents who believe their children are physically punished unjustly or too severely will go to the administration. If the complaint can be justified (and this depends more upon the status of the offended party than the facts of the case) the superintendent may censure the offending teacher, suspend him/her for a day, with or without pay, apologize, make promises, perhaps warn the assembled faculty about the close call they had had, and polish his P.R. image with some conspicuous display.

7. If the administration fails to mollify the outraged parent, the school board is approached next. The relative numbers are probably comparable to the California survey which showed that for every 7 families who actually went to court, another 63 were stopped at the school board level and 535 had been mollified by the superintendent (Riles, 1974). School boards usually set aside a block of time for community input. Parents with complaints about abuse in a specific case may or may not get the floor but quite a few try. If the school board takes them seriously, makes a genuine investigation, and takes appropriate action (reprimand, transfer, termination after hearing), that may be the end of it. A number of reported cases were withdrawn from the courts when the school board handled them well.

8. If neither the administration nor the school board handles the matter to the satisfaction of the parents, they may go public. A parent in Fremont, California, whose retarded daughter came home black and blue could get no sensible answers from the teacher, the principal, the school psychologist, the superintendent, or the school board. Finally she went to the police. They promised to look into her complaint but on the advice of counsel

turned her off with a laconic, "Lady, it's legal." The mother and I visited the office of State Senator Nicholas Petris who was easily persuaded to sponsor a bill protecting handicapped children from corporal punishment. In spite of opposition from a representative of the Council for Exceptional Children, the bill, amended to read "except with parental permission," was passed. It seemed a small step to forbid teachers to hit blinded, crippled, retarded children unless mama says OK, but it had far-reaching effects. Not only did the special class which this parent's daughter attended get a new teacher, but they also got an enriched program with field trips, handicrafts, cooking, and a speech therapist. The regional centers that have custody of the retarded who have no families were able to enforce a blanket "no" against corporal punishment of their charges and this in turn all but eliminated the problem for the state of California.

9. Occasionally parents with few options try to take matters into their own hands. This is uniformly unsuccessful. Direct assault upon a teacher, even if that teacher has assaulted one's child, calls for immediate action by the police. For a shove that would go unnoticed in a crowded bar, a parent can spend time in jail. The story is told elsewhere of the mother, whose five-year-old son thought he had been sentenced to death. She tried to still his hysterical crying by attacking his teacher with a kindergarten chair, and was accused of being a dupe of the Black Panthers set to murdering white teachers ("Don't Kill the Teacher," 1973). More recently a grandmother in East Dallas shot and killed a custodian who had spanked her eight-year-old grandson. Details at this writing are unclear but Mrs. Georgia Reeves, who had stood on the schoolhouse steps awaiting the police after the shooting was in the city jail for investigation of murder (Dallas *Times Herald*, April 27, 1978).

Direct retaliation by paddled pupils is usually reported as vandalism and labeled senseless violence. The antecedent attack by the teacher is rarely mentioned except by implication ("he resented being disciplined"). When teachers report that they feel they have to carry a gun to protect themselves against students, one can be sure that that teacher's discipline has been physical, excessive, and unfair ("I was a schoolboy," 1976).

10. The last resort of the parents whose child has been battered in school is to go to court. Like other last resorts it is rarely successful. Many lawyers prefer not to take such cases since they are difficult to win. Many judges require that permanent injury and malice must be proved before an "ordinary paddling" becomes assault or abuse. This varies widely, of course, since $3,000 was awarded a family after their son had a tuft of his Afro snipped off and was insulted (United Press, 1977).

A victory in this kind of suit cheered long-suffering families in Portland, Oregon. They read in the *Oregonian* of April 1, 1978, that Rene

Silguero had won $10,000 from the vice principal and the wrestling coach of David Douglas High School in a suit alleging assault and battery that resulted in the fracture of the boy's left elbow.

It is generally believed that before they abolished corporal punishment Los Angeles School Board attorneys had the task of talking irate parents out of bringing suit at the rate of two a week. If parents cannot be talked out of it they may run into a "catch 22" situation. As in rape cases, the court may spend more time investigating the moral character of the victim than in investigating the alleged crime. A family from Oregon found themselves saddled with mountainous dental bills after their son received an uppercut by a teacher. The family told me:

> Our son was not being punished at the time he was hit. He was an innocent bystander. This teacher took out his frustration on our son after he separated two boys who were having a verbal argument. It was proven in court to be an unprovoked assault. My son's favorite teacher . . . went on the stand and stripped him of all dignity and degraded his character. My son's character then became the issue and not the assault. By the court's allowing it to be turned into a corporal punishment case, it was then covered by government immunity from lawsuits. My husband and I were both told we would be witnesses and must stay out in the hall during court. My husband testified for about five minutes and then was sent back out. I was never asked to testify or permitted in the courtroom from the time it started until after the verdict came in. (personal communication)

Not being a lawyer I am not quite clear as to the meaning of "double jeopardy." I thought it meant that you couldn't be tried twice for the same offense; if you were acquitted, you were free. But what if your lawyer makes a mistake? This is what happened in Gastonia, North Carolina. The coach (the coach again!) was charged with picking up a fifteen-year-old student by the neck and slamming his head against the bleachers for refusing to do some extra push-ups. He was charged with child abuse, a crime under a new statute that applies to parents and anyone acting in place of the parent. District Court Judge Ramseur ruled that the coach was charged under the wrong statute and dismissed the charge. He said that, while there might be evidence of assault, he did not see enough evidence to support the charge of child abuse. The parents, Mr. and Mrs. Lanny Drum, took out a second warrant charging simple assault. Both charges are misdemeanors. District Court Judge Mason ruled the coach could not be tried on the assault charge because that would constitute "double jeopardy." There was to be an appeal (*Gastonia Gazette*, 1977). But appeals can take years.

Although individuals who hire their own attorney have not been particularly successful, the public advocates have done a bit better if recent cases are typical. The American Civil Liberties Union and Rural Legal

Assistance have had a certain number of victories, but more of these have been out of court settlements than outright wins. In the California case, *Zamora* v. *Riles* (1974), it was charged and admitted that the principal had strapped the student and bruised his testicles. The case was settled when the defendant agreed to pay $2,000 damages and the school district agreed to cease strapping without parental permission. Originally it had been planned to challenge the constitutionality of the whole concept of corporal punishment, but this, of course, came to nothing when the suit was settled.

Rural Legal Assistance pursued the Guadalupe case. The town was found to be a feudal enclave where the 5 percent Anglo owners ran roughshod over the 95 percent Mexican-Americans by threatening them with loss of jobs and deportation hearings when they protested the treatment their children were receiving in school. One child told that he had been held head down in the toilet bowl while the teacher flushed it. Another teacher was accused of grabbing the children around the neck with the hook he used as a prosthesis for a missing hand. That case too was settled amicably when the school board agreed to get rid of the three most punitive teachers, hire a new superintendent and add bilingual counseling (*Ortega* v. *Guadalupe*, 1973).

The Chicago school system after almost a hundred-year tradition of "never lay a hand on a child" became embroiled with the problem at the Mosely Social Adjustment School. Northwestern (University) Legal Assistance Clinic obtained a consent decree which restored the policy of no corporal punishment (*Chicago Tribune*, 1976).

It takes outrageous actions by educators to break the tenacious American belief that schools are the royal road to success and that the teacher is always right. That being true, we are justified by this evidence to conclude that corporal punishment is an ubiquitous evil even though middle- and upperclass children are comparatively immune.

It should also be clear from this recital that the offenses of the children are so minor as to not even be considered status offenses: forgotten gym clothing, tardiness, unfinished homework, taking both cherry pie *and* a cookie on the lunch tray. To my knowledge, in no case was a child who was violent paddled. A fourteen-year-old fired a gun out an open window of a school bus. The driver turned the bus around and drove back to school. Security officers confiscated the gun and took the boy into custody (*Louisville Times*, 1976). Another gun incident involved a fifteen-year-old who shot the principal after he had been humiliated by a public paddling (Associated Press, 1975a). The defense of corporal punishment on the basis of its being needed because of school violence is thus seen to be without merit.

The "back to basics" movement, however, has begun to gain a certain amount of popularity. Public reports about local school ratings below the national average in reading scores never explain that the tests are so rigged that half of all students fall below grade level by definition. Instead they leave the impression that the local teachers are incompetent and that children are being allowed to waste their time dawdling foolishly or playing inconsequential games instead of being educated. Parents panic and listen to the first siren song of "Back to the Three Rs" although assurances soon follow that music and athletics will not be neglected either. The main appeal is almost always that there will be "Discipline" with a capital *D*. Dress codes, marching in straight lines, silence, instant obedience, and noses dutifully pressed into books, with a quick swat for any who strayed— these reminders of their own schooling gratify clumps of less successful parents who lack confidence in their ability to handle their children and who hope desperately that someone else can force them up the ladder of success that they failed to climb. The nostalgia for traditional schools is based on the belief that "permissiveness" had eliminated punishments, thus leaving teachers at the mercy of drug-crazed, illiterate vandals bent solely on destroying the school building and raping and murdering the teachers. This weird nightmare has only the flimsiest backing in fact in that a few inner city schools have suspended or expelled too many teenagers who, being unemployed and unemployable, return to the school for mischief. Now, on the basis of a collective fright, Taft Green, for example, principal of a middle school in Fort Lauderdale, Florida, can sit back in his office and complacently boast to an interviewer, "We paddle students all the time. The only reason you don't hear it now is the dean is at lunch" (Pompano Beach *Sun-Sentinel*, February 28, 1978).

Letters to the editor on this subject split about fifty-fifty. Those in favor of physical punishment are generally less grammatical and more angry. Those opposed (with exceptions) tend to be longer, more thoughtfully organized, and better expressed. Editorials are less evenly divided. Most (perhaps 75 percent) are calmly hopeful that physical punishment can be avoided yet discipline maintained. The 25 percent that favor more and stiffer punishment quote Proverbs, often incorrectly, evoke the good old days, or expand on the destructive nature of youth in a permissive society. Editorials in the newspapers of the larger cities—the *New York Times, Wall Street Journal, Los Angeles Times, Washington Post*, etc.— are strongly and eruditely in favor of total abolition. The *Sacramento Bee* headlined, "Thousands of Better Ways" in answer to the tiresome question, "What's the alternative?"

To quote President Jimmy Carter, schoolmen as well as nations need to be reminded that "a quiet strength need not be proven in combat."

REFERENCES

Associated Press dispatch (Butte, Montana), October 23, 1975 (a).
―――― (Atlanta, Georgia), November, 1975 (b).
Bartow (Florida) *Ft. Meade Democrat and Leader*, February 14, 1978.
――――, *Polk County Democrat*, February 13, 1978.
Brunswick News (Georgia), December, 1976.
Canyon News (Texas), January, 1977.
Chicago Tribune, July 12, 1976.
Corry, Pennsylvania, *Journal*, March 28, 1978.
Courier (Houma, Louisiana), December 21, 1976.
Daily Local News (West Chester, Pennsylvania), January 6, 1977.
Daily Town Talk (Alexandria, Louisiana), January, 1977.
Dallas Times-Herald, April 27, 1978.
――――, September 13, 14, and 19, 1977.
"Don't kill the teacher," *Freedom News*, January, 1973.
Duncan, C. "They beat children, don't they?" *Journal of Clinical Child Psychology*, 1973, 2(3), p. 13.
Dymally, M. (chairman). Testimony of children at hearing held by senate select committee on children and youth. Guadalupe, California, August, 1973.
Flint (Michigan) *Journal*, March 5, 1978.
Fresno Bee (California), September, 1974.
Gastonia Gazette (North Carolina), January, 1977.
Holland Evening Sentinel (Michigan), December, 1975.
Ingraham v. *Wright*, 45 U.S.L.W. 4364 (4/19/77).
"I was a school boy." *Last ? Resort*, September–October, 1976, 5 (1).
Jacksonville Journal (Florida), September 26, 1976.
Lakeland (Florida), *Ledger*, February 23, 1978.
Last ? Resort, March, 1974, 2(4).
――――, November–December, 1974, 6(2).
――――, September–October, 1976, 5(1), p. 1.
Leader Telegram (Eau Claire, Wisconsin), November 20, 1976.
Los Angeles Times, January 31, 1977, et seq.
Louisville Times (Kentucky), November, 1976.
Maurer, A. Personal Communication, 1976.
Memphis Scimitar, May 13, 1976.
Miami News, December 10, 1976.
Nashville Tennessean, October 15, 1976.
Nevada Herald (Missouri), December 19, 1976, et seq.
News-Star (Shawnee, Oklahoma), November 2 and December 7, 1976.
New York Post, November 16, 1977.
Olean (New York) *Times-Herald*, February 23, 1978.
The Oregonian (Portland, Oregon), April 1, 1978.
Ortega v. *Guadalupe Union School District*, No. SM 12821 (Cal. Super Ct., Santa Barbara County, filed June 4, 1973). Clearinghouse No. 14,457.

Oskaloosa Herald (Iowa), October 23, 1976.

Pompano Beach (Florida) *Sun-Sentinel*, February 28, 1978.

Record Chronicle (Renton, Washington), January, 1977.

Round Lake (Illinois) *News*, March 9, 1978.

Riles, W. Administration of corporal punishment in the California public schools (a report to the California legislature as requested by ACR 6). Sacramento: California State Department of Education, 1974.

San Diego (California) *Tribune*, March 27, 1978.

San Francisco Examiner and Chronicle, March 14, 1976.

Seattle Post Intelligencer, November 19, 1973.

Sunday Bulletin (Philadelphia), March 20, 1977.

Tampa (Florida) *Tribune*, February 23, 1978.

Times Observer (Warren, Pennsylvania), December, 1976.

Tucson Star (Arizona), November 17, 1976.

United Press dispatch (Mt. Clemens, Michigan), December, 1976.

_____, (Lenoir, North Carolina), February, 1977.

_____ (Blacksburg, Virginia), March 27, 1978.

Wilmington (North Carolina) *Star*, March 11, 1978.

Zamora v. *Riles* (Civil No. 8752, Superior Court, San Benito). Settled out of court, August 6, 1974.

15

Corporal Punishment and School Suspensions: A Case Study

Justine Wise Polier,

Luis Alvarez, Vincent L. Broderick,

Phyllis Harrison-Ross, Robert C. Weaver

With an Introduction by Kenneth B. Clark

•

Introduction

On re-reading *Youth in the Ghetto*, the report of the Harlem Youth Opportunities research project, and *Dark Ghetto*, I was forced to remember that a number of the teachers—white and black, who were interviewed for these studies in the early 1960s—made the following comments:

> The children are not taught anything. They are just slapped around and nobody bothers to do anything about it.

> I soon learned that the boys liked to be beaten. . . . When I learned to say things to them that, to me, would be absolutely insulting and to hit them when they needed it, I got along all right and they began to like me.

> Here, both the Negro and white teachers feel completely free to beat up the children, and the principal knows it. They know he knows it and that nothing will be done about it.

On May 20, 1974, when Leonard Buder of the *New York Times* broke the story that children in Jordan L. Mott Junior High School 22 in the Bronx were being subjected to corporal punishment, these quotes came back most disturbingly. Like many of my friends and associates I pretended to be shocked and amazed that corporal punishment was taking

This essay is part of MARC Monograph #2, The Report of the Citizens' Commission to Investigate Corporal Punishment in Junior High School 22.

237

place in any public school in New York City in the latter part of the twentieth century. But memory of these casual admissions by teachers, who had made these statements protected by the cloak of anonymity-covered social science research subjects, blocked me from accepting my own pretense of ignorance. For over ten years I knew and had published statements by teachers in the New York City public schools that they had inflicted corporal punishment upon children in ghetto schools because "they are accustomed to it and they like it."

As the person who directed the HARYOU research project, I cannot plead ignorance of the fact that children were victims of physical punishment in the New York City public schools. After publishing the verbatim comments of these teachers, I, like many others, remained silent and permitted this evil to persist. With the publication of this new set of charges concerning corporal punishment in Junior High School 22, the time for silent acceptance of this disgrace has come to an end.

In addition to the stories in the *New York Times*, the specific charges of corporal punishment in Junior High School 22 were brought to the attention of the Metropolitan Applied Research Center corporation by the persistent pressure of Ira Glasser, the executive director of the New York Civil Liberties Union. Subsequently MARC joined the New York Civil Liberties Union, the Puerto Rican Legal Defense and Education Fund, the National Association for the Advancement of Colored People, the NAACP Legal Defense and Educational Fund, and ASPIRA of America in seeking to set up a commission of independent citizens to investigate the facts.

As can be seen by this report, the commission placed the problem of physical and psychological violence inflicted upon children in the New York City public schools within the context of other violations of the rights of students such as the illegal suspensions of students. They also demonstrated that the specific problem of corporal punishment in the New York City public schools exists within a total pattern of disregard for the rights of children and parents who are perceived as powerless. This remains a fact in spite of the evidence that some black parents sought to justify the use of corporal punishment even as they were denying that it was used. The fact that the individuals who inflicted corporal punishment on the children in this school were themselves black does not in any way make this illegal act any more acceptable. In a democracy, teachers and school officials have the responsibility of helping children to understand that human problems can be solved without resorting to violence.

The message of this report—which must not be forgotten or ignored —is that inflicting corporal punishment and violating other rights of students, such as illegal suspensions, are dehumanizing and cannot be tolerated in a civilized society.

I. A Case of Corporal Punishment: History and Setting

In May 1974 a series of articles by Leonard Buder in the *New York Times* reported the extensive use of corporal punishment with a thick wooden paddle known as the "smoker," leather straps, and fists at the Jordan L. Mott Junior High School 22, District 9, the Bronx, New York City. Denials by the two deans charged with these actions, denials by the principal, denials by the district superintendent, and denials by the local community board were issued. It appeared that although the chancellor of the central board of education for the city had requested an investigation by the local community board and district superintendent, this request had not been pursued with energy. Furthermore, the chancellor's representatives were excluded by the local community board from its "hearing" which was held to investigate the charges.

The newspaper articles reported harassment of Irving Sandrof, the guidance counselor who had made the initial complaints, as well as harassment of the teachers and students who supported his charges. Letters by the guidance counselor to the district superintendent and the chancellor had been left unanswered until he went to the press with his charges. Moreover, he was called to a meeting and threatened with trouble if he continued his charges. Finally he had been transferred to the office of the district superintendent and then out of the district to the central office of the board of education.

Meanwhile, the guidance counselor had sent copies of his letters to the New York Civil Liberties Union (NYCLU). The NYCLU in turn had written to the superintendent about the charges of corporal punishment reported to them. By the time the story had broken in the *Times*, the NYCLU had been aware of the inaction or limited action on the part of local and central school board officials for a period of three months.

Following the publication of the *New York Times* articles, the guidance counselor, students, parents, and teachers contacted the NYCLU and Kenneth B. Clark, president of the Metropolitan Applied Research Center (MARC) to secure their support. Further harassment was described and some of the persons asked that their names not be disclosed. There was no indication that the charges or denials had been or would be subjected to a thorough and unbiased investigation.

Creation of Citizens Commission. Kenneth Clark of MARC and Ira Glasser, director of the New York Civil Liberties Union, decided that the situation demanded an investigation by independent citizens who had been connected in various ways with the problems of children and youth in the city. At their request and supported by the sponsorship of the National Association for the Advancement of Colored People, the NAACP Legal

Defense and Educational Fund, and the Puerto Rican Legal Defense and Education Fund, a group of citizens undertook to investigate the charges of corporal punishment at Junior High School 22.

The appointment of a Citizens Commission to Investigate Corporal Punishment at Junior High School 22 was announced at a press conference on June 10, 1974. At that conference Kenneth Clark expressed his concern over the alleged physical abuse of children in the school, the alleged harassment of those who had challenged such abuse, and over the procrastination by both local and central school authorities in their investigation of the charges and the reporting of findings. In view of subsequent questions directed to the commission, it is significant that Kenneth Clark at that time stated:

> I am convinced that this serious matter would not be dealt with so casually if the victims were not black and Puerto Rican. I do not believe that the fact that these charges involved black deans and a black principal make the matter any less grave. And the fact that some parents have supported the use of brutal corporal punishment of their children can be viewed merely as another example of the extent to which past victimization leads to the acceptance and perpetuation of cruelty.

Citizens Commission Sets Scope of Investigation.   At its first meeting the citizens commission reviewed the available reports on the situation at J.H.S. 22 and agreed that it would be necessary to hold public hearings so that both those who alleged the abuse of children and those who denied it could be heard in the open. It was also agreed that representatives of the school administration and others concerned with the problem be invited to appear.

The question was immediately raised as to whether the commission should limit its inquiry to what had occurred at J.H.S. 22 in view of reports that the use of corporal punishment was widespread in the city schools. Because of the limited time and staff available, the commission agreed, with one member dissenting, that it would have to confine its inquiry to J.H.S. 22. It was, however, agreed that, if there were evidence of similar charges in other schools, an appropriate public or private agency should be requested to make a subsequent city-wide investigation. In developing plans for its inquiry, the commission agreed to the following:

> It would examine the laws applicable to the use of corporal punishment of students in the public schools in New York City as well as the relevant court decisions.
> It would seek to determine the responsibility of public agencies or officers for the enforcement of existing protections against abuse of students.

It would explore the methods of discipline which are alternatives to corporal punishment and bring together a summary of what has been learned in this field.

It would issue a report that would include findings of fact, conclusions, a summary of relevant material collected, and recommendations.

It would publish the report in both English and Spanish.

Citizens Commission at Work. The commission started its investigation by examining the newspaper reports of the charges, the answers to the charges by school representatives, the reports of interviews with the district superintendent, the chancellor, parents, students, and teachers. It held hearings for two days in June at which testimony was taken from Irving Sandrof, the guidance counselor who had lodged the complaints, as well as from students, teachers, and parents who volunteered to testify. Unfortunately, no member of the school administration appeared except a school aide who was employed by the principal and was also president of the parents association at J.H.S. 22. No representative from the United Federation of Teachers appeared.

Following the hearings, the commission reviewed the credibility of the testimony by various witnesses. It also reviewed the available literature on the use of corporal punishment, the reasons why corporal punishment was used, and the alternatives to the use of corporal punishment. Finally, it examined the pertinent law, the emerging recognition of children as persons with rights to due process under the Constitution, and the issues of violation of law as presented in this case.

History of the Case at Junior High School 22. The facts elicited concerning the use of corporal punishment at J.H.S. 22 must be seen within the framework of the conditions in the community, the past history of the school, and the attitudes of parents toward the school. According to some testimony, alleged past disorders in the school including acts of vandalism had brought about conditions in the school that obstructed learning. Legitimate fears of parents that their children would be deprived of opportunities for learning and achievement in a "chaotic" school situation or become involved in delinquent behavior caused many parents to regard the establishment of law and order within the school as the first priority. Following the appointment of Acting Principal William E. Green, reported improvements in these conditions created confidence in the new principal on the part of the parents and the community.[1]

In addition to this, a sense of pride and hope had developed as a result of the election of a community board to operate the school and the subsequent appointment of black staff members to administrative positions in the district and in J.H.S. 22 (as district superintendent and as principal). The parents anticipated a greater understanding of community problems and more consideration for the educational needs of the children. As a consequence there was a real sense of relief when parents knew that a new acting principal was exercising control and achieving order in the school. One mother testified that conditions in the school under the new principal compared favorably with those which existed when her older children attended the same school. Corporal punishment of those students who misbehaved was not too high a price for the order that had been achieved, according to some witnesses. On questioning, however, these witnesses stated that their own children had not been subjected to corporal punishment and acknowledged they would object if it were imposed on their children.

Some viewed the investigation of corporal punishment in J.H.S. 22 where the children came almost entirely from minority groups and where a black principal and two black deans were involved as a potential attack on community control of the school. This concern was fed by distrust of the United Federation of Teachers (UFT). Allegations of anti-black attitudes surfaced.

Thus both the legitimate concerns of parents for an orderly school as well as hostile reactions to an airing of the charges that corporal punishment of students at J.H.S. 22 had become institutionalized confronted the commission as it proceeded to its fact-finding task.

The published record established that a guidance counselor at J.H.S. 22, Irving Sandrof, had written to the superintendent of District 9, John Greene, on March 11, 1974, to request an investigation of the use of corporal punishment at the school. Copies of his letter were sent to Chancellor Irving Anker and to the New York Civil Liberties Union. In the absence of any response from the district superintendent or the chancellor, Sandrof sent five additional letters during the following two months to the superintendent and to the chancellor urging an investigation. He also sent several letters directly to the chancellor from whom he received no response. The sole response during this period was a summons to Sandrof to appear before a community school board committee for a hearing on April 17, where he was warned that his allegations might cause him trouble, including an action for libel.

When the guidance counselor finally went to the *New York Times* and produced a heavy wooden "smoker" allegedly used by the deans to paddle students, an investigation was begun. On May 20, 1974, the first of the series of articles by Leonard Buder appeared in the *Times*. The *Times* series reported the charges of use of a thick, wooden paddle, leather straps and fists by the two deans at J.H.S. 22 to enforce discipline. It reported that the principal, William Green, and the two deans denied the allegations. It also reported that the district superintendent, John S. Greene, said "he had received no complaints from parents and knew about this matter only through the Sandrof charges." When asked about the charges, Chancellor Irving Anker is reported to have said that his office had sent three letters to the district asking for a full report but had not received any report. Later on the same day he said he had at that point "invited" members of the District 9 Community School Board to meet with him that evening to "discuss" the situation.[2]

After refusing permission to three representatives of the central board to gather information at the school on Monday, May 20,[3] members of the local board agreed to meet with Chancellor Anker. At this time it was decided that the district would continue the investigation with the central headquarters aides present during interviews. Following this meeting of May 21 the superintendent of District 9 directed the two deans to report to the district office until the investigation was completed.[4] However, they were restored to their posts within two days[5] and then again transferred to the district office on May 28 on the request of the principal.[6]

The *Times* articles also reported that Chancellor Anker said on May 22 that he would issue a new directive within days to all 950 city schools with respect to enforcing the school system's ban on corporal punishment.[7] The date of the last issuance of the ban was not known, and one official speculated that some people in the system did not know about it and that others might not want to know about the ban.

By May 29, as citizens, officials, and organizations expressed criticism not only of the use of corporal punishment at J.H.S. 22, but of what seemed to be a cover-up by the community board and inaction by the chancellor, there was an angry response from the district superintendent. He now charged "trial by the press" and said that the individual who should be charged with covering up was Sandrof, the guidance counselor (who had filed complaints repeatedly) for not revealing the alleged situation earlier.[8]

When the community school board once more refused admission to all observers from the central board to attend their investigation, the chancellor stated he wanted a full report by Friday, June 7, 1974.[9]

On June 4 the chancellor wrote a letter to the *New York Times* asserting his unequivocal opposition to corporal punishment in New York City schools and his disapproval of the recommendation by Superintendent Greene that the law banning corporal punishment be modified. He also noted the responsibility of the community school board to make a thorough investigation of the charges and stated that, if it failed in its responsibility, he would conduct an independent investigation. He concluded that "there had been no negligence on the part of the Central Board of Education or its staff, nor has there been any abatement of its responsibility in this matter."[10] It was reported that the chancellor regarded the decentralization school law as preventing his prompt and effective intervention.

Amid repeated denials of the use of corporal punishment by the two deans and by the principal, witnesses including students, teachers, and parents came forward to support the charges. They volunteered statements to the NYCLU, to MARC, to the *New York Times* and to the commissioner of investigations for the city of New York.[11] These statements included charges of harassment of those who opposed corporal punishment.

At noted above, on June 10 the Citizens Commission to Investigate Corporal Punishment at Junior High School 22 was announced. Its members were Luis Alvarez, national executive director of ASPIRA; Vincent L. Broderick, former New York City police commissioner and attorney; Phyllis Harrison-Ross, M.D., child psychiatrist, pediatrician, and director of the Community Mental Health Center at Metropolitan Hospital; Hon. Justine Wise Polier, director of the Juvenile Justice Project of the Children's Defense Fund, as chairman of the commission; and Robert C. Weaver, distinguished professor of urban affairs at Hunter College of the City University of New York.[12] The stated purpose of the commission was to conduct an independent and impartial investigation of the facts and submit a public report including findings of facts, conclusions, and recommendations.

Two days later, on June 12, the *New York Times* reported that Chancellor Anker had disclosed a ten-page "preliminary report" from the community school board of District 9 confirming allegations that students at J.H.S. 22 had been beaten and that he expected a full report the following Monday.[13] This was reported to be the first official confirmation of the allegations concerning the use of corporal punishment at J.H.S. 22 and contrasted with an earlier report by a district committee that found no apparent evidence of corporal punishment.

On June 13, three days after the appointment of the commission, a special circular signed by the chancellor (No. 119, 1973–4) was addressed to community school board chairmen, all superintendents, executive directors, heads of bureaus and principals of all day schools. This circular was entitled "Pupil Behavior and Discipline." It requested that attention of all staff be directed to section 90, subdivision 15 of the by-laws of the board of education: "No corporal punishment shall be inflicted in any of the public schools, nor punishment of any kind tending to cause excessive fear or physical or mental distress."

On June 17, twent-eight days after the publication of the first *New York Times* article on corporal punishment at J.H.S. 22 and one week after the appointment of the citizens commission, the community school board—

which had first denied the charges—found that corporal punishment had in fact been inflicted on students.

The community school board voted to discipline the two deans, John Mathis and Oscar Smith, as well as to place a "strong reprimand" in the file of Acting Principal William E. Green. The president of the community school board of District 9 stated it had voted "to accept the recommendations and findings of the Community Superintendent as to the nature and degree of punitive action."[14]

The citizens commission decided to proceed with public hearings that had previously been scheduled for June 20 and 21. This decision was based on certain facts and circumstances:

1. No clear and adequate findings of the scope or severity of corporal punishment used at J.H.S. 22 had been presented to parents or to the public by the responsible educational authorities.

2. No explanation had been given of how corporal punishment had come to be used in violation of New York City law; of what steps would be taken to ensure that such practices would not be allowed at this school or any other school in New York City by the central board of education; of the reasons for the initial denial of facts by the deans and the principal and for the alleged ignorance of facts by the district superintendent.

3. There was no indication that meaningful steps had been taken by the central board to develop conditions at public schools conducive to the use of needed alternative methods of discipline or to train school personnel in the use of such alternatives.

On June 20 and June 21 the commission held lengthy hearings at the Findlay Auditorium in the Bronx. Witnesses came to testify about the use of corporal punishment at the school either in support of the principal or in opposition to the system of punishment. Witnesses included students, parents, teachers, the president of the parents association,[15] the New York City Youth Board, Irving Sandrof, and others interested in J.H.S. 22 or in the use of corporal punishment in the public schools. Unfortunately Acting Principal Green, the two deans, members of the community school board, the office of the district superintendent, and the central board of education failed to respond to the invitation to appear as witnesses and failed to send representatives.

It must be noted that the UFT also failed to appear either to oppose the use of corporal punishment or to support teachers who were harassed because they came forward to oppose its use. One teacher testified that when the union failed to take a stand on the issue of corporal punishment, she went to the Civil Liberties Union.

Racial Issues at J.H.S. 22. Unlawful use of corporal punishment or of school suspensions in the public schools of New York cannot be ad-

dressed in isolation. Responses to such practices were found closely inter-
twined with discrimination against minority groups in the public schools,
with fear on the part of parents, teachers, and professional groups, with
suspicions of persons not belonging to the minority groups, and with resentment over the low expectations for the education of the children and
insensitivity to their feelings.

Discrimination in educational and career opportunities fed suspicion
that any investigation into the charges of wrongdoing by black administrators, teachers, or the local community school board was intended as
or would be used as a weapon against minority groups and school
decentralization.

An open unsigned letter from the Ad Hoc Committee of Concerned
Black Educators dated June 17, 1974, raised the question of what "hidden
agenda" lay behind attacks on black and Puerto Rican public school administrators. It claimed direct knowledge of extensive use of corporal punishment against black children at the hands of white teachers and administrators but gave no facts to substantiate the charge. It asserted that no
fact-finding committees or investigative bodies had been created and no loud
protest had ever appeared in the press because of the widespread abuse of
"our children." It referred to having been surrounded by "multiple and
varied accents, usually mid-European" and charged that the "established
white professional majority feels its power and job control threatened by
the newly arrived minority who are now in a few decision-making
positions."

The Inter-Boro Council of Black Women addresssed a letter to Kenneth Clark in which they insisted that corporal punishment was not the
real issue at J.H.S. 22 but rather an "opening salvo in a war for the highly
remunerative supervisory jobs in the school system." The letter spoke of the
corporal punishment that had continued for many years in the public
schools and of the physical abuse of black children by whites that, it
alleged, continues in the majority of public schools of New York City. The
attack on the principal was seen as part of an overall plan to discredit,
remove, or limit appointments of more minority group members to supervisory positions.[16]

At the hearing, suspicions of those who did not belong to minority
groups also surfaced. To some witnesses, the fact that the guidance counselor, who had brought the use of corporal punishment to light, was white
made him suspect or was used to discredit him. Irving Sandrof testified
that at the first hearing before a committee of the community district board,
he was treated as a defendant and questioned as to whether he directed
children who were black or Puerto Rican to vocational high schools.

Fortunately there were witnesses who rejected such suspicions and
reverse racism. One fifteen-year-old black student testified to the corporal

punishment she had received. In her criticism of those responsible, she defended the counselor and said simply, "Color doesn't have anything to do with it—if you were wrong, you are wrong." A black teacher testified that she had never heard any criticism of the counselor until he raised his voice against corporal punishment. Then she heard that he must be removed from the school.

Fear was expressed by some parents that criticism of the principal or placing a check on his power to administer discipline would engulf the school in the disorder and violence which were all too common in public schools in poor areas. Their first concern was that their children should learn enough to achieve greater opportunities than they had known, and that their children should not be truant, misbehave in school, or become delinquent. Fear that their children would not be educated or would become involved in delinquent behavior caused parents to condone the unlawful use of force without recognition of the resulting injury to their or other children. To what extent such honest concerns had been exploited by those charged with unlawful corporal punishment and school suspension is not known.

That students in poor areas or in ghetto schools were more accustomed to corporal punishment for misconduct at home crept into the picture as a rationale for seeing its use at school as less traumatic. Such a position was reminiscent of reasons given for not providing adequate medical care to the poor on the grounds that they suffer less or can tolerate pain better than those who are more privileged.

It also seemed that some of the parents who had suffered many deprivations had been conditioned to accept low expectations for their children without realizing they were condoning a strategy for educational failure. They were not demanding the entitlement of their children to effective teaching based on good teacher-child relationships as an essential ingredient or their entitlement to order *not* based on fear. Not having been able to command these from white administrators in the past, they seemed to feel that to require them of black administrators would be unjust or prejudicial. That corporal punishment of non-white children was imposed by non-white teachers may also have seemed a step forward to those who had suffered at the hands of white teachers.

Defenders of the conditions at J.H.S. 22 failed to confront the larger racial issue: that both corporal punishment and school suspensions have been used most widely against children of minority groups. Although concerned with advancing racial or ethnic equality, they did not appreciate that to condone school practices which denied non-white students equal protection under law would be counter-productive.

Corporal punishment has been found to be most widely used in ghetto and barrio schools,[17] and is rarely used in middle class or suburban areas. In a memorandum urging the abolition of corporal punishment, the Black

Education Commission of Los Angeles wrote: "We see corporal punishment as one of those intimidating and demeaning factors which must be removed in order for young Black people, especially young Black men, to be totally free and responsive to the process of learning."[18]

In similar fashion suspension of school students has been found to be most widely used against children of minority groups.[19] Data collected by the Office for Civil Rights of the U.S. Department of Health, Education and Welfare showed this to be true not only in other parts of the country, but in New York City. In May 1974, the director of the Office for Civil Rights, Peter E. Holmes, testified before a subcommittee of the House of Representatives that minority pupils were suspended far more often than other pupils. The data showed that while New York City had a 64.4 percent minority enrollment, 85.9 percent of all pupils suspended came from minority groups. This pattern, according to the director, was to be found in almost all major cities analyzed.[20]

There is, therefore, special significance in the struggle for human and equal rights for all children in Justice Robert Jackson's statement of 1943 that school authorities "have, of course, important delicate and highly discretionary functions, but none that they may not perform within the limits of the Bill of Rights."[21]

In fairness to principals and others responsible for the administration of ghetto schools, it must be added that resources for children with special problems are fewer and less adequate than those generally available for white or middle-class children. Diagnostic, out-patient treatment and residential treatment services are all inadequate. The *Fleischmann Report on Handicapped Children*[22] found that a handicapped child's ethnic background and social class in many instances had substantial influence on his placement. The figures, in fact, showed that comparatively few children from minority groups were receiving the benefits of state funding for residential special schooling. Inevitably a higher proportion of black, Puerto Rican, and poor white children who could benefit by special schooling is therefore left to buffet and be buffeted about in public schools without appropriate help or is exiled from school and left in the community without specialized services.

II. The Citizens Commission's Findings of Fact

1. The evidence established that some parents sincerely felt that when Acting Principal Green was appointed, he was confronted with the dual task (a) of imposing control and order in the school and (b) of improving the quality of education.

Some witnesses alleged that conditions at J.H.S. 22 had been chaotic prior to the appointment of the new principal. The commission was not able to make an independent investigation of these allegations. However, it felt that the allegations of past acts of violence, including arson and serious vandalism committed in the school by students and outside gangs were relevant to the attitudes of parents who endorsed the use of corporal punishment. These witnesses claimed that children and parents had become fearful of conditions in the school, and that school authorities had been unable to control the situation or impose conditions necessary for learning.

2. Witnesses who supported as well as those who opposed the use of corporal punishment testified that the improvement in conditions at J.H.S. 22, after Acting Principal Green's appointment, was initially achieved without the institution of corporal punishment.

3. The weight of the credible evidence established that promptly upon appointment of the two deans, Oscar Smith and John Mathis, what may have been the occasional use of corporal punishment (prior to their arrival) became widespread and institutionalized. Its use was not limited to correcting violent or dangerous behavior.

Thus one twelve-year-old boy testified to being hit five times with the large wooden paddle known as the "smoker" for running in the hall. He received a second paddling when he and five other students were reported for failing to bring their books to class.

Another twelve-year-old testified that he and six other students had been hit with a belt because they had been disruptive in class, although his teacher told the dean she only wanted to have him sent home with a letter to his parents.

A girl student who had been graduated testified she had been hit for being late or forgetting her books on a number of occasions with the smoker or a belt, beginning with the time when Mr. Green was appointed acting principal.

A boy student who had been graduated testified that he had been hit with the smoker by one of the deans and described how the two deans regularly walked the halls of the school with smokers in hand.

A teacher testified that, after she had learned of the corporal punishment administered to those students she had referred to the deans for disruptive behavior, she ceased making such referrals. She thereafter reported only minor forms of misbehavior on the assumption that corporal punishment would not be administered for such offenses, only to learn that children referred for such offenses had also been subjected to corporal punishment. She then ceased reporting all misbehavior.

Additional students and teachers testified that paddling and beating of students had developed into an everyday occurrence during the administration of Mr. Green as acting principal. It had come to be regarded as a normal procedure.

One student testified that he saw both deans physically punish students who failed to do push-ups properly.

4. The testimony established that the deans, on receiving students with teachers' reports of misconduct, required them to sit in the office of the deans, sometimes for as long as a day waiting their turn for their names to be called for punishment, while they witnessed the physical punishment of other students.

5. Students, when called by the deans for their punishment were repeatedly given a choice of five "licks" or "strokes" or five days' suspension. There was no indication that notice was ever sent to parents or that a hearing was held before suspension was threatened or imposed.

Thus one student testified he was given the choice of receiving five licks with the paddle or a five-day suspension. On a second occasion when he chose the five licks he received them and was also suspended.

A second student, a girl, testified she was given the choice of five licks or five days' suspension, and that on several occasions, though she opted for the licks and received them, she was also suspended.

6. The evidence established that public humiliation was part and parcel of the discipline used by the deans.

Thus, one student spoke of how humiliated he was made to feel by the public nature of the proceeding.

Students testified to being hit in front of other students, teachers or whoever happened to be in the deans office.

Students were required to autograph the smoker used to punish them.

One student testified that he was hit twice for running in gym class by one of the deans in front of the whole class of approximately fifty students.

There was testimony that, in addition to being hit, on at least one occasion, two boys were required to walk through the school halls holding hands, thus finding themselves subjected to ridicule and humiliation.

7. Evidence established that the institutionalization of widespread corporal punishment seemed to lead to sadistic enjoyment on the part of the perpetrators.

Thus, one boy testified that the deans (who were also the gym teachers) would either hit the student with the smoker or step on the students' fingers while they were attempting the push-ups, if they did not do the push-ups properly.

Several witnesses described the deans as smiling while they hit the students.[23]

8. The evidence clearly established that Smith and Mathis who were hired by Acting Principal Green as two deans in charge of discipline dis-

pensed institutionalized corporal punishment at J.H.S. 22. The evidence established that corporal punishment was not widespread until their arrival at the school. The evidence is inconclusive as to whether the acting principal participated in the imposition of corporal punishment. However, the commission finds on the basis of evidence submitted that the acting principal knew of the use of corporal punishment by the deans and approved such disciplinary treatment of students at J.H.S. 22.

9. With respect to why such pervasive violations of law were tolerated for two years without corrective action, the commission finds that some teachers did not know it was a violation of law, that other teachers and parents believed it the best way to maintain order, and that some teachers feared to object to a procedure clearly condoned and approved by the principal at J.H.S. 22. It is significant in this connection that some students who testified only came forward when they became upset at hearing that their principal denied the charges of the use of corporal punishment which they themselves had either experienced or witnessed. They were shocked that he lied and at his unjust attack upon the guidance counselor who complained.

10. The evidence established that there was harassment of members of the school staff who opposed corporal punishment. Thus immediately after the first article appeared in the *New York Times*, Irving Sandrof was relieved of his duties as a guidance counselor, assigned to the office of the district superintendent, and then transferred to headquarters of the central board of education.[24] A second teacher who spoke out against corporal punishment was promptly transferred out of J.H.S. 22 and assigned to the district office for the remainder of the school year to carry out some clerical assignments. A third teacher who testified to the use of corporal punishment was asked if she would not prefer a transfer.

11. The evidence established that the community board committee initially denied the use of corporal punishment and sought to make a scapegoat of the complainant. Representatives from the chancellor's office were refused admission by the community school board to subsequent hearings. The use of corporal punishment was only acknowledged after the press reports, the appointment of this citizens commission, and the insistence of a full report by the chancellor. Even when the committee of the community board finally found that corporal punishment had been used, the sanctions it invoked were ten days' suspension for the two deans who had employed it and a reprimand for the principal who had condoned it. There was no public reprimand or sanction with respect to the fact that the deans and the principal had previously falsely denied the use of corporal punishment.

12. The evidence clearly established that, despite a turnover in school personnel, there was no ongoing orientation of teachers in how to deal with

misbehavior of students other than to send them to the deans for punishment. The teachers were not advised of the law prohibiting corporal punishment. Fortunately some teachers found the ongoing procedure so wrong that they failed to follow it even though they felt they could not openly oppose it.

13. The president of the parents association alleged that she knew nothing about the use of any corporal punishment in the school and insinuated that the guidance counselor, who made the original complaint, might have had the smoker made. In addition to being the president of the parents association, she was a paid aide in the school. The commission found her testimony not credible.

14. The commission found that children were sent to the deans for discipline without information about their physical or emotional problems. Parents were not notified or consulted. The use of corporal punishment became an automatic response by the deans to reports of misbehavior they had not witnessed and in regard to which the child had no chance of an explanation or a hearing.

Apart from the law and the inadvisability of using corporal punishment against students, this procedure led to extreme abuse through ignorance. Thus, evidence was heard that one girl who had received corporal punishment was later found to be in need of special mental health services and was transferred to an agency for emotionally disturbed adolescents.

15. The commission is fully satisfied that Irving Sandrof, a guidance counselor of ten years' experience, including over two years at J.H.S. 22, acted responsibly when he sought an investigation of the use of corporal punishment through the district superintendent and the chancellor. His testimony was convincing and fully supported by the weight of the other evidence.

We find no basis for Superintendent Greene's attempt to shift responsibility for failing to respond to or investigate Sandrof's charges by alleging that Sandrof should have brought the matter to light sooner. It is indeed regrettable that the district superintendent and the chancellor both procrastinated in examining the charges when they were received, and that they waited until the public press forced them to confront the facts.

The harassment and unfounded attacks against Irving Sandrof by individuals and the district board committee were unjustified. He is to be commended for his concern for children and his courage in opposing abuse of them at J.H.S. 22.

III. The Law on Corporal Punishment in New York City

In the absence of laws prohibiting corporal punishment of students, court decisions have held that such punishment must be administered without malice, be reasonable in the light of the child's age, sex, size, and physical strength, be proportionate to the child's offense, and be employed to enforce reasonable rules. When parents challenged the use of corporal punishment as a disciplinary measure in the public schools of Boston, a consent decree was issued under which such punishment was ended so long as the school board remained in office.[25]

Increasingly where the use of corporal punishment is challenged, constitutional issues of cruel and unusual punishment are now being raised. The provisions in the by-laws of the board of education prohibiting the use of corporal punishment have made these constitutional issues academic in New York City. Where the law is not implemented, these constitutional issues are, however, present. They must be confronted squarely, as well as the question of the effects on children of corporal punishment and the reasons or excuses preferred for violating the law.

Over 120 years ago the Supreme Court of Indiana expressed its disapproval of the discriminatory treatment accorded students:

> The public seems to cling to the despotism in government of schools which has been discarded everywhere else. . . . The husband can no longer moderately chastise his wife nor . . . the master his servant or apprentice. Even the degrading cruelties of the naval service have been arrested. Why the person of the schoolboy . . . should be less sacred in the eye of the law . . . is not easily explained.[26]

In 1968, the U.S. Supreme Court wrote in defending the right of students to express themselves about political events, "Students . . . are 'persons' under our constitution. They are possessed of fundamental rights which the state must respect."[27] In a series of cases the courts have required that, before taking certain types of disciplinary action, public schools must provide students with an opportunity to hear and rebut charges before the proper authorities.[28]

Who Is Responsible for Enforcement?   While only a few states have enacted laws to prohibit the use of corporal punishment in public schools throughout the state, New York City, like many other important metropolitan areas,[29] has prohibited its use by regulations that have the force of law.[30]

Principals and *school personnel* have primary responsibility for obedience to the law prohibiting the use of corporal punishment in the public schools of New York City.

District superintendents and *community boards* have the duty to exercise their supervisory powers to assure enforcement of the law, promptly to investigate charges of violations, and to act in appropriate fashion where violations are found.[31]

The central *board of education* is not relieved of its responsibility to assure compliance with the law throughout the school system of New York City by reason of the provision of the education law which created community boards.[32]

The central *board of education* has the responsibility to implement the by-laws, to monitor their enforcement, to investigate charges of violation promptly, and to provide aid needed to translate policy into reality.

That the central board recognizes its responsibility for monitoring a wide range of laws and regulations is evidenced by the publication of special circulars distributed to community school board chairmen, superintendents, executive directors, directors, heads of bureaus and principals. Such circulars give instructions that cover a wide range of subjects including "Safety in the Schools,"[33] "Drug Abuse Education,"[34] "Child Abuse and Maltreatment,"[35] and "Pupil Behavior and Discipline."[36]

The special circular on "Pupil Behavior and Discipline"—the subject of this report—was reissued by Chancellor Irving Anker on June 13, 1974, three days after the announcement of the appointment of this panel.[37] It was addressed to community school board chairmen, all superintendents, executive directors, heads of bureaus and principals of all day schools. The circular began by requesting that attention of all members of the staff be brought to section 90, subdivision 15 of the by-laws of the board of education which forbid the use of corporal punishment.

The circular stated that this by-law remains in full force and effect and that "the use of corporal punishment to enforce discipline is not only contrary to regulations; it is counter-productive. The dehumanizing results of harsh and punitive treatment will inevitably lead to further disruption."

The effect of this special circular on "Pupil Behavior and Discipline" appeared however to be undermined by a letter from the chancellor to the president of the community school board of District 9, dated June 19, 1974, six days after publication of the circular. In this letter the chancellor acknowledged the belated findings of the community school board to the effect that corporal punishment was administered to pupils at J.H.S. 22. The chancellor noted that the two individuals determined to have committed the acts were to be suspended for the balance of the school year (less than two weeks) and that a letter of reprimand was to be placed in the principal's file. After referring to difficulties in conducting the investigation, the chancellor stated, "While the judgment as to the nature of the penalties to be imposed is placed by law with your Board, I urge that your Board give consideration to the following steps":

1. to consider carefully whether to request the renewal of the temporary licenses of the two teachers assigned as Deans;

2. to instruct the Community Superintendent to monitor closely supervisors at the school and to take steps to guard against recurrence throughout the District;

3. to instruct the Community Superintendent that a copy of the investigatory record and letter be placed in the files of the three persons involved with copies to the Division of Personnel and the Board of Examiners.

In conclusion, the chancellor reiterated that "corporal punishment is in violation of the By-Laws of the Board of Education, is counter-productive, is dehumanizing and in my judgment, has no place in the City School System. Your Board should take those steps necessary to ensure that corporal punishment is not inflicted by staff of your district." One finds no reference to the residual or ultimate responsibility of the central board and no steps through which assistance will be rendered by the central board to encourage use of alternative forms of discipline.

The position of the chancellor in regard to penalties for violation of the ban against corporal punishment was at sharp variance with his actions and the position taken ten days later when an assistant principal at a Brooklyn elementary school was charged with instructing teachers to withhold low reading scores. In the latter instance the chancellor sent in his own investigators under supervision of his special assistant who made findings. While stating that the community school district board would determine the disciplinary action to be taken, the chancellor was quoted as having said that he regarded the matter of test scores as "very serious" and that he would review the disciplinary action imposed by the district superintendent to see if it was appropriate. While dishonesty about test scores is unquestionably a "very serious" offense, it surely should not be regarded as more serious by the chancellor than the infliction of corporal punishment on students.

The special circular on "Pupil Behavior and Discipline" contained hortatory language about the negative effects of corporal punishment, and it asserted that sound discipline is "based on creative teaching, skillful guidance and effective supervision." It also contained various recommendations for action including the development of a "ladder of discipline" and an appropriate referral system. This special circular failed, however, to fix responsibility on the principal; it failed to require adequate reporting; and it failed to acknowledge responsibilities of the central board similar to those recognized in circulars concerning school safety, drug abuse, and child abuse.

Responsibility was not placed on community school boards to provide sound alternative measures to corporal punishment as was done in the circular regarding safety in the schools. Nor were minimum standards of responsibility set for the principal in regard to preventing the use of corporal punishment such as those set in regard to matters of safety. Reporting of incidents was not required, as was required in the safety circular concerning injury to any person. Thus responsibility of the central office for school safety was detailed, but reference to no similar responsibility of the central office in regard to pupil behavior and discipline is to be found in the circular on that subject. There was no indication that a central board administration existed to develop and administer a city-wide information system with regard to school discipline or that any person at the central board was charged with using such information for operational assignments including monitoring in the community schools, such as was required by the circular addressed to "Safety in the Schools."

The circular concerning drug abuse was also far more concrete than the circular concerning "Pupil Behavior and Discipline." Steps were detailed for the implementation of the drug abuse curriculum, including availability of audio-visual aids, inservice training courses, institutes and workshops, availability of resource personnel, etc. Under suggested procedure, students were to be given the opportunity of informing their parents, but if they did not wish to do so, the school experts, after informing the student, was authorized to contact the parent.

Again, under the special circular on "Child Abuse and Maltreatment," the principal was required to establish procedures for all staff members to report to him, and copy is to be sent to the district office. Moreover, each principal or bureau head was required to conduct an educational program for all staff members in order to encourage the fullest degree of reporting.

The state *commissioner of education* is also responsible. In addition to the obligations of school staff, principals, district superintendents, the local community board, and the central board of education, the commissioner of education for the state of New York has responsibility to see that corporal punishment shall not be inflicted on students in New York City. As chief executive officer of the state education system and of the board of regents (by whom he is appointed),[38] the commissioner is given responsibility for general supervision over all schools and the duty to advise and guide school officers of all districts and cities of the state.[39] He has the duty to cause to be instituted such proceedings as may be necessary to properly enforce general or special laws pertaining to the school system or "to any school district or city."[40]

Violation of Corporal Punishment Law at J.H.S. 22. New York law prohibits corporal punishment of public school students and punishment of any kind tending to cause excessive fear or physical or mental distress. This law was violated in J.H.S. 22 by the two deans with the knowledge of the principal.

The record provides clear and convincing evidence that, beginning with occasional infractions of the law, the tolerance and use of corporal punishment or suspensions from school carry within themselves the evil seeds that grow into institutionalized excesses.

While the corporal punishment at J.H.S. 22 did not involve physically crippling acts, it entailed the infliction of pain, fear, and public humiliation on students. It provoked loss of respect for teachers and the principal who violated the law and lied about what had become known practices in the school in order to cover-up their wrongdoing. Students saw teachers who opposed corporal punishment harassed and removed.

The unlawful infliction of corporal punishment was compounded by the further violation of law in forcing students to choose between corporal punishment and suspension from school. Respect for law and due process was thus undermined by the arbitrary use of power which denied to students and parents the right to notice, the right to a hearing, and the right to enforcement of the law restricting the use of suspensions from school.

The central board of education, the community school boards, district superintendent, principals and all school personnel must be held responsible for enforcing and complying with the law. Students cannot be taught to respect the law when they observe or are subjected to violations of law by the state through actions of public officials.

Violations outside J.H.S. 22. The commission was originally requested to make an independent investigation of charges of the institutionalized use of corporal punisment in J.H.S. 22 in the Bronx and of the use of such punishment in other public schools. On consideration of what would be required in terms of staffing and time to make a city-wide study, the commission decided that it could not, at this time, make an investigation of such scope. However, information concerning the use of corporal punishment in other schools did reach the commission and requests were made to testify.

The material that reached the commission concerning conditions or allegations of conditions in schools other than J.H.S. 22 included:

• Dean of School 33, Brooklyn, David Silver, published a letter stating: "Corporal punishment in greater or lesser degree takes place in many intermediate and junior high schools that are in economically depressed areas." He charged that the central board of education, most local boards, elected officials, political leaders of both parties, and the Shanker leadership of the UFT "encouraged the notion that schools such as J.H.S. 22 should be basically custodial whose graduates will provide a cheap labor pool."[41]

• While the commission was investigating the situation at J.H.S. 22 Bronx, charges of the use of corporal punishment against students in three other schools in District 9 were forwarded for investigation by Chancellor Anker to a district superintendent for full inquiry. The schools named were P.S. 53, P.S. 133, and P.S. 63.[42]

• At the commission hearing, Jerome M. Becker, chairman of the New York City Youth Board, stated that he was convinced that corporal punishment was covertly practiced in many city schools. He added that "the practice unfortunately appeared most prevalent in minority group areas of the city."[43]

• The *New York Times* reported that a sixth grade teacher in P.S. 46 who used corporal punishment to stop a fight between two boys was ordered to report to the community school board of District 5 on June 5, 1974, pending a hearing on charges brought by the parents of one boy. Two other alleged incidents at the same school were reported to be under investigation.[44]

• The commission received a letter from the mother of an eight-year-old child alleging she had been suspended from the free lunch service on the basis of misconduct in a Queens school.

There appeared to be rather general agreement that corporal punishment is practiced primarily against poor children and therefore against a disproportionate number of non-white children. There were charges that it is practiced by white teachers and administrators against black children. At the same time fear was expressed by some black groups that the investigation by this commission had a secret agenda, namely, to undermine blacks who had achieved administrative positions.[45]

In view of the serious complaints, the suspicions, and the evidence submitted, this commission recommends that a city-wide study by an independent body be initiated without delay to determine the extent of corporal punishment in the city schools and to make appropriate recommendations to secure its abolition in fact as well as in law.

IV. The Law on School Suspensions in New York City

The federal courts have held that before a public school may suspend or expel a student, the student must be afforded a hearing that complies with due process requirements of the Fourteenth Amendment of the United States Constitution. While the requirements in various circumstances have varied in these decisions, certain basic requirements for due process have been established. These include the right to adequate notice of specific charges in advance of a hearing; sufficient time to prepare a defense and present witnesses prior to a hearing; notice to the parent or guardian as well as the student; information concerning "the nature of the evidence to be presented." It is further required that the hearing shall be more than an informal interview and that the student must be allowed to present his defense to the person authorized to take disciplinary action. None of these due process requirements was met at J.H.S. 22 when the deans suspended students without notice, without specific charges, and without a hearing.

The law of New York City in regard to school suspensions has been cited as a model by the American Civil Liberties Union.[46] The law permits the use of suspension only when the student's behavior "prevents the orderly operation of the class or other school activities, or presents a clear and present danger of physical injury to school personnel or students." It places the emergency power to suspend a student in the principal only and requires daily review of the suspensions by the principal, directing that the suspension "shall last only so long as the conditions continue to prevail, but in no case shall exceed five days." Detailed requirements include immediate notice to parents of any emergency suspensions, with notice of the reasons for the action and with a request for a parent conference. When suspended a student shall remain under the supervision of the principal until the end of the school day or until the parent claims the child. Plans to provide maximum educational experience for the student during suspensions are required.

Detailed procedures for the implementation of the New York City law were spelled out in a special circular (No. 103, 1969–70) by the board of education on June 24, 1970. In addition to the procedures for due process, this circular states that "the school . . . must take all possible steps in the educative process to prevent the suspension of children. . . . Each principal and teacher has a responsibility to identify pupils in need of help and to enlist the aid of the Board of Education's pupil personnel services as well as the resources available in the community." The New York City Board of Education has also expressed its commitment to the right of due process including a fair and impartial hearing whether the hearing be administrative or judicial.[47] That a child's interest in schooling is entitled to the protections of due process is therefore no longer an issue in New York, except where the law is violated.

Unfortunately, violations of the model school suspension law of New York have been continuous since its adoption. A 1971 study by the New York Civil Liberties Union[48] concluded that "the legal rights established by the state legislature and the New York City Board of Education have been nullified by the failure of school officials to comply with their own laws."

The NYCLU study showed that "in *every single one* of the more than 100 suspensions we were able to check, either the state law or the Board of Education by-law had been violated. In 77 percent of the cases, we found that students were suspended for illegal reasons; in 99 percent of the cases, neither students nor the parents were even told what the specific reasons for the suspension were, despite the fact that the by-law specifically requires it. Other provisions of the law have been violated with similar frequencies." The study went on to make specific recommendations:

> The failure to comply with the new laws has created a disrespect for the rule of law itself that can only be destructive of our schools and our students. We believe that the Board of Education should immediately initiate the following steps:
>
> 1. Conduct a full and independent investigation of the extent of compliance with the new laws in *all* 14,000 suspensions imposed during 1969–1970. Records of all suspensions are kept by law, and should not be difficult to check.
>
> 2. Conduct public hearings to allow all interested parties to inform the Board of their own experiences with the new laws governing suspensions.
>
> 3. Create machinery to receive and investigate complaints involving non-compliance in the future.
>
> 4. Take action to ensure that school employees obey the law, including if necessary the filing of charges of insubordination against particular officials.

Following the release of the NYCLU study, the *New York Times* urged the New York City Board of Education to reveal the facts concerning what it called "the staggering total of 14,000 suspensions" and called upon the board "to cease high-handed violations of student rights."[49]

The board of education never responded to the report or recommendations of the NYCLU. No machinery was developed and lawlessness continued. Meanwhile, the total number of suspensions continued to rise.

The flagrant city-wide complicity of the central board of education in refusing to enforce its own laws must be seen as the backdrop against which particular violations of student rights took place at J.H.S. 22.

Violations of Suspension Law at J.H.S. 22. Despite the law, the 1970 special circular, and public pronouncements, all protective safeguards for students and parents were violated at J.H.S. 22 when the deans forced students to choose between five "licks" or five days of suspension. In effect, children were put out of school by the deans. They were not sent to the principal. Their parents were not notified immediately, if at all. The children were not kept in the principal's office until the end of the day or until their parents claimed them. There were no plans for educational experience while the children were out of school. No arrangements were made for early conferences with parents. The suspensions were not reviewed daily to determine if continuation was necessary under the emergency power of suspension. Indeed, the emergency power of suspension was offered as an alternative to corporal punishment even for minor misconduct such as lateness, failure to bring books, or running in the halls. In addition, in some instances after the student chose the five licks and received them, he or she was also suspended.

Who Is Responsible?   What is possibly most disturbing is that in all the reported statements of the district superintendent, the community school board, and the chancellor concerning the situation which was exposed at J.H.S. 22, one does not find a single reference to the violation of the law controlling the use of suspension, the harm done to students through its abuse, or what, if any, action would be taken to end such abuse at J.H.S. 22 and all other schools in the city of New York. Surely the state education law, the by-laws of the board of education, and the special circular all bespeak concern for the destructive consequences to students of the widespread or casual use of school suspension as a method of school discipline.

Injury to Students from School Suspension and Discrimination.   The abuse of the power of school suspension does serious harm to a student in many ways beside depriving him of his right to education. Where the procedure is not fair the student senses the injustice, and anger and distrust may result. The student is humiliated. He is marked as deviant which threatens his self-esteem. All too often, suspension, in fact, means pushing a student who needs special services out of school, losing sight of him, and failing to secure for him services that could be beneficial. The suspension must be recorded in his cumulative record, and if he moves to another school district within the city, the pertinent information must be forwarded to the new district.[50] In this computerized age such entries in his record may result in subsequent denials of educational and career opportunities. The consequences of school suspensions thus carry potential harm to students far beyond those realized by students or their parents.

Deans for Discipline.   Deans in public schools should not be persons designated to administer discipline. The title of dean has long been honored in the educational world and should remain so. A dean should be selected for his knowledge of education of young people and for his ability to enrich the educational life of a school. To give persons designated to administer discipline the title second only to that of principal mistakenly places the focus on custodial control rather than education.

The consequences of such action were found at J.H.S. 22 where two tall and powerful men with only temporary licenses for physical education were appointed as the deans in charge of discipline. There were no requirements for the position with respect to knowledge of, or training in, children's behavioral problems, and the procedures used in exercising discipline were not based on knowledge of the child or consideration of his intelligence, his emotional problems, or his family situation. No respect was shown for the rights of the child or his parents to due process before the deans inflicted corporal punishment or suspended a child from school in violation of law. Such uninformed and impersonal use of punishment violates all that has been learned about the right of every child to appropriate care and treatment in the educational process.[51]

Studies have shown that causes of delinquency may be found in the existence of physical problems or of neurological impairment, in the absence of parental affection coupled with family conflicts and inconsistent discipline at home. Certainly the public school must not superimpose on such problems punishment inflicted without knowledge of or concern for the child's difficulties.

The situation at J.H.S. 22 cannot be dismissed as a sport because it reflects all too common procedures in handling disciplinary problems here and in other parts of the country. Disciplinary officials have been elevated to posts of deans or assistant principals. This reflects the growing custom of assigning power without requiring appropriate qualifications to assure its beneficial exercise. It raises discipline to a separate and specialized function with no appropriate requirements for knowledge of human behavior, and with few safeguards against discipline being applied sadistically. As one additional consequence, it reduces the role of teachers, guidance counselors, school medical and mental health personnel, and the principal in the handling of complex student problems.

The commission recommends that the title of dean shall not be employed for persons designated to exercise discipline. It recommends that no person shall be authorized to discipline a child who has not at least received certification in guidance.[52]

This commission further recommends that teams shall be established in every school to provide initial diagnosis and referrals for specialized help where a teacher finds he or she cannot work out the problems directly with a student, or where a student's behavior appears to endanger others or himself.

Recognizing that crisis situations do occur which require immediate separation of a student from others, the commission recommends provision that a student so separated shall be seen promptly by the specialized team.

V. Alternatives to the Use of Corporal Punishment

Until progressive services and programs are adequately provided, school officials will continue to resort to expeditious and ill-advised devices to control the school environment.

> John Greene, District Superintendent, Community School Board, District 9[53]

This statement made by the district superintendent during the controversy over the use of corporal punishment at J.H.S. 22 in his district presents a valid challenge that demands a valid response. Neither teachers nor parents can be expected to reject corporal punishment or the abuse of school suspensions wholeheartedly until alternative remedies for maintaining conditions necessary to learning and to helping children with behavioral problems are made available. No statements about the dangers or injuries resulting from corporal punishment or the abuse of suspension procedures can satisfy the need for alternative remedies.

Problems of discipline in school will continue to evoke anger and to invite impetuous and hurtful discipline so long as the schools fail to help teachers to meet behavioral problems; fail to provide the avenues through which tense situations in the classroom may be relieved; and fail to provide special services for children. The schools should provide in this connection: means for identification of medical and mental problems, opportunity to secure appropriate remedial help, timely mental health services when needed, guidance to teachers in handling difficult problems, encouragement of parent and teacher consultations, and relief assistance when needed.

The commission, recognizing these needs, explored what studies had been done in this field.[54] In addition, Dr. Phyllis Harrison-Ross, director of the Community Mental Health Center of Metropolitan Hospital and a member of the commission prepared a paper on "Suggested Resources for Children with Disruptive Behavior within the New York City Public School System."

The findings and recommendations published by the Task Force on Corporal Punishment (1973) of the National Education Association[55] were most helpful in the consideration of alternatives to corporal punishment and school suspensions. The task force expressed the belief that corporal punishment was used in schools only when school conditions for dealing with discipline were so poor that school staff reached a point of total frustration. Lack of needed inservice training programs to assist in identifying, developing, and practicing alternatives to the infliction of pain was seen as a causative factor in preventing teachers from securing education in alternative disciplines.[56] Teacher training and time for teachers to secure inservice training for this purpose were recommended.

The task force concluded that physical punishment is ineffective, is subject to repetitive use, may increase disruptive behavior, and hinders learning. It fails to develop self-discipline, develops aggressive hostility, and teaches that might is right. It is detrimental to the educator who uses it and discourages the search for more effective means of discipline.[57]

The task force found that temporary removal from classroom detention after school, withdrawal of privileges, imposition of special tasks, and even physical restraint when necessary were appropriate methods for the control of behavior. It stated that none of these measures should be used to correct student mistakes, unintentional happenings, or trivia. Emphasis was placed on the positive effects of rewards for good behavior as compared with the limited short-term effects of punishment for bad behavior. Forced conformity was seen as failing to provide stimulus either to learning or to positive conduct. It was also noted that the effects on the person using corporal punishment too often showed a sequence from feeling disturbed about its use, to indifference to using it, and finally to learning to enjoy its use.

The commission recognizes that, in considering alternative remedies to the use of corporal punishment or school suspensions, it is necessary to consider different types of misconduct that occur within a public school. They cannot be treated as though they were one homogenized thing to be dealt with in one way.

In these days when increasing violence is reported in all areas of life, it is important that a distinction be drawn between violence that comes from outside the school and the violence of students. A clear distinction must also be drawn between criminal conduct by students in a school, with the consequent right and duty of school authorities to invoke the protection of the law, and the wide spectrum of noncriminal student misconduct.

When misconduct involves drug abuse or sex offenses, corporal punishment or school suspension will only drive such activity further underground and will help neither the student nor those with whom he or she is involved. In such situations, a procedure is needed for teacher referrals and for appropriate specialized help.

In the majority of cases children engage in the garden variety of misbehavior such as talking in class, failing to do their work, running in the hall, ignoring directions of teachers, flaring up, name calling, or fighting with other students. In all such situations it is of first importance that teachers by reason of training and understanding of pupils be able to work out the problem directly with pupils whenever possible. Dr. Harrison-Ross stressed in our discussions the importance of students feeling their teachers know them and understands how they feel, and that the teachers respect them enough to want to understand their interests and their problems. The referral for misconduct to a third person for discipline when such a referral is not needed is an admission by teachers of weakness or inability to handle the situation. This must reduce the stature of and respect for the teachers in the eyes of the students. It also diminishes the teachers' capacities for handling the class and their sense of mastering responsibilities as a teacher.

There are, however, situations where continuing misconduct of a student is too disturbing to other children to enable the classroom teacher to handle the resulting problems alone. In such cases temporary removal from the classroom is necessary with immediate referral to a guidance counselor for work with the student. The guidance counselor may then make recommendations to the teacher or refer the student for further and more specialized help where indicated.

Formal and informal structures involving teachers, parents, and students in the neighborhood councils to consider school problems including discipline have been created in some areas. In New Jersey, student courts were established to hear cases and make recommendations. These courts were designed and implemented by law school students who were teaching contemporary law to junior high school pupils. This program was successful because it dealt with law and legal practices as they related to the specific problems of junior high school pupils and their families. The possible application of such structures in the New York City schools should be studied.

In her memorandum to the commission Dr. Harrison-Ross urges the teacher first to try to learn from the child as much as possible; if the problems cannot be solved on this basis, then the teacher should *meet with the parents and child together.* She states that procedures for referrals to medical or mental health professionals on the consent of child and parents should include provisions for explanation to the child and parents of why such help should be sought.

Employment of alternative remedies requires that teachers and administrators have knowledge of the specialized resources available within the school itself, within the school system, and in the community. Guidance counselors should provide counseling to the child, the family, and the teacher, screening examinations when learning disabilities are suspected, and where indicated should make recommendations for specialized assistance. The Bureau of Child Guidance should be used for diagnostic studies, individual or family therapy, and counseling and consultation services. The commission is not in a position to say what resources or special services were actually available or the extent to which those available were used by the teachers or the principal at the time corporal punishment and suspensions were institutionalized as methods of discipline at J.H.S. 22.

The commission fully agrees with the position taken by Dr. Harrison-Ross that a massive increase of inservice training of teachers is needed to help them to recognize learning or behavioral problems, including those which are reactive to poor teaching.

The commission is further agreed that a key ingredient, without which the concept of alternative remedies will be meaningless rhetoric, must be the availability of adequate resources within the school and in the community on which the school can call for help with behavioral and learning problems.

Responsibility for Alternative Remedies.   In the provision of alternatives to corporal punishment or school suspensions, the classroom teacher is on the front line. Training, teaching ability, knowledge of pupils, concern for their needs, all play an essential role. The teacher must also be supported by the provision of ongoing information concerning resources within the school system or the community available to the child or his family. In handling problems, the teacher must also be conscious of the school's responsibility to parents for the welfare of their children.

The principal is responsible for providing a staff education program, for encouraging open discussion about class problems, and for developing current material on the use of special resources. Close contact with the parents association should prove helpful in this area. With the cooperation of students, parents, and teachers the principal should also seek to develop a fair code of behavior so that there will be full understanding of school rules and of how the school will handle violations. When casual and arbitrary treatment is eliminated, students will come to know what to expect and will anticipate that they will be treated fairly.

If it is found that services are inadequate to meet the special problems of children, the facts concerning needs and the lack of appropriate resources should be identified and brought to the attention of the parents association and, through the district superintendent, to the community district board so that they, in turn, can present the unmet needs of the school to the central board of education and to such citizens or organizations as can be helpful in obtaining the needed services. Utmost care must be taken to provide safeguards against the abuse of corporal punishment and suspension of children who do not present behavior problems or do not require special services because of their independent thought or political dissent.

The central board of education should not wait for complaints or grievances. It should immediately undertake the creation of a city-wide information service so that it will know not only about violations of law but about the alternative remedies that various schools are using. It has the duty to develop inservice programs, including institutes and workshops to improve the handling of disciplinary problems in the schools, and also to develop city-wide operational programs to provide additional service resources where needed.[58]

The commission is aware of the realistic budgetary problems that face local district boards and the central board. However, to move toward meeting the needs of children in the city, especially in deprived areas, the central board must engage in fact finding and the presentation of needs in New York City to both the state and federal authorities. It must also undertake to investigate and correct any lack of services due to discrimination on the basis of ethnic background or poverty, such as was reported in the *Fleischmann Report* on special schooling for children who are poor or non-white. No single school can fill gaps in the existing mental health services for students who need out-patient treatment, hospital care, or residential treatment services. However, every school administrator is responsible for making the fullest use of the best available services, and for presenting the facts concerning the gaps to those responsible for services and to those agencies or groups who will act as advocates for more adequate services.

VI. Recommendations

1. Corporal punishment of children—an inheritance from the English common law and traditions under which children were not treated as persons entitled to any rights—must be recognized by all personnel of the public school system as archaic and violative of human dignity and of rights of students as persons. School authorities must, in the words of the Supreme Court, perform their duties "within the limits of the Bill of Rights."

2. The law in New York City prohibiting the use of corporal punishment in the public schools must be published and widely disseminated to teachers, parents, and children. It must be closely monitored and strictly enforced by school administrative officers at all levels. Principals, district superintendents, the chancellor, and the New York State commissioner of education all bear responsibility for the enforcement of law. The decentralization law does not relieve the central board of education or the commissioner of education from responsibility for the enforcement of laws enacted to protect students.

3. The law in New York City prohibiting school suspensions except as an emergency measure and with restrictive safeguards to assure due process, including notice, a fair hearing, and alternative education must be enforced.

4. It is recommended that an independent ombudsman be appointed with the power to receive, investigate, and report on all complaints of violation of the laws outlawing corporal punishment and restricting the use of school suspensions. The alleged ignorance of and procrastination in dealing with the violations of law at J.H.S. 22 by the principal, the district superintendent, and the chancellor demonstrate that there is need for an independent investigative ombudsman with an independent voice to protect the rights of students. The appointment of the ombudsman should in no way relieve those responsible by law of their primary obligations.

5. The findings of this commission and the charges submitted concerning widespread violations of the law prohibiting corporal punishment and

its disproportionate use against poor and non-white children warrant an immediate investigation by the central board of education.

6. The board of education should establish a city-wide informational service and a monitoring service to protect the rights of students in regard to both corporal punishment and school suspensions.

7. The public school system must provide substantive support for alternatives to the use of corporal punishment and school suspensions so as to increase order in the public schools, develop appropriate methods of discipline, and provide the fullest access to services by children with special needs.

• Such support should include ongoing education of teaching staff including open discussions, institutes, and workshops with the support of the central board of education.

• The lack of knowledge of the laws on the part of teachers, parents, and students who testified before the commission evidenced the importance that they be made known. In order to secure understanding and support, schools should involve teachers, parents, and students in both the development of rules and procedures for their enforcement.

• Community school boards should establish procedures for open communication with students, parents, teachers, and the principal in each school so that problems can be explored openly and measures taken to prevent the festering of grievances.

• The parents association should be encouraged to become a vital and representative group that can work with teachers and students. It should be helpful in the development of constructive methods of discipline and serve as an advocate for special services needed by the students. Compensation to elected officers of the association, when needed, should be made from funds outside the school district to assure independence. No officer of the association should serve as an employee of the school district, or of any school or unit thereof.

8. Effective use of alternative remedies to corporal punishment and school suspensions require:

• Teachers shall know their students, identify their problems, and seek to work directly with the child and with parents where that is appropriate.

• Teachers shall make appropriate referrals to guidance counselors for professional conferences, screening, and recommendations when they cannot resolve learning or behavioral problems.

• Removal from a classroom shall be used only when conduct cannot be controlled and is injurious or threatening to the other students or teacher. Such removal shall be used as a temporary measure and the student shall receive prompt aid from specialists, including the guidance counselor during the period of removal.

• Parents must be notified immediately and parent-teacher conferences must be arranged without delay whenever disciplinary measures are invoked.

• Copies of evaluations and recommendations for disciplinary action for a child shall be sent together with the educational plan for the child to the district superintendent.

9. Effective alternative remedies require the use of specialized services within the school or appropriate referral for professional services outside the school when needed.

• Teachers and parents must be informed in regard to all special services within the school, available through the school system (e.g., Bureau of Child Guidance) and of special services in the community.

• Teachers and parents must be informed of the entitlement of children in need of special education under the New York State provision for $2,500 annually for such schooling. Lists of available schools for this purpose should be kept current by the principal.

• Parents and teachers must be informed in regard to out-patient and residential treatment services available when a full study of the child and family situation warrant a recommendation for such services.

10. When specialized services prove inadequate or unavailable to students with special needs, or when there is evidence of discrimination in access to them, the principal shall report such facts to the superintendent of the district community school board, the chancellor, and to other appropriate city and state agencies for investigation and corrective action.

NOTES

1. "School Board Votes to Discipline Three in Student Paddlings," *New York Times*, 15 June 1974, p. 41.

2. Leonard Buder, "Two at Bronx School Accused of Paddlings," *New York Times*, 20 May 1974, p. 1.

3. Ibid., "Local Officials in Bronx Bar Investigators in Paddlings," *New York Times*, 21 May 1974, p. 1.

4. Ibid., "Two Deans in Paddling Case Removed," *New York Times*, 22 May 1974, p. 1.

5. Ibid., "2 Paddling-Case Deans Back at School," *New York Times*, 24 May 1974, p. 14.

6. Ibid., "City Enters the School-Paddling Inquiry," *New York Times*, 29 May 1974, p. 27.

7. Ibid., "Anker to Issue a Directive Restating Ban on Beating," *New York Times*, 23 May 1974, p. 48.

8. Ibid.

9. Ibid., "Anker Sets Paddling-Inquiry Deadline," *New York Times*, 31 May 1974, p. 65.

10. Irving Anker, Letter to the Editor, *New York Times*, 8 June 1974, p. 30.

11. Leonard Buder, "Citizens' Group Formed to Study School Beatings," *New York Times*, 11 June 1974, p. 45.

12. Ibid.

✓ 13. Ibid., "Anker Confirms Bronx Paddling," *New York Times*, 12 June 1974, p. 49. It was in this report that the president of the District 9 school board first acknowledged that "obviously the two deans were involved."

14. St. Clair Marshall to Chancellor Irving Anker, New York City Board of Education, 17 June 1974.

15. Parents' Association of Community Junior High School 22, Executive Board, "Position Paper Re: Rebuttal and Counter-Charges," 6 June 1974, 4 pp.

16. Inter-Boro Council of Black Women to Kenneth B. Clark, Metropolitan Applied Research Center, 14 June 1974, 2 pp.

17. The Task Force on Corporal Punishment found that "corporal punishment is more common in ghetto and barrio schools," National Education Association, *Report of the Task Force on Corporal Punishment*, Washington, D.C., 1972, p. 13.

18. Black Education Commission, Los Angeles City Schools, "Abolition of Corporal Punishment," (Memorandum), 27 January 1972. Quoted in the National Education Association *Report of the Task Force on Corporal Punishment*, Washington, D.C., 1972, p. 13.

19. See Brief Amicus Curiae by Children's Defense Fund in *Goss* v. *Lopez* in Supreme Court of the U.S., October term 1973, pp. 21–23, 59 and Appendix A. In Columbus, Ohio, when there was a confrontation between white and black students following Black History Week, many black children were suspended from school without a notice or hearing. The suspensions were found to be in violation of due process by the lower federal court, which also ordered that all references to suspensions should be removed from the public school records. *Lopez* v. *Williams*, 372 F. Supp. 1279 So. Dist. Ohio (1973). This case was then on appeal to the Supreme Court.

20. *Lopez* v. *Williams*, 372 F. Supp. 1279 So. Dist. Ohio (1973) pp. 21–23.

21. *West Virginia State Board of Education* v. *Barnette*, 319 U.S. 624, 637, (1943).

22. New York State Commission on the Quality, Cost, and Financing of Elementary and Secondary Education, *Fleischmann Report*, Albany, N.Y.: University of the State of New York, State Education Department, 1972, chap. 9.

23. Such conduct by the deans is all too reminiscent of what has been described as the "really unmistakable kind of satisfaction which some teachers

feel in applying the rattan." Jonathan Kozol, *Death at an Early Age*, Boston: Houghton Mifflin, 1967, pp. 16–17.

✓ 24. Leonard Buder, "Two Deans in Paddling Case Dismissed," *New York Times*, 22 May 1974, p. 1.

25. Peter S. Aron and Martin L. Katz, "Corporal Punishment in the Public Schools, *Murphy* v. *Kerrigan*." *Harvard Civil Rights–Civil Liberties Law Review*, vol. 6, no. 1, 1970, pp 583–594.

26. *Cooper* v. *McJunkin*, 4 Ind., 290–293 (1853).

27. *Tinker* v. *Des Moines Independent Community District*, 393 U.S. 503, 511 (1968).

28. *Ingraham* v. *Wright*, 498 F. 2d 248 (5th Cir. 1974). This decision reviews the constitutional provisions applicable to corporal punishment.

29. These cities include Baltimore, Boston, Chicago, Philadelphia, Pittsburgh, San Francisco, St. Paul, and Washington, D.C.

30. "No corporal punishment shall be inflicted in any of the public schools, nor punishment of any kind tending to cause excessive fear or physical or mental distress." *By-Laws of the Board of Education*, City of New York, section 90, subdivision 15.

31. "Each community board shall have all the powers and duties invested by law . . . but ". . . not inconsistent with the . . . policies established by the city board . . ." New York State *Education Law*, Article 52–A "New York City Community School District System"; section 2590–e "Powers and duties of community boards."

32. "The city board shall have the power and duty to hold public hearings on any matter relating to the educational welfare of the city school district . . . wherever in its judgement the public interest will be served." Ibid., section 2590–g, "Powers and duties of the city board."

33. Board of Education, City of New York, "Special Circular No. 23," 1973–74, October 15, 1973. This circular states that the regulations regarding safety in schools, in keeping with decentralization, place responsibility on community school boards to provide for safety in schools under their jurisdiction (section IB). These regulations establish minimum standards in regard to the "Responsibility of the Principal in Matters of Safety" (section II). The eighth standard set forth requires that "all cases involving assaults on teachers must be reported to the Office of the Counsel (for the Board of Education) by telephone immediately" (section IIH). Under Section III, procedures are set forth for "Reporting Incidents in Schools or on School Property" and section IV provides procedures involving "Injury to a Person—Report of Accidents" including pupils. Section V defines the "Responsibility of the Central Office of School Safety." Such responsibility with regard to schools in the community school districts includes informing, aiding, and advising school community boards in regard to employment of safety personnel, providing training programs, reviewing and approving school safety plans, and providing technical assistance as requested by community boards (section VA2). It further requires the chief administrator for school safety to develop and administer a city-wide information system with regard to school safety. The city administrator is charged with

using such information systems for operational assignments including "to monitor school safety in the community school districts" (section VB1).

34. Ibid., "Special Circular No. 75," 1973–74, 11 February 1974.

35. Ibid., "Special Circular No. 31," 26 October 1973.

36. Ibid., "Special Circular No. 119," 1973–74, 13 June 1974.

37. Ibid.

38. New York State, *Education Law*, Article 7, Commissioner of Education," section 302, "How chosen."

39. Ibid., section 305.2, "General powers and duties."

40. Ibid., section 308, "Other powers."

41. David Silver, Letter to the Editor, *New York Times*, 22 June, 1974, p. 28.

√ 42. Leonard Buder, "Second School in Bronx District Charged with Whipping Pupils," *New York Times*, 22 June 1974, p. 59. "Paddling Inquiry May Be Widened," *New York Times*, 25 June 1974, p. 41. Bert Shanas, "Board Refuses to Fire Paddling Deans," *Daily News*, 25 June 1974, p. 5.

43. Gene I. Maeroff, "Corporal Punishment," *New York Times*, 23 May 1974, p. 48.

44. See note 16 above.

45. Ad Hoc Committee of Concerned Black Educators, "An Open Letter to the Whole Community of the New York Public School System," 17 June 1974, 2 pp.

46. Board of Education, City of New York, *By-Laws*, section 90, subdivision 42. Also, New York State, *Education Law*, article 65, "Compulsory Education and School Census," section 3214-6, "Suspension."

47. American Civil Liberties Union, Brief in *Goss* v. *Lopez*, Supreme Court of the United States, October term 1973, No. 73–896.

48. New York Civil Liberties Union, *Suspension Procedures in the New York City Public Schools: A Report on the Failure to Implement Legal Rights of Students*, New York, February 1971, 21 pp.

49. "Illegal School Suspensions," *New York Times* editorial, 20 February 1971, p. 26.

50. Board of Education, City of New York, "Special Circular on School Suspensions, No. 103," 1969–70, III (5), (6).

√ 51. "Paddling," *New York Times*, 8 September 1974, p. 35.

52. "Deans, like other pupil personnel workers, are required to have state certification in guidance as set forth in 'Special Circular No. 138,' June 19, 1973." Board of Education, City of New York, "Special Circular No. 119," 1973–74, 13 June 1974.

53. John S. Greene, Letter to the Editor, *New York Times*, 19 June 1974, p. 44.

54. National Education Association, *Report of the Task Force on Corporal Punishment*.

55. Ibid., p. 3.

56. Ibid., p. 27.
57. Ibid., p. 7.
58. Ibid.

REFERENCES

Board of Education, City of New York, *Special Education and Pupil Personnel Services*. Office of Educational Information, Board of Education, 110 Livingston Street, Brooklyn, N.Y. 11201. 1971.

Harrison, Phyllis Anne. *Getting It Together: A Psychology Book for Today's Problems*. New York: Globe Book Company, 175 Fifth Avenue, New York, N.Y. 10010. 1973. A teachers guide is available.

Harrison-Ross, Phyllis, and Wyden, Barbara. *The Black Child—A Parent's Guide*. New York: Peter H. Wyden, 750 Third Avenue, New York, N.Y. 10017. 1973.

Kozol, Jonathan. *Death at an Early Age*. Boston: Houghton Mifflin, 1967.

Levine, Alan H., with Eve Cary and Diane Divoky. *The Rights of Students: The Basic ACLU Guide to a Student's Rights*. Avon Books, 250 West 55 Street, New York, N.Y. 10019. 1973.

Loe, Roy. "IS 201." The University of the State of New York, State Education Department, Albany, N.Y. 12224. A film made at IS 201 over a period of one year by an anthropological photographer who was at the Division of Family Studies, Bronx State Hospital, Albert Einstein College of Medicine. A limited number of copies is available at the archives of the Fleischmann Commission.

National Education Association, *Report of the Task Force on Corporal Punishment*. National Education Association, 1201 Sixteenth Street, N.W., Washington, D.C. 20036. 1972.

New York State Commission on Quality, Cost and Financing of Elementary and Secondary Education. *Fleischmann Report*. The University of the State of New York, State Education Department, Albany, N.Y. 12224. 1972.

✓ Reitman, Alan, Fellman, Judith, and Ladd, Edward T. *Corporal Punishment in the Public Schools: The Use Of Force in Controlling Student Behavior*. American Civil Liberties Union, 22 East 40 Street, New York, N.Y. 10016. 1972.

✓ Roberts, Francis J. *Taking a Beating: Some Observations on Corporal Punishment*. Bank Street College of Education, 610 West 112 Street, New York, N.Y. 10025. 1974.

Special Action Office for Drug Abuse Prevention. *Coming Home: A Thoughtbook for People*. Executive Office of the President, Special Action Office for Drug Abuse, Washington, D.C. 20506. 1973.

Special Circulars and Directives may be obtained by writing to the Office of Education Information, Board of Education, 110 Livingston Street, Brooklyn, N.Y. 11201.

Student Rights Project of NYCLU. *Student Rights Handbook for New York City*. New York Civil Liberties Union, 84 Fifth Avenue, New York, N.Y. 10011.

————. *Suspension Procedures in the New York City Public Schools: A Report on the Failure to Implement Legal Rights of Students*. New York Civil Liberties Union, 84 Fifth Avenue, New York, N.Y. 10011. 1971.

16

The Paddle in the School:
Tool or Weapon–
The Case of Pittsburgh Public Schools

Carolyn Schumacher

•

On October 21, 1975, the Pittsburgh Board of Education had before it a proposal from a board subcommittee to reinstitute corporal punishment in the Pittsburgh public schools, where a total ban had been in effect since 1973. The Pittsburgh school board frequently votes on corporal punishment. While other school districts have reviewed paddling from time to time in the past hundred years, Pittsburgh has reviewed it six times in the past eight years. By coincidence, the Supreme Court had just ruled on a corporal punishment case earlier that same month. The only effect of that decision on the Pittsburgh schools was to delay the board vote until November when they decided to keep the ban.

I first saw a school paddle when I taught in a Pittsburgh school. I was asked to be a witness to a beating. To my surprise the teacher swung with all of her might at a small fourth grade boy whom I knew and whom I had never known to be in any trouble. He braced himself against a heavy desk so he would not fall flat on his face when she slammed him five times with the standard thirty-six-inch paddle. I don't know what the boy had done. The teacher straightened up as she finished, puffing and winded from the exertion, and explained authoritatively that this was an approved procedure, just so you had a witness. She was wrong of course: our board of education rule then stated that this procedure was supposed to be done in the office by the principal or vice principal, or by the teacher in the presence of the principal or vice principal, or by the teacher in the presence of the principal. Its use by teachers in the classroom had long been forbidden. Neither I nor anyone else in that school seemed to know the exact rule, but in spirit the board regulation had said that hitting was right if it was done right, so the teacher wasn't too far off base.

First published in *Pitt*, Vol. 31, no. 3, Feb. 1977.

Corporal punishment was partially abolished in Pittsburgh early in 1970 in response to a movement that was started by a citizens' committee formed to investigate corporal punishment in the city schools. It was a problem that had never been discussed here publicly before 1967. That year the Public Affairs Committee of the Unitarian Church called a meeting on "Corporal Punishment in the Schools," just to see if there was any interest in the subject. About fifty parents from all over the city came to express their anger and frustration because their children were being slapped, pushed, and poked by teachers, and constantly threatened with a paddle. Sometimes principals carried a paddle when they patrolled the halls; frequently the teachers kept a paddle handy in their desks. The parents who came to the meeting felt they had been unfortunate in their choice of schools. It was a shock to all of us to learn that almost every school in the city was using physical pain as punishment.

The ad hoc Committee for the Abolition of Corporal Punishment in the Schools was formed at that first meeting at the Unitarian Church in April 1967. Parents, psychologists, social workers, teachers, lawyers, and other professionals joined us in the investigation of corporal punishment in Pittsburgh schools, and in other city schools as well. Petitions were passed, a list of cases was compiled, and a report with recommendations was prepared to present to the board of education. Abolition in the Pittsburgh public schools was our goal, which was accomplished at least temporarily when the Pittsburgh Board of Education banned all corporal punishment in the schools in the fall of 1973.

We gathered ample evidence that corporal punishment was widely used and frequently abused, and prepared a strong case to present to the board. We assumed that they would gratefully recognize our work as a service to the community. After pointing out the alarming situation (of which they must have been unaware), we expected the board to abolish corporal punishment immediately. We estimated that the whole problem would be solved in three or four months. Almost ten years later we are still returning to the board of education almost every two years to support the ban on corporal punishment against the repeated efforts, mainly from the Pittsburgh Federation of Teachers, to return the paddle to the classroom.

We did not understand the complexity of the issue until we started to talk to our friends and neighbors to get signatures on petitions. Some people we spoke to were convinced that discipline was synonymous with punishment, and the paddle was the symbol of adult authority; without physical punishment there would be no discipline. Some people, usually native Pittsburghers, took corporal punishment for granted and never questioned the practice; those who had moved here from areas where corporal punishment had not been used were incredulous. We spent an average of half an hour per signature trying to convince people not only that corporal punishment was widely used, but that the punitive atmosphere that pervaded the schools was being sustained by the paddle. That atmosphere could never change until teachers and principals stopped beating the children.

The ad hoc committee met for the first time with the board of education in a private session in July 1967. (School board open hearings did not exist yet.) We were given what amounted to an audience, where we gave a ten-minute presentation outlining our findings: the excessive use of corporal punishment, the danger of psychological and physical damage to children, and the legal fiction of the teacher as parent. After a few questions we were coolly dismissed. The board seemed unmoved, uninterested. In the days before sunshine laws and public hearings, people who came to the board with suggestions were treated like intruders. We were puzzled by our reception, but undaunted.

Who Gets Beaten?

We perceived a certain amount of reluctance on the part of the school administrators to deal with the issue, but we continued to press until Superintendent Sidney P. Marland finally created a staff committee on discipline to conduct a survey of the teachers and principals on the subject. The survey, released in spring 1968, revealed that 80 percent of the teachers in grades one through four were paddling children right in the classrooms at least several times a year, contrary to clearly stated board rules. Most of the paddling by the teachers was done in large schools receiving Title I funds: that is, in the poor neighborhoods and the ghetto neighborhoods. In other words, the small children, the poor children, and probably the black children received the most beatings. It should be added here that, although it was not part of this survey, boys were generally thought to be more likely to be beaten than girls.

More than 50 percent of the teachers favored liberalizing the board rule to permit more freedom to hit the students right in the classroom, but 66 percent favored inservice training in effective alternatives to paddling. Many teachers have been afraid to lose the paddle, but they usually have been willing to look for alternatives.

The board was able to gather the impersonal, statistical evidence to show the scope of the problem. Our committee gathered documented cases to show how corporal punishment was actually used on a practical level. One of the cases we submitted to the board of education involved a boy who was in the third grade at a school that had a reputation for being one of the "best" in town. The boy came home with stripes on his back from a paddling administered by the principal for the boy's refusing to say why he did not have his homework. He had been beaten once before in the previous year, and the parents had informed the school principal that they

were eager to cooperate with the school to help the boy improve his performance, but they did not want him to be beaten.

In the case affirmed by the Supreme Court in October 1975 (*Baker* v.
Owen), it was declared constitutional for the teacher to hit the plaintiff
(Russell Carl Baker), even over the mother's previously expressed objections. In that case the boy had been paddled for throwing a kick-ball at a
time other than a designated play period. By this standard the teacher is not
just *in loco parentis* (in place of the parent), but *above* the parent. A federal ruling establishes a minimum standard, however, and does not prevent
states from enforcing higher standards. The Commonwealth of Pennsylvania
does maintain a higher standard. The new Pennsylvania School Code prohibits the use of corporal punishment on a child in any public school in the
state if the child's parents have notified the school authorities that they
prohibit such discipline for their child.

Another case submitted by our committee in our first report involved
a boy who was punished for making a paper airplane. He was given a choice
of eating the airplane or getting paddled; after choosing to eat the airplane
he was paddled anyway. I should add that the boy in this case was a foreign visitor. He had a withered hand and he did not have complete command of our language. His father, a visiting scientist, had recently been
hospitalized because of a serious automobile accident. The superintendent,
in a letter to the attorney who protested this treatment of the boy, said that
the teacher had placed the airplane in the boy's mouth, but he had not been
asked to eat it. The superintendent went on to say that he had "mixed feelings" about spanking children in school, but that "an accustomed practice
. . . cannot be quickly set aside."

Other cases were included in our report of abuse. One junior high
school vice principal routinely paddled all of the five or six children sent to
him in the course of each day. (As he told us, that was his job, that was
what the teachers expected him to do when they sent children in for punishment.) A social worker in another school testified that he was forced to
do his paper work at home rather than listen to the noise emanating from
the adjacent office of the principal, where a constant stream of children
came in to be paddled. The theory that corporal punishment might be nice
to have as a last resort is impossible to maintain, because in practice it becomes the line of least resistance.

The Debate Continues: Abolition and More Abolition

In June 1968 the Pittsburgh Board of Education took their first vote
on corporal punishment. It was not long after they had released their
teacher-survey showing how much corporal punishment was used in the

Pittsburgh schools. They announced that corporal punishment was used even more than we had led them to believe, and that abolition was a long-range goal. The first step was a two-year trial ban on corporal punishment in grades one through three and in kindergarten, beginning in September 1968. We saw this as progress. Since corporal punishment was most heavily used in the lower grades, we agreed that this was a good place to start. Superintendent Marland was authorized to implement this reform with in-service training and to provide administrative support and encouragement to ensure the success of the experiment.

At the end of two years, in 1970, a complete review of corporal punishment was conducted by a subcommittee chaired by board member Frank Beal. The ad hoc committee resumed the campaign of public testimony and private conferences with the board of education. As the initial two-year trial period drew to a close in 1970, the Pittsburgh Federation of Teachers became a powerful advocate for reinstating corporal punishment. The president of the PFT began to speak in favor of corporal punishment at open hearings, and it was a bargaining issue in all subsequent PFT contract negotiations. It was unfortunate that they did not concentrate more heavily on alternatives to corporal punishment, because that was the area that was most neglected after corporal punishment was abolished. No real system-wide measures have been instituted by the central staff to help teachers develop new classroom management techniques, and to relieve the frustrations that were in many ways built into the school system.

At their July 21, 1970, meeting the board of education had before them a proposal to phase out corporal punishment in three steps. Beginning in fall 1970, corporal punishment would be forbidden in kindergarten through the fourth grade; the ban would be extended upward each year by one grade until fall 1973, when all remaining grades would be included.

The majority of the board seemed to be swayed by the argument, eloquently expressed by then–board president Robert Kibbee, that the increase in violence in this country is a threat to our way of life, and that the use of physical punishment in the schools serves to teach children that violence is a solution to problems. After an hour and a half of heated public debate, some members still felt that the teachers should be able to hit the children if they wanted to, but the majority of the board voted to accept the subcommittee proposal to phase out corporal punishment.

In a sense we considered this a great victory. Up to that point it may have been the most successful citizen effort to change a school policy in Pittsburgh. On the other hand, we could not help feeling that it was cowardly to condemn a practice and then allow it to go on just a little longer for the benefit of those who were addicted to it, at the expense of the children who would suffer from it. A ten-year-old child, when she heard that corporal punishment was to be phased out by grade level, suggested that it might have been just as reasonable to phase it out alphabetically—all those whose names began with "A" through "F" in the first year. . . .

Six months later, on January 1, 1971, the board of education signed a contract with the Pittsburgh Federation of Teachers that included a discipline clause requiring the board to "review and evaluate its existing policy relating to corporal punishment, including its action of July 21, 1970 [the plan to phase it out]." After four years of work we went through the whole campaign all over again. We gathered new evidence and presented testimony with the help of many other civic and professional groups who testified. We were again successful. The initial effort of the ad hoc group called attention to corporal punishment, but other organizations were as active in the campaign in subsequent years. Women in the Urban Crisis, the American Civil Liberties Union, the Pittsburgh Psychological Association, the National Organization for Women, the National Association for the Advancement of Colored People, and many other organizations and individuals did the real work in the campaign. Without community support the board would not have given serious consideration to the issue. This time the board reviewed corporal punishment, but it came up as an information item rather than an action item and they did not take a formal vote.

In April 1973 the board of education did vote on the issue of corporal punishment, again in compliance with a Pittsburgh Federation of Teachers contract agreement, and again they voted, for the third time, to maintain the ban. In 1975 a new subcommittee of the board reviewed discipline in the schools and recommended that corporal punishment be reinstated. This time the recommendation was to allow principals to hit only those children whose parents would specify in writing that they would permit the school personnel to use corporal punishment on their children. Each time a review has come up, the ad hoc Committee for the Abolition of Corporal Punishment has been supported by the community with letters and testimony, and each time there have been more community and professional organizations added to the list of supporters. At a board hearing in November 1975, twenty-five parents, professionals, and citizens representing community organizations testified against the use of corporal punishment. The PFT president and three parents testified on the side of corporal punishment. It was a close, eight-to-seven vote against lifting the ban. The November 1975 vote was the fourth one on this issue. It had been reviewed five times, but it had actually come to a vote only four times since 1968.

Almost as soon as the fourth vote was taken, the fifth vote was already being planned by the five people who formed the solid pro–corporal punishment block on the board.

In January 1976 the PFT ended the longest teacher's strike in Pittsburgh history. Money was the most important factor, but class size, reading specialists, job security, and discipline were also considered important. Included in the union demands was the provision that the board reinstate corporal punishment. The board agreed, as part of the contract settlement, to vote on corporal punishment again by March 1976.

They went through the whole review process again, wrote a new proposal on corporal punishment procedures, and held an open hearing on the issue. The hearing drew about twenty-five speakers, with all but five opposing corporal punishment. The board devoted another few hours to debating the issue and then voted to retain the ban for the fifth time in eight years—a world record. The reinstatement proposal drew more opposition this time, for a nine-to-six vote, because it stipulated that corporal punishment be permitted for all students unless the parent sent in an objection form. One board member suggested that we call the objectors "P.O.s" (paddling objectors), like C.O.s (conscientious objectors).

Who Supports Corporal Punishment?

Some parents have supported corporal punishment in the past on the grounds that the paddle is necessary to beat *other* children so that *their* children would not be prevented from getting an education. This position is usually held by parents who are certain that their own child behaves well enough to avoid being affected. The Bill of Rights was created because it was well known that we can only be sure of protecting our own rights by protecting the rights of all. It is naive to believe that only the "deserving" children will be beaten. In our interviews with principals we found that all agreed that it was usually the same children who were beaten over and over. The principals were not having a positive effect on the children who were being beaten (else why would they need repeated beatings?): they were using a few children as examples to frighten the other children.

All children suffer in a punitive atmosphere. Those who never get beaten may suffer more from the pain of anxiety than those who suffer from the physical pain. The more problems a child has in school and out of school, the more likely he or she is to be singled out for beatings; the more timid the child the less likely he or she is to be struck, but the more likely he or she is to suffer from fear. Teachers never really know the ultimate effect of striking a child because children are passed from teacher to teacher over many years and damage is difficult to assess.

It is both unfortunate and puzzling that some parents ask the teacher to beat their own children. In most cases they are responsible, loving parents who truly believe that their children will benefit by beatings. William

Grier and Rice Cobbs deal with this very problem in *Black Rage*. They are speaking about black parents, but in this discussion, as in many others in their book, the argument applies to any parents.

> The black parent approaches the teacher with the great respect due a person of learning. The soaring expectations which are an important part of the parent's feelings find substance in the person of the teacher. Here is the person who can do for this precious child all the wonderful things a loving parent cannot. The child is admonished to obey the teacher as he would his parents and the teacher is urged to exercise parental prerogatives, including beating. In this the parent yields up his final unique responsibility, the protection of his child against another's aggression. The child is placed in the teacher's hands to do with as she [*sic*] sees fit, with the sole requirement that she teach him. The meaning of this gift is not lost on the teacher, who is alternately touched by the parent's trust and staggered by the responsibility, for the teacher knows best of all that much has gone on before she gets the child and knows that, even as the parent urges her not to spare the rod, that same parent is telling volumes about the life that child has led up to this moment. The parent tells of a child both beloved and beaten, of a child taught to look for pain from even those who cherish him most, of a child who has come to feel that beatings are right and proper for him, and of a child whose view of the world, however gently it persuades him to act toward others, decrees for him that he is to be driven by the infliction of pain.
>
> Pity that child.[1]

Like the southern slaveholders before the Civil War who said slavery shouldn't be abolished, just the abuses of slavery, the Pittsburgh Federation of Teachers supports the position that corporal punishment shouldn't be abolished, just the abuses. The president of the Pittsburgh Federation of Teachers said, "Until somebody comes up with an alternative, we'll support it. It's a quick way to show disapproval—like the city giving me a ticket when I park illegally."[2] (Actually, it would be more like permitting policemen to punch him in the nose for illegal parking.)

A black principal charged that the Committee for the Abolition of Corporal Punishment was conspiring to destroy the education of black children. He believed that if he could not hit the children in his school he would have to expel them, and then they would not be in school getting an education. Of all the problems in education that we face today, the most serious one may be the poverty of ideas emanating from the people who are running our public schools. Corporal punishment doesn't work: It does not have a long-lasting effect on behavior, although it creates all kinds of side-effects. The teacher, acting as a model, teaches that hitting is a solution to problems and that people can hit if they are big enough and in a position of power. Teachers discount systematic evidence of the ineffectiveness of corporal punishment in the literature. Such evidence is often scorned as impractical and theoretical. They ignore their own practical evidence that corporal punishment does not have the desired effect on discipline in a school. There is no evidence that discipline is better when corporal punishment is used, and in many places the schools with the most corporal punishment have had the worst discipline.

Many kinds of data have been produced to show how much corporal punishment has been used, and the ineffectiveness of physical pain for punishment.[3] I would argue simply that the use of pain for punishment is anachronistic. It is inconsistent with modern concepts of individual human rights.

The answer must lie with the teacher-training colleges and the university schools of education. Many training programs may deal directly and effectively with discipline, but most teachers, especially those trained in isolated, rural schools, are totally unprepared for the problems they encounter in the city, where the majority must go to find jobs. For example, one young teacher just out of a rural Pennsylvania teachers' college challenged me to suggest what she could do to disobedient children if she could not hit them. She was just out of school; what had she been taught about discipline techniques? She learned in the teachers' college that "if you are teaching in a system that permits corporal punishment you can hit them, and if corporal punishment is not permitted you cannot hit them." That was the sum of her preparation for the myriad problems in the modern school. She is not alone in her need. Clearly, schools of education should be devoting a major portion of the program to teach effective techniques for dealing with children in groups. Group dynamics and classroom management are the weakest areas in the school because they are the weakest areas in the training program. There is yet much to be learned about classroom management, but there are many humane techniques available that could be included in training programs.

Conclusion

Children face as many as one hundred teachers of varying ability and temperament during their twelve years in school. The shortness and changeability of the contact between child and teacher break down the historic meaning of the teacher as parent. The use of corporal punishment is a special kind of deprivation for children as distinct from adults, because its use as an official policy is not extended to any other public bureaucracy with compulsory subjects.

Until the 1975 Supreme Court decision, the signal from the High Court had been to increase the rights of juveniles as persons under the Constitution. In *Tinker* v. *Des Moines Independent School District*, the United

States Supreme Court said that "school officials do not possess absolute authority over their students. Students in school as well as out of school are 'persons' under our Constitution. . . ."[4]

In an earlier decision the Court, in a classic statement on the responsibilities of the school to teach students the meaning of the Bill of Rights by example, said that the board of education has ". . . important, delicate, and highly discretionary functions, but none that they may not perform within the limits of the Bill of Rights. That they are educating the young for citizenship is reason for scrupulous protection of Constitutional freedoms of the individual, if we are not to strangle the free mind at its source and teach youth to discount important principles of our government as mere platitudes."[5]

Corporal punishment may come before the Court again. Standards change and courts change. In another era the Supreme Court ruled that separate but equal facilities did not violate the Fourteenth Amendment right of blacks to equal protection under the law. Fifty-eight years later, in 1954, that decision was reversed in *Brown* v. *The Board of Education*, after half a century of school segregation, based on the doctrine of separate but equal, had deprived black children of equal education. In the *Brown* case Chief Justice Earl Warren concentrated on the social and psychological evidence that segregation imposed a feeling of inferiority on Negro children. The Supreme Court has yet to consider the psychological effects of corporal punishment on children.

In the long run this problem may be ended by the professionals themselves. The North Carolina decision, affirmed by the Supreme Court, stated that "school officials are free to employ corporal punishment for disciplinary purposes until in the exercise of their own professional judgment, or in response to concerted pressure from opposing parents, they decide that its harm outweighs its utility."[6]

A few years ago I carried an old school paddle across campus to the University Book Store, where it was to be used to decorate a display of books on violence. I was diffident about being seen with a paddle, so it was inevitable that I should meet most of my friends and acquaintances on the way. Professors, deans, students, and even the president of the board of education greeted me without seeming to notice the paddle. Five high school boys sitting on a park bench spied it immediately. "Hey, Miss," shouted one of the boys, "are you a teacher?"

NOTES

1. William Grier and Rice Cobbs, *Black Rage* (New York: Basic Books, 1968), pp. 137–138.

2. *The Wall Street Journal,* June 16, 1970, p. 1.

3. See "Report of the Task Force on Corporal Punishment," National Education Association, 1201 Sixteenth St., N.W., Washington, D.C. 20036.

4. *Tinker* v. *Des Moines Independent Community School District,* 393 U.S. 503, 511 (1969).

5. *West Virginia State Board of Education* v. *Barnette,* 319 U.S. 624 (1943).

6. *Baker* v. *Owen,* 395 F.Supp. 294 (1975).

17

Discipline in Soviet Schools:
The Observations of an American
Teaching in the USSR

Kenneth Cassie

●

> *Discipline is a product of the sum total of the educative*
> *efforts, including the teaching process, the process of*
> *political education, the process of character shaping, the*
> *process of collision—of facing and settling conflicts in*
> *the collective, the process of friendship and trust, and the*
> *whole educational process in its entirety.*
>   A. S. Makarenko (1965, p. 56)

Three years ago, as a guest of the Soviet Ministry of Education, I taught in two Soviet schools—Special School No. 157 in Leningrad, and Experimental School No. 4 in Moscow. My assignment in each school lasted six weeks. Both schools are ten-year schools (*desyatiletki*) and are attended by students from age seven to sixteen. The very titles of these schools suggest that they are not what the Russians sometimes call "schools for the masses" (*massovye shkoly*).

These special schools differ from the schools for the masses, or ordinary schools, in two ways. Specifically, they provide a nine-year course in English. Other special schools specialize in German, Spanish, Japanese, and so forth. In addition, children whom I asked, although I took no formal census, had parents who were professionals or white collar workers.

Since my return to America a paradox has disturbed me. In our society, where we claim respect for the individual and his rights, only four states fully outlaw corporal punishment. Yet in the Soviet Union, a nation scored for its brutal penal system and severe limitations on what we in the West consider essential civil rights, corporal punishment is illegal and is frowned upon in the homes and schools.

Closer examination may expose the proscribing of corporal punishment in Soviet schools as an aberration in a sea of disregard for the individual. Or it may reveal the Soviet system of discipline as harmoniously woven into larger social patterns. In either case value judgments of Soviet social ideals will be avoided.

My purpose here will be to outline Soviet theory, methods, and attitudes regarding school discipline, supported by my personal experiences and those of other first-hand observers. From the resultant composite image some inferences might be drawn that may aid in suggesting directions a study of discipline and corporal punishment in America could take.

I first had to question the degree to which my own observations represent conditions in Soviet schools at large. Certainly a Soviet educator visiting an American inner-city school might easily make generalizations about school discipline that would not apply to a school in an affluent suburb.

To illustrate by a reversed situation, an American teacher visiting Soviet schools made the following observation: ". . . as a corrective disciplinary measure in one school, an unruly student was not permitted to wear the uniform as a punishment and was so disgraced in the eyes of his classmates that day" (Downey, 1972, p. 30). The statement is valid when applied to younger children. But from my observations of fifteen- and sixteen-year-old students of the ninth and tenth forms, they made constant efforts to add unique touches to their uniforms. A few avoided wearing them, using the standard ploy that the uniforms were being laundered. Girls wore various Peter Pan collars, ribbons, colorful sweaters. Some wore drastically shortened skirts. Boys were less demonstrative, although now and then a pair of Levis would be substituted for the standard gray pants. In two situations I saw students reprimanded for too conspicuously modifying their uniforms. In short, spurred by Ms. Downey's observation, the reader could make an unwarranted generalization about the role of the uniform as an implement of negative reinforcement.

While granting that generalization is the thin ice of observation, the visitor to a Soviet school is on somewhat firmer footing than his Soviet counterpart. First, the Soviet system of education is centralized, from philosophy to aims, curriculum, and even textbooks. Second, the teacher-student relation is standardized and far more ritualized than in an American school. Third, the role of the student in the disciplinary structure has been stable for over forty years. Since 1917 two basic changes have occurred (Nettl, 1967, p. 112). During the twenties, "the traditional and disciplinarian relationship between teachers and students gave way to new forms of collaboration; 'the teacher must be an organizer, an assistant, an instructor, and above all an older comrade, but not a superior officer.'" Then in the early thirties, under Stalin, an essentially traditional discirplinary format was instituted. This shift corresponded chronologically to the social-political cataclysms of collectivization, begun in 1929, and to the great purges, begun in 1932. All three changes reflected Stalin's desire to exert tight control over the Soviet citizenry. Since that time the teacher-student relationship has been stable. For these reasons I suggest that from careful observations judicious generalizations can be made.

Inferences drawn from limited observations are even more hazardous than generalizations with regard to the Soviet Union. To illustrate, several years ago I served with the United States Information Agency in the Soviet Union. Over a six-month period I spoke with literally thousands of Soviet citizens. Occasionally I would be asked whether slums exist in America. Upon hearing the affirmative reply, the Soviet would say, "Just as I thought. Thank you." After several of these concise conversations I began to realize that given the Soviet's point of reference my well-meaning yes was actually a distortion. So I would reply in the following way: "Would you consider the houses on N. Street (dilapidated log structures with open wells in front) to be slums?" Upon receiving the invariably negative reply, I would say, "Then on that basis we have no slums." Having approached a better common understanding of what a slum is or is not, I could better give the questioner an accurate idea of the slum problem in our country.

By the same token, to conclude that because the Soviets do not employ corporal punishment or that Soviet schoolchildren are polite their system of discipline is *in toto* better than ours leads nowhere. The American observer should seek to understand the context in which Soviet school discipline functions. First, Soviet education should be viewed in terms of the historical imperatives laid upon it. Second, the role of education in the highly centralized Soviet society should be considered. The concept of a single, unchallenged power base and its ideological control over all facets of life is especially difficult for an American to grasp. Third, the unique relationship of the individual to the group in Soviet schools as it affects positive and negative reinforcements must be understood.

Historically, Soviet education was charged with the task of (1) conquering an 85 percent illiteracy rate, (2) preparing people for specialized roles in the rapidly burgeoning industrial economy, and most uniquely, (3) to create "Soviet man"—the scientifically developed human product and perpetrator of socialism. He is the instrument through which, with the guidance of the Communist party, the most advanced society in the world will be led to communism.

The weight of this responsibility is felt in the expectations and demands placed upon student behavior. As the future Soviet man, he faces the urgent

and monumental task of building a new society. In this context misbehavior cannot be seen as an individual or isolated problem.

The ideological implications with which misbehavior is fraught echoes
the attitude of the Communist party toward each member.

> In Bolshevik theory one cannot be a passive doubter and merely go away
> quietly into political oblivion and simply sit, having lost one's faith. . . .
> This belief provides the rationale of the relentlessness with which the Soviet
> Union persecutes any Party member who appears to have faltered, devi-
> ated, or doubted in the slightest degree. This is not to be compared with the
> attitude of the Spanish Inquisition, which tortured the erring soul for that
> individual soul's sake to save it from Hell, for the individual is not regarded
> as valuable in the Soviet system. . . . So, by Bolshevik doctrine, the back-
> slider cannot be let alone, because such a one will not merely backslide into
> harmless activity but will become transformed almost instantaneously into
> an active enemy. (Mead, 1951, p. 23)

Revolutionary thought carries with it the following indispensable axiom—
if you are not actively and wholeheartedly with us, then you are our enemy.
The enemy is thus readily visible. The choice is clearly drawn between the
revolutionary cause, which is good, and everything else, which is evil. The
perimeters of acceptable behavior are clear and narrow.

The concept of morally charged and carefully channeled behavior
filters into the schools. When asked whether all children opt to join the
Pioneers (the youth organization which serves as the stepping stone for
entry to the Komsomol or Communist Youth), a teacher replied:

> It is not an issue. The Pioneers and the Soviet children believe in peace,
> truth and friendship, so why should there be any doubts? It is like choosing
> between good and evil. There is no question as to which is better and
> should be chosen. (Downey, 1972, p. 30)

We would find it quaint to hear a teacher urging our children to join the
Boy or Girl Scouts on the strength of this reasoning. The point emerges that
a child's behavior is a crucial social, political, and moral issue rising from
the historical imperative of his building a new society and in so doing being
actively on the good side.

The Soviet schools have selected a specific approach to guide the child
in making the right choice of behavior:

> Upbringing must develop in the child the qualities of personality which,
> combined, form the moral countenance of a future for communism: ideo-
> logical purposefulness, strong convictions, patriotism, sense of duty, cour-
> age, generosity combined with the care of property, modesty, neatness,

politeness, and sensitivity to the needs of others. Obedience is seen as the first step toward developing a disciplined will. Anxiety related to performance of duty is viewed as a virtue. Qualities are regarded as virtues if they are socially oriented; they are undeserving of approval when used to further purely personal interests. (Calas, 1951, p. 108)

Key words are obedience and anxiety, suggesting that the student is expected to fill a designated role. Guilt and shame are the results of failure. Obedience is directed both to the teacher and to the "collective":

> From an early age a child should be trained to value highly a feeling of responsibility to the collective and in upholding [sic] the honor of the group (his class or Pioneer brigade). The child should be trained to honor highly the approval of the collective and to fear its disapproval. (Calas, 1951, p. 108)

Self-image is built into the child through his contribution to the group and its subsequent recognition and approval:

> Children learn discipline by what is psychologically called "love withdrawal." The child is threatened with loss of acceptance, and guilt feelings are engendered for wrongdoing with the effect that the youngster acquires a set of ethics that guide his behavior. (Rumstein, 1959, p. 2)

Performance for the Soviet student carries implications that extend far beyond teacher or group approval: "Children reported that their 'labor obligations' consisted of studying hard; for to be a good student was a sacred duty for their country" (Rumstein, 1959, p. 3). By contrast, teaching in American schools has shown me that the child needs recognition of his personal worth as a thing apart from his academic performance. Occasionally, such recognition is a prerequisite to academic achievement. But in the Soviet anthropology of the child, he is identified and rewarded for his performance in a social and even national context.

Within the Soviet anthropology of the child, individualism is not only irrelevant, it is the enemy. One rule of the Komsomol states that every Komsomol member is obliged to fulfill irreproachably the decisions of the Party. In reporting on his experiences at a Soviet boarding school, a former student said:

> . . . . the invasion of privacy was complete—every thought and act of each student was the active interest of everyone else and especially of fellow brigade members. It stressed that privacy or egocentrism as it was called, was a vicious transgression of Communist morality; whereas "collectivism," or the total submersion of individuality and the repudiation of private thought, was the ideal. (Rumstein, 1959, p. 1)

Soviet children are expected to behave perfectly in school, for which they receive a behavior grade of "5." Should the grade for behavior slip to a "4," the student may be placed on probation. Awards given to graduating students are based on both academic performance and behavior.

A member of the Komsomol told me that the student is expected to be "self-standing but not independent." He must strive to seek rewards within the group's concept of achievement. He must be an active contributor to the social collective; and he internalizes its successes or failures. He is expected to display enthusiasm and motivation along with power, self-discipline, and a singularity of purpose. The student's commitment to a collective, be it to his class, youth group, or to his "homeland," must be both of the body and of the mind.

To inculcate this type of group commitment, formidable pressure is brought to bear on the child through a harmonized effort of politically oriented groups. Their desire as expressed in the Eleventh Komsomol Congress through the official organ of the Komsomol (*Komsol'skaya pravda*) is that "millions of Soviet boys and girls carry in their hearts the images of the great creators of our party and State" (March 31, 1949, p. 3). This desire is supported by school and family: "Now the school and the family are joined in one wish: to nurture in us the traits of real Soviet man, to make us educated persons for our people, for our mother country" (Stories by graduates of Moscow, 1947, p. 8). The price paid for refusing to fulfill the role requirements assigned by these pressure groups is a diffuse sense of guilt, unworthiness, and shame. Two factors make these feelings difficult to escape: the absence of alternative socially acceptable roles, and the burden placed on the child of balancing repressive behavior—obedience, punctuality, neatness, and the clearly defined rituals associated with them in Soviet schools on the one hand, with spontaneous behavior—self-confidence, enthusiasm, and optimism on the other.

My awareness of the historical imperatives, centralized ideology and power, and the anthropology of the student armed me with certain rather generalized preconceptions when I went to teach in the Soviet Union. I expected that the human interaction of teacher and student would be kept at a rigid minimum, that discipline would be swift and harsh, and that the student would be an automaton.

Certain surprises awaited me. I was to learn that simplistic "factual" answers to questions in which the United States and the Soviet Union are compared are inadequate and sometimes misleading. This was especially true concerning the teacher-student relationship and the discipline in Soviet schools.

Although I don't consider myself educationally hardened from my fifteen years of high school teaching, I was quite curious about how order is in fact maintained in my Soviet school. I saw no equivalent vice-principal in charge of discipline, no detention system. In fact substitute teachers are not even called in except for extended absences. One day I dropped into a class, and seeing no teacher present, asked the students where she was. A student replied that Olga Ivanovna was not in school. He explained that the students have the option of sitting in their class or going to another.

With none of our usual paraphernalia of order and punishment in evidence, I was sorely tempted in the beginning to ask one of the teachers, "How do you keep order? How do you punish the bad kids?" I did not ask because I feared that my questions would reveal more about our schools than the answer would about Soviet schools. I recalled a Russian once asking me if we Americans carry internal passports. When informed that we do not, he asked in dismay, "How are the police going to know where you are?"

My first school principal, Ludmila Petrovna, told me that correct discipline should lead to positive self-discipline. Retribution is destructive. All forms of abuse, even of the verbal kind, must be constrained and in no way serve as a catharsis for the adult's feelings. A child's misbehavior occurs when he loses his self-control. The teacher must set a behavioral model of self-control, "not by punishment but by example." If either the teacher or the child is too overwrought to be rational, then the teacher should wait for the right moment to approach the problem. Repeated misdeeds by the child should be a sign to the teacher that he/she should examine his/her own treatment of the problem and the ways in which he/she may have been inadequate to the task.

The outward signs—the rituals of teacher-student relationships—suggest a more archetypal and less introspective teacher. Certainly the rituals are strikingly apparent. I came to appreciate, however, that to evaluate the dynamics of discipline by students' rising when the teacher enters the class, standing when speaking, younger students lowering their heads when I pass, keeping their elbows on the desks when raising their hands, and wearing uniforms would be simplistic. A great deal of humanity and positive motivation is possible for a concerned teacher even within the rigorous program of building "Soviet man."

But all too easily within this program the blade of ostracism from the group can be bared. Short of this, shame and humiliation in the form of public disapprobation lay in wait for the student.

School behavior can affect the student's standing in two types of "collective": the elite or special school which he attends and the political youth group to which he belongs. The student passes through three politically oriented groups during his school career: the Oktyabryata, or Children of the Revolution, in which the youngsters are considered the symbolic grandchildren of Lenin, the Pioneers, to which the Oktyabryata graduate in the third grade, and the Komsomols, which only certain children may join at age fourteen at the recommendation of their teachers. The following recollection by an American student attending a Soviet school reveals the leverage expulsion from any of these groups may have:

> One day during recess my friends Maxim was caught hitting Boris, though Boris had hit him first. The teacher came over to Maxim and grabbed him by the collar. She told him to stand against the wall until recess was over. When . . . everyone else was in their classrooms, she grabbed him again and dragged him into our classroom. She shoved him in the corner and started yelling at him about how he could not be a child of Lenin if he misbehaved. She tore off his Oktyabryata pin and his uniform jacket. She told him he could not wear the uniform of an Oktyabryata if he did not live up to his pledge to be a good citizen. (Schecter, L. and J., 1975, p. 136)

Another Schecter child reports: "From the first grade boys and girls share in the cleaning of the school. Some skip, but if they do it too often they run the risk of losing their Pioneer scarves" (p. 138). When a student cheated, "punishments ranged from being moved to another seat to automatic failure: in the background always lurked the loss of the Pioneer scarves" (p. 133). The shame and humiliation of expulsion from a group to which most children belong are terrifying negative incentives.

Another device which furthers the student's sense of social responsibility and through which he is evaluated is the "dezhurny" system. Students in the tenth, or highest, form, are required on a rotated basis to regulate the behavior of the younger students during non-class time. Evelind Schecter recalls:

> . . . my whole homeroom had to keep the school in order for one or two weeks in every six. We had to arrive punctually at eight in the morning for a line-up reviewed by the directress. . . . The directress would take roll and check to see that our uniforms and hair were in place. (p. 138)

When I first saw the young dezhurnys, distinguished by red arm bands, performing their functions, I reflected on the dismal failure in my own school of attempts at a peer monitor system in our halls and cafeteria. In our schools resentment toward authority is a perceptible current which runs especially strong when authority is not backed by power. Even in our classes men like Thoreau and Martin Luther King, Jr., are admired partly for their defiance of the legal power structure. The possibility that a law is morally attackable exists in America.

But it is vital to understand three realities of power in the Soviet Union. First, it is inadmissable to doubt the correctness of authority. Second, one must display respect for authority in specific ways, for example, through the social rituals, including membership in the political youth groups. Third, the school and its opinion of a student's behavior significantly determine his chances of success in later life.

Severe consequences can follow seemingly minor lapses in the performance of one's dezhurny responsibility. On one occasion in Moscow I was sitting in the cafeteria with a fellow teacher. Not far from us a class of eight-year-olds had just finished lunch and had raced out of the cafeteria, with most of them leaving their trays at the tables. A senior girl had been in charge of the children. The teacher called the girl to our table. In stern tones she informed the student that the misbehavior of the children was a black mark on her record. The girl cleaned up the trays herself, stunned and on the verge of tears. Disapprobation by even a minor functionary in a centralized, all-pervasive power structure lends enormous weight to the threat of a "black mark."

Formal interaction between teacher and student is one-directional. The teacher instructs or asks questions, and the student records information or answers. Although I did not specifically note it at the time, I cannot remember a student ever asking a question. My residual recall is supported by the Schecter children's mother: "In their life they added to their knowledge but not to their intellectual development. In Soviet classrooms they never had the opportunity to ask questions, argue a position, test their powers through to a conclusion" (p. 401). One day I observed a history class. The teacher asked questions. The children raised their hands, stood, and answered in rapid-fire order. It was a lively class, sparked by the eager, spirited responses of the students. Afterwards I complimented the teacher and asked whether they ever have discussion periods. She replied, "We just had one." I would surmise that the far-reaching implications of teacher disapproval partly explains the passivity of students in class.

Whenever possible I used the last ten minutes of class to let the children ask me questions about America. In most cases we carried on lively exchanges. It was amply demonstrated to me that the Soviet student does not lack curiosity. But it seems to me that curiosity is the natural enemy of ritual.

The implications of ritual are twofold. First, the student performs because he believes that he thereby demonstrates implicit if not explicit support of his group's ideology, from the smallest unit—family, class, youth group, to the largest—his motherland. Second, even if he rejects in whatever degree the ideology, he still must contend with the power behind the rituals. No distinction is necessary in effect between the child who rejects the ritual and the child who rejects the reason behind the ritual. Both correct thought as well as action are required of the student.

I noted a few instances where students evidenced implicit opposition either to ideology or to ritual. In one of my classes the question of religion arose. I was asked what young people in America though about religion. They asked about new religious directions and about their expression in art forms, for instance, *God-Spell* and *Jesus Christ Superstar*. The curiosity was genuine and positive; this surprised me, as one of the school's tasks is to inculcate atheism.

After class three students approached me. In confidential tones they expressed a desire to discuss religion further with me. We met three times after school in one of the classrooms in a conspiratorial atmosphere which, though I tried, I could not dispel. They were torn between their interest in religion and their fear of the "black mark." According to one boy, acceptance at the university could hang in the balance if one acted indiscretely.

By contrast to this somber example of ideological chaffing, while teaching at the Moscow school I observed a saucy and sophisticated display of ritual chaffing. A sixteen-year-old student, Vanya, had attended public school in New York while his father worked at the Soviet Consulate. Vanya despised the gray, characterless uniforms. Every day he wore his Levis along with the standard jacket. Twice in my presence his teacher asked him about the Levis. Both times he gave a saccharine smile of compliance, but kept wearing the Levis. One day the teacher stopped Vanya in the corridor and told him that she was upset by his insolent manner. She insisted that he apologize. He turned on his smile, lowered his eyes contritely, and switched to English, which he spoke better than his teacher, saying, "From the bottom of my heart, I apologize." He slipped a mischievous glance in my direction. The teacher seemed befuddled. She told him that she would let him go this time: he had after all obeyed. I suspected that in the way he adroitly parried this authoritarian thrust he had brought home more than a mastery of English.

Vanya's performance implies that the narrow perimeters of student behavior limit the way one can cope with authority if for no other reason than because he or she sees fewer variations around to serve as examples.

I have described ways in which students are contolled in Soviet schools through institutions that show authority as always right, unavoidable, and omnipotent. The individual's sense of worth is gauged by the group's approval. Ritual plays a central role in exacting from the student the outward tributes to authority and the beliefs it represents.

Parenthetically, while corporal punishment is forbidden, there is evidence that it occasionally occurs. One former Soviet student told me that a teacher had once severely beaten him. I have also heard of "rough" treatment of children in the lower grades. But I would consider such incidents exceptional.

Most frequently guilt, humiliation, and fear of exclusion are the negative motivants for acceptable behavior. Anxiety is considered a positive emotion, apparently because it spurs the student's efforts. It is difficult to ascertain to what degree negative motivants are balanced by or mingle with the desire to build a new society or to forge Soviet man.

Methods of controlling and motivating students are consistent with Soviet attitudes toward the individual and the shaping of his need to be a "self-standing but not independent" member of a goal-oriented collective.

One more vital element needs to be expanded upon in order to complete my composite image of Soviet school discipline. I soon became aware of a strong affection many teachers, most of whom were women, had for their students. A teacher has the same class for many years and functions as a kind of homeroom or class mother. She takes the students on extended class trips, consults with parents, and in general displays a deep concern for her "kids."

In some cases the limits of acceptable behavior are stretched. A former American exchange teacher told me that in her school the teachers overlooked one boy's unruly behavior because his mother was in a hospital dying of cancer. The strongly maternal attitude of several teachers I knew seems to be an important motivational factor.

At a teachers' meeting in the Leningrad school, the principal told the teachers that they must be firm, but above all they must love the children: "If you do not love the children, you should not be a teacher."

Finally, I noted an unexpected positive element in the clear-cut roles students were designated to play. In general students showed a lack of shyness or false modesty. They readily recited, spoke and performed in front of groups. I had the impression that they were kept in the incubator of childhood longer, nurtured with a patient consistency. They seemed more accepting of whatever age they were at, and were less burdened by the need for false sophistication, cynicism, boredom, or insecurity as to social roles than their American counterparts.

To conclude, without resorting to corporal punishment, Soviet educators achieve an impressive degree of student discipline, the veneer of which comprises the social rituals between student and teacher.

Examination beyond this highly developed system of protocol reveals that positive reinforcement in Soviet schools differs from ours. While we stress personal success as reflected in grades, the Soviets establish group approval as the major positive reinforcement. More striking is the ideological baggage that accompanies service to the group. The ultimate goal of every group is to advance, however modestly, the cause of communism.

Group approval rewards the individual's service to this cause with a sense of identity and security.

Negative reinforcement evolves logically from the failure to live up to the group's expectation. Guilt results from not having served the cause adequately, and fear of ostracism from the group looms as a result of serious misbehavior.

While the aims of Soviet discipline may not fit American needs, the principle of logically relating positive with negative reinforcement deserves further study as a fundamental alternative to the so-called swift justice of the paddle, in which American education has placed substantial faith.

REFERENCES

Bronfenbrenner, Y., *Two Worlds of Childhood.* New York: Russell Sage Foundation, 1970.

Calas, E., "Summary of Conclusions of Research on Soviet Child Training Ideals and Their Political Significance," in Mead, M. (ed.), *Soviet Attitudes toward Authority.* New York: McGraw Hill, 1951.

Cantril, H., *Soviet Leaders and Mastery over Man.* New Brunswick: Rutgers University Press, 1960.

DeGeorge, R., *Soviet Ethics and Morality.* Ann Arbor: University of Michigan Press, 1969.

Dmytryshyn, B., *USSR: A Concise History*, 2d ed. New York: Scribner's, 1971.

Downey, B., "Student Discipline," in Lane, G. (ed.), *Impressions of Soviet Education.* Washington: George Washington University Press, 1973.

Jacoby, S., *Inside Soviet Schools.* New York: Hill and Wang, 1974.

Komsomol'skaya pravda, March 31, 1949.

Makarenko, A., *Problems of Soviet School Education.* Moscow: Progress Publishers, 1965.

Mead, M., *Soviet Attitudes toward Authority.* New York: McGraw Hill, 1951.

Nettl, J., *The Soviet Achievement.* Norwich, England: Harcourt Brace, 1967.

Schecter, L. and J., *An American Family in Moscow.* Boston: Little, Brown, 1975.

Stories by Graduates of Moscow. Moscow: Detgiz, 1947.

Weaver, K., *Lenin's Grandchildren.* New York: Simon and Schuster, 1971.

PART VI

•

SURVEYS AND OPINION

This section presents two formal surveys and three opinions regarding the use of corporal punishment in the schools.

"A Survey of Attitudes toward Corporal Punishment in Pennsylvania Schools" by Reardon and Reynolds represents one of the most extensive and adequate examples of survey research yet discovered in the literature on corporal punishment. Reardon and Reynolds conducted the survey for the State Board of Education and collected some interesting figures indicating attitudes of various groups toward the use of corporal punishment in the schools. Their findings of 70 and 80 percent agreement among different groups of adults for the use of corporal punishment reflect data gathered by others and suggest that our society is well entrenched in its belief that corporal punishment is an effective means of discipline.

Following the Supreme Court decision on Ingraham v. Wright, there was a several-week period which witnessed the publication of many editorials around the country. Through the use of a press-clipping service, McDowell and Friedman conducted a regional analysis of the opinions expressed by the writers. The results are interesting but not surprising and further support the contention that conservative political and religious beliefs encourage the use of physical force against children.

The next two essays by Skinner and Friedman offer contrasting views concerning the effects of corporal punishment. Interestingly, Skinner has been misquoted as believing in the use of corporal punishment whereas it is clear that he has always proposed the use of reward rather than punishment. Friedman, a prominent pediatrician, describes some of the physiological consequences of the use of corporal punishment.

The final essay by Reinholtz represents the only pro corporal punishment chapter in this book. While critics might suggest that this evidences an unfair balance of presentation, an examination of the arguments in support of corporal punishment reveals them to be extremely limited and lacking in supportive objective data. Further, the arguments most often based

299

on religion, tradition, or personal experience are presented throughout the book where they are continually refuted. The myths regarding the effectiveness of the practice are discussed in detail in the Introduction and the facts regarding punishment are analyzed further in Part VII.

Without further discussion, it is obvious that this book considers the weight of evidence clearly against the use of corporal punishment in the schools.

18

A Survey of Attitudes
toward Corporal Punishment
in Pennsylvania Schools

Francis J. Reardon

Robert N. Reynolds

•

Introduction

The Student Bill of Rights and Responsibilities was adopted by the (Pennsylvania) State Board of Education after spirited debate. One of the most controversial portions of the bill was that concerning corporal punishment. Despite some strong support for abolishing it entirely, a majority of the board members voted to continue it. The minority requested a study specifically aimed at answering these questions:

1. What kinds of corporal punishment are used in Pennsylvania schools?
2. What variations of corporal punishment regulations are common in Pennsylvania schools?
3. What are the positive and negative effects of corporal punishment from the viewpoint of parents, students, and school personnel (teachers, administrators, school board)?
4. What, if any, types of corporal punishment result in desired changes in student behaviors?

The study should consider these questions in terms of: school policies, court cases, due process, and basis for hearings.

Review of the Literature

Spare the rod, spoil the child? This question seems to be the essence of a long-running debate on the subject of corporal punishment. Hapkiewicz

This is a shortened version of a report entitled *Corporal Punishment in Pennsylvania.* Harrisburg: Pennsylvania State Department of Education, 1973.

(1975) conducted an extensive review of the literature concerning corporal punisment and arrived at the following conclusions:

1. The incidence of corporal punishment has increased in the last 20 years and is widely used in some districts.
2. Research on corporal punishment cannot satisfactorily answer questions about its direct or indirect effects.
3. Due to ethical problems in investigating the effects of corporal punishment, it is unlikely that research will ever provide satisfactory answers.
4. The frequency with which corporal punishment is used, combined with the absence of research support, suggests that its continued use is justified and protected on grounds other than scientific.

Ebel (1975), Geisinger (1974) and Myers (1975) are other authors who, after reviewing the literature on various aspects of corporal punishment, support Hapkiewicz's conclusion that empirical research has not, and probably will not, provide definitive answers on the effectiveness of corporal punishment.

Although there is an absence of empirical studies on the effects of corporal punishment, there is no such scarcity of writings which discuss the issue and, generally, oppose its use. Perhaps the most prominent is the Report of the Task Force on Corporal Punishment of the National Education Association (1972). After reviewing the literature, conducting site visits to schools, interviewing many educators and otherwise gathering, examining and evaluating all the reasons it could identify in support of and in opposition to the use of corporal punishment, the task force concluded: "The weight of fact and reasoning was against infliction of physical pain as an attempt to maintain an orderly learning climate." Therefore, the NEA recommended that corporal punishment be abolished.

Other organizations have agreed with the National Education Association's opposition to corporal punishment. Bard (1973) reports that over sixty groups are working to eliminate the practice. A 1972 National Conference on Corporal Punishment, sponsored by the American Orthopsychiatric Association and the American Civil Liberties Union, attracted representatives from sixty-two national organizations. One result of the conference was the formation of a consortium to oppose the use of corporal punishment (Benedict, 1974). More recently, the Commission on Administrative Behavior Supportive of Human Rights of Phi Delta Kappa, a prestigious professional education fraternity, prepared a Model Student Code which comprehensively discussed such matters as student discipline, records, suspension, and student rights. Corporal punishment was addressed with the brief statement, "Students will not be subject to corporal punishment" (Children's Defense Fund, 1975, 255).

As noted before, it is difficult to find statements from prestigious national organizations *supporting* the use of corporal punishment. However, a number of surveys concerning the incidence of corporal punishment and the attitudes of various school officials and the general public are reported. The results of these surveys are somewhat surprising considering the organized opposition to corporal punishment reported above. A nationwide poll of administrators conducted by *Nation's Schools* (1971) indicated that 74 percent of the respondents applied corporal punishment in their district and 64 percent believed it had proved to be an effective instrument in assuring discipline. Patterson (1974) reported that 55 to 65 percent of school officials see corporal punishment as effective and favor its use. A *Good Housekeeping* (1972) panel of one thousand consumers in 1972 was asked the question, "Should teachers spank their pupils?" The vote was 66 percent yes, 31 percent no. When the National Education Association polled its membership (NEA *Research Bulletin*, 1970), two-thirds of the members favored the use of corporal punishment at the elementary level, and one-half favored its use at the secondary level. These results are somewhat in contrast to the report of the NEA task force. Queer (1971) sought the opinions of parents, principals and teachers in the Pittsburgh school district. In spite of some ambivalent feelings about administrative support, parents' apathy and other concerns, a majority of all three groups supported the use of corporal punishment. There appears, then, to be a difference of opinion between committees of national organizations and various individuals participating in the schooling process as to the efficacy of corporal punishment.

An increasingly important consideration in the debate over corporal punishment has been the recent court decisions which address the issues of due process and parental rights.

As part of the current emphasis on students' rights to due process, three courts have recognized that students are entitled to due process prior to the administration of corporal punishment (*Mahanes* v. *Hall*, C.A. No. 304–73–R, E.D. Va., May 16, 1974; *Ingraham* v. *Wright*, 498 F.2d 248, 5th Cir. 1974; *Baker* v. *Owen*, 43 U.S.L.W. 2451, M.D.N.C., Apr. 23, 1975).

The principle of *in loco parentis*, the traditional source of the schools' right to administer corporal punishment, has been modified and narrowed rather extensively in recent court decisions. In *Glaser* v. *Marietta*, 351 F. Supp. 555 (W.D.Pa. 1972), the court held that corporal punishment cannot be administered when a parent has specifically requested that it not be used. In *Mahanes* v. *Hall*, C.A. No. 304–73–R (E.D. Va., May 16, 1974), the court went further and ruled that the schools' failure to obtain consent for corporal punishment from the student's mother violated her parental rights.

The literature on corporal punishment, then, reveals three major findings. First of all, empirical research has not, and probably will not, provide conclusive answers on the effects of the practice. Second, the intense debate over its use continues, with extensive organizational opposition countered by reports of educators and public belief in its effectiveness. Third, the trend of recent court decisions has been to narrow the independence of schools in their freedom to administer corporal punishment.

Procedure

To answer the questions posed by the State Board (see Introduction) the Pennsylvania Department of Education (PDE) developed a study that would collect information in two different ways. Initially a Basic Education Circular (BEC) was sent out requesting that all school districts forward their written policies on corporal punishment to the Division of Research.

The second type of information collected involved the production of a questionnaire and the cooperation of several statewide groups to solicit responses of their members to the questionnaire. The department felt that this was the most efficient and effective way to reach groups whose members constituted the most significant viewpoints on the subject. The groups involved were: Pennsylvania Association of Elementary and Secondary Principals, Pennsylvania Association of School Administrators, Pennsylvania Congress of Parents and Teachers, Pennsylvania School Boards Association, Pennsylvania State Education Association, IU student forums— which select representatives to the secretary of education's Student Advisory Board.

The procedure for disseminating the questionnaires was as follows. The students on the secretary's Student Advisory Board were given packets of questionnaires and were asked to administer them to their respective intermediate forums. The Research Division of the Pennsylvania State Education Association selected a random sample of their membership and mailed questionnaires to this sample together with a follow-up postcard mailed to the entire group. Members of the remaining four organizations received the questionnaire and a letter on the organization's stationery explaining that the study was a cooperate one involving the PDE and the organization. Questionnaires for these four organizations were mailed out by the department. Response rates varied from 39 to 68 percent, with the total group response over 53 percent. This exceptionally high response rate is probably related to the fact that the study was done in cooperation with the various organizations.

Results of the Survey of School District Policies

Responses to the BEC broke down as follows. Of the 292 school districts responding, 269 permit the use of corporal punishment, 16 prohibit it, and 7 were uncertain at the time of the survey. The uncertain districts were in the process of developing their policies and hoped to complete them by the end of the school year or shortly thereafter. This development process often involved conscientious work by committees of students, parents, faculty, and other concerned citizens.

Policies were examined for their congruence to the State Board policy. There were about equal numbers in three categories: those that allow it (no elaboration), those whose policies approximate or supersede the board regulations and those that differ from board regulations.

Many policies suggested guidelines which go beyond those in the regulations. Among the more frequently suggested were: witnessing by another professional (teacher or principal); written notification to principal by teacher, never administering to child known to be under psychological or physical treatment for disabilities; regarding as a last resort (extreme cases); *not* administering in presence of other students; clear understanding by student of seriousness of offense; not degrading; notification to parents/guardian; paddle not displayed in the classroom; being aware that the older or more sensitive the child, the more aggravated the results of such punishment; and allowing student to speak in own defense before paddling (due process).

Other guidelines dealt with narrowing the definition of corporal punishment: not more than one paddling on any given day; striking, slapping or shaking student with open hand or fist entirely indefensible as a means of corporal punishment; no striking above the shoulders; paddle on buttocks, "back end," proper place only; no striking about the face or head; paddling only acceptable form of corporal punishment; no striking above the waist; hitting, pushing, slapping or other physical abuse prohibited except as specified; not more than three swats of the paddle; slapping a pupil around the head, pulling hair, pinching, hitting with a ruler or subjecting a pupil to sarcasm or ridicule not defended by administration; student paddled only once in a week; administering corporal punishment when other measures have proved ineffective, but never with any type of paddle or other implement; girls beyond the primary grades not to be paddled by *anyone*, for any reason, at any time; other methods, and male professional employees *never* paddling female students. In summary these suggest that corporal punishment should be delivered on the back of the *male* student, below his waist. In addition the student should not be struck more than three times and not be exposed to punishment more than once in a given period of time (day, week).

Three guidelines attempted to deal with parental prohibition. (1) Parents/guardians prohibiting corporal punishment should include suggested alternative methods of discipline in their letter to the principal. These parents must accept full responsibility for their child's behavior. (2) Section on parental prohibition shall not be interpreted to mean that punishment for a violation will be waived; instead, a different but comparable penalty will be imposed. (3) Any student who refuses to take corporal punishment or is excused by the provisions of the Student Bill of Rights and Responsibilities shall receive detention time not to exceed ten (10) hours.

Problems engendered by this regulation have been recognized, and an effort has been made to spell out alternatives. Either parents take the responsibility, or other measures (e.g., detention, suspension) are employed.

Questionnaire Responses—Attitudes

Questionnaires were administered to six groups. Only the principal questionnaire is presented since all adult questionnaires used the same questions. Response to the questionnaire was as follows; *606* students, *558* parents, *972* teachers, *1,278* principals, *461* administrators, and *216* school board presidents. Analysis of responses to the attitude questionnaire indicated that the five adult groups were somewhat similar, but the student group was slightly different. Since a few of the questions on the student form were modified, their data will be presented separately. Table 1 shows the correlations among groups in their agreement with the attitude items. The teacher-parent and administrator-principal correlations are sufficiently

Table 1.   Correlations of Attitude Responses

Group	Principals	Administrators	Teachers	School Board Presidents	Students
Parents	.84	.84	.98	.77	.69
Principals	—	.96	.91	.90	.53
Administrators		—	.90	.81	.68
Teachers			—	.84	.63
School Board Presidents				—	.35

high to suggest that these groups are virtually the same in their response to these attitude items.

Responses of the five adult groups are presented in Table 2. A number of respondents pointed out that such questions cannot be answered in a vacuum. The responses, therefore, will be discussed together with some modifying comments that appeared.

Corporal Punishment Will Cause Changes in Behavior.

About three out of four members in each group agreed with this statement. Some people would modify it to say "can" rather than "will." Others pointed out that the change in behavior may be a negative one.

Corporal Punishment Builds a Student's Character.

Disagreement with this item was fairly general, but one group, school board presidents, was more in agreement than disagreement. Comments on this item were "sometimes" (by several people) and "under the right circumstances."

Students Learn Self-Discipline from Corporal Punishment.

There was general agreement with this item, but some groups were stronger in their agreement than others. Here again comments were of the "in some cases" type.

Discipline Cannot be Maintained Without Corporal Punishment.

There was substantial disagreement with the item. Again the school board presidents were the only group with a higher percentage of agreement than disagreement. One comment pointed out that "In some schools this may be true, sad, but true." Another suggested that it is the availability of corporal punishment and not the exercise of it which helps to maintain discipline.

Corporal Punishment is Less Harmful than Other Forms of Humiliation.

The item brought a substantial amount of agreement. One individual suggested that it is not a form of humiliation. Indeed, if the student is removed from the presence of his or her peers, as one of the additional guidelines above suggests, this individual's point becomes quite valid. Another comment suggested that this depends on individual's personality.

Teachers use Corporal Punishment When They Have no Other Way to Respond to Difficult Situations.

The large amount of agreement with this item suggests that the groups believe punishment is used only as a last resort. That two parents amended the questionnaire to say "hopefully" supports this interpretation.

Table 2. Total Group Response (Agreement, Disagreement) to Attitude Questions

Item	N=558 Parents		N=1,278 Principals		N=461 Administrators		N=972 Teachers		N=216 School Board Presidents	
	% A	% D	% A	% D	% A	% D	% A	% D	% A	% D
Corporal punishment will cause changes in behavior.	74.9	17.5	75.6	15.7	76.0	17.8	75.8	13.6	75.0	17.6
Corporal punishment builds a student's character.	35.5	50.1	30.9	50.6	32.3	52.3	29.5	49.3	45.1	42.8
Students learn self-discipline from corporal punishment.	54.9	38.8	52.3	37.3	49.1	42.9	49.7	37.7	61.9	29.8
Discipline cannot be maintained without corporal punishment.	43.8	50.7	36.7	55.9	37.8	55.1	38.9	52.9	58.4	36.9
Corporal punishment is less harmful than other forms of humiliation.	57.0	27.5	61.3	25.0	61.6	25.3	58.4	23.6	67.3	21.8
Teachers use corporal punishment when they have no other way to respond to difficult situations.	63.8	26.0	62.1	30.8	62.9	29.7	64.9	26.6	57.8	35.6

Statement										
Corporal punishment is the only thing that will work with some students.	76.0	20.4	70.3	23.7	66.4	28.4	76.8	17.3	81.9	14.9
Student attitudes are generally made worse by corporal punishment.	28.8	59.4	24.1	66.0	31.7	60.8	19.8	67.6	15.8	76.3
Most of the people in the community served by my school support the use of corporal punishment.	36.9	23.9	65.6	19.4	62.0	14.1	42.0	23.4	73.2	11.7
Complete elimination of corporal punishment would have serious consequences.	73.1	20.1	71.8	20.3	67.0	24.5	76.2	14.3	79.2	14.9
Corporal punishment is not effective unless administered at the time of the incident.	83.5	12.0	74.1	17.7	69.6	21.4	81.5	12.7	83.3	13.5
Some students receive corporal punishment while others do not for the same offense.	72.1	12.1	63.7	25.3	73.7	16.6	68.5	19.2	66.7	20.2

Corporal Punishment is the Only Thing That Will Work With Some Students.

This statement brought the highest rate of agreement from several groups. A student commented here that it is a very, very small minority, and this is probably true.

Student Attitudes Are Generally Made Worse by Corporal Punishment.

The worsening of student attitudes as a result of corporal punishment is something that has little, if any, credence among the groups. In fact, even a majority of the students didn't agree that this happens. Very few comments were elicited by this item, the most notable one pointing out that resentment can be a problem.

Most of the People in the Community Served by My School Support the Use of Corporal Punishment.

Interestingly enough, when asked about community support, the parents, students and teachers failed to produce a majority in agreement with the item. The other three groups, in positions of more responsibility and authority, had substantial majorities here. What must be determined is whether people in such positions are more attuned to the will of the community. If they are, then this marked split in group responses is very meaningful.

Complete Elimination of Corporal Punishment Would Have Serious Consequences.

Strong feelings were elicited by the suggestion of complete elimination. Only students disagreed substantially, one replacing the word "serious" with the word "good."

Corporal Punishment is Not Effective Unless Administered at the Time of the Incident.

Large majorities of all groups felt that the punishment must occur at the time of the incident to be effective. A student pointed out the need for the teacher to be calm and not angry in this situation. Some local district guidelines also stress this common-sense factor. A parent dichotomized elementary and secondary students, feeling the older children can associate punishment and offense over a wider temporal range.

Some Students Receive Corporal Punishment While Others do Not for the Same Offense.

This final attitude item was interesting in that it, for the only time on the questionnaire, brought out a larger percentage of agreement among students than any of the adult groups. This suggests that students are more sensitive to unjust application of the practice. This item also elicited a wide range of comments.

> Student: Are any two incidents the same?
> Board President: For some it is a first offense.
> Parent: Fact, but not desirable.
> Parent: Parental prohibition regulation is encouraging this.
> Teacher: Not in my room!
> Teacher: Inconsistency does exist.

The student responses are presented in Table 3. Several of them have been mentioned already. The students reversed the trend of adult responses on only four items, learning self-discipline, forms of humiliation, no other way to respond and the consequences of elimination. In general the students were the most liberal and the school board presidents were the other extreme of the spectrum.

Questionnaire Responses—Situations

Fifteen situations which covered a broad range of disciplinary problems were developed. Respondents were given the following instructions:

> It has been suggested that corporal punishment should be used only in certain circumstances. What follows is a list of circumstances under which it might be employed. If you feel that it should be employed, put a check under *Yes*; if you feel it shouldn't, put a check under *No*; if you are not sure, put a check under *Not Sure*.

Situations and the responses of all six groups are presented in Table 4. This portion of the questionnaire probably brought the strongest reaction. Members of all groups strongly criticized the idea of having a standard punishment applied automatically for a given offense. They strongly asserted that the application of corporal punishment must be based on incident-specific circumstances and that the discretion of school officials must enter into it.

The series of situations had been designed to determine if there were levels of offenses generally deemed to demand corporal punishment as a response. A number of comments suggested alternatives, for example, parental responsibility, suspension, expulsion, and handling by law enforcement authorities.

The general feeling was that possession of drugs, alcohol, or weapons is a matter for law enforcement agencies to deal with. This explains the large number of individuals responding "no" to these items. Other of-

Table 3.   Total Group Response to Attitude Questions (Students)

Questions	% Agree	% Disagree
Corporal punishment will cause changes in behavior.	57.6	35.2
Corporal punishment builds character.	11.4	61.6
Students learn self-discipline from corporal punishment.	27.1	55.4
Discipline cannot be maintained without corporal punishment.	16.0	50.1
Corporal punishment is less harmful than humiliation.	40.6	49.1
Teachers use corporal punishment because they have no other way to respond to difficult situations.	37.0	45.3
Corporal punishment is the only thing that will work with some students.	59.5	32.9
Student attitudes can only be made worse by corporal punishment.	44.5	50.6
Most of the people in the community served by my school support the use of corporal punishment.	23.4	49.0
Complete elimination of corporal punishment would have serious consequences.	34.2	58.3
Corporal punishment is not effective unless administered at the time of the incident.	61.9	34.6
Some students receive corporal punishment while others do not for the same offense.	80.0	17.4

fenses thought to be within the jurisdiction of a law enforcement agency were vandalism, truancy, and theft. There was also some support for turning over cases of physical assault, smoking, and fighting to a law enforcement agency. Situations considered within the province of the school were insubordination, disrespect, disobedience, disruptive behavior, and profanity. These five, as well as the two physical assault situations, were the only areas in which a small majority of adult responses favored the use of corporal punishment. It is interesting to note that the student group rarely responded in large numbers on either side of the fence. The predominant response of students to this entire portion of the questionnaire was in the "not sure" category, although about half felt that the physical assault situations might warrant corporal punishment.

The exceptionally strong feelings expressed in the comments that corporal punishment is situational are typified by these comments:

Teachers

"It was very difficult to complete this portion with such general terms; so much is dependent on the seriousness of the incident, the attitudes of,

Table 4. School Discipline Situations: Should Corporal Punishment Be Used?

				GROUPS					
Situations	Parents	Principals	Administrators	Teachers	School Board Presidents	Students
	Y N ?	Y N ?	Y N ?	Y N ?	Y N ?	Y N ?
Possession or use of drugs at school	35 55 10	6 86 8	6 82 12	14 74 12	28 60 12	22 12 66
Insubordination	57 32 11	66 24 10	62 26 12	63 24 13	70 19 11	26 30 43
Disrespect	51 36 13	64 25 11	56 29 15	58 29 13	63 26 11	27 18 54
Physical assault on other students	65 27 8	56 34 10	56 31 13	62 26 12	77 19 4	50 14 36
Physical assault on school employe	67 26 7	49 42 8	55 36 9	64 26 10	79 17 3	56 15 30
Vandalism	46 45 8	26 65 9	26 62 13	33 55 12	38 54 9	31 15 54
Possession or use of alcohol at school	35 56 9	7 84 9	9 78 13	17 70 13	28 62 10	19 14 66
Truancy	13 75 12	12 79 8	10 77 13	11 79 10	14 72 13	8 15 77
Smoking	18 72 9	15 77 8	15 74 11	15 73 12	18 73 9	10 12 78
Fighting	47 39 14	51 39 10	45 41 14	48 38 14	61 32 7	32 20 48
Theft	37 54 8	14 77 9	13 74 13	22 64 14	31 61 7	29 14 57
Disobedience	48 36 15	61 26 12	56 33 11	54 31 15	65 24 10	24 24 52
Continual disruptive behavior in class	62 27 10	69 23 8	63 26 11	69 21 10	72 19 8	33 23 44
Profanity	44 45 11	47 42 11	39 46 14	40 47 13	41 47 11	18 19 63
Possession or use of weapons at school	48 44 8	18 72 10	20 65 14	30 55 16	40 49 11	41 14 45

and the child himself; however, as a teacher, I feel I should have the right to determine whether corporal punishment is needed."

"Too many questions cannot be put on paper. I don't look on these 15 circumstances as being able to generate hard and fast rules. Considered must be age, sex, temperament, parental attitudes, and other conditions."

Administrators

"This is difficult with elementary pupils when parents are not available or won't take responsibility. Provision to monitor pupils during the interim needs attention if corporal punishment is deleted."

"This tends to make the punishment fit the crime rather than to have the punishment fit the offender. Corporal punishment can be both bad and good. How, why and type are the important factors."

"Generally no, but corporal punishment may prove valuable in any one of these situations where it is used to emphasize society's dissatisfaction with the act or to reassert the authority of the teacher or the school."

"This is all relative. Each person (student) is different and requires treatment accordingly. Also depends on what other means of discipline are approved. Corporal punishment should be an approved method as a last resort. Some of these listed acts should call for suspension and in some cases expulsion."

"Perhaps in these instances, suspension and parent conference could be a requirement, if such offenses do not occur too frequently and require far too much administrative time. It has been my experience that violations of the items listed are occurring much too frequently since there has been a gradual reluctance on the part of teachers and administrators to utilize measures to maintain good discipline in the schools."

Parents

"I do not feel that corporal punishment is the answer in all cases where I have checked 'yes.' I believe that it depends upon the nature of the child. For some children corporal punishment is definitely not effective."

"If corporal punishment is available, I think it would be helpful to know what type of punishment is administered at home. Also school administrators should be aware of psychological attitudes and effects on each student. I believe this should be administered by one in higher authority than the teacher."

"I'd have to qualify most of these. I'm for much stricter penalties for the disrupting of education by halfwit forces. As long as there is special privilege instead of equality, this to me is all a farce!"

"You need to get to the root of the problem. 'Clout' doesn't solve situations for a very long period of time. Force may be necessary to handle assault-type cases, but I don't consider that corporal punishment."

"Expulsion or fine. I'd have to qualify all these. I'm for much stricter penalties for disruptions of educational processes. Keep state and national out of education. Let locals handle their own problems. Too much liberalism."

Students

"All should be handled by the police. Corporal punishment will not alleviate any of these situations."

Who Should Administer Corporal Punishment?

The question posed to explore this area was: When corporal punishment is administered, it should be done by: (Check the lowest level of the continuum that applies. It will be assumed that you feel it can be applied by all levels above that one.)

1. only the principal   ———
2. principal and vice-principals   ———
3. the teacher and other professional ———
4. teacher alone   ———

The results are presented in table 5.

On this item, as in other parts of the questionnaire, a large proportion of students did not take a position. This also could relate to general opposition to the concept of corporal punishment. Of the adult groups, most don't want to see the power confined to the principal. The largest proportion would have the teacher, observed by a witness, administer it. Very small proportions would have the teacher do it alone, particularly among the principals and administrators, who may have been exposed to the administrative problems that can arise from such a situation.

Comments associated with this question often were from people who said no one should be allowed to use it. Beyond these, however, there were some insightful points made.

Table 5.   *Who Should Administer Corporal Punishment?*

Group	Principal	Vice Principal Principal &	Witness Teacher &	Teacher	NR
Students	20	23	28	0	29
Parents	14	21	36	18	11
Principals	5	35	46	9	5
Administrators	8	32	42	7	10
School Board Presidents	6	26	46	15	7
Teachers	5	19	58	18	3

Parents

"I feel the punishment should be dealt with by whomever is in charge at the time of what the punishment is for."

"*Only parents* have right to punish children."

"Corporal punishment should never be administered by an angry person."

"Physical punishment is usually done in the heat of anger—yet if you let anyone higher than the teacher do it, corporal punishment will be delayed and applied by someone not involved in the situation at its start."

"This could include notification of parent before corporal punishment is administered. Person administering punishment should not be vengeful!"

Students

"Teacher, but not when upset terribly—the teacher should be rational."

"Noninvolved personnel, no personal involvement."

Administrators

"If at all by the one of these closest to the offense."

"The teacher and other professional—if not, the principal and vice-principal will become the executioners. Teachers will request corporal punishment freely knowing that they need not participate."

"If it is administered, it should be done by the person who feels it is necessary and beneficial."

"The individual in charge of the offender at the time of the incident."

Current Regulations

A news story published shortly after the Steelton-Highspire school district abolished corporal punishment suggested that this step was taken "in order to be fair to all." The superintendent was quoted, "When you have two kids throwing spitballs, and one has a note from his parents and the other doesn't—what do we do?" This points up the feeling of a great many people that the present board regulation leads to unfairness. The groups were asked to respond to this situation. Table 6 shows how they responded.

Considering all groups, there is probably a small majority which feels that the present situation is unfair. A parent's comment may sum up the reaction: "My opinion is that only irresponsible parents make such demands of our school authorities. Therefore, the unfairness to the other students comes from the fact that they have to put up with the criminal acts of the undisciplined students. Just another example of our courts' desire to protect the criminals and forget the law-abiding citizen."

Table 6.   *Unfairness of Current Regulations*

Group	% Yes	% No	% ?	% Omit
Teachers	54	38	7	1
Students	48	30	19	4
Parents	56	32	7	5
Principals	42	46	10	2
Administrators	46	41	8	5
School Board Presidents	53	37	5	6

Personal Attitudes

The final question on the form asked each person what his or her own attitude toward corporal punishment was. Results are shown in table 7.

These results indicate that a substantial portion of the adults favored continued availability of corporal punishment. Again there is the possibility that mediating factors may exist. Examination of comments is again helpful.

Many individuals began to define an age dichotomy, pointing out that it is often impractical, if not impossible, to administer corporal punishment to the senior high school student or, in some cases, the junior high student. There was some confusion of the reasonable force principle with corporal punishment. Other respondents indicated that they are aware of this distinction. It certainly is a question that results in a great deal of thought and some mixed feelings. As evidence:

Administrators

"In favor of. I personally do not favor it; *however*, under certain circumstances a reasonable form of corporal punishment might be appropriate

Table 7.   *Personal Attitudes of the Six Groups*

Group	% Favor	% Oppose	% Not Sure
School Board Presidents	81	12	6
Principals	78	13	8
Administrators	68	25	6
Teachers	74	16	9
Parents	71	21	7
Students	25	51	25
Total	67	22	11
Total (Adults)	75	17	8

for a particular child. I feel it should be discouraged but not prohibited even if it is never used."

"Opposed to because it does not apply equally to all pupils. Equality before the law is an objective—seldom achieved—in adult legal procedure. It should be no less vital in juvenile cases."

"In favor of. Depends on individual student and circumstances. Should be used very sparingly and as a last resort as a matter of professional judgment. The fact that it *can* be used will mean that it will hardly ever *need* to be used."

"Opposed to, in general. However, in some cases, and with some students, it may be effective. An all-inclusive yes or no is virtually impossible."

"In favor of if conditions are spelled out. Can be used with some students and not with others (sure it's unfair), but conditions may differ and so might pupils. Must be used judiciously but not eliminated."

Teachers

"(1) Discipline must be meaningful; without it there will be anarchy. (2) If no discipline, then I want a teacher 'Bill of Rights.' (3) I don't want my child going to a school that is a madhouse."

"In 24 years of teaching, I have found it is not the use of corporal punishment, as much as the students know you (teacher) have 'the right' to do so if necessary, and if it is necessary the effect usually lasts for three or four years. . . . If two students are fighting and a teacher takes both by the arm to separate them and is told, 'take your hand off me—you have no right to touch me,' how can discipline be maintained?"

"What about age? I don't believe in corporal punishment for students over 14. They should be suspended!"

"In favor of. However, in 15 years of teaching I have never had to resort to corporal punishment."

"There is a correct way to administer corporal punishment. In fact, I believe there is an art to administering it correctly. Too many teachers are not skilled in the correct skill which should be demonstrated—you paddle a student, not beat him or her."

Parents

"I feel that a continual discipline problem should be looked into by teacher and parent and the method of discipline decided by both parties. I personally prefer to administer punishment to my children myself if I am made aware that there is a problem."

"Opposed to, but no offense should go unpunished. Make the punishment fit the crime—if vandalism that can be repaired, make them repair it; if not, make them earn the money by working at school to pay for it; if injure another, make them work to pay for doctor visit; truancy, theft, drugs, alcohol, etc., *have* to involve the parents or the law."

"I am opposed because I will have no control over the teacher with a short fuse. Corporal punishment meted out in home discipline is in a different category because the parent is in a better position to administer love and give added guidance to a situation than a teacher before the day is over. We need to get to the root of the problem so that our discipline leads to self-discipline. A positive reward system rather than a negative one is more to my liking."

"I strongly believe in it because if I'd be notified by a teacher or principal, you may be certain the children would receive it again when they got home. I believe if some of us older ones stop to think of the punishment we got when we got home and our parents found out, you'd never do it again!!"

"I cannot answer this question 'yes' or 'no.' I am definitely not in favor of corporal punishment. However, I feel there are times when it is necessary. How long can we continue to sacrifice the majority of our children by leniency toward the disruptive?"

"There should be more done by parents; then it would not be as necessary in the schools."

"I do feel in certain instances that only corporal punishment works. However, I do fear that there are certain professionals who might abuse it."

"In favor of—for entire student body. Those students with immunity are aware of their status and use it accordingly. In my opinion the schools are operating with little or no discipline. Learning lessons is impossible."

General Comments

An exceptionally large number of individuals felt moved to add a general comment, either on the questionnaire, the issue of corporal punishment or the incidence of use of corporal punishment. These comments add significantly to the data of the report. They are subdivided by category and group membership within categories.

Questionnaire

Principals

"I think this questionnaire was drafted by a person who is against corporal punishment."

"I find that this questionnaire is impossible to use and still permit me to accurately reflect my opinion. It would be extremely unfair to base any decision on the use of corporal punishment on the basis of this instrument."

"I don't like your questionnaire! It reeks of built-in bias. Where is there a place for the moderate who hates the use of corporal punishment but has found it necessary and even beneficial in isolated cases to respond?"

"If principals are going to be asked their opinion and if the opinions expressed are going to be used for some purpose, please be objective in writing the questions. This questionnaire is absolutely biased. The real question involved is much more complex than these first-year law school questions indicate."

School Board

"We believe the results of your poll will be very misleading! First of all, the definition of 'corporal punishment' is not totally clear. Second, we feel differently about it for minor infractions among elementary students and secondary students. A slap on the fingers may solve a problem in third grade, but it's highly questionable if any kind of physical treatment would help a senior who is drug-addicted. To repeat, we do not think your poll will be meaningful, for the answers cannot be that clearly given."

Parents

"I feel there should have been two sets of questions—grades 1 to 6 and grades 7 to 12. Also, the degree of physical punishment certainly differs with the various circumstances."

"Your tool for collecting information is difficult to mark. Each child is an individual. Some come to school each day beaten—a bit more corporal punishment is not the answer. It depends on the individual, and any professional will take this into consideration. Maybe we should make school for those who want it and let the rest suffer the consequences. They will get little education anyway and it only cheapens a diploma for those who work for it!!! School should be a privilege!!!"

Students

"This questionnaire is too vague. My opinion is that corporal punishment should be maintained in elementary and junior high school. Senior high school is a completely different matter."

Administrators

"The questionnaire regarding use of corporal punishment in the schools is designed in my opinion to elicit a negative response to corporal punishment. The questions are couched in the 'Why do you enjoy beating your wife?' sort of tenor, extremely prejudicial in tone."

Teachers

"I do not believe that this survey really will bring out how teachers really feel about the situation at present. Try eliminating compulsory attendance for the misfits and you will have good schools. Give the 'hoods' apprentice training."

"Thank you for providing the opportunity to comment on the *IMPORTANT* issue."

Issue of Corporal Punishment

Principals

"I *do not* feel the State Board of Education has a place in this matter. *Individual rights* have been protected by such regulations already to the detriment of groups and their rights."

"I favor corporal punishment not in the sense that I want students physically punished capriciously or unreasonably. I favor it because of the *broad interpretation* that corporal punishment takes *when totally prohibited*, especially at the junior high and high school levels. My experience in New Jersey schools proved that one cannot even lightly touch a student to get him moving without the retort, 'You can't touch me.'"

"I believe that the people with the infinite wisdom to advocate the elimination of corporal punishment should get out of the PDE and other selected professions and into the public schools on a full-time basis for at least five years, and we can take a poll of their opinions. Perhaps an exchange program would be appropriate."

"In this time of disagreement, I say if the courts would stay out of the schools and school officials would stick to their guns of expulsion or suspension, I feel we would be doing a favor to all concerned, but when the courts render a decision and then they don't have to worry about its enforcement, this is disastrous and places many restrictions on schools and their administrators. Let's leave schools to school personnel, politics to politicians, and other work to their respective personnel."

"A prohibition of corporal punishment may lead to taunting of teachers by students. I discourage the use of corporal punishment by my staff. The repercussions from the use of corporal punishment may cause an unpleasant situation for the professional as well as the student and his family. It does cause alienation. Do people realize that they are dealing with professional people when they legislate the prohibition of corporal punishment? The school code still permits the teacher to act in 'loco parentis.'"

"It is time to come back to basic education and stop playing politics."

"The fact that you can and the student knows you might is the deterrent needed to keep order. Can't run a school without this fear being available for some students. Otherwise you have a zoo. The *authority* must be there. Use must be weighed by principal's judgment. Each school makes its own policy. Should not be governed by blanket state prohibition!"

"In many incidences and in many ways, kids are telling us to 'go to hell.' Many have the attitude, "Alright, I did something wrong—so what!' Even after talking with parents involved, child ends up feeling, 'All they do is talk," so the kid just bears with us."

"I have worked in an urban center when corporal punishment was eliminated and saw a complete disrespect for teaching personnel, other students and administrative personnel take place. I am currently in the suburbs and could see that an occasional use of corporal punishment would definitely settle some students and make for a much better teacher-learning situation for all children. Why should the good students be denied an appropriate education while the negative ones are permitted to continually disrupt classes and destroy school property? Corporal punishment acts as a deterrent for many who might otherwise act out. I do not agree with the ACLU that a great number of children are getting permanent injuries from corporal punishment. The damage academically to other children far outweighs any minor bodily injuries."

"If corporal punishment is seen as a license to beat kids, it has no excuse for existing in a public school. If it is *one* of a number of techniques which *might* be used, it could have considerable value in limited instances. I see nothing in the Student Rights and Responsibilities regulations which alters what we have been doing all along!"

"I can still keep good control over the student body by use of the paddle. I informed the Sup't. if he takes the paddle away from me, he can have my job also."

"Readin' 'ritin' 'rithmetic to the tune of the hickory stick!!!"

School Board

"Quit playing psychological games. If student knows he will be punished for an act, he probably won't do it."

"This survey is perfectly ridiculous. Everyone knows what's wrong with our schools today—lack of discipline and the 'old hickory stick' when necessary. You don't need a survey to know this if you've worked in education for *40* years. (Bring back the old hickory stick.)"

"When I went to school, if you came home with a sore butt, you took one back to school the next day. It should still be that way."

Parents

"These items to be checked don't leave me a clear way to answer, but I believe limited use of corporal punishment is not harmful to growth of the child and might have positive effects."

"I feel that the whole question of corporal punishment would be irrelevant if the *parents* would be more responsible with their children. A school system cannot change a pupil with irresponsible parents. The dreadful 'rot' that has fallen over our society falls back on home conditions."

"Corporal punishment in itself is not a total answer under any circumstances; many problems need total parental understanding with school officials. The problem, as I see it, with corporal punishment is that its authority can fall into the wrong hands and do more harm than good. Many of our children nowadays do need a great deal of discipline due to their *total lack of respect towards authority*, and many times school officials are helpless as far as a solution. Unfortunately, it's the children who need the most discipline who have the parents who don't care and won't allow schools to help out."

"You cannot make generalized statements about corporal punishment. Guidelines must be set up and strictly adhered to. This avenue *must* remain *open* to the teacher or professional involved in difficult situations. Only the parties involved can know if corporal punishment would help in the situation."

"I am learning from my church classes there are better ways to handle or treat children than spankings. They need understanding why they do the things they do; if they are disruptive there is a reason behind their disruption. However, teachers do not have time for this, which is not their fault. If a teacher felt my child should receive a spanking, I would not ridicule the teacher in front of my child."

"The answers given apply to elementary school. The answers are different for junior high and high school. This questionnaire shows evidence of lack of thought. An 8-year-old who gets mad and strikes a teacher is not the same as an 18-year-old high school student who physically attacks a teacher—the former should be paddled, the latter charged with assault."

"In favor of. I am not representing the PTA in the above answers, but I know my people are fed up to their neck with the irresponsible guidance we have been getting the past few years. Let us have the courage to begin speaking and acting for right."

"Violence breeds violence, some of these children are aggressive and undisciplined because of their abuse at home or complete lack of caring and love. Understanding is needed, not corporal punishment."

Students

"Corporal punishment makes it possible for the student who has committed a minor offense to have another form of punishment other than suspension. This means that the student's grades will not have to suffer for what he did."

Administrators

"I *do* believe this *is* a matter for local district determination and not State Board regulation."

"It should be outlawed by state law."

"The question is really of assault and battery—using the excuse of discipline. In other states where I have been employed it is outlawed or forbidden, and serious problems have not become the case as far as discipline is concerned."

"To eliminate corporal punishment as a 'possibility' is the problem— I hope there is never a need for it—already we are having reactions from students, 'You can't touch me!' Corporal punishment is an absolute last resort, but without the possibility we will have difficulty."

"The fact we must take verbal, physical, mental abuse from students is absurd, especially in upper secondary levels. Why are the public schools forced to baby-sit youths who do not want to be in school?"

Teachers

"I believe we must have the right to use corporal punishment. I am also convinced it must be used more wisely than what I have observed in my 19 years' experience. Its proper usage depends on the offense, age of student, personality of student, and whether other punishments have proven to be effective. It also depends on the individual teacher."

Number of Occasions Used

Principals

"Three parents involving four students out of approximately 800 have requested no corporal punishment on signed forms."

"We are using corporal punishment less and less. I personally have not used it in two or three years. However, this does not say I won't use it tomorrow."

"In the 11 years I have taught and the three years I have served as principal, I have yet to use corporal punishment. I feel that when the situation comes up that it would be appropriate, it should be allowed. If it would be needed a *third* time with the same student, then obviously it isn't working for him and an alternative must be found."

"I have noticed an increase in misbehavior since the 'student rights' package was released. Corporal punishment in a reasonable form is the last line of resistance. Parents cannot control their children for the most part. Discipline takes 60 percent of my time."

"I am not sure I could require it for each offense. I think a choice should be given as each teacher may not favor the same punishment. In my present position (junior-senior high principal), I have not had to speak to a pupil in 10 years, but I do not favor its removal as a means of punishment."

"Corporal punishment is administered probably less than 10 times a year with our 1,050 students. However, *not* to have the right binds the hands of school personnel too tightly."

"We have used it only two times in the nine years I have been a principal. However, I know the fact that it can be used does make a difference. We intend never to use it unless *all* other ways have been explored to help the student."

Administrators

"My views on corporal punishment are not based on conjecture. In 38 years of school administration I administered corporal punishment but once—and that instance failed to achieve its objectives. My school systems were noted for correct conduct."

"The above may be *incorrectly* interpreted that I am in favor of a great amount of corporal punishment. How paddling is administered is much more important (as to its effectiveness) than why or by whom. There is a 'law of diminishing returns.' There have been years when I did not use the paddle at all, and other years it was used a handful of times. We must never abolish this form of punishment—but by all means it must be controlled."

Discussion and Conclusions

The response to the Basic Education Circular indicates that a majority of school districts in Pennsylvania permit the use of corporal punishment. Perhaps the most striking feature is the conscientious approach that most school districts have taken in developing policies. The wide range of additional guidelines points up the fact that the administration of corporal punishment is not taken lightly. Some efforts also have been made to define corporal punishment in terms of who may be hit, on what parts of the body, the striking implement and the amount of exposure. The response definitely indicates that frequent or frivolous use of this type of punishment is not strongly advocated, but that its availability is desirable.

The outstanding feature of the attitude responses is the high degree of agreement among the adult groups. Corporal punishment was supported on the basis of these beliefs:

It will cause changes in behavior.
Students learn self-discipline from it.
It can be less harmful than some other forms of humiliation.
There are situations where it is the most appropriate technique.
It is the only thing that will work with some students.
There is no harmful effect on student attitudes.

Its elimination could seriously affect the learning atmosphere in the school. On the other hand, the groups generally didn't feel that it builds character.

Three items are worthy of more extensive discussion. There was fairly general agreement that corporal punishment loses its effectiveness if it is temporally removed from the offense. Such a belief has implications for determining who should administer it and the administrative guidelines on its use.

Although there was substantial agreement with the statement "Some students receive corporal punishment while others do not for the same offense," the clarifying comments suggest that responses may have been based on two differing interpretations of the statement. First of all, some respondents felt that this represented unjust and inconsistent use of the practice. Also, some respondents indicated that the state board regulation allowing parental prohibition created instances of inconsistency. The second, and perhaps more common interpretation, was that this resulted from consideration of circumstances, for example, ability of a particular child to benefit from corporal punishment whether or not it is a first offense, and so forth.

The item dealing with perceived community support for use of corporal punishment presents some difficulties in interpretation because it was the only item which did not show a substantial degree of agreement among groups. A substantial majority of three groups (principals, administrators and school board presidents) believed that their communities support corporal punishment. The other three groups, while not agreeing with this, did not disagree either. This finding suggests an uncertainty about their perception of community feeling. More investigation would be required to determine whether people in the three groups with generally more authority are more sensitive to the beliefs of their community.

The portion of the questionnaire which presented fifteen different situations and requested responses as to whether corporal punishment should be applied revealed several significant findings. The most strongly emphasized of these, and an idea which appears frequently throughout the report, is that a rigid specification of any punishment runs counter to the philosophy of the educational system. The application of corporal punishment should, according to the respondents, occur only after a thorough analysis of all components of the situation. Much of the sentiment of the group was that professionals are capable of the necessary judgment.

In relation to the specific situations presented, there was quite strong agreement that certain offenses are beyond the province of the school and should be handled by other agencies, most often law enforcement agencies. Insubordination, disrespect, disobedience, disruptive behavior and profanity were perceived as school matters, and small majorities were in favor of corporal punishment in these situations if the circumstances warranted it. This section of the questionnaire received the strongest criticism. Again, those surveyed were critical of the attempt, as they perceived it, to obtain simple, clear-cut responses to very complex situations.

Responses to the question on who should administer corporal punishment, along with the added comments, indicate that there were two somewhat conflicting concerns of importance to the respondents. First, there appeared to be a strong feeling that the number of people empowered to administer it be kept small. However, there was also a strong general belief that corporal punishment, in order to be effective, should be administered at or near the time of the offense. The compromise chosen by the largest number of respondents was to allow the teacher to administer the punishment, but only in the presence of a witness, who could be the principal.

The item on whether the present state board regulation permitting parental prohibition creates situations perceived as unfair produced a somewhat ambivalent response. The responses indicate that a small majority considered the differential administration of corporal punishment unfair. The crucial consideration here seems to be the conflict between the desire for consistency, which can only mean the total elimination of corporal punishment, and the feeling that corporal punishment is effective and therefore should not be eliminated.

When asked bluntly about their personal attitudes toward the use of corporal punishment, a substantial portion of the respondents said they favored it. If students are excluded and only those responses of adults are considered, 75 percent of the respondents favored the use of corporal punishment. Many of the respondents, however, felt constrained by the simplicity of this question and added conditional and limiting statements to amplify their response.

The following comment by an administrator illustrates the dilemma posed by this very complex issue: "In favor of. I personally do not favor it; *however*, under certain circumstances a reasonable form of corporal punishment might be appropriate for a particular child. I feel it should be discouraged but not prohibited even if it is never used."

The many general comments were sorted into three broad areas. The first pertained to the questionnaire itself. Several respondents charged bias and felt that the people constructing the questionnaire were attempting to shape the responses to produce results supporting the abolition of corporal punishment. If the results already presented are used as an indication, this venture was an abysmal failure.

The second area into which comments were categorized was broadly defined as "the issue of corporal punishment." Gathered into this catchall category were:

> The determination of whether corporal punishment is used should be determined at the district level, not by the State Board, state legislature, state department of education or the courts.
> Corporal punishment is necessary to "stem the tide" of increasingly disrespectful student behavior.
> Even if never used, the deterrent value of corporal punishment mitigates against its abolition.
> Support for the use of corporal punishment definitely should not be equated with support for child abuse.
> Parents/guardians must assume responsibility which is removed from the school. If they prohibit the use of corporal punishment, then it is up to them to assume more responsibility for control of their children's behavior.

The third category involves several kinds of comments dealing with incidence of usage, parental prohibition and perceived effect of the student rights and responsibilities regulations. Individuals commenting on incidence of usage emphasized the rarity of its employment (e.g., "10 times a year with our 1,050 students," "two times in nine years"). The frequency of parental prohibition is indicated by a principal's response that parents of four out of 800 students had written requesting that their children not be punished. One principal commented, "I have noticed an increase in misbehavior since the 'student rights' package was released."

The overall response to this study emphasizes the complexity of this issue and the strong feelings that surround it. The careful consideration displayed by the respondents indicates their concern with this issue and provides a comprehensive examination of its many facets.

REFERENCES

Baker v. *Owen,* 43 U.S.L.W. 2451 (M.D.N.C., April 23, 1975).

Bard, B. Shocking facts about corporal punishment in the schools. *Education Digest,* 1973, 38, 46–48.

√ Benedict, E. *A study of corporal punishment.* Ohio Division, American Association of University Women, Dayton, 1974.

Children's Defense Fund. *School suspensions: Are they helping children?* Cambridge, Mass., 1975.

Corporal punishment: Teacher opinion. *NEA Research Bulletin,* 1970, 48(2), 48–49.

Ebel, R. L. The case for corporal punishment. Paper presented to Annual Meeting, American Educational Research Association, Washington, April 1975.

Geisinger, R. W. Corporal punishment in public schools: A review of literature. Pennsylvania Department of Education, October 1974.

Glaser v. *Marietta,* 351 F. Supp. 555 (W.D.Pa., 1972).

Hapkiewicz, W. G. Research on corporal punishment effectiveness: Contributions and limitations. Paper presented to Annual Meeting, American Educational Research Association, Washington, April 1975.

Ingraham v. *Wright,* 498 F.2d 248 (5th Cir., 1974).

It's time to hang up the hickory stick. *Nation's Schools,* 1972, 90, 8–9.

Mahanes v. *Hall,* C.A. No. 304–73–R (E.D. Va., May 16, 1974).

Myers, C. Punishment: Problems in definition. Paper presented to Annual Meeting, American Educational Research Association, Washington, April 1975.

National Education Association. *Report of the task force on corporal punishment.* Washington, 1972.

Patterson, J. How popular is the paddle? *Phi Delta Kappan,* 1974, 56, 707.

Queer, G. E. Discipline study. Pittsburgh Public Schools, Office of Research, Pittsburgh, Pa. (ERIC Document Reproduction Service No. 063660).

√ Should teachers spank their pupils? *Good Housekeeping,* September 1972.

*These four court decisions were summarized in *Inequality in Education,* Center for Law and Education, Harvard University, No. 20, July 1975.

19

An Analysis of Editorial Opinion
Regarding Corporal Punishment:
Some Dynamics of Regional Differences

Eileen McDowell

Robert H. Friedman

•

April 19, 1978, is the first anniversary of the Supreme Court's decision regarding the corporal punishment of schoolchildren (*Ingraham* v. *Wright*, 1977). One year ago, the majority of Supreme Court justices claimed that corporal punishment does not violate the Eighth Amendment's prohibition against cruel and unusual punishment. This landmark decision provoked debate between and within various sectors of society. Child advocates felt that it thwarted their movement toward upholding children's rights as citizens. Many parents felt that it denied them absolute domain in the disciplining of their children. Some teachers claimed that they deserved this added measure of protection. Others felt that it was a necessary step if we were to return to basic educational procedures. Even those students who were being punished corporally were divided on this issue.

While anecdotal evidence clearly is indicative of a division in public sentiment, a systematic investigation appeared to be warranted. The present authors undertook the task of analyzing opinion throughout the country. During an effort to sample these opinions, it was discovered that editorial opinion is often thought to be a barometer of public thinking on sensitive issues. Therefore, a decision was made to collect and analyze editorial opinion throughout the country which related to the landmark Supreme Court decision. Further, it was felt that a regional analysis would allow for the integration of findings on the opinion with other information related to variations throughout the regions.

This essay was presented as a paper at the annual meeting of the National Association of School Psychologists, New York City, March 23–26, 1978.

The present study represents an attempt to analyze the editorial opinion on the Supreme Court decision regionally and to relate these findings to other educationally relevant data available about these regions.

Method

Newspaper articles related to corporal punishment were received from a major newspaper clipping service (LUCE). Those expressing editorial opinion were separated and rearranged according to state. These were then combined into regions in accordance with the U.S. Department of Commerce, Bureau of the Census classifications (Statistical Abstract, 1976).

The investigators then identified as positive ($+$) those editorials which were supportive of the Supreme Court decision; identified as negative ($-$) those against the Supreme Court decision; identified as neutral (0) those articles not expressing a discernible position. All opinions were summed categorically. The percentages $+$, $-$, and 0 within a region were then computed, and a chi square was performed on the respective proportions. Coincident with this, the authors collected data on the money spent on education as a percentage of personal income (U.S. National Center for Education Statistics, 1975), the percentage of people over 25 completing high school within a region (U.S. Bureau of the Census, 1970), rates of illiteracy within a region (U.S. Bureau of the Census, 1976), and psychological personnel as a percentage of total instructional staff within a region (U.S. Department of Health, Education and Welfare, 1974). A set of rankings was computed for each factor and a Spearman Rank Order correlation was used to compare these rankings with rankings of editorial opinion.

Results and Discussion

Table 1 presents a summary of the regional distribution of the percentages of editorial opinion following the Supreme Court decision. The significance of the differences was tested by chi square for all regions. The result of this analysis indicated that a significant difference does exist among regions ($X^2 = 28.48$, df $= 16$, p .05).

Further, groups with significant differences were analyzed. The editorial opinion of the New England and Mid-Atlantic states was least supportive of the Supreme Court decision. It is interesting to note that the two states which have clearly abolished corporal punishment, Massachusetts and New Jersey (Friedman and Hyman, 1977) are in the New England and Mid-Atlantic regions respectively. While not a subject of our analysis, a hypothesis which needs further exploration is the relationship between

Table 1. *Percentage of Editorial Opinion within a Region Given by +, —, and 0 Designations*

	REGION*								
Position	*NE*	*MA*	*ENC*	*WNC*	*SA*	*ESC*	*WSC*	*MT*	*PAC*
+	11	21	55	56	62	68	61	45	47
0	22	26	19	20	19	5	13	36	27
—	67	53	26	24	19	26	26	19	26

*New England: ME, NH, VT, MA, RI, CT
Mid-Atlantic: NY, NJ, PA
East North Central: OH, IN, IL, MI, WI
West North Central: MN, IA, MO, ND, SD, NB, KS
South Atlantic: DE, MD, DC, VA, WV, NC, SC, GA, FL
East South Central: KY, TN, AL, MS
West South Central: AR, LA, OK, TX
Mountain: MT, ID, WY, CO, NM, AZ, UT, NV
Pacific: WA, OR, CA, AK, HI

the practice of corporal punishment and opinion regarding it. It is certainly possible that, where it is not practiced, other more effective methods of discipline have been found, and thus opinion about corporal punishment has become less favorable. The Mountain and Pacific states are next with 45 percent and 47 percent of editorials being pro opinion, followed by East North Central, West North Central, West South Central, South Atlantic, and East South Central.

Condensing the data, we found that regional differences on a larger scale are apparent. When NE, MA, and ENC are combined to represent northern states and SA, ESC, and WSC to represent southern states, the percentages of pro opinion are 30 percent and 76 percent respectively, and negative opinion was 70 percent and 26 percent. A chi square was performed ($X^2 = 10.78$, df $= 1$, p $< .005$), and an inference can be made that southern states are more in favor of corporal punishment than are northern states. This is consistent with anecdotal evidence. The southern city of Houston was at one time considered to be the corporal punishment capital of the country (Hyman et al., 1977).

A further analysis was done on west coast states versus east coast states. When NE, MA, and SA were combined to represent east coast states, 47 percent of editorial opinion was considered to be pro and 53 percent was negative (excluding neutral data). In contrast west coast states, consisting of PAC and MT, had 67 percent for the opinion and 33 percent against the decision. A chi square was computed, and significance was found ($X^2 = 3.01$, df $= 1$, p $< .05$). An inference made from this data is that the west coast views corporal punishment more positively than does the east coast. However, recent efforts directed toward the elimination of corporal punishment have emanated from the west coast.

Spearman Rank Order correlations were used to compare the percentage of those editorial opinions supporting the Supreme Court decision (+) within a region with the factors listed in Table 2. Four correlations, comprising three categories, were chosen to compute. It was hypothesized that

Table 2.   Spearman Rank Order Correlations between + Editorial Opinion and Related Factors

Factors	Spearman r
1. Expenditure for Public Education as a Percent of Personal Income	.750*
2. Percent of Population Over 25 Not Completing High School	.717*
3. Percent Illiterate within a Population	.650*
4. Psychological Personnel as a Percent of Total Instructional Staff	.417

*p < .05.

opinions about corporal punishment would have strong positive relationships with attitudes toward education and children as measured by money spent for education, the level of education within a region, and the decision to hire supportive personnel.

The strength of association between total expenditures for public education as a percentage of personal income within a region and the percentage of pro Supreme Court decision editorials is given by $r_s = .750$ (p < .05). As the percentage of opinion against the Supreme Court decision goes up, the percentage of income spent on education also goes up.

There are various explanations for this phenomenon. Corporal punishment is an inexpensive means of discipline. Other methods aimed at reducing disruptive behavior, such as the hiring of support personnel, in-service presentations, outside consultations, and so forth involve an initial outlay of more money. Another issue is that school has been a negative experience for those children who were punished corporally. As adults, they may vote against the allocation of increased funds for education.

The strength of association between the percentage of pro Supreme Court decision editorials and the percentage of those not completing high school is given by $r_s = .717$ (p < .05). As the percentage of those not completing high school (dropouts) goes up, the percentage of editorial opinion pro the Supreme Court decision goes up. In addition, a correlation of r_s — .650 ($p < .05$) was found between the percentage of pro Supreme Court decision editorials and the percentage of illiteracy within the population. The greater the percentage of illiteracy within a region, the greater the percentage of pro Supreme Court decision editorials. The above findings are interesting because they indicate a relationship between the extent of education within a region and opinion regarding corporal punishment toward children.

Descriptively, in regions where corporal punishment is not endorsed editorially, children are staying in school longer. In reviewing the effects that teacher criticism had on learning, Rosenshine and Furst (1971) conclude that "teachers who use extreme amounts and forms of criticism usually have classes which achieve less in most subject areas." It would be appropriate to view corporal punishment as an extreme form of criticism. Further, the findings in this study show that in those regions which editorially endorse corporal punishment, the literacy rates are relatively lower. Similarly, in those regions which endorse corporal punishment (severe criticism), the number of dropouts is relatively high.

The strength of association between psychological personnel as a percentage of total instructional services and percentage of pro Supreme Court decision is given by $r_s = .417$. That is, as the regions showed an increase in psychological personnel proportionally, there was a tendency for the editorial opinion in those regions to be less favorable toward corporal punishment. This is consistent with the hypothesis that the use of professional support personnel provides a viable alternative to the use of corporal punishment for disciplinary purposes.

In summary, the aggregate of correlations suggests that as a region becomes less editorially in favor of corporal punishment, they are spending proportionally more money on education, they are more educated, and they employ proportionally more psychological personnel.

REFERENCES

Friedman, R. and Hyman, I. An analysis of state legislation regarding corporal punishment. Paper presented at the Conference on Child Abuse, Children's Hospital National Medical Center, Washington, D.C., February 1977.

Hyman, I., Bongiovanni, A., Friedman, R., and McDowell, E. Paddling, Punishing and Force: Where do we go from here?, *Children Today*, September–October 1977.

Ingraham v. *Wright*

Rosenshine, B. and Furst, N. Research in Teacher Performance Criteria. In B. O. Smith (ed.), *Research in Teacher Education*, Englewood Cliffs, N.J.; Prentice Hall, 1971

United States Bureau of the Census, *Census of Populations*: 1960 and 1970, vol. I, part C.

United States Department of Health, Education, and Welfare, National Center for Educational Statistics, *Statistics of State School Systems*, 1973–74.

United States Department of Commerce, Bureau of the Census, *Statistical Abstract of the United States,* 1976.

United States National Center for Educational Statistics, *Advance Statistics of Public Schools*, Fall 1975.

20

Corporal Punishment

B. F. Skinner

•

Corporal punishment has, of course, a very long history. The Egyptians, the Greeks, and the Romans all flogged their schoolboys—there were no schoolgirls then. In medieval times it was the same. In England, even today, teachers' magazines contain advertisements for the taws—a leather strap preferred to the cane because it leaves no marks.

If you believe that what has always happened is going to happen, then history is certainly on the side of corporal punishment. But you might as well argue that it is also on the side of tyranny, despotism, military dictatorship, and police states. Almost every nation in recorded history has controlled its citizens through punitive measures, and issues between nations have almost always been resolved by that particular form of punishment called war.

We are proud of our efforts and occasional achievements in moving toward other ways of dealing with each other as people, and with other nations as nations. If education cannot lead in that movement, it can at least follow. The mistake has been to suppose that the alternative to punishment is permissiveness. If you take away the teacher's rod, the teacher feels helpless. Over the years, through the last half or three-quarters of a century, in the name of progressive education, education has abandoned one task after another because the teacher lacked the power to teach, and we come at last to a desperate situation. Those who support education must ask education to do something for them, and teachers must return to more effective methods. Many people suppose that there must therefore be a return to the aggressive, violent, punitive method of corporal punishment. A more effective alternative, which we are now pretty clear about, is hard to implement. We are *naturally* aggressive, for nature operates through aggressive techniques, as you will see if you watch any animal society. Moreover, we quickly learn to treat each other adversely because the results are quick.

This is an edited version of an essay presented at the Annual Meeting of the American Psychological Association in Washington, D.C., August 1976.

There are positive methods which produce what used to be called discipline. They need to be learned and they need to be taught by schools of education. The reason we are not ready to abandon corporal punishment is that alternative methods are still unfamiliar to a very large part of the world of education. The task of schools of education, and the task for all of us, is to make teachers aware of the possibilities of nonpunitive methods of interpersonal control and to promote all this at every opportunity.

But what about that "really tough student"—one who has been taught that there is only one way of getting along in the world and that way is to cause trouble? There are problem people of all ages who have been created by bad environments and who probably cannot greatly be changed. When that's the case a person does not belong in an ordinary educational environment. But it is worth asking whether or not a school is *producing* problem students, not only by the use of corporal punishment but by punitive or aggressive methods in general. It's so easy to resort to criticism, complaint, fault finding, ridicule, and all the other less than corporal forms of punishment. They all generate in the student the kind of problem behavior which in desperation the teacher tries to eliminate by even more violent punitive control, which turns out to be corporal.

The problem is not what you can now do with the disruptive student who causes trouble. We must look to the future. Can we create a school environment which will not produce these problems? I don't mean to say that all problem behavior is due to schools, but much can be done in the classroom by avoiding practices which through carelessness and ignorance create the problems which build up to the point at which corporal punishment is needed. The alternative is to replace *all forms* of punitive control— even the simple practice of marking wrong answers as wrong, rather than right answers as right. You can at least start by stopping corporal punishment. The punishing teacher who punishes teaches students that punishment is a way of solving problems. There are better ways and the school is the place where we all should learn them.

21

Pediatric Considerations
in the Use of Corporal Punishment
in the Schools

David B. Friedman

Alma S. Friedman

●

Children and their parents progress through social and emotional developmental stages in relation to each other. For school-aged children and their teachers, these stages become developmental tasks which they must accomplish to assure optimal cognitive development. Discipline is necessary for the accomplishment of these tasks. Discipline is also important for the safety and physical well-being of the child as well as for his or her social, emotional, and cognitive development.

However, discipline and punishment are not synonymous. Some parents and teachers who are strict disciplinarians seldom resort to punishment. Some punitive parents and teachers are poor disciplinarians. The aim of discipline is to provide the child with outside control until he or she can develop the inner or self-control necessary to function as a mature adult. Punishment is what adults resort to when discipline fails. The former headmaster of a well-known Eastern preparatory school commented recently, "When you resort to corporal punishment, you win the battle, but you lose the war!" We are defining corporal punishment as the deliberate use of physical force such as impulsive shaking, hitting, choking, swatting, head banging, caning, or paddling. We are not talking about the bare-handed swat on the clothed buttocks of a preschool child although even this, uncontrolled, may have its dangers.

There are five major developmental tasks of school-aged children and their teachers. Corporal punishment inhibits the accomplishment of each of these tasks.

By school age, the child should have developed what Erikson calls basic trust (Erikson, 1950). The parallel developmental task of the teacher

337

is to learn the cues; that is, to learn how to interpret the needs of each of his or her pupils. Corporal punishment erodes the youngster's basic trust, stimulates mistrust, anger, and resentment. The child learns that the adult world not only will not protect him from assault and battery, but also will sometimes be a party to it. Corporal punishment undermines the teacher's ability to interpret a pupil's basic needs and to provide an environment of mutual trust conducive to learning.

By school age the child should also have developed a feeling of autonomy or "I-ness." The teacher, therefore, has the task of accepting growth and development and learning to delegate some control to the students. Teachers must accept some loss of control while maintaining necessary limits. Again, corporal punishment slows the development of a child's feeling of autonomy and produces some degree of shame and doubt. The child's teacher fails in this developmental task, showing, at least in this one interaction, an inability to accept any loss of control.

By school age most children have achieved some degree of what Erikson calls initiative, that is, to be able to move out in the world and appropriately assert himself or herself. Another developmental task of teachers is to separate themselves from their pupils and to allow the children to develop independently while the teacher models optimal behavioral standards. Corporal punishment is demeaning, inhibits initiative, and stimulates in many children the development of feelings of shame, guilt, anger, and the wish to retaliate. The teacher shows his or her inability to accept independent development and models the big and strong controlling the small and weak by force rather than a mutual respect relationship. Ralph Welsh (1976), Adah Maurer (1976), and others are uncovering data which show a direct relationship between severe corporal punishment in early childhood and delinquency later in the life cycle. In these situations the child's initiative appears to be misdirected by the lifestyle modeled by important adults.

The school-age child must learn to learn and to develop industry or the ability to learn, work, and accomplish. His or her teacher has the task of accepting some degree of rejection and loss of control yet managing to be there when needed without intruding unnecessarily. Corporal punishment interferes with these processes by producing in the child some feeling of inferiority, helplessness, and inability to accomplish while thrusting the teacher into the role of intruder rather than learning facilitator or teacher.

The school-age child explores roles and relationships and struggles to develop his or her own identity, that is, who he or she is in relation to others. The teacher, therefore, must adjust to changing classroom roles, relationships, and interactions. Once again, corporal punishment interferes. The youngster may see himself or herself in relation to the authority figure administering the corporal punishment, in a number of ways depending on othcr life experiences. However, the child's own identity becomes diffused and the message is "might makes right." The teacher loses some flexibility in interrelating with the individual student and with the class. The teacher also loses the ability to develop and to model a variety of alternative coping and controlling mechanisms made possible by an atmosphere of mutual respect.

In addition to interfering with the developmental tasks of both teacher and pupil, corporal punishment may be physically harmful to the child. There are a number of recorded incidents of severe tissue damage, CNS hemorrhage, lower spine injuries, sciatic nerve damage, and even blood clots due to paddling. Recent evidence leads to the suspicion of possible whiplash injury especially in younger children. Other types of corporal punishment such as strapping also have the potential for physical harm.

Adah Maurer kindly has given permission to quote from her research (1976).

> In sworn testimony for the prosecution in a trial of a teacher accused of using excessive force and bizarre punishments, Dr. Moses Grossman of San Francisco gave a deposition:
>
> > From the medical point of view, corporal punishment, unless very strictly controlled, always involves the risk of bodily damage which at times might be severe. This is particularly the case when punishment is being administered in the heat of anger—when the person administering the punishment may not be fully in control of his emotions and might apply more force than he intended.
> >
> > In my opinion any kind of blow on the head must be absolutely banned. Any blow to the head whether delivered by a fist, open hand, book, or that results from being shoved into a wall can result in the production of either an epidural or subdural hemorrhage.
> >
> > Similarly, choking should have no place in the methods of punishment used. Choking can result in a decrease of supply of oxygen to the brain, or might even result in vomiting and aspiration of vomited contents into the lungs.
> >
> > Blows about the chest, over the genitalia and kidney areas might also produce unexpected and serious physical difficulties.
> >
> > Punishment which is capable of producing such injury should simply not be allowed. Although blows upon the buttocks have been known to cause broken blood vessels, massive fat emboli, and sciatic nerve damage, it is generally thought to be the safest area because no vital organs are located there. This, of course, presupposes that the skin is not broken and that the genitalia are protected.
>
> Dr. Frederick L. Goodwin, an orthopedic surgeon of Portland, Oregon, was asked to review and give an opinion on a school paddle that measured 33" including a 17" handle. The base was 10 3/4" across and 15/16" thick,

weighing 4 lbs. It had 26 holes, each the size of a penny drilled through the base. He refers to it as a "so-called paddle," more in the category of a club or a semi-brutal weapon. His statement in part:

> From an orthopedic standpoint this would be considered a very dangerous weapon. . . . There are multiple reasons for this. The length of the paddle would give it such leverage that the impact on the buttocks of a child could be such that it could give him several of the following: (1) It could cause a subdural hematoma from the contracoup effect. (2) It could cause particular hemorrhages in the brain from the same type of traumatic jar, as well as subarachnoid hemorrhages. (3) Also in reference to the gluteal muscles of the buttocks, it could do considerable damage to these and to the underlying bones of the pelvis. (4) If the paddle did not hit quite sharply, and was turned slightly obliquely, this paddle could cause severe damage to the sciatic nerves in the gluteal area. . . . If it happened to hit in the right place, it could cause a fracture of the bones of the pelvis and/or the femoral femur. If the above is not enough, (5) it could knock even a grown adult of my size, something like 200 lbs., off his feet and the damage could be multiple if the child was knocked off his feet to the floor or into a wall.

> The above considerations and opinions are given at this time on the basis of (1) as a human being with consideration for other human beings, (2) also as a father in consideration of children and (3) as a professional orthopedist in consideration of true medical injuries which could result from the use of such an instrument.

Just as the reported incidence of child abuse varies with public and professional awareness, so we believe increased public and professional awareness of injuries due to corporal punishment will demonstrate an increased number of reports of injuries due to school paddling and other forms of corporal punishment.

Child abuse has been defined as any interaction or lack of interaction between a caregiver and a child resulting in nonaccidental harm to the child's physical or developmental state. Paddling and other forms of corporal punishment may cause tissue damage and we believe that any punishment which causes such damage clearly falls in the category of child abuse.

Corporal punishment is one teacher-child interaction harmful to children. Corporal punishment inhibits learning, interferes with the accomplishment of each of the important developmental tasks of children and their teachers, and has the potential for physical harm to the child. Corporal punishment should be considered as child abuse and prohibited in all our schools.

REFERENCES

Caffey, J. The whiplash shaken infant syndrome. *Pediatrics*, vol. 54, no. 4, October 1974.

Chess, S. Temperament and learning ability of school children. *Am. J. of Public Health*, vol. 58, no. 12, December 1968.

Erikson, E. H. *Childhood and society*. New York: W. W. Norton, 1950.

Feshbach, N. D. Personal communication, July 1976.

Foster, H. L. *Ribbin, jivin and playin the dozens*. Cambridge, Mass.: Ballenger, 1974.

Friedman, A. S. and Friedman, D. B. Parenting: a developmental process. *Pediatric Annual*, vol. 6, September 1977, pp. 564–578.

Group for the advancement of psychiatry: Joys and sorrows of parenthood. New York, G.A.P., Report #84, 1973.

Helfer, R. Personal communication, June 1976.

Langner, T. S. Epidemiology of mental disorders in children, symposium. "A critical appraisal of community psychiatry," Kittay Scientific Foundation, New York, March 28, 1976.

Maurer, A. Personal communication, July 1976.

Welsh, R. S. Personal communication, July 1976a.

———. Severe parental punishment and delinquency: A developmental theory. *J. of Clin. Child Psychol.*, vol. 5, no. 1, Spring 1976, pp. 17–20.

22

A Practical Defense of Corporal Punishment in the Schools

Lansing K. Reinholz

●

I'm speaking as a school administrator and as a parent. I have three children, ages sixteen, fourteen, and twelve. The oldest is a boy and the younger two are girls. I've been a school administrator for eleven years; prior to that I was a teacher for three years. I'm not a psychiatrist, I'm not a psychologist, I'm not a counselor, I'm not a lawyer. I'm not anything except a "practitioner" that faces 6,000 children a day, 12,000 parents, a school board of 13 from a community of 40,000 that employs 400 professional teachers. Burlington is a Democratic city in a state that is viewed as a conservative state. But, in fact, Vermont is probably the second or third most liberal state in the country in terms of its political attitudes. Therefore, my point of view and point of reference are that there is a practical defense of corporal punishment.

An attorney by the name of Kelly Frels (1975) from Houston wrote:

> The authority of a teacher to use corporal punishment as a disciplinary technique is an element of the common law doctrine of "in loco parentis." Under the doctrine, a teacher stands in the place of the parent and has the right to use reasonable physical punishment to secure acceptable behavior. Standing alone as an abstract concept and unsupported by the requirements of securing and maintaining an educationable environment "in loco parentis" loses some of its Blackstonian vitality. The doctrine's loss of relevancy is particularly evident when a parent in whose place the teacher stands does not want the child physically punished. The concept of "in loco

This essay is based on a speech presented at the National Invitational Conference on Child Abuse, Feb. 18, 1977, sponsored by Children's Hospital National Medical Center. It was then published in *Proceedings: Conference on Corporal Punishment in the Schools: A National Debate*, by the National Institute of Education, 1977 (NIE–P–77–0079).

parentis" has almost universally been rejected at the university and college level. Teachers and administrators of public schools stand in some degree "in local parentis" to the students. The degree to which teachers and administrators stand "in loco parentis" appears directly related to the maturity of the individual student and his ability to function independently, conditioned somewhat by his parents' expectations. These factors, together with the existence of compulsory education, the nature of public school scheduling, the financing of the school through local property tax and other environmental factors peculiar to the public school setting are contributing factors to the existence of "in loco parentis." (p. 149)

On the other hand, the necessity for the use of corporal punishment as a means of managing behavior in schools arises from two particular sources. First, education is compulsory; children between the ages of six and sixteen must attend school unless otherwise excused by local or state statute. Secondly, there is often no positive alternative institution to which a child can turn when he/she is suspended from school. In this instance I think the word suspension is appropriate to describe the state of many of these youngsters. If they are suspended from school, where are you going to suggest the parents or the child go for assistance in obtaining a public education for that child? All of us recognize that public education is desirable; it is desirable for children to learn the basic skills that they need to support themselves and to be contributing members of society. The basic knowledge must come from the public school in this country, for there isn't any other source. Therefore, if we suspend a child from school as a possible alternative to corporal punishment, there is no place to send him/her except to the street. In Burlington, suspensions total about one hundred per year, all in the secondary schools. Suspended children under the age of sixteen do not end up back in the public school system for the most part. They go to an institution called Weeks School. Weeks School is a quasi-reform school for wayward youngsters. Wayward in this case means some behavior which may or may not be described in state statutes.

I think that as public school administrators or public school teachers we're being derelict in our responsibilities as public employees if we haven't used the alternative of corporal punishment prior to permanently suspending the student and sending him/her down a road where return to the public institution is impossible. Not having a place to send students when we suspend them from school results in a great cost, not only to society, but to the individuals involved. We recognize that.

The difference between what people refer to as the abuse of children and corporal punishment is not the only distinguishing factor with regard to touching children or disciplining children in school. Another term that is thrown about loosely is "physical restraint." There are qualifications that need to be exercised when corporal punishment is about to be considered as a means of punishing the child for inappropriate behavior. Those qualifications are necessary so that the corporal punishment has a beneficial effect and is not a destructive tool. Punishment should not physically harm a child for a long period of time. I'm not talking about abusing the child. I'm talking about leaving marks on the child. In fact, if a force beyond that which is reasonable results in physical harm to the child, then by all means that individual should be tried for criminal assault. I don't think you can find an educator in the country who would say that a person who inflicts such harm should be allowed to stay in the school. By the way, I was not the public school administrator in Vermont, referred to by another speaker, who in 1974 kicked a kid in the stomach. Kicking that kid in the stomach resulted in a court case which the teacher won, interestingly enough. The child was not kicked in the stomach; that was the alleged incident. Those people who are advocating the abolition of corporal punishment consistently put the term abuse right out in the front where the public sees it as being the norm rather than the extreme form of corporal punishment in public schools.

Corporal punishment should not be applied with malice. Again, we are talking about the reasonable use of discipline on a student in the public schools. The grievant, in my opinion, should not do the punishing. In the school the grievant is usually a teacher. As a parent, I don't believe that parents should inflict corporal punishment, spank their child or shake their child at the time that they are grieved. At that time the parent is angry, just as the teacher is angry when the child is disruptive in the classroom. When the parent is angry, he/she is not going to be reasonable. Under normal circumstances he/she is not going to inflict the kind of punishment that he/she would inflict if he/she took five minutes and calmed down and assessed the situation to determine whether, in fact, what the child had done really required as stringent a method of discipline as corporal punishment. The same thing should be true of the teacher. If the teacher is the grieved party, then the teacher should not be the person to inflict corporal punishment.

It's not even necessary to say, but I will, because people advocating the abolition of corporal punishment fail to recognize it, that rarely is corporal punishment ever used as the first means of punishment in the school. I've been in public education for thirteen years and I've never seen, never, not one time, a teacher or administrator or nonprofessional employee of the public school system hit a child the first time that a child does something that he/she is not supposed to do in school. I am not going to say that there are not instances of that. I do know of football coaches that have used forearm blows to a player who doesn't do what he is supposed to do on the football field and I think that is abuse. That is not corporal punishment. However, corporal punishment is not the first means of punishment in the school and it should not be. Corporal punishment should, in most cases, be a last resort after all means of appropriate punishment have been used and evaluated. It should be used when all other alternative means of punishment have been tried and have failed. The child should know beforehand why he/she is being punished and what he/she is being punished for.

The student receiving the punishment might be given a choice of corporal punishment or suspension if a professional, other than the grievant, deems that this would be a meaningful decision. If we rely so heavily on independence of students today, if we think that they are capable of making all those decisions that people in this country would like to have the students making for themselves, then maybe we should give them the chance to make this decision. Do you wish to receive corporal punishment or do you wish to be suspended from school? Suspension, in this case means not to return. Those are the last two alternatives when you get to the bottom line in a situation that demands corporal punishment as appropriate. Which one do you want? I can tell you that I have used that approach. In the thirteen years that I have been a school administrator and a schoolteacher, I can recall and document at least two hundred instances where I've administered corporal punishment and that's not all whacking. That's not just using paddles in every instance, but if you shake a student, if you grab a student, if you wash a student's mouth out with soap, that's corporal punishment under the definition of the law. If a teacher grabs a pupil by the ear to make him/her do something, that's corporal punishment. We're not talking about those things just limited to spanking. In all of those instances where I paddled children, as a high school principal, I never once failed to offer the child the alternative of being suspended from school permanently. We're not talking about a three-day suspension or a ten-day suspension. We're talking about a bottom-line permanent suspension by a school board. We've already been through the three-day and ten-day suspension route. Never once has an independent-thinking child chosen to be suspended from school because in most of those instances he/she wants an education. He/she wants to be some place where people care what happens to him/her. In most instances students choose corporal punishment because they know that we do care. In many of those instances, they come from homes where parents don't care.

The child should not be restrained in order to receive corporal punishment. If you use restraint, you then get into a situation where a child could get injured. Use of corporal punishment should not involve, needless to say, racial, sexual, social, or economic discrimination. The argument that "that's the only language they understand" or that "that child was always beaten at home" is circular. If beating worked, then the child wouldn't be in trouble now. A pampered child from an affluent home would be a more likely person to benefit from a "slap on the ass." Corporal punishment should be used no more than once for a child in a particular school. If the occasion arises where corporal punishment as an alternative is considered but has already been tried, chances are it's not going to be successful the second time. In my experience, I have never found it necessary to use it more than once on the same child.

With the above qualifications, I feel that corporal punishment is a necessary tool for educators. We should stop getting hysterical about the stimulus and concentrate on the needs of the individual and the organization serving that child and thousands of other individuals. The alternatives to corporal punishment are usually less attractive and, in my opinion, much less effective. I am more concerned about the continuous pain caused by boredom, fear, and anxiety among our students. These are things that they face more often than a single occurrence of corporal punishment. In addition, my concern rests with the right of all students to receive an education uninterrupted by a single, individual, disruptive student.

I'd like to take just a minute to tell you what happened in Burlington, Vermont. I was invited to speak as an advocate of corporal punishment on the "Good Morning, America" show with Alan Reitman, one of the speakers on the podium this morning. In the state of Vermont, three times, the relatively conservative legislature turned down legislation to abolish corporal punishment. As a sidelight, this term of the legislature, which started January 3, also had from the State Board of Education a bill for the abolition of corporal punishment. It lasted three days in committee and was killed. Subsequently, the state board deemed it appropriate to regulate corporal punishment by setting up a series of regulations for reporting the instances of corporal punishment which, in itself was not a bad procedure. No one objected to reporting instances of corporal punishment to the state to prove sufficient cause and documenting the occurrence rate in order to establish a data base. However, the legislature also attached a regulation which stated that if somebody used corporal punishment and failed to report it, that person could lose his/her teaching license. The administrator responsible in the school could lose his/her teaching license, the superintendent could lose his/her license. You know where that went! The National Education Association opposes corporal punishment, the Vermont Education Association opposes corporal punishment, the Burlington Education Association, as an association, opposes corporal punishment. However, the teachers do not oppose corporal punishment. Unfortunately, after I got back from New York and the "Good Morning, America" show, my board abolished corporal punishment when the majority of the community was up in arms over the state board's regulation. The Burlington Education Association leadership stood up and applauded. However, of the 401 professional staff employed by the Burlington Public School System, my personal estimate is that 90 percent of those professional employees insist that it be used as a means of discipline, when necessary, if teachers and administrators are effectively to deal with some of the students that are in the Burlington schools.

The deterrent nature of corporal punishment is inescapable. In 1975–76, there were forty-six instances of corporal punishment reported to the state from the city of Burlington (State Department of Education, 1976). Eight girls received some form of corporal punishment; the rest were boys. It was not all paddling. Of all the cases that have gone to court in the state of Vermont on charges of criminal assault, not one has been decided in favor of the complainant. The teacher or administrator has been upheld in every single instance. And so, although corporal punishment has been abolished, I work for the school board and therefore I'm not distraught at the fact that it's abolished. I'll work to get it reinstated because I believe in it as a means of disciplining, because we have found that problems have arisen since we've eliminated corporal punishment. For instance, a seventh grade student in Burlington stood up in front of a teacher after being disruptive and told the teacher he could "go plain to hell" because he knew he couldn't be touched. You can see that we have problems in the public schools.

I think it is important to establish the fact that there are alternatives to corporal punishment. There are probably two thousand or two million alternatives, on the bottom line, to corporal punishment. But as other speakers here have said, they are rather expensive because for each individual child, if you're going to have an alternative that you deem more appropriate than corporal punishment, it will be necessary to have people trained in how to implement those alternatives. The university instructors today are not prepared to train the future teaching professionals coming out of college in how to deal with some of our children in the classroom. Until those alternatives are available and used, until the funding is available, then this society must deal with the problems it is faced with currently. Society must get its head out of the clouds and get its feet on the ground in the public schools.

REFERENCES

Frels, Kelly, Corporal punishment—1975 style. *NOLPE School Law Journal*, 1975, *4*(2), 149+.

State Department of Education. *Annual report*. Montpelier, Vermont: Author, 1976.

PART VII

•

RESEARCH

One of the greatest problems in rationally discussing corporal punishment in the schools is the lack of hard research data. In order to obtain convincing data to examine the effectiveness of this practice, it would be necessary randomly to assign children to paddling and non-paddling with pre and post measures of behavior. Problems in methodology are numerous since there would be different rates of misbehavior which might or might not be affected by the paddling but would not be observable. While design problems in experimental settings would be simpler than those in the field, it is unlikely that such research will ever be conducted because of an interesting paradox. While most Americans favor the use of corporal punishment, the funding of such research would be unlikely because of controls for the protection of human subjects which are maintained by most responsible funding agencies and research organizations. Therefore, much of the discussion of the effects of corporal punishment must be based on either correlational or retrospective studies or on inference from related research. This section presents the first attempt known to the editors systematically to gather most of the data available which are pertinent to the problem. A number of research issues are discussed in less depth in the Introduction, but the essays presented here offer overwhelming data to discourage the use of corporal punishment in the schools.

The first one resulted from an exhaustive review of the research on punishment over the last ten years. At the time of the review the writer was a graduate student in school psychology who did not have strong biases about the issue. In fact, because of his own background, he tended to be mildly in favor of the "moderate" use of the practice. A thorough examination and analysis of the subject convinced Bongiovanni that the weight of the evidence indicates that corporal punishment in the schools is not only ineffective, but probably counterproductive.

In contrast to the review of research on punishment, Wise offers an argument in favor of the use of reward to change behavior. Despite the

*overwhelming data supporting the use of reward to shape and change be-
havior, many educators still cling to the belief that battering is better than
bribery.*

*The third essay is a review of studies which compare the effects of
punitiveness on achievement. If one conceptualizes punitiveness on a continuum, it is obvious that hitting will be some place on the end representing
an extreme. This is not to argue that excessive sarcasm, ridicule, and other
forms of verbal abuse are any better than the use of physical force; in fact,
the two often go hand in hand. The acceptance of this proposition resulted
in the review presented. Since most educators and the public appear to
agree that hitting is only a "last resort" to promote learning, it is important
to examine the effects of this extreme form of punitiveness on the learner.*

*The final essay by Hyman represents an attempt to examine some tra-
ditional assumptions regarding the need for the use of corporal punishment
in American education. As pointed out by Piele in Part II, the majority of
the Supreme Court in the case of* Ingraham v. Wright *used traditional beliefs and assumptions to justify their decision. The writers' examination of
the evidence and their ongoing research casts grave doubts about the wisdom
of the Court's approach to the problem.*

23

An Analysis of Research on Punishment and Its Relation to the Use of Corporal Punishment in the Schools

Anthony F. Bongiovanni

•

In recent years we have witnessed an increase in concern over the reported lack of discipline in American schools. It is not uncommon to attend a school board meeting where the discussion focuses on school violence, vandalism, and lack of respect for authority. A commonly suggested solution to the problem is to return to the practices "of the good old days" when corporal punishment was the usual fate of recalcitrant pupils. In fact, many proponents of the "back to basics" movement support the conservative ideology of stern discipline as a necessity for learning and the development of good character. However, despite protestations of lax discipline and the need to return to the use of corporal punishment and other punitive methods, a review of the literature will reveal that the practice is still thriving. Corporal punishment is still a widespread and officially sanctioned form of discipline in home and school (Hyman, 1976; Maurer, 1974). Yet while debate over the use of corporal punishment in the schools has continued for years, it is clear that little scientific data have been used to resolve the issue. A major problem is to determine how corporal punishment, as practiced in schools, affects the behavior of pupils. This is obviously a difficult question to answer. Central to the issue are questions of the effectiveness of corporal punishment in producing durable behavior change, the various factors which influence its outcome, and the incidence and effect of negative side-effects.

An examination of the empirical research on punishment reveals that the answers to these questions have not been clearly delineated. The lit-

This is a revised version of an essay which appeared in *Proceedings; Conference on Corporal Punishment: A National Debate*, National Institute of Education, 1977.

erature offers two major sources of information which may be utilized in formulation of answers. These are the systematic body of empirical data from the laboratories of experimental psychology and the field studies which focus upon the effects of discipline and punishment on the development of children. An analysis of the literature reveals very complex issues which often suggest contradictory conclusions. This paradox is in part due to the conceptualization of the punishment procedure, theoretical differences, and the limitations of our present experimental designs to isolate, control, and measure the numerous factors which combine to influence the ultimate outcome (Azrin & Holz, 1966; Church, 1963; Estes, 1944; Johnston, 1972; Solomon, 1964; Walters & Grusec, 1977).

As in any area of research, it is important clearly to define what one is attempting to measure. The conceptualization of the research problem and the experimental design rely on such a definition. While defining punishment may appear to be an easy task, it is the very lack of a universal definition which is primarily responsible for many of the paradoxes within the punishment literature.

Punishment has long been associated with the familiar dictionary usage which infers pain, suffering, penalty, and retribution. The intention of punishment is assumed to be the maintenance of authority or order (Mauer, 1974). In 1967 at a conference on punishment and aversive control, twenty-one experts were unable to agree on an acceptable definition of punishment (Campbell & Church, 1969). It is no wonder that those who look to the research for answers are often confused and discouraged.

The present literature appears to maintain two major definitions of punishment which differ primarily on the issue of aversiveness. One definition calls for "a reduction of the future probability of a specific response as a result of the immediate delivery of a stimulus for that response" (Azrin & Holz, 1961, p. 381). Such a definition makes no reference to aversiveness but focuses upon the future occurrence of the response in question. The other definition which is more prevalent subscribes to "the presentation of an aversive stimulus consequent upon a response" (Myers, 1975, p. 4). The latter definition makes no reference to response-reduction but focuses upon the aversive properties of the applied stimulus. A major problem of the latter is the failure of most researchers to actually demonstrate the existence of the aversive properties of the stimulus (Bercez, 1973). Therefore, due to this inherent inadequacy one cannot universally define the success or failure of most punishment procedures. If aversiveness is indeed a necessary requisite of punishment, it is vital to evaluate its presence and intensity when applying punishment to humans (Bercez, 1973).

The present concern about the use of corporal punishment poses a particularly difficult problem. Experimental psychology and field studies have not been successful in defining or clearly delineating the effects of punishment. As one looks specifically to the issue of corporal punishment in the schools no research has been reported. Thus, the effort empirically to define and categorize corporal punishment in the schools is difficult and is not without its own controversial aspects (Mauer, 1974).

The attempts which have been made are confounded by distinctions between pain and aversiveness, and whether such pain is physical, psychological, or both. Johnston, in a recent comprehensive review of the punishment research (1972), writes: "It should be noted that there is neither stated nor intended any implication that the consequent stimulus must be in any way painful to the subject or experimenter" (p. 1034). Yet, the majority of the experiments under review include the presentation of electrical shock ranging from mild to severe in intensity. If it is not for the presence of "pain," discomfort, or some other unpleasant quality, what is the mechanism of behavior change?

Myers (1975) makes some noncommittal attempts to classify corporal punishment into the existing punishment research. He alludes to the painful quality of corporal punishment and defines it as "pain inflicted upon the body of a person by another with or without some sort of painful instrument" (p. 9). He hints at grouping corporal punishment within a "presentation of stimuli" (p. 9) along with electrical shock. Such a classification is also at the more severe end of an implied continuum of intensity. However, he does refrain from doing so due to the paucity of research. No attempts are made to clarify the physical/psychological dimension.

Since corporal punishment, like the presentation of shock, includes the administration of a physical stimulus upon the body it seems plausible that they are similar types of stimulation. In addition, since it is typically applied to reduce the future probability of a behavior, some degree of aversiveness or pain appears to be the behavior change mechanism. Therefore, corporal punishment is conceptualized as sharing the two major definitions of punishment and is restricted to mean aversive stimulation.

Having defined corporal punishment we are still faced with the absence of empirical research from which to draw conclusions. It is appropriate, therefore, to turn to the massive laboratory research on animals and the limited field studies which examine the effects of other forms of punishment on children. Even with such an approach a conceptual gap remains. It appears that laboratory researchers have failed to recognize or have underemphasized the reality of education and human customs, while those involved in field research have underemphasized the scientific findings from the laboratory. Such an approach has inevitably resulted in misunderstanding and problems in generalizability (Mauer, 1974). In effect, dual approaches to research on punishment have results which are mutually exclusive at times.

Inherent to the problem of duality is the question of generalizing the results of animal research to humans, especially to the issue of corporal punishment. It is obvious that one must exercise full caution and a sense of conservatism when applying the results of animal studies to human interaction. Yet there is no valid reason not to utilize the massive amount of knowledge gained in animal studies. This appears particularly true because of the lack of literature in this problem area.

While at first glance the gap between animal and human research on punishment may appear large, there is some evidence to the contrary. Walters and Grusec in their extensive review of punishment (1977) note that, in fact, many principles derived from the animal laboratories have been successfully applied to humans, especially in the area of behavior modification. In addition, the authors note that several researchers are working in both areas attempting to integrate their findings. Of special importance is their following statement:

> It is also true that a parent or a teacher can turn to a rather straightforward set of principles developed in the animal laboratory for precise suggestions for the suppression of certain unwanted responses. Because the technology associated with the operant approach can be effective, practioners have been eager to borrow and apply it to human problems. Interesting enough, we might add that research in child development has not afforded the same degree of help for those who need to solve practical problems. (pp. 242–43)

Needless to say, corporal punishment represents a major practical problem for which little help has been offered.

The solution to the problem of generalizability would be to conduct research on corporal punishment within our schools. Such research would allow for appropriate experimental designs which would help to define variables and measure outcomes. Such research would, of course, permit some students to be physically struck. Only with this type of research could we begin to approximate the knowledge we have gained with animals. This research would, however, be extremely limited in application due to the stated moral, social, and ethical taboos of the American society (Baer, 1970; Johnston, 1972; Solomon, 1964). While this type of field research is not being advocated, one finds the logic involved with this issue to be ironic. We state that research which allows children to be physically punished is morally and ethically wrong. In addition, by not permitting this type of research we are protecting children from physical harm. Such a policy is indeed admirable. However, the reality is that society legally allows and often advocates the use of corporal punishment in the schools despite research ethics.

After reviewing and analyzing the literature, I recommend that corporal punishment not be allowed as a method of discipline in the schools. The remainder of the chapter will systematically review selected research on punishment to support this point of view. Unlike other reviews (Azrin & Holz, 1966; Church, 1963; Estes, 1944; Johnston, 1972; Solomon, 1964; Walters & Grusec, 1977) the findings will be directly applied to the issue of corporal punishment and its efficacy in changing undesirable behavior in the schools. This material is not intended to serve as an exhaustive survey of the punishment research. The interested reader is referred to the above stated references for this purpose.

As previously stated, the use of corporal punishment in the schools is viewed as the application of aversive stimulation upon the body for the purpose of reducing the future probability of a specified behavior. The application is that of operant conditioning within the social context of the school environment. In this respect, social learning is an important part of the punishment process.

The basic assumptions of educational philosophy in the use of corporal punishment within the school cannot be ignored. The research findings will, therefore, be applied in light of two basic educational concepts. First, any educational method (discipline) should be used in the form most effective to insure that the child maximizes his or her potential. Second, the best interest and welfare of the student should always be of paramount concern to school personnel. In light of the reviewed research on punishment, this chapter will demonstrate that corporal punishment cannot be effectively applied in the schools, and that the use of corporal punishment is potentially harmful to both students and school personnel, and thus contrary to the best interest and welfare of the student.

The Punishing Stimulus and Its Application

The characteristics of a punishing stimulus itself have been found to influence the ultimate effectiveness of punishment (Azrin & Holz, 1966). Five such characteristics, which should be adhered to as closely as possible, even with humans, have been identified. First, the punishing stimulus should be accurately described and measured. To the extent that such preciseness is not possible, the future use of the same stimulus may yield different results. School personnel would find it extremely difficult if not impossible to define and measure the intensity of a slap or blow. Second, during the application of punishment the stimulus should have consistent contact with the subject. Such contact or impact would again be all but impossible for a teacher to obtain. In fact, this concept is most difficult to even imagine within the context of any human interaction. Third, the punishing stimulus should not allow for any escape or behavior which would minimize the effect of application. Therefore, any escape behavior such as running away or even flinching on the part of the student would tend to minimize the true effect of the blow. Such control is not even achieved within the confines of the laboratory, let alone within a classroom. Fourth, the punishing stimulus should be able to vary in intensity to produce differential effects. Again, such control would prove to be unlikely. It is likely that, when one individual is striking another, he or she does not stop to consider whether the second blow is of the same intensity as the first.

Therefore, from an experimental view it would prove to be impossible for school personnel to administer an effective punishing stimulus. Even if one were able to control all the characteristics, there would surely be question about such a "person" within our schools. It appears as if proponents of corporal punishment are dealing with a method which they cannot adequately control.

Once the punishing stimulus has been specified, the manner in which it is applied has received much attention in the literature (Azrin & Holz, 1966). The most effective means of introduction appears to be complete surprise, with no anticipation of the occurrence of punishment. When application is sudden the elimination of undesired behavior is greatest. As punishment is introduced more gradually, the subject has opportunity to become habituated and may continue the undesired behavior at a high level regardless of any subsequent increase in punishment (Azrin, Holz, & Hake, 1963; Masserman, 1946). The degree of response suppression is also contingent upon the manner of introduction. It has been demonstrated that gradual introduction produces less suppression (Azrin, 1959a; 1959b). These findings suggest that school personnel should apply corporal punishment with the element of surprise. The child should receive no anticipatory cues. Such capability would be highly limited within the classroom. The typical procedure of yelling at the student first, and then having him or her come to the front desk for the deserved paddling, contradicts this research principle.

Related to the manner of introduction is the immediacy of delivery or the timing of the punishment with the undesired behavior. The most effective use of punishment calls for its application almost simultaneously with the occurrence of the behavior to be reduced (Azrin, 1956; 1958; Azrin & Holz, 1966; Parke & Walters, 1967). Any delay in the delivery of punishment leads to a lowered degree of effectiveness which assumes the form of a delay of punishment gradient. Effectiveness is inversely proportional to the length of time delay (Banks & Vogel-Sprott, 1965; Butler, 1958; Camp, 1965). Therefore, school personnel would need to be like minute men, ready to jump at the detection of unwanted behavior. One may wonder how a teacher would be able to demonstrate such a capacity. Even if this was achieved, it would seem plausible to suspect that he or she is really not concentrating on teaching behaviors.

The issue of timing poses a complex and potentially dangerous problem for school personnel. Human behavior is not simple and isolated. Rather, it occurs in complex sequences of events or motions with each motion capable of influencing the next. The execution of an undesirable act consists of initial or preparatory behaviors which may be very subtle and undetectable. As the sequence continues these behaviors may become associated with different degrees of reinforcement, which will tend to maintain or facilitate the development of the behavior sequence (Mower, 1960*a*; 1960*b*; Solomon, 1964; Walters & Demkow, 1963). To suppress an act, it is, therefore, beneficial to apply the punishment stimulus during the initial stages of the behavioral sequence to achieve maximal effectiveness. This appears to be particularly true with human behavior (Aronfreed, 1965; Aronfreed & Reber, 1965; Birnbauer, 1968; Walters & Demkow, 1963; Walters, Parke, & Crane, 1965). As one waits for the act to be completed prior to administering the punishment, the risk of having its effects counteracted by the presence of concurrent reinforcement increases with time (Walters & Demkow, 1963). In administering corporal punishment school personnel would experience problems, it appears, in attempting to adhere to immediate application. The detection of the initial preparatory behaviors may prove to be impossible. This is especially true in light of the number of children in a classroom and the busy agenda of the classroom teacher.

Still another problem in relation to timing and delay is present. Research (Johnston, 1972) indicates that many behaviors which may be separate from the undesirable behavior can occur during the delay in the application of punishment. Therefore, delayed delivery of punishment increases the likelihood of actually punishing a behavior quite different from the behavior in question. The behavior which ultimately receives the punishment may be an appropriate behavior. To illustrate this point, a child may have committed a transgression (talking) at 11 o'clock. However, he is not punished for that behavior until 3 o'clock. It just so happens that the child is sitting quietly at the time he is punished. What may actually happen is that the child is punished for sitting quietly. The common method of punishing a child after school for behavior which occurred in the morning is doomed to failure.

The intensity or strength of a punishing stimulus has been a factor which has received much attention in testing the effectiveness of punishment. In general, the greater the intensity the greater the response suppression (Azrin & Holz, 1966; Church, 1963; Johnston, 1972; Solomon, 1964; Parke & Walters, 1967). At lower levels of intensity the punishing stimulus may serve as a cue to future behaviors, a discriminative stimulus, a response intensifier, or a secondary reinforcer. The implication of this is frightening! If a blow is to be most effective it should be as intense as possible. Inherent in such application is the danger of inflicting physical damage. While most teachers and administrators do not intend to inflict physical damage on a child, one cannot deny that corporal punishment is often administered while angry. Under this heightened emotional state the results may be more severe than intended.

Research on the intensity of punishment on children has demonstrated that the effects of various intensities may well depend upon the task or behavior in question (Aronfreed & Leff, 1963; Feldman, 1961). In general, the greater the intensity the greater the response suppression provided that the task is relatively simple in nature. On tasks which are more complex, high intensity punishment tends to be less effective. One explanation is that at high levels of intensity, the punishment of complex behaviors may lead to a level of anxiety which is counterproductive for learning. Thus, intensity poses a very practical problem for the schools. There is no simple or efficient manner of knowing how intense a blow is, nor is the human control of such behavior consistent over time. Further, fear aroused even in nonrecipients of punishment may interfere with their learning as a result of a "ripple effect."

The scheduling of punishment or how often punishment should be applied is another important aspect to be considered. Studies have demonstrated that punishment is most effective when it is applied to each and every occurrence of the undesired behavior (Azrin, Holz, & Hake, 1963). Varying the application over ratio or interval schedules yields less effective results (Azrin & Holz, 1966). Studies of interval punishment have demonstrated that responding will continue at lower levels until just prior to the anticipated punishment, at which time it will approach a rate of zero (Appel, 1968; Azrin, 1956). Therefore, the anticipatory effect related to the onset of punishment allows for the maintenance of the behavior when punishment is not imminent. Research with humans on the effects of various schedules of punishment (even nonphysical types) is lacking. Such research would prove helpful to those concerned with the application of punishment (Johnston, 1972). At present, the implication for school personnel is that undesired behavior should be punished at each occurrence for the most effective results. Any application less often will allow for the continuance of the behavior at some consistent rate. The ability of students to anticipate when they are, in fact, to be punished detracts from maximal effectiveness. To be constantly aware of undesirable behavior, and to take the time to punish that behavior on each occurrence would require the major portion of school personnel time and attention. The focus of education would be upon undesirable behavior rather than learning and the fostering of desirable behaviors.

When employing a punishment procedure as a means of reducing undesirable behavior, we must ascertain how long and to what extent that behavior has been maintained by reinforcement. In short, how strong is the behavior to be eliminated? The fact that such behavior exists is evidence that it has a history of prior and concurrent reinforcement. Under such circumstances punishment is usually employed to counteract the concurrent reinforcement with the intention of decreasing the frequency of the behavior (Azrin & Holz, 1966). In general, the greater the history of reinforcement (especially concurrent reinforcement) of a behavior, the more resistant that behavior will be to the effects of punishment. Therefore, any reduction in the reinforcement of an undesired behavior will serve to facilitate punishment. To the extent to which concurrent reinforcement is allowed to exist, there will be resistance to punishment (Azrin, 1956; 1959b; 1960a; 1960b; Azrin, Holz, & Hake, 1963; Brethower & Reynolds, 1962; Holz & Azrin, 1961). Behavior maintenance by sources of reinforcement presents a major problem in utilizing corporal punishment in such settings as schools. It is highly impractical and probably impossible for school personnel to control and eliminate the numerous sources of reinforcement of a particular behavior deemed as inappropriate in schools. Many behaviors such as talking, laughing, and moving about are frequent, daily behaviors which occur at various times and in numerous settings. Such behaviors typically result in pleasure or reinforcement which tends to strengthen or perpetuate them. For example, talking to friends at lunch is a consistent behavior which offers the individual much social reinforcement. It, therefore, becomes a very strong behavior which is difficult to suppress. Within the school setting, such behaviors are not only required at various times but are permitted and encouraged to varying degrees by different personnel. It is evident that teachers allow different amounts of "free talk" in class. To control and attempt to minimize the reinforcement of such behaviors in order to maximize the punishment of them in a particular class would require a comprehensive analysis of the child's life. Such a task is beyond realistic expectation for a classroom teacher.

The availability of a second response or alternative behavior, which is reinforced and not punished, has been found to facilitate the reduction of a punished behavior (Herman & Azrin, 1964; Holz, Azrin, & Ayllon, 1963). It appears that in a punishment situation where a previously reinforced behavior is being punished, the presence of an alternative behavior, which is capable of earning similar reinforcement, will make the individual less likely to behave in a manner which will be punished. In the majority of cases where corporal punishment is used, the child is not offered an alternative response which is appropriate and reinforced. A typical example is the student who expresses anger by slamming books on the desk. More often the student is punished for "undesirable and disruptive" behavior rather than given the opportunity to leave class or discuss his feelings. Once again, the focus is upon undesirable behavior rather than promoting acceptable coping behavior which would be conducive to education.

A punishing stimulus may come to serve as a discriminative stimulus or signal for some forthcoming event which may ultimately hinder or facilitate the effects of punishment (Azrin & Holz, 1966; Holz & Azrin, 1961; 1962a). When punishment signals the subsequent occurrence of reinforcement within the environment the effects of punishment tend to be negated. As a result of signaling reinforcement humans have demonstrated both maintenance of punished behavior (Ayllon & Azrin, 1966) and an increase in the rate of that behavior (Azrin, 1958) in order to receive the subsequent reinforcement. In such instances, the individual actually works for punishment and seemingly enjoys doing so. It is, therefore, always preferable to have punishment signal that no reinforcement is forthcoming in order to produce the intended effects of punishment. Such a situation requires both a thorough knowledge of what is reinforcing to the individual and the ability to control such events (Lovaas & Simmons, 1969). It appears as if the school situation is particularly resistant to such safeguards since a number of social reinforments may maintain or even increase undesirable behaviors. Teachers may have to control such possible contributors to undesirable behavior as peer attention and laughter. A student who does not enjoy participating in a certain class or exercise may actually come to enjoy a paddling which keeps him or her from having to participate. In such a situation a student who does not want to attend a particular class may purposefully misbehave, receive physical punishment, and then be dismissed from class. He has indeed accomplished his mission. In such a case, the behavior which led to the paddling may be strengthened since it has been demonstrated to be effective. School personnel would be inadvertently working toward reinforcing the child's avoidance behavior.

As stated previously, it is preferable to have punishment signal the absence of reinforcement. However, this situation may be to the disadvantage of the child if he or she must be kept from participating in enjoyable activities that facilitate the educational process. By isolating a child after paddling, the child is kept out of the educational process and is placed within a situation which may acquire reinforcing properties. A typical situation would be paddling a child, then placing him in the hall to avoid the snickering and approval of his peers. Although the principle of the absence of future reinforcement has been met, the child cannot very well learn arithmetic while in the hall.

The Effectiveness of Punishment

Thus far the discussion has focused on specific variables which influence the effectiveness of punishment. Research has also identified characteristics of the operant conditioning paradigm which may be applied to certain questions about the outcome of punishment (Azrin & Holz, 1966). A frequently asked question is: How rapid are the effects of punishment? If it is indeed effective, the effects are immediate and drastic in reducing the rate of undesirable behavior. This phenomenon has been well documented in animal studies (Azrin, 1956; 1959a; 1959b). With humans, the initial effect is even more dependent upon the control of the variables discussed. Such a strong dependence makes a general statement regarding the rapidity of response reduction more tentative (Johnston, 1972).

The duration of effect and the permanence of response suppression are other major concerns. The permanence of suppression appears to be a direct function of the intensity of the punishing stimulus. Depending upon the intensity the duration can range from slight to absolute zero (Azrin & Holz, 1966).

The recovery of punished behavior has been demonstrated to occur both during and following the punishment procedure and is primarily a function of intensity and the schedule of punishment. Recovery during punishment is primarily a function of punishment intensity. With intense levels applied to each occurrence little or no recovery may be expected. Lower levels can be expected to yield varying rates and degrees of recovery (Azrin, 1956; Holz & Azrin, 1962a; Hake & Azrin, 1963; 1965). Even under well-controlled conditions, unexplainable increases in behavior have been observed (Azrin & Holz, 1966). When punishment is actually terminated, there is generally an increase in punished behavior. Such increases should be expected unless specific steps have been taken to avoid postpunishment rate increase (Johnston, 1972). Following the termination of continuous punishment, increases in response rate may actually exceed the original level. However, such a phenomenon is usually temporary (Azrin, 1960b).

In contrast to the immediate recovery of behavior which has been punished continuously, intermittent punishment tends to produce a more gradual increase in the recovery of punished behavior (Azrin, Holz, & Hake, 1963). In studies performed on humans the recovery response rates following the termination of punishment varied from being immediate (Baer, 1962; Barrett, 1962), to gradual (Risley, 1968), to none at all (Banks & Locke, 1966; Hamilton & Allen, 1967; Lovaas & Simmons, 1969). The type of recovery will depend upon the control of all the variables discussed and the amount of concurrent reinforcement available. In light of the difficulty in controlling such a number of variables within the school setting, educators should expect the recovery of the undesirable behavior treated by means of corporal punishment. The general implication of the research in this area is that corporal punishment is not the sure method of eliminating unwanted behavior which many proponents claim.

The generalizability of the effects of punishment is yet another major concern. Will the behavior punished in one situation generalize to other situations in which it is not actually punished? In general, the effects of punishment tend to be specific to the situation in which the behavior has been in fact punished. Initially, there may appear to be a lowered level of responding in other situations. However, such an effect is temporary and may lead to a higher level of responding within the nonpunished situations (Azrin & Holz, 1966). Therefore, the sharpening of the difference between the presence of the punishing stimulus and its absence tends to decrease the probability that a behavior will be reduced in situations where the punishment is not present (Terrace, 1966). Since behavior is maintained by the flow and sequence of stimuli within the environment it is inappropriate to expect the effects of punishment to generalize to different settings (Baer, Wolf, & Risley, 1968; Birnbrauer, 1968; Risley, 1968).

Johnston in his review of punishment research (1972) alludes to the problems a teacher may encounter when using punishment to decrease the out-of-seat behavior of a child. With the appropriate control of variables the teacher may be successful in reducing the behavior within the room in which he or she is in charge and is able to administer the punishment. However, to decrease such behavior in following classes, special arrangements of the environments will be necessary and other teachers will have to implement the same procedure. The results cannot be guaranteed, nor should they be expected. When corporal punishment is the method of choice the child may need to be physically punished in a number of classes and by a number of teachers. Such coordination may be difficult to establish and the social controls all but impossible to maintain.

In addition, the question of generalizability poses a difficult conflict within the school. For example, we may or may not want the reduction of a certain behavior to generalize to other situations. A teacher may not want a child to talk in class during a test. This same talking behavior may be required for another class which tends to focus on class discussions. Therefore, while the effects of punishment do appear to be situation-specific, there is still the risk that they will generalize.

As stated previously, an educational practice should be used as effectively as possible. By reviewing some of the primary principles of maximally effective punishment procedures it should be possible to create a hypothetical procedure for utilizing corporal punishment effectively in the schools. It should be made clear that the purpose for doing so is to illustrate that its use is impractical and to demonstrate the inhumane and potentially harmful consequences of such an approach to school discipline. Needless to say, the following procedure should never be used with a student: (1) The individual administering the punishment should arrange the environment so as to prevent the student from escaping. (2) The individual delivering the punishment should use as intense a blow as possible in order to inflict severe pain. (3) For each and every occurrence of that particular behavior the student should receive that same intense blow. (4) The blow should be delivered immediately without any form of discussion or explanation. (5) The blow should not be given gradually, but very quickly and with the element of surprise. (6) Extended periods of punishment should be avoided so as to avoid any increase in the unwanted behavior. (7) In order to avoid having the blow become a discriminative stimulus for pleasure, no pleasurable event should follow the beating. (8) Strict control over any source of reward for that behavior should be exercised. (9) Alternative behaviors which are capable of earning the same reinforcement as the unwanted behavior should be created and offered.

Beyond the absurdity of the above procedure it must be stressed that the successful use of punishment cannot be reduced to these few basic principles within such a setting as the school. Each case is unique and requires an individual analysis of the behavior in question. To the extent that a comprehensive analysis cannot be made, the ultimate effectiveness of corporal punishment will be decreased.

Negative Side-Effects

Inherent in the use of punishment is the potential of producing a number of negative side-effects. These effects may serve to hinder the effectiveness of the punishment procedure and to facilitate the development of socially disruptive behavior.

In the school setting, punishment may result in uncontrollable changes in the environment which affect the frequency of the undesirable behavior once the punishment has been terminated (Johnston, 1972). Several studies have demonstrated the sudden increase in new behaviors following punishment (Lovaas & Simmons, 1969; Risley, 1968; Wolf, Risley, Johnston, Harris, & Allen, 1967). Although the reported changes in behavior were positive in nature, they were also uncontrolled, unexpected, and fortuitous. Therefore, it appears that negative behaviors may also follow the termination of punishment. The post-punishment behavior patterns must always be considered since they may serve to facilitate or complicate the reduction of undesirable behaviors (Johnston, 1972). School personnel should attempt to anticipate classroom changes following punishment. However, it should be made clear that there are no sure methods of doing so. The teacher would appear to have to guess as to what changes will occur. This may prove to be a dangerous decision.

The use of punishment has been shown to produce strong emotional side-effects (Brady, 1958; Maier, 1959; Solomon & Wayne, 1954). The effects of aroused anxiety and stress may have a profound influence on subsequent behaviors and the ability of the student to learn and perform. Illustrative of the potential strength of conditioned anxiety is the prominence of behavior therapy techniques such as aversion therapy, sensitization, and implosion therapy all used to inhibit undesirable behaviors (Wolpe, 1958). Research on punishment often depends upon the gross observation of behaviors designated as "emotional." Such behaviors are often considered important for discussion only if they result in chronic behavior disturbances (Azrin & Holz, 1966). Emotional disturbance does not have to appear in observable behavior, especially in the case of human emotions.

In discussing the possibility of emotional disturbance as a negative side-effect of punishment Walters and Grusec (1977) state: "The question to be answered, however, is not whether bizarre behavioral changes can be produced by a punishment procedure, but whether such changes are a typical outcome of its use" (p. 158). While the authors do not intend to de-emphasize the possibility of emotional side-effects, there is cause to ponder such a casual attitude when applying a potentially dangerous technique to children. The point of whether such possibilities are "typical" is a statistical concept which should not be applied when the emotional well-being of a child is at stake.

Of prime importance is the potential of punishment to produce socially disruptive behavior. "It is in the area of social disruption that punishment does appear to be capable of producing behavioral changes that are far-reaching in terms of producing an incapacity for an effective life" (Azrin & Holz, 1966, p. 439). When a specific behavior is punished we usually expect that behavior to decrease and no change in other related behaviors. However, punishment tends negatively to reinforce any behavior which is successful in terminating or avoiding that punishment. In this respect any behavior which a child finds to be successful in terminating physical punishment will be strengthened. Such a side-effect may appear especially relevant to increasing incidences of truancy, tardiness, and dropping out of school (Azrin & Holz, 1966). To the extent that a student employs one or more such behaviors, he or she may be successful in avoiding all punishment at school. Since the school offers a major source of personal, social, and cognitive development, such a disruption represents a major social concern. Azrin and Holz (1966) state:

> The end result would be termination of the social relationship, which would make any further social control of the individual's behavior impossible. This side-effect of punishment appears to be one of the most undesirable aspects of having punishment delivered by one individual against another individual since the socialization process must necessarily depend upon continued interaction with other individuals. (p. 440)

For obvious reasons such an incident within the school could have devastating effects upon the student-teacher relationship which in turn would negatively affect the educational development of the student. The formation of avoidance or escape behavior plays a major role in running away from school and home.

Aggressive behavior as a form of retaliation against punishment is another potential negative side-effect which warrants much concern. Research has identified two types of social aggression which often result from the use of painful punishment. The first type, called operant aggression (Delgado, 1963), is a direct attack against the source of the punishment, with the intent of destroying or immobilizing the punisher. It appears that such aggression is maintained by the potential favorable consequence of terminating the punishment. When such behavior is successful, it becomes a negative reinforcer and is more apt to occur in the future under similar circumstances. The implication for school personnel using corporal punishment is obvious, especially at the junior and senior high school levels.

The second type of aggression is termed elicited aggression (Ulrich & Azrin, 1962). Elicited aggression appears to occur when an individual is physically punished in the company of others. Unlike operant aggression, elicited aggression is directed toward others in the environment, and not at the source of the punishment. The incidence of elicited aggression has been demonstrated to exist in several species and to be elicited by several forms of painful stimuli (Azrin, 1964; Azrin, Hutchinson, & Sallery, 1964; Hutchinson, Ulrich, & Azrin, 1965; Ulrich & Azrin, 1962; Ulrich, Wolff, & Azrin, 1964). Therefore, elicited aggression appears to be a general response to painful stimulation. Azrin and Holz (1966) state: "Since physical punishment requires the delivery of aversive stimulation, this social aggression would be expected as an elicited reaction to physical punishment" (p. 441). Again, the implication for school personnel is obvious. However, with elicited aggression, innocent classmates who have no relationship to the undesired behavior under punishment may be the target of physical aggression. The safety and welfare of other students should be a major concern of school personnel who use corporal punishment.

In addition, inanimate objects have also been demonstrated to be the targets of elicited aggression (Azrin, Hake, & Hutchinson, 1965; Azrin, Hutchinson, & Sallery, 1964). Therefore, the damage of physical property, such as books, desks, and windows, may also be expected as a result of corporal punishment. This issue warrants particular concern in light of the current increase in the cost of school vandalism across the nation.

When considering the potential for avoidance behavior, operant aggression, and elicited aggression as side-effects, Azrin and Holz (1966) state: "These three disadvantages seem to be especially critical for human behavior since the survival of the human organism appears to be completely dependent upon the maintenance of harmonious social relations" (p. 441). Developmental research has consistently pointed to the conclusion that children of parents who use physical punishment tend to be more aggressive than the children of parents who use other forms of discipline. Thus, the side-effects appear to have long-term influence upon the development of certain behaviors (Bandura & Walters, 1959; Eron, Walder, Tiogo, & Lefkowitz, 1963; Sears, Whiting, Nowlis, & Sears, 1953; Sears, Maccoby, & Levin, 1957). While such research focused upon parents there is no reason to believe that teachers would not have a powerful influence upon pupils' aggressive behavior.

Finally, the use of corporal punishment by teachers and other school personnel provides the child with a real-life model of aggressive behavior. Research tends to be quite conclusive and in agreement over the imitation behavior of children (Bandura, 1962; Bandura, Ross, & Ross, 1961; 1963; Bandura & Walters, 1963). Not only do children imitate such aggressive behavior from adults and other children, but many tend to utilize such behavior when faced with frustration in their own lives. In a study in which children observed another model being punished, a learned fear reaction was demonstrated to have occurred, although they were not personally the recipient of any punishment (Berger, 1962). The implication for school personnel is quite clear. The teacher who uses hitting provides a live model of aggressive behavior for the child to learn from and to imitate. Such a model may provide the child with a problem-solving method which he or she can use in a variety of situations.

Proponents of Corporal Punishment

Those who defend the use of corporal punishment as an effective method of discipline in our schools generally do so on grounds other than empirical research. The defense that it is a practical approach is often stated. However, those who utilize this argument view the practicality issue from the standpoint of the school only. After all, it can be applied by anyone, there is no need for special training, no expensive equipment is needed, and it can be applied within any setting at any time. The fact that most school personnel are physically stronger than the students makes the use of corporal punishment even more attractive. This defense makes no mention of the recipient of the punishment.

Killory (1974), in defense of corporal punishment, cites four criteria of punishment which should be considered and met: First, it should result in the greatest behavior change; second, it should demand the least effort on part of the user; third, it should result in behavior that is relatively permanent; and fourth, it should produce minimal side-effects. The research presented refutes each of these criteria.

In one article Leviton (1976) called for the need to individualize discipline by considering the match between the discipline strategy and the unique characteristics of the student involved. He then presented a tentative child-type and intervention technique strategy to deal with disciplinary problems. It is interesting to note that the only recommendation for the use of corporal punishment is with disorderly pupils. These students were characterized by: "restlessness, attention-seeking behavior, disruptiveness, irresponsibility, disobedience, incooperativeness, hyperactivity, impertinence, physical and verbal aggression, dare-devil behavior, bossiness, etc." (p. 447). It is ironic that corporal punishment be recommended for such students in that it often elicits the very same behaviors which already characterize them. In addition, it is with such students that corporal punishment is often used repeatedly with minimal behavior change (Bongiovanni & Hyman, 1978). Later (1978) Leviton states: "After reading through their brief article [Bongiovanni & Hyman, 1978] I feel their arguments make sense and that perhaps corporal punishment is not an appropriate disciplinary procedure for conduct-disordered children" (pp. 291–92). Once again we are faced with the potential danger behind the risk of the "ifs" and the "perhaps." Others defend its use on the superficial concept: "It's the only thing kids understand." This belief has been refuted (Hyman, McDowell, & Raines, 1977).

Conclusion

The available research on punishment when applied to the use of corporal punishment in the schools suggests: Corporal punishment is ineffective in producing durable behavior change; it is potentially harmful to students, school personnel, and property; it is highly impractical in light of the controls required for maximal effectiveness. As demonstrated, the maximal effectiveness of corporal punishment can only be achieved by strict adherence to the basic factors and principles which have been identified in empirical research. In light of the environment which exists in our schools, it is impossible to adhere to such principles and to establish the necessary controls. When we consider the stated role of school personnel in education the use of corporal punishment appears to be time-consuming and contrary to the best interests and welfare of the students.

The potential for negative side-effects, especially that of social disruption, constitutes the greatest danger. In light of this danger the possible reduction in any undesirable behavior should be secondary in importance. We must consider the ultimate cost involved in the temporary suppression of behavior. The remarks of Azrin and Holz (1966) seem especially appropriate: "At the institutional level, it would seem to be quite possible to eliminate the use of physical punishment. Conceivably, administrative regulations could be altered such that public punishment in the form of flogging, spanking, or other physical abuse would be excluded" (p. 438).

Some readers, especially the proponents of corporal punishment, may argue that the research is not conclusive but is at best questionable. While they are correct in noting the many contradictions in the literature, our main concern should not be with waiting for conclusive findings. Like a jury, those who deal with children must ethically question whether employing such a technique as corporal punishment can produce harm. Certainly, enough evidence points to this danger. In light of the many other alternatives to the use of corporal punishment, why even take the chance?

REFERENCES

Appel, J. B. Fixed-internal punishment. *Journal of the Experimental Analysis of Behavior,* 1968, *11,* 803–808.

Aronfreed, J. Punishment learning and internalization: Some parameters of reinforcement and cognition. Paper presented at the Biennial Meeting of the Society for Research in Child Development, Minneapolis, March 1965.

_____, & Leff, R. The effects of intensity of punishment and complexity of discrimination upon the learning of an internalized inhibition. Manuscript, University of Pennsylvania, 1963.

_____, & Reber, A. Internalized behavioral suppression and the timing of social punishment. *Journal of Personality and Social Psychology,* 1965, *1,* 3–16.

Axline, V. M. *Play therapy.* New York: Ballantine Books, 1974.

Ayllon, T., & Azrin, N. H. Punishment as a discriminative stimulus and conditioned reinforcer with humans. *Journal of the Experimental Analysis of Behavior,* 1966, *9,* 411–419.

Azrin, N. H. Effects of two intermittent schedules of immediate and nonimmediate punishment. *Journal of Psychology.* 1956, *42,* 3–21.

_____. Some effects of noise on human behavior. *Journal of the Experimental Analysis of Behavior,* 1958, *1,* 183–200.

_____. A technique for delivering shock to pigeons. *Journal of the Experimental Analysis of Behavior*, 1959, *2*, 161–163 (*a*).

_____. Punishment and recovery during fixed-ratio performance. *Journal of the Experimental Analysis of Behavior*, 1959, *2*, 301–305 (*b*).

_____. Sequential effects of punishment. *Science*, 1960, *131*, 605–606 (*a*).

_____. Effects of punishment intensity during variable internal reinforcement. *Journal of the Experimental Analysis of Behavior*, 1960, *3*, 123–142 (*b*).

_____. Aggressive responses of paired animals. Paper read at Symposium on Medical Aspects of Stress. Walter Reed Institute of Research, Washington, April 1964.

_____, Hake, D. F., & Hutchinson, R. R. Elicitation of aggression by a physical blow. *Journal of the Experimental Analysis of Behavior*, 1965, *8*, 55–57.

_____, & Holz, W. C., Punishment. In W. K. Honig (ed.), *Operant Behavior*. New York: Appleton-Century-Crofts, 1966.

Azrin, N. H., Holz, W. C., & Hake, D. F. Pain-induced fighting in the squirrel monkey. *Journal of the Experimental Analysis of Behavior*, 1963, *6*, 620.

Azrin, N. H., Hutchinson, R. R., & Sallery, R. D. Pain-aggression toward inanimate objects. *Journal of Experimental Analysis of Behavior*, 1964, *7*, 223–228.

Baer, D. M. Laboratory control of thumbsucking by withdrawal and representation of reinforcement. *Journal of the Experimental Analysis of Behavior*, 1962, *5*, 225–228.

_____. A case for the selective reinforcement of punishment. In C. Neuringer & J. L. Michael (eds.), *Behavior Modification in Clinical Psychology*. New York: Appleton-Century-Crofts, 1970.

_____, Wolf, M. M., & Risley, T. R. Some current dimensions of applied behavior analysis. *Journal of Applied Behavior Analysis*. 1968, *1*, 91–97.

Bandura, A. Social learning through imitation. In M. R. Jones (ed.), *Nebraska Symposium on Motivation*. Lincoln: University of Nebraska Press, 1962, 211–269.

_____, Ross, D., & Ross, S. A. Transmission of aggression through imitation of aggressive models. *Journal of Abnormal Social Psychology*, 1961, *63*, 575–582.

_____. Imitation of film-mediated aggressive models. *Journal of Abnormal Social Psychology*, 1963, *66*, 3–11.

_____, & Walters, R. H. *Adolescent aggression*. New York: Ronald Press, 1959.

_____. *Social learning and personality development*. New York: Holt, Rhinehart & Winston, 1963.

Banks, M. & Locke, B. J. *Self-injurious stereotypes and mild punishment with retarded subjects*. (Working paper no. 123) Parsons Research Project, Parsons, Kansas, 1966.

Banks, R. K. & Vogel–Spratt, M. Effect of delayed punishment on an immediately rewarded responses in humans. *Journal of Experimental Psychology*, 1965, *70*, 357–359.

Barrett, B. H. Reduction in rate of multiple tics by free operant conditioning methods. *Journal of Nervous and Mental Disease.* 1962, *135*, 187–195.

Bercez, J. Aversion by fiat: The problem of face validity in behavior therapy. *Behavior Therapy*, 1973, *4*, 110–116.

Berger, S. M. Conditioning through vicarious insigation. *Psychological Review*, 1962, *69*, 450–466.

Birnbrauer, J. S. Generalization of punishment effects: A case study. *Journal of Applied Behavior Analysis*, 1968, *1*, 200–211.

Bongiovanni, A. F., & Hyman, I. Leviton is wrong on the use of corporal punishment. *Psychology in the Schools*, 1978, *15(2)*, 290–291.

Brady, J. V. Ulcers in "executive monkeys." *Scientific American*, 1958, *199*, 95–103.

Brethower, D. M. & Reynolds, G. S. A facilitated effect of punishment on unpunished behavior. *Journal of the Experimental Analysis of Behavior*, 1962, *5*, 191–199.

Butler, D. C. Two choice behavior as a function of the delay between response and punishment. Doctoral dissertation, Northwestern University, 1958.

Camp, D. S. Response suppression as a function of punishment intensity and response-punishment contiguity. Paper read at the annual Meeting of the Eastern Psychological Association, Atlantic City, New Jersey, April 1965.

Campbell, B. A. & Church, R. M. (eds.). *Punishment and aversive control.* New York: Appleton-Century-Crofts, 1969.

Church, R. M. The varied effects of punishment on behavior. *Psychological Review*, 1963, *70*, 369–402.

Delgado, J. M. R. Cerebral heterostimulation in a monkey colony. *Science*, 1963, *141*, 161–163.

Eron, L. D., Walder, L. O., Tiogo, R., & Lefkowitz, M. M. Social class, parental punishment for aggression, and child aggression. *Child Development*, 1963, *34*, 849–867.

Estes, W. K. An experimental study of punishment. *Psychological Monographs*, 1944, *57* (3 whole no. 263).

Feldman, S. M. Differential effects of shock in human maze learning. *Journal of Experimental Psychology*, 1961, *62*, 171–178.

Hake, D. F., & Azrin, N. H. An apparatus for delivering pain-shock to monkeys. *Journal of the Experimental Analysis of Behavior*, 1963, *6*, 297–298.

_____. Conditioned punishment. *Journal of Experimental Analysis of Behavior*, 1965, *8*, 279–293.

Hamilton, J. & Allan, P. Ward programming for severely retarded institutionalized residents. *Mental Retardation*, 1967, *5*, 22–24.

Herman, R. L., & Azrin, N. H. Punishment by noise in an alternative response situation. *Journal of the Experimental Analysis of Behavior*, 1964, *7*, 185–188.

Holz, W. C. & Azrin, N. H. Discriminative properties of punishment. *Journal of the Experimental Analysis of Behavior*, 1961, *4*, 225–232.

_____. Recovery during punishment by intense noise. *Psychological Reports*, 1962, *11*, 655–657 (a).

————. Interactions between the discriminative and aversive properties of punishment. *Journal of the Experimental Analysis of Behavior*, 1962, *5*, 229–234 (*b*).

————, & Ayllon, T. Elimination of behavior of mental patients by response-produced extinction. *Journal of the Experimental Analysis of Behavior*, 1963, *6*, 407–412.

Hutchinson, R. R., Ulrich, R. E., & Azrin, N. H. Effects of age and related factors on the pain-aggression reaction. *Journal of Comparative Physiology*, 1965, *59*, 365–369.

Hyman, I. A. A bicentennial consideration of the advent of child advocacy. *Journal of Clinical Child Psychology*, 1976, *5* (3) 15–20.

————, McDowell, E., & Raines, B. Corporal punishment and alternatives in the schools: An overview of theoretical and practical issues. Paper presented at the Conference on Child Abuse, Children's Hospital National Medical Center, Washington, D.C., February 20, 1977. Partially funded by the National Institute of Education Contract NIE–77–0079.

Ingraham v. *Wright* 525 F. 2d 909 (1976).

Johnston, J. M. Punishment of human behavior. *American Psychologist*, 1972, *27*, 1033–1054.

√ Killory, J. F. In defense of corporal punishment. *Psychological Reports*, 1974, *35*, 575–581.

Leviton, H. S. The individualization of discipline for behavior disordered pupils. *Psychology in the Schools*, 1976, *13*(4), 445–448.

————. Response to Bongiovanni and Hyman. *Psychology in the Schools*, 1978, *15*(2), 291–292.

Lovaas, O. I., & Simmons, J. B. Manipulation of self-destruction in three retarded children. *Journal of Applied Behavior Analysis*, 1969, *2*, 143–157.

Maier, N. R. F. *Frustration: The study of behavior without a goal.* New York: McGraw-Hill, 1949.

Masserman, J. H. *Principles of dynamic psychiatry.* Philadelphia: Saunders, 1946.

√ Mauer, A. Corporal punishment. *American Psychologist*, 1974, *29*(8), 614–626.

Mower, O. H. *Learning theory and behavior.* New York: Wiley, 1960(*a*).

————. *Learning theory and the symbolic processes.* New York: Wiley, 1960(*b*).

Myers, C. Punishment: Problems in definition. Paper presented at the American Educational Research Association's Annual Meeting (60th), Washington, D.C., March–April 1975.

Parke, R. D. & Walters, R. H. Some factors influencing the efficacy of punishment training for inducing response inhibition. *Monographs of the Society for Research in Child Development*, 1967, *32*, (1, serial no. 109).

Risley, T. R. The effects and side-effects of punishing the autistic behaviors of a deviant child. *Journal of Applied Behavior Analysis*, 1968, *1*, 21–24.

Sears, R. R., Maccoby, E. E., & Levin, H. *Patterns of child rearing.* New York: Row, Peterson, and Co., 1957.

_____, Whiting, J. W. M., Nowlis, V., & Sears, P. S. Some child-rearing antecedents of aggression and dependency in young children. *Genetic Psychology Monographs*, 1953, *47*, 135–234.

√ Solomon, R. L. Punishment. *American Psychologist*, 1964, *19*, 239–253.

_____ & Wynne, L. C. Traumatic avoidance learning: The principles of anxiety conservation and partial irreversibility. *Psychological Review*, 1954, *61*, 353–385.

Terrace, H. S. Stimulus control. In W. K. Konig (ed.), *Operant Behavior*. New York: Appleton-Century-Crofts, 1966.

Ulrich, R. E. & Azrin, N. H. Reflexive fighting in response to aversive stimulation. *Journal of the Experimental Analysis of Behavior*, 1962, *5*, 511–520.

_____, Wolff, P.C., & Azrin, N. H. Shock as an elicitor of intra and inter species fighting behavior. *Animal Behavior*, 1964, *12*, 14–15.

√ Walters, G. C. & Grusec, J. E. *Punishment*. San Francisco: W. H. Freeman and Company, 1977.

Walters, R. H. & Demkow, L. Timing of punishment as a determinant of response exhibition. *Child Development*, 1963, *34*, 207–214.

_____, Parke, R. D., & Cave, V. A. Timing of punishment and the observation of consequences to others as determinants of response inhibition. *Journal of Experimental Child Psychology*, 1965, *2*, 10–30.

Wolf, M. M., Risley, R. T., Johnston, M., Harris, F., & Allen, E. Applications of operant conditioning procedures to the behavior problems of an autistic child: A follow-up and extension. *Behavior Research and Therapy*, 1967, *5*, 103–111.

Wolpe, J. *Psychotherapy by reciprocal inhibition*. Stanford, Calif.: Stanford University Press, 1958.

24

The Carrot Not the Stick: Comparing the Use of Reward to Corporal Punishment in Promoting Discipline, Learning, and Human Relationships in the Classroom

James H. Wise

●

The judge said to the prisoner, "You are to be hanged, and I hope it will be a warning to you."

The judge's statement usually understood by most children by age eleven as a verbal absurdity may be no less irrational than the firm belief held by a significant segment of the general public (Gallup, 1976), including the educational community (Reardon & Reynolds, 1975; Shaffer, 1968; NEA, 1972), that corporal punishment is a legitimate tool for teaching appropriate behavior or maintaining school discipline. The widely held view that corporal punishment is effective as a last resort is refuted by research which shows that it is the *same* children who appear to receive paddlings again and again (Shaffer, 1968). Consequently, the "logic" in the notion that corporal punishment is an effective *last* resort finds itself in close company with the above judge's sentencing remark.

Bongiovanni's review of the literature on the effects of punishment in the schools (1977) states that corporal punishment is "ineffective in producing desirable behavior change, is potentially harmful to students and personnel and is highly impractical in light of controls necessary for maximum effectiveness" (p. 35).

If the literature provides little support for the use of corporal punishment as a method of behavioral control in the classroom setting, what about its opposite, reward? The intention of this paper is to provide several comparisons of reward to punishment in general, and corporal punishment in particular, as related to their respective effects and efficacy in the management of behavior, particularly as applied to the classroom setting.

For the purposes of consistency and clarity the following definitions will be used:

1. PUNISHMENT: A negative incentive capable of arousing displeasure or pain. *Corporal punishment* involves pain inflicted on another's body.

2. REWARD: A positive incentive capable of arousing pleasure or satisfying a drive.

I (a) *A reward approach to behavioral management focuses on appropriate behaviors.*
   (b) *A punishment approach to behavioral management focuses on inappropriate behaviors.*

According to principles of learning theory, those behaviors followed by a positive reward or reinforcer tend to be strengthened or repeated. Reward here may refer to positive social verbal reinforcers such as praise or teacher attention; earned activity reinforcers or activity privileges such as games, trips, or "fun" jobs; primary reinforcers such as food or treats; token reinforcers such as reimbursable tokens or money; and other "ego" rewards such as merit awards or good grades.

There is today a considerable body of research literature on the effects of teacher attention on student behavior (O'Leary & O'Leary, 1972). Research studies have found that teacher attention is a particularly powerful factor in the management of children's behavior. Unless these studies are fully understood, teachers may actually "teach" children to misbehave without realizing their own role in the process. For example, Madsen et al. (1968) demonstrated that teachers who systematically increased the number of times they said "sit down" to out-of-seat first grade children actually increased out-of-seat behavior significantly. The children's out-of-seat behavior decreased only when teachers began to systematically quit telling (attending to) the children to sit down, and instead praised sitting and working. In another related study (1968), Thomas et al. demonstrated that when a teacher no longer praised (verbally rewarded) on-task behavior, off-task behavior increased from 8.7 percent to 25.5 percent. The teacher then criticized (verbally punished) off-task behavior. When the teacher then systematically further increased criticism of off-task behavior, off-task behavior actually increased to 31.2 percent and on some days was found to be above 50 percent! Only a return to praising brought back good working or on-task behavior. It is commonly assumed by many teachers that good behavior is its own reward. Unfortunately, the "good" or appropriate behavior may go unacknowledged while misbehavior receives teacher or peer attention. Thus with a punishment orientation—that is, attending primarily to inappropriate rather than appropriate behavior—the teacher may paradoxically increase the probability or frequency of occurrence of the inappropriate or punished behavior. The lesson for teachers here seems to be "catch them being good."

It has also been observed that some children seem to seek out punishment. These children may see themselves as "bad" and develop an identity of self which includes behaviors that are clearly aimed at receiving punitive attention. For example, observations of physically abused children indicate that many seem to seek out physical punishment from adult figures (Milowe & Lourie, 1964). Theoretically, it is thought that such children may see physical punishment as a confirmation of their own existence or self-perception. In effect, the child may be saying to him/herself, "I'm a bad person who will be recognized and confirmed as such by an adult figure through provoking physical beatings by them." Related to this is the apparent gratification described in the masochistic personality where pleasure or reward is found contingent upon one's experiencing physical pain or punishment (Freud, 1933). From a learning standpoint, punishment may signal forthcoming rewards (Ayllon & Azrin, 1966; Azrin 1958). Sadly, some children may only get hugged or attended to after beatings by the assaulting parent or caretaker, perhaps to assuage guilt on the part of the punishing adult. Paradoxically, therefore, for some of these children teachers attending to inappropriate behavior through acts of verbal or physical punishment may potentially increase rather than decrease the likelihood of future repetition of the punished behavior.

On the other hand, several studies have documented how the selective use of positive reinforcement or incentives contingent upon appropriate behaviors can enhance favorable behavior in children and youth who are particularly a risk for antisocial behaviors such as juvenile delinquent populations (Buchard & Harig, 1976).

II (a) *A reward approach to behavior management can shape and strengthen new or appropriate behaviors incompatible with inappropriate behaviors.*

(b) *A punishment approach to behavior management can suppress inappropriate behaviors although not necessarily shaping new or appropriate behaviors.*

When incentives, rewards, or other forms of positive reinforcement are used, the goal is typically to build or increase a particularly approved or appropriate behavior. Under such conditions the child is usually motivated to work at the rewarded behavior whether sitting in a chair, completing classroom assignments, or participating in cooperative peer relations or other approved behaviors. Development of appropriate behavior may initially be difficult for some children, as, for example, hyperkinetic students whose impulse controls are typically quite poor. Through a process of rewarding ever increasing amounts of appropriate behavior (shaping), a child may learn to sit still in his/her chair for longer periods of time, keep from talking out for longer periods of time, increase greater amounts of peer cooperation, increase on-task school work performance, or complete more classroom assignments. A number of studies have demonstrated how principles related to behavioral shaping with animal populations can be transformed to the human learning situation (Ferster, 1971; Skinner, 1957).

Related to the development or shaping of new behaviors is the concept of rewarding incompatible behaviors. The student who wanders around the classroom or frequently talks out may be rewarded for completing academic work since the latter behavior (on-task) is incompatible with the former (off-task). The elementary school student who habitually steals may be assigned as a special safety patrol monitor in the classroom. To continue stealing would be incompatible with the student's assigned responsibility and new found status.

While utilization of a positive reinforcement approach can develop and strengthen new or appropriate behaviors through gradually shaping them, the usual result of punishment alone is to temporarily suppress, through fear, those behaviors which the child has full control over. The assumption that a hyperkinetic student, for example, *knows* how to control his/her excess energy and only needs to be motivated by fear of punishment to suppress the child's activity level over extended periods of time is not supported by the literature on punishment (Bongiovanni, 1977). If punishment serves any purpose at all it is probably as a discriminative stimulus when a student has an alternative, acceptable, and previously unpunished response currently available that can be reinforced promptly (Holz & Azrin, 1962). Typically, unacceptable behavior has been observed to return to its original unpunished level after punishment is discontinued (Ferster, 1958; Powell & Azrin, 1968). While the same outcome may be argued (i.e., a recurrence of unacceptable behavior) when rewards which previously reinforced appropriate behavior are withdrawn, the likelihood of such an event occurring decreases when the rewarded acceptable behavior has a history of intermittent reinforcement (Ferster & Skinner, 1957).

III (a) A reward approach to behavioral management involves approach-type conditioning where desire for attainment for rewarded behavior motivates performance.

(b) *A punishment approach to behavioral management involves avoidance-type conditioning where fear of physical discomfort motivates performance.*

Related to the previous discussion on the influence of reward verses punishment and the shaping of new or appropriate behaviors is the difference each approach yields in the psychological set for the child. Use of an aversive event to punish a student is tantamount to giving the instruction, "Stop!" following an unacceptable response. On the other hand, the use of a reward procedure encourages a repeat performance of an acceptable response. Clarke, Montgomery, and Viney (1971) point out that if the intended outcome of punishment does not coincide with the student's value system, he copes by avoiding detection in order to continue to maintain the behavior unacceptable within the school authority. When the student is successful in avoiding detection and thus avoids punishment, the student therefore effectively reinforces (on an intermittent schedule) the undesired behavior so as to increase the probability of the ineffectiveness of the punishing stimulus permanently to suppress or extinguish the inappropriate behavior.

Conversely, the student who is rewarded for exhibiting particularly approved behaviors should ordinarily seek out and spend increasing effort at accomplishing those behaviors for which rewards are contingently made available. Although it happens that some students may perform "just enough" to reach criteria for earning rewards, the fault lies not so much with the concept but in its programming or systematization. Typically, over time, greater amounts of target or acceptable behaviors should be required of the student prior to receiving reinforcement. By sensitive scheduling of reinforcement beginning with fixed continuous rates of rewarding leading to intermittent or partial reinforcement rates, positive motivation for maintaining reasonably high levels of appropriate behavior should be ensured.

IV (a) *A reward approach to behavioral management may lead to positive feelings toward the reinforcing agent or others.*
   (b) *A punishment approach in behavioral management may lead to hostile feelings toward the punishing agent or others.*

Razran (1938) first studied the phenomenon which he called the positive or negative "spread of affect" or "affective association." Simply put, those things associated with pleasurable feelings tend to be responded generally in a more positive light; and conversely, those things associated with pain or discomfort tend to be seen affectively in a more negative light. However, it does not take more than common sense to realize that most students prefer to be with teachers or principals who focus in on the positive, who emphasize the rewarding of acceptable behavior rather than emphasize the punishing of unacceptable behavior. At the same time, students predictably will avoid or express hostility toward those associated with infliction of psychological or physical pain (Bakan, 1971).

In addition to differential feelings aroused under conditions of reward and punishment is the very real probability of creating antisocial behavioral changes under conditions of physical punishment. Response to physical punishment may trigger the following: (1) retaliatory direct physical aggressive acts toward the punishing agent (teacher or principal); (2) indirect aggression in the form of displaced acts of violence or hostility toward weaker peers (scapegoating); or (3) acts of vandalism against school property (HEW, 1977; Curtis, 1963). It is interesting to note that recent statistics from the Safe Schools Study by the National Institute of Education (HEW, 1977) indicate that 36 percent of all secondary schools reported paddling students in a typical month with many localities reporting very high incidence rates. At the same time the average monthly reports of physical attacks in schools by students against teachers is estimated slightly over five thousand. While a cause and effect relationship cannot be readily supported by the data, one must wonder what is actually being "learned" in some of our schools today with respect to human relations when so many teachers and administrators choose physical acts of violence against students as a legitimate method of behavioral management.

V (a) A reward orientation to behavioral management teaches students that praise and other forms of positive reinforcement are powerful tools for controlling or managing others' behavior.

(b) A punishment orientation to behavioral management teaches students that physical violence is a legitimate tool for controlling or managing others' behavior.

There is now a significant body of literature on how children learn through observation of the modeling of behavior by others (Bandura, 1973). In a classic series of studies by Bandura and his coworkers, it has been shown that children regularly imitate aggressive behavior of a model in the presence of the model (Bandura & Huston, 1961). Children will also generalize the modeled aggressive behavior to new situations where the original model may be absent (Bandura, Ross, & Ross, 1963). Hyman et al. (1977) note that in school environments where corporal punishment is condoned, "the basic message that violence is a way to solve problems is not lost on the children" (p. 4).

The notion that violence seems to be learned and passed on from one generation to another is seen in analyses of violence approval in our society (Owens & Straus, 1973) as well as in the current child abuse literature where it has been found that a high percentage of child abusers were, in fact, themselves victims of abuse as children (Kempe & Helfer, 1972). To this writer's knowledge no research exists today supporting the notion that the use of rewards or incentives instills or provokes violence in schoolchildren. Rather, there is now a wealth of research on the use of positive reinforcing approaches to increase prosocial behaviors in classroom settings (O'Leary & O'Leary, 1976).

VI (a) *A reward approach to behavioral management requires the availability of positive reinforcing agents such as tangible incentives or fun activities, approving teachers or administrators. This approach has not been found injurious to students' health.*

   (b) *A punishment approach to behavioral management requires punishing agents such as paddles, clubs, sticks, tough disapproving teachers or administrators. It may be injurious to students' physical or mental health.*

We have already covered such differences between a reward and punishment orientation in behavioral management with respect to differential focus or attention to positive versus negative student behaviors; the acquisition or shaping of new behaviors; differential psychological set, motivational consequences and differential feelings or actions toward the rewarding versus the punishing agent or others; and differential behavioral modeling effects found with each approach. Finally now we come to a practical common sense differential. Reward does not result in hurting the child physically or mentally. In contrast, the intention of punishment, and particularly corporal punishment, is to control behavior through fear of or actual application of physical or mental discomfort to the student.

Expert opinion on the medical risks of corporal punishment is provided by Dr. David Friedman in Part VI of this book. Friedman's testimony on the cases documented by Maurer in Part V certainly offer convincing proof of the potential harm that may be inflicted every time an educator raises a paddle. And research has shown that the paddle is the most popular method for applying corporal punishment in school settings (HEW, 1977). What can be said of the physical or medical risks involved in the selective use of a reward orientation in motivating appropriate student behaviors? While this writer has not yet heard of a case of a student being satiated or overloaded with M&M candy with resultant belly- or toothache by an overzealous (nonselective rewarding) teacher, the possibility of such an occurrence cannot be totally dismissed. Beyond that, one is pressed to find other physical-medical contraindications for utilization of a reward orientation to behavioral management.

Conclusions

This paper has attempted to make several comparisons of punishment, in particular, corporal punishment (the stick) to reward (the carrot) with respect to motivating appropriate student behavior in the classroom setting. In brief, these two approaches were differentiated with respect to: (1) the types of behavior attended to; (2) the capability of each orientation with respect to teaching or developing new appropriate behavior repertoires; (3) differential effects of approach versus avoidance-type learning; (4) the differential psychological set, feelings, and potential resultant behaviors produced by each approach; and finally (5) the physical-medical risks involved with two behavioral management approaches.

Does rewarding appropriate behavior always work to motivate and produce desired classroom behavior? The answer here must be an honest *no* (Varenhort, 1969). Does punishment and, in particular, corporal punishment sometimes work effectively to eliminate inappropriate behavior? The answer here too must be an honest *yes* (Lovaas, 1965).

It is generally recognized that corporal punishment frequently provides a cathartic release for pent-up anger and frustration on the part of the punisher. Corporal punishment therefore has specific reinforcing properties for the punisher increasing the probability of its future use on occasions. This is the paradoxical problem described by many teachers or parents who often find themselves reluctantly "hooked" on using a belt or paddle as a disciplinary technique. The sequence typically goes as follows: The child's misbehavior increases the teacher's or parent's frustration which, in turn, increases the teacher's or parent's anger which leads to the teacher's or parent's increased discomfort which leads to a discharge of anger in the form of physical assault upon the child. The child then stops the misbehavior, at least temporarily. The teacher's or parent's anger is spent and the teacher's or parent's discomfort is reduced until the next episode of child misbehavior occurs when, sadly, the cycle is most likely to be repeated again.

Ultimately, the case against the use of corporal punishment as a disciplinary method must be attacked on moral grounds. Simply to show, as attempted in this paper, that corporal punishment should not be used because of its relative ineffectiveness or unwanted side-effects really begs the question. For what would one's position be if research studies actually showed that corporal punishment was a more efficient or effective method for behavioral management? Should we then reverse our position? One is reminded here of a well-known long-standing "treatment" for the crime of stealing in a number of Middle Eastern countries. The guilty party simply has his/her hand amputated by the state. To what extent should our opinion on the merits of implementing this particular approach as a deterrent to crime be based on evidence that the incidence rates for stealing are significantly less in those countries that utilize that method of punishment? Clearly, we must draw the bottom line on the issue of human dignity and the worth of the individual human being. Sanctioning the use of corporal punishment in our schools only undermines this basic human tenet. Choosing the carrot, not the stick, is advocated in the interest of promoting positive classroom attitudes and behavior, while, at the same time, preserving the individual human dignity of both teacher and student.

REFERENCES

Ayllon, T., & Azrin, N. H. Punishment as a discriminative stimulus and conditioned reinforcer with humans. *Journal of the Experimental Analysis of Behavior*, 1966, 9, 411–419.

Azrin, N. H. Some effects of noise on human behavior. *Journal of the Experimental Analysis of Behavior*, 1958, 1, 183–200.

Bandura, A. *Aggression: A Social Learning Analysis.* Englewood Cliffs, N.J.: Prentice-Hall, 1973.

_____ & Huston, A. C. Identification as a process of incidental learning. *Journal of Abnormal and Social Psychology*, 1961, 63, 311–318.

_____, Ross, D. & Ross, S. A. A transmission of aggression through imitation of aggressive models. *Journal of Abnormal and Social Psychology*, 1961, 63, 575–582.

_____. Imitation of film-mediated aggression. *Journal of Abnormal and Social Psychology*, 1963, 66(1), 3–11.

Bankan, D. The effects of corporal punishment in school. *Journal of the Ontario Association of Children's Aid Societies*, 10–15, November 1971.

Bongiovanni, A. *A review of research on the effects of punishment: Implications for corporal punishment in the schools.* In J. H. Wise (ed.), *Proceedings: Corporal punishment in the schools: A national debate.* U.S. Department of Health, Education and Welfare, National Institute of Education, 1977.

Buchard, J. & Harig, P. *Behavior modification and juvenile delinquency* in H. Leitenberg (ed.), *Handbook of behavior modification and behavior therapy.* Englewood Cliffs, N.J.: Prentice-Hall, 1976.

Clarke, A. M., Montgomery, R. B. and Viney, L. I. The psychology of punishment and its social implications. *Australian Psychologist*, 1971, vol. 6, no. 1.

Curtis, G. C. Violence breeds violence—perhaps? *American Journal of Psychiatry* 120: 386–387, October 1963.

Ferster, C. B. *Transition from animal laboratory to clinic.* In A. M. Graziano (ed.), *Behavior therapy with children.* Chicago: Aldine-Athenton, 1971.

_____. Reinforcement and punishment in the control of human behavior by social agencies. *Psychiatric Research Reports*, 1958, 10, 101–118.

_____ and Skinner, B. F. *Schedules of reinforcement*. New York: Appleton-Century-Crofts, 1957.

Friedman, D. B. Corporal punishment in the schools. In R. S. Welsh (ed.), The Supreme Court spanking ruling: An issue in debate. Papers presented at the annual convention of the American Psychological Association in Washington, D.C., 1976.

Freud, S. A child is being beaten (1919). *Collected papers vol. II*. London: Hogarth Press, 1933.

Gallup, G. H. Eighth annual Gallup poll of the public attitudes toward the public school. *Phi Delta Kappan*, October 1976, 187–200.

Holz, W. C. & Azrin, N. H. Interactions between the discriminative and aversive properties of punishment. *Journal of the Experimental Analysis of Behavior*, 1962, 5, 229–234 (*b*).

Hyman, I. A., McDowell, E., and Raines, B. *Corporal punishment in the schools: An overview of theoretical and practical issues*. In J. H. Wise (ed.), *Proceedings: Corporal punishment in the schools: A national debate*. U.S. Department of Health, Education and Welfare, National Institute of Education, 1977.

Kempe, C. H. & Helfer, R. E. *Helping the battered child and his family*. Philadelphia: J. B. Lippincott Company, 1972.

Lovaas, O. I., Schaeffer, B. and Simmons, J. B. Building social behavior in autistic children by use of electric shock. *Journal of Experimental Research in Personality*, 1965, 1, 99–109.

Madsen, C. H., Becker, W. C., & Thomas, D. R. Rules, praise and ignoring: Elements of elementary classroom control. *Journal of Applied Behavior Analysis*, 1968, 1, 139–150.

Milowe, I. D. and Lourie, R. S., The child's role in the battered child syndrome, *Journal of Pediatrics*, 1964, 65, 1079–1081.

National Education Association. *Report of the task force on corporal punishment*. Washington, D.C. Author, 1972. (Library of Congress no. 22–85743).

O'Leary, S. G. & O'Leary, K. D. Behavior modification in the school. In H. Leitenberg (ed.), *Handbook of behavior modification and behavior therapy*. Englewood Cliffs, N.J.: Prentice-Hall, 1976.

O'Leary, K. D. & O'Leary, S. G. *Classroom management: The successful use of behavior modification*. New York: Pergamon, 1972.

Owens, D. J., & Straus, M. A. The social structure of violence in childhood and approval of violence as an adult. Paper presented at the meeting of the American Orthopsychiatric Association, 1973.

Powell, J. & Azrin, N. The effects of shock as a punisher for cigarette smoking. *Journal of Applied Behavior Analysis*, 1968, 1, 63–71.

Razran, G. Conditioning away social bias by the lunchroom technique. *Psychological Bulletin*, 1938, 35, 693.

Reardon, F. J., & Reynolds, R. N. *Corporal punishment in Pennsylvania.* Department of Education, Division of Research, Bureau of Information System, November 1975.

Shaffer, S. M. *Corporal punishment survey.* Pittsburgh: Board of Education, Office of Research, June 13, 1968.

Skinner, B. F. *Verbal behavior.* New York: Appleton-Century-Crofts, 1957.

Thomas, D. A., Becker, W. C., & Armstrong, M. Production and elimination of disruptive classroom behavior by systematically varying teacher's behavior. *Journal of Applied Behavior Analysis*, 1968, 1, 35–45.

Varenhort, B. B. Reinforcement that backfired. In J. D. Krumboltz & C. E. Thoresen (eds.). *Behavioral counseling: Cases and techniques.* New York: Holt, Rinehart & Winston, 1969. Pp. 49–51.

Violent Schools–Safe Schools. The safe school study report to the Congress: Executive summary. U.S. Department of Health, Education and Welfare, National Institute of Education. December 1977.

25

The Effects of Punishment
on Academic Achievement:
A Review of Recent Research

John Lamberth

•

The usual rationale for the use of punishment in educational settings focuses on the need to maintain order and a proper atmosphere for learning. The immediate and practical implications are to stop undesirable behaviors which are interpreted by educators as being disruptive. While there are a variety of methods to eliminate disruptive behavior, punitive methods are still widely used. Practices such as corporal punishment, suspension, and expulsion are historically rooted in American educational tradition. Earlier sections of this book document the use of physical abuse of children based on the Judeo-Christian belief that "sparing the rod" will retard or prevent proper moral development. Corporal punishment is just one extreme type used by educators.

Although punishment has historically been accepted pedagogical procedure there is relatively little research to demonstrate its effectiveness. Other essays in this section of the book examine the merits of punishment and reward as educational strategies to change behavior but do not present in depth analyses of the effects of punishment on academic achievement. The purpose of this paper is to examine the literature which focuses on the relation between the use of punitive educational methods and academic achievement.

Since there are no studies specifically examining the effects of corporal punishment in school on academic achievement, the investigator chose to review studies of punishment in general. By conceptualizing corporal punishment as one facet of the broader category, it is possible to speculate upon the results which might be obtained from the type of research which will probably never be adequately conducted. There is a body of literature which reports the effects of teacher behaviors on students' learning and achievement. Specifically, investigations have revealed that teacher use of approval, praise, and mild forms of criticism are more effective in enhancing various aspects of learning in students than are the use of disapproval and severe criticism.

Rosenshine and Furst (1971) reviewed seventeen studies which considered teachers' use of criticism. The great majority of these studies revealed a negative relationship between teacher criticism and students' school achievement. They concluded that the use of severe criticism generally results in less achievement for schoolchildren. The more current literature appears to support these conclusions. The following are brief summaries of a number of recent studies which investigate the relation between punishment and other teaching strategies to educational outcomes.

A study by Tikunoff, Berliner, and Rist (1975) analyzed the classrooms of a selected sample of teachers. Forty teachers who varied in their measured effectiveness as educators were chosen. The study was designed to obtain qualitative information concerning the effective teaching of reading and mathematics in the second and fifth grades. Graduate students trained in ethnographic data collection techniques observed each of the forty teachers in the sample continuously for one week. The higher achieving classrooms were noted as being cooperative, democratic, convivial, and warm; the lower achieving classes were viewed as being more belittling, shaming of students, and sarcastic.

Solomon and Kendall (1976) conducted a factor analytic study of teacher behavior and pupil outcomes. A broad sampling of classrooms at the fourth grade level was obtained in order that important classroom characteristics and classroom "types" could be determined. Fifty fourth grade classes, in twenty-six schools spread among five of a school district's six administrative areas, were observed. They were observed on eight separate one-hour occasions throughout the school year by eight different trained observers. A structured observation system was utilized to tally the occurrences of a number of specific classroom activities, teacher behaviors, and student behaviors. A set of global ratings was made at the end of each visit concerning general classroom atmosphere and quality of the teacher and student activities. Separate factor analyses were conducted with each section of the observation form. Also, a questionnaire wherein the teachers described their classroom organization and activities was also factor analyzed. In all, six factors were eventually obtained. They were considered to represent basic dimensions of classroom organization and activity.

Solomon and Kendall cluster analyzed the fifty classrooms into groups with like profiles in terms of their factor scores on the six factors. This cluster analysis resulted in six classroom types. There were approximately thirteen hundred fourth grade students in the fifty classrooms studied. Sets of parallel questionnaires administered to the children at the beginning and end of the school year measured creativity, inquiry skill, self-esteem, and a number of school-related attitudes and values. At the close of the school year, the students were asked to evaluate their classes. Further, they took achievement tests. The results were compared with achievement test scores administered the previous year. Finally, at the close of the school year, the teachers made ratings concerning the classroom behaviors of each of the children in their classes. The investigators concluded that teacher criticism of student behavior, shouting, scolding, ridicule, and sarcasm were consistently negatively related to achievement gain.

Taffel, O'Leary, and Armel (1974) conducted a study in which some children were given reasons (reasoning condition) for engaging in academic behavior, some were given praise (praise condition), some were given both reasons and praise (reasoning and praise condition), and some were given neither praise nor reasons (control condition). Subjects were second grade children from a public elementary school who were randomly assigned to one of the four conditions. The effects of reasoning and praise were measured by assessing the subsequent independent maintenance of that task behavior. One result of this study was that the reasoning and praise subjects worked longer and completed more problems correctly than those who received neither reason nor praise.

A 1974 study by Ludy investigated the effect of structure and praise on the performance of the retarded and nonretarded. Thirty retarded (fifteen educable and fifteen trainable children) and fifteen nonretarded children from institutionalized settings were given equivalence formation tasks using structured administration of tasks with praise for reinforcement. The author concluded that the retarded as well as the nonretarded possess the potential for the utilization of functional or action based concepts (linguistically based concepts essential for association and recall processes) within a framework of structured administration of tasks with praise for performance.

Fish (1974) examined how the effectiveness of verbal reinforcement is influenced by task interest and task performance level. Three verbal reinforcement conditions were utilized: approval, disapproval, and a neutral statement. Based on subject ratings, school tasks of high, medium, and low interest to fifth grade subjects were developed. At each interest level was one task with high performance feedback and one task with low performance feedback. Students within each class were selected randomly to receive one of the tasks. Also, task interest was determined and the subject's rating of the task was completed. Each subject had a pre- and post-test score for the number of items correct and items completed as well as pre- and post-test rating of interest for the task the student took. It was revealed that the greatest increase in number completed occurred when middle and low interest tasks were coupled with verbal approval and when high performance feedback tasks were paired with verbal approval. The study also found that verbal approval appeared to maintain and increase interest in a task. Therefore, children's attitudes toward a task were affected by the type of verbal reinforcement presented to them. If it is assumed that maintenance of and increase in interest of a task aids in improved study habits and academic attending behaviors, then it may be implied that school achievement would also increase.

A study of music teacher behavior (Dorow, 1973) was conducted for the purpose of obtaining evidence with regard to pupil music selection behavior and concert attentiveness as influenced by rates of teacher approval or disapproval. Seventy-six fourth and fifth graders were pre- and post-tested. The subjects were exposed to selected piano music under teacher high/low approval conditions. Approval ratios were controlled by approval/ disapproval cues given to the teacher at predetermined time intervals. A similar, second, experiment with twenty-eight first grade students was also conducted.

Dorow concluded that music taught under the high approval condition will be more reinforcing. That is, the time spent listening will increase for fourth and fifth graders and that music taught under the low approval condition will become less reinforcing. It was found, then, that teacher behavior (approval/disapproval) does effect such important aspects of learning as attentiveness.

Hughes (1973) investigated the effects of pupil responding and teacher reacting on pupil achievement. The subjects in this study were form II (seventh grade) pupils from thirteen classrooms in five intermediate schools in Christchurch, New Zealand. Three forty-minute experimental science lessons were taught; the topic of the lessons was assumed to be unfamiliar to the pupils since it was not a topic to be studied as part of the regular science program. However, efforts were made to ensure that the experimental lessons were similar to a typical classroom lesson. Variables being investigated were pupil response and teacher reaction. Pretest and post-test measures of achievement were obtained.

The two treatment groups in the teacher reacting portion of the study were termed reacting and no reacting. Pupils in the reacting group received frequent praise for correct answers, were supported when incorrect answers were given, but were urged or mildly reproved when it was warranted by the specific instance. Pupils in the no reacting group generally received little more than a statement of the correct answer.

The results of Hughes's investigation indicated that positive teacher reactions facilitate pupil achievement more than minimal teacher reactions. Furthermore, the reacting group's achievement increase over the no reacting group seemed to be the result of the generalized effect of positive teacher reactions and not the effect of the reinforcement of particular pupil response.

In 1976, Walker and Hops examined three groups of sixteen subjects selected from regular primary grade classes at three different times during the school year (September, December, and March). Subjects were selected in pairs and one child from each pair was assigned randomly to the experimental group. The experimental group received treatment in an experimental class setting; control children remained in the regular classroom. Group one children were reinforced for behaviors facilitative of academic performance. Attending, volunteering, and complying behaviors, as well as predetermined, classroom appropriate behaviors were reinforced for this group of students. Group two was reinforced for correct academic performance. Correct academic responding included such things as papers finished, problems completed, and tests passed. Group three children were reinforced for both facilitative behaviors and correct academic performance. Teacher praise for each group described exact behavior and/or response categories. For example, reinforcing statements such as "I like the way you followed my command," or "You've completed your assignment again. Very good" were employed.

No significant differences were found among the three experimental groups. However, there was a significant difference between the experimental and control groups. The experimental groups fared better with regard to reading achievement, math achievement, and level of appropriate behavior.

Jackson and Cosca (1974) measured teacher behaviors as a factor in the quality of educational opportunity offered to students of differing ethnic backgrounds within the schools of the Southwest United States. Four hundred and ninety-four classrooms were visited. The authors examined the relationship between student achievement and teachers' behaviors involving specific forms of praise, the acceptance and use of students' ideas, and the questioning of pupils. A slightly modified Flanders (Amidon & Flanders, (1967) interaction coding system was employed for the purpose of coding teacher verbal behaviors with reference to the ethnicity of the students to whom each behavior was directed.

This study found significant differences involved in all three of the teacher behaviors which were examined. Teachers praised or encouraged Anglos 35 percent more often than Chicanos, accepted or utilized Anglo students' ideas 40 percent more often than Chicano students' ideas, and directed 21 percent more questions to Anglos than to Chicanos. "Thus, Chicanos in the Southwest receive substantially less of those types of teacher behavior presently known to be most strongly related to gains in student achievement" (p. 227).

According to a study by the U.S. Commission on Civil Rights (1971), school achievement of Chicanos is below that of Anglos in the Southwest. The proportion of Chicano students who are reading below their grade level is nearly twice that of Anglos; also, 40 percent of Chicanos, compared with 15 percent of Anglos, do not complete high school. Other sections of the present book indicate that minority children often are the recipients of more corporal punishment than are Anglos. While comparison data are only suggestive, they are worth speculation.

Although Jackson and Cosca admit that their 1974 study may, in fact, fail to prove that the disparity of teacher behavior is a cause of disparity in student achievement between ethnic categories of students, they do suggest that the behavior of teachers in the Southwest are partially contributing to the poor academic achievement of many Chicano students.

Firestone and Brody (1975) conducted a longitudinal study which investigated the role of teacher-student interactions as a predictor of success in school. The subjects included seventy-nine kindergarten children and their six teachers. The children were observed over a period of one year in their four kindergarten classes; they were also observed during the first half of their first grade school year. Systematic recordings of the interactions which occurred between the teachers and the children were made by observers who employed a modified version of a category system which Flanders (Amidon & Flanders, 1967) originated.

The Lorge-Thorndike Form A IQ test was administered prior to classroom observation. The Primary Academic Sentiment Scale and the Metropolitan Achievement Test (MAT) were administered as post-test measures. Through the use of a multiple regression analysis, the authors found that knowledge of interactions between teacher and students significantly increased one's capacity for predicting academic performance independently of IQ.

Firestone and Brody concluded that "it is clear that children who experienced the highest percentage of negative interactions with their kindergarten teacher were also children who did more poorly on the MAT at the end of the first grade. Since these results exist with IQ controlled, it removes the possibility that negative interactions relate negatively to achievement solely because the 'duller' students were also those who received negative interactions" (p. 548). The authors suggest the interpretation that frequent exposure to negative reactions from the teacher hinders children in their attempts to feel competent or successful in the classroom.

Pritchett (1974) investigated the relationship between student perception of teacher-pupil control behavior and student attitudes toward school. Helsel and Willower's Pupil Control Behavior form, an instrument designed to measure an educator's behavior with regard to pupil control, was given to students. The PCB utilizes a continuum ranging from "custodialism" to "humanism." Also, Coster's High School Student Opinion Questionnaire, part 1, was administered to students and provided information concerning student attitudes toward school. These two instruments were administered to students from metropolitan area secondary schools.

An important conclusion was that custodial teacher-pupil control behavior was positively related to negative student attitudes toward school. Also, the attitudes of students toward teachers were shown to be a predominant factor in the determination of student attitudes toward school. The high correlation between student attitudes toward teachers and teacher-pupil control behavior stressed the importance of interpersonal relationships in determining students' attitudes toward school.

Pusey (1974) designed a study to examine the relationship between an environmentally realistic punitive threat and levels of high and low anxiety within the milieu of an Indian boarding school to expressions of behavioral hostility among the school's senior high school students. In other words, does the use of punitive threat serve to elicit forms of hostile behavior which it attempts to control or reduce?

Subjects were dichotomized into high and low anxiety groups. The students were then assigned to threat or no threat conditions. Both experimental and control groups were administered a projective testing device in order to ascertain level of hostility.

The investigator found that punitive threat acted to elicit significantly greater amounts of hostile expression in the treatment group as compared to the control group. Punitive threat by teachers, then, increases hostile behavior in their students. The use of punitive threat in the school situation is, therefore, seriously questioned by this investigation.

Rollins, McCandless, Thompson, and Brassell (1974) observed that teachers of inner-city students generally utilize negative or punitive techniques as their predominant mode of behavior control and incentive for academic learning. Their study, entitled "Project Success Environment," attempted to move teachers from their predominant use of negative techniques to a predominant use of positive incentives. Appropriate students' behaviors were rewarded, inappropriate behaviors were ignored, and almost no aversive measures were employed. The study's emphasis was on the preservice and inservice training of teachers in the use of positive behavior modification through contingency management techniques.

Subjects included 367 male and 363 female black students enrolled in a public middle school and three of its feeder elementary schools. The study's population came from pupils in the first, second, third, fourth, sixth, and eighth grades. The population was divided into an experimental group of sixteen classes and a control group of fourteen classes. With the exception of the first grade students, the experimental and control subjects were matched on the basis of reading scores.

The experimental teachers were trained during a three-week workshop held by psychologists and educators. The training was designed to provide instruction in the theory and implementation of operant conditioning techniques in the classroom. In the classroom the experimental teachers followed a policy of "ignore and praise"; that is, they rewarded appropriate behaviors and ignored inappropriate conduct. None of the control teachers were trained in the use of behavior modification techniques. All of the control classes were conducted in a traditional manner. A primary goal of this project was to accelerate both academic aptitude and achievement. These objectives were assessed by the experimenters.

The experimenters concluded that, through positive contingency management, inner-city teachers can be instrumental in controlling behavior, accelerating academic achievement and, as a function of accelerating academic achievement, increase IQ test scores. All sixteen teachers who participated in the study reduced the amount of punishment they had administered and increased their use of positive reinforcement, which included the use of praise. Within these sixteen classes, disruptive behavior dropped and task involvement increased.

In conclusion, the information presented here represents an update of the reviews conducted by Rosenshine and Furst (1971). The more recent research on teacher behavior and pupil outcome supports Rosenshine and Furst's finding that extreme forms of punishment are counterproductive to learning. The reader may question whether corporal punishment is really the same as the kinds of punishment reported in the studies reviewed. It may be that there are subtle outcome differences among verbal threats, sarcasm, ridicule, and actually hitting a child. However, until these differences are clearly demonstrated, the overwhelming evidence presented here suggests that extreme punishment in any form is counterproductive to good academic achievement and the development of positive attitudes toward school. Most important, it has been demonstrated here and in many essays in this book that teachers can be trained to use effective positive methods of discipline.

REFERENCES

Amidon, E. J. & Flanders, N. A. *The role of the teacher in the classroom.* Minneapolis: Association for Productive Teaching, 1967.

Dorow, L. G. The effects of teacher approval/disapproval ratios on student music selection behavior and concert attentiveness (doctoral dissertation,

Columbia University, 1973). *Dissertation Abstracts International,* 1973, *34,* 2157A–2158A (University Microfilms no. 73–25, 157).

Firestone, G. & Brody, N. Longitudinal investigation of teacher-student interactions and their relationship to academic performance. *Journal of Educational Psychology,* 1975, *67* (4), 544–550.

Fish, M. C. The effects of verbal reinforcement, interest, and performance feedback on task performance (doctoral dissertation, Columbia University, 1974). *Dissertation Abstracts International,* 1975, *35,* 4248A. (University Microfilms no. 74–28, 491).

Hughes, D. C. An experimental investigation of the effects of pupil responding and teacher reacting on pupil achievement. *American Educational Research Journal,* 1973, *10* (1), 21–37.

Jackson, G. & Cosca, C. The inequality of educational opportunity in the Southwest: An observational study of ethnically mixed classrooms. *American Educational Research Journal,* 1974, *11* (3), 219–229.

Ludy, I. E. The effects of structure and praise on the use of action concepts in retarded and non-retarded children (doctoral dissertation, Southern Illinois University, 1974). *Dissertation Abstracts International,* 1975, *35,* 4287A. (University Microfilms no. 75–129)

Pritchett, W. The relationship between teacher pupil control behavior and student attitude toward school (doctoral dissertation, Pennsylvania State University, 1974). *Dissertation Abstracts International,* 1974, *35,* 1929A–1930A. (University Microfilms no. 74–21, 022)

Pusey, P. F. The effects of punitive threat and levels of anxiety on hostility among Indian high school students (doctoral dissertation, Oklahoma State University, 1973). *Dissertation Abstracts International,* 1974, *34,* 6459A. (University Microfilms no. 74–8103)

Rollins, H. A., McCandless, B. R., Thompson, M., & Brassell, W. R. Project success environment: An extended application of contingency management in inner-city schools. *Journal of Educational Psychology,* 1974, *66* (2), 167–178.

Rosenshine, B. & Furst, N. Research in teacher performance criteria in Smith, B. O. (ed.), *Research in teacher education.* Englewood Cliffs, N.J.: Prentice-Hall, 1971.

Solomon, D. & Kendall, A. J. *Final report individual characteristics and children's performance in varied educational settings.* Chicago: Spencer Foundation Project, May 1976.

Taffel, S. J., O'Leary, K. D., & Armel, S. Reasoning and praise: Their effects on academic behavior. *Journal of Educational Psychology,* 1974, *66* (3), 291–295.

Tikunoff, W., Berliner, D. C., and Rist, R. C. *An ethnographic study of the forty classrooms of the Beginning Teacher Evaluation Study known sample.* Technical Report no. 75–10–5. San Francisco: Far West Laboratory for Educational Research and Development, October 1975.

U.S. Commission on Civil Rights. *The unfinished education.* (Report II of the Mexican American Education Study.) Washington, D.C.: U.S. Government Printing Office, 1971.

Walker, H. M. & Hops, H. Increasing academic achievement by reinforcing direct academic performance and/or facilitative non-academic responses. *Journal of Educational Psychology*, 1976, 68 (2), 218–225.

26

A Social Science Analysis
of Evidence Cited in Litigation
on Corporal Punishment
in the Schools

Irwin A. Hyman

•

During the twentieth century American society through its judicial and educational establishments has recognized increasingly that children are citizens. While parents' and citizens' groups have lobbied and worked for reform legislation, there is little question that the judicial system has aided in the recognition of the rights of children. However, it is becoming increasingly obvious that the Nixon appointees to the Supreme Court, in concurrence with earlier conservative appointees, has moved away from the recognition of children's rights as citizens within the context of the public schools. Perhaps one of the most far-reaching decisions in the current backward spiral of the Supreme Court attitude occurred on April 19, 1977, when the United States Supreme Court ruled that the cruel and unusual punishment clause of the Eighth Amendment did not apply to the use of corporal punishment on public school children. In the case of *Ingraham* v. *Wright*, 45 L.W. 4364, the Supreme Court not only refused protection (under the Constitution) for children against corporal punishment but they held that the due process clause of the Constitution does not require notice and hearing prior to the imposition of corporal punishment. The minority opinion written by Justices White, Brennan, Marshall, and Stevens outlines the obvious legal inconsistencies apparent in the majority opinion.

The legal and educational implications of the Supreme Court decision in *Ingraham* v. *Wright* have far-reaching effects. However, the purpose of

This essay was presented as a paper at the 55th Annual Meeting of the American Orthopsychiatric Association, San Francisco, California, March 31, 1978.

this essay is not to present an extensive legal analysis of that decision but rather to discuss underlying assumptions that appear to have led the majority to rule against plaintiffs.

Assumption: Corporal Punishment Is Rarely Abused

Underlying the assumption of the rarity of abuse of corporal punishment is the opinion suggested in the brief of the Miami Dade County School Board which indicated that "moderate use of corporal punishment is a rare alternative to more drastic exclusionary devices" (Howard, p. 11). Although this was not directly stated in the majority opinion written by Justice Powell, he does indicate the belief that physical injury rarely occurs as a result of corporal punishment and that when physical injury does occur it is rarely severe.

In order to understand Powell's statement it is important to define "physical injury" and the actual meaning of "rare." Is redness of skin tissue as a result of paddling considered injury? Depending on the force and number of blows, the redness increases and eventually hematoma results. Dr. David Friedman (1977) presented an excellent paper outlining the many physical dangers inherent in the use of corporal punishment. Included are broken blood vessels, massive fat emboli, sciatic nerve damage, damage to gluteal muscles, and even hemorrhages in the brain. In a case in Michigan a child suffered hearing loss because of paddling (Lee, 1977). In most cases of corporal punishment the damage does not require hospitalization; however, abuse may be defined as the actual infliction of bodily changes as the result of force rather than by the need for medical attention.

Powell's statement about "rareness" was analyzed. Webster's New Collegiate Dictionary defines rareness as "infrequent or seldom occurring events" (Webster, 1973, p. 957). If one assumes that any bodily changes which occur as a result of a physical blow may be considered abuse of the body of the recipient, then data should indicate the extent and severity of the use of corporal punishment in order to answer Powell's contention. Under the assumption that corporal punishment is rarely abused are the statements of Powell which indicate that there is little risk of error in paddling. Research on teacher behavior in disciplinary situations indicates that there are many teachers who are poor disciplinarians. Their classroom management is often characterized by the use of incorrect targeting of students for discipline. Findings by Kounin (1970) and others (Hyman, 1972) suggest that there is a great deal of error in disciplinary practices by teachers.

At the National Center, two efforts have begun in order to test the assumptions concerning the severity and extent of corporal punishment.

We have begun the development of a casebook in which all incidents of corporal punishment are categorized by type. This casebook has been made possible by the use of a press clipping service by Adah Maurer in the production of her newsletter, *The Last Resort*. Further, we have a national network of Friends of the Center who send us clippings and information concerning legal cases where corporal punishment has been used to the extent of severe physical harm. While the actual statistical incidence of reported severe abuse is small, there is enough evidence from the reported cases, which are just the tip of the iceberg, to indicate that abuse is not rare.

In reference to the extent of the use of corporal punishment, a number of studies show that large numbers of children are corporally punished each year (Hyman, McDowell, Raines, 1978). However, in an effort to gather more data, staff at the National Center has conducted a study using information collected by the Office of Civil Rights in their most recent survey of school practices regarding suspensions and corporal punishment with minority children (Glackman, Martin, Hyman, McDowell, Berv, & Spino, 1978). In this study, the investigator examined the raw data available at the Federal Regional office in Philadelphia. Because of the large number of returns, it was decided to draw a random sample which represented 1.5 percent of 7,673 public schools in the five-state area including Pennsylvania, Maryland, West Virginia, and Delaware. This sample represented 73,643 students from the schools selected. Unfortunately, the data did not indicate whether students were hit more than once but only recorded number of corporal punishments per school. If one assumes, however, for statistical purposes that each incident reported was for a different child, it was found that out of 73,643 enrolled students, there were 4,335 incidents of corporal punishment. This indicates that 5.9 percent of students or one out of every seventeen students may have received corporal punishment during the year of the report. However, the data varied among schools. For example, one elementary school reported 205 incidents of corporal punishment for a student population of 375 while another reported only 2 incidents for 550 students. It is obvious that a figure of 6 percent, while not massive, certainly does not suggest the rarity of occurrence indicated in the thinking of many of the lawyers and friends of the court who supported the use of corporal punishment in the case of *Ingraham* v. *Wright*. The Center is currently planning a larger study and hopes that the Office of Civil Rights will publish national figures based on their computerized data. In summary, it appears that the Supreme Court's assumption about the rarity of the abuse and, underlying this, about the rarity of its use is not supported by the data available.

Assumption: Corporal Punishment Is an Effective Form of Discipline Serving Important Educational Interests

Unfortunately, the evidence reviewed by the Supreme Court did not indicate that they did a comprehensive review of educational research on punishment. At the time of the writing of the brief on behalf of the APA Task Force on the Rights of Children and Youth, the time limitation and early development of the Center did not make possible the presentation of the data now available. In order to test the assumption regarding the effectiveness of punishment, two doctoral graduate students in school psychology reviewed the literature on punishment for the last ten years. This literature included both animal and human studies. A paper written by Bongiovanni (1978) and published by the Center and National Institute of Education seriously challenges the efficacy of the use of corporal punishment in the schools. While it is obvious that physical punishment, especially as it becomes more severe, tends to suppress the punished behavior, there are many undesirable consequences. There is research evidence that the infliction of pain often results in operant and elicited aggression which is counter-productive in terms of "important educational interests." Although there has been no research using experimental and control groups with corporal punishment as the independent variable, there are studies which have examined other forms of punitiveness (Rosenshein & Furst, 1971; Lamberth, 1978). These studies indicate that student achievement is negatively correlated with the use of criticism, threats, and the resulting punitive atmospheres created by these teacher behaviors. Corporal punishment may be readily conceptualized as the extreme form of expression of criticism and anger (Hyman, Bongiovanni, Friedman, and McDowell, 1977).

Some evidence indicates that the increasing use of corporal punishment is correlated with increasing vandalism in schools. A study supporting this contention was conducted by a group in Portland, Oregon. The researchers were a committee of citizens, and unfortunately the results are not published in a scientific journal. However, at the Center, several students are currently pursuing a similar study which will lead to at least one doctoral dissertation. We are attempting to obtain a small grant to support its completion. In this study, data from the Office of Civil Rights are being gathered which indicate the rate of corporal punishment in schools. This will be correlated with insurance rates for vandalism by use of a mailed questionnaire. If the suggested correlation between corporal punishment and vandalism is found, this will further reinforce animal and human studies suggesting that the use of violence only leads to counter-violence (Bongiovanni, 1978).

It is apparent from the reviews of the Court's decision in *Ingraham* v. *Wright* that Powell cannot cite the scientific literature to support his assumption concerning important educational interests served by the use of corporal punishment. However, there is another way to conceptualize his concerns. Implicit in the Supreme Court's decision is the historical and moral value system of what was and to some extent still is essentially a Puritan society. This thinking was apparent in the statement by Justice Powell who notes that "paddling of recalcitrant children has long been an acceptable method of promoting good behavior and instilling notions of responsibility and decorum into the mischievous heads of school children" (*Ingraham* v. *Wright*, 45 L.W. 4366). If Justice Powell's assumptions are correct, the elimination of corporal punishment should result in a lack of "responsibility and decorum" which would affect the learning climate. Powell reinforces this assumption by quoting previous litigation which indicated that the states may impose corporal punishment "for the proper education of the child and the maintenance of group discipline" (*Ingraham* v. *Wright*, 45 L.W. 4367).

One way to test the assumption of the necessity of the use of corporal punishment is to examine those schools which do not use it and compare the disciplinary atmosphere between the times of the use and elimination of corporal punishment. In order to examine the assumption, a two-stage study has been conceptualized. The first stage has been completed and will be reported here. Farley, Kreutter, Russell, Blackwell, Finkelstein and Hyman (1978) developed a list of fifty-nine school districts which were reported to have eliminated corporal punishment as a practice in their schools. The schools were contacted by telephone and those which responded were interviewed by use of a structured questionnaire. The person most often responding was the superintendent. However, in some cases the assistant superintendent or director of pupil personnel services responded. Thirty-three school districts were interviewed. While many others returned the calls, the schedule of interviewers available was such that many could not be questioned. The responding schools represent about two million students who function in educational atmospheres without the use of corporal punishment. Approximately 69 percent of the responding schools had eliminated corporal punishment within the last ten years. Without presenting this whole study here, we can report some of the interesting findings.

While there were differing responses regarding changes in the frequency of disciplinary problems following the elimination of the use of corporal punishment, only one district reported a belief that increase in problems resulted from the elimination of corporal punishment. Fifteen districts (42 percent) reported no change in the number of disciplinary problems; twelve districts (33 percent) were unable to respond to the question; 5 percent reported a decrease in the number of disciplinary problems. This data would certainly suggest that there were no noticeable changes in discipline as a function of the elimination of corporal punishment. While the major aspect of this study was to test the assumption of the Supreme Court that corporal punishment is necessary for effective discipline, we also questioned the respondents as to alternatives which they were using. Each school responded with an average of three methods of discipline most often used in their school district. These included suspension, parent conferences, counseling, and such preventive measures as problem committees, crises information centers, social workers, core teams, in-service training, teacher consultation. Also listed were the use of detention, chores, student rights and responsibility programs, special education services, expulsion, behavior modification, discussion, court referral, rehabilitation, and lectures. While, unfortunately, 69 percent of the schools responded most frequently with the use of suspension as an alternative to corporal punishment, it is obvious that many schools have a more sophisticated repertoire of disciplinary procedures.

A study recently completed by two Center staff members suggests some other interesting consequences of the use of corporal punishment which challenge Justice Powell's assumptions regarding the effectiveness of corporal punishment. McDowell and Friedman (1978) conducted a regional examination of editorial opinion following the Supreme Court decision. The complete study is presented in another section of this book. However, one finding of interest is reported here. A chi square analysis indicated statistical significance for differences among regions. The northeastern and mid-Atlantic states reflect more editorial opinions against the Supreme Court decision and the southern and southwestern states are more favorable in terms of editorial opinion. Whether this reflects actual population opinion is another question which we hope to investigate.

The evidence thus far presented suggests that Justice Powell is incorrect in his assumptions about the use of corporal punishment as an efficacious way of maintaining order and decorum. In fact, the research indicates that use of corporal punishment may well be counter-productive.

Assumption: Corporal Punishment Is an Accepted Form of Discipline and There Is No Trend toward Its Elimination

The Supreme Court's decision concerning corporal punishment, which constituted a violation of the Eighth Amendment, relied heavily on historical and contemporary approval of reasonable corporal punishment. The

Court considered few scholarly opinions on this subject because they did not have an integrated body of data. Powell indicates "yet we can discern no trend towards its elimination" (*Ingraham* v. *Wright*, 45 L.W. 4366). Powell makes a strong argument for the continuation of corporal punishment because there is no trend away from its use.

However, as part of the study on alternatives to corporal punishment mentioned previously (Farley et al., 1978), the National Center is determining whether or not it is true that there is no discernible trend toward the elimination of corporal punishment. Although we are currently observing a movement for "back to basics" and a more conservative trend toward discipline, the study conducted by the Center indicates that historically there is a trend away from the use of corporal punishment. We are able to identify over fifty school districts, some of them the largest in the country including New York, Chicago, and Baltimore, which have eliminated the use of corporal punishment. Many of the school districts in the survey had eliminated it within the last ten years while the oldest elimination was in New Jersey which occurred in 1867. More recently, Maine and Hawaii have eliminated the use of corporal punishment; therefore, four states plus many schools and districts have now eliminated the use of corporal punishment (Friedman and Hyman, 1977). Data indicated that, of the districts surveyed, there was a distribution of all socio-economic classes and that there were a number of reasons for the elimination of corporal punishment. Twenty-two percent of the districts reported that corporal punishment was felt to be ineffective. Additionally, 9.8 percent felt that there are better ways to achieve positive discipline, and 7.3 percent of the districts felt that there are equally effective measures. The commonly stated reasons for its elimination included community pressure, reactions to bad incidents, legal administrative decision, protection of the school from lawsuits, the conviction that corporal punishment is inhumane, and the commitment to student's rights. Therefore, the data available and ignored or unknown to the Supreme Court, are that there has been a gradual turning away from the use of corporal punishment and therefore one might discern a societal trend.

In order to conduct a more thorough study of what is occurring in school districts where corporal punishment has been eliminated, the Center is currently developing a study which will use questionnaires. While the original study depended upon responses by high school officials, the current questionnaire will be sent to the vice principals, disciplinarians, and those who have an actual on-line role in discipline. The survey will be sent for comparison purposes to a sample of districts using corporal punishment and those which have eliminated it. The survey instrument describes specific discipline situations and lists alternatives so that respondents will indicate the likelihood of various disciplinary measures being used in the situations described. In this manner the Center, for the first time in educational history, as far as we can determine, will survey the extent and use of a variety of methods used in public schools to discipline children. This will provide a great deal of data as to accepted and effective forms of discipline which the Supreme Court ignored.

Assumption: Schools Are Open Institutions

Justice Powell's decision suggests the assumption that schools are open institutions and therefore children do not need protection under the Eighth Amendment. While this assumption is somewhat harder to test from a research point of view, it certainly could be investigated by attitude or opinion surveying of parents of children in the schools. This is an area which must yet be investigated by the Center. However, Justice Powell seems to believe that all schools are open to public scrutiny and that they are in some sense supervised by the community. After twenty years of experience at every level in the public schools, the present writer would certainly challenge the assumption. Within ongoing practices it is the exception rather than the rule that a school district has active participation of parents and community members. The files of the American Civil Liberties Union have many examples of schools repeatedly, often secretly and often without fear, violating already established liberties of children (Hyman & Schreiber, 1974).

Material already cited relates to a social science analysis of the Supreme Court decision on *Ingraham* v. *Wright* developed by Virginia Lee of the Center for Law and Education. Other questions which may be investigated have to do with due process issues raised by the majority opinion of Justice Powell. However, the Center has not yet attended to these as it is examining other litigation involving corporal punishment.

An important area of litigation has to do with civil rights. There is evidence that minority children receive corporal punishment more often than their peers. A study in California tended to support this as did some work in the Pittsburgh schools (Hyman et al., 1977). In order to take a closer look at the data, the Center organized a study, which is partially reported earlier in this essay, in regard to the extent of the use of corporal punishment. The survey data of the Office of Civil Rights were analyzed in terms of the use of corporal punishment by race. From the data available, the analysis revealed very clearly that minority children, particularly males, are corporally punished far more than their white peers, sometimes at a ratio of four to one. Further, the analysis changes from elementary to secondary school indicating that the rate for whites drops as they reach secondary school but it does not drop for minority males or black females. It does drop for females of minority groups other than black. The figures suggest that (a) teachers may be less tolerant of the kinds of behavior exhibited by minority groups, (b) that minority group members may exhibit more inappropriate behavior as defined by society, or (c) the rates of inappropriate behavior of all racial groups may be about equal but corporal punishment is used to a greater extent to "correct" the transgressions of minority groups.

Another legal issue has to do with minority rights vis-à-vis sex differences. The data from the study indicated a large difference in the frequency of corporal punishment use for males as against females suggesting that either males misbehave more than females or that society feels males as a group are more able to "take" corporal punishment. Certainly there appears to be a case for sex discrimination.

In the brief by Frank Howard on behalf of the Dade County School Board, it was stated that "the moderate use of corporal punishment is a rare alternative to more drastic exclusionary devices" (Howard, p. 11). This argument implies that not only is corporal punishment used rarely, as has been discussed previously, but that it is often used in preference to suspension which is considered by most educators to be more drastic. The argument is often stated that it is better to paddle children than to suspend or to expel them. While this argument is not based primarily on legal issues, it does form an underpinning for the societal support of the use of corporal punishment. Is it then true that corporal punishment is often used instead of more serious exclusionary measures? If this were true, one would expect a negative correlation between the use of corporal punishment and the use of suspension. In order to examine this question, the data collected from the Office of Civil Rights survey was utilized. When the overall rates of corporal punishment and suspensions for each of the schools sampled were determined, they were analyzed by the use of a Pearson Product Moment correlation. The resulting correlation coefficient was $+.23$ indicating a small positive correlation between the use of corporal punishment and suspensions, that is, that schools which use a high rate of corporal punishment tend also to use a high rate of suspension. This finding offers serious doubt that corporal punishment is used as an alternative to suspension. Rather it suggests that the atmosphere of punitiveness toward children in school results in the use of both methods, each of which is considered by many educators to be counter-productive to learning.

For the present, there is little doubt that the Supreme Court decision in *Ingraham* v. *Wright* has eliminated the major method of constitutional grounds to abolish corporal punishment. However, it is important to examine some of the assumptions underlying the Supreme Court decision so that eventually court cases will find their way to a constitutional solution to this problem. Meanwhile, the testing of the assumptions underlying the legal interpretations certainly forms the basis for the accumulation of knowledge in this very important area. It is hoped that the efforts of the Center in cooperation with the Center for Law and Education and other legal groups including the American Civil Liberties Union will result in a massive amount of data for use in various cases of litigation and legislative change throughout the country. The Center with its research potential is interested in the identification of other social assumptions which underlie litigation in the area of school discipline. Whenever possible, within the financial limitations of the Center, questions will be examined by use of appropriate scientific methods.

REFERENCES

Bongiovanni, A. A review of research on the effects of punishment: Implications for corporal punishment in the schools in *Proceedings of Conference on Corporal Punishment in the Schools: A National Debate*. National Institute of Education, NIE P–77–0079, 1977.

Farley, A., Kreutter, K., Russell, R., Blackwell, S., Finkelstein, H., and Hyman, I. The effects of eliminating corporal punishment in schools: A preliminary survey. *Inequality*, published by The Center for Law and Education, Cambridge, Mass., No. 23, Summer 1978.

Friedman, D. Corporal punishment in the schools. Paper presented at Annual Convention of the American Psychological Association, Washington, D.C., September 4, 1976.

Friedman, R. and Hyman, I. An analysis of state legislation regarding corporal punishment in the schools. In J. Wise (ed.), *Conference on Corporal Punishment in the Schools: A National Debate*. National Institute of Education, Contract NIE–P–77–0079, 1977.

Glackman, T., Martin, R., Hyman, I., McDowell, E., Berv, V., and Spino, P. Corporal punishment in the schools as it relates to race, sex, grade level and suspensions. *Inequality*, published by The Center for Law and Education, Cambridge, Mass., No. 23, Summer 1978.

Howard, F. Brief filed in support of Dade County Florida School Board in the U.S. Supreme Court Case of *Ingraham* v. *Wright*, decided April 19, 1977.

Hyman, I. Consultation in classroom management based on empirical research. Paper presented at the Annual Meeting of the American Psychological Association, Honolulu, September 3, 1972.

————, Bongiovanni, A., Friedman, R., and McDowell, E. Paddling punishing and force. *Children Today*, vol. 6, no. 5, September 1977, 17–25.

————, McDowell, E., and Raines, B. In J. Wise (ed.), Conference on Corporal Punishment in the Schools: A National Debate. National Institute of Education, Contract NIE P–77–0079, 1977.

_____, and Schreiber, K. The school psychologist as child advocate. *Children Today*, vol. 3, no. 2, March 1974, 21–23.

Ingraham v. *Wright*, 45 L.W. 4364.

Kounin, J. *Discipline and Group Management in Classrooms*. New York: Holt, Rinehart and Winston, 1970.

Lamberth, R. The effects of punitiveness on academic achievement: A review of recent literature. Department of School Psychology, Temple University, 1978.

McDowell, E. and Friedman, R. A national analysis of editorial opinion regarding Ingraham vs. Wright. Paper presented at the Annual Convention of the National Association of School Psychologists, New York City, March 24, 1978.

Rosenshein, B. and Furst, N. Research in teacher performance criteria. In B. O. Smith (ed.), *Research in Teacher Education*. Englewood Cliffs, N.J.: Prentice-Hall, 1971.

Webster's New Collegiate Dictionary. Springfield, Mass.: G. & C. Merriam Co., 1973.

PART VIII

•

ALTERNATIVES

The final section of this book represented the greatest problem in terms of selection of articles. Because of page limitations, the vast literature on alternatives could only be meagerly represented. Yet no book on the topic of corporal punishment should omit discussion of the plethora of approaches available which offer positive techniques for changing behavior, building good character, and developing good citizens who will behave appropriately because they want to rather than because they are afraid. The problem that faces modern society is to help young people develop internalized controls rather than external controls represented by authority. The result of the two types of controls on the behavior of unsupervised fifth graders is described in the lead essay by Hyman. It presents a conceptual scheme for understanding discipline in the classroom.

The second essay by Ladd furthers the argument for internalized control through the use of "influence strategies." Ladd speaks to the teacher who wishes to move toward positive approaches with students who have been accustomed to punitiveness. Attempts by beginning teachers to be friendly and open are often mistaken by pupils as signs of weakness. Ladd tells teachers how to become friendly and still maintain discipline.

The following essay by Jacob Kounin represents one of the few empirical studies of discipline that have effectively identified good management techniques. Kounin's findings regarding "with it" techniques and other appropriate desist behaviors should be included in the training of all teachers in the United States. The techniques do not require a particular philosophical approach and may be learned easily. They certainly offer a basic approach to classroom management.

The following two essays discuss the problems of inner-city schools and methods to eliminate violence. The Sanders and Yarbrough essay offers research support for a multifaceted approach drastically to eliminate the use of corporal punishment in an inner-city middle school. Jackson, in his article dealing with violence in high schools, stresses the importance of the principal. While this essay is based on observation and opinion, it clearly supports research findings which point to the need for an orderly, predictable atmosphere to enhance learning. The structure and order can vary and may not often be evident. Open education may have as much structure as a punitive authoritarian approach. Behind the structure is the leader who determines the ambiance which will set the tone for learning. Jackson tells us that, even in the most difficult situations, punitiveness is not a determinant of success.

The final selection of the section describes a year-long experiment with tokens for good behavior and tickets for bad. It explains how students and staff perceived the effect of the procedures implemented on the system of justice. Elardo presents a readable example of positive approaches to discipline based on the developing technology of behavior modification.

It should be noted in conclusion that this section could be a book in itself. Many promising positive approaches are currently available for those interested in positive, effective, and humane approaches to discipline. Among these are Glasser's Reality Therapy, Gordon's Teacher Effectiveness Training, and programs based on Transactional Analysis, Rational Emotion Therapy, and so forth. There is a whole literature on behavior modification and token economies. The pioneering work of Fritz Redl, Rudolf Dreikurs, Bruno Bettelheim, Haim Ginott, and Carl Rogers represents only a few of the theorists who have given us practical applications of their work from a variety of perspectives.

Those seeking alternatives to corporal punishment will find a treasure-trove of knowledge if they are willing to open their minds and, when necessary, challenge tradition.

27

Is the Hickory Stick out of Tune?

Irwin A. Hyman

•

Last April, the United States Supreme Court, in the case of *Ingraham* v. *Wright*, decided in a five-to-four decision that schoolchildren are not entitled to constitutional protection from cruel and unusual forms of corporal punishment. The meaning of the decision requires extended discussion. Immediately, a groundswell of renewed debate arose concerning the need for and effectiveness of corporal punishment as a method of school discipline.

At the same time, many educators are concerned about the results of recent Gallup polls which indicate that school discipline is the number-one educational concern of citizens. In a developing struggle which relates to many concerns besides discipline, two camps of parents and educators are emerging.

On one side are parents and educators who have greeted the Supreme Court ruling as further reinforcement for the "back to basics" movement. They view the decision as a sign that the Court is stepping back from the kinds of constitutional positions it took in the *Goss* v. *Lopez* case, which entitled children to due process before suspension. They insist that courts should not meddle in the everyday affairs of local educators. This group tends to harbor an almost religious faith in the proverbial warning "Spare the rod and spoil the child." They believe that love and physically painful punishment are compatible and effective adjuncts to the development of good moral character and the desire to learn.

At the other end of the educational-political continuum are parents and teachers who view the Supreme Court decision as a step backward in the establishment of children as citizens legally entitled to full constitutional protection. They cite the massive psychological and educational literature which demonstrates that punishment, especially physically painful punishment, only serves temporarily to suppress behaviors and that reward and internalized incentives are vastly superior in encouraging learning. They emphasize the research on modeling which demonstrates that children

This essay first appeared in *Today's Education* April–May 1978.

who are punished physically learn that force is an acceptable method of solving problems in the society in which they live.

Viewed with a dispassionate eye, evidence of this type suggests that corporal punishment should not be a last resort for punishing errant students. Rather, it should be eliminated universally as it already has been in the states of New Jersey (for over one hundred years), Massachusetts, and Maine and in many school districts. The NEA Task Force on Corporal Punishment made similar recommendations in its report in 1972.

Surveys have consistently revealed that the vast majority of teachers—even those who would retain corporal punishment—want to develop a large repertoire of ways to maintain order and promote learning without the use of force. In fact, teachers consistently complain about the lack of appropriate preservice and inservice training in this area.

At the National Center for the Study of Corporal Punishment and Alternatives in the Schools, we have been studying classroom discipline methods to help teachers. Theory, research, and practice suggest three aspects of the classroom situation that bear on discipline problems and their solutions: (1) teacher-child personality interactions, especially those involving anger, guilt, and fear of "loss of face"; (2) techniques gleaned from the teacher's own experience and from other teachers; and (3) classroom systems, based on the teacher's theory, whether conscious or unconscious, about what promotes learning. Classrooms organized on the basis of specific theoretical orientations such as open education, reward systems, or democratic teaching result in distinct classroom climates. Two additional factors which are not discussed in this essay are (4) the past experiences of the child in relation to discipline and (5) social-emotional climate in the school.

All aspects of classroom management are mediated through the personality of the teacher. When dealing with aggressive kids, teachers can be their own worst enemies. Under the stress of continuous classroom problems, they may feel anger, guilt, insecurity, and contempt—all these easily detected by students, although the teachers themselves often aren't even aware of these feelings.

One clear example occurred while I was a consulting school psychologist for a nursery program. Johnny was a hyperactive child who was at times aggressive. His teacher denied being angry about his behavior and said she felt sorry for him. We started a program of parent consultation, modified day, behavior modification, and individual therapeutic tutoring that combines counseling with one-to-one teaching. The teacher did not like using a system of rewards: despite her denials, she was very angry at the child.

For several days, Johnny kept threatening to bite the tutor. One day she foolishly dared him, and to her dismay, he instantly bit her thumb.

After a moment of shock and anger, she realized she had done something wrong and asked the teacher what to do. Rather than try to find out the circumstances of the incident, the teacher told her to go back and bite Johnny, and the tutor followed this advice.

Without realizing it, the teacher had vented her anger through the tutor. It is true that Johnny didn't bite the tutor any more; it is also true, however, that he learned that the aggression he displayed toward the tutor and other children is a method sanctioned for use by adults.

Teachers who are insecure may resort to sarcasm, overreact to minor infractions, and engage in a constant battle with children. Teaching is such a personal, all-consuming task that teachers with discipline problems often find it helpful to obtain outside, objective consultation. School psychologists, counselors, other teachers, and often students can help a willing teacher understand what his or her feelings really are.

Ms. Bach is a slender, sensitive music teacher from a white, middle-class background. She loves music, and during her first two years of teaching in an elementary school, she did an excellent job. Then she was transferred to an inner-city junior high where most students were black children from poor homes. In the new school, she began to have discipline problems.

A discipline clinic conducted by the Center considered Ms. Bach's situation. When she role-played a typical discipline situation, the videotape immediately revealed several problems.

First, Ms. Bach was afraid of some of the children and afraid to admit this to her principal. She felt that as a good teacher she should be able to control, by physical force if necessary, classroom disruptions or fights between children. She was stronger than she looked and had taken some karate lessons; still, on several occasions, she was hit and pushed aside while trying to separate children.

After several months in the school, Ms. Bach became extremely angry with some of the students. Her thoughts of retaliation and revenge for what they were doing to her made her feel guilty. A knowledgeable, sensitive, and caring person, she understood the violence and deprivations in the lives of many of the children, so she felt she shouldn't blame them. But things got worse, and the angrier she became, the guiltier she felt. As a result, she was inconsistent in her techniques of classroom management and some of the kids knew that they had "gotten her goat."

The first thing we had to do was stop the guilt-anger cycle. The clinic leader, supported by participants, pointed out that nowhere in the teachers' manual or negotiated contract does it say that teachers have to be bigger and stronger than their students or that they aren't allowed to be afraid. We told Ms. Bach to find a teacher or administrator near her class who was physically capable of breaking up fights. It was all right to let students know that authorities were nearby whom she would call on if things got too rough. This would not be losing face; besides, the students already knew her physical limitations. Her lack of physical strength did not mean she couldn't manage her class of adolescents.

For Ms. Bach, relieving her guilt, accepting her own anger, and realizing that her problem was not unique provided important relief. We went on from there.

Although a healthy personality is important in creating a positive learning atmosphere, good techniques also are needed. Our next step with Ms. Bach was to examine how she could change her teaching techniques to adapt them to junior high rather than elementary students.

It appeared that Ms. Bach needed only a relatively simple change in technique. The pupils in her classes needed to take part in planning their activities.

Ms. Bach had determined what music would interest inner-city black adolescents. She was trying to impose what turned out to be an irrelevant curriculum, and the children resisted. Role playing, especially by two black administrators who were participating in the clinic, showed Ms. Bach that her predetermined attitudes and curriculum could easily be construed as contemptuous of the kids' culture.

Mutual planning by the teacher and students does not mean turning the curriculum over to the kids. It is *mutual*, and a teacher may easily introduce the learning she knows is important by making it more palatable.

When Ms. Bach returned to school, she was less guilty and more able to face directly her anger with herself and with the few students who were constantly causing problems. She met with her classes and restructured the curriculum by combining her goals with their needs.

Although the techniques available to improve classroom management are numerous, their use and effectiveness are limited by the availability of resources, the quality of individual teacher-pupil interaction, and the personalities of some children. No matter what techniques are used, teachers, administrators, and school boards must recognize that a small percentage of behavior problems are caused by children with characterological problems. Many of these children come from families whose emotional rejection and neglect cause disruptive behavior in school, destructive to both themselves and others.

Some children need special classes until they are able to change their behavior. Others stay in regular classes but require constant supportive help in such forms as therapy or family counseling. A headlong rush to integrate certain types of exceptional children into regular classrooms might lead to disaster if schools don't provide teachers with adequate support. Personnel such as school psychologists, social workers, special educators, and psychiatrists are needed to provide both direct service to children and ongoing teacher consultation and training.

Considering the proportion of children who are estimated to be emotionally disturbed or disruptive, the average middle-class school district should have at least one school psychologist and one social worker for each 1,500 children, in addition to adequate numbers of special education and other special staff. The ratio should be much higher in areas of poverty, where the incidence of disruptive behavior increases.

Adequate support services should be negotiated in every contract. Otherwise, a board of education may attempt to use the new federal mandate of the "least restrictive environment" to save money, eliminating special classes by integrating handicapped children into classrooms with unprepared and untrained regular teachers. Teachers need the help of school psychologists and other specialists as well as training in effective techniques if they are to teach children with special discipline problems in regular classrooms.

Another way to help improve classroom discipline is the consistent application of particular theoretical systems. This usually requires extensive training for the teacher, who must first learn the theory and then learn to apply it consistently.

Behavior modification is one such approach that has been shown to be especially helpful with some disruptive children. William Glasser's reality therapy, which he describes in *Schools without Failure* and in *Today's Education* for November–December 1977, has become quite popular. Transactional analysis, rational emotive therapy, and humanistic psychology are other theoretical approaches that have been applied in the classroom.

No existing theory, however, offers the universal answer; most seem to offer a modest amount of success. Each makes particular assumptions about personality development, learning, and change. To apply it successfully, a teacher must understand it thoroughly.

My own approach applies to the classroom the findings of social psychology about the democratic and the authoritarian personality. John Dewey considered a democratic approach appropriate for our society because citizens in a democracy need internalized controls. Children should learn to behave in the correct way just because it is correct, rather than because they are afraid of the consequences of not being "good."

Scales available at our Center operationally define democratic and authoritarian classrooms. In studying the two types, I have found that authoritarian teachers tend to be less secure, more in need of rigid structure, more likely to feel moral guilt, and more fearful of loss of control. As a result, they tend to make more errors in classroom management and generate more anxiety and hostility among children. Democratic teachers tend to be more secure and flexible personally, more tolerant of change, and more liked by children; most important, their students gain internalized controls.

Democratic doesn't translate into *permissive*. Democratic classrooms, like democratic societies, provide structure and order—whose nature the constituents help determine.

In one study, teachers of each type were absent from their classrooms for forty-five minutes. The authoritarian classrooms became scenes of utter chaos: students were yelling, bullying, hitting, scapegoating, threatening to "tell," and trying to find the teacher. In the democratic classes, children were slightly better behaved and more task-oriented than the children in the authoritarian classes.

The problem of discipline is multifaceted. The high rate of divorce, the current economic strains on intact families, the emotional stress of our pace of life, and the overwhelming poverty of many in both cities and rural areas all affect the relations among children, parents, and school authorities.

Returning to the hickory stick sounds like a simple solution for the resulting problems, but it won't work. Teachers need more training and more supportive help. Disruptive students need more direct service, as do their families. These should be major concerns in contract negotiations as we round out the decade of the stressful seventies.

28

Moving to Positive Strategies for Order-Keeping with Kids Accustomed to Restrictions, Threats, and Punishments

Edward T. Ladd

●

Kids in elementary and secondary school who are accustomed to being controlled within narrow limits by means of reprimands, reproaches, threats, and punishments—that is, through aversive approaches—present a special problem to the teacher who prefers to regulate behavior more liberally, and to do so through influence strategies which enhance kids' morale and initiative, improve student-teacher relations, and lead to the kids' sharing substantially in the governing of their own behavior.

This essay endeavors to explore the source of that problem and to propose a solution. There are important questions with which it does not attempt to deal: whether regulating student behavior is necessary at all; if so, how much regulation is beneficial; whether aversive methods of regulating behavior—that is, restrictive and punitive methods—are good or bad; and to what extent students as groups, rather than teachers, can do the regulating. It simply presupposes that regulation is necessary; that the extent of regulation should be much less than is customary; that teachers should prefer compliance practices that are not aversive (for a discussion of restrictive-punitive approaches see Ladd, 1971); and that wherever the problem at issue arises, the turning over of regulatory powers to kids must await its solution.

"Moving to Positive Strategies for Order-Keeping with Kids Accustomed to Restrictions, Threats, and Punishments" by Edward T. Ladd is reprinted from *Urban Education* Vol. 6, No. 4 (January 1972) pp. 331–348 by permission of the publisher, Sage Publications, Inc. The author is deceased; the editors have attempted to update the essay where possible and to eliminate sexist language, but have left some original male pronouns intact for readability.

Typically, when a teacher suddenly changes the way kids are dealt with from a largely aversive one to a positive one, they become wild. A serious effort to be humane may lead, depending in part on their age, to their walking or running around the room during what are supposed to be whole-class activities, leaving the room when they are not allowed to, destroying property, throwing things, insulting or threatening one another or the teacher, or fighting. Even a friendly wisecrack from the teacher may produce disruptive guffaws and behavior.

There are situations where this is all right, where kids may indulge themselves in free, impulsive behavior without doing serious harm, and where, therefore, requirements may suddenly be liberalized and punishments and threats may suddenly be discontinued, at no particular risk of damage. Indeed, it may well be that, from a strictly educational point of view, an abrupt transition from being controlled by aversive means to being free from them is sometimes good for kids. However, in most school settings, this should not happen. Sometimes the process can be dangerous to the kids themselves or to other persons. Usually teachers, principals, fellow students, and in fact the subculture of the school strongly condemn "wildness," and in ways that are subtle or not so subtle make kids who behave "wildly" suffer for it. Insofar as the kids' suffering takes the form of fears of their own aggressiveness or strong feelings of guilt or shame, it may seriously injure them. Also, serious injury may be done to the mental equilibrium of the teacher, who may find himself hating his kids, or to his standing in the school system.

Thus it is important to identify ways in which teachers new to a class of such kids can avoid a period of disorder when they start to put more positive strategies into effect. Is there some sort of withdrawal program teachers can use, analogous to a program of withdrawal from an addictive drug? And can a program of this kind be carried out in such a way that during it he does not do continued harm to the kids? In principle, the answer to these questions seems to be "yes."

It is sometimes said of the kids in question that they are different from other kids, and that tight restrictions and aversive approaches are "the only language they understand." The point is proven, it is believed, when a switch to more humane treatment triggers intolerable behavior.

That argument overlooks the fact that because aversive approaches are powerful, fear-inspiring ways of motivating, anyone suddenly freed from them is almost bound for a time to release pent-up feelings and impulsive behaviors.[1] Still, in the situations under discussion, the wildness usually lasts for weeks or months, well beyond the normal backlash period. So there must be something else at work, defeating the teacher's efforts to keep order in the new way. What is it? When the teacher tries to be friendly, why do not the kids respond by being orderly?

How Friendliness Precipitates Wildness

There is a body of research supporting the notion that being generous and kind tends to increase one's power over those who receive one's favors (see Blau, 1964). So the kids' continued wildness in the face of a friendly teacher can hardly be the result of the new, positive approach itself. The explanation seems more likely to lie in some unarticulated line of thinking which the unaccustomed friendliness presumably provokes in the kids, some such line as:

(1)   The only reason for complying with rules, requests, or orders, is that if you don't the teacher may act mean, and a proper teacher is ready and able to act mean to get kids to comply with rules, requests, and orders.

(2)   This teacher doesn't act mean.

(3a)   ∴This teacher must be not a real teacher but a friend.

and/or

(3b)   This teacher must lack the ability to act mean.

(4)   In either case this teacher will not act mean no matter what we do.

(5)   ∴With this teacher there is no reason for complying with rules, requests, or orders.

Informal observation suggests that kids in the middle grades may be more likely to make assumption (3a) and junior high school kids assumption (3b). In either case the effort to be friendly logically invites unrestrained behavior.

The root of the trouble, of course, is proposition (1), and disabusing the kids of that belief is, after all, one of the teacher's purposes. But, whether this be easy or hard, it is unlikely to be done in an instant. So, during the interim, the teacher must allow for the fact that the kids believe proposition (1): this is part of "starting with the kids where they are." Yet as long as the kids continue to believe proposition (1) and also see that proposition (2) is true, the only way to keep them from drawing conclusion (5) seems to be for the teacher to avoid leading them to believe proposition (4), which means avoiding sending either message (3a) or (3b). And the best way for the teacher to do that is *for the time being to refrain from appearing particularly friendly and from appearing incapable of acting mean.*

For the teacher who overflows with friendliness for kids this will not be easy. But the state of affairs need not last long.

Can a friendly teacher keep from appearing particularly friendly, even appear capable of being mean without being untrue to himself? It depends on what "untrue" means. By virtue of the kids' previous experience, the teacher presumably starts out with an image that is somewhat ogre-like. It may be possible then for teachers to start out acting in a way that, though not mean, still conceals how nice they are and *to program their behavior to let the kids discover how nice they are bit by bit*, so that the kids do not get the message of (3a) all at once but only gradually. And it may be possible for teachers to *avoid sending any messages at all about his capability or incapability of being mean*, so that they do not get message (3b).

This program requires, then, that the news that there is nothing to fear be broken gradually, that even though a new era is dawning, the teacher not communicate this fact immediately, either by his words or by his manner. It suggests that if former teachers figuratively or literally kept a stick in the corner of the room, however tempted the new teacher may be to break it in two with a flourish, he should leave it right where it is. So the kids who begin their encounter with him expecting him to rule by fear do not yet have any convincing reason to believe that he will not or cannot sooner or later do so. Only as time goes by, and they find him not doing so, will they come to recognize that that is not his style, will they learn their new lesson, and will their fears evaporate.

If our analysis and conclusions are correct, the teacher's initial dealings with kids should be carried on in a manner which is neither unpleasant nor pleasant, neither unfriendly nor friendly.

When the teachers cut back on restrictions, they should convey the idea they are doing so deliberately rather than out of unthinking generosity or ineptitude. To this end they would do well to make it clear just what they do and do not require or permit. At the beginning teachers should probably not do away with restrictions which over time have become strong symbols of authority, such as calling teachers "Miss," "Mrs." or "Mr." They should drop requirements and restrictions only piecemeal, doing so in a manner suggesting that they are still quite willing and able to restore them if necessary. This means they must not ignore noncomplying behavior, at least not in a way that makes them appear confused or inept.

James Herndon's and Herbert Kohl's experiences along these lines show what this may mean in practice. Not knowing for sure what to do with his ninth grade class on the first day of school, Herndon left them entirely alone: he gave them a "free gift" of a period's liberty. The next day, however, the class, "having received the free gift, wasn't about to let go of it as easy as that." They paid little, if any, attention to the teacher.

Verna's explanation was, "You should have made us get to work yesterday. All the other teachers made us get to work. If you want us to do work, why didn't you make us yesterday" (Herndon, 1969: 26, 35–36)?[a]

On Kohl's first day, a test seemed to have tired everyone out. "Take ten minutes to talk and then we'll get back to work," he said. The class talked quietly for ten minutes and then did go back to work. The next day Robert raised his hand.

"Mr. Kohl, remember that ten minutes you gave us yesterday? Couldn't we talk again now? We're tired after all this reading."

Kohl gave them the ten minutes ("and then we'll move on to social studies"), found them reluctant to return to their work after it was over, but quickly brought them around by insisting that there had been a bargain which they must keep. He reports feeling that it was essential that he not suffer a "failure of will at that moment."

Over the weeks "the ten-minute breaks between lessons grew until, in my eyes, the lessons were secondary. Everything important happening in the class happened between lessons" (Kohl, 1968: 17, 20–21, 26).

As to the style in which the teacher tries to influence kids' behavior—that is, gives briefings, instructions, and reasons for doing things—if it is to communicate neither niceness nor unfriendliness, it should be respectful and businesslike and cool, calm, and neutral, even bureaucratic, with few emotional overtones (see Waller, 1932). Dealing with kids in this way, the teacher implicitly uses some of the same aversive power as his or her predecessors. As has been pointed out, although the kids do not know that teachers will be mean to them, neither do they know that teachers will not, so it is partly to avoid unpleasant consequences which teachers may be inclined to visit on them that they behave the way teachers want them to. Still, if all works as it should, the teacher has put an end to the counter-educational process of fear-building and fear-reinforcing, and has stopped teaching the old lesson; indeed, insofar as it begins to dawn on the kids that, while a teacher insists on order, he or she actually cuts back on restrictions and does not use aversive approaches; they have begun to learn a new lesson. And the teacher has done all this without precipitating wildness.

If things do not work out quite this well, the teacher may on occasion have to forestall kids' learning proposition (3b) or prematurely learning proposition (3a) by doing something he does not want to do: he may have to say or do something that actually carries the message that he is willing or able, if necessary, to "act mean." This is not to say that he or she must act mean: there may be other ways, such as facial expressions and quiet words of warning, by which these messages can be relayed. In any case, these approaches should be necessary only during the interim withdrawal period.

A Different Kind of Power

While this is going on, how can the teacher start building a new, positive base of power for influencing kids' behavior—either to use over them himself or to use to get them to govern themselves?

Establishing or keeping order always implies the use or potential use of some form of power. A situation of the type in question can be looked upon as one in which a transition is to be made from the use of one kind of power to the use of another. What kind of power is to be discarded and by whom it has been used are clear. Even if the teacher wanted to coast along on the kids' fear that he or she, too, may use it, it will not be long before they find out that he or she will not. With what power is it to be replaced?

In part, the answer will depend on whether or not somewhere the kids already have developed the attitudes and skills needed for an acceptable kind of self-direction. Insofar as they have, after the danger of an initial backlash subsides, it should take little power on the teacher's part to get them to govern themselves. In the more common case, where the kids have not yet developed the attitudes and skills needed to control their own behavior properly, there will be that much greater a need in the transition stage for power exercised by the teacher.

There are many kinds of power teachers can use to influence kids' behavior. For our purpose here, it is helpful to classify them very roughly under four headings:

(a) power to manipulate punishments—the aversive approach our teacher is trying to discard,

(b) power to change physical and other environmental circumstances,

(c) power to educate,

(d) power to manipulate rewards.

Category (b), exemplified by the confiscating of an object or changing of seating arrangements, can be extremely useful. One experienced elementary school supervisor who has worked largely in ghetto situations has claimed that most disorder can be cut out merely by arranging kids' desks in face-to-face groups. Many experts insist that developing smooth, efficient routines and rituals for classroom activities is the answer. But changing physical and other environmental circumstances require that the teacher have a kind of awareness and sometimes a skill which some teachers, especially beginners, do not have. For this and other reasons, it seems not nearly adequate by itself for preventing wildness in the kind of situation under discussion.

Category (c), exemplified by getting kids to think about the long-range consequences of their behavior, is ordinarily effective only if there is a good deal of tranquillity on the kids' part; it often takes time for it to affect behavior; it often requires credibility on the part of the teacher; and it usually requires skill. So by itself it, too, is unlikely to be adequate for the immediate task under discussion.

Category (d), the power to manipulate rewards, is a most formidable kind of power and one with which every human being has had a lot of experience. Contrary to the assertion that the kids we are talking about here do not respond properly to rewards, in these kids' free behavior—that is, their behavior away from an adult whom they expect to try to control them with aversive approaches—the vast majority of them show that they do. These kids are as open as any other human beings to motivation by rewards, real or prospective—in short, to the good things of life, fun and games, affection, respect from others, self-respect, and so on. Category (d) power may be the kind our teacher will have to rely on most.

The teacher's possible repertoire of rewarding approaches would seem to be about as varied as all the things kids like. Because teachers often find it hard to think of many such approaches, we digress at this point to list a number of them, roughly in the order in which it might be practical for a teacher to use them (on this subject, more below).

- looking attractive
- smiling and otherwise appearing cheerful
- calling kids by the names they like
- being polite to kids (within the limits of attending to one's duties)
- having kids do work that they like doing
- accentuating the positive rather than the negative (e.g., saying, not "we can't do this until . . ." but "as soon as . . . we can do it"; not "you mustn't be that noisy," but "lets see if we can be a bit quieter")
- explaining requirements and the reasons for them
- helping kids, as a friend might do, to meet the demands one has put on them in one's capacity as a teacher
- praising kids' performance
- making their work into a game
- showing a personal interest in kids as individuals, their clothes, possessions, families, interests, feelings, ideas, problems
- talking of the class as a very special group
- identifying oneself as a "member" of the class
- standing near kids who need attention
- displaying kids' work
- showing kids ways to stay out of trouble

• showing sympathy when kids are in trouble, even if the trouble they're in is trouble with oneself
  • protecting kids when they are in trouble or might get into trouble
  • establishing various roles or assignments for members of the class
  • playing games with kids
  • allowing kids free time
  • giving kids candy or redeemable tokens
  • visiting kids at their homes
  • teasing them in a friendly way
  • making wisecracks
  • laughing with them
  • telling kids interesting or amusing tidbits about oneself
  • admitting some of one's own shortcomings and mistakes
  • taking kids on trips, and so forth

There are, it should be noted, psychological circumstances which may restrict a given teacher's repertoire in a given situation.

First, some of the approaches listed presuppose a teacher who is a certain kind of person, a teacher who has empathy, a sense of humor, charm, or an easy way with people. Except insofar as a teacher is that sort of person, these approaches will not be available for him to use. Even if he is that sort of person, on occasion he may not be in the mood to use a particular approach, and he may have to fake it, that is, dramatically act it, or forgo its use. In either case, a teacher will have to tailor his repertoire to fit himself.

Second, any teacher can expect to encounter emotional difficulties in using rewarding approaches when he suffers from frustration. In such a situation, even though the teacher may wish to be pleasant with the kids, he or she may be impelled to respond to them aggressively. This tendency may be reinforced, in fact, by subtle pressures which kids put on him— very likely without either his or their knowledge—to play the aggressive role they expect a teacher to play. So the teacher emotional response to the situation he or she is in may make it difficult or impossible to do the rewarding or pleasant thing he or she knows would be most effective for the achieving of his or her goal.

Teacher's repertoire having been established, there are in principle at least three ways in which they can use it as a form of power with which to influence kids' behavior. First, one can give out good things freely and unconditionally. Such generosity tends to increase his influence over the kids for two reasons: because of the good will it builds, and because what he gives away acts as a free sample, suggesting that more can be got out of the old guy if one keeps him in a good frame of mind.[3] A teacher cannot give all his goodies away free, however, since he needs to save some for the second strategy: using them as a form of payment for desired behavior. ("As soon as you're all settled and quiet, we can talk about the question you asked.") The third strategy is a negative one: it consists of withholding or withdrawing good things previously offered or given, as a mild form of aversive approach, should such appear to be needed. If the teacher feels he must threaten or punish the kids, withdrawing or withholding privileges or rewards is likely to be just as effective as causing them pain or some other kind of punishment ("punishment" strictly defined), and perhaps more so; it is less likely to set them back in their program of withdrawal from fear; and it avoids other disadvantageous side-effects. More on this subject later.

Kindness without Wildness

We now come to the central question of how a teacher can use his repertoire of rewards without communicating the unwanted messages which produce disorder. Operationally, providing rewards comes close, after all, to being friendly.

Three generalizations seem justified.

First, the unwanted communications may be less likely to occur if the teacher introduces the rewards not all at once but bit by bit. As has been suggested, putting on an attractive appearance can start right away, while joking will probably have to wait. The rewarding of specific desired behavior—for example, praising a kid for carrying out a request—is unlikely to be interpreted as general friendliness, so the teacher should be able to move into that kind of practice right away. More generalized rewarding, and the free handing out of clearer evidences of friendliness may have to come by more gingerly steps. The schedule will be different in different situations. With one class, a teacher may be able to go a long way in an hour; with another the same distance may take several weeks. The teacher will have to feel his way warily, trying to sense how ready the majority of kids are to receive the message that the teacher is benevolent and to distinguish it from a message that anything goes.

Every year, hundreds of new teachers are advised by their principals and their colleagues to "start out tough, and later ease up on them," and every year this advice gets beginners into unnecessary conflicts with both their kids and their natural inclinations. Dangerous though the prescription is, it contains a partial wisdom, which this analysis would seem to sift out and explain.

Second, rewards can be provided in a way which keeps the kids from attributing them to the teacher's being a nice person or simply an inept one. ("So that you can do better work, I want you to move your desks and chairs into a circle.") Experiments with systematic contingent reinforcement or "behavior modification" in the classroom have had fabulous success with the use of rewards, and part of the explanation may be that, except when dealing with very little children, teachers typically set up systems and routines which make the dispensing of rewards impersonal and almost mechanical (see Madsen & Madsen, 1970, and Meacham & Wiesen, 1969).

Third, rewards can be given under conditions when the kid sees the teacher as something other than a keeper of order. A teacher can save nice things he or she might say to a kid until he or she can say them in a private conversation before work starts again, after it is done, or at lunch.

All three of these approaches should help convey to kids a distinction which it is essential for them to understand, the distinction between the issue of personal friendliness versus unfriendliness and the issue of the teacher's governance behavior in the classroom. In principle, all the actions a teacher takes vis-à-vis his kids and the things he says to them can be divided into two categories. The first is the things he does pursuant to his function as a teacher, a member of a profession employed by a school board, governed both by the standards of his profession and by the policies of the board. This category includes teaching behavior of all kinds and behavior under the loose heading of classroom governance, regardless of the kind of requirements set and the strategies used to gain compliance with them. The second is the things the teacher does freely as an individual human being, a private person with feelings and social relationships, such things as expressing irritation to a kid or chatting with him about a TV show seen the night before.[4] When a teacher is acting as the kids' friend, he is playing his free private role. When he liberalizes the requirements or hands out rewards to keep order, he is carrying out the demands of his official role.

The more friendly the teacher-as-person becomes, the greater the consequent risk that the kids will view him as *only* a friend, and the more he needs to emphasize the distinction between his roles, showing himself to be clearly professional about playing his role and meeting his obligations as teacher—in this case, as the person responsible for seeing that whatever kind of order he believes to be essential prevails.

For most kids, this distinction is not difficult to grasp. If the teacher himself is clear about it, they will probably absorb it intuitively. If he talks about it, he may make it that much easier. A teacher may have intuitive skill in getting the distinction across by such a device as putting on an entertaining "ferocious tiger" act (Smith & Geoffrey, 1968), or by ribbing kids gently about misdemeanors, both being ways of saying, "I'm your friend, and we can have fun together, even while I insist on your doing what I have to make you do."

An example of this is provided by an episode reported by a white teacher who was on hall duty in a Chicago ghetto school, when four boys came down a staircase "sounding like a rhythm and blues record."

"Look man," the teacher said, "I really dig your sound, but I'm afraid it's going to get all five of us in trouble. So why don't you rehearse somewhere else?"

"OK, man," they said, and the problem was solved (Canfield, 1970: 32).

Part of what the teacher presumably communicated might be put this way: "As human beings we share a feeling for good music. As members of this organization, however, we have to tailor our behavior to our roles in the organization, mine being to keep such behavior on your part from taking place."

Insofar as the kids in a given situation see that the teacher allows for the distinction between person and institutional role and grasp it themselves, two consequences will flow, which will help the kids to discriminate friendliness from permissiveness. First, the kids will tend to see that praise and other rewards which he gives out in conjunction with their classroom performance, academic or otherwise, are calculated manifestations of his professional posture and say nothing necessarily about his personal friendliness. Second, when the friendliness he shows is personal friendliness, they will tend to accept and enjoy it for what it is, without drawing inferences about what he may or may not do in his professional capacity. He has laid the groundwork for their understanding that, while he may be a friend, he still has a job to do which he is committed to doing, and which sometimes requires him, however little he may enjoy it, to set limits and requirements and even, perhaps, to give kids he likes a hard time. He has also laid the groundwork for their trusting him to be fair and temperate in his official actions.

Ups and Downs in the Withdrawal Program

If the teacher is fortunate, the withdrawal program may proceed steadily without setbacks. It may be, though, that in the course of the program, or even right at the start, the kids will reveal doubts that the teacher will really insist on order. For the typical teacher, such occasions may arise more than once, requiring him, then, to reinforce his credibility by going back to restrictions, reprimands, reproaches, threats, or punishments. The distinctions he is asking the kids to grasp may take a series of experiences to get across. Besides, kids are unpredictable: now they shoot ahead, now they drop back; and a teacher who is trying to move as fast as possible will sometimes get ahead of them. Furthermore, the teacher is likely at times to get aggravated and become psychologically unable to use patient, positive approaches. And, especially if he is inexperienced, there will probably be times when he runs out of positive approaches and is simply unable to think of new ones that might work. Whatever the explanation, no matter how careful he is, the kids are likely to revert occasionally to a wild, impulsive state which appears controllable only by aversive means. In such a situation, not only to control wildness, but also to preserve the credibility of his insistence on order, the teacher must be prepared to use such means.

When the teacher reverts to aversive means, it will obviously be less damaging to his long-range purpose if he can stick with low-voltage ones, such as the withdrawal of privileges mentioned above, reprimands ("I'm getting sick and tired of that, Mary"), or veiled threats ("I'd hate to have to do something really unpleasant just because we can't seem to get this behavior under control"), rather than going to high-voltage ones, such as publicly humiliating a kid, punishing him severely, or going to his parents about him.

If the teacher falls back on negative approaches a great deal of the time, he may, of course, defeat his purpose, and perhaps even worsen the kids' fear and negativism. But doing so occasionally is unlikely to have serious consequences. It will probably upset the teacher a bit, and it will probably extend the withdrawal period. But, if limited, any harm it may do should be small. In fact, after such an episode, the teacher may be able to explore with the kids what happened, and how his and their emotions influenced what they did; if he can do this with skill and without reproaches, he may be able to turn a minor defeat into something of a victory (see Morse & Wineman, 1965; Kohl, 1968: 24–26).

To the extent that the withdrawal program is successful, though, the new basis for order will be built, the process will reinforce itself, and the degree of friendliness can be increased. Eventually the relationship between the teacher and the kids may become warmly personal and frank.

NOTES

1. Even laboratory animals usually respond to the discontinuance of punishment by doing more of what they have been punished for doing, except when the punishment has been so severe as to cow them (Reese, 1966: 32).

2. See also Herndon's account of the disturbing wildness that followed in another junior high school class after a sudden radical relaxing of restrictions (Herndon, 1971).

3. Even though no obligations are specified, handing out benefits free may build a formidable power base (Blau, 1964).

4. For the classic statement of this distinction, see Cooley (1909: esp. chap. 28). See also Hughes (1937). The overlapping of the two kinds of role in school-teaching, particularly great in the lowest grades, need not concern us here.

REFERENCES

Blau, T. M. (1964) Exchange and Power in Social Life, New York: John Wiley.

Canfield, J. (1970) "White teacher, black school," in K. Ryan (ed.), Don't Smile until Christmas. Chicago: The University of Chicago Press.

Cooley, C. H. (1909) Social Organization: A Study of the Larger Mind. New York: Scribner's.

Herndon, J. (1971) How to Survive in Your Native Land. Riverside, N.J.: Library of Contemporary Education.

———— (1969) The Way It Spozed to Be. New York: Bantam.

Hughes, E. C. (1937) "Institutional office and the person." Amer. J. of Sociology 43 (November): 404–13.

Kohl, H. (1968) 36 Children. New York: New American Library.

Ladd, E. T. (1971) "Disciplinary practices and behavior changing drugs." Inequality in Education 8 (June): 2–10.

Madsen, C. H. and Madsen, C. (1970) Teaching/Discipline: Behavioral Principles Toward a Positive Approach. Boston: Allyn & Bacon.

Meacham, M. L. and Wiesen, A. E. (1969) Changing Classroom Behavior: A anual for Precision Teaching. Scranton: International Textbook.

Morse, W. C. and Wineman, D. (1965) "Group interviewing in a camp for disturbed boys," pp. 374–380 in N. J. Long et al. (eds.), Conflict in the Classroom: The Education of Emotionally Disturbed Children. Belmont, Calif.: Wadsworth.

Reese, E. P. (1966) The Analysis of Human Operant Behavior. Dubuque, Iowa.

Smith, L. M. and Geoffrey, W. (1968) The Complexities of an Urban Classroom: An Analysis toward a General Theory of Teaching. New York: Holt, Rinehart, & Winston.

Waller, W. (1932) The Sociology of Teaching. New York: John Wiley.

29

Observing and Delineating Technique of Managing Behavior in Classrooms

Jacob S. Kounin

•

If all observations have a locus in reality, records or reports of observations should be evaluated on two bases: (1) their objectivity, and (2) their completeness.

The degree of objectivity of an observational record is conventionally determined by some measure of the degree of agreement among independent observers. Do different people seeing the record agree on what happened? If a record, for example, reads that "John caused trouble in school today" and one observer "sees" John throwing spitballs while another observer "sees" John urging other boys to smoke in the washroom then this record lacks objectivity. An objective record must enable all who see it to see the same thing or event.

Completeness is another matter. Does the observation report everything that happened at the time and place? A record may be objective yet incomplete. Thus, sixty different children, a teacher, and a principal may all agree in reporting that "John was in school today." This record may be adequate for an attendance record but it is not a complete record of all that happened to John in school that day and of everything that John did while there. A good record, then, should not only tell the truth but should tell the whole truth.

This author and his colleagues spent five years studying desist techniques—techniques used by teachers in attempts to stop a child's misbehavior. We accumulated many objective records but they were not complete records. The very selection of misbehavior-desist events as a unit of study and the neglect of all other events in classrooms constituted a lack of completeness. Apparent differences in findings about desist events ob-

This essay appeared in *Journal of Research and Development in Education*, vol. 4, no. 1, Fall 1970, of the College of Education, University of Georgia, Athens, Georgia.

tained in different settings or with different methods of research forced us into an ecological frame of reference. In order to make more certain that important variables were not overlooked in favor of unimportant ones (no matter how testable and statistically significant these latter might be in experiments) we decided that a naturalistic, ecologically oriented approach was called for; that is, the study of many coexisting events in real settings. Our further research in behavior management in classrooms was then to be conducted in a spirit of inquiry to see what could be learned rather than in a spirit of debate to see what hypothesis or theory was to be tested.

With a focus upon "emotionally disturbed" children in regular classrooms, Dr. A. E. Norton and the writer spent several months observing approximately one hundred different elementary school classrooms containing what principals, teachers, and school diagnosticians labeled as emotionally disturbed children. We were always armed with pencils and notebooks. At different times, we were accompanied by experts from fields other than our own—curriculum, elementary school methods, guidance, social group work.

At the end of several months we had accumulated some impressions and several filled notebooks but had very little scientific data that would enable us to fill in some numbers in a simple table of results pertinent to the question of behavior management in classrooms.

The main difficulty behind the failure to obtain usable data pertinent to the research problem was the inadequacy of the data-gathering medium— the human observer. Some of our deficiencies as data-gathering media were:

1. An inability to obtain complete records of what happened. In spite of many combinations of divided responsibilities in record taking and synchronization, we were never satisfied that our records contained *all* that happened. We may have recorded, with a reasonable degree of completeness and objectivity, the behavior of one child. But there is more than the behavior of one child to be considered in a study of a classroom. At a minimum, there are activities, props, other children, and a teacher.

The behavior of the teacher was especially impossible to record with any satisfactory degree of completeness. Teachers simply have a large behavior volume—they do many different things, in many ways, and direct their behaviors at too many targets to allow an observer to record their behavior with completeness.

2. A tendency selectively to notice and record events that were impressive, contrasting, in line with some pre-existing hypotheses or concerns, intense, or otherwise perceptually outstanding to the point of the exclusion of other mundane and less noticeable events. Thus, if a child was tossing

paper airplanes in the air at the back of the room, this event would be in our notes. However, the notes would contain little description of what the other children were doing.

3. A propensity to include labels, evaluations, judgments, pseudo-interpretations, summaries, and other types of nonobjective and nondescriptive entries. To write that children are "attentive," "well-behaved," "disorderly," "apathetic," and the like, is not to provide descriptions of actual behaviors. These are judgments made by an observer and are not behavior facts.

4. An inclination to arrive at premature interpretations about the management of children's behavior. An example from the notes: "The teacher was reading the story with high enthusiasm, changing voice inflection and 'hamming it up,' paused, leaned forward in her seat, and visually swept all the children in the reading group, and said, 'The next part is a *real* surprise. What do you think he'll find,' looked around suspensefully and then . . . all the children were waving their hands to be called on, including five 'preemies' [children who raised their hands even before the question was asked]."

In addition to an incomplete description, our notes contained the interpretation that these teachers who are enthusiastic and suspenseful produce enthusiasm in children. A few days later we observe a teacher who was labeled as matter-of-fact and calm, and who simply raised a question while remaining seated in her chair. Children waved hands "enthusiastically" to be called on, including six "preemies." What happened to our previous interpretation that enthusiasm in children is produced by enthusism in teachers? Evidently there must be something else that both teachers are doing, or that is occurring, which is less noticeable than the histrionics and that has the effect of inducing x-degree of volunteering on the part of children.

The above, as well as additional inadequacies in the records of events and behaviors in classrooms, led us to conclude that answers to the kinds of questions one might raise about classroom management require a better data-gathering medium than the human observer. Such a data-gathering medium must record *all* events that occur in a classroom whether perceptually intense or barely noticeable, whether interesting or dull, or whether supportive or nonsupportive of a particular theory or point of view. These events must include activities, children, and teacher. Moreover, the data-gathering method should not only provide factual bases for measuring preselected events (i.e., desist events) or provide ways of checking existing hypotheses, but should also provide data for ideas or hypotheses not thought of at the time of data-gathering. It should provide data that would allow for repeated study of the same events by different persons. These criteria would preclude check lists, rating scales, and other secondary data. For once the ratings are made, the original events are over and no longer available for study. All that remains are the ratings that are pre-selected and sifted out from many other events by the original observer.

We decided to use videotapes. The combination of a camera and videotape recording meets the criteria of a good observer and recorder. The lens has no biases, theories, preconceptions, needs, or interests. It takes in all that is occurring in its field and makes no distinctions between what is boring or interesting, major or minor, important or unimportant, outstanding or ordinary, good or bad. And the videotape records it all without forgetting, exaggerating, theorizing, judging, interpreting, or eliminating.

Two TV cameras were mounted in boxes and placed on stands in a classroom. Since a TV camera may also be incomplete by means of selecting, one camera was placed in a stationary position to record the largest possible area of the classroom continuously and without editing or selecting. The second camera, equipped with a remote-controlled pan-tilt mechanism, enabled the engineer, at the direction of the project director, to record various positions in the classroom and to superimpose this picture on some part of the major picture that would not conceal the behaviors shown on it. Priority was given to videotaping the teacher and next the emotionally disturbed children when they were lost from the main picture. Two microphones were used to record sound—the main source being a wireless transmitting microphone worn by the teacher that produced a recording of everything she said on the videotape. All recording was accomplished by remote-control using equipment in a truck parked outside the school building.

Thirty self-contained elementary school classrooms were videotaped for a half-day each and forty-nine classrooms were videotaped for a full day each.

Since this research pertains to the management of overt behavior, the behavior of the children was coded for work involvement and deviancy. Managerial success in a classroom is defined as producing a high rate of work involvement and a low rate of deviancy in academic settings.

Only behavior in academic activities (reading, arithmetic, social studies, science, etc.) was scored. Children's behavior during nonacademic activities (attendance, milk time, nonacademic games, etc.) was not coded. Scores were kept separately for seatwork settings (where children engage in some kind of seatwork without direct supervision by the teacher, and recitation settings (where the teacher is actively engaged in conducting some sort of recitation with an entire class or subgroup of children).[1]

The Effects of Desist Techniques

The first question to answer dealt with the effects of "direct" managerial techniques—the techniques of dealing with misbehavior as such. These were called *desist* events. (These events were in line with an existing interest of ours and tended to be more perceptually outstanding than most other events in a classroom.) Does the manner in which a teacher handles a misbehavior affect the reactions of children to this event or not?

Every time a teacher did something to stop a child's misbehavior, the incident was coded for the type of misbehavior, how the teacher did it, and the degree of success she had in stopping that misbehavior and inducing proper behavior.

Having developed reliable measures of both desist techniques and of children's behaviors, we could answer the question of whether variations in desist techniques make any difference in the behavior of children. There are two methods of ascertaining the relationship between desist techniques and managerial success with the data available. One method is to see whether, for any one teacher, there is a relationship between his or her desist technique and his or her degree of success in handling a particular deviancy. Another is to see whether teachers who differ in their general style of handling deviancies have different degrees of general managerial success.

An answer to the first kind of question was obtained by correlating a specific teacher's scores for each of his or her desists with his or her scores for the degree of success in handling each of the corresponding deviancies. This produced 300 different correlations: thirty teachers x five desist qualities x two measures of the degree of success. There were only two correlations that were significant at the .05 level—a result that can be obtained by chance alone. The remaining 298 correlations were insignificant. One must conclude that there is no relationship between the qualities of a teacher's desist techniques and the degree of success in handling a deviancy. Thus, for any teacher, neither the degree of clarity, firmness, and intensity of the desist effort; nor whether the teacher focuses on the misbehavior, or on the legal activity, or on both; nor whether the teacher treats the child positively, negatively, or neutrally; makes any difference for how readily a child stops the deviancy or gets on with the prescribed task.

The second method of seeing whether desist techniques make any difference in how children behave is to correlate teachers' average scores for desist techniques with their scores for managerial success. Thus, all of a teacher's desist scores for clarity, intensity, firmness, focus, and child treatment were averaged. Each teacher would thus be scored for the general degree of clarity, firmness, etc. of desists. These scores were correlated with three scores of managerial success: work involvement, deviancy rate, and the degree of deviancy contagion. There were also two sets of scores for work involvement and deviancy rate; one set for the emotionally disturbed children and one for the nondisturbed children. These scores were further separated for seatwork activities and for recitation activities.

None of the correlations between teachers' desist styles and managerial success was significant. This finding held true for the emotionally disturbed children as well as for the nondisturbed children, and for seatwork settings as well as for recitation settings. As far as this research is concerned, it must be concluded that the techniques of dealing with misbehavior, as such, are not significant determinants of how well or poorly children behave in classrooms, or with how successful a teacher is in preventing one child's misbehavior from contaging others.

For purposes of research, records were not limited to desist events. Relatively complete and objective videotapes were a permanent record which could be played many times over to see whether there was anything that could be related to managerial success. As can be noted in Table 1, there are dimensions of teacher behavior that correlate with children's behavior.

With-it-ness and Overlapping

Occasionally, while observing the videotapes and scoring the teachers' desist techniques, we noticed that a teacher would sometimes desists the "wrong" child. A question was posed as to whether this might be an issue in managerial success rather than the manner in which she handled misbehavior. This dimension was defined as *with-it-ness* and a code was developed to obtain scores that would measure this category during the replay of the videotapes.

With-it-ness was defined as teachers' communicating to the children that they know what the children are doing, or have the proverbial eyes in back of their heads. What kinds of teacher behaviors, and in what circumstances, provide cues to pupils as to whether the teachers do or do not know what is going on? It is not adequate to measure what teachers know in order to obtain a score for the degree of their *with-it-ness*. It is necessary to measure what they *communicate* they know. The children, after all, must get the information that they know or don't know what they are doing.

Desist events are examples of incidents where teachers do something that communicates to the children whether they do or don't know what is happening. In such incidents the teacher engages in some overt action that may demonstrate this. In desist events a child is doing something and the teacher does something about it. Does the teacher pick the correct target

Table 1.   Correlations Between Teacher Style and Children's Behavior in Recitation and Seatwork Settings*

	RECITATION *Work*		SEATWORK *Work*	
Style	*Involvement*	*Deviancy*	*Involvement*	*Deviancy*
Momentum (Absence of Overtalk, Target and Prop Fragmentation, Overdone, Actone Overemphasis)	.656	.641	.198	.490
With-it-ness	.615	.531	.307	.509
Smoothness (Absence of Thrusts, Dangles, Stimulus-Boundedness)	.601	.489	.382	.421
Group Alerting	.603	.442	.234	.290
Accountability	.494	.385	.002	—.035
Overlappingness	.460	.362	.259	.379
Valence and Challenge Arousal	.372	.325	.308	.371
Seatwork Variety and Challenge	.061	.033	.516	.276
Recitation Variety and Challenge	.238	.162		
Overall Variety and Challenge	.217	.099	.449	.194
Average Duration of Seatwork Activities ("Attention Span")			.231	.005
Maximum Multipliers	.812	.720	.686	.741

*N = 49 classrooms (r of .276 significant at .05 level)

and do it on time? Or, does he or she make some kind of mistake that communicates the information that the teacher doesn't know what is happening?

Each separate and distinguishable desist was categorized as being correct and incorrect for both the *target* of the desist and for its *timing*.

The child or subgroup that the teacher desisted constituted the target. The teacher could pick on the correct target or the incorrect target. The target was correct if the teacher desisted the correct deviant or subgroup of deviants (two or more children talking together).

Target mistakes consisted of:

1. The teacher desisted the wrong children for a deviant act, or desisted an onlooker or contagee rather than an initiator.

2. The teacher desisted a less serious deviancy and overlooked a more serious deviancy that was occurring at the time or that had occurred between the time of this desist and the previous one. Thus, if a teacher desisted a child who was whispering to a neighboring child while two children were running around chasing each other, the event would be categorized as a wrong target due to "more serious ignored."

Whether the teacher used correct or incorrect timing was determined by whether or not the deviancy became clearly more serious before the teacher acted. A desist was categorized as correct in timing if the misbehavior was no more serious at the time of the desist than at the time it started. The issue here is not how much time elapsed between the initiation of the deviancy and the teacher's doing something to stop it. Rather, the issue is whether the deviancy increased in seriousness between the time it started and the teacher desisted.

Timing mistakes, or being too late, consisted of:

1. The deviancy spread before it was desisted. Thus, if two children started to whisper illegally, then a third joined them, then a fourth joined them and then the teacher desisted for talking, the desist was categorized as being "too late" by reason of its having spread before the teacher stepped in.

2. The deviancy increased in seriousness before it was desisted. Thus, if John turned around and whispered to Jim, then Jim poked John, then John poked Jim, then Jim started to pull off John's shirt and John started to pull off Jim's shirt, and then the teacher desisted, the desist was coded as "too late" by reason of having increased in seriousness before the teacher did something about it.

Overlapping was a dimension that correlated highly with *with-it-ness*. *Overlapping* refers to what the teachers do when they have two matters to deal with at the same time. Do they somehow attend to both issues simultaneously or do they remain or become immersed in one issue only, to the neglect of the other? These kinds of "overlapping" issues occur in both desist events and in child intrusion events.

An overlapping issue is present at the time of a desist event when the teacher is occupied with an ongoing task with children at the time that he or she desists a deviancy. Thus, if the teacher is in a recitation setting with a reading group and notes and acts upon a deviancy occurring in the seatwork setting, he or she is in an overlapping situation. Overlapping may also occur when the teacher is involved in a recitation setting and the desist occurs in the recitation setting. At this time the teacher is confronted with two issues: one is the ongoing recitation activity he or she is involved with and the other is the deviancy he or she is desisting.

An overlapping issue is also present during child intrusions and child "bring ins" when these occur at the time the teacher is engaged in some activity with a subgroup of children. Thus, if a child from the seatwork setting approaches the teacher with a paper in hand to show while the teacher is working with a reading group, this event constitutes an overlapping situation. At this time, the teacher has two issues to deal with: the ongoing reading task and the child with the "bring in."

The code for overlapping was designed to answer one question: When teachers are confronted with two issues simultaneously do they attend to both during the event or do they not? In this code, we were not concerned with coding how they handled the issues, or with whether they handled them successfully or unsuccessfully, or wisely or unwisely, but merely with whether they manifested some act that evidenced their paying attention to both issues or to only one of either of the two issues. The act of "attention to" might be a remark, a direction, or a simple look.

Movement Management: Smoothness and Momentum

There were appreciable and measurable differences among teachers in how they initiated and sustained the activity-flow of a classroom that related to the amount of work involvement and deviancy of children. These techniques of managing movement were categorized as *momentum* (the absence of slowdowns) and as *smoothness* (the absence of jerkiness).

Momentum concerns the behavior of teachers having to do with the rate of flow of activities. Do they sustain momentum or do they do things that slow down the rate of activity, hold movement back, and produce dragginess? The latter were labeled slowdowns and were categorized as *overdwelling* and *fragmentation*.

Overdwelling was scored when the teacher dwelled on an issue and engaged in a stream of action or talk that was clearly beyond what was necessary for most children's understanding or getting with an activity. Following are categories of overdwelling:

1. *Behavior overdwelling* ("nags") refers to behavior of teachers focused upon how the children were behaving and which could be characterized as "nagging" or "preaching" and overdwelling upon misbehavior beyond what was adequate to get a misbehavior stopped or to produce conformity.

2. *Actone overdwelling* consists of concentrating on a sub-part of a more inclusive behavior unit. Thus, "getting black pencil," "reading prob-

lem," "writing an answer" are sub-parts of the behavior unit "doing an arithmetic problem." In actone overdwelling a teacher would focus on how to hold a pencil, how to sit, where to put a book, and the like, to a degree that would detract from getting on with the major task.

3. *Prop overdwelling* was coded when the teacher overemphasized the props (pencils, books, crayons) use in an activity to the point of temporarily losing the focus on the activity.

4. *Task overdwelling* is the same as behavior overdwelling but as applied to the task rather than to the behavior of children. Here the teacher overelaborates directions and explanations beyond what would be required for most children to understand, to the point where they would be held back from progressing with the task if they were listening.

The other type of slowdown consisted of *fragmentation*, which is a slowdown produced by a teacher's breaking down an activity into sub-parts when the activity could be performed as a single unit.

1. *Group fragmentation* was coded when a teacher had single members of a group do something singly and separately that a whole group could be doing as a unit and at one time. For example, having children go to the reading group one at a time when the total reading group could very well do so at one time. This group fragmentation would produce significant "waits" for individuals and thus slow down the movement.

2. *Prop or actone fragmentation* was coded when the teacher fragmented a meaningful unit of behavior into smaller components and moved through these components as separate steps when the behavior could have been performed as a single, uninterrupted sequence.

The *smoothness* code delineates various behaviors initiated by teachers that interfere with the smoothness of movement in academic activities. This code includes perceptible actions initiated by a teacher which produce stops or jarring breaks in the activity flow. These may be short, momentary jerks or relatively long episodes. The categories are:

1. *Stimulus-boundedness* may be contrasted with goal-directedness. Does the teacher maintain a focus upon an activity goal or is he or she easily deflected from it? In a stimulus-bound event, teachers behave as though they have no will of their own and react to some unplanned and irrelevant stimulus as an iron filing reacts to a magnet: They get magnetized and lured into reacting to some minutiae that pull them out of the main activity stream. The conditions for coding a stimulus-bound event occur when teachers are engaged in some ongoing activity with a group of children, happen to become aware of some stimulus or event that is minor and unrelated to the ongoing activity, become distracted by this stimulus, and react to it with sufficient involvement to warrant that they are immersed in it to the point of dropping their focus on the ongoing activity.

2. A *thrust* consists of a teacher's sudden "bursting in" on the children's activities with an order, statement, or question in such a manner as to indicate that the teacher's own intent or desire was the only determinant of the timing and point of entry. That is, the teacher evidenced no sign (pausing, looking around) of looking for, or of being sensitive to, the group's readiness to receive the message. A thrust has a clear element of suddenness as well as an absence of any observable sign of awareness or sensitivity to whether the target audience is in a state of readiness. An everyday example of a thrust would be someone's "butting in" on a conversation of two or more people without waiting to be noticed or attempting to "ease in" by listening to find out what was being discussed. A thrust is the equivalent (in the sense of jerkiness) of a stimulus-bound event except that in stimulus-boundedness the event is started by a stimulus outside of the teacher, whereas in a thrust the event is initiated by an intent of the teacher.

3. A *dangle* was coded when a teacher started or was in some activity and then left it hanging in mid-air by going off to some other activity. Following such a "fade away" the teacher would then resume the activity.

4. A *truncation* is the same as a dangle, except that in a truncation the teacher does not resume the initiated, then dropped, activity. One might say that a truncation is a longer-lasting dangle.

5. *Flip-flops* were coded only at transition points. A transition entails terminating one activity ("put away spelling papers") and starting another ("take out your workbooks and turn to page 190"). In a flip-flop a teacher terminates one activity, starts another, and then initiates a return to the activity that had been terminated.

Maintaining Group Focus: Group Alerting and Accountability

In videotape replay differences were noted among teachers with respect to their tendencies to become immersed in single children and "losing" the group as compared to attending to individual children without losing some focus on the group. Since a classroom teacher is not a tutor working with one child at a time, we thought this dimension, which we labeled *group focus*, might be related to work involvement and deviancy. It became necessary to delineate concrete behaviors that would compromise a measurement of this dimension. Two related categories were found that made a difference in how children behaved: *group alerting* and *accountability*.

Group alerting refers to the degree to which a teacher engages in actions that involve nonreciting children in the recitation task, maintain their attention, and keep them "on their toes" or alerted. Anything the teacher does that indicates an effort on his or her part to get more than the reciter or performer involved was considered a group alerting cue. A score for a teacher was obtained by counting concrete positive and negative (or anti) group alerting behaviors.

Positive group alerting cues consisted of such teacher behaviors as: creating "suspense" before calling on a child to recite by pausing and looking around to "bring children in" before selecting a reciter; keeping children in suspense in regard to who will be called on next by selecting reciters "randomly" so that no child knows whether he will be called on next or not; alerts nonreciters that they might be called on in connection with what a reciter is doing; creates suspense or challenge into an issue by saying, "Let's put our thinking caps on; this might fool you," and similar techniques used to create alertness on the part of nonreciters (and prereciters).

Negative group alerting cues were those behaviors of teachers during a child's recitation, or preceding the selection of a reciter, that reduced the involvement of nonreciters in a recitation session. These consisted of such behaviors as: becoming completely immersed in a reciter without any signs of awareness of the group or subgroup; directing a new question to a single new reciter only; prepicking a reciter before the question is even asked; having reciters perform in a predetermined sequence of turns so that each child knows when he or she will or will not be called on.

Accountability refers to the degree to which the teacher holds the children accountable and responsible for their task performances during recitation sessions. This entails doing something to get to know what the children are actually doing at the time and to communicate to the children that the teacher knows what they are doing or accomplishing. While concrete behaviors comprising this dimension could be delineated, a simple measure of the number of *different* reciters per unit of time was adequate: the more different reciters per unit of time, the higher the degree of accountability.

As can be noted in Table 1, the above dimensions of teacher style correlated significantly with both work involvement and freedom from misbehavior in recitation settings. The pattern for seatwork was different. In seatwork, for example, the single highest correlation with the degree of work involvement obtained for variety and intellectual challenge. This was a score based not only upon programmed variety in content (arithmetic, science, "subjects") but also for variety in intellectual challenge (simple perseveration, skill rehearsal, problem solving), geographical location, work companions, and other aspects of activities that describe the degree of similarity or difference between activities and which tend to avoid or retard the rate of satiation.

In summary, it is possible to delineate what teachers do that makes a difference in how children behave. The role of a teacher and the dynamics of a classroom milieu are not haphazard phenomena. And even within a classroom, the dynamics of seatwork settings vary from the dynamics of recitation settings. There is evidently a lawfulness to classrooms which should make interrelationships potentially discoverable.

NOTE

1. The results pertaining to the management of the emotionally disturbed children are presented in Kounin et al. (1966) and Kounin & Obradovic (1968). Since the results regarding the management of these children are no different from the results pertaining to management of the nondisturbed children, they will not be presented separately here. More complete details about coding and scoring are presented in Kounin (1970).

REFERENCES

Kounin, Jacob S. *Discipline and Group Management in Classrooms.* New York: Holt, Rinehart and Winston, 1970.
_____, Friesen, Wallace V., and Norton, A. Evangeline. Managing Emotionally Disturbed Children in Regular Classrooms. *Journal of Educational Psychology*, 57: 1–3, 1966.
_____ and Obradovic, Sylvia. Managing Emotionally Disturbed Children in Regular Classrooms: A Replication and Extension. *Journal of Educational Psychology,* 2: 129–135, 1968.

30

Bringing Order to an
Inner-City Middle School

Stanley G. Sanders

Janis S. Yarbrough

•

For seven of the past eight years, the public's number one concern with respect to American public schools has been discipline, according to the annual Gallup polls of attitudes toward education.[1] The problem is most acute in secondary schools, especially in metropolitan areas. Its persistence indicates that, in general, school administrators have found no workable solutions.

However, one inner-city middle school in a poverty area of a large metropolis has been the object of a complete reorganization aimed at developing an atmosphere of constructive and orderly student behavior in which learning can occur.[2] This school's neighborhood attests to the low socio-economic environment of most of its students. The student body is 99 percent black; 92 percent of the students qualify for the free lunch program. It is typical of inner-city schools stereotyped as violent and disorderly.

The reorganization began as a pilot project funded under the Emergency School Aid Act, U.S. Office of Education. It was called Project ORDER (Organization for Responsibility, Dependability, Education, and Reality). Its general aim is to overcome adverse effects of minority group isolation. More specific objectives include: (1) improving the general school atmosphere as perceived by faculty, students, and parents; (2) improving pupil behavior; and (3) improving the teaching/learning environment so that affective objectives can be achieved and eventually contribute to greater cognitive gains.

The program design incorporates a systems approach based on four assumptions. The first assumption is that much misbehavior results from a feeling of impersonalness and anonymity due to large enrollments and lim-

This essay first appeared in the *Phi Delta Kappan* 58 (1976), no. 4, pp. 333-334

ited teacher contact. We attacked student alienation and teacher helplessness by organizing students and teachers into relatively small clusters. Small groups of students (from 100 to 300) spend most of the day within one area of the building under the supervision of a small group of teachers and a team leader. The clusters foster feelings of identity and personal responsibility.

The second assumption is that lack of instruction in attitudes, values, and behavior within the school contributes to the disciplinary problems. Project ORDER has used numerous techniques to develop proper attitudes and values in varied classroom settings. The teachers have borrowed from transactional analysis, Individually Guided Education, reality therapy, values clarification, etc., in pursuit of a particular blend that will satisfy student needs.

The third assumption is that a majority of any school's serious behavior problems are caused by a small minority of the students. Therefore Project ORDER provides a Crisis Intervention Center or CIC for students with behavior problems too severe to be handled in the regular classroom. Teachers and cluster teams handle most of the discipline problems, so the CIC is a last resort after an admission and dismissal committee has reviewed the situation. The CIC holds suspensions to a minimum while alleviating student disruptions. A special teacher and aide provide individual attention for the student while in the CIC. Not only does the student work on daily assignments provided by his classroom teachers; also he is helped to improve in his attitudes and behavior through reality therapy and other appropriate psychological methods. Once the student develops his own approved plan of conduct, he is allowed to return to his regular classes on a temporary basis, made permanent if his behavior proves acceptable.

Assumption four is that much alienation and misbehavior is caused by a faulty curriculum. A strong effort is made in Project ORDER to adjust the curriculum to the daily needs of children, with emphasis on affective needs. Teachers are reminded to use cognitive objectives appropriate to the learning levels of their pupils.

Project ORDER was typical of many federal programs in that funding approval was not forthcoming until July 1974. This left only one month for final preparation before school began.

The program demanded complete planning and preparation. Fortunately, much of the planning had been completed by the proposed developers. Also, flexibility had been built in; the project evolved and adapted as necessary.

Preschool inservice workshops gave us time to gain full cooperation of the faculty and staff. Teachers were paid for this program, but participation was voluntary. The concepts of Project ORDER were introduced during this period, and additional inservice training has been continued throughout the program.

The inservice program was based on two distinct yet complementary themes. First, modern approaches to educational psychology and sociology —transactional analysis, reality therapy, values clarification, etc.—were emphasized, with special emphasis on classroom implementation. Second, curriculum improvement and teaching methods were studied.

After extensive work sessions, the administrators realized that faculty and staff can easily be overburdened with inservice meetings. Some resistance became evident. Consequently, the workshops were made more intensive than extensive.

The Project ORDER grant amounted to $158,000 per year for each of the first two years, or approximately $175 per pupil annually. It was a significant sum. The North Forest Independent School District, in which the project operated, was one of the poorest urban districts in Texas, with a very limited tax base and below-average ($702) per-pupil expenditures in 1974–75. For the year 1975–76, our first of the project, expenditures rose to $861.

The additional expenditures went chiefly for salaries of four team leaders ($46,744), two counselors ($28,652), one CIC teacher ($9,524), five teacher aides ($20,581), and three half-time administrative interns ($16,527). Most of these expenses were to continue for the life of the project. Other expenditures—for consultant services, inservice training, printing, travel, etc.—were chiefly one-time or start-up costs. In the future they will be much smaller.

Thus it is apparent that Project ORDER is not prohibitively expensive. It demands reorganization of personnel to a greater extent than it does additional personnel. In a school which already has favorable pupil/teacher and pupil/counselor ratios, it could operate with no additional personnel and little extra cost.

The project has been thoroughly evaluated, and results have been encouraging beyond the planners' expectations. Behavior problems were greatly reduced in one year. The number of discipline problems handled by teachers decreased by 63 percent. The number of cases referred to the principal's office dropped by 77 percent. The use of corporal punishment was reduced by 93 percent. The number of suspensions was significantly lower—by 20 percent.

Teachers now have the means of coping with behavior problems themselves, before the problems become serious or insoluble. At the end of the first year, teachers filled out a survey instrument without identifying themselves, to encourage frankness. Sixty percent of them saw the curriculum as becoming more relevant, 71 percent perceived an overall improvement in instruction, and 80 percent saw evidence that student achievement had increased significantly. Improved attendance over the previous year, which can be attributed to improved morale, was evident in every grading period.

The results of a Student Sentiment Index[3] administered in the fall and again in the spring indicated that students had a positive feeling about the total school environment. The survey covered feelings about peers, teachers, and administrators. Even the parents absorbed a more positive feeling about the school and its activities. Parents of students who had spent time in the CIC were questioned about the value of this means of behavior adjustment. A large majority supported the program and felt that the CIC had helped the children adjust in a positive way.

Project personnel have developed a slide-tape presentation and brochure, both of which summarize the program's objectives, design, and achievements. We have presented the slide program often, at local, state, and national levels, before a great variety of audiences. It has also been used in university classes, serving as an example of an application of the systems approach to a very practical organizational problem. These presentations have prompted high interest and numerous requests for additional information.

A functional description of Project ORDER, more detailed than this article, has been prepared for distribution to interested administrators from other districts. It will outline the project's purposes, means of implementation, and achievements and should be useful to educators considering similar programs.

In summary, Project ORDER has been effective in developing constructive, orderly, and acceptable behavior through reorganization. The systems model has provided a structure and guide for the planning, implementation, and evaluation of all aspects of school reorganization, along with an adaptability that has allowed for changes as the project developed. Organizational and administrative arrangements aimed directly at the number one secondary school problem, poor discipline, were highly successful.

NOTES

1. George H. Gallup, "Eighth Annual Gallup Poll of the Public's Attitudes toward the Public Schools," *Phi Delta Kappan*, October 1976, pp. 187–200.

2. B. E. Elmore Middle School in the North Forest Independent School District, Houston, Texas.

3. Student Sentiment Index, adapted from combined elementary and secondary versions, *Attitude toward School*, Instructional Objectives Exchange, Los Angeles, California, 1972.

31

Schools That Change:
Success Strategies for Dealing with
Disruption, Violence, and Vandalism
in Public High Schools

Maurice A. Jackson

•

A New Responsibility

During the 1975–76 school year, I became one of the many pilgrims moving across the United States looking for insights and perhaps revelations on the causes and cures for crime, disruption, and violence in the public schools of our nation.

My quest was not inspired as of old by religious or ideological conviction and zeal, but by the more contemporaneous forces which now create causes or pursuits: the power of public concern supported by the federal funding establishment.

School violence has become an issue transcending the traditional sphere of responsibility of local school systems and is now also the subject of concern of many federal agencies. My role is not ordinarily that of a pilgrim on quest or a knight on crusade. I am a principal, of long experience, in a large urban high school in Washington, D.C. During the summer of 1975, the National Institute of Education invited me to become part of their team of investigators working on the "Safe School Study" mandated by an act of Congress. The consensus of the Institute personnel designing the study was that it would be essential to have some person-to-person contact with the school administrators, teachers, and students who had developed successful strategies for dealing with violence and disruption.

The charge given me was to identify and visit those secondary schools which had experienced recent incidents of violence but which were on their way toward stabilizing and containing the disruptive situation.

The decision to join the NIE study group and take a year's leave-of-absence from my high school was not an easy one. However, personal confidence in my school's students, administrative team, the majority of teachers, and the custodial staff, made it possible to accept the assignment. Yet another reason for becoming a participant in the study was the opportunity to view firsthand how other secondary schools were operating, and to learn more about new trends in school organization and curriculum. And finally, the most compelling motivation came from the conviction that it was essential to have a school person work with researchers, statisticians, social scientists, demographers, and surveyors—a school person who would be a voice for the thousands of people who live and cope with the daily problems of school administration, and who would continue to do so long after the outside investigators and the media moved on to a new focus for their studies and attention.

On September 1, 1975, I reported not to the vibrant, active halls of a high school but to the subdued atmosphere of a federal office building. The question foremost in my mind that first day was: "How is it possible for people who work in such an isolated, individualistic environment ever to understand the complexities and responsibilities of school administration?" I have now become accustomed to and somewhat envious of the quiet, lengthy, uninterrupted time intervals that researchers have at their disposal as they make decisions and form policy.

My year's assignment was spelled out in an intergovernmental personnel directive. As a research associate on a twelve-month leave from the District of Columbia Public Schools, I was to complete the following tasks:

1. Through literature search, telephone contact, and other relevant means, identify public schools that have had exemplary success in dealing with school crime.

2. Consulting with other members of Safe School research staff, select 12–15 schools to be investigated personally.

3. Visit each exemplary school to collect information having to do with the reasons for the success the schools have had in preventing or reducing school crime.

4. Write a case study of each school visited from the perspective of an investigative reporter.

5. After all the exemplary schools have been investigated and all the case studies written, prepare a summary analysis on the subject which will constitute a chapter in NIE's report to Congress.

Selecting the Schools

My first task was to identify public schools that had exemplary success in dealing with school crime, incidents of violence, disruption, or vandalism. The process used for identifying the "success" schools was one that took almost six months. The first step was, of course, to agree on what we at the National Institute of Education meant by "success" or "exemplary" schools. Typically, we defined and redefined our concept, accepted and rejected lists of schools, and solicitated nominations from a wide variety of sources. In the end we agreed on the following description and canvassed the country for recommendations: " 'Success' schools would be those which had stemmed, diminished, or completely eradicated the chaos and had established an environment where the educational process could resume."

The cooperation with and concern for our efforts provided by all of the people we contacted were heartwarming. The educational community and the agencies which provide supportive services to that community said that they valued our efforts to discover the sources of success, and viewed this approach as more positive and potentially productive than one that would seek only data on schools in turmoil and disruption.

From an abundant list of "success" schools we narrowed the possibilities down to fifteen. Our objective was to obtain some geographic, rural/urban, racial, and economic distributions in our choices. The final selection cannot of course be proffered as a scientifically controlled selection, but is made up of mutually agreed upon choices that resulted from long hours of contemplation, discussion, and analysis on the part of the NIE staff.

Meeting the School People

As I began my field work the efforts of the first six months of the NIE assignment took shape. The visits to the schools were exhilarating and demanding. Each visit required interaction with a minimum of ten individuals. The content of these interactions included (1) giving information about the NIE study; (2) giving information on my background as a high school principal and my role as an interviewer and observer; (3) seeking information about the interviewer's perception of the study; (4) seeking information on past history of violence, vandalism, and disruption; (5) seeking information on the current situation and people's conceptions on why or how the conditions at the school had changed; and (6) seeking data from a cross section of the school's professional staff, student body, and custodial staff, and integrating all of the material.

As an observer I spent all of my time at the schools (two days per institution) engaged in face-to-face relationships with the school officials whose activities I was to analyze. In gathering data I first relied on a prepared questionnaire, then asked questions which grew out of responses to the questionnaire. During the later visits I often asked permission to tape record responses so that I could refer to something other than memory and notes in preparing my summary report. In short, the process used in collecting information was one of registering or listening, recording, and interpreting.

The school people I met were open and gracious. Typically, they expressed satisfaction at being singled out by the National Institute of Education to become part of the study. While all the site visits were noteworthy, I particularly recall my visit to Central High School in Little Rock, Arkansas, because of its place in the history of school integration. Sometime after this high school had experienced a good deal of disruption and chaos, a young black principal was appointed. He was the youngest principal ever appointed to a high school in Arkansas.

The principal at Little Rock Central High School seemed to be successful because he has developed strategies for reaching all segments of the school community. When he was first appointed, he spent many hours listening to teachers, students, parents, custodians, cafeteria workers, and all who would come to talk to him about what they saw as problems.

He demonstrated an uncanny ability to get things done. He developed an excellent organization. The policies for the building were written out for students and staff alike. A policy not followed by an individual resulted in a face-to-face conference followed up with a written report.

The success of Little Rock Central High School, according to the principal, had to do with the student involvement in shared leadership and in their total involvement in every aspect of student campus life.

A student interviewed said of "our principal": "He has gained the respect of all students and teachers. He has proven himself fair to all and willing to listen to what anyone has to say. He has expanded student rights and responsibilities. He has constantly met with teachers and has sent various letters of updated information to the students' parents, thus keeping them informed of current events, procedures, and rules of our school."

The Individual Schools: Case Studies

The following represents a compendium of my impressions, audio tape recordings, notes, and written responses to prepared questionnaires.

The methodological problems presented in synthesizing all of the data were immense. The "how to" of organizing and analyzing material that almost exclusively reflected the subjective interpretations of those interviewed, as filtered through my own subjective screen, made me uneasy and often reluctant to set words to paper.

I have therefore elected to use some simple observational indicators to illustrate or report on very complex, social, and institutional structures and interactions. Rather than presenting interpretive data in the case studies themselves, I have reserved the option to make summary comments only in the "Coming to Conclusions" section of this report as it would indeed be unfair to burden any one of the schools visited with the responsibility of my subjective conclusions.

The classification of data for the case studies reflects the way I, an experienced high school principal, look at and compare schools. Without the benefit of my experience the tendency would be to be too analytical and too enumerative, a posture I could not and would not assume after just a day or two in any secondary school in this country.

Coming to Conclusions

Since starting my assignment for NIE in September 1975, several major studies and reports have been published and numerous conferences, seminars, and workshops have been held on the general topic of school violence, crime, and disruption.

The school people I visited during the year gave little indication that they had read the reports, researched the literature, attended the conferences, or contributed much data to the studies. Rather, they attributed most of their success to the fact that they were spending twelve to fifteen hours each day on the job responding to the oceanic demands of their work situation.

In summing up my impressions of the year's activities, I found much to support some of my own long-held views.

School Leadership

When a school is operating well the job looks easy. Anyone who has served as a school administrator or, for that matter, taught in a classroom, knows that all schools have a great potential for disharmony, confusion, and disorganization. Secondary schools with their large adolescent and pre-adolescent populations are particularly prone to discord and disruption.

The school visits have confirmed my opinion that the single most crucial factor in determining whether or not (or how much) violence, crime, and chaos occur in a school is the presence or absence of competent leadership at that school.

The principal and the people to whom authority is delegated determine the quality of education, the condition of life, and the characteristics of the school climate. The responsibility is awesome. The methods of selection for the position of school principal are at best empirical, at worst political and casual.

Principals assigned to the successful schools which I visited came in all sizes, ages, colors, religions, ethnic origins, and sexes. They had one similarity, however: *All* were grossly underpaid for the magnitude of demands and the numbers of hours and days of the week they were expected to give to their jobs.

The complexity of the position leaves a wide spectrum of leadership styles as possible success models for the principal's role. Indeed, Redden[1] and other sources suggest that the more flexible and adaptable to situations a person is, the better that person's leadership. Sensitivity, problem-solving capability, goal-oriented behavior, efficiency, and the like are familiar terms to anyone who has tried to employ or attempted to fire a school administrator.

In addition to having all of the above characteristics, the principals I visited at the successful schools had in one way or another acknowledged their responsibility for everything that happened in their school. They made decisions that were firm but not rigid. They were able to delegate responsibility without abdicating their position of authority and, perhaps most important of all, they were able to take steps that were not universally popular. Like it or not, everyone knew who was in charge and the person in charge (the principal) knew how much the cooperation and support of every adult and student in the school building was needed.

The significance of the principal's role in stemming violence and disruption was evident. In almost all situations pupils, parents, and teachers reported that important visible changes were made in the school anywhere from two days to two weeks after the arrival of the new principal.

In listening carefully to what assistant principals, teachers, counselors, students, and security officers were saying, I heard that a school functioned relatively free from violence if the principal assumed the responsibility for resolving conflicts; initiated structure in administrative and interpersonal interactions; was sensitive to the social and emotional needs of all the groups residing in the school; and was successful in procuring materials, personnel, and services for the school.

Simply put, by providing effective leadership and backing it up with a responsive support system, a chaotic, violent situation can quickly, efficiently, and effectively be contained, thus permitting the school to function normally.

School Climate

Much could be said about the climate or social environment of the "success" schools. What was evident to me, a transient observer, was that each school, no matter what its specific approach, was attempting to generate cohesiveness, trust, respect, and concern for all the residents of the school. Great efforts were made to identify and attend to those things which would give the student population a sense of satisfaction and a feeling of productivity. In the most successful of the schools, the similar needs of the teachers and other staff were also considered and attended to.

The messages seemed to be out and up front. There was a school that had adults who cared, who controlled and commanded. The key success factor lay in making the students and the teachers believe the message which came via curriculum and program contributions, process and interaction contributions and management and material support contributions.

Some schools relied very heavily on curriculum changes and innovations to improve school climate. These program changes gave students an opportunity for many experiential or active learning experiences. They also provided more varied and challenging learning opportunities for students. Several curricula changes took the students out of the confines of the classroom or school building and multiple learning environments were created. The curriculum innovation took into account the level of maturity and the gradation of skills and ability of all of the students in the school and provided for a variety of performance expectations. These schools set up a reward system that also valued things other than high grades or tests and so most of the students were assured some success experience at the school.

Often in conjunction with curriculum changes, but sometimes as the only new strategy for getting at the causes of violence and disruption, the schools initiated process, functional or administration changes. Ineffective principals were removed and new leaders with greater problem-solving capabilities were installed. The administration, teachers, students and often parents became involved in goal clarification for the school. Everyone was given an opportunity to participate in decision making activities. The channels of communication were opened, and, most important of all, a process for acknowledging and working with conflict was established. Accountability was established and responsibility for the form and flow of school functions was assumed by adults and students alike.

In practically all situations, attendant material support was provided to the schools. Additional personnel, funds for new curriculum material, staff training, security hardware and personnel, and increased maintenance services were some examples of the material support systems put into effect as the school moved toward improving school climate. The most successful of the "success" schools retained this material support even after the crisis subsided.

Outside Forces

Although the principal and the school staff have great potential for creating or correcting situations leading to vandalism, violence, and disruption, the social environment of the school is in large measure determined by outside forces and conditions. Lacking the power and often the training, time, and inclination to modify those external forces, school administrators and staff must know what the operating, economic, social, psychological, safety, achievement, recognition, and self-actualization needs of the school's student population are. They then must attempt to fill and work with these needs as fully as possible within the school program. The sphere of influence of the school administrator falls away sharply beyond the schoolhouse door. The support and interest of the school system in providing resources and adequately trained personnel; of the police in apprehending outsiders who enter the school to commit illegal acts; of the economic system to supply employment and decent wages; of the family to set controls and standards of behavior; and of the community to reinforce the moral and ethical values, are obligations owed but often not paid to the schools of our country.

School personnel feel strongly that they are expected to be the medicine men or witch doctors of modern-day society. They are given too few tools and very little usable scientific knowledge with which to face epidemic problems. The traditional remedies of suspension, detention, transfer, dress codes, physical punishment, and "I shall not" written a thousand times have been wiped out by court orders, parental ire, and student rights, as well as new social realities.

At a minimum, school personnel feel they should receive prompt, effective, supportive services from the school system and school board. A few of the requirements are:

- supplies and materials delivered on time
- repairs made promptly
- adequate building and ground maintenance
- alternative schools or placement for students who cannot or will not respond to the educational standards set for the majority of students
- training for teaching and administrative personnel to upgrade and maintain skills
- an adequate but prompt system for evaluating and removing inadequate teachers and administrators from the school
- security personnel and security devices for keeping vandals and burglars out of the schools after hours.

School people want a responsive and cooperative police force and court system; law officers who respond promptly to calls for removal of outsiders and students who have committed illegal acts; police who show a sensitivity to the individual student and to student groups and understand their potential for violence and vandalism when dealt with improperly; recognition by the courts of the unique and difficult role of the school in shaping the character and behavior of students, and recognition of the school's need to establish controls, boundaries, and limits, and to maintain discipline; parents who view the efforts of the school positively and who have expectations for and control over their children; and communities that value their schools and provide the fiscal resources necessary for operating them.

What Works and Why

Many schools in this country have operated for a long, long time under conditions of chaos, confusion, and violence. In these unfortunate situations, no individual or group seems to feel it has the power or responsibility for doing anything about the problems that are victimizing generations of young people. It is only when someone cares or is outraged by excesses that transcend acceptable limits, or when the opinion-making media get into the act that something seems to happen.

The larger socio-economic conditions affecting the schools are almost never modified or touched. All efforts focus on in-school, school-people solutions. These solutions take the form of changing leadership, curriculum reform, organizational modifications, tougher controls and rules, student participation in decision making, increased resources, security system devices and hardware, increased counseling services, and intergroup relationship workshops. School people are really quite impotent when it comes to changing outside forces, but when what works in schools themselves is analyzed, we see that the exact nature of the change strategy does not matter too much. What does seem essential is that these in-school solutions activate strategies of *caring*, *control*, and *increased* or *improved communication*.

The literature on school crime and violence is replete and somewhat redundant with descriptions of activities initiated and conducted to reduce incidents in the schools. The categorization of these programs usually describes the materialistic end-product rather than the social, emotional, and psychological needs of the so-called perpetrators of the antisocial acts.

It is significant, I think, that the Law Enforcement Assistance Administration (LEAA) Research for Better Schools report, "Planning Assistance to Reduce School Violence, and Disruption," developed four major categories of activities that schools are using to control violence, and the first was "Security Systems."

I contend that as long as politicians, taxpayers, and school administrators ignore the needs, frustrations, and humanity of the students who attend public schools, the incidence of violence and disruption in the schools will grow.

A more helpful and generic organization of remedial activities would be one that organized programs into the general categories of *Caring*, *Control*, and *Communication*. Some elements of all three must be present if a school is to succeed as a viable educational institution.

Caring

There are many strategies that show students that people care; good teachers and school administrators have used them for years, and each one of us can cite at least one school incident where caring made the difference. Showing care and concern for students is of course easier in smaller schools —a good reason perhaps to keep populations down to 1,100 or less. Caring strategies include knowing each student by name, where the student belongs during a given period, knowing his/her family and who the student's friends are.

Caring means providing opportunities for active learning, flexible, varied curriculum, multiple learning environments, and an inclusive rather than exclusive reward system. It means providing bus tokens to get to a job, a counselor who helps you find a job, advice on how to plan a program, nonjudgmental extra help in reading and math, and a strong adult who knows how to say "No" or "Hold it." Caring means schools that have supplies, books, clean halls, and teachers who come on time and work with you. It means school dances, plays, traditions, and a football team with uniforms. The list can grow longer and longer without significantly adding to the basic idea. Students need to feel a sense of personal satisfaction and recognition from the school and this includes needs for inclusion, affection, and control. The principal needs the help of students, co-administrators, custodial force, teachers, and parents. Also in many ways the principal needs to develop caring strategies for the adults on the scene as well as for the students. These approaches are not much different from the ones described for the adolescents in the building, although they might be even more demanding of the principal's effort and time.

If the school board and central administration are wise, they will value and support their school principals as much as possible. Caring by the board and administration means frequent public and private recognition of a job well done, and prompt responses to requests for maintenance, repairs, supplies, and personnel.

While control and communication are discussed with some detail in the next paragraphs, it is important to say here that caring also means that the school board and central administration value the individuals and groups in their system enough to establish controls and protection for the rights of all. To care means that individuals and groups are given the opportunity to know what is going on in the school, to have some influence on the process, and to be able to express dissatisfaction without being excluded, ostracized, or punished in some other manner.

Control

The school administrator is expected by students, parents, and teachers to be in control of a large number of things: traffic and buses, repairs and windows, instruction and books, curriculum and courses, good nutrition and the cafeteria food, the safety of individuals, and all the things that go on in and around the school. The control is wanted, needed, and, of course, often resented at one time or another by everyone concerned. It therefore must be present but unobtrusive.

The wisdom of Solomon, the insight of Dr. Spock, and the authority of Solon are the trinity of virtues needed to institute and maintain control successfully. The control mastery of the most successful principals, while largely unseen, is not unknown. Strength and success lie in communicating to faculty and students the knowledge that when their personal control systems fail, that of the principal will remain safely and reassuringly intact —that they may not abdicate their responsibilities, but should they falter, the strength, firmness, and common sense that will help them reassert their better selves will be supplied by their principal.

To this is added the delicate balance of a stern, uniform, but flexible code of discipline or behavior expectation that is well known to all, firmly enforced, and only gradually relaxed.

Communication

One of the most successful principals I met during my visits said that the key to the lack of violence and disruption at his school was the fact that he and his team of administrators knew before most of the student body did when and where the trouble was brewing. "The kids come and tell us what's happening. They want help but often can't ask for it directly."

It is obvious that most of the teachers, administrators, and counselors in the "success" school laugh, joke, and show satisfaction when communicating with students in the hallways, classrooms, and other meeting places. Good communication in these schools takes place on the personal, group, and intergroup level. Adults talking with children are courteous, open, and spontaneous. There is much expression and acceptance of feelings. The tone set in these one-to-one communications is warm, friendly, and sincere. Students are encouraged to be open, polite, and supportive of one another and of their teachers.

At the group level there are in-depth, ongoing discussions. Individuals are given an opportunity to express feelings, to share information, and, most important of all, to develop group feelings by supporting one another. Group goals are expressed and tested for consensus and commitment.

At the intergroup level there is much opportunity for collaboration with other groups. People are encouraged to enter a conflict situation with the understanding that compromise and consensus are the goal rather than outright concession. Individuals and groups are involved *in* rather than excluded *from*.

Daily news bulletins, weekly school newspapers, and of course the ubiquitous loudspeaker are other devices used to keep people in close communication.

Any method that enables people to know, to be heard, and to be included helps the situation. Rumor monitoring, open parent and community meetings, student councils, open-door policies, parent participation in school and classroom activities, and intergroup relationship workshops and conferences are familiar tactics employed by schools to open up or improve communications.

What works and why? Analyze any of the success schools and you will find an adroit school administrator that knows how to concoct a delicate, delectable stew from some combination of the ingredients of *caring*, *control*, and *communication* that is generously offered to students, teachers, and parents as they all work toward making their school free of disruption, violence, and vandalism.

The professional life of the school principal is prolonged and his continued productivity ensured if the people in the central administration provide some nurturing by way of real support services and public recognition. Certainly not all the problems are solved by this formula, but in place of rampant violence and crisis, it provides everyone with a chance for survival and growth.

NOTE

1. William J. Redden, *Managerial Effectiveness* (New York: McGraw-Hill, 1970).

32

Behavior Modification
in an Elementary School:
Problems and Issues

Richard Elardo

•

Since 1969 the Center for Child Development and Education has been running a unique experiment in the Kramer School of Little Rock, Arkansas. A large grant from the federal Office of Child Development enabled the project's director, Bettye Caldwell, to devote five years to improving and humanizing all aspects of this inner-city school. The goal was to produce a working model of an ideal educational institution for children—not just a school but a comprehensive child development center offering day care, early childhood and elementary education, and a range of other family support services.[1]

This report centers on just one aspect of this project: how problems of school discipline were dealt with. What follows is a report of a year-long case study of the implementation of a token economy in an entire elementary school. The effort was intended to provide teachers with an alternative to corporal punishment. I shall describe both the successful and unsuccessful procedures in chronological fashion and trace the evolution of the school justice system that ensued.

The School and the Problem

In 1972 the Kramer School population consisted of approximately 175 elementary children (grades 1 through 5) in seven classrooms, with a 60:40 black/white ratio. No busing was employed, since the school was located in an integrated area.

This essay, reprinted from the January 1978 *Phi Delta Kappan*, is condensed from a paper presented at the annual convention of the American Educational Research Association in April 1977.

There were nagging discipline problems. A group of the older children were always fighting. There was excessive school property abuse. And there were instances of disrespect toward teachers. For control, certain teachers depended on the threat of corporal punishment and on occasion actually paddled offenders. Generally, paddles were kept out of sight, but both the staff and the children were well aware of their frequent use.

Project personnel discussed discipline problems with the entire staff. The black teachers pointed out that corporal punishment was what the black children were used to when they misbehaved at home. These teachers felt the same form of discipline should be continued at school, so the children would "understand." Certain other teachers—taking seriously their courses in child development—questioned the approach. Working with me (a consultant) and Ms. Caldwell (the principal), this small group of dissenters developed a plan that would make corporal punishment in the classroom unnecessary, or so they hoped. The core of the plan was a schoolwide behavior modification system. Because they knew it would fail if some of the initiative and planning did not come from the total group, these teachers spent a good deal of time in discussions with other teachers. Finally, a survey showed that most of the staff were eager to try a behavior modification or reward system plan.

The Discipline System

The plan eventually adopted called for token rewards in the entire school, grades 1 through 5. This decision was made after our task force considered whether it would be better to introduce the system to one room at a time. To avoid charges of favoritism and divisiveness, we opted for the all-school approach. After familiarizing ourselves with the literature on token systems,[2] we outlined the following plan:

1. Discuss class rules with children on the first morning of school. Children themselves can help compose some of the rules about what type of behavior is acceptable in the classroom. The teacher should also explain the token system rules listed below.

2. Each day, a child may earn up to fourteen tokens. He may earn one for the morning class meeting, four more during reading time, four more during math time, four more during social studies, and one more in physical education.

3. Tokens will be given both for good behavior and for good academic work. If a child completes a reading task but runs around the room without permission, a token may be given for academic work but not for good behavior.

4. There will be penalties for misbehavior at lunch and at recess. Supervisors will carry a ticket book, and if they observe a child misbehaving they may issue a ticket. These tickets will be given for starting a fight, destroying property, ignoring a request by a supervisor, etc. One copy of the ticket will be given to the child, and one will be placed in the ticket box in the principal's office as soon as possible. The principal will then talk with the child and decide how many tokens the child must give up for his offense.

5. Tokens should be deposited in the bank every day. Banking hours will be from 2:30 to 3:15 p.m., Monday through Wednesday, and at noontime on Thursday and Friday. The bank will be at the west end of the upstairs hall.

6. Tokens may be exchanged for tickets to participate in many types of activities. Various staff members and volunteers will offer different things to do each Thursday (for primary children) or Friday (for intermediate). Among the activities will be a beauty parlor treatment, an unbirthday party, a rocket launching, an ice cream–making party, a dance, a tennis lesson, a sewing lesson, and a trip to the airport. A price list for each activity will be posted near the bank, and children may sign up for an activity when they have earned enough tokens. A "surprise store" will visit each room occasionally, with various items for sale.

7. Children who do not earn enough tokens to participate in an activity are to spend the Thursday or Friday activity period (2:00 to 3:00 p.m.) in a quiet "helping room." They should bring something to do (perhaps a book to read). A supervisor will be available and will be in charge during this time.

Before school convened for the fall term, we scheduled training and orientation for the entire staff. There were approximately four hours of lecture and discussion on methods of implementing the behavior management system. While we believed this was not enough time for the teachers to master behavior modification principles, we pointed out that help would be available in classrooms after school began and reminded the teachers that we intended to discuss the behavior modification system at our weekly inservice meetings.

Most teachers and students began the year with high interest in and curiosity about the token system; it was a novelty for both groups.

Teacher reactions were summarized in the middle of October, after a six-week trial. A sample:

> Mrs. N. enthusiastically supports the system and feels we should keep it. She mentioned several problem areas, however, and offered these comments:

1. Introducing the entire school to the system may have been too much for this year.

2. Reward activities are not really more rewarding than other classroom activities going on at the same time.

3. Children do not value the tokens and will give them away at times.

4. Children need less delay between tokens and other reinforcers.

5. Teachers are put in the role of punishers when they are required to stay with the "left-over" children on Thursday afternoons.

6. We should not allow 10 to 12 children out of 175 to disrupt the school; i.e., we should separate these children and use an extensive behavior modification system with them.

7. We should do something about disruption in the halls and on the playground.

Another teacher, Mrs. J., felt that the system was valuable and that we should continue using it. But she suggested that we needed more immediate primary rewards, in addition to the activities on Thursday and Friday. She suggested that we terminate bank balances every week, so that only children who accumulated enough tokens for that same week could receive rewards.

The teachers concluded that part of the system's inefficiency was traceable to inadequate administrative procedures. They also pointed to some difficulties we were all aware of; e.g., some children bought activities but somehow missed participating in them. In general, however, the staff wanted to see the system continued—with some changes.

Beginning early in November, we decided to conduct a more formal series of discussions on behavior modification principles. (We had been holding informal weekly discussions.) It was not clear at that time whether inadequacies in application of the principles arose from teacher forgetfulness or a lack of motivation. For example, one teacher would wait several hours before giving out any tokens—then would give nearly every child five of them. Most of the staff felt that everyone needed a better understanding of the basic principles of reinforcement, especially after a teacher made this comment: "I didn't give out many tokens, because I was too busy teaching." Some teachers still had the attitude that you can or should ignore good behavior.

Following these interviews and other discussions, we concluded that some changes were needed. Several teachers observed that many of their children were acquiring and saving enough tokens to buy activities several weeks in advance. Some of these students then felt more free to misbehave. In an attempt to overcome this problem, the staff decided that all bank balances would return to zero at the end of each week. This was considered a more desirable alternative than penalizing the children by subtracting tokens from their bank balances; we wanted to avoid a "demerit" system.

Consequently, on November 2 we announced this alteration to the children.

Many of our fifth-graders were quite upset over this new rule. Several spoke to me about it. Their view was that the change was arbitrarily imposed, without their involvement in the decision-making process. I communicated their feelings to several staff members, and we decided that the protest was a desirable type of behavior, showing initiative and concern worthy of reward. We perceived in these reactions an answer to the criticism that behavior modification systems involve only externally imposed control. The children, we realized, were entirely capable of indicating to us their own objectives for behavioral change; thus they were participating in the control process. We therefore invited the fifth-graders to plan their own token system rules. These children and their teacher developed a new system, and on November 9 I asked their representative, a ten-year-old named David, to write a description of what occurred.

His reply:

> The old token system worked like this: You got the tokens during the day and turned them in to the bank. Some people would not buy anything for a while, so they had a whole lot in the bank. So they could be real good for one week and get a lot of tokens, but the next week they could be bad, but they would still be able to buy things with their tokens. Then the *teachers* went to a meeting and thought up a new program where the kids go back to zero at the end of each week.
>
> So we went to Dr. Elardo and told him how that makes us kids feel. We said, the next time you decide to change the token system take some of us. So we, the teachers and the kids, went to a meeting and worked out a new token system that we all like. What we do is we get the tokens during the week, and at the end of the week when we buy things with our tokens, the left-over ones go into a savings account. Now with those tokens in the savings account we may buy things during the week. Some things like the spool [an old wire spool used as a table] where we read books and comic books and the art table where we have various kinds of art supplies like paper, stencils, and art games. We also have a TV where we may watch our favorite show, or we can use a record player.
>
> But to keep all the kids in order while at these special activities we have a judge and an assistant judge. The job of these people is to figure out punishment for the children who misbehave. They are also in charge of the work turned in. When a kid turns in his work to the judge or assistant, his name is checked off a list, and he is asked, "Want to buy something?" The kids in our room love the new system for the simple reason that they're tired of being boared [*sic*]. Mrs. B.'s room is the only room with the new system, but we think it might go on to other classrooms.

Although we did not perceive the children in Mrs. B.'s room as being "boared" very often, we were happy to see them stimulated by involvement in planning and living under the new system. We now see this involvement as crucial to the success of an alternative discipline system of this kind.

Further Developments

During January each child in the elementary school was polled to determine what price should be charged for each reward activity. A price list was prepared for each room. Here is the list for Mrs. B.'s fifth grade room: assembly (staff provides entertainment)—38; ball game—25; bingo—30; bus ride (double-decker)—40; candy—35; canister set making—23; caramel apples—38; coin collecting—25; cookies—38; crafts: Christmas tree— 30, Christmas wreaths—30, ice candles—31, Indian crafts—23; doll clothes—23; embroidery party—33; gourmet picnic—39; grooming class— 23.

Also in January, teachers reported that their token supply was diminishing; some extortion was suspected, many tokens were simply lost, and a great number were chewed beyond recognition by the children. As a remedy, we shifted to a system of tokens using checkmarks instead of plastic chips. Each child's name was posted in front of the room, along with checks to indicate his daily earnings.

A schoolwide discussion began over rules of behavior. Children felt that some classes had unfair rules. The staff consequently asked all children to hold discussions and arrive at a uniform set of rules for the entire school. The following list resulted:

Kramer School Rules
Suggested by the Children of Kramer

Penalty: Loss of tokens (amount varies from room to room). (1) No fighting anywhere; (2) no running in building; (3) no throwing paper in building; (4) no cursing anybody; (5) no eating in building, except in cafeteria; (6) no pushing; (7) no breaking into lines; (8) no throwing rocks; (9) no yelling in halls; (10) no using things you haven't bought; (11) no pencil sharpening after 8:30; (12) no littering in or out of the building; (13) no letting your neighbor get you in trouble; (14) no running in room; (15) no walking around room unless you're getting work, putting work away, or going from one group to another; (16) no name calling; (17) no talking back to teachers; (18) no taking things from others unless they give them to you; (19) no writing, scratching, or coloring on walls or desks; (20) no interrupting people while they're talking; (21) no sliding down the stair-rails; (22) no leaving school grounds without permission; (23) no meddling or bothering others; (24) no bothering the intercom system; (25) no wasting time; (26) no standing on the swings.

Following this change, most of the students and teachers agreed that the remainder of the school year unfolded harmoniously and without any corporal punishment.

Broader Issues

1. *Opposition to the philosophy of reward.* I maintain that if we could only supply teachers with a knowledge of behavioral principles and techniques (such as shaping, contingency management, etc.), they would come to rely more and more on positive means of behavior control and less and less on physical punishment and other forms of aversive control. As B.F. Skinner has said, "Most teachers are humane and well disposed. They do not want to threaten their students, yet they find themselves doing so."[3] Skinner explained that aversive techniques have been so prevalent in education because effective alternatives were slow in coming. Currently, I believe the field of behavior modification (operant conditioning) can supply these alternatives. Yet one still hears arguments to the effect that "our children are reared with physical punishment at home; therefore the school should continue it for disciplinary purposes." I hope we can now change teacher attitudes on this point.

When I discussed discipline with several of Little Rock's elementary school principals recently, two of them expressed the view that spanking is O.K. and "makes kids respect you." I suggested that they ask Kramer School teachers how they handle discipline. We called Mrs. B and Mrs. A to a meeting. They reported that they do not spank but withhold privileges as punishment. The visiting principals asked what the children thought about the system. I suggested asking the youngsters directly. Accordingly, we called in children from Mrs. B.'s room: Tim, Mickey, David, and Dwight.

As the boys entered, Tim made a spontaneous remark, "Oh, I know you," he said, addressing one of the principals. "I used to go to your school, and you whipped me four times." Encouraged by the laughter that ensued, Tim added, "Seventeen licks each time."

This reminiscence illustrated more dramatically than anything we could have said at least one effect of frequent use of corporal punishment: It makes for vivid memories.

Our boys enjoyed themselves immensely while expounding to these principals on our system of discipline. In a good-natured way, the visiting principals baited the youngsters, trying for some indication that the boys considered spanking appropriate at times. Wouldn't they at least respect their principal more if she paddled the unruly? Mickey replied, "Oh, no. She's a sweet lady and it wouldn't seem right for her to paddle any of the kids." Mickey added that sometimes it might be a good idea for the principal to call the parents and tell them to paddle a child, adding that "your parents always spank harder anyway."

All the boys expressed the opinion that some kids would probably prefer to get a spanking to "get it over with" but that spankings did no good at all. Finally Mickey, the most articulate of the four, added an interesting insight: "Sometimes you get accused falsely of doing something. If you get paddled and later prove you did not do it, you can't get unpaddled. But if you lose an activity, maybe by the time the activity should occur you can prove your innocence and still get your activity."

2. *Problems with the schoolwide approach.* As mentioned earlier, before we began this system in August we discussed the pros and cons of beginning a token system in one or two rooms versus all elementary rooms simultaneously. We decided upon the latter approach because we felt it would help insure a more unified school. However, it has been impossible to install *exactly* the same system in each of our seven elementary classrooms. As noted, our fifth grade class requested much more control over their token system than did the younger groups; we were pleased by this request and granted it.

We found that some teachers would not distribute as many tokens (or checks) as others, which led to the differential pricing of reward activities in each room.

Finally, we found that at least two teachers tended to go along with this approach only half-heartedly. This leads to the next point.

3. *The problem of teacher incentives.* What motive will lead a teacher to adopt a token system—or any other education innovation, for that matter?

This is a question that young advocates of behavior modification never hear while, as undergraduate or graduate students, they study rats in Skinner boxes or children in a special lab school. In the real world, it seems that many teachers are not beating a path to the door of the behavior modifier, so it becomes necessary to convince skeptical, twenty-year-veteran teachers of the value of behavior modification. How can this be done? Present them with the research evidence? Let them read a copy of the *Journal of Applied Behavior Analysis*? We all know this is not the answer.

What we all would like to see is this: A teacher tries some behavior shaping; it works, so he or she uses it again. To get the teacher to this point, however, may require a great deal of time and effort. We should remember that a teacher's monetary reward—his salary—is not truly contingent upon his teaching skill. After ten years or so, when the teacher has reached peak salary and has tenure, it is too late to think about using salary as an incentive to improve the quality of teaching; and before this point is reached there seems also to be no built-in way of shaping teacher behavior with monetary rewards. At one point, when we wanted to pay our Kramer School teachers some extra money for learning about behavior modification, the school district said that to do so would violate "certain guidelines."

In most schools the problem of how to get and maintain higher teacher motivation for innovation will persist.

4. *The question of evaluation.* We have not had as our main purpose the design of one or two classroom token economies. Rather, we have been working on a comprehensive, schoolwide discipline plan, and we have tried to implement this plan in a typical public elementary school, with 175 elementary students and several teachers, most of whom were not selected by our senior research staff. Nevertheless, we believe we have achieved these objectives for our program: (1) the establishment of a system of behavior modification with (2) significant input from the children and (3) evidence that classroom teachers can learn to implement the program and rely on it as an alternative to physical punishment as a form of discipline.

5. *Problems with the more difficult children.* As mentioned earlier, our main purpose in implementing a schoolwide discipline plan was to offer teachers an alternative to corporal punisment. In our case the alternative was a loss of privileges: Children who did not earn enough tokens or checkmarks to attend a reward activity had to stay behind in their rooms. This procedure brought several problems within our system into focus. First, it was often the case that children with the most severe behavior problems did not earn enough checkmarks to pay for a reward activity. Their teachers were simply not able to "catch them being good" often enough or to isolate enough improvement in their behavior or their schoolwork—in spite of our help as researchers. So quite often we saw the same youngsters being left behind. Second, problems arose in the rooms in which the detained children were to remain. Since the teachers were free to attend a staff development meeting at this time, we typically used research assistants or student helpers to supervise the children being "punished." Children were told to remain quiet, stay in their seats, and to find something to work on during the two-hour detention. Often the children would misbehave in the detention room—running around, throwing erasers or pencils, or talking to children outside by leaning out the window.

One incident should be highlighted. Perhaps students of behavior modification can learn from it.

I had been left in charge of a fourth grade room while several students who had not earned a reward activity were to remain behind. When I arrived at the room, the teacher was just leaving, and student teachers and research assistants were gathering children into groups to leave for the reward activities. There were eight children to supervise (two or three from an adjoining room were included). At this point a tall girl, who was in quite a bad mood, stated that she was leaving the room. She started using foul language. It became difficult to tolerate. She went to the window and said she was going to climb down to the playground two stories below. She put a leg outside. At this juncture it appeared that she might fall, so I dragged her back to her seat. In a minute she was up again. I stood between her and the door. Then she said, "My uncle has a gun and he'll get you," and tried to push me away and run out the door. I grabbed her and yanked her back into the room. She fell down, tripping over a desk. Just then some staff members walked by and got a revealing glimpse of the way a consultant provides teachers with an alternative to corporal punishment.

This was not the only such incident that occurred during the year's experiment. The luxury of hindsight has led us to conclude that perhaps some of the difficulties could have been relieved if the children had been allowed to earn small rewards toward the end of the two-hour detention period—perhaps the opportunity to listen to records.

Conclusion

It is my opinion that research in behavior modification via operant conditioning has reached a crucial point. The need for more knowledge of the principles involved is being surpassed by the need for knowledge of how to implement successfully those techniques that have already worked under controlled conditions. As I have shown, it is not enough for a school psychologist or counselor to be knowledgeable about behavior modification principles. He must also know how to *implement* them in the schools. We need more implementation studies of the kind done by N. Dickon Reppucci and James Saunders, who have reported on difficulties encountered in employing behavior modification in natural settings.[4]

In the continuing effort to eliminate negative systems of school discipline, we need to find out more about designing school justice systems involving both children and adults. We have attempted to make our elementary classrooms more democratic and have found that the older children (ages 9 through 11) are able to assume much responsibility for planning and supervising the token system.[5] This type of classroom may be more difficult to launch than the traditional autocratic one, but it affords children a priceless opportunity to learn firsthand the problems of treating each other fairly.

NOTES

1. Phyllis Elardo and Bettye Caldwell, "The Kramer Adventure: A School for the Future?" *Childhood Education*, January 1974.

2. K. Daniel O'Leary and Ronald Drabman, "Token Reinforcement Programs in the Classroom: A Review," *Psychological Bulletin*, vol. 75, 1971, pp. 379–98; see also K. Daniel O'Leary and Susan G. O'Leary, *Classroom Management: The Successful Use of Behavior Modification* (New York: Pergamon Press, 1972).

3. B. F. Skinner, "Why Teachers Fail," *Saturday Review*, October 16, 1964.

4. N. Dickon Reppucci and James Saunders, "The Social Psychology of Behavior Modification: Problems of Implementation in Natural Settings," *American Psychologist*, vol. 29, 1974, pp. 649–60.

5. Phyllis Elardo and Mark Cooper, *Aware: Activities for Social Development* (Menlo Park, Calif.: Addison-Wesley, 1977).

Index

•